Evolutionary Psychology

BPS Textbooks in Psychology

BPS Blackwell presents a comprehensive and authoritative series covering everything a student needs in order to complete an undergraduate degree in psychology. Refreshingly written to consider more than North American research, this series is the first to give a truly international perspective. Written by the very best names in the field, the series offers an extensive range of titles from introductory level through to final year optional modules, and every text fully complies with the BPS syllabus in the topic. No other series bears the BPS seal of approval!

Each book is supported by a companion website, featuring additional resource materials for both instructors and students, designed to encourage critical thinking, and providing for all your course lecturing and testing needs.

For other titles in this series, please go to **www.bpsblackwell.co.uk.**

Evolutionary Psychology

A Critical Introduction

**EDITED BY
VIREN SWAMI**

The British Psychological Society | BPS BLACKWELL

Library of Congress Cataloging-in-Publication Data:

Evolutionary psychology : a critical introduction / edited by Viren Swami.
   p. cm.
Includes bibliographical references and index.
ISBN 978-1-405-19122-7 (pbk.)
1. Evolutionary psychology.   I. Swami, Viren, 1980-
BF698.95.E957 2011
155.7—dc22

                                                                    2010036848

A catalogue record for this book is available from the British Library.

Set in 11/13pt Dante by MPS Limited, a Macmillan Company

Printed in Great Britain by TJ International, Padstow, Cornwall

The British Psychological Society's free Research Digest e-mail service rounds up the latest research and relates it to your syllabus in a user-friendly way. To subscribe go to www.researchdigest.org.uk or send a blank e-mail to subscribe-rd@lists.bps.org.uk

Commissioning Editor:	Andrew McAleer
Assistant Editor:	Georgia King
Marketing Managers:	Fran Hunt and Jo Underwood
Project Editor:	Nicole Burnett

Brief Contents

About the Contributors   xi

1   **Evolutionary approaches to behaviour**   1
Thomas E. Dickins

2   **The evolution of cognition**   31
Kayla B. Causey and David F. Bjorklund

3   **Cooperation as a classic problem in behavioural biology**   73
Michael E. Price

4   **Mate choice and sexual selection**   107
David Waynforth

5   **The evolutionary psychology of human beauty**   131
Viren Swami and Natalie Salem

6   **Life history theory and human reproductive behaviour**   183
David W. Lawson

7   **Parenting and families**   215
Rebecca Sear

8   **Personality and individual differences**   251
Adrian Furnham

9   **Evolution, cognition and mental illness: The imprinted brain theory**   281
Christopher Badcock

10   **Interactions between cognition and culture**   311
Jeremy Kendal

11   **The future of evolutionary psychology**   343
Kevin N. Laland and Gillian R. Brown

Index   367

Contents

About the Contributors   xi

1   Evolutionary approaches to behaviour   1
A brief introduction to evolutionary theory   5
Fitness, sociobiology and life history theory   16
Evolutionary psychology   21
Conclusion   25
Acknowledgements   27
References   27

2   The evolution of cognition   31
Why are we so smart?   33
How did we get so smart?   38
What, exactly, are we so good at? And when did we 'get it'?   46
Conclusions   60
References   61

3   Cooperation as a classic problem in behavioural biology   73
Why has cooperation been such a biological puzzle?   74
Individual-level solutions to the puzzle: Selfish replicators,
    cooperative vehicles   76
Cooperation via genic self-favouritism (kin selection and
    greenbeard altruism)   77
Cooperation via return benefits (reciprocal altruism, indirect
    reciprocity and costly signalling)   82
Summary of individual-level theories of cooperation   86
Group selection   87
Complex human cooperation: Collective action   91
Conclusion   98
Acknowledgements   100
References   100

4   Mate choice and sexual selection   107
Sexual selection   108
Which human traits are sexually selected signals?   115
Sexual selection and within-sex differences   116
Time allocation   122
Conclusion   125
References   126

5   **The evolutionary psychology of human beauty**   **131**
   Facial attractiveness   134
   Bodily attractiveness   145
   Conclusion and future directions   162
   References   164

6   **Life history theory and human reproductive behaviour**   **183**
   Trade-offs in human life history   185
   The optimisation of family size in traditional societies   193
   The optimisation of family size in modern societies   196
   Conclusions and future directions   204
   Acknowledgements   205
   References   206

7   **Parenting and families**   **215**
   What is parental investment?   216
   Who invests in offspring?   217
   Familial conflict   227
   What is invested?   228
   Who is invested in?   230
   Conclusion   242
   Acknowledgements   243
   References   243

8   **Personality and individual differences**   **251**
   The current state of differential psychology   254
   Personality and the evolutionary imperative   257
   A cost-benefit analysis of the Big Five   262
   Authoritarianism   267
   Ability and intelligence   268
   'Dark-side' disorders   271
   Conclusion   276
   References   276

9   **Evolution, cognition and mental illness: The imprinted
   brain theory**   **281**
   The illnesses that made us human   282
   Antitheses of mentalism in autism and psychosis   288
   The imprinted brain   294
   Implications for evolutionary psychology   303
   Acknowledgements   305
   References   305

10 Interactions between cognition and culture   **311**

Social transmission   315

Gene-culture co-evolution of cognition and culture (mainly) in the
    hominid lineage   325

Conclusion: A niche construction framework of multimodal inheritance   333

References   334

11 The future of evolutionary psychology   **343**

A brief historical perspective   344

Can the EEA be made workable?   347

Universals and the challenge of explaining variation   351

Hypothesis testing: Alternative approaches   354

A vision of the future   359

Acknowledgements   361

References   362

Index   **367**

About the Contributors

Christopher Badcock was born in 1946 and graduated from the London School of Economics with First Class Honours in Sociology and Social Anthropology in 1967. He obtained his PhD with a thesis on structuralism in 1973 and since 1974 has taught at the LSE, where he is currently Reader in Sociology. From 1978 until her death in 1981, he had a private didactic analysis with Anna Freud, and in 1985 introduced the first course on evolution and social science to be taught at the LSE since before World War Two. Since 2004, he has collaborated with Bernard Crespi, and recently published a summary of their joint work on the genetics of mental illness in *The Imprinted Brain: How Genes Set the Balance between Autism and Psychosis*.

David F. Bjorklund is Professor of Psychology at Florida Atlantic University, and currently the editor of the *Journal of Experimental Child Psychology*. He is the author or editor of numerous books, including *Why Youth is* Not *Wasted on the Young, Children's Thinking, The Origins of Human Nature: Evolutionary Developmental Psychology* (with Anthony Pellegrini) and *Origins of the Social Mind: Evolutionary Psychology and Child Development* (with Bruce Ellis). He has published more than 150 scholarly articles on various topics relating to child development and evolutionary psychology. He has received financial support for his research from the National Science Foundation, the Spencer Foundation and the German Research Foundation. His current research interests include children's cognitive development and evolutionary developmental psychology.

Gillian R. Brown obtained a PhD in Zoology from the University of Cambridge in 1997 and is currently a Lecturer in Psychology at the University of St Andrews. Her research focuses on sex differences in animal behaviour from neuroendocrine, developmental and evolutionary perspectives, with a particular interest in the role of hormones in infant and adolescent mammals. She also investigates sex-biased parental investment, adaptive birth sex ratio biasing and sex differences in mating strategies. Together with Kevin Laland, she is the co-author of *Sense and Nonsense: Evolutionary Perspectives on Human Behaviour*.

Kayla B. Causey is a PhD candidate at Florida Atlantic University and researches human cognition and behaviour from the perspective of evolutionary developmental psychology. Her research focuses on early childhood cognitive development. Her dissertation examines the developmental relationship between metacognition and prospective memory (and mental time travel, more broadly). Her research interests also include grandparental investment and children's deontic reasoning about precautionary and permission rules. She is currently co-editing a special issue on evolutionary psychology and evolutionary developmental psychology for the Spanish journal *Psicothema*.

Thomas E. Dickins is a Principal Lecturer in the School of Psychology at the University of East London and a Research Associate in the Centre for the Philosophy of Natural and Social Science at the LSE. He received an education in both psychology and the philosophy of science before receiving a PhD on the evolution of language from the University of Sheffield in 2000. Since then, he has worked on theoretical aspects of evolutionary behavioural science and evolutionary approaches to sexual orientation, social dominance and, more recently, fertility decisions. In 2006, he began a series of European conferences for the human evolutionary behavioural sciences. In collaboration with Rebecca Sear, David Lawson and Kevin Laland, this conference series has blossomed into the European Human Behaviour and Evolution Association (www.ehbea.com) for which he currently acts as Treasurer. Since 2007, he has been the Editor-in-Chief for the *Journal of Evolutionary Psychology*.

Adrian Furnham was educated at the London School of Economics, where he obtained a distinction in an MSc Econ, and at Oxford University, where he completed a doctorate (DPhil) in 1981. He has subsequently earned a DSc (1991) and a DLitt (1995) degree. Previously a lecturer in Psychology at Pembroke College, Oxford, he has been Professor of Psychology at University College London since 1992. He has lectured widely abroad and held scholarships and visiting professorships at, amongst others, the University of New South Wales, the University of the West Indies, the University of Hong Kong and the University of KwaZulu-Natal. He has also been a Visiting Professor of Management at Henley Management College. He has recently been made Adjunct Professor of Management at the Norwegian School of Management (2009). He has written over 60 books and 700 papers on a wide variety of topics mainly in applied social psychology, psychometrics and differential and evolutionary psychology.

Jeremy Kendal is an RCUK Academic Research Fellow in the Department of Anthropology, Durham University. He completed his PhD (2003) on animal social learning from the University of Cambridge under the supervision of Kevin Laland. Since then, he has developed an increasing interest in human cultural evolution, developing mathematical models of human cultural niche construction and the evolution of costly social norms as a post-doctoral researcher with Marc Feldman (Stanford University), before carrying out experimental and theoretical analysis on the evolution of social learning strategies with Kevin Laland (University of St Andrews). His current research interests include social learning, cultural evolution, gene-culture co-evolution and niche construction.

Kevin Laland is Professor of Behavioural and Evolutionary Biology at the University of St Andrews. His research encompasses a range of topics related to animal behaviour and evolution, particularly social learning, gene-culture co-evolution and niche construction. He has published six books and 150 articles on these topics and has been elected a Fellow of the Royal Society of Edinburgh.

David W. Lawson is a Leverhulme Early Career Research Fellow at the Department of Psychology, University College London. He classifies himself as a Human Behavioural Ecologist and holds a PhD in Anthropology (University College London) along with research degrees in Evolutionary Psychology and Biological Sciences. He has broad interests in evolutionary models of human and animal behaviour. His research focuses on the behavioural ecology of the family, particularly resource competition and cooperation between siblings, and the co-evolution of reproductive and parental investment strategies.

Michael E. Price is currently Lecturer in Psychology at Brunel University and previously held academic positions at Indiana University, the Santa Fe Institute and Washington University in St Louis. He has a BA in Psychology from Duke University and a PhD in Biosocial Anthropology from the University of California, Santa Barbara. His research on the evolutionary psychology of cooperation and social cognition has been conducted among indigenous Amazonian groups in Venezuela and Ecuador as well as among US and UK study populations.

Natalie Salem is a PhD candidate in Evolutionary Psychology at University College London, where she received her BSc and MSc degrees in Psychology. Her research explores whether mating strategies can be accurately inferred using bodily cues alone, namely the waist-to-chest ratio, the waist-to-hip ratio and body mass index. She has particular research interests in the effect of the male and female sex hormones on both physiological and behavioural development, and their consequences for human mate choice.

Rebecca Sear is a Reader in Evolutionary Anthropology at Durham University. She has degrees in Zoology and Biological Anthropology and obtained her PhD from University College London in 2001. She is interested in the application of evolutionary theory to the social sciences, particularly demography. She has published a number of articles on the subject, mainly focused on two areas: the impact of kin on demographic phenomena and interrelationships between health and demographic outcomes. Her research so far has been focused on high fertility populations in the developing world, specifically sub-Saharan Africa, but she also has interests in the demographic transition and low fertility regimes. She is vice-president and co-founder of the European Human Behaviour and Evolution Association, and a Council Member of the Galton Institute.

Viren Swami is a Reader in Psychology at the University of Westminster and part of the adjunct faculty at HELP University College in Malaysia. He obtained his BSc and PhD, both in Psychology, from University College London, and has previously held an academic position at the University of Liverpool. The main foci of his research are on the psychology of interpersonal attraction, particularly from cross-cultural perspectives, and issues relating to body image, including the promotion of positive body attitudes. He is an associate editor for the journal *Body Image* and is the author of *The Missing Arms of Vénus de Milo* and *The Psychology of Physical Attraction* (with Adrian Furnham). He has also translated works by Jorge Luis Borges, Roberto Bolaño, Franz Kafka, George Orwell and Federico García Lorca, among others, into Malay.

David Waynforth is presently Senior Lecturer in Human Behaviour in the School of Medicine at the University of East Anglia, Norwich. His academic background is in anthropology, and after completing his PhD in the Human Evolutionary Ecology programme in anthropology at the University of New Mexico, he lectured for several years in psychology at Durham University. His research interests include the evolution of conditional and alternative mating strategies, paternal care and evolutionary medicine.

1 Evolutionary approaches to behaviour

THOMAS E. DICKINS

CHAPTER OUTLINE

A BRIEF INTRODUCTION TO EVOLUTIONARY THEORY 5

    Plasticity and evolution 12

FITNESS, SOCIOBIOLOGY AND LIFE HISTORY THEORY 16

EVOLUTIONARY PSYCHOLOGY 21

CONCLUSION 25

ACKNOWLEDGEMENTS 27

REFERENCES 27

Evolutionary theory was first applied to the behavioural sciences by Darwin (1871, 1872). Since then the field of evolutionary behavioural science has blossomed. The history of this field is detailed and well-rehearsed within the literature (e.g. Buss, 2008; Dennett, 1995) and it would not be possible to do it justice within the confines of a chapter. Instead, this chapter will introduce a particular perspective on evolutionary behavioural science in the hope that it will act as a stimulus to discussion and help the reader to unravel subsequent chapters in this volume. Inevitably, there is some historical detail in order to contextualise certain points, but this chapter is far from a complete history. I hope that historically minded readers will forgive this.

This volume is about evolutionary psychology, but I have chosen to write a chapter about evolutionary behavioural science. Psychology is, of course, a behavioural science and much activity within the discipline is solely about measuring behaviour. However, psychology is also interested in endocrine, neurological and cognitive mechanisms that all cause behaviour, and these mechanisms are discussed in computational or information-processing terms. These mechanisms can be said to mediate input–output relations, with the final outputs being behavioural. Evolutionary theory is used in order to discuss the functions of behaviour – what any given behaviour is designed to achieve – and to determine the functional limits for underlying psychological mechanisms. Evolutionary theory, then, gives us an ultimate explanation (Tinbergen, 1963) that helps us to develop accounts of the kinds of proximate mechanisms that constitute, in this case, the psychology of an organism; it does not tell us the detail of those mechanisms, which is a task left to the proximate methods of the discipline of psychology. This chapter discusses the breadth of this application, hence its focus on evolutionary behavioural science as a whole.

Evolutionary theory is a theory of design. Before moving on to discuss the process of evolution, it is important to clarify this key notion of design. Design is not confined to organic life, and an unnatural example will help to abstract the fundamental features of this concept. Think of a simple robot with the task of moving across a room whilst avoiding various obstacles (see Dickins and Dickins, 2008, for a fuller treatment of this example; and also Braitenberg, 1984). One possible design for such a robot would be based around a simple car chassis. It would have four wheels, two at the front and two at the back. The back wheels would be attached to a motor each, to power them independently. At the front of the robot, there would be two depression paddles. The left paddle would be connected to the back right motor; the right paddle would be connected to the back left motor. These connections would be inhibitory, such that depressing the left paddle would stop the right motor. As the left motor is still going, the robot would turn to the right (see Figure 1.1). In the same way, depressing the right paddle would cause the robot to turn left.[1] In this way, obstacles would be avoided and the robot could continue its travels across the room.

---

[1] There are obvious design flaws in this robot. First, if the robot hits an object straight on then both paddles could potentially be depressed and then both motors would stop. There are various ways around this, including angled paddles that will not make such a contact. Second, in a closed room the robot will eventually find a wall and begin a jerky kind of wall-following behaviour until it powers down. Again, more design is needed to resolve this and I leave it to the reader's imagination to improve the robot.

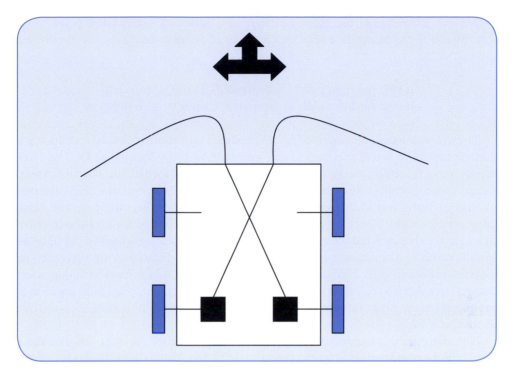

Figure 1.1. *A robot with two depression paddles at the front of its basic chassis design.*

These paddles are linked to rear motors such that when the left paddle is depressed it inhibits, or stops, the back right wheel, and when the front right paddle is depressed the back left wheel stops. In this way the robot can avoid most obstacles. This simple design is like those found in biological organisms in that it is a conditional architecture – if (P1: left sensor depressed) then (Q1: stop back right wheel).

The robot clearly has a function and has been designed, by an engineer, to meet this function. The depression paddles are an essential part of this design for they are the robot's only source of inputs from the outside world and, to this extent, they act as a sensory system. The only knowledge this robot has of the outside world, through which it has to move, is through these paddles. To this end, its only experience of the world is tactile and such inputs are the only inputs of any importance. The robot could be bathed in light and sound but such things will have no effect because the robot has not been designed to use them.

There is much discussion about the relationship between function and knowledge in the philosophical literature (e.g. see Millikan, 1993). I am using the term loosely in this chapter to imply a meeting of design and environment such that the robot, in this case, can deliver its functions. So, if a design provides a good fit to the environment the design embodies facts about that environment and in this sense represents something about the environment. This relates to the difference between environment and ecology that is mentioned later. I am not seeking to discuss notions of content, concepts, meta-representational states and all else associated with high-order cognition. However, the astute reader will realise that there is a relationship to be drawn out.

We can characterise the robot's design as a series of conditional rules, such that the robot's architecture embodies a number of possible decisions. Informally, we can say:

If (P1: the right paddle is depressed) then (Q1: turn left)
If (P2: the left paddle is depressed) then (Q2: turn right)

These conditional rules can readily be translated into more technical terminology that captures the actual mechanical actions made to move from P to Q. This may appear superfluous or, worse still, an exercise in artificial formalism. It is certainly a simple point that this robot can be described in this way. However, the point extends to all organisms and all biological systems. Think of a bat; bats navigate and hunt using echolocation. They emit pulses of sound and listen for a returning echo in order to locate the distance and direction of moths. Distance is easy enough to calculate as sound travels at a constant speed; so, simply timing the duration from utterance to received echo and then dividing it by two will give the distance. Bats have cognition that enables them to calculate the distance and, to some extent, you could argue that bat cognition encompasses this simple mathematical algorithm; it represents a truth about the world.

Bats determine direction of prey by calculating whether the echo reaches their right or left ear sooner. Folds within the ear help to determine the vertical positioning of the bat owing to the angle at which the sound hits the ear. Smaller objects reflect sound less intensely than larger ones and inbuilt knowledge of the sizes of suitable prey determines whether the bat will treat the echo as indicative of food. The sounds that bats emit are at very high frequencies, often too high for human ears. They are also at extremely loud volumes – indeed, if they were within the human frequency range but at the same volume, they would be damaging. This is clearly an issue for the bats. To counter this, they temporarily deafen themselves whilst emitting the sound, and then switch their hearing back on to receive the echo.

There is more to say about the biology of bat echolocation (see Altringham, 1999), but from this account you can see that we are dealing with systems that deliver outputs and that they are describable in terms of decision rules. So, for example, horizontal location during hunting can be characterised as follows:

If (P1: left ear input first) then (Q1: dip left wing and raise right wing)

Bats, just like robots, are clearly designed to process inputs and deliver outputs. When we discuss bats, we might refer to them as processing information about the outside world in order to navigate and hunt. That information is processed by conditional systems, and the relationship between the inputs and the processing systems captures truths about the world. Note that 'information' refers to the functional relationship between an input and a system. If the system is designed to take this input, designed to have a conditional response, then the input is informative. If not, then it is an empty input. Information is not something in the world to be captured; it is a consequence of design.

Bats, unlike robots, have no engineer, no designer who has intentionally built them to capture moths. To this end, we need an account of the design of organic life that does not rely upon any kind of agency: evolutionary theory delivers this.

A BRIEF INTRODUCTION TO EVOLUTIONARY THEORY

Darwin's interest was in the diversity and variation found in life. He noted that the various traits he observed in species appeared fit for purpose, as if they were designed to do a specific job, and he sought to explain this. His explanation was the theory of evolution through natural selection.[2]

The Darwinian view sees organisms as engaged in a struggle for life. They face numerous problems that can deleteriously affect their survival and reproductive chances. However, the heritable traits that organisms possess can help them to solve these problems and, if this happens, those traits can be passed onto their offspring. As traits vary between individuals, such that one individual may deliver a solution to a problem more effectively than the next, some organisms thrive relative to others. Those with a variant of a trait better suited to the struggle for life are more likely to survive and to reproduce than those with less-well-suited variants, and gradually this 'better' variant will come to dominate in the population because of its heritability. Just so long as the problem remains a stable aspect of the environment, this variant will reach fixation.

It is the problems of survival and reproduction that provide selection pressure for particular variants. Natural selection is, therefore, an economic consequence of the interaction between problems of survival and reproduction and heritable traits. Those traits that are selected can be termed 'adaptations'. Darwin's own formulation of the natural selection of adaptations can be distilled into a number of key principles. First, the principle that there is a struggle for life, an idea seeded by Darwin's reading of Malthus's (1798) *An Essay On the Principle of Population*, in which the consequences of geometric rates of reproduction relying upon finite, and at best gradually linearly increasing, resources, were discussed. Malthus's stark prediction was that population growth will exceed resources and will then be checked by famine, disease and war.[3] The second principle is that of trait variation. From these Malthusian catastrophes, some

---

[2] Darwin also established sexual selection. Sexual selection is a special form of natural selection in which the ecology of sexual reproduction establishes key selection pressures. Indeed, sexual selection is sometimes rephrased as sex-dependent selection (for recent discussions, see Carranza, 2009; Clutton-Brock, 2008).

[3] Malthusian tensions between population growth and resources are not regarded as the only form of struggle in modern times. More technically, what the Malthusian idea captured was the notion of differential survival and reproduction within a population.

individuals will emerge and continue their lives. The traits that enable them to survive can be passed on, which is the third principle of inheritance. Darwin draws the three principles together in the following passage of *The Origin* (1859/1985, pp. 169–170):

> If during the long course of ages and under varying conditions of life, organic beings vary at all in the several parts of their organisation, and I think this cannot be disputed; if there be, owing to the high geometrical powers of increase in each species, at some age, or year, a severe struggle for life, and this certainly cannot be disputed; then, considering the infinite complexity of the relations of all organic beings to each other and to their conditions of existence, causing an infinite diversity in structure, constitution, and habits, to be advantageous to them, I think it would be a most extraordinary fact if no variation ever had occurred useful to each being's own welfare, in the same way as so many variations have occurred useful to man. But if variations useful to any organic being do occur, assuredly individuals thus characterised will have the best chance of being preserved in the struggle for life; and from the strong principle of inheritance they will tend to produce offspring similarly characterised. This principle of preservation, I have called, for the sake of brevity, Natural Selection.

The Origin was published on 24 November 1859, and the impact of this elegant process of selection was immediately felt. Darwin had provided an explanation for design that required no hidden hand, no grand designer, and he demonstrated this through detailed and exhaustive natural history. What was lacking, however, was a theory of inheritance; how were traits passed on from generation to generation in a manner that would permit selection to do its work?

Many histories of Darwin (see Dennett, 1995) note that he had not read Mendel's paper on particulate inheritance published some two years before *The Origin*. One can only speculate as to how Darwin might have put this to use, although Darwin was not alone. Mendel's work on garden peas and other plants, and his notion of inheritance, was effectively ignored until the twentieth century, when chromosomes became the focus of attention for research on heredity (see Fox Keller, 2000). Then, in 1953, the structure and character of DNA was revealed, with the authors of that key paper laconically noting at the end that their discovery may have some impact upon theories of heredity (Watson and Crick, 1953). Genetics had come of age.

Genes code for proteins,[4] and in so doing build traits; genes vary in trait expression and genes are inherited. What is more, genes can become altered through mutation[5]

---

[4] In fact, genes code for polypeptide chains (see Box 1.2) that in turn become proteins and enzymes (which are a subcategory of proteins) and some genes control the expression of other genes.

[5] I am focusing upon mutation in this chapter for ease of exposition. However, there are a number of random events that can lead to the emergence of new forms. For example, because of the random nature of the allocation of genes during gamete formation it is possible for genes (or alleles) to become over- or underrepresented within a population. Changes in relative gene frequencies as a consequence of such action are referred to as 'genetic drift'. Clearly, genetic drift can change the available traits within a population and this is like evolutionary change. However, it is worth noting that those genes are still subject to selection pressure. Recombination, founder effects and hybridisation can also introduce new forms (see Ridley, 2004, for a full discussion).

and in this way new trait variation can be introduced.[6] Monod (1972) famously described evolution as a process of chance and necessity. Mutation is the main aspect of evolution that is reliant upon chance. Once a beneficial mutation is produced, that gives some competitive advantage in the struggle for life, selection will 'take hold' of it and this blind process will take that trait to fixation within a population.

During the 1960s, much theoretical work made it clear that selection at the level of the gene best explained the main effects of evolution. Genes could be conceptualised as functionally eternal, replicating themselves through the generations just so long as natural selection permitted it. In this way, an adaptation was defined as any trait that causes its underlying genes to increase in relative frequency within the gene pool. Dawkins (1976) captured the essential logic at work in his book *The Selfish Gene*.[7] Genes were to be seen as self-interested, seeking their replication through the vehicles that carried them. If this replication is best served by building traits that make the organism bearing them selfish, then selection will see to it. Equally, if it is beneficial to build organisms that cooperate to attain resources, then genes for cooperation will be selected for. Nothing in selfish gene theory implies selfish behaviour in the organisms carrying those genes.

This theoretical innovation had fruitful consequences. First, it has been possible to separate biochemical accounts of molecular genetics from functional discussions where it is useful to talk of *genes for* a particular trait (Haig, 2006). Second, it allows genes to be seen as strategists, and their strategies, their traits, account for the changes in gene frequencies over time. In the final analysis, a complete biological science will provide the full biochemistry but evolutionary biology can productively move forward without this knowledge. These consequences were mathematically realised in the form of evolutionary game theory (Maynard-Smith, 1982). Traits, as competing strategies, could be modelled to see which would come to be stable over time, such that they could not be shifted by the arrival of a new mutant strategy, even if other strategies could survive in the population (so-called evolutionarily stable strategies; see Box 1.1).

The biochemistry of genes does have some theoretical impact. Genes are best understood as functionally described portions of DNA. Their function is to build polypeptide chains, that later become enzymes or proteins, or to control the expression of other genes. During protein synthesis, DNA unravels, the code is transcribed and translated through the action of various types of RNA, leading to the formation of a polypeptide chain (see Box 1.2), which is folded into a protein. In the now classical formulation, information is regarded as flowing in one direction only, from DNA to protein. There is no information flowing back from the protein, or any other intermediate stage in the process, to the DNA. In other words, DNA is unaffected by

---

[6] Most mutations are neutral in effect; the next most likely outcome is that the mutation is deleterious to the organism, and the least likely outcome is that the mutation is beneficial.
[7] Dawkins' book effectively summarises the canonical work of George C. Williams, William H. Hamilton, John Maynard Smith and Robert L. Trivers, as he openly acknowledges.

BOX 1.1.   EVOLUTION AND GAMES

The Prisoner's Dilemma is one of the best-known games used in evolutionary theory. In its original incarnation, the game is set in a prison. Two prisoners are planning an escape, but the authorities become suspicious and decide to interrogate both prisoners separately. The authorities have no firm evidence, so they suggest a deal to each of the prisoners – if they reveal the escape plot, the authorities will treat them well and even reduce their sentence. However, if both prisoners stay quiet, their plot will be safe and they can potentially escape, even though the act of escape may carry risks. So, each prisoner has to decide whether to stay quiet and cooperate with the other, keeping their plan a secret, or to cheat on the other by revealing the plot. They have to weigh the costs and benefits. If one decides to remain quiet whilst the other talks to the authorities, they will be a sucker and get nothing for their efforts. If both decide to reveal the plot, then the authorities will punish them but not too heavily as the regulations reward realisation of wrongdoing even at this late stage.

The Prisoner's Dilemma is a game about cooperation, and the simple version above is about cooperation in a one-shot game where each player has only one strategic move that they can make. Cooperation is a trait seen in many species, and evolutionary biologists have been keen to understand how such behaviour can become a stable strategy within a population. Your intuitions, whilst reading the preceding paragraph, probably told you that the prisoner should defect and reveal the plot. Even if they both keep quiet, there are still risks associated with trying to escape, but a confession will secure either earlier release or at least minimal punishment.

Axelrod and Hamilton (1981) used the Prisoner's Dilemma to reveal the underlying game-theoretic dynamics in natural cooperation. Table 1.1 is a version of the original pay-off matrices used in their key paper. It represents the pay-offs for two possible one-shot game scenarios. In other words, each player has only one move to make, either cooperate or defect, and the matrix maps the consequences. The values in the matrix can be thought of as the fitness gain in each interaction for player A. Fitness could be measured directly in terms of offspring, or indirectly in terms of useful resources that will later enhance fitness.

Table 1.1. The Prisoner's Dilemma Game.

		Player B		Player B	
		Scenario 1		**Scenario 2**	
		Cooperate		Defect	
Player A	Cooperate	R = 3 Reward for mutual cooperation		S = 0 Sucker's pay-off	
	Defect	T = 5 Temptation to defect		P = 1 Punishment for mutual defection	

The pay-off to player A is shown with example values.

Source: Based on Axelrod and Hamilton (1981).

Scenario 1

If player A encounters B, who always cooperates and A cooperates too, then A increases her fitness by 3. But if A defects – that is cheats B – she increases her fitness by 5; if B always cooperates, it therefore is in A's interests to defect.

Scenario 2

If player B always defects and A cooperates, A's fitness is unchanged. If A defects, she increases her fitness by 1; if B defects, it benefits A to defect also.

The overall conclusion is that, whatever the other player's choice, it pays A to defect. This means that cooperation is not what is termed an Evolutionarily Stable Strategy (ESS). If there were a population of cooperators, a mutant defector would soon spread. Furthermore, this strategy would be the best response to itself and any other strategic move and therefore unbeatable. Defect strategies are an ESS, as a mutant cooperator will not spread. The values used are exemplars. However, using the notation in the matrix above (Table 1.1), the expression for the requisite conditions to maintain this ESS is:

$$T > R > P > S \text{ and } R > (S + T)/2$$

If the two individuals play only once, a one-shot game, then defection is always the best response. Defection is also the best policy if the number of interactions is known in advance. Once the last move is reached, an individual should defect (think of that last move as a one-shot) and this means defect will also be best on the penultimate move and so on all the way back to the very first. But, if the series of encounters goes on with no end in sight, or there is a possibility, however small (w), that the individuals will encounter one another again, then more complex encounters and strategies can emerge.

Axelrod (1984) tested this by running a computer contest in which various scientists played their strategies against one another, against themselves (unwittingly) and against random defector/cooperator strategies (with equal probability of cooperation or defection). The pay-offs were as in Table 1.1 and were iterated between pairs of contestants with w = 0.99654.

The winning strategy was the tit-for-tat strategy. This cooperated on its first move and thereafter did whatever its opponent did on the previous move. This means that tit-for-tat becomes a strategy of cooperation based on reciprocity. The strategy succeeded because it was punishing, and this discouraged defection, and it was forgiving after one punishment, which restored cooperation.

Tit-for-tat was an ESS provided w was large (Axelrod and Hamilton, 1981). It did not allow a mutant defector to take advantage. However, if an always-defect strategy emerged first this would win out, whatever the value of w, as a mutant tit-for-tat strategy would quickly get forced to the suckers pay-off where it would not get future compensation. So how could tit-for-tat ever get started as an ESS? This is still an open research question.

Whatever the answer to this question, it is the case that this strategy exists in natural populations. Wilkinson (1984) studied vampire bats (*Desmodus rotundus*) in Costa Rica that reciprocally feed one another. Individuals who did not secure a blood meal at night would beg for food from other bats and this situation could be reversed later, such that the benefactors later became altruists. Bats lose weight markedly with increasing time since their last meal. If a fed bat gave up just a small percentage of its meal to an unfed bat, this would benefit the unfed bat enormously in terms of staving off weight loss at very little cost to the fed bat. His cost-benefit asymmetry is essential to establishing tit-for-tat. Regurgitation occurred between close relatives but also between unrelated individuals who shared a roost. What is more, these bats were companions for many years, giving the opportunity for reciprocation. It could be that the bats are acting as if their neighbours are kin (Dunbar and Shultz, 2007).

BOX 1.2.   DNA

DNA, or deoxyribonucleic acid, is the molecule that forms our genetic material. DNA is found in the nucleus of the cell and has a double helix structure – two strands of sugar and phosphoric acid wind about each other and held apart by pairs of four bases: Adenine (A), Thymine (T), Guanine (G), and Cytosine (C). The structural properties of these bases mean that A always pairs with T and G always with C, as follows:

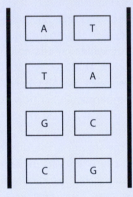

The base pair structuring allows DNA to replicate during cell division. The double helix unwinds into two strands, separating the base pairs and each strand then attracts the appropriate bases to construct its complement. Two complete helices are formed.

DNA encodes the various sequences of 20 amino acids that make up the many specific enzymes and proteins. RNA (ribonucleic acid) is also involved in this process. The message is decoded in two steps – *transcription* and *translation*. Information only goes from the DNA to the phenotype; it does not run the other way. This is the central dogma.

During transcription the sequence of base pairs on one strand of the double helix is copied to mRNA (messenger RNA). mRNA is single stranded and is formed in a similar fashion to DNA replication except that uracil substitutes for thymine such that A pairs with U. mRNA then leaves the cell nucleus, enters the cytoplasm and connects with the ribosomes, which are the location of protein formation. The next stage is translation in which the mRNA is translated into amino acid sequences. tRNA (transfer RNA) transfers amino acids to the ribosomes; each tRNA is specific to one amino acid. tRNA, with the attached amino acid, pairs up with the mRNA in a sequence dictated by the base sequence of the mRNA as the ribosome moves along the mRNA strand. Each of the 20 amino acids found in proteins is specified by a codon made up from three sequential mRNA bases. So, the mRNA triplet code GUA attracts tRNA with the complementary code CAU, and this tRNA transfers its attached amino acid, valine, which is then bonded to a growing polypeptide chain of amino acids. The next mRNA codon, say UAC, then attracts tRNA with the complementary codon AUG, which has the amino acid tyrosine attached and so on:

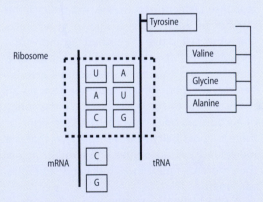

The sequence of amino acids determines the initial shape and function of the proteins.

the subsequent stages of the process. This is known as the 'central dogma of molecular biology' (Crick, 1970).

The central dogma effectively deals with a view often referred to as 'Lamarckian evolution': the idea of the inheritance of acquired characteristics as formulated by Jean-Baptiste Lamarck. If information only flows one way in order to synthesise a protein, in order to build a trait, then whatsoever happens to that trait later in terms of its development cannot affect the substrate of inheritance. So, the children of a weightlifter will not be born with bigger muscles as a consequence of their father's exercises. If he is successful at weightlifting, it is likely that he has genes that build muscles with a lot of developmental scope. His children may well inherit these genes, and if they exercise too they will resemble him in this trait, but they have only inherited the predisposition to develop muscle in a certain way.

Biological evolution relies upon genes, as we have seen, and the central dogma is a crucial aspect. For evolutionary change to occur, there must be new variation as a consequence of mutation and this variation needs to be selected. Other kinds of change can be seen over time, and one can even discuss other notions of inheritance. It could be argued that the children of the weightlifter have inherited his gym and this has led to their developing their muscles. Their children, too, inherit the gym and so on down the generations such that the characteristic of large muscles appears stable within the population. If the generations of muscle-building people are in some way favoured, perhaps because having big muscles allows more resources to be accessed through farming, then this family's descendants will increase in relative frequency. If this ability is absolutely crucial, then they could come to dominate the population.

Dickins and Dickins (2008) discuss this kind of change and draw a distinction between intrinsic and extrinsic inheritance. The children extrinsically inherit gyms, for gyms are not part of the children. Gene variants that code for relatively more muscle development in response to exercise are intrinsically inherited, for they are a part of the children. Indeed, the children are just the latest in a long line of vehicles that these particular replicators have been using. If the children inherited the gym but not the gene variants for muscle development, they would not thrive in the manner described. If the children inherited the gene variants but not the gym, they equally might not thrive, but they would have the potential to should circumstances change. Thus, there is a fundamental asymmetry at work here, which is captured by the central dogma. Extrinsic inheritance cannot alter the intrinsically inherited facts. There is no potential for true biological evolution in such systems.

The division between intrinsic and extrinsic inheritance is the key to evolutionary biology and, as we shall see, has implications for the behavioural sciences. Strict adherents to the central dogma of molecular genetics will see anything outside the genes, so any gene product or gene expression modifier, as extrinsic. The strategies that genes create are the cause of their selection, and genes effectively live or die by their strategies; but the strategies never cause the genes to change thereby altering the strategy for subsequent generations.

Plasticity and evolution

The preceding discussion may lead one to assume that evolutionary biologists believe that genomes contain all the responses to the ecology[8] that an organism will ever need. In some sense they do, as discussed in the opening comments of this chapter, but such a statement requires a qualification with regard to the granularity of the argument.

Genomes provide a capability to deal with a specific ecology, but that can mean anything from the production of rigid and fixed responses to the ability to learn. In 2001, when the first human genome was published, scientists were surprised that it consisted of between 20 and 25 000 functional genes (Venter *et al.*, 2001), not least because simpler organisms have comparable, if not larger, genomes. For example, the nematode worm (*Caenorhabditis elegans*) has a genome of 20 000 functional genes (*C. elegans* Sequencing Consortium, 1998) organised on six chromosomes. However, simpler organisms are arguably defined as simpler by dint of the restrictions upon their ecological niche. Nematode worms live in the soil in temperate environments and feed on bacteria found in decaying vegetation. They do far less, and exploit a much narrower band of resources. To this end, natural selection has built all (or many) of the solutions to the relevant ecological problems into the genome. By this definition of complexity, more complex organisms have greater ecological bandwidth as well as greater day-to-day variation in ecological change. The amount of information involved in broad bandwidth ecologies is large and would make it difficult for natural selection to incorporate into a genome whilst still maintaining coherent development. Indeed, for the most complex of organisms, those often termed 'generalists', such as rats and humans, this may be computationally intractable at the level of the genome. However, the solution has been to build mechanisms that essentially store information outside of the genome and permit learning. These include epigenetic mechanisms and nervous tissue, especially brains.

Psychologists are well aware that brains store many, many more bits of information than the human genome (Pinker, 1997). We will return to the proximate detail of psychology later in the chapter, but for now we should note that learning mechanisms, which take account of specific aspects of ecology, have been selected for. This allows for great flexibility and the overall generalist strategy that typifies humans, accounting for their wide dispersal across the planet.

Epigenetic mechanisms are increasingly drawing attention in evolutionary biology (e.g. Jablonka and Lamb, 2005). Epigenetics, as a discipline, is primarily concerned with the development of organisms. In this way, epigenetics contributes to discussions and theories about how final adult form is produced. It is not specifically an evolutionary

---

[8] The term 'environment' refers to everything that is outside of something else, what that something is surrounded by. The term 'ecology' refers to that aspect of the environment something is adapted to use. So, the human eye has been selected to deal with a portion of the electromagnetic spectrum and that portion defines its visual ecology. Birds use other portions of the same spectrum and thus inhabit different visual ecologies. The electromagnetic spectrum is part of a shared environment for avian species and humans. Therefore, the term 'ecology' is an evolutionary one, whereas 'environment' is not. Behavioural scientists who discuss environmental effects are most likely not evolutionarily minded.

theory, but rather the study of particular proximate mechanisms involved in development. However, a number of researchers think that epigenetic processes have implications for our understanding of evolution.

Epigenetics literally means 'above genetics', implying that there is something operating above the standard genetic inheritance that has been discussed so far in this chapter. More crucially, researchers in this field often refer to the notion of epigenetic inheritance, which, on the surface, can appear to be a Lamarckian process. The core idea is that the expression of genes can be affected by extrinsic factors and that sometimes these effects can be passed along generations without any changes to the DNA sequence that constitutes the genes in question. For example, Jablonka and Lamb (2005) note that liver cells, kidney cells, skin cells and so on all have identical DNA but, all things being equal, they continue to produce daughter cells of the same kind, so skin cells beget skin cells in spite of the potential in the DNA to do otherwise. Jablonka and Lamb (2005) see the extrinsic factors affecting gene expression as epigenetic inheritance systems. These include systems that alter RNA functions, and therefore transcription, systems that alter the chromatin packaging of DNA and systems that attach methyl groups to cytosine.

To the behavioural scientist, these epigenetic inheritance systems could appear to be of distant relevance to their topic. Crews (2008) refers to these concerns as 'molecular epigenetics', which he contrasts with molar epigenetics which emerged from the move to functionalism within psychology. Specifically, Crews discusses how comparative psychology became focused upon the interaction of genetic endowments and other biological systems with the environment, and how these interactions led to species-typical behaviours developing from conception to death. In so doing, Crews is also referring to the origin of epigenetics in debates about preformation, which began with Aristotle (see Depew and Weber, 1996).

Molar epigenetics, of course, relies on molecular effects at some point. Where functional psychologists are interested in particular environmental (and therefore ecological) effects upon development, they must assume that the environmental aspect of concern is, to all intents and purposes, acting as an input for the organism and affecting development. As can be seen from work on the effects of maternal care upon offspring stress response (see Box 1.3), it would seem that epigenetic mechanisms allow organisms to track key, yet changeable, aspects of the ecology across generations without irreversibly altering DNA. In times of risk, as in the maternal care example, increasing the sensitivity of stress response in one's offspring, as well as oneself, is useful. In this way, the epigenetic mechanisms are processing information and solving problems for the organism and, therefore, can be seen as candidate adaptations.

As extrinsic factors can lead, through epigenetic inheritance, to the introduction of different variants of form, and these variants can then be carried across generations at some increased frequency, it looks like an evolutionary change. But, by the definitions given above, this is not so. Given that there is no change to the DNA, the central dogma of molecular genetics remains intact. Gene-level selection has not been challenged and, as said, we can think of epigenetic mechanisms as possible adaptations and therefore as selected precisely to track specific kinds of ecological change

BOX 1.3. MATERNAL CARE AND EPIGENETICS

Champagne (2008) has reviewed the literature on maternal care and epigenetic inheritance. Much work has been conducted in rodent models, investigating the role of licking and grooming behaviour (henceforth grooming) in the development of pups. In mice, when pups are prevented from attaining the normal amount of interactions with their mothers it has been shown that those pups go on to nurse their own pups less and engage in less grooming behaviour toward them. In short, the maternal strategy is inherited. In Long-Evans rats the amount of grooming engaged in by mothers varies between individuals but is a stable individual trait; it is also inherited by their offspring such that daughters of low-frequency grooming mothers will in turn be low frequency grooming mothers to their offspring. Fostering studies indicate that this inheritance is not genetic but rather modified by behaviour. This would appear to be a candidate for molar epigenetic explanation and Champagne's overview is worth examining in detail:

A number of nuclei in the brain have been associated with the activation of maternal care but the medial preoptic area in the hypothalamus appears to be crucial. Female rats that are low on grooming and are lactating have relatively low oxytocin receptor binding in the medial preoptic area in contrast to high grooming females. Oxytocin is a neurohormone implicated in reducing social inhibition and facilitating affiliative and kin bonding. Champagne notes that experimentally introducing an oxytocin receptor binding antagonist reduces grooming in previously high grooming females.

There is a role for mesolimbic dopamine in grooming. Dopamine increases evenly prior to the onset of grooming in high grooming females. This is released in the nucleus acumbens. The amount of dopamine released directly predicts how long the mother will engage in grooming, and upon cessation the dopamine level returns to baseline. In those mothers who are low in grooming there is no substantial increase in dopamine activity and the behaviour is short-lived. The current hypothesis is that the hypothalamic oxytocin neurons mediate this mesolimbic response and cause the stable individual differences between mothers in terms of maternal care.

Grooming will affect stress response in pups. The hypothalamic-pituitary-adrenal axis (HPA-axis) delivers what is sometimes referred to as a passive stress response. Corticotropin-releasing factor (CRF) is synthesised, stored and released by neurons in the hypothalamus – specifically at the paraventricular nucleus (PVN). Neurons elsewhere in the brain, which respond to fear stimuli, stimulate these hypothalamic neurons to secrete CRF into a local blood vessel. This then travels a short distance to the pituitary gland, which contains CRF receptors, and this in turn stimulates the secretion of adrenocorticotrophic hormone (ACTH). ACTH is a classical hormone and is distributed throughout the entire blood stream, targeting the distant adrenal gland where ACTH stimulates a class of hormones known as 'corticosteroids'.

Corticosteroids are released from the outer layer of the adrenal gland. Corticosteroids are involved in responses to threat and help to mobilise energy by releasing stored glucose. More precisely they break down proteins (from muscles and other tissues) into amino acids that are then used in the liver to synthesise glucose at critical times. This energy is directed to key sites. Corticosteroids also cause the release of fatty acids, or lipids, which are another source of energy.

The release of corticosteroids from the adrenal gland sends an inhibitory signal back to the hippocampus, which in turn inhibits PVN activity. This negative feedback loop, when functioning properly, sees to it that just enough corticosteroid action is produced to remove the stressor or remove the organism from the stressful situation. If this malfunctions it can lead to a prolonged stress response in the absence of any stressor as well as neurotoxic effects.

Champagne (2008) notes that pups of mothers who are low in grooming have a particular HPA response. They maintain heightened adrenocorticotropin and corticosterone levels after exposure to stressors. These pups also have a reduction in hippocampal glucocorticoid receptor mRNA and an increase in hypothalamic CRF mRNA thereby making the maintenance of baseline corticosteroids problematic once a stressor is removed. Thus the stress response is prolonged and there is the potential for neurotoxic effects. Those pups that receive less grooming have relatively elevated corticosteroid levels after exposure to a stressor. It is known that this has behavioural effects such as a reduction in exploratory behaviour and an increase in inhibition. In short, it leads to behavioural depression.

The individual differences in hypothalamic activity associated with high and low grooming are found in the pups of high and low mothers such that the pups of low grooming mothers have relatively low oxytocin receptor binding in the postpartum period. The pups of low grooming mothers also display low oestrogen sensitivity. Oestrogen normally increases the expression of the oxytocin receptor gene, and at parturition pups are normally exposed to high oestrogen, which in turn should lead to increased oxytocin receptor binding. The insensitivity in the pups of low grooming mothers is like that found in mice that lack a functioning copy of the oestrogen receptor alpha, which is involved in affecting gene expression, thus causing a reduction in the ability of oestrogen

affect upon that expression. In the offspring of low grooming mothers the expression of oestrogen receptor alpha is reduced relative to that of high grooming mothers, which potentially will affect the oxytocin activity in the medial preoptic area. What is more, fostering experiments have revealed that this alteration to gene expression is affected by postnatal maternal care – low-grooming mothers cause a reduction in the level of oestrogen receptor in the medial preoptic area of the hypothalamus. This has been linked to high levels of methylation at a number of sites in the promoter region of oestrogen receptor alpha.

Stressed mothers expose their *in utero* offspring to higher levels of glucocorticoids and the offspring in turn have increased levels of plasma corticosterone and CRF mRNA in the amygdala. This leads to behavioural depression as noted above. Normally high-grooming mothers that are experimentally stressed in the final week of pregnancy produce low-grooming behaviours of the sort associated with a reduction in hypothalamic oxytocin action. The relationship between stress exposure and low grooming remains unknown but the low grooming will induce the effects discussed.

In summary: Low maternal care affects the expression of a gene that is crucial to the development of the neurobiology of maternal care. In so doing, low maternal care is inherited. The affect of low maternal care is to alter the passive stress response in offspring and through the epigenetic inheritance of maternal care this response can also be passed along a number of generations. Methylation is not irreversible and there is evidence that postnatal behaviours, such as social enrichment, can switch the low maternal care lineage back to high maternal care by attenuating the HPA response. In this way, the organism can react to the environment and prepare its offspring for a similar future but not irreversibly so. This is a form of transgenerational learning, not an evolutionary change.

(Dickins and Dickins, 2007). Indeed, epigenetic mechanisms can be compared with brains as they are effectively designed to learn about specific aspects of the ecology and to respond to them. The flexibility of epigenetic learning relative to neural learning is unknown, and epigenetic mechanisms clearly affect brain development. To this end, epigenetic mechanisms can perhaps be referred to as a 'pre-brain'.

FITNESS, SOCIOBIOLOGY AND LIFE HISTORY THEORY

Fitness is a much used concept in evolutionary biology and it has at least five different senses (Dawkins, 1983). The sense of most relevance to this chapter is that of 'classical fitness', as Dawkins labels it, which originated within the discipline of ecology. Classical fitness (henceforth, fitness) is a property attributed to an individual organism and is 'often expressed as the product of survival and fecundity' (Dawkins, 1983, p. 183). Put crudely, the longer one survives and the more one reproduces, the fitter one is. Indeed, the empirical application of this notion is often referred to as 'baby-counting'. Fitness, then, captures the fundamental dynamic at the heart of Darwin's formulation of evolution through natural selection: traits only reach fixity through successful reproduction, and the more offspring an individual has, the more copies of its genes it gets into the gene pool. Dawkins (1983, p. 184) discusses the limitations of this concept and arrives at the following:

> Ideally we might count the relative number of descendants alive after some very large number of generations. But such an 'ideal' measure has the curious property that, if carried to its logical conclusion, it can take only two values; it is an all-or-none measure. If we look far enough into the future, either I shall have no descendants at all, or all persons alive will be my descendants . . . If I am descended from a particular individual male who lived a million years ago, it is virtually certain that you are descended from him too. The fitness of any particular long-dead individual, as measured in present day descendants, is either zero or total.

In spite of this caution, we can attribute fitness to an organism within a limited timeframe and in so doing use it to model the evolutionary success or failure of its behaviours. Moreover, we can discuss the strategies implemented by genes as more or less fit. Fitness has a central place in evolutionary behavioural science, as is evident from the early developments in sociobiology. Sociobiology was a term applied by Wilson (1975/2000) to an amalgamation of proximate biology, behavioural ecology, ethology and a number of other disciplines. Wilson had paid close attention to various theoretical innovations in evolutionary biology and noted the success of gene-level explanations. Wilson also understood that social behaviour was a fertile ground for the 'new' evolutionary explanations and in particular he focused upon the problem of altruism. If genes were to be understood as self-interested replicators, then what could altruism have been selected for? Altruism is, by definition, an act that confers a benefit on another at some cost to oneself. In fitness terms, an individual altruistic act, understood in isolation, is bad news for the altruist and good news for the benefactor.

The initial explanations for altruism centred on kin selection. Given that relatives share some genetic variants[9] (or alleles) with you, an investment in a relative is a proportional investment in your own genes. The degree of relatedness is expressed as r. A full sibling has an r of 0.5, as they share 50% of their gene variants with you; a nephew or niece has an r of 0.25. It is the same for descendant kin. A child shares 50% of its gene variants with its parent, and a grandparent shares 25% of its gene variants with its grandchild. As genetic relatedness decreases, it might be predicted that the willingness to invest and the amount invested would also decrease. Haldane famously quipped that he would jump into a river to save two brothers or eight cousins, thereby capturing the logic of this argument. However, the real issue is when altruistic and, therefore, costly behaviour would emerge and stabilise within a population; that is, under what conditions would altruism benefit fitness? It was Hamilton (1964) who brought the mathematical precision of game theory to the notion, expressing the relationship between costs, benefits and relatedness as follows:

$$C_a < r_{ab} B_b$$

where C is the cost, B the benefit, r relatedness, a the donor and b the recipient. So, the cost to individual a has to be less than the product of the relatedness of a to individual b and the value of the benefit. So, if I am in the business of benefiting my brother at a cost of one unit (say £1) to me then the benefit must be worth more than two units (say £2.10) to him. For example:

$$C \, (\pounds1 \text{ from Tom}) < r(0.5)B(\pounds2.10 \text{ to Ben})$$

What this means is that altruistic behaviour will stabilise in a population whenever the cost of the act is offset by the indirect fitness benefits of assisting a relative. If this is not the case, then selection will not permit such altruism. Hamilton's rule captures the parameters of this relationship.

Kin selection is not a complete account of altruistic behaviour, for we see altruism between non-relatives. Hamilton and colleagues applied game theory here too, most

---

[9] My father, David Dickins, taught me a valuable pedagogical trick when I was younger. If you ask a group of students how much genetic commonality they have with chimps, they usually report a figure between 95 and 98%. Then, when you ask them how much genetic commonality they have with their brother or sister, they unflinchingly state that it is 50%. So, you conclude aloud, you have more in common with a chimp than your own sibling. This focuses the subsequent discussion. The students are conflating two uses of genetic commonality. On the one hand, we do have about 95% of the same *kinds* of genes as chimps, whilst on the other hand we have 50% of the exact same *variants* of genes as our siblings. This is a type-token distinction.

notably with the Prisoner's Dilemma (see Box 1.2 for details). As we have seen with this game, one-shot interactions favour defection but iterated games with an uncertain number of interactions spread across time allow for the emergence of a tit-for-tat strategy. This notion of incurring a cost for another individual's benefit, and in the future attaining a benefit from them, is referred to as 'reciprocal altruism' (Trivers, 1971).

As the vampire bat example demonstrates, reciprocal altruism is in essence a form of trade and it flourishes when each individual gains more in benefits than it cost them to be altruistic. Giving up a small portion of a blood meal to another is low cost to the donor but extremely significant to the future fitness of the benefactor. Given this asymmetry, it means that the future fitness benefits for the initial donor, when that individual is in need of a donation from the initial benefactor, far outweigh the costs first accrued. To this end, altruism will stabilise in the population, as it will be selected for. Ecologically, this is dependent upon a high degree of uncertainty over resource acquisition such that any bat could find itself unfed.

The problem of altruism firmly established evolutionary game theory as an essential tool for assessing the fitness of competing behavioural strategies. However, the fitness of successful strategies is understood in terms of the average pay-off over an extended period. This does not capture the dynamic nature of 'lived strategies' over the course of an organism's lifetime. This issue is addressed by life history theory, which has also emerged from the discipline of Ecology (Stearns, 1992).

The core assumption of life history theory is that organisms are fitness maximisers: they seek optimal fitness. Fitness maximisation is not a one-shot game. Organisms develop to adulthood, reproduce, grow old and die.[10] Across all of these stages, organisms have access to different kinds and differing levels of resources, owing to changes in local ecological conditions, which they can invest in their fitness and decisions have to be made about what, when and how much to invest. These decisions are the outcome of naturally selected strategies.

Strategically, organisms can either attempt to delay mortality, and thereby buy more time for reproduction, or alter the onset of fertility, where 'fertility' refers to the amount of reproduction rather than the biological capacity to reproduce. Given this, fitness maximisation is changeable across lifespan and can be characterised by a set of energetic trade-offs (Kaplan and Gangestad, 2005). These are current versus future reproduction, quantity versus the quality of offspring and mating versus parenting effort.

Work on clutch size in bird populations provides a good example of such trade-offs. Each egg represents a possible chick and therefore a possible reproducing adult. In this way, an egg is an investment in future fitness for the adult pair that produces it. Each egg also represents a number of costs: they are energetically, and hence

---

[10] Life history theory explains why organisms senesce and therefore die (Kirkwood, 1997). Put briefly, in order to maintain a body the organism has to invest energy. If this investment led to perfect maintenance, then any extra energetic investment would not alter maintenance and would be wasted. At this point it would make sense to redirect that investment to reproduction, thereby increasing fitness. Given this, it is in an organism's interests to let the body decay and allocate resources to reproduction instead. This is referred to as the 'disposable soma theory'.

nutritionally, expensive to produce; any chicks represent further energetic investment in terms of feeding, which has to be balanced against effort to feed oneself; the more eggs and chicks one has, the more such resources have to be divided. Resources are finite and differ between ecologies such that one would expect to see different decisions reached in different circumstances.

David Lack (1947) was perhaps the first to discuss the clutch size issue for birds in these terms. His initial hypothesis was that the number of chicks that survived would be in a linear and inverse relationship to the number of eggs in a clutch. So, as clutch size went up, chick survivorship went down. This would be a consequence of the finite nature of resources and the division across mouths.

Casual observation of wild birds would indicate that Lack's hypothesis was correct, and indeed a number of clutch size manipulation experiments have appeared to support him (Stearns, 1992). However, it appears that there are complexities that Lack overlooked. Boyce and Perrins (1987) reported on a 22-year study of 4489 clutches of great tits (*Parus major*) in an Oxfordshire woodland. They found that the average clutch size was 8.53 eggs, but the clutch size with the highest rate of chick survivability was 12. Furthermore, the results of clutch size manipulation experiments, where clutch sizes were increased by three, again showed 12 to yield the best survivorship. It would appear that the great tits could have laid more eggs, and this violates Lack's initial hypothesis.

Boyce and Perrins (1987) have revealed some assumptions at the heart of Lack's hypothesis. First, great tits have a lifespan of three years on average (though the oldest recorded, according to the British Trust for Ornithology, was almost 14 years), begin reproducing at one year and can potentially produce more than one brood in a season. So, great tits can produce somewhere between two and four clutches before death, and if predation and other risks are reduced, many more. This means that any investment in a current brood needs to be traded off against future investments. A current versus future trade-off is likely to alter the outcome of Lack's initial hypothesis and will lead to clutch size varying according to the resource richness of the ecology, the ability of the adults to capture these resources and their ability to begin a new brood in short order after the first has fledged. There is also the issue of the quality of the offspring. It is possible that, given resources, producing fewer eggs and fewer chicks will improve their quality and that they will in turn be more likely to successfully reproduce. So, there may be a quantity/quality trade-off to consider. Indeed, the initial measure of chick survivorship may not be the best measure of fitness, but perhaps the reproductive success of the parents' chicks is.

As these avian examples show, life history theory sees an organism's task as that of capturing energy and using it to maintain itself and to reproduce (Kaplan and Gangestad, 2005). This job leads to one of the key trade-offs, that between current and future reproduction, with only three possible outcomes: no current reproduction, some energy allocation in the present and some in the future, and total reproduction in the present followed by death. All of these outcomes are seen in natural populations.

A strategy of no current reproduction is rare and is generally a consequence of resource stress. In anorexic girls, poor nutrition will lead to cessation of menstruation whilst the body directs what resources there are to maintain life (see Chan and Mantzoros, 2005); there are clearly mechanisms for switching fertility off. It is also worth noting that in economically stressed populations, such as those in Addis Ababa, Ethiopia, the fertility rate is declining and is now below replacement fertility (1.9[11]; Gurmu and Mace, 2008).

Pacific salmon (*Oncorhynchus spp.*) spawn in their natal river, with females producing thousands of eggs in a number of nest sites, which are then fertilised by the males. During their long journey from the ocean back to these freshwater rivers, the salmon deplete their fat stores and general somatic capital dramatically, with many adults not surviving the journey. Spawning marks the end of the adult life cycle and within a couple of days the adults die. This is a case of total current fertility.

Allocating energy across current and future reproduction is the typical pattern of fertility in humans, and many other species, including great tits. This strategy is not without variation between individuals, and a large part of this variation is the result of facultative or conditional responses to ecological conditions. The literature on teenage pregnancy provides an excellent case study of such effects.

Teenage pregnancy is generally defined as pregnancy under the age of 18 years. The United Kingdom has the highest rate of teenage pregnancy in Western Europe. In England, in 2007, 41.7 in every one thousand girls aged between 15 and 17 years had a conception and 50.6% of those conceptions were terminated.[12] Girls from low socioeconomic status backgrounds are at least four times more likely to have a teenage conception than girls from wealthier backgrounds, and poorer girls are far less likely to abort should they become pregnant (Lee *et al.*, 2004). Given that socioeconomic status is a key indicator of ecological conditions, the fact that there are distinct differences across these groups indicates a possible adapted fertility strategy. It is possible that the ecological conditions faced by these women are prompting them to favour current reproduction. To this end, we may wish to think about teenage pregnancy as the extreme end of a general early fertility strategy.

There are a number of theories about what it is that prompts females to early fertility. These theories assume that particular aspects of the environment inform developing females about a likely future. If these cues lead to the prediction that there is an uncertain or poor trajectory, development is hastened and these females enter into a fast life history. This will include growing smaller bodies, diverting resources to reproductive physiology and beginning sexual behaviours sooner (Hawkes, 1994; Hill, 1993). Such cues would appear to induce development.

A candidate developmental inducement is father absence. Belsky, Steinberg and Draper (1991) propose that attachment is related to judgements about possible futures. Specifically, they see puberty as the beginning of independence for an individual: they are readying themselves to be a sexual adult. According to Belsky *et al.*, any perception of risk in the current childhood environment is more likely

---

[11] A fertility rate of 1.9 means that every 100 mothers produce 190 children; replacement fertility is usually agreed to be 2.2.

[12] Statistics taken from the Teenage Pregnancy Unit; available online at http://www.everychildmatters.gov.uk/teenagepregnancy/.

to cause earlier puberty. So, what they found is daughters raised in a single-parent, father-absent family are more likely to reach menarche sooner than those raised by both a mother and father are. The reasoning behind this is that father absence suggests a lack of resources, such that an optimal decision would be to reproduce sooner rather than later whilst still healthy, and so on. Risks other than father absence will also lead to this effect.

Chisholm (1999) places this social and developmental psychological theory within the context of life history theory and interprets early puberty, as a consequence of exposure to risk, as a fitness maximising strategy. Various behavioural aspects of earlier sexual behaviour are clearly candidates for psychological decisions, albeit unconscious according to Belsky *et al.*, but menarche looks to be a physiological decision. Belsky *et al.* also note that risk is not necessarily the only factor. They point, for example, to clear heritable variation in onset of menarche, such that maternal age of menarche is a good predictor.

A number of studies (Cater and Coleman, 2006; Lee *et al.*, 2004) have also demonstrated conscious decision-making about fertility that indicates reasoning in terms of current versus future reproduction. It would seem that a number of teenage pregnancies are in fact planned and that many young women in high-risk, low-socioeconomic status positions realise that the best time for them to reproduce is now rather than later. In part, this is because they are young and as healthy as they are going to be, but it is also because they can call upon their own parents for support. All told, girls in poorer environments are more likely to allocate effort and resources to current reproduction (Dickins, 2006; Wilson and Daly, 1997). More recently, in an extension of the Belsky *et al.* argument, Nettle, Coall and Dickins (2010) have shown that lack of paternal involvement and low birth weight predict both intended and actual early fertility in a British population.

Life history theory enables scientists to make predictions about and explain population level patterns of behavioural and general trait variation. Understanding how organisms are likely to react to their ecology is clearly of enormous use and it helps to guide a subsequent set of questions about the proximate mechanisms that may deliver behaviour. Indeed, life history theory is fundamentally a black-box approach to the proximate mechanisms that lead to optimal fitness. There is no need to say or assume anything about these mechanisms when discussing the fitness benefits of particular behavioural strategies; but we can be assured that mechanisms do exist to deliver evolved strategic behaviour, and once we have evidence for maximisation this then becomes the focus of evolutionary psychology.

EVOLUTIONARY PSYCHOLOGY

In its simplest guise, evolutionary psychology is the application of evolutionary theory to psychology. Historically, evolutionary thinking led to the emergence of comparative psychology and many modern psychologists rely on animal models in order to explain behaviour, often generalising their conclusions to humans. In recent years, however, evolutionary psychology has become strongly associated with a particular school of thought emerging from the laboratory of Leda Cosmides and John Tooby at the University of California at Santa Barbara. This school sought to provide proximate explanations of key findings from sociobiology at the cognitive level.

As we have seen, game theory has helped us to understand the selection parameters for cooperative altruism. Once cooperation emerges within a population, other strategies can co-exist including defection, or cheating. This does not mean that cheating can beat the strategy of cooperative altruism, for this is an evolutionarily stable strategy. But the existence of an evolutionarily stable strategy does not imply that there are no other strategies available, and it is possible to have more than one evolutionarily stable strategy within a population (for a discussion see Maynard-Smith, 1982).

Cheating can operate in a number of ways within a generally cooperative population. For example, sociopathy can be understood as an example of a cheating strategy embodied in a stable personality variable (Mealey, 1995; see also Nettle, 2006). Sociopathic individuals rely on cooperative first moves of individuals within the population and they defect. After a while, the reputation of a sociopath precedes them and they shift populations. In this way, sociopathy is a parasitic life history strategy and is also evolutionarily stable. Another and more common way in which cheating exists in populations is by happenstance. If we assume that individuals are interested in benefiting their own fitness, we can further assume that if they see an opportunity to defect and feel that they can get away with it, they will. Intuitively, you can predict that within large modern populations, such as our own, there are numerous occasions when we effectively have only one-shot interactions with people. If individuals encounter such an opportunity on the off-chance, then they are more likely to defect. Furthermore, such situations should be a rich hunting ground for confidence tricksters and will be subject to stringent laws, should the potential costs be significant.

I am reminded of an occasion whilst on holiday in France. My friend and I had travelled across to France from the United Kingdom in her car, which was a right-hand-drive vehicle. She was driving and I was in the passenger seat. As we entered a motorway, we approached the tollbooth, which was on my side. Fresh arrivals, we only had large denomination notes and I was sorting through them as we pulled up to the booth. The man in the booth said something fast in French and I saw ten francs come up on the display. I handed him a note and he said something else that I could not decode rapidly. At the same time, he hit the switch, the light went green, the barrier went up and my companion moved off – before I could receive any change. I only lost ten francs but I remember both of us being annoyed. The man had relied on my poor French, my unfamiliarity with the currency and my companion's focus upon the road to defect on what should be a cooperative strategy of maintaining France's highways. He also knew I would never see him again as I was clearly heading away from his neighbourhood. It was a perfect defection.

Our annoyance was not just at the loss of money but also at my gullibility. In discussion, it was felt that I should have made it clear I was expecting change and told my companion to wait until I received it. We both clearly felt that I should have been more sensitive to the possibility that we could be cheated in this situation; we both had a sense that a social contract had been violated.

Cosmides and Tooby argue that, given the possibility of being cheated in the manner just described, humans should have evolved psychological mechanisms that make them sensitive to situations where they may be cheated (Cosmides, 1989; Cosmides and Tooby, 1992). Put more colloquially, Cosmides and Tooby (1992) argue that humans should have psychological mechanisms for cheater detection. Such strategies would be selected for as they reduce costs and benefit fitness.

Cosmides and Tooby note that cooperation between individuals is a form of social contract, just as my companion and I did. Individual *a* agrees to do *x* for individual *b* on the understanding that at some point in the future *b* will do *y* for *a*. This is the logic of tit-for-tat: if you scratch my back, I'll scratch yours. This structure is that of a conditional rule. In order to be sensitive to cheating, one must be able to check that a conditional rule, a social contract, is being followed and not violated.

There is a large literature on people's ability to detect violations in conditional arguments and much of it centres upon the Wason Selection Task (WST). Wason (1966) developed a card selection task in order to see whether people will, when asked to check the veracity of a conditional rule, attempt to falsify or verify it. Wason's interest stemmed from Popperian notions about the demarcation of science from non-science and he was curious to see if falsification was a natural human ability. The basic task is presented in Figure 1.2a.

The WST consists of variants about a core problem that focuses upon four marked cards, only one side of which can be seen. In the original version, two of the cards had letters marking them, one vowel and one consonant, and two had numbers, one even and one odd. The task was to say which of the cards it was essential to turn over to check the rule 'If a card has a vowel on one side then it has an even number on the other'. The logical way to do this is to attempt to falsify the rule by turning over the vowel card and the odd-number card. If the vowel card has an odd number on the back, then the rule is falsified, if the odd-number card has a vowel on the back, the rule is again falsified. On average, less than 9% of people make the correct choice in this form of the WST (see Evans, Newstead and Byrne, 1993, for a discussion).

People seem poorly equipped for abstract conditional reasoning and much experimental effort has been spent trying to facilitate performance by making the problems less abstract. Cosmides (1989; Cosmides and Tooby, 1992) hypothesises that placing the WST within the context of a social contract should lead to significant facilitation, because human psychology should be biased towards this kind of reasoning, given

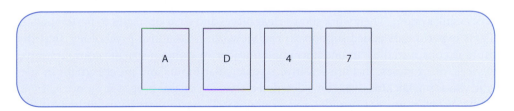

Figure 1.2a. *Wason Selection Task: Abstract Form.*

Task: Which of the cards is it essential to turn over to check the rule? If a card has a vowel on one side then it has an even number on the other.

Answer: A and 7.

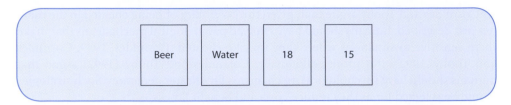

Figure 1.2b. *Wason Selection Task: Social Version.*

Task: You are a member of bar staff in a pub. Each of the cards above represents an individual customer in the bar. There is information about age on one side and chosen drink on another. Which of the cards is it essential to turn over to check the rule: if a person is drinking alcohol they must be 18 years or older.

Answer: Beer and 15.

Source: Based on Cosmides (1989).

the arguments above. To this end, a series of experiments was conducted in which social contracts were used (an example is given in Figure 1.2b) and, as predicted, performance was massively enhanced: on average people make the correct choice in the task and will uncover any potential defection. It would seem that this aspect of psychology is designed to take and process specific inputs in a specific way.

Game theory tells us of parameters for selection of particular traits. From this, we have been able to tell much about the nature of cooperation at the population level. The innovation of Cosmides and Tooby has been to realise that, for those strategies to stabilise, there must be specific psychology in place. In other words, they have sought to uncover the proximate psychological mechanisms that would prevent rampant cheating from threatening the cohesion of a cooperating group. Sociopaths move on because people eventually realise what they are doing and even if they are not punished they lose their opportunity to parasitise. Given the nature of our ecology, the uncertainty over quite how many interactions we are to have with others and uncertainty about the stability of resource acquisition our fitness is maximised through cooperation, on average. This effect has been replicated many times, across cultures, and there is some evidence for specific neurological sites of action (Stone *et al.*, 2002; Sugiyama, Tooby and Cosmides, 2002).

Cosmides and Tooby (1992) go further than simply demonstrating a social contract facilitation effect. They also use this set of experiments to make a number of theoretical claims about evolved psychology. First, they argue that the specificity of response in their experiments is evidence against the idea that cognition is a general processing system. Their work shows clear biases and clear obstacles to performance. Their experiments added support to the view, from cognitive psychology, that the mind is constituted by an undetermined number of domain-specific computational devices, or modules, that are sensitive to particular inputs and process them in specific ways (see Dickins, 2003, for a detailed discussion of this proposal; Samuels, 1998, 2000). What is more, Cosmides and Tooby (1992) argue that the modularity claim made sense from the perspective of natural selection. Selection resolves particular contingent problems for organisms at particular points in evolutionary time as those problems arise. This means that selection builds isolable and discrete traits one by one. The mind will be structured in the same manner, with new psychological mechanisms, or modules, bolted on as and when selection pressures demand.

These latter arguments about cognitive organisation are secondary to the task of evolutionary behavioural science. Experimental manipulations of human participants, or subjects from other species for that matter, that can demonstrate the nuts and bolts of evolved conditional strategies are the main work of evolutionary psychology, and this area has thrived since the early work of Cosmides and Tooby, as the chapters in this book attest.

CONCLUSION

This chapter has not aimed to be exhaustive and has merely scratched the surface of evolutionary approaches to behaviour. What this chapter has done is to reinforce the purpose of applying evolutionary theory within the behavioural sciences, and that is to account for design. In so doing the basic mechanics of evolution have been described and the influence of gene-level thinking, notions of fitness and game theory have been shown at work in life history theory, the main theoretical framework of behavioural ecology and evolutionary psychology.

The kind of evolutionary psychology discussed can be seen as very narrow in its focus. Psychology, as a discipline, covers many areas such as social psychology, developmental psychology, health psychology, clinical psychology and so on. It is really only cognitive psychology that attempts to model the mind, and the proximate mechanisms that cause behaviour. The other subdisciplines are all behavioural, but also proximal, in their focus.

One of the key problems that the behavioural sciences face is the individuation of behaviours and subsequently of the mechanisms that cause them. The adoption of evolutionary theory resolves this issue. It will not inform scientists about the detail of mechanisms, but it will inform them about what the organism needs to achieve and, in so doing, will give information about the kinds of mechanisms the organism must have. To this end, the project of evolutionary psychology, as captured in this book, can be seen more broadly than in the previous section; indeed, it should be seen as an amalgamation of population-level modelling and proximate-level theorising and experimentation.

This broad approach sees organisms as calibrating to their ecology by capturing information. As said at the beginning of the chapter, those inputs that are informative are so simply because of the evolved design of the system using them. What genetics, epigenetics, life history theory and evolutionary psychology show us is that organisms are a hierarchy of calibrating, conditional mechanisms that afford facultative responding to key aspects of the environment at appropriate times. Systems that permit heritable change operate on a generational timescale and can help organisms to forecast the future (Bateson *et al.*, 2004); systems, such as proximate physiological and psychological responding, can afford day-to-day calibration, much as our robot can avoid new obstacles when they are encountered and we are sensitive to new possibilities for defection. Natural selection has built the constraints to all these mechanisms and in so doing has captured facts about change and the parameters of change.

When discussing life history theory and early fertility, general population level distinctions were made using socioeconomic status as an index of ecological hardship and risk. The general argument was that females in harder, higher-risk ecologies would be more likely to opt for an early fertility strategy and this would be embodied within physiological development and behavioural decisions. The evolutionary reason for this is that early reproduction under these circumstances would maximise fitness as current risk is informative of future risk and, therefore, the accumulation of resources cannot be relied on. As this is a black-box approach, the nature of information processing was not discussed in very much detail, but this is clearly something that evolutionary behavioural science should address. How might we begin to do this?

First, the hypotheses of Belsky, Steinberg and Draper (1991) require further work. Is it the case that early menarche is indicative of early reproduction? It certainly affords the opportunity for early reproduction, but it is also possibly a side effect of other aspects of low socioeconomic ecologies. The recent work of Nettle et al. (2010) has begun to address this issue. Second, it is worth noting that it is not the case that the majority of girls in low socioeconomic status groups have teenage pregnancies; it is very much a minority. Given this, it would be fair to argue that teenage conceptions represent the extreme end of an early fertility strategy. What is it that is different about teenage girls in this minority? Psychology has a strong tradition of individual differences research,[13] and personality differences would be the place to start.

Nettle (2006) argues that the 'Big Five' personality traits of Extraversion, Neuroticism, Openness to Experience, Conscientiousness and Agreeableness capture heritable life history strategies. Central to his thesis is the idea that these strategies are held in the population through frequency-dependent selection. The earlier example of sociopathy is also a probable case of frequency-dependent selection (Mealey, 1995). As noted, sociopaths rely on the cooperative first moves of others and they then defect. One constraint on sociopaths is the number, or frequency, of sociopaths in the group. If the frequency of sociopaths is too high, there will be insufficient people to parasitise as too many will be waiting to defect and not cooperating. Because of this, sociopathy is capped within the population; it can never go to saturation, even though it is a candidate evolutionarily stable strategy. This is the essence of frequency-dependent selection. Nettle argues that the Big Five personality traits are held in the population in the same way and represent particular ecological niches.

Nettle's (2006) treatment of Neuroticism is pertinent to early fertility. According to Nettle, Neuroticism conveys particular advantages, including vigilance to dangers as well as increasing striving and competitive behaviours. There are, of course, costs, and these are typically stress and depression. Those girls who become teenage mothers may well be more sensitive to the risks in their ecology than others are,

---

[13] Research into individual differences has been a core component of psychology since Darwin, as scientists were keen to measure trait variation, because variation is a core component for natural selection, as we have seen.

and this may be what shifts them into very early fertility. Such sensitivities may well put females in low-socioeconomic environments ahead of the curve in terms of their fitness and one may predict a higher occurrence of Neuroticism within these populations more generally. What is more, there is an association in the literature between teenage pregnancy and depression (Azar *et al.*, 2007). This has been related to hypothalamic-pituitary-adrenal axis (HPA-axis) dysregulation, presenting the possibility for an endocrine explanation focusing upon cortisol function. Cortisol dysregulation is also associated with Neuroticism (McCleery and Goodwin, 2001; Oswald *et al.*, 2006). Such things will be genetically heritable, but there is every reason to investigate epigenetic possibilities too given the preceding discussion.

Cognitive psychological questions can also be investigated as we may predict differences in performance on reasoning about the future. This can be captured in terms of the consideration of future consequences (Strathman *et al.*, 1994), time preference and future discounting (Frederick, Loewenstein and O'Donoghue, 2002). There is also reason to look to genetic differences between early- and late-fertility females (Mendle *et al.*, 2009).

This discussion is merely presenting the reader with loose hypotheses. They will need much refining before a proper research programme can be undertaken and results collected. However, they serve to demonstrate how the evolutionary behavioural scientist can begin with population-level concerns, ask questions from a life history perspective and refine knowledge about the patterns of behaviour in and between groups. This work provides a basis for evolutionary psychologists with interests in proximate mechanisms to begin their investigations. Their enquiries are not too distant from those of other, non-evolutionary, psychologists, but they are informed by a theory that places the function and design of such mechanisms at its centre. If a psychological theory does not make sense in light of evolutionary biology then it is false.

ACKNOWLEDGEMENTS

This chapter has benefited from the critical scrutiny of Ben Dickins, David Dickins, Fatima Felisberti, David Hardman, Barbara Johnson, David Lawson, Rebecca Sear, Max Steuer, Paul Taylor, Richard Webb, Andy Wells and Jonathan Wells. I am enormously grateful for their efforts and, of course, any errors of content or exposition are still my own.

REFERENCES

Altringham, J. D. (1999). *Bats: Biology and behaviour*. Oxford: Oxford University Press.
Axelrod, R. (1984). *The evolution of cooperation*. New York: Basic Books.
Axelrod, R. and Hamilton, W. D. (1981). The evolution of cooperation. *Science, 211*, 1390–1396.

Azar, R., Paquette, D., Zoccolillo, M. *et al.* (2007). The association of major depression, conduct disorder, and maternal overcontrol with a failure to show a cortisol buffered response in 4-month-old infants of teenage mothers. *Biological Psychiatry, 62,* 573–9.

Bateson, P., Barker, D., Clutton-Brock, T. *et al.* (2004). Developmental plasticity and human health. *Nature, 430,* 419–21.

Belsky, J., Steinberg, L. and Draper, P. (1991). Childhood experience, interpersonal development, and reproductive strategy: an evolutionary theory of socialization. *Child Development, 62,* 647–70.

Boyce, M. S. and Perrins, C. M. (1987). Optimizing Great Tit clutch size in a fluctuating environment. *Ecology, 68,* 142–53.

Braitenberg, V. (1984). *Vehicles: Experiments in synthetic psychology.* Cambridge, MA: MIT Press.

Buss, D. M. (2008). *Evolutionary psychology: The new science of mind,* (third edition). Boston, MA: Allyn & Bacon.

Carranza, J. (2009). Defining sexual selection as sex-dependent selection. *Animal Behaviour, 77,* 749–51.

Cater, S. and Coleman, L. (2006). *'Planned teenage pregnancy': Perspectives of young parents from disadvantaged backgrounds.* Bristol: Joseph Rowntree Foundation and Policy Press.

C. elegans Sequencing Consortium (1998). Genome sequence of the Nematode *C. elegans*: A platform for investigating biology. *Science, 282,* 2012–18.

Champagne, F. A. (2008). Epigenetic mechanisms and the transgenerational effects of maternal care. *Frontiers in Neuroendocrinology, 29,* 386–97.

Chan, J. L. and Mantzoros, C. S. (2005). Role of leptin in energy deprivation states: Normal human physiology and clinical implications for hypothalamic amenorrhea and anorexia nervosa. *Lancet, 366,* 74–85.

Chisholm, J. S. (1999). Attachment and time preference: Relations between early stress and sexual behavior in a sample of American university women. *Human Nature, 10,* 51–83.

Clutton-Brock, T. (2008). Sexual selection in males and females. *Science, 318,* 1882–5.

Cosmides, L. (1989). The logic of social exchange: Has natural selection shaped how humans reason? Studies with the Wason selection task. *Cognition, 31,* 187–276.

Cosmides, L. and Tooby, J. (1992). Cognitive adaptations for social exchange. In J. H. Barkow, L. Cosmides and J. Tooby (eds), *The adapted mind: Evolutionary psychology and the generation of culture* (pp. 163–228). Oxford: Oxford University Press.

Crews, D. (2008). Epigenetics and its implications for behavioural neuroendocrinology. *Frontiers in Neuroendocrinology, 29,* 344–57.

Crick, F. H. C. (1970). Central dogma of molecular biology. *Nature, 227,* 561–3.

Darwin, C. (1859/1985). *The origin of species by means of natural selection or the preservation of favoured races in the struggle for life.* London: Penguin Books.

Darwin, C. (1871/1998). *The descent of man.* New York: Prometheus Books.

Darwin, C. (1872/1998). *The expression of the emotions in man and animals.* London: HarperCollins.

Dawkins, R. (1976). *The selfish gene.* Oxford: Oxford University Press.

Dawkins, R. (1983). *The extended phenotype: The long reach of the gene.* Oxford: Oxford University Press.

Dennett, D. C. (1995). *Darwin's dangerous idea: Evolution and the meanings of life.* London: Allen Lane.

Depew, D. J. and Weber, B. H. (1996). *Darwinism evolving: Systems dynamics and the genealogy of natural selection*. Cambridge, MA: MIT Press.

Dickins, T. E. (2003). What can evolutionary psychology tell us about cognitive architecture? *History and Philosophy of Psychology*, *5*, 1–16.

Dickins, T. E. (2006). Evolutionary health psychology. *Health Psychology Update*, *15*, 4–10.

Dickins, T. E. and Dickins, B. J. A. (2007). Designed calibration: Naturally selected flexibility, not non-genetic inheritance. *Behavioral and Brain Sciences*, *30*, 368–9.

Dickins, T. E. and Dickins, B. J. A. (2008). Mother Nature's tolerant ways: Why non-genetic inheritance has nothing to do with evolution. *New Ideas in Psychology*, *26*, 41–54.

Dunbar, R. I. M. and Shultz, S. (2007). Evolution in the social brain. *Science*, *317*, 1344–7.

Evans, J. St. B. T., Newstead, S. E. and Byrne, R. M. J. (1993). *Human reasoning: The psychology of deduction*. Hove: Lawrence Erlbaum Associates.

Fox Keller, E. (2000). *The century of the gene*. Cambridge, MA: Harvard University Press.

Frederick, S., Loewenstein, G. and O'Donoghue, T. (2002). Time discounting and time preference: A critical review. *Journal of Economic Literature*, *40*, 351–401.

Gurmu, E. and Mace, R. (2008). Fertility decline driven by poverty: The case of Addis Ababa, Ethiopia. *Journal of Biosocial Science*, *40*, 339–58.

Haig, D. (2006). The gene meme. In A. Grafen and M. Ridley (eds), *Richard Dawkins: How a scientist changed the way we think* (pp. 50–65). Oxford: Oxford University Press.

Hamilton, W. D. (1964). The genetical evolution of social behaviour, I. *Journal of Theoretical Biology*, *7*, 1–16.

Hawkes, K. (1994). On life-history evolution. *Current Anthropology*, *35*, 39–41.

Hill, K. (1993). Life history theory and evolutionary anthropology. *Evolutionary Anthropology*, *2*, 78–88.

Jablonka, E. and Lamb, M. (2005). *Evolution in four dimensions: Genetic, epigenetic, behavioral, and symbolic variation in the history of life*. Cambridge, MA: MIT Press.

Kaplan, H. S. and Gangestad, S. W. (2005). Life history theory and evolutionary psychology. In D. M. Buss (ed.), *The handbook of evolutionary psychology* (pp. 68–95). New York: John Wiley & Sons, Ltd.

Kirkwood, T. B. L. (1997). The origins of human ageing. *Philosophical Transactions of the Royal Society B*, *352*, 1765–72.

Lack, D. (1947). The significance of clutch size. *Ibis*, *89*, 302–52.

Lee, E., Clements, S., Ingham, R. and Stone, N. (2004). *A matter of choice? Explaining national variation in teenage abortion and motherhood*. York: The Joseph Rowntree Foundation.

McCleery, J. M. and Goodwin, G. M. (2001). High and low neuroticism predict different cortisol responses to the combined dexamethasone-CRH test. *Biological Psychiatry*, *49*, 410–415.

Malthus, T. (1798/1985). *An essay on the principle of population*. London: Penguin.

Maynard-Smith, J. (1982). *Evolution and the theory of games*. Cambridge: Cambridge University Press.

Mealey, L. (1995). The sociobiology of sociopathy: An integrated evolutionary model. *Behavioral and Brain Sciences*, *18*, 523–41.

Mendle, J., Harden, K. P., Turkheimer, E. *et al.* (2009). Associations between father absence and age of first sexual intercourse. *Child Development*, *80*, 1463–80.

Millikan, R. G. (1993). *White Queen psychology and other essays for Alice*. Cambridge, MA: MIT Press.

Monod, J. L. (1972/1988). *Chance and necessity: An essay on the natural philosophy of modern biology*. New York: Random House.

Nettle, D. (2006). The evolution of personality variation in humans and other animals. *American Psychologist, 61*, 622–31.

Nettle, D., Coall, D. A. and Dickins, T. E. (2010). Birthweight and paternal involvement affect the likelihood of teenage motherhood: Evidence from the British National Child Development Study. *American Journal of Human Biology, 22*, 172–179.

Oswald, L. M., Zandi, P., Nestadt, G. *et al.* (2006). Relationship between cortisol responses to stress and personality. *Neuropsychopharmacology, 31*, 1583–91.

Pinker, S. (1997). *How the mind works*. London: Allen Lane.

Ridley, M. (2004). *Evolution*, (third edition). Oxford: Blackwell Publishing.

Samuels, R. (1998). Evolutionary psychology and the massive modularity hypothesis. *British Journal of the Philosophy of Science, 49*, 575–602.

Samuels, R. (2000). Massively modular minds: The evolutionary psychology account of cognitive architecture. In P. Carruthers and A. Chamberlain (eds), *Evolution and the human mind: Modularity, language and meta-cognition* (pp. 13–46). Cambridge: Cambridge University Press.

Stearns, S. C. (1992). *The evolution of life histories*. Oxford: Oxford University Press.

Stone, V. E., Cosmides, L., Tooby, J. *et al.* (2002). Selective impairment of reasoning about social exchange in a patient with bilateral limbic system damage. *Proceedings of the National Academy of Sciences USA, 99*, 11531–6.

Strathman, A., Gleicher, F., Boninger, D. S. and Edwards, C. S. (1994). The consideration of future consequences: Weighing immediate and distant outcomes of behavior. *Journal of Personality and Social Psychology, 66*, 742–52.

Sugiyama, L. S., Tooby, J. and Cosmides, L. (2002). Cross-cultural evidence of cognitive adaptations for social exchange among the Shiwiar of Ecuadorian Amazonia. *Proceedings of the National Academy of Sciences USA, 99*, 11537–42.

Tinbergen, N. (1963). On the aims and methods of ethology. *Zeitschrift für Tierpsychologie, 20*, 410–433.

Trivers, R. L. (1971). The evolution of reciprocal altruism. *The Quarterly Review of Biology, 46*, 35–57.

Venter, J. C., Adams, M. D., Myers, E. W. *et al.* (2001). The sequence of the human genome. *Science, 291*, 1304–51.

Wason, P. (1966). Reasoning. In B. M. Foss (ed.), *New horizons in psychology* (pp. 135–51). Harmondsworth: Penguin.

Watson, J. D. and Crick, F. H. C. (1953). A structure for deoxyribose nucleic acid. *Nature, 171*, 737–8.

Wilkinson, G. S. (1984). Reciprocal food sharing in the vampire bat. *Nature, 308*, 181–4.

Wilson, E. O. (1975/2000). *Sociobiology: The new synthesis*. Cambridge, MA: Harvard University Press.

Wilson, M. and Daly, M. (1997). Life expectancy, economic inequality, homicide, and reproductive timing in Chicago neighbourhoods. *British Medical Journal, 314*, 1271–4.

2   The evolution of cognition

KAYLA B. CAUSEY AND DAVID F. BJORKLUND

CHAPTER OUTLINE

WHY ARE WE SO SMART? 33
    Different types of problems require different
      types of solvers 35
    Information-processing systems 37

HOW DID WE GET SO SMART? 38
    Smarts aren't just for sociality 41

**WHAT, EXACTLY, ARE WE SO GOOD AT?
AND WHEN DID WE 'GET IT'?** 46
    Executive function 47

Explicit awareness and mental time travel 52
Social learning 55
Representing others' intentions is not necessary,
    but it is efficient 57

CONCLUSIONS 60

REFERENCES 61

E = Mc². It was a flawed equation, as far as I was concerned. There should have been an 'A' in there somewhere for Awareness – without which the 'E' and the 'M' and the 'c'. . . could not exist.

Kurt Vonnegut, Breakfast of Champions *(1973, p. 247)*

Humans differ from all other animals in their ability to use language, pass on material culture with great fidelity and reason scientifically, among other things. While other species adapt over time to meet the challenges of their environment, humans have been successful in adapting the world to satisfy their needs, for better or for worse. Despite these distinctions, biologists since Darwin have believed there is a continuity of mental functioning across species. In this sense, the cognition of a species such as *Homo sapiens* should share many features with species with which they recently shared a common ancestor, such as chimpanzees (*Pan troglodytes*) and bonobos (*Pan paniscus*). However, there is significant scientific and philosophical debate regarding discontinuities in human and primate cognition.

The evolution of conscious awareness, or more specifically *self-awareness*, defined here as 'that naturally occurring cognitive representational capacity permitting explicit and reflective accounts of the – mostly causative – contents of mind, contents harboured by the psychological frame of the self and, as a consequence, also the psychological frames of others' (Bering and Bjorklund, 2007, p. 598), has been argued to represent one such discontinuity in cognitive abilities between humans and other species (see Bering and Bjorklund, 2007). Armed with this capacity to reflect on personal experiences, imagine future scenarios and examine current and future needs and desires, humans are able to overcome implicit drives, form metarepresentations of the world, and reason about the long-term effects of their decisions (Boyer, 2008). In this way, humans changed the nature of selection pressures by becoming a selection pressure themselves and sending human social cognition spiralling upwards. This is a feat unique to *Homo sapiens*.

In this chapter, we examine the evolution of human intellect and consciousness, considering the continuities and discontinuities between humans and other animal species by asking the following questions: *What* is special about human intelligence, if anything? *When* did these unique abilities evolve? *How* have these higher-level cognitive abilities emerged from lower-level cognitions over phylogeny? And *why* did these abilities evolve in the line that led to *Homo sapiens*? While we address each of these questions in separate sections, we emphasise that these issues are not mutually exclusive and that a full account of human cognitive evolution must be able to address all of these concerns.

We begin by asking why humans have the mind that they have. We approach this question from the perspective of evolutionary psychology (Buss, 2005; Tooby and Cosmides, 1998), which holds that the human mind has adapted over geological time, by means of natural selection, for life in a social group (Bjorklund and Pellegrini, 2000, 2002). We discuss the unique selection pressures that humans faced in the environment of evolutionary adaptedness (EEA) and use this as our basis for predicting the cognitive mechanisms built therein. Next, we examine explanations for how changes in higher cognitions occurred as a result of changes in lower-level abilities. We outline these specific abilities in the third section, examining those that represent continuities and discontinuities in cognitive evolution and describing comparative work to suggest *when* these abilities emerged over humans' phylogenetic history.

WHY ARE WE SO SMART?

The answer to this question is neither simple nor concrete and has fuelled many scientific debates. Figure 2.1 illustrates the phylogenetic relation between humans and some extant primates. Humans last shared a common ancestor with chimpanzees and bonobos about five to seven million years ago, yet humans have many cognitive skills not possessed by their nearest primate relatives, including language, mental time travel and the capacity to reason about the beliefs and desires of others (even if we do not always do so accurately). There are several explanations for why humans have some of the cognitive skills that their nearest primate relatives do not.

One hypothesis is that a general increase in brain size and plasticity over hominid evolution enabled our ancestors to perform general cognitive operations more effectively than other species, allowing us to learn more over our lifetimes (Harvey, Martin

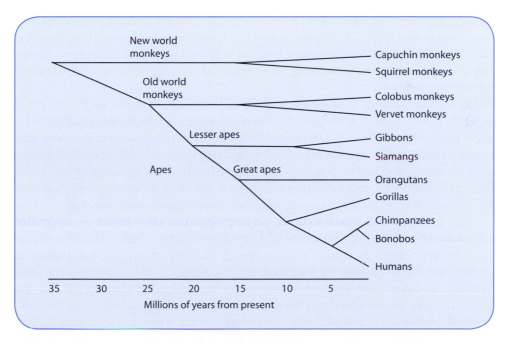

Figure 2.1. *Phylogenetic relations among extant primates.*

Source: From Bjorklund, D. F., and Pellegrini, A. D. (2002). *The origins of human nature: Evolutionary developmental psychology.* Washington: American Psychological Association, p. 139.

and Clutton-Brock, 1987; Jerison, 1973). According to this view, there is continuity in learning across many species, given that the basic laws of association are available to all animals, ranging from reptiles to rodents to humans (Mackintosh, 2000; Thorndike, 1911). In other words, the 'general intelligence hypothesis' proposes that only quantitative changes, such as a general expansion of brain structures and increases in computing power, are responsible for hominid cognitive evolution, and that the human mind is a general processor of experience. A strict form of this view fails to take into account relative differences in brain organisation between humans and non-human primates, especially differences in areas associated with social cognition (e.g. Premack, 2007).

An opposing hypothesis, and the mainstay of evolutionary psychology, argues that the human mind is modular, consisting of highly constrained cognitive abilities that evolved in response to specific recurrent adaptive problems, producing a mind that is qualitatively different from that of other species and a fast and efficient processor of invariant information in the environment (Cosmides, 1989; Cosmides and Tooby, 1994). According to this 'massive modularity hypothesis', the human mind can be thought of as a Swiss-army knife, with many inherently specialised tools, or modules, that evolved *de novo* in humans and need not function interdependently (Tooby and Cosmides, 1992). These modules have been designed by natural selection to operate with little experiential input.

There is no single conceptual definition of 'what is a module', however, and use of the term often varies with the level of analysis. We describe the four basic forms of modularity in Table 2.1 (adapted from Geary and Huffman, 2002), based on how they have been explored in the literature (e.g. Cosmides and Tooby, 1994; Elman *et al.*, 1996; Fodor, 1983; Krubitzer and Huffman, 2000). Each form represents a different level of information processing, all of which seem important for understanding human cognitive evolution.

To account for each of these levels of modularity, a third model of the mind has been proposed and suggests that the brain's domains are best described as being organised hierarchically (e.g. Geary, 2005; Marcus, 2004, 2006). As an organism's environment becomes more complex, so does the brain system, by using existing lower-level modules, designed to process less complex information, as building blocks for multiple higher-level, more complex modules. In this way, information processed at lower levels is integrated, allowing complex skills and cognitions to emerge.

This notion of 'soft modularity' (Geary and Huffman, 2002) stands in contrast to notions of massive modularity by imposing a template of information exchange between modules, providing a framework for how specific abilities are adapted descendants of general abilities, and accounting for experiential modification. In contrast to the general learning hypothesis, soft modularity invokes constraints on the learning process that guides relevant information down the appropriate processing pathway.

While terms like 'module' and 'modularity' have been used to describe the brain's organisation in the past, we argue that this terminology may be obsolete. The persistent use of this type of language implies compartmentalisation (e.g. Fodor, 1983) and thus precludes conceptualising brain function and organisation as interdependent hierarchical systems. According to Geary, the human mind consists

Table 2.1. *Forms of modularity.*

Form	Description
Neural module	At the lowest level, modularity describes the relation between sensory regions and corresponding parts of the body and environment. For example, regions of the somatosensory cortex that support sensation in the five digits may be considered a neural module. Each module provides only limited information regarding the environment.
Perceptual module	Perceptual modules are those that integrate information from neural modules, resulting in a more complex representation of the organism's interaction with the environment. Coordination of the neural modules representing the digits results in the perception of a grasped object, for example.
Cognitive module	At a more complex level of abstraction, meaning-based representations are formed from perceptual modules. The ability to imagine the manipulation of an object without any sensory input is one such cognitive module.
Functional module	Lower-level modules are integrated with affective and motivation systems that *function* to guide behaviours that will increase survival and reproduction, for example approaching food but avoiding enemies. For humans, the integration is across a complex mix of modular systems.

Source: Adapted from Brain and cognitive evolution: Forms of modularity and functions of mind, by D. C. Geary and K. J. Huffman (2002), *Psychological Bulletin*, 128, p. 698. © 2002 American Psychological Association.

of brain and cognitive systems that are open to experiential modification as a result of variant information patterns in the environment *and* gene-driven constrained modules that evolved in response to invariant information patterns (Geary, 1998, 2005; Geary and Huffman, 2002). In order to present the most accurate description of these mechanisms, we refer to problem-solving *systems*, some of which are relatively open to experience and others for which the input is more constrained. We use the term 'domain' when distinguishing different types of input, such as that which is social from that which is ecological.

Different types of problems require different types of solvers

An organism's mind, shaped by natural selection, is a problem solver. Much like a computer, it should evolve to receive or detect input from its environment relevant to its reproduction and survival (problem identification), perform a decision rule (means) and produce the appropriate behavioural output (end) (Tooby and Cosmides, 1992). As such, characteristics of the problem-solving mechanism will depend on the variability in problems the environment poses to the organism. We can hypothesise about the structure and function of the human mind by identifying the type of environment that was pertinent to our ancestors' survival and reproduction.

The efficiency of a particular information-processing system will be a direct function of the variability of the information in the environment. Specifically, implicit systems should evolve in situations where the organism's environment is relatively invariant over time. These systems should involve fast and frugal responding, even at the cost of accuracy (Gigerenzer and Selten, 2001), and input detection should be constrained insofar as the information that the mechanism is designed to process is invariable. That is, if an organism's survival covaries with its ability to process certain unchanging features of its environment, that organism should possess information-processing systems that constrain its attention and guide decision-making and behavioural responses in a manner that is efficient (Cosmides and Tooby, 1994; Gallistel, 1995). These fast and frugal heuristics (Gigerenzer and Selten, 2001; Simon, 1955, 1956; Tversky and Kahneman, 1974) result in behavioural outputs that are 'good enough' – they are accurate *most* of the time, but not always, owing to limitations on the amount of information that can be processed and manipulated. For humans, these biases often lead to systematic errors in judgement when people draw inferences about an evolutionary novel situation based on 'intuitive' understanding, or 'folk knowledge' that evolved in a natural ecology (Geary, 2003; Geary and Huffman, 2002).

For example, based on an availability heuristic, most people judge the probability of events based on the frequency with which they have been exposed to those events. When the frequency and probability of an event match, usually the case in natural settings, the resulting judgement of risk is relatively accurate. However, in modern settings, the frequency with which information is presented in the mass media is much greater than would be available in a natural setting. Because these heuristics led to near optimal and good-enough decisions for our ancestors, we still rely on them today when asked to make quick, implicit judgements. As a result, people tend to judge the probability of a terrorist attack or dying in a plane crash as greater than it really is (Lichtenstein *et al.*, 1978; see also Gigerenzer, 2001; Todd, 2001).

In summary, if an organism is required to solve recurring problems to survive, it will evolve implicit, automatic problem-solving abilities that do not require conscious awareness. If these problems are recurrent over generations, then these abilities will be narrowly constrained to this information and require little experience or learning.

In contrast, relatively open systems should evolve in situations where an organism's survival covaries with its ability to effectively deal with fluctuating information. The processes of these systems are likely less efficient (i.e. more effortful and require more experience), more accurate and involve the generalisation of previously acquired information to novel situations. To the extent the organism possesses a great deal of knowledge about the problem domain, it can solve a novel problem by generalising this knowledge. Many if not all animals are capable of implicit associative learning, and thus it is not surprising to find substantial continuities in such cognition across the animal kingdom. However, the ways in which animals represent these associations and generalise them to novel problems constitutes a discontinuity among animals (e.g. Tomasello, 2000), one that is likely the result of a qualitative change in 'the way we think', such as conscious, declarative representation and fluid intelligence.

Unlike other 'generalist' species, such as rats and pigeons that are capable of implicit generalisation, humans, and perhaps some other species, have evolved explicit cognition in response to the pressure to generalise learned behaviours and cognitions, which allows us to bring to mind relevant information and move fluidly through the problem space (i.e. problem identification – means – end; Geary, 2005). Information that can be explicitly recalled is referred to as 'declarative knowledge' and is stored in long-term memory. The extent to which an organism has access to declarative knowledge is referred to as 'crystallised intelligence' (Cattell, 1963). The ability of the organism to apply this knowledge when solving novel problems is referred to as 'fluid intelligence' (Cattell, 1963) and involves the integration of crystallised intelligence across domains and cognitive systems, or modules.

Information-processing systems

As we mentioned previously, there is debate among evolutionary psychologists about how best to describe the systems, or modules, that characterise the human mind and how they might have evolved. Figure 2.2 illustrates Geary's (2005) taxonomy of the folk psychology, folk biology and folk physics systems, argued to have evolved in response to social and ecological pressures. The highest tier represents the information processors that house the implicit and explicit systems responsible for the integration of information from the social and ecological environment needed to solve novel problems. This system manages the flow of information through

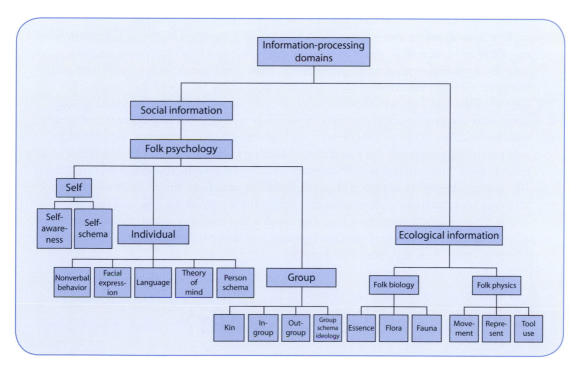

Figure 2.2. *Geary's (2005) taxonomy of modular domains that captures the areas of folk psychology, folk biology and folk physics.*

Source: From Geary, D. C. (2005). *The origin of mind: Evolution of brain, cognition, and general intelligence.* Washington: American Psychological Association.

operations of executive functions such as attention, inhibition and working memory, and is often referred to as 'the central executive' (Baddeley and Logie, 1999; Cowan, 1999). The social and ecological domains constitute the second tier and are subdivided into three functional systems, illustrated in the third tier (described in Table 2.1), that encompass different types of folk knowledge, or knowledge that is implicit and heuristic-based. These include folk psychology, folk biology and folk physics (although Geary notes there may be more, such as intuitive mathematics) and are subserved by lower-level cognitive, neural and perceptual systems, such as self-awareness and kin recognition.

These systems are the product of distinct selection pressures faced by our ancestors. Following Geary's model, might changes in one domain have been more critical to the evolution of the modern human mind than others? While humans are undoubtedly more innovative and technologically advanced than non-human primates, much of *Homo sapiens'* success in gaining access and control over their ecology (Geary, 2005) is not attributed to our technological brilliance but to our ability to cooperate with others when our interests overlap (Trivers, 1971) and to outmanoeuvre individuals with whom our interests do not (Humphrey, 1976). Previously, we (e.g. Bjorklund and Bering, 2003; Bjorklund, Causey, and Periss, 2009), as many others (e.g. Alexander, 1989; Dunbar, 1995, 2009; Humphrey, 1976), have proposed that human intellectual evolution was driven by selection for social skills (i.e. the social brain hypothesis). As such, human social cognition, meaning the capacity to track the mental states of others, can be viewed as the more principal form of thought from which *Homo sapiens'* impressive suite of intellectual abilities is derived.

It is hypothesised that a geological shift led to a drastic change in the environment five to eight million years ago, making resources such as food scarce and unreliable. By evolving explicit brain systems (i.e. fluid intelligence) that could track and integrate variable information patterns across ecological and social domains (Geary's Tier 1), ancestral humans increased their chance of survival. The pressure to gain ecological dominance supported selection of folk biology, folk physics and a motivation for sociality. This in turn created a social struggle for resources, supported by folk-psychology systems, the formation of kinship networks and reciprocal relationships (Geary, 2005). In this way, humans created their own selective force: themselves. By evolving the ability to reason about the contents of others' minds, humans created an arms race between cooperation and competition, mind-reading and deception, and truth and fallacy, to name a few. The result was a runaway selection for complex social-cognitive abilities and the rapid exchange of information that uniquely serves humans, more than any other social species.

HOW DID WE GET SO SMART?

While most agree that quantitative changes in brain size, at least increases in prefrontal cortical regions, are responsible for some advances in hominid intelligence, it remains muddled just how these changes in quantity led to changes in quality, and in particular the emergence of consciousness. Another issue concerns the extent to which changes in asocial cognitions, such as the understanding of relational categories in the physical world or the ability to represent one's own intentions, preceded the cognitive advances in the social domain, such as the understanding of social relations and theory-of-mind abilities.

Reader and Laland (2002) report that social learning, relative executive brain size and innovative tool use, but not social complexity, are correlated across a number of species. In other words, species with larger brains are better and more innovative tool users and social learners than those with smaller brains. These findings are interpreted to reflect that asocial and social learning underwent correlated evolution, but are also interpreted to support arguments that the evolution of technical intelligence in response to ecological conditions is responsible, at least in part, for the evolution of primate intelligence. However, given the impressive suite of distinctly social-cognitive abilities unique to humans, we feel that an explanation based solely on asocial learning, just as one based solely on social learning, is insufficient.

More specifically, we have proposed that modern human intelligence evolved as a result of the co-evolution of an enlarged brain, an extended juvenile period and life in socially complex groups (e.g. Bjorklund and Bering, 2003; Bjorklund and Rosenberg, 2005). In confluence with an increase in social complexity, we argue that an increase in brain size provided the quantitative increases in computing power necessary for qualitative changes in cognition since humans last shared a common ancestor with non-human primates. Additionally, we argue that humans' prolonged juvenile period (Bogin, 1999, 2003) allowed brain development to extend into adolescence and young adulthood (e.g. Gould, 1977), enabling comparatively prolonged synaptogenesis, glial cell growth, myelination of axons and dendritic growth in the cortex. In contrast to claims that the increase in brain size over hominid evolution was driven by an addition of specific problem-solving modules (i.e. the massive modularity hypothesis; Cosmides and Tooby, 1994), we argue that the extension of the juvenile period substantially influenced human cognitive evolution by stipulating an increase in plasticity and flexible learning across many brain regions, resulting in humans' disproportionately enlarged prefrontal cortex, the area most associated with general executive functioning and fluid-like intelligence (e.g. Zelazo, Carlson and Kesek, 2008). Humans' protracted development also meant that we were reliant on our caregivers for a longer time, which provided the time and opportunity to learn and perfect the skills necessary to navigate complex social and asocial worlds.

Joffe (1997) provides important evidence that social complexity, brain size and an extended juvenile period are three important, yet non-dissociable, influences on human intellectual change. Joffe reports that the relationship between brain size and social complexity among 27 primate species is further influenced by the length of a species' juvenile period. The co-occurrence of large brains, longer juvenile periods and large social groups within these primate species indicates that these factors likely co-evolved, enabling a runaway selection for intellectual abilities capable of solving problems across multiple domains (see Box 2.1).

BOX 2.1.   INVENTING LANGUAGE: CHILDREN'S GIFT TO HUMANKIND

When did our ancestors become language users and what survival advantages did having a language afford its early (and later) users? The fossil record can only tell us so much, in part because most of the anatomical features associated with language are soft tissue, specific parts of the brain and throat musculature, for example, that do not fossilise. Thus, we do not have precise answers for these questions. However, we can make some educated guesses about the origins of language; the inner shapes of fossilised skulls indicate the shape of the brains they held, and the bones surrounding the mouth and throat can give us some clues about our ancestors' ability to speak. After examining this evidence, some experts suggest that the first humans to use rudimentary language lived about two million years ago, and that more complex language was used by humans about 40 000 years ago (Bickerton, 1990) and perhaps much earlier (see MacWhinney, 2005).

The adaptive benefits of language seem obvious. Ancient humans with linguistic ability were better able to communicate with one another and thus better able to coordinate their actions and transmit information across generations (Pinker and Bloom, 1990). Language alone would not be enough to make this more sophisticated communication possible, for it must be accompanied by an advanced ability for social learning. Yet, language provides a more efficient means of transmitting information between people than imitation or other forms of social learning (Donald, 1991). Similarly, the emergence of language can be seen as an expression of a new cognitive capacity, symbolic thought, that provided its bearers with advantages beyond those associated with better communication (Deacon, 1997).

Although the evolutionary origins of language must remain speculative, it seems likely that it was children, not adults, who first 'invented' language. For example, physician and science writer Lewis Thomas (1974) suggests that the enlarged brains of ancient humans provided the capacity to use language, but adults likely made little use of it, continuing to communicate with grunts, gestures and individual words to express ideas. Children learned these words from their parents, but discovered how to put them together into sentences while playing with other children. From this perspective, language was the emerging product of groups of youth who 'played with' these new sounds in 'purposeless' ways, leading to a useful new ability.

We know that children easily *acquire* their mother tongue (see discussion of a sensitive period for language, Box 2.2), but this seems a stretch from proposing that children *invent* language. Some support for this controversial claim comes from observations of children who invent a real language from the non-language communication systems that adults around them use. Linguist Derek Bickerton (1990; Calvin and Bickerton, 2000) notes that throughout history people of different language groups have come together, often to work, and have had to communicate with one another. While gestures are useful, typically the language of the majority group or the language of the 'bosses' serves as the basis for communication, with words from other languages sprinkled in. The result is a 'pidgin', which includes terms from a variety of languages, with a simple and often inconsistent word order and little in the way of a grammatical system. A pidgin is not a true language, but serves to convey necessary information within the group (the 'workers') and between the group and the bosses. This is the way many tourists speak when in a foreign country. They know a few words, may know how to make (some) nouns plural, typically use only the present tense, frequently sprinkle in words from their own language and keep the word order simple. It is not grammatical, but it often serves to get basic messages across. Based both on historical evidence and on his own research of the Hawaiian language, Bickerton showed that children of pidgin speakers transform the language of their parents into a true language, termed a 'creole', often in a single generation. That is, these children do not *acquire* language in the usual sense, but *create* a language.

One may question whether the transformation of pidgins into creoles in the hands (or mouths) of youngsters is truly evidence of children 'inventing' language. Recent research supporting the creative role of children in language comes from studies of deaf children who invented Nicaraguan Sign Language (*Idioma de Señas de Nicaragua*). Until the opening of a school for the deaf in the 1970s, Nicaragua had no deaf culture and no recognised sign language. At this school, deaf children lived together and learned to read Spanish, but they were not taught to sign. Children had developed idiosyncratic 'home signs' they had used to communicate with friends and family and used these signs to communicate with other deaf children. From these interactions, a true sign language began to emerge. Over the course of three cohorts of students, children created a 'true' sign language (i.e. with syntax). Nicaraguan Sign Language was systematically modified from one cohort of children to the next, with children aged 10 years and younger generating most of the changes. In other words, sequences of children created a new sign language from the incomplete forms used by their predecessors (Senghas and Coppola, 2001; Senghas, Kita and Ozyurek, 2004).

Effective communication is useful for anyone, but the adaptive value of language has typically been focused on what it does for adults, from enhancing social cooperation to wooing members of the opposite sex (Miller, 2001). Might language be especially useful (and adaptive) for children? One proposal is that language improves the communication between preschool children and their parents at a time when children are particularly in need of assistance, specifically during the preschool years (Locke, 2009; Locke and Bogin, 2006). Barry Bogin (2001) proposed that humans 'invented' a new stage of development – childhood – when children were no longer nursing but still not able to prepare their own food or otherwise fend for themselves, making effective communication between parent and child especially important in humans. The adaptive value of language became particularly important again in adolescence, being related to same-sex competition and courtship.

Although these ideas are based on a wealth of evidence on language development, how people in different cultures use language today, communication systems in other species and fossil evidence, they must remain speculative. Nonetheless, we are confident that natural selection related to the evolution of language operated on *children*, and that it was something about children's brains and cognitive systems that made possible the invention of language and language's many advantages.

Smarts aren't just for sociality

Advanced technological skills required for dealing with variability in the environment were likely important selection pressures for both an extended juvenile period and increased brain size, but the pressure to transmit this information faithfully across generations necessarily selected for social intelligence. In other words, asocial and social learning processes evolved concurrently, but may be represented in separate domains (i.e. social information and ecological information; see Figure 2.2), which were largely dealt with by separate systems that, as a result of an extension of the juvenile period and the emergence of consciousness, became connected in modern humans (i.e. through information-processing systems, or the central executive, the highest tier of Geary's model). For example, Box 2.2 describes research on how early exposure to language, as a system of representation and redescription, is crucial to the development of theory of mind. In this section, we discuss how changes in neocortical capacity may have led to the emergence of self-consciousness and finally advanced social-cognitive abilities, such as theory of mind, and social learning.

How does a mind built on implicit associations become explicitly aware? Earlier, we discussed what types of cognitive machinery are necessary for an organism in variant versus invariant environments. That is, implicit, heuristic-based systems are adaptive in relatively invariant environments, whereas explicit fluid systems that allow integration across lower-level systems are adaptive in those that are more variable. However, the amount of variability in an ancestral environment was not all-or-none and differed across domains. In some domains, such as the ecological domain, variability was likely less than in the social domain. In less variable domains, or domains in which an organism can rely on a lot of pre-existing knowledge to solve a problem, the organism may be able to move through a problem space with a relative amount of ease and implicit responding. However, if an organism is presented with a novel problem, then the organism must develop a system of making knowledge from other systems explicit and generalisable to the novel problem (Geary, 2005).

We argue that humans' changing ecological world (e.g. tool-use, hunting, foraging) provided the sort of halfway house between a largely invariable physical domain (e.g. gravity) and a largely variable social domain. It is in reasoning causally about the self in relation to the ecological world that general fluid intelligence thrived and consciousness emerged in the human lineage. A corresponding increase in social complexity then locked in these capacities and allowed them to flourish into advanced social cognition and social learning.

Organisms with fluid intelligence may have been able to exploit the environment in innovative ways, gaining exposure to novel selection pressures as a result (Reader and Laland, 2002). As we discussed in previous sections, fluid intelligence, insofar as it involves directing attention to relevant pieces of information and performing operations on them, is controlled by the central executive system, including working memory and inhibition (Baddeley and Logie, 1999; Cowan, 1999). This system implicates the prefrontal cortex, particularly the dorsolateral region, and the anterior cingulate cortex for planning (e.g. Duncan, 2001; Kane and Engle, 2002; Miller and Cohen, 2001). These areas appear to be particularly active in problems that cannot be solved by heuristics (Ranganath and Rainer, 2003).

Expansion and reorganisation of the brain

Evidence suggests that the prefrontal cortex in humans is proportionally larger than it is in non-human primates, has more neural connections with subcortical regions

BOX 2.2.   HOW IMPORTANT IS IT TO BE A NATIVE 'THEORY OF MIND' SPEAKER?

As we mentioned, theory of mind allows an individual to reason about the mental states of others. Often we think, *Sally thinks that X* when reasoning about Sally's false beliefs, for example. How important is this linguistic construction in our reasoning about the beliefs and desires of others? Are there some aspects of theory of mind that require language? Are there others that are robust against language deprivation?

Some consider language as crucial to theory of mind development (e.g. Lohmann and Tomasello, 2003), arguing that language allows children to redescribe, or represent, the otherwise ambiguous mental states of others. In the same way that language may enable theory of mind, however, theory of mind may be a prerequisite for conversational communication. Fleshing out this relationship is difficult given that language development and theory of mind are inextricably linked in the typically developing child. However, some evidence suggests that the two are causally related: research has indicated that exposure to early verbal interaction, around age 3 to 4 years, specifically that involving mental-state words like *think*, *know* and *want*, predicts children's later theory of mind development (Harris, de Rosnay and Pons, 2005; Ruffman, Slade and Crowe, 2002; Siegal, Varley and Want, 2001).

Morgan and Kegl (2006) note that the delayed language development of deaf children may provide an interesting avenue by which to investigate the relationship between language and theory of mind because most (90–96%) are born to hearing parents and thus are delayed in acquiring their first language (Spencer, 1993). These researchers recruited a sample of Nicaraguan signers (deaf individuals who have acquired Nicaraguan Sign Language, see Box 2.1 for more information) and compared theory of mind performance across individuals who had been exposed to the sign language by 10 years of age (early learners) with those who had acquired it later in life (late learners). Participants were both children (as young as 8 years old) and adults (as old as 39 years old).

Morgan and Kegl (2006) used two tasks to assess participants' theory of mind: a modified false-belief task, similar to the Sally task described above, and a moral dilemma narrative. For the false-belief task, participants were shown four scenarios of different characters engaging in various activities. For example, participants saw a picture of a boy fishing who thinks he caught a fish. An object (grass, in the fishing example) obstructed the character's view of the desired object in the scene (the fish) and was constructed on a flap that could be moved to reveal the occluded object. Participants were instructed to cover the fisherman's eyes while the flap was removed to reveal the object that the fisherman was 'catching'. To examine reasoning about *false* beliefs, the researchers presented a scene in which removal of the flap revealed that the fisherman was actually catching a boot, rather than a fish. Participants were then asked to point out the object that the fisherman *thought* he was catching in a separate picture displaying an array of objects. Participants passed this task if they correctly identified the fish and not the boot. To examine participants' ability to reason about *true* beliefs, the flap revealed that the fisherman was catching a fish and participants were then asked to point out what the fisherman *thought* he had caught (the fish). Participants passed this task if they correctly identified the fish and not the boot.

The moral dilemma narrative was elicited from participants after they viewed a 1.5-minute nonverbal cartoon, which follows the moral dilemmas of 'Mr Kourmal' as he struggles with the decision to return some money he found after a rich lady accidentally dropped it. Participants were asked to retell the events of the story to a fluent adult signer and were scored for references to mental states.

The results of the study revealed that early language learners of Nicaraguan Sign Language performed significantly better on the false-belief tasks than did later language learners. Importantly, it was not years of language exposure that predicted performance on the false-belief tasks, but only whether participants had been exposed to language during the sensitive period, before age 10. The early- and late-language groups were not statistically different in the number of mental states they included in their narratives (second theory of mind task), but early signers mentioned a mean of 6.55 mental state propositions and late learners mentioned an average of 5.64. The amount of exposure was related to the number of mental state references participants made in this latter task, suggesting that more experienced signers were simply able to say more (including signs about mental states) than those who were less experienced. The results confirmed that early language exposure predicts deaf children's performance on false-belief tasks, but that late exposure does not preclude a child from developing these theory of mind abilities. The narrative task offered a more nuanced measure of participants' appreciation of behaviour-relevant language, but did not distinguish between groups based on age of language acquisition.

However, participants who passed the false-belief tasks were more likely to receive a perfect score on the narrative task (according to the researchers' criterion, eight out of eight mental state references), relative to those who failed the false-belief task. Moreover, the narratives of those participants who had failed the false-belief tasks differed in a qualitative way from those participants who had passed: those who did not receive a perfect score consistently lacked statements like 'lack of knowledge' or 'deception' – statements that were included by most participants who passed the false-belief task. Because deception and false belief are situations where appearance and reality differ, they may rely more heavily on access to conversations about mental states during an early period in development when the child begins to use his or her own mental states to understand others' mental states. Thus, the authors propose that the complexity of false-belief situations is difficult for late-language learners whose theory of mind and language did not develop in tandem. Late-language learners may need to learn about these instances 'by rote,' relying on observational learning and active reasoning, while early-language learners are able to reason about others' false beliefs fluently and effortlessly.

According to Morgan and Kegl (2006, p. 818). 'In this framework, the nature of computing false belief is much like doing grammaticality judgements in language tests. Early exposed speakers perform perfectly and effortlessly on grammaticality tasks compared with late learners whose knowledge, when put in demanding situations, appears superficial and errorful . . . In the same way it may be the case that the false-belief task requires you to be a native "ToM speaker". Native in this sense means having developed an understanding of the mental states of others through a natural process of language acquisition beginning at some time period before 10 years of age.'

and greater gyrification (i.e. more folds; Preuss, 2000, 2004). Moreover, the anterior cingulate cortex is larger in primates than in other groups of mammals (Vogt, 1987).

There is also evidence of modularisation in the dorsolateral prefrontal cortex. This area is larger in the right than the left hemisphere in humans, while no such asymmetries exist in chimpanzees (Zilles *et al.*, 1996). The right dorsolateral region is associated with processing of visuospatial information, while the left is associated with language (Stephan *et al.*, 2003), suggesting that there has been reorganisation within the prefrontal cortex in the primate line since humans last shared a common ancestor with chimpanzees (see Holloway, 1969; Holloway and de la Coste-Lareymondie, 1982; Semendeferi *et al.*, 2001; Zilles *et al.*, 1996).

In addition, evidence indicates localisation and specialisation of the posterior regions of the brain. Lewis and Carmody (2008) report that the left temporo-parietal junction is most related to self-representational behaviour whereas the right hemisphere is involved when comparing the self to others. An increase in overall brain size, coupled with a protracted period of development and the disproportionate increase and specialisation of the prefrontal cortical areas responsible for self-awareness, behavioural planning, maintenance of attention and episodic memory likely resulted in enhanced executive control over information pertaining to the self in time and an increased ability to integrate information across frontal and posterior regions through a process of interactive specialisation.

Interactive specialisation

Johnson, Grossmann and Kadosh (2009) present a developmental model of how the brain moves towards specialised systems through a process of interactive specialisation. While theirs is a developmental model, it provides an appropriate analogy of how brain specialisation may have occurred over primate evolution.

Based on their research, Johnson and colleagues concluded that brain organisation takes place via a knowledge-based cascade, in which new networks recruit previously functional networks when required during learning. They report that the prefrontal cortex is more active in children than in adults when engaging in mentalising or social-cognitive tasks and that this activation shifts to more posterior regions associated with the social brain in adulthood. They infer that brain networks become more specialised as they become more localised over development. Prefrontal cortex activation decreases because it no longer must engage in solving a new problem, but only in guiding attention to the now-specialised regions of the posterior cortex.

'Self'-reliance

The need to differentially attend to information to move through a complex problem space, facilitated by the expansion of the prefrontal cortex, likely created a situation in which an organism became able to represent his or her own intentions and sensations. Eventually, the variability of the environment rendered insufficient the evolved heuristics, once so useful to our ancestors, and it became advantageous to mentally represent 'what is happening'. For example, at one time, it would have been adaptive to possess the following implicit algorithm: 'If I encounter a log, I should tear it open and eat grubs'. However, as environments became more variable and scarce, the likelihood that a poisonous critter lay therein instead of a grub increased, and the behavioural output no longer had any adaptive value, but in fact may have become *mal*adaptive (i.e. was too costly). Because these processors were hard-wired, the organism still fired an automatic response to the appropriate input or command signal (e.g. log = food = satisfy hunger motivation by tearing open log). While the generated outputs (tear open log) were no longer relevant, monitoring the input of the environment was (log = potential food). Thus, the motivation became activated and notified the organism of 'what is happening to me'. If the organism possessed enough computing power to differentially inhibit and active at multiple pieces of information, it was able to represent itself in the problem space, gain access to the motivations of its own behaviour and decide whether the behavioural output in question was appropriate. In this way, sensation became short-circuited, or privatised, as perception (see Humphrey, 2000). Given the degree of behavioural plasticity endowed by an extended juvenile period, in response to a complex environment the organism was able to explore alternative means for reaching the goal, such as investigative probing (for a review of this behaviour in chimpanzees, see McGrew, 1992). An increase in behavioural plasticity and flexibility meant individuals likely encountered species-atypical environments, altering the nature of selection pressures and epigenetic processes (Bjorklund, 2006).

The ability to self-represent was advantageous in that, as executive functions increased, it allowed an organism to recall itself in past scenarios (episodic memory) as well as reason about future ones, or engage in 'mental time travel' (Suddendorf and Busby, 2005; Suddendorf and Corballis, 1997, 2007; Tulving, 1985). This type of representation and intentional reasoning does not implicate social cognition. Self-representation and causal understanding could be extrapolated to form predictions of others' intentions, infer their goal states and acquire information vicariously. The scarcity of resources and increase in group size and behavioural flexibility created a situation in which it became advantageous to learn by watching others (social learning), teach one's own offspring (social referencing) and reason about others' beliefs and desires so as to cooperate and compete.

This, we believe, is the crux of human intelligence: the ability to pass on behaviours and information epigenetically has endowed humans with advanced intellectual abilities through cumulative cultural evolution (Richerson and Boyd, 1976, 2005). Although apes and cetaceans have been shown to transmit acquired knowledge across generations (a minimum definition of culture; see Bender, Herzing and Bjorklund, 2009; Rendell and Whitehead, 2001; van Schaik et al., 2003; Whiten et al., 1999), no other species transmits so much information and with such high fidelity as humans. The faculty to build on the knowledge of past generations is an arguably unique human ability that results in the rapid evolution of increasingly complex adaptations.

WHAT, EXACTLY, ARE WE SO GOOD AT? AND WHEN DID WE 'GET IT'?

Chimpanzees and bonobos provide the best models for what the cognition of our ancestors may have been like. In addition to sharing greater than 98% of DNA with humans by some estimates (Chimpanzee Sequencing and Analysis Consortium,

2005), like humans, chimpanzees and bonobos have disproportionately big brains, an extended juvenile period and live in socially complex communities. We should thus see hints of some of the cognitive and social-cognitive abilities that we see in young humans in our close genetic relatives. If the abilities possessed by contemporary chimpanzees were also possessed by humans' and apes' common ancestor, they may have served as a solid foundation for the emergence of the suite of cognitive and social-cognitive skills that characterise modern people. Understanding when and how these abilities evolved over ancestral history can help us gain insight into the function of modern human cognition.

In this section, we first discuss the executive capacity necessary for self-awareness and the processing of social and asocial information. Next, we describe evidence that non-human primates possess any kind of explicit knowledge necessary to reason about the self and others. Finally, we describe the social-cognitive precursors of the unique human ability to transmit non-genetic information across generations and discuss whether these abilities are available to non-human primates.

Executive function

Executive function refers to the processes involved in regulating attention and in determining what to do with information just gathered or retrieved from long-term memory. It involves a related set of basic information-processing abilities, including how quickly one can process information, how much information one can hold in the short-term store (and 'think about') at a time, and how well one can selectively attend to relevant information, switch between different tasks inhibit responding and resist interference (Jones, Rothbart and Posner, 2003; Wiebe, Espy and Charak, 2008). As we discussed earlier, an organism must evolve content-free, general mechanisms that enable the integration of sensory and perceptual information in order to operate on conscious representations (Baddeley and Hitch, 1974; Geary, 2005). Executive functions, such as inhibitory control and working-memory capacity, are features of general intelligence and likely evolved in response to the need to mentally simulate potential future social scenarios or changes in ecological conditions and rehearse appropriate responses (Geary, 2005). In this section we discuss briefly the role of executive function in human cognition and examine some executive-function abilities in non-human primates.

Inhibitory control

An initial step in evolving a human-like form of intelligence would include an increased ability to inhibit prepotent responding. Delaying gratification and planning future scenarios requires inhibiting current drives. Moreover, as social complexity and brain size increased, greater requirements to cooperate and compete with conspecifics and the ability to predict future scenarios required greater voluntary inhibitory control of sexual and aggressive behaviours, which contributed to increased social harmony and delay of gratification (see Bjorklund, Cormier and Rosenberg, 2005; Bjorklund and Harnishfeger, 1995; Bjorklund and Kipp, 2002). Neural circuits initially involved in the control of emotional and appetitive behaviours could then be co-opted for other purposes, playing a critical role in the evolution of the cognitive architecture of modern humans. Over time, inhibitory mechanisms became increasingly under cortical (and thus intentional) control.

A number of researchers have documented a relationship between children's developing theory of mind and executive function abilities, particularly inhibition (e.g. Flynn, O'Malley and Wood, 2004; Hughes and Ensor, 2007). For example, Clements and Perner (1994) suggest that children's inhibition is important for developing an explicit theory of mind. While most children do not pass explicit false-belief tasks before the age of four, children's looking behaviour suggests that they implicitly understand others' false beliefs much earlier. Thus, their failure on explicit forms of this task may not indicate a theory-of-mind deficit, but rather an inability to inhibit a prepotent response (see also Frye, Zelazo and Palfai, 1995; Peskin, 1992).

Chimpanzees and other primates obviously are able to inhibit their actions in some contexts. For example, a number of researchers have shown that great apes are able to engage in deception in some contexts by inhibiting a behaviour (see Byrne and Whiten, 1988) and that male chimpanzees will inhibit a distinctive cry during orgasm while copulating with a favourite female so as to avoid sharing the oestrous partner with others (see Whiten and Byrne, 1988). In addition, Gibson, Rumbaugh and Beran (2001) presented a series of studies in which chimpanzees learned to press a particular lever, ignoring another lever, to receive food. The chimpanzees were then able to switch this rule and press the second lever, ignoring the first. Their success at this task suggests that chimpanzees are capable of inhibiting some prepotent responses.

However, other research indicates that chimpanzees' inhibitory abilities are substantially less sophisticated than those of humans. For example, Boysen and Bernston (1995) placed two chimpanzees on opposite sides of a partition. One chimp, the 'selector', was shown two boxes with different amounts of candy in them. The box the selector chose was given to the other chimp (the 'observer'), and the selector received the contents of the box not chosen. To get the greatest amount of candies, the selector would have to choose the box with the fewer candies in it. Similar to young children (e.g. Hala and Russell, 2001; Peskin, 1992; Russell et al., 1991), the chimpanzees could not inhibit their primary response of selecting the array with the larger portion, thus they consistently received the lesser quantity of food. (As an aside, one of these chimpanzees had been trained to associate quantities with numerical symbols [e.g. '3' corresponds to three entities], and she was able to 'pass' the task when these symbols were used. Presumably, the use of symbols made it possible for this highly trained chimpanzee to inhibit her tendency to select the larger quantity.) These studies and other research suggest that the last common ancestor shared by chimpanzees and humans likely possessed inhibitory mechanisms that, given the right circumstances, may have aided in advancing human social cognition.

Working memory

Working memory is the name used to describe the memory system responsible for the activation of memory representations held in the short-term store and the capacity to bring them into focus or maintain attention on them (Baddeley, 1986; Baddeley and Hitch, 1974). There is debate regarding whether working-memory capacity is best described in terms of the amount of information that can be attended to and managed or in terms of the amount of time information can be held active (see Cowan and Alloway, 2009). What is clear is that individuals with higher working-memory capacities perform better on advanced problem-solving tasks and have higher IQs (see Frye and Hale, 2000). Increases in working-memory capacity may be responsible for the evolution of a qualitative change in human cognition – cognitive fluidity, that is, the ability to combine knowledge across different domains in new ways (see Mithen, 1996, 1999).

Working-memory capacity seems to underlie the understanding of categorical and causal relationships. For example, humans are capable of making spontaneous first-order classifications at around 12 months, grouping objects of the same colour together (Spinozzi et al., 1999). At 3 years, children can form three or more contemporaneous groups, sorting objects into three categories of different shapes, demonstrating that they are capable of focusing on the similarity relationship between three different groups of objects at once (Langer, 1980, 1986; Poti et al., 1999). However, adult chimpanzees rarely demonstrate a spontaneous formation of three or more contemporaneous groups (e.g. sorting objects into three groups based on three different colours; Langer, 1980, 1986), suggesting that chimpanzees' working-memory capacity is constrained to two to three items.

If extant chimps have insufficient working-memory capacities to allow the tracking of third-party relations, for example, then the expansion of working memory that led to qualitative changes, such as the acquisition of language and advanced social-cognitive abilities, must have happened some time along the *Homo* line. Read (2008) summarises data on chimpanzees' nut-cracking behaviour: he reports that few chimps are able to perform a three-step sequence of nut-cracking, such as manipulating a hammering stone, nut and anvil (Matsuzawa, 1994, 1997), and that this is a relatively late-developing ability, observed only in chimps older than 3 years. This behaviour suggests that successful chimps are able to keep three pieces of information in working memory. However, because nut-cracking involves placing the nut on the anvil (action 1) and then coordinating the hammer to strike the nut (action 2), some researchers have argued that nut cracking only entails a sequence of two actions and thus is best characterised as requiring a working-memory capacity of only two (Greenfield, 1991; Parker and McKinney, 1999). Regardless, the ability to sequence three objects appears to be at the limits of chimpanzees' ability, developing in only a few juveniles and adults.

Additionally, Visalberghi and Limongelli (1996) demonstrated limits to chimpanzees' working memory in a more controlled setting. When presented with the contraption pictured in Figure 2.3, apes were able to infer that force could be transmitted from themselves to the treat through the stick. However, when a trapdoor was introduced, apes could not integrate this information with their causal understanding of gravity and their understanding of the affordances of holes to avoid pushing the food down the trapdoor. Only after substantial practice were they able to understand that they should always push the food away from the trap, which meant entering the stick

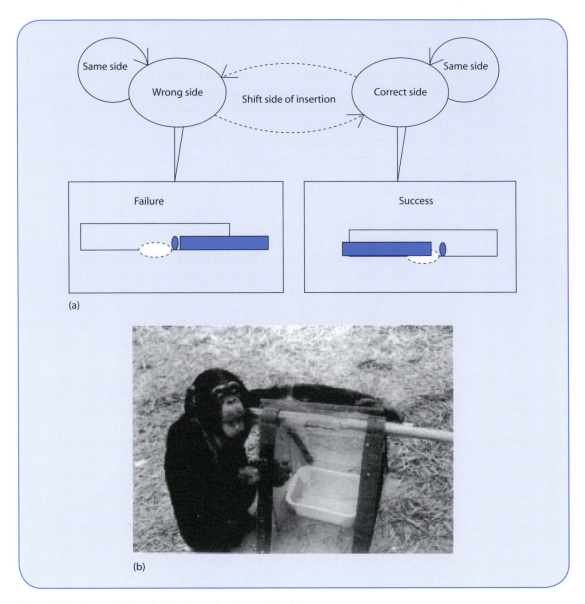

Figure 2.3. *Cause–effect relations in tool-using task by chimpanzees.*

The illustration on the left (a) depicts the possible sequences of insertions of the stick into the trap tube. In both examples a reward is placed on the right side of the trap. The choice made by the subject when inserting the stick for the first time is described in the oval. The first insertion may be correct or incorrect; if the subject pushes the stick all the way through, the correct insertion leads to success, whereas the wrong insertion leads to failure. Arrows indicate retrieval of the stick, and a new insertion in the same side of the tube. Dashed lines indicate retrieval of the stick and a shift in the side of insertion. The illustration on the right (b) portrays Bobby opening his mouth while pushing the reward with the stick. In this case the reward (placed on the right-hand side of the trap, furthest from Bobby) is going to fall into the trap because the stick has been inserted in the wrong side of the tube.

Source: Modified from Visalberghi, L., Boysen, S., and Visalberghi, E. (1995). Comprehension of cause–effect relations in tool-using task by chimpanzees (*Pan troglodytes*). *Journal of comparative psychology, 109*, pp. 20, 21.

on the end furthest away from the food (see Limongelli, Boysen and Visalberghi, 1995). Two- to 3-year-old human children, in contrast, were able to solve this problem from the very earliest trials. These findings, consistent with Read's (2008) reports of nut-cracking behaviour, indicate that, while chimps have an understanding that their actions cause events to occur in the world, this capacity is limited and they are not able to hold multiple causal representations in mind to allow them to mentally work through a problem-space in a manner comparable to young human children.

In addition, Read (2008) reports that chimpanzees' number-span recall does not exceed these limits. However, one could argue that this evidence only represents chimpanzees' working-memory capacity as it is assessed for non-social cognition, but cannot speak to their social abilities. In other words, if the social domain is so important to chimpanzees, perhaps they evolved specialised systems to process this information more efficiently and so their true working-memory capacity will be featured there.

Working memory and social relations

Life in a complex social group requires that an organism recognise and distinguish between members and non-members of a group or alliance. For example, humans must represent different categories of relationships among individuals, such as mothers and offspring, enemies and friends (Dasser, 1988a; Tomasello, 2000). Understanding triadic relations (how these individuals relate to the self and others) requires that an organism track at least three pieces of information. There is evidence that non-human primates understand third-party relationships (Tomasello and Call, 1994). For example, Dasser (1988a) found that longtail macaques are capable of understanding categories of social relationship, reliably choosing photos of mother–offspring pairs and sibling pairs over photos of unrelated group mates (Dasser, 1988b). Tomasello (2000) reports that chimpanzees in the wild will choose allies who outrank an opponent, demonstrating the ability to track the relationships between other members of the group and understand how these relationships pertain to the self.

However, Tomasello (1998) notes that chimpanzee gestures are almost exclusively used in dyadic relationships and do not exceed a sequence of two to three gestures or word-token combinations (for those language-trained apes) and rarely, if ever, do chimpanzees, even mother–infant pairs, engage in shared attention (Herrmann et al., 2007; Tomasello and Carpenter, 2005), in which one member of the dyad points out an object to the other member, an interaction that, according to Read (2008), requires a working-memory capacity of at least three items (see more in-depth discussion of shared attention below). These findings suggest that, even in the social domain, chimpanzees' abilities are constrained to the processing of no more than two to three pieces of information.

We should not be too hasty in discounting chimpanzees' abilities, however. Consistent with other evidence (Herrmann et al., 2007), these findings suggest that the minimal underlying quantitative capacity necessary for advanced social cognition may have been available to our last common ancestor with chimpanzees. In addition, while the findings of Visalberghi and Limongelli suggest that the ability to reason about multiple covert causes of actions, such as intentions in the social world or forces in the physical world, is not available to chimpanzees, these findings and others indicate that chimpanzees are able to reason that their own actions are a causal force in achieving a goal. The representation of the self as causally related to the environment was perhaps the most critical transition in the mind's evolution because it allowed for the emergence of explicit awareness (i.e. the ability to represent one's own perspective).

Explicit awareness and mental time travel

As Kurt Vonnegut noted, without conscious awareness, Einstein would have never arrived at a theory of relativity. While the physics would still undoubtedly exist in the natural world, it would not exist in his mind (or ours for that matter). Conscious awareness essentially reflects an awareness of self – the ability to experience one's own feelings, desires and behaviour – and correspondingly the realisation that other individuals have the same insight. While we try to avoid philosophical existentialist debates on the issue, we do feel that a discussion of consciousness is crucial to include in a chapter on the evolution of human cognition, as it is the foundation of uniquely human cognitive abilities distinguishing the rudimentary behaviour of non-human primates from the insightful behaviour of modern *Homo sapiens*.

Humphrey (1976) was the first psychologist to suggest the significance of self-awareness in human cognitive evolution, recognising that self-consciousness allows one to interpret and predict the feelings and behaviours of the self and others, a valuable tool for a social animal. With self-awareness, experiences can be redescribed, permitting knowledge that was once implicit to become explicit, or generating new insights by reflecting on what one already knows (Karmiloff-Smith, 1991, 1992).

As with other aspects of cognitive development, there seems not to be a definitive point in time before which self-awareness is not present and after which it is. Perhaps the classic demonstration of self-awareness is mirror self-recognition, in which children realise that it is themselves and not another child whom they see in the mirror. Children 'pass' this task, usually by pointing to a mark on their face that was surreptitiously placed there rather than pointing at the mirror, around 18 months of age (e.g. Brooks-Gunn and Lewis, 1984; Nielsen, Suddendorf and Slaughter, 2006). Chimpanzees, orang-utans, a few gorillas (Gallup, 1979; Suddendorf and Whiten, 2001), dolphins (Reiss and Marino, 2001), elephants (Plotnik, de Waal and Reiss, 2006) and magpies (Prior, Schwarz and Güntürkün, 2008) have also been found to pass mirror self-recognition tasks. However, 'passing' this task reflects only a rudimentary understanding of self. For example, when researchers placed stickers on children's heads, most 2- and 3-year-olds failed to reach for the stickers when shown photographs or videos of themselves (e.g. Povinelli, Landau and Perilloux, 1996; Povinelli and Simon, 1998), suggesting that children's sense of self develops gradually over the preschool years, as their ability to deal with different modes of representation (mirrors, photos, videos) develops (see also Skouteris, Spataro and Lazaridis, 2006; Zelazo, Sommerville and Nichols, 1999).

Other research suggests that some aspects of self-awareness and explicit cognition develop much earlier. For example, infants as young as 9 months old display deferred imitation (see Bauer, 2007), which entails imitating a modelled behaviour after a delay, and has been proposed to be a non-verbal form of explicit memory. Corroborating evidence comes from studies of adults with hippocampal damage, who are unable to acquire new explicit knowledge but can learn new implicit knowledge. For instance, when given a mirror-drawing task (trace figures while watching one's hand in a mirror), adult patients with hippocampal damage do not remember performing the task from day to day (explicit memory) but nonetheless improve their performance as a result of practice (implicit memory) (Milner, 1964), indicating a dissociative deficit in explicit memory, but not implicit memory, in these patients. When these patients are given deferred-imitation tasks similar to those used with infants in Bauer's studies (e.g. observe a novel behaviour and then reproduce it a day later), they perform much as they do on verbal explicit memory tasks: they are unable to remember seeing the task performed and fail to reproduce the modelled behaviour (McDonough et al., 1995). These findings support the argument that infants' deferred imitation is demonstrative of non-verbal explicit memory.

Humans' ability to explicitly recall, or re-experience, the what, where and when aspects of an event is called 'episodic memory', or 'mental time travel', and is differentiated from other forms of explicit memory, such as semantic memory, in that it relies on an autonoetic component, or an explicit retrieval of the self's experience of a particular episode (Tulving, 2005). This type of memory is often described as autobiographical because it is from the perspective of the self. Currently, there is scarce evidence suggesting that mental time travel is available to non-human primates, and this issue remains a topic of intense debate (e.g. Suddendorf and Busby, 2003).

An exception seems to be for enculturated chimpanzees that are capable of demonstrating deferred imitation (e.g. Bering, Bjorklund and Ragan, 2000; Bjorklund et al., 2002; Tomasello, Savage-Rumbaugh and Kruger, 1993). Enculturated chimpanzees (and other apes) are raised much as human children are raised, with their 'parents' speaking to them, pointing out things for them to see and attempting to teach them child-like behaviours, such as eating with a spoon (Call and Tomasello, 1996). Compared to mother-reared animals, they experience a species-atypical rearing environment, and as a result may develop cognitive or social-cognitive skills similar to those displayed by human preschool children (see Bjorklund and Rosenberg, 2005; Call and Tomasello, 1996). For example, with respect to deferred imitation, in several experiments, chimpanzees observed a human model display specific actions on objects (e.g. placing a plastic nail in a form board and striking it with a plastic hammer), and after a 10-minute (Bering, Bjorklund and Ragan, 2000; Bjorklund, Bering and Ragan, 2000) or 24-hour (Tomasello, Savage-Rumbaugh and Kruger, 1993) delay, were given the objects again. In all studies, the enculturated chimpanzees displayed greater-than-chance levels of deferred imitation, unlike mother-raised animals (Tomasello, Savage-Rumbaugh and Kruger, 1993).

Using a generalisation of imitation task, Bjorklund and colleagues (2002) modelled a target behaviour with one set of objects (e.g. musical cymbals) for enculturated chimpanzees and then subsequently gave the apes similar but not identical objects (e.g. trowels) to determine if they would generalise the observed actions. The chimpanzees displayed above-chance levels of deferred imitation of actions on objects (although at lower levels than for deferred imitation when the same objects were used in the modelling and imitation phases). That chimpanzees could generalise previously learned behaviour suggests that they recalled their intentions at the time of the initial episode and were able to use this information with novel objects. Enculturated chimpanzees' ability to use representations of their own intentions and prior mental states to infer how they should behave in different situations parallels the way humans infer and represent others' intentions and use this information to predict behaviour. This is a strong indication that precursory social cognition was available to our last ancestor with chimpanzees.

Others argue that mental time travel is available to animals other than primates. For example, Clayton and colleagues (Clayton, Bussey and Dickinson, 2003; Clayton, Dally and Emery, 2007; Clayton and Dickinson, 1998; Emery and Clayton, 2004) contend that the food-caching behaviours of western scrub jays are indicative of mental time travel. While it seems difficult to explain birds' behaviour in a way that does not posit autonoetic experience, it is unlikely that they are engaging in mental time travel in the way that humans do. It has been suggested that jays' caching behaviours may be based on a series of conditionals and do not require that the birds represent any kind of goal when moving through this problem space. For most animals, the means of achieving the goal (i.e. retrieving food) is not separate from the goal itself (assuaging hunger).

Future mental time travel may provide the sought-after distinction between human and non-human cognition. Like the generalisation of deferred imitation, future mental time travel is like a stepping-stone from being self-aware to reasoning about the intentions of others, as it involves hypothesising about how one's mind will be similar or different in the future.

The capacity to mentally time travel into the future may allow an animal to predict, shape and respond flexibly to the environment. Imagining future scenarios means conceiving of possibilities. This was likely advantageous for our ancestors when adapting to a variable environment: if individuals can manoeuvre their current environments to match the who, what, when and where of their envisioned scenarios, they have effectively adapted the environment to meet their needs, instead of the contrary. Engaging in mental time travel to envision a future goal may also provide the organism with motivation to delay gratification, encouraging restrained choices and a decrease in the extent to which the future is 'discounted' (Boyer, 2008). Thus, it is likely facilitated by the inhibitory capacity we discussed earlier. Moreover, rehearsal allows one to think through a problem space, representing an initial state, a means and an end, and may be evidence that an animal is capable of representing causal relationships. Likewise, this type of reasoning may be available to chimpanzees, as it can be carried out with a minimum working-memory capacity of three items. In situations where an organism must cooperate and compete ad nauseam, it is important for an organism to stay 'one step ahead'.

Mulcahy and Call (2006) report that bonobos and orang-utans select, transport and store tools that they will use later for retrieving food. Because tool selection, transport and storage is removed from the goal of food retrieval, these behaviours imply that this sequence of tasks involves mental time travelling through a problem space to identify a goal, and then representing it long enough to work backwards and construct the means with which to achieve it. However, it is unclear that the goal of obtaining food must be represented by these apes. These behaviours may be associated with a hunger drive that persists throughout the problem space and not represented as a distinct goal of the future self (Suddendorf, 2006). Thus, it is unclear from this study whether apes' behaviour in these situations involves an autonoetic, or time-travelling, component.

If an animal demonstrates evidence of rehearsal, however, we might argue that it is capable of mental time travel into the future. To test whether enculturated apes benefit from an opportunity for rehearsal, researchers presented one chimp and one orang-utan (O'Connell, 1995) and 3- to 7-year-old children (McAdam, 1996) with a puzzle box. When children and apes were allowed to 'study' the puzzle box for a period prior to opening it, they opened the puzzle box significantly faster than when they were not given this time to 'look but not touch'. These effects, though significant, were only marginal for the chimpanzee and orang-utan, and given the small sample size, more studies are needed before we conclude with confidence that non-human primates are capable of benefiting from advance rehearsal. However, this evidence is consistent with conclusions drawn by Read (2008) that these abilities, requiring larger working-memory capacity, are at the fringe of chimpanzees' competencies.

In summary, these studies provide preliminary evidence that at least some of our closest relatives are capable of explicitly recalling previous episodes and reasoning about future ones. Comparative research has provided evidence that non-human primates possess explicit memory in some contexts and may be capable of reasoning about their own past and future intentions. In other words, they act as if they can make use of their own past perspective. The ability to generalise one's own goals and intentions to non-present novel situations requires explicit representation, self-awareness and mental time travel. These abilities seem to represent different sides of the same coin, that is the basis for taking the perspective of others and forming theories of their minds.

Social learning

As we mentioned, the epitome of human intelligence is our ability to transmit non-genetic information across generations with great fidelity via language and other processes of social learning. This is the basis of modern human culture. Social learning refers to 'situations in which one individual comes to behave similarly to others' (Boesch and Tomasello, 1998, p. 598). In groups where there is a steep 'information gradient' (Dennett, 1983), meaning individuals vary a great deal in what they know, an individual will thrive based on his or her ability to use others as sources of information about the world. Comparative psychologists differentiate between different types of social learning, based on presumed underlying mechanisms, including local enhancement, mimicry and emulation (see Tomasello, 1999; Tomasello and Call, 1997; Want and Harris, 2002). These forms of social learning are contrasted with what Tomasello and his colleagues refer to as 'true imitation', which uniquely requires that one take the perspective of another to represent his or her goal and faithfully copy the observed means with which the goal is met (Tomasello, 1999; Tomasello, Kruger and Ratner, 1993).

The most sophisticated way to transmit knowledge is through teaching, which involves a bidirectional process that requires that the teacher understand what the learner knows and his or her goals, and that the student appreciate the teacher's goal (Caro and Hauser, 1992; Tomasello, Kruger and Ratner, 1993). At the core of these abilities is the capacity to take on the perspective of another and view others as intentional beings (i.e. they do things 'on purpose'; see Bandura, 2006; Tomasello and Carpenter, 2007). The term used to describe such phenomena is 'theory of mind', based on the assumption that people possess a 'theory' of how their and other people's minds work. According to Wellman (1990), people's theories are based on belief-desire reasoning. People understand that one's behaviour is a function of what one knows or believes, and what one wants or desires, and that different people can have different, and often conflicting, beliefs and desires. Belief-desire reasoning, as assessed by the false-belief task (understanding that someone can have a false belief, for example believing that a crayon box contains crayons when it really contains candles) is not reliably observed in children until about 4 years of age (e.g. Wellman, Cross and Watson, 2001). A critical basis for reasoning about others' intentions, beliefs and desires is the ability to reason about one's own intentions as differing over time, an ability built on self-consciousness.

We know that chimpanzees (e.g. Whiten et al., 1999), orang-utans (van Schaik et al., 2003) and cetaceans (Bender, Herzing and Bjorklund, 2009; Rendell and Whitehead, 2001) transmit non-genetic information across generations, including forms of greeting, grooming and foraging, a characteristic of human culture. Importantly, chimpanzees' considerable social-learning ability indicates that they possess the behavioural plasticity necessary for the acquisition of new cognitive skills (e.g. Call, Carpenter and Tomasello, 2005; Horner and Whiten, 2005). However, chimpanzees seem less likely to use the more cognitively advanced form of imitation, displayed by young children, but use cognitively less demanding, but sometimes more efficient, methods. For example, after observing a model demonstrate a series of relevant and irrelevant actions to open a transparent puzzle box, 3- and 4-year-old children imitated irrelevant actions to open the box and obtain a treat, even though they could see that the actions were irrelevant (Horner and Whiten, 2005). In contrast, when given the same task, chimpanzees used goal emulation, imitating only relevant actions (see also Nagell, Olguin and Tomasello, 1993). There is less evidence that chimpanzees are able to take the perspective of others necessary for true imitation or engage in teaching (see Fouts, 1997; Tomasello and Call, 1997; Whiten et al., 2004).

For example, Premack and Woodruff (1978) inferred that the chimpanzee, Sarah, understood a human's goal because, after observing a video of a woman attempting to exit a locked door, Sarah chose a picture of a key. However, Savage-Rumbaugh, Rumbaugh and Boysen (1978) report that their apes chose a picture of a key after seeing a picture of a lock, with no human present in the scene, suggesting that Sarah's performance may only demonstrate associative learning and not the ability to reason about others' intentions and goals as causing their behaviour. Thus, it is not clear that apes are capable of assessing information about others' intentions, but only the abilities that allow them to appear 'as if' they are reasoning in this way.

Representing others' intentions is not necessary, but it is efficient

Some animals seem capable of learning causal relationship by associating a specific stimulus with its subsequent response. For example, rats learn to avoid a food pellet that has been poisoned once it makes them sick, behaving as if they understand that this particular type of pellet causes illness (Garcia and Koelling, 1966). The sociality of humans mandates that we apply the ability to reason about causes to predict behaviour. Any given behaviour can be effectively predicted by learning the association between stimulus and response, in the same manner rats learn the association between poisoned food and vomiting. However, when the demands to predict behaviour increase, it is no longer sufficient to learn the association between each environmental stimulus and each behavioural output. For example, any behavioural output, such as aggression, could be caused by a number of inputs, such as the presence of food, the presence of out-group members and/or aggressive advances by a rival, and so on. The task of learning all of these stimulus–response associations is arduous, at best. Rather, in variable social environments, where a number of stimuli can trigger a number of behavioural responses, positing that a single hidden variable, such as an intention, or goal, is the cause of a behaviour provides a more efficient route through which to predict others' actions.

Besides addressing the issue of variability of the social environment, understanding others as intentional agents helps an organism to navigate an environment where information is translucent (Sterelny, 2000), meaning individuals' behaviours are not always true reflections of their inner states. In other words, an individual's ability to avoid being deceived by conspecifics depends on how well he or she can track others' motivations (Whiten, 1996), especially when the mixture of cooperation and competition is ever-changing. For instance, inferring that aggressive behaviours are demonstrated by a conspecific with playful intentions allows one to respond appropriately, and potentially avoid disaster. Thus, the more socially complex an organism's group, the more adept he or she should be at perceiving the relationship between others' intentions and their behaviour. Tracking others' intentions is most efficiently achieved by adopting the perspective of another (i.e. 'What would I do/think in this situation?'). This ability also subserves the transmission of social information, especially when engaged in teaching, as mentioned above. In humans, evidence of this capacity begins to appear in the first years of life, as reflected by young children engaging in shared (or joint) attention (e.g. see Brooks and Meltzoff, 2002; Gergely *et al.*, 1995; Gergely, Bekkering and Király, 2002; Liszkowski *et al.*, 2006; Liszkowski, Carpenter and Tomasello, 2007; Meltzoff, 1995; described below). However, belief-desire reasoning, as we mentioned, is not reliably observed until about 4 years of age (e.g. Wellman, Cross and Watson, 2001).

We are unaware of any evidence to suggest that either mother-reared or enculturated chimpanzees pass false-belief tasks, at least under controlled conditions (Call and Tomasello, 1999; Herrmann *et al.*, 2007). However, there are several lines of research examining the manners in which they reason about others' intentions. For example, shared (or joint) attention involves a triadic interaction between the observer, another individual and an object. For example, I might try to draw my dog's attention to her toy by pointing or gazing at the object, a form of referential communication. If my dog is able to follow my gaze or pointing finger and detect the toy, it might indicate that she infers that I see something that she does not (she is able to imagine another perspective) and that I intend to draw her attention to it. The understanding that others possess knowledge differing from one's own and have intentions underlying their behaviour is at the basis of theory of mind abilities. Unfortunately, my dog does not pass this task.

While there is some evidence that chimpanzees and even monkeys will follow the gaze of another individual in some contexts (Bering and Povinelli, 2003; Bräuer, Call and Tomasello, 2005), there is much debate about whether this means they grasp the concept, 'seeing is knowing'. Most researchers argue that there is no evidence that either mother-reared or enculturated chimpanzees engage in shared attention (Herrmann et al., 2007; Tomasello and Carpenter, 2005). Others disagree, noting, for example, that captive chimpanzees point to food only in the presence of a caretaker (Leavens, Hopkins and Bard, 2005). Additional research supporting the idea that chimpanzees understand that the 'eyes have knowledge' has been reported in a food-competition task (Hare, Call and Tomasello, 2001; Hare et al., 2000). In these studies, lower-ranking chimpanzees retrieved food placed in a room only when it was placed out of sight of a higher-ranking animal. This implies that chimpanzees understand that if another conspecific is looking at something the other individual 'sees' it (i.e. has knowledge of it), and they can use this information adaptively, in this case to retrieve the food (or not).

This ability is more limited than it is in humans, however. For example, Povinelli and Eddy (1996) demonstrated that chimpanzees would choose to beg for food from a human trainer who was facing them as opposed to one facing away from them. However, they chose randomly when both trainers faced them but one had her eyes occluded (by a blindfold, for example). Believing that Povinelli and Eddy's experiments may have been ecologically invalid, Gomez (1996) trained chimps to attract the trainers' attention. In a natural setting, if a conspecific is facing another, it is likely that, eventually, he or she will spot the other. Thus, tracking whether the face is visible may be sufficient for primates to infer attention (or at least potential attention). Gomez found that his chimps performed better than Povinelli and Eddy's, concluding that chimps have implicit, context-bound knowledge about how to manipulate and use attention, but they do not have explicit access to represent that others see and thus cannot take on another's perspective to reason about blindfolded individuals (Sterelny, 2000; see Brooks and Meltzoff, 2002, 2005, for evidence that 10- to 12-month-old human infants can do this and Box 2.3 for a description of recent work).

An exception to this seems to be for enculturated apes that have demonstrated generalised imitation following a significant delay (e.g. Bjorklund et al., 2002, discussed earlier) and rational imitation immediately after viewing a model's behaviour (e.g. Buttelmann et al., 2007). For example, Buttelmann and colleagues used a procedure in which enculturated chimpanzees observed a human model using an unusual body part to operate an apparatus (such as using his forehead to turn on a light), both with his hands free and occupied. A similar paradigm was used by Gergely, Bekkering and Király (2002) with 14-month-old human infants. Similar to Gergely et al.'s findings with 14-month-old human infants, the enculturated chimpanzees imitated rationally,

BOX 2.3.   DOES SEEING REQUIRE KNOWING?

Infants will no longer follow an adult's eye gaze once she closes her eyes, yet will continue to follow her gaze if she is blindfolded (Brooks and Meltzoff, 2002). Why is there a difference?

Meltzoff and Brooks (2008) suggest this is because eye blinking is a biological motion, one that infants have experience with, while the visual occlusion caused by a blindfold is unfamiliar to most infants. Infants' experience opening and closing their own eyes yields a framework upon which they can map others' blinking, while their inexperience with blindfolds makes this a novel situation, one they are incapable of simulating when observing others. Meltzoff and Brooks examined the importance of self-experience for understanding others, predicting that providing infants with 'blindfold self-experience' (i.e. placing the blindfold on the infant) would allow the infant to understand that when another individual was blindfolded his or her vision was occluded. In their study, 12-month-old infants wore an opaque cloth or a windowed cloth blindfold for approximately three minutes. Infants who were provided with the experience of being truly blindfolded (wore the opaque cloth) were able to later generalise this experience and did not follow the gaze of the blindfolded adult, while infants who wore the windowed blindfold were significantly more likely to later follow the gaze of a blindfolded adult.

In a second experiment, 18-month-old infants had their eyes covered by a trick blindfold, one that seemed opaque from the outside but was actually transparent when worn. Unlike the truly blindfolded infants, these trick-blindfolded infants followed the gaze of a blindfolded adult, treating him or her as if she could see. These findings add to those of the first study because they suggest that infants' development is not simply 'accelerated' down a normally developing pathway by experience (e.g. understanding the properties of opaque barriers), but that training with a novel 'trick' blindfold (one that appears opaque but actually is not) yields them a basis for interpreting the behaviour of others wearing a blindfold.

Together, these findings suggest that infants map their own experience onto the experience of others in social learning. This mapping is not simply an unfolding of a predetermined developmental plan, however, but Meltzoff and Brooks argue that 'self experience provides a mechanism of change in social understanding: As children's self-experience broadens, their appreciation of others' minds and behavior is enriched and refined' (p. 1264). Infants' may map information onto an abstract framework in a way that is bidirectional, meaning infants learn about the psychological attributes associated with behaviour by mapping the self onto others (based on first-person experience) and others onto the self (based on third-person observation). This demonstration is important because it illustrates the significant role of plasticity and novel self-experience in shaping social learning early in development.

using the unusual body part when the model's hands were free and the more convenient hands when the model's hands had been occupied. These findings indicate that enculturated chimpanzees may be capable of representing others' goals, at least in some very controlled circumstances (but see Wood *et al.*, 2007).

Even if the social-cognitive abilities of chimpanzees are less than those of human preschool children (e.g. Herrmann *et al.*, 2007), research reviewed here makes it clear that chimpanzees have some understanding of the psychological states of other individuals. This research also makes clear that chimpanzees, and thus likely humans' common ancestor with them, possess the roots of a human-like cognitive system and that they have the neural plasticity to modify their behaviour and cognition in response to environmental contingencies. We believe that such cognitive plasticity was a necessary component for the cognitive changes that occurred in the hominid line over the past five to seven million years. Moreover, the fact that the most human-like forms of cognition (or at least social cognition) are displayed by enculturated apes – animals raised much like human children and very differently from the way their own mothers would raise them – indicates early experience, likely at the hands of their mothers, was the most probable impetus for such changes (Bjorklund, 2006; Bjorklund, Grotuss and Csinady, 2009). Research with a variety of mammals has demonstrated the epigenetic transmission of behaviour (e.g. styles of attachment, reactions to stress) acquired early in development across generations (see Champagne and Curley, 2009; Meaney, 2001; Suomi, 2004), making mothers an especially likely candidate for the source of environmental change.

As we have noted, we believe that humans' unique suite of cognitive abilities emerged via the confluence of an enlarged brain, an extended juvenile period and life in socially complex groups. We also believe that early hominids' neural and cognitive flexibility afforded the opportunity for behavioural and cognitive modification that, as a result of early experience, created new phenotypes, which were then subject to natural selection. Moreover, because of the ubiquity of maternal effects in mammalian development (see Maestripieri and Mateo, 2009), they are the most likely candidates for the source of epigenetic inheritance in human social-cognitive evolution. Ecological conditions that promoted changes in behaviour in only a handful of mothers could have resulted in offspring with enhanced social-cognitive skills. Should these individuals realise a selective advantage, their greater abilities for dealing with conspecifics could have been passed onto their own offspring and spread through the population.

CONCLUSIONS

In writing this chapter, we strove to transmit information and knowledge to the reader, in hopes that it will provide the foundation upon which future knowledge can build. By reflecting on the arguments and evidence we have conveyed, becoming aware of how this information relates to his or her previously acquired knowledge and the knowledge that he or she will obtain in the future, the reader obtains knowledge in a cumulative manner. During this process of transmission, we made efforts to take the perspective of the reader and understand what knowledge he or she already possesses, and what he or she may wish to gain.

In this way, this chapter is just as much an example of what makes humans uniquely intelligent as it is of how we came to be this way: the ability to consider the perspective of others is fundamental to humans' capacity to transmit cultural information, survive in a social group and accrue an amassed intelligence that trumps that of other species. The passage of knowledge in this way – in which one generation's intelligence mounts directly on the intelligence of the previous generation – is not seen in any other species, at least to the extent it is in humans, and must have evolved some time in human phylogeny following the separation of the line that led to modern-day humans from those of contemporary chimpanzees and bonobos.

We have argued that variable ecological and social conditions allowed for the emergence of an extended juvenile period, large brains and a general intelligence superior to that of any other species. As a result, we were able to evolve the explicit, conscious self-awareness necessary for advanced problem-solving and the ability to take another's perspective and reason about the state of our own mind and those of others. In turn, increases in the sophistication of social-cognitive abilities within a population yielded increases in social complexity, resulting in a within-species arms race for social intellect, one that still carries on today (as evidenced by this chapter, the purpose of which is to further our knowledge of these processes). An increasingly intricate social environment in which information is transmitted faithfully and at a rapid pace serves to reciprocally drive intellectual abilities spiralling upwards today, just as it did along the path of human phylogenetic history.

REFERENCES

Alexander, R. D. (1989). Evolution of the human psyche. In P. Mellars and C. Stringer (eds), *The human revolution: Behavioural and biological perspectives on the origins of modern humans* (pp. 455–513). Princeton, NJ: Princeton University Press.

Baddeley, A. D. (1986). *Working memory*. New York: Oxford University Press.

Baddeley, A. D. and Hitch, G. J. (1974). The psychology of learning and motivation. In G. A. Bower (ed.), *Recent advances in learning and motivation* (pp. 47–89). New York: Academic Press.

Baddeley, A. D. and Logie, R. H. (1999). Working memory: The multiple component model. In A. Miyake and S. Priti (eds), *Models of working memory: Mechanisms of active maintenance and executive control* (pp. 28–61). Cambridge: Cambridge University Press.

Bandura, A. (2006). Toward a psychology of human agency. *Perspectives on Psychological Science, 2*, 164–80.

Bauer, P. J. (2007). *Remembering the times of our lives: Memory in infancy and beyond*. Mahwah, NJ: Lawrence Erlbaum Associates.

Bender, C. E., Herzing, D. L. and Bjorklund, D. F. (2009). Evidence of teaching in Atlantic Spotted Dolphins (*Stenella frontalis*) by mother dolphins foraging in the presence of their calves. *Animal Cognition, 12*, 43–53.

Bering, J. M. and Bjorklund, D. F. (2007). The serpent's gift: Evolutionary psychology and consciousness. In P. D. Zelazo, M. Moscovitch and E. Thompson, E. (eds), *Cambridge handbook of consciousness* (pp. 595–627). New York: Cambridge University Press.

Bering, J. M., Bjorklund, D. F. and Ragan, P. (2000). Deferred imitation of object-related actions in human-reared, juvenile great apes. *Developmental Psychobiology, 36*, 218–32.

Bering, J. M. and Povinelli, D. J. (2003). *Comparing cognitive development*. In D. Maestripieri (ed.), *Primate psychology* (pp. 205–33). Cambridge, MA: Harvard University Press.

Bickerton, D. (1990). *Language and species*. Chicago: University of Chicago Press.

Bjorklund, D. F. (2006). Mother knows best: Epigenetic inheritance, maternal effects, and the evolution of human intelligence. *Developmental Review, 26,* 213–42.

Bjorklund, D. F. and Bering, J. M. (2003). A note on the development of deferred imitation in enculturated juvenile chimpanzees (*Pan troglodytes*). *Developmental Review, 23,* 389–412.

Bjorklund, D. F., Bering, J. M. and Ragan, P. (2000). A two-year longitudinal study of deferred imitation of object manipulation in an enculturated juvenile chimpanzee (*Pan troglodytes*) and orangutan (*Pongo pygmaeus*). *Developmental Psychobiology, 37,* 229–37.

Bjorklund, D. F., Causey, K. and Periss, V. (2009). The evolution and development of human social cognition. In P. Kappeler and J. Silk (eds), *Mind the gap: Tracing the origin of human universals*. Berlin: Springer Verlag.

Bjorklund, D. F., Cormier, C. and Rosenberg, J. S. (2005). The evolution of theory of mind: Big brains, social complexity, and inhibition. In W. Schneider, R. Schumann-Hengsteler and B. Sodian (eds), *Young children's cognitive development: Interrelationships among executive functioning, working memory, verbal ability and theory of mind* (pp. 147–74). Mahwah, NJ: Lawrence Erlbaum Associates.

Bjorklund, D. F., Grotuss, J. and Csinady, A. (2009). Maternal effects, social cognitive development, and the evolution of human intelligence. In D. Maestripieri and J. Mateo (eds), *Maternal effects in mammals*. Chicago: Chicago University Press.

Bjorklund, D. F. and Harnishfeger, K. K. (1995). The role of inhibition mechanisms in the evolution of human cognition and behavior. In F. N. Dempster and C. J. Brainerd (eds), *New perspectives on interference and inhibition in cognition* (pp. 141–73). New York: Academic Press.

Bjorklund, D. F. and Kipp, K. (2002). Social cognition, inhibition, and theory of mind: The evolution of human intelligence. In R. J. Sternberg and J. C. Kaufman (eds), *The evolution of intelligence* (pp. 27–53). Mahwah, NJ: Lawrence Erlbaum Associates.

Bjorklund, D. F. and Pellegrini, A. D. (2000). Child development and evolutionary psychology. *Child Development, 71,* 1687–708.

Bjorklund, D. F. and Pellegrini, A. D. (2002). Evolutionary perspectives on social development. In P. Smith and C. Hart (eds), *Handbook of social development* (pp. 44–59). London: Blackwell.

Bjorklund, D. F. and Rosenberg, J. S. (2005). The role of developmental plasticity in the evolution of human cognition. In B. J. Ellis and D. F. Bjorklund (eds), *Origins of the social mind: Evolutionary psychology and child development* (pp. 45–75). New York: Guilford.

Bjorklund, D., Yunger, J. L., Bering, J. M. and Ragan, P. (2002). The generalization of deferred imitation in enculturated chimpanzees (*Pan troglodytes*). *Animal Cognition, 5,* 49–58.

Boesch, C. and Tomasello, M. (1998). Chimpanzee and human cultures. *Current Anthropology, 39,* 591.

Bogin, B. (1999). Evolutionary hypotheses for human childhood. *Yearbook of Physical Anthropology, 40,* 63–89.

Bogin, B. (2001). *The growth of humanity*. New York: John Wiley & Sons, Ltd.

Bogin, B. (2003). The human pattern of growth and development in paleontological perspective. In J. L. Thompson, G. E. Krovitz and A. J. Nelson (eds), *Patterns of growth and development in the genus Homo* (pp. 15–44). Cambridge: Cambridge University Press.

Boyer, P. (2008). Evolutionary economics of mental time travel? *Trends in Cognitive Sciences, 12,* 219–34.

Boysen, S. and Bernston, G. (1995). Responses to quantity: Perceptual versus cognitive mechanisms in chimpanzees (*Pan Troglodytes*). *Journal of Experimental Psychology*, *21*, 82–6.

Bräuer, J., Call, J. and Tomasello, M. (2005). All great ape species follow gaze to distant locations and around barriers. *Journal of Comparative Psychology*, *119*, 145–54.

Brooks, R. and Meltzoff, A. (2002). The importance of eyes: How infants interpret adult looking behavior. *Developmental Psychology*, *38*, 958–66.

Brooks, R. and Meltzoff, A. (2005). The development of gaze and its relation to language. *Developmental Science*, *8*, 535–43.

Brooks-Gunn, J. and Lewis, M. (1984). Maternal responsivity in interactions with handicapped infants. *Child Development*, *55*, 782–93.

Buss, D. M. (ed.) (2005). *The evolutionary psychology handbook*. Hoboken, NJ: John Wiley and Sons, Ltd.

Buttelmann, D., Carpenter, M., Call, J. and Tomasello, M. (2007). Enculturated chimpanzees imitate rationally. *Developmental Science*, *10*, F31–F38.

Byrne, R. W. and Whiten, A. (eds) (1988). *Machiavellian intelligence: Social expertise and the evolution of intellect in monkeys, apes, and humans*. Oxford: Clarendon Press.

Call, J., Carpenter, M. and Tomasello, M. (2005). Copying results and copying actions in the process of social learning: chimpanzees (*Pan troglodytes*) and human children (*Homo sapiens*). *Animal Cognition*, *8*, 151–63.

Call, J. and Tomasello, M. (1996). The effects of humans on the cognitive development of apes. In A. E. Russon, K. A. Bard and S. T. Parker (eds), *Reaching into thought: The minds of the great apes* (pp. 371–403). New York: Cambridge University Press.

Call, J. and Tomasello, M. (1999). A nonverbal false belief task: The performance of children and great apes. *Child Development*, *70*, 381–95.

Calvin, W. H. and Bickerton, D. (2000). *Lingua ex machina*. Cambridge, MA: MIT Press.

Caro, T. M. and Hauser, M. D. (1992). Is there teaching in nonhuman animals? *Quarterly Review of Biology*, *67*, 151–74.

Cattell, R. B. (1963). Theory of fluid and crystallized intelligence: A critical experiment. *Journal of Educational Psychology*, *54*, 1–22.

Champagne, F. A. and Curley, J. P. (2009). Epigenetic mechanisms mediating the long-term effects of maternal care on development. *Neuroscience and Biobehavioral Reviews*, *33*, 593–600.

Chimpanzee Sequencing and Analysis Consortium (2005). Initial sequence of the chimpanzee genome and comparison with human genome. *Nature*, *437*, 69–88.

Clayton, N. S., Bussey, T. J. and Dickinson, A. (2003). Can animals recall the past and plan for the future? *Nature Reviews Neuroscience*, *4*, 685–91.

Clayton, N. S., Dally, J. M. and Emery, N. J. (2007). Social cognition by food-caching corvids. The western scrub-jay as a natural psychologist. *Philosophical Transactions of the Royal Society B: Biological Sciences*, *362*, 507.

Clayton, N. S. and Dickinson, A. (1998). Episodic-like memory during cache recovery by scrubjays. *Nature*, *395*, 272–4.

Clements, W. A. and Perner, J. (1994). Implicit understanding of belief. *Cognitive Development*, *9*, 377–95.

Cosmides, L. (1989). The logic of social exchange: Has natural selection shaped how humans reason? Studies with the Wason selection task. *Cognition*, *31*, 187–276.

Cosmides, L. and Tooby, J. (1994). Origins of domain specificity: The evolution of functional organization. In L. A. Hirschfeld and S. A. Gelman (eds), *Mapping the mind: Domain specificity in cognition and culture* (pp. 85–116). Cambridge: Cambridge University Press.

Cowan, N. (1999). *Attention and memory: An integrated framework*. Oxford: Oxford University Press.

Cowan, N. and Alloway, T. (2009). Development of working memory in childhood. In M. L. Courage and N. Cowan (eds), *The development of memory in infancy and childhood* (pp. 304–42). New York: Psychology Press.

Dasser, V. (1988a). A social concept in Java monkeys. *Animal Behaviour, 36*, 225–30.

Dasser, V. (1988b). Mapping social concepts in monkeys. In R. W. Byrne and A. Whiten (eds), *Machiavellian intelligence: Social expertise and the evolution of intellect in monkeys, apes, and humans* (pp. 85–94). Oxford: Clarendon Press.

Deacon, T. (1997). *The symbolic species: The co-evolution of language and the brain*. London: W. W. Norton.

Dennett, D. (1983). Intentional systems in cognitive ethology: The 'panglossian paradigm' defended. *Behavioral and Brain Sciences, 6*, 343–90.

Donald, M. (1991). *Origins of the modern mind*. Cambridge, MA: Harvard University Press.

Dunbar, R. I. M. (1995). Neocortex size and group size in primates: A test of the hypothesis. *Journal of Human Evolution, 28*, 287–96.

Dunbar, R. I. M. (2009). The role of cognition in primate brain evolution. In P. Kappeler and J. Silk (eds), *Mind the gap: Tracing the origin of human universals*. Berlin: Springer Verlag.

Duncan, J. (2001). An adaptive coding model of neural function in prefrontal cortex. *Nature Reviews Neuroscience, 2*, 820–829.

Elman, J. L., Bates, E. A., Johnson, M. H. *et al.* (1996). *Rethinking innateness: A connectionist perspective on development*. Cambridge, MA: MIT Press.

Emery, N. J. and Clayton, N. S. (2004). The mentality of crows: Convergent evolution of intelligence in corvids and apes. *Science, 306*, 1903.

Flynn, E., O'Malley, C. and Wood, D. (2004). A longitudinal, microgenetic study of the emergence of false belief understanding and inhibition skills. *Developmental Science, 7*, 103–115.

Fodor, J. A. (1983). *The modularity of mind*. Cambridge, MA: MIT Press.

Fouts, R. (1997). *Next of kin: My conversations with chimpanzees*. New York: William Morrow and Company.

Fry, A. F. and Hale, S. (2000). Relationships among processing speed, working memory, and fluid intelligence in children. *Biological Psychology, 54*, 1–34.

Frye, D., Zelazo, P. D. and Palfai, T. (1995). Theory of mind and rule-based reasoning. *Cognitive Development, 10*, 483–527.

Gallistel, C. R. (1995). Insect navigation: Brains as symbol-processors. In S. Sternberg and D. Scarborough (eds), *Conceptual and methodological foundations. Vol. 4 of An invitation to cognitive science*. Cambridge, MA: MIT Press.

Gallup, G., Jr. (1970). Chimpanzees: Self-recognition. *Science, 167*, 86–7.

Garcia, J. and Koelling, R. A. (1966). Relation of cue to consequence in avoidance learning. *Psychonomic Science, 4*, 123.

Geary, D. C. (1998). *Male, female: The evolution of human sex differences*. Washington: American Psychological Association.

Geary, D. C. (2003). Learning disabilities in arithmetic: Problem solving differences and cognitive deficits. In H. L. Swanson, K. Harris and S. Graham (eds), *Handbook of learning disabilities* (pp. 199–212). New York: Guilford Press.

Geary, D. C. (2005). *The origin of mind: Evolution of brain, cognition, and general intelligence*. Washington: American Psychological Association.

Geary, D. C. and Huffman, K. J. (2002). Brain and cognitive evolution: Forms of modularity and functions of mind. *Psychological Bulletin*, *128*, 667–98.

Gergely, G., Bekkering, H. and Király, I. (2002). Developmental psychology: Rational imitation in preverbal infants. *Nature*, *415*, 755.

Gergely, G., Nadasdy, Z., Csibra, G. and Bíró, S. (1995). Taking the intentional stance at 12 months of age. *Cognition*, *56*, 165–93.

Gibson, K. R., Rumbaugh, D. and Beran, M. (2001). Bigger is better: Primate brain size in relationship to cognition. In D. Falk and K. R. Gibson (eds), *Evolutionary anatomy of the primate cerebral cortex* (pp. 79–98). Cambridge: Cambridge University Press.

Gigerenzer, G. (2001). Are we losing control? *Behavioral and Brain Sciences*, *24*, 408–9.

Gigerenzer, G. and Selten, R. (2001). *Bounded rationality: The adaptive toolbox*. Boston: MIT Press.

Gomez, J. C. (1996). Ostensive behavior in great apes: The role of eye contact. In A. E. Russon (ed.), *Reaching into thought: The minds of the great apes* (pp. 131–52). Cambridge: Cambridge University Press.

Gould, S. J. (1977). *Ontogeny and phylogeny*. Cambridge, MA: Harvard University Press.

Greenfield, P. M. (1991). Language, tools and brain: The ontogeny and phylogeny of hierarchically organized sequential behavior. *Behavioral and Brain Sciences*, *14*, 531–95.

Hala, S. and Russell, J. (2001). Executive control within strategic deception: A window on early cognitive development? *Journal of Experimental Child Psychology*, *80*, 112–141.

Hare, B., Call, J. and Tomasello, M. (2001). Do chimpanzees know what conspecifics know? *Animal Behaviour*, *61*, 139–51.

Hare, B., Call, J., Agentta, B. and Tomasello, M. (2000). Chimpanzees know what conspecifics do and do not see. *Animal Behaviour*, *59*, 771–85.

Harris, P. L., de Rosnay, M. and Pons, F. (2005). Language and children's understanding of mental states. *Current Directions in Psychological Science*, *14*, 69–73.

Harvey, P. H., Martin, R. D. and Clutton-Brock, T. H. (1987). Life histories in comparative perspective. In B. B. Smuts, D. L. Cheney, R. M. Seyfarth, R. W. Wrangham and T. T. Struhsaker (eds), *Primate societies* (pp. 181–96). Chicago: University of Chicago Press.

Herrmann, E., Call, J., Hernández-Lloreda, M. V. *et al.* (2007). Humans have evolved specialized skills of social cognition: The cultural intelligence hypothesis. *Science*, *317*, 1360–1366.

Holloway, R. L. (1969). Culture: A human domain. *Current Anthropology*, *10*, 395–412.

Holloway, R. L. and de la Coste-Lareymondie, M. C. (1982). Brain endocast asymmetry in pongids and hominids: Some preliminary findings on the paleontology of cerebral dominance. *American Journal of Physical Anthropology*, *58*, 101–10.

Horner, V. and Whiten, A. (2005). Causal knowledge and imitation/emulation switching in chimpanzees (*Pan troglodytes*) and children (*Homo sapiens*). *Animal Cognition*, *8*, 164–81.

Hughes, C. and Ensor, R. (2007). Executive function and theory of mind: Predictive relations from ages 2 to 4. *Developmental Psychology*, *43*, 1447–59.

Humphrey, N. K. (1976). The social function of intellect. In P. P. G. Bateson and R. A. Hinde (eds), *Growing points in ethology* (pp. 303–17). Cambridge: Cambridge University Press.

Humphrey, N. K. (2000). How to solve the mind-body problem, *Journal of Consciousness Studies*, *7*, 5–20.

Jerison, H. J. (1973). *Evolution of the brain and intelligence*. New York: Academic Press.

Joffe, T. H. (1997). Social pressures have selected for an extended juvenile period in primates. *Journal of Human Evolution*, *32*, 593–605.

Johnson, M., Grossmann, T. and Kadosh, K. (2009). Mapping functional brain development: Building a social brain through interactive specialization. *Developmental Psychology*, *45*, 151–9.

Jones, L. B., Rothbart, M. K. and Posner, M. I. (2003). Development of executive attention in preschool children. *Developmental Science*, 6, 498–504.

Kane, R. J. and Engle, R. W. (2002). The role of prefrontal cortex in working-memory capacity, executive attention, and general fluid intelligence: An individual-differences perspective. *Psychonomic Bulletin and Review*, *9*, 637–71.

Karmiloff-Smith, A. (1991). Beyond modularity: Innate constraints and developmental change. In S. Carey and R. Gelman (eds), *The epigenesis of mind: Essays on biology and cognition* (pp. 171–98). Hillsdale, NJ: Lawrence Erlbaum Associates.

Karmiloff-Smith, A. (1992). Constraints on representational change: Evidence from children's drawing. In G. Hatano (ed.), *Handbook of cognitive science*. Tokyo: Kyoritsu Shuppan.

Krubitzer, L. and Huffman, K. J. (2000). A realization of the neocortex in mammals: Genetic and epigenetic contributions to the phenotype. *Brain, Behavior and Evolution*, *55*, 322–35.

Langer, J. (1980). *The origins of logic: Six to twelve months*. New York: Academic Press.

Langer, J. (1986). *The origins of logic: One to two years*. New York: Academic Press.

Leavens, D. A., Hopkins, W. D. and Bard, K. A. (2005). Understanding the point of chimpanzee pointing: Epigenesis and ecological validity. *Current Directions in Psychological Science*, *14*, 185–9.

Lewis, M. and Carmody, D. P. (2008). Self-representation and brain development. *Developmental Psychology*, *44*, 1329–34.

Lichtenstein, S., Slovic, P., Fischhoff, B. *et al.* (1978). Judged frequency of lethal events. *Journal of Experimental Psychology: Learning, Memory, and Cognition*. 4, 551–78.

Limongelli, L., Boysen, S. T. and Visalberghi, E. (1995). Comprehension of cause–effect relations in a tool-using task by chimpanzees *(Pan troglodytes)*. *Journal of Comparative Psychology*, *109*, 18–26.

Liszkowski, U., Carpenter, M. and Tomasello, M. (2007). Pointing out new news, old news, and absent referents at 12 months of age. *Developmental Science*, *10*, F1–F7.

Liszkowski, U., Carpenter, M., Striano, T. and Tomasello, M. (2006). 12- and 18-month-olds point to provide information for others. *Journal of Cognition and Development*, *7*, 173–87.

Locke, J. L. (2009). Evolutionary developmental linguistics: Naturalization of the faculty of language. *Language Sciences*, *31*, 33–59.

Locke, J. L. and Bogin, B. (2006). Language and life history: A new perspective on the development and evolution of human language. *Behavioral and Brain Sciences*, *29*, 259–80.

Lohmann, H. and Tomasello, M. (2003). The role of language in the development of false belief understanding: A training study. *Child Development*, *74*, 1130–44.

McAdam, D. (1996). Conceptual origins, current problems, future directions. In D. McAdam, J. D. McCarthy and M. N. Zald (eds), *Comparative perspectives on social movements: Political opportunities, mobilizing structures and cultural framing* (pp. 23–41). Cambridge: Cambridge University Press.

McDonough, L., Mandler, J. M., McKee, R. D. and Squire, L. R. (1995). The deferred imitation task as a nonverbal measure of declarative memory. *Proceedings of the National Academy of Sciences*, *92*, 7580–7584.

McGrew, W. C. (1992). *Chimpanzee material culture: Implication for human evolution*. Cambridge: Cambridge University Press.

Mackintosh, N. (2000). Abstraction and discrimination. In C. Heyes and L. Huber (eds), *The evolution of cognition* (pp. 123–43). Cambridge, MA: MIT Press.

MacWhinney, B. (2005). The emergence of linguistic form in time. *Connection Science, 17,* 191–211.

Maestripieri, D. and Mateo, J. (eds) (2009). *Maternal effects in mammals.* Chicago: Chicago University Press.

Marcus, G. (2004). *The birth of the mind: How a tiny number of genes creates the complexities of human thought.* New York: Basic Books.

Marcus, G. (2006). Cognitive architecture and descent with modification. *Cognition, 101,* 443–65.

Matsuzawa, T. (1994). Field experiments on use of stone tools by chimpanzees in the wild. In R. W. Wrangham, W. C. McGrew, F. B. M. de Waal and P. G. Heltne, (eds), *Chimpanzee cultures* (pp. 351–70). Cambridge, MA: Harvard University Press.

Matsuzawa, T. (1997). Phylogeny of intelligence: A view from cognitive behavior of chimpanzees. *IIAS Reports,* No. 1997-004, 17–26.

Meaney, M. J. (2001). Maternal care, gene expression, and the transmission of individual differences in stress reactivity across generations. *Annual Review of Neuroscience, 24,* 1161–92.

Meltzoff, A. N. (1995). What infant memory tells us about infantile amnesia: Long-term recall and deferred imitation. *Journal of Experimental Child Psychology, 59,* 497–515.

Meltzoff, A. N. and Brooks, R. (2008). Self-experience as a mechanism for learning about others: A training study in social cognition. *Developmental Psychology, 44,* 1257–65.

Miller, E. K. and Cohen, J. D. (2001). An integrative theory of prefrontal cortex function. *Annual Review of Neuroscience, 24,* 167–202.

Miller, G. (2001). *The mating mind: How sexual choice shaped the evolution of human nature.* London: Vintage.

Milner, B. (1964). Some effects of frontal lobectomy in man. In J. M. Warren and K. Akert (eds), *The frontal granular cortex and behavior* (pp. 313–334). New York: McGraw-Hill.

Mithen, S. (1996). *The prehistory of the mind: The cognitive origins of art, religion and science.* London: Thames & Hudson.

Mithen, S. (1999). Handaxes and ice age carvings: Hard evidence for the evolution of consciousness. In S. R. Hammerhof, A. W. Kazsniak and D. J. Chalmers (eds), *Towards a science of consciousness III* (pp. 281–96). Cambridge, MA: MIT Press.

Morgan, G. and Kegl, J. (2006). Nicaraguan Sign Language and Theory of Mind: The issue of critical periods and abilities. *Journal of Child Psychology and Psychiatry, 47,* 811–819.

Mulcahy, N. J. and Call, J. (2006). How great apes perform on a modified trap-tube task. *Animal Cognition, 9,* 193–9.

Nagell, K., Olguin, R. and Tomasello, M. (1993). Processes of social learning in the tool use of chimpanzees (*Pan troglodytes*) and human children (*Homo sapiens*). *Journal of Comparative Psychology, 107,* 174–86.

Nielsen, M., Suddendorf, T. and Slaughter, V. (2006). Mirror self-recognition beyond the face. *Child Development, 77,* 176–85.

O'Connell, S. M. (1995). *Theory of mind in chimpanzees.* PhD Thesis, University of Liverpool.

Parker, S. T. and McKinney, M. L. (1999). *Origins of intelligence: The evolution of cognitive development in monkeys, apes, and humans.* Baltimore: The Johns Hopkins University Press.

Peskin, J. (1992). Ruse and representations: On children's ability to conceal information. *Developmental Psychology, 28,* 84–9.

Pinker, S. and Bloom, P. (1990). Natural language and natural selection. *Behavioral and Brain Sciences, 13,* 707–84.

Plotnik, J., de Waal, F. B. M. and Reiss, D. (2006). Self-recognition in an Asian elephant. *Proceedings of the National Academy of Sciences, USA, 103*, 17053–7.

Poti, P., Langer, J., Savage-Rumbaugh, S. and Brakke, K. E. (1999). Spontaneous logicomathematical constructions by chimpanzees (*Pan troglodytes, Pan paniscus*). *Animal Cognition, 2*, 147–56.

Povinelli, D. and Eddy, T. J. (1996). Factors influencing young chimpanzees' (*Pan troglodytes*) recognition of attention. *Journal of Comparative Psychology, 110*, 336–45.

Povinelli, D., Landau, K. R. and Perilloux, H. K. (1996). Self-recognition in young children using delayed versus live feedback: Evidence of a developmental asynchrony. *Child Development, 67*, 1540–1554.

Povinelli, D. J. and Simon, B. B. (1998). Young children's understanding of briefly versus extremely delayed images of the self: Emergence of the autobiographical stance. *Developmental Psychology, 34*, 188–94.

Premack, D. (2007). Human and animal cognition: Continuity and discontinuity. *Proceedings of the National Academy of Sciences, 104*, 13861–7.

Premack, D. and Woodruff, G. (1978). Does the chimpanzee have a theory of mind? *Brain and Behavioral Sciences, 1*, 515–26.

Preuss, T. M. (2000). What's human about the human brain? In M. S. Gazzaniga (ed.), *The new cognitive neurosciences* (pp. 1355–63). Boston: MIT Press.

Preuss, T. M. (2004). Specializations of the human visual system: The monkey model meets human reality. In J. H. Kaas and C. E. Collins (eds), *The primate visual system* (pp. 231–361). Boca Raton, FL: CRC Press.

Prior H., Schwarz, A. and Güntürkün, O. (2008). Mirror-induced behavior in the magpie (*Pica pica*): Evidence of self-recognition. *PLoS Biol 6*: e202.

Ranganath, C. and Rainer, G. (2003). Cognitive neuroscience: Neural mechanisms for detecting and remembering novel events. *Nature Reviews Neuroscience, 4*, 193–202.

Read, D. W. (2008). Working memory: A cognitive limit to non-human primate recursive thinking prior to hominid evolution. *Evolutionary Psychology, 6*, 676–714.

Reader, S. and Laland, K. (2002). Social intelligence, innovation, and enhanced brain size in primates. *Proceedings of the National Academy of Sciences, 99*, 4436–41.

Reiss, D. and Marino, L. (2001). Mirror self-recognition in the bottlenose dolphin: A case of cognitive convergence. *Proceedings of the National Academy of Sciences, 98*, 5937–42.

Rendell, L. and Whitehead, H. (2001). Culture in whales and dolphins. *Behavioral and Brain Sciences, 24*, 309–82.

Richerson, P. J. and Boyd, R. (1976). A simple dual inheritance model of the conflict between social and biological evolution. *Zygon, 11*, 254–62.

Richerson P. J. and Boyd, R. (2005). *Not by genes alone: How culture transformed human evolution*. Chicago: University of Chicago Press.

Ruffman, T., Slade, L. and Crowe, E. (2002). The relation between children's and mothers' mental state language and theory of mind understanding. *Child Development, 73*, 734–51.

Russell, J., Mauthner, N., Sharpe, S. and Tidswell, T. (1991). The 'windows tasks' as a measure of strategic deception in preschoolers and autistic subjects. *British Journal of Developmental Psychology, 9*, 331–49.

Savage-Rumbaugh, E. S., Rumbaugh, D. and Boysen, S. T. (1978). Sarah's problems in comprehension. *Behavioral and Brain Sciences, 1*, 555–7.

van Schaik, C. P., Ancrenaz, M., Borgen, G. and Galdikas, B. (2003). Orang-utan cultures and the evolution of material culture. *Science, 299*, 102–5.

Semendeferi, K., Schleicher, A., Zilles, K et al. (2001). Prefrontal cortex in humans and apes: A comparative study of area 10. *American Journal of Physical Anthropology*, *114*, 224–41.

Senghas, A. and Coppola, M. (2001). Children creating language: How Nicaraguan sign language acquired a spatial grammar. *Psychological Science*, *12*, 323–8.

Senghas, A., Kita, S. and Ozyurek, A. (2004). Children creating core properties of language: Evidence from an emerging sign language in Nicaragua. *Science*, *305*, 1779–82.

Siegal, M., Varley, R. and Want, S. C. (2001). Mind over grammar: Reasoning in aphasia and development. *Trends in Cognitive Sciences*, *5*, 296–301.

Simon, H. A. (1955). A behavioral model of rational choice. *Quarterly Journal of Economics*, *69*, 99–118.

Simon, H. (1956). A comparison of game theory and learning theory. *Psychometrika*, *21*, 267–72.

Skouteris, H., Spataro, J. and Lazaridis, M. (2006). Young children's use of a delayed video representation to solve a retrieval problem pertaining to self. *Developmental Science*, *9*, 505–17.

Spencer, P. E. (1993). Communication behaviours of infants with hearing loss and their hearing mothers. *Journal of Speech and Hearing Research*, *36*, 311–321.

Spinozzi, G., Natale, F., Langer, J. and Brakke, K. E. (1999). Spontaneous class grouping behavior by bonobos (*Pan paniscus*) and common chimpanzees (*Pan troglodytes*). *Animal Cognition*, *2*, 157–70.

Sterelny, K. (2000). Primate worlds. In C. M. Heyes and L. Huber (eds), *The evolution of cognition* (pp. 143–62). Boston: MIT Press.

Suddendorf, T. (2006). Foresight and evolution of the human mind. *Science*, *312*, 1006–7.

Suddendorf, T. and Busby, J. (2003). Mental time travel in animals? *Trends in Cognitive Sciences*, *7*, 391–6.

Suddendorf, T. and Busby, J. (2005). Making decisions with the future in mind: Developmental and comparative identification of mental time travel. *Learning and Motivation*, *36*, 110–125.

Suddendorf, T. and Corballis, M. C. (1997). Mental time travel and the evolution of the human mind. *Genetic Social and General Psychology Monographs*, *123*, 133–67.

Suddendorf, T. and Corballis, M. (2007). The evolution of foresight: What is mental time travel, and is it unique to humans? *Behavioral and Brain Sciences*, *30*, 299–351.

Suddendorf, T. and Whiten, A. (2001). Mental evolution and development: Evidence for secondary representation in children, great apes and other animals. *Psychological Bulletin*, *127*, 629–50.

Suomi, S. J. (2004). How gene-environment interactions shape biobehavioral development: Lessons from studies with rhesus monkeys. *Research in Human Development*, *1*, 205–22.

Thomas, L. (1974). *The lives of a cell: Notes of a biology watcher*. New York: Viking Press.

Thorndike, E. L. (1911). *Individuality*. Boston: Houghton-Mifflin.

Todd, P. M. (2001). Fast and frugal heuristics for environmentally bounded minds. In G. Gigerenzer and R. Selten (eds), *Bounded rationality: The adaptive toolbox* (pp. 51–70). Boston: MIT Press.

Tomasello, M. (1998). Uniquely primate, uniquely human. *Developmental Science*, *1*, 1–30.

Tomasello, M. (1999). *The cultural origins of human cognition*. Cambridge, MA: Harvard University Press.

Tomasello, M. (2000). Two hypotheses about primate cognition. In C. M. Heyes and L. Huber (eds), *The evolution of cognition* (pp. 165–84). Boston: MIT Press.

Tomasello, M. and Call, J. (1994). The social cognition of monkeys and apes. *Yearbook of Physical Anthropology*, *37*, 273–305.

Tomasello, M. and Call, J. (1997). *Primate cognition.* New York: Oxford University Press.

Tomasello, M. and Carpenter, M. (2005). The emergence of social cognition in three young chimpanzees. *Monographs of the Society for Research in Child Development, 70* (1, Serial No. 279).

Tomasello, M. and Carpenter M. (2007). Shared intentionality. *Developmental Science, 10,* 121–5.

Tomasello, M., Kruger, A. C. and Ratner, H. H. (1993). Cultural learning. *Behavioral and Brain Sciences, 16,* 495–552.

Tomasello, M., Savage-Rumbaugh, S. and Kruger, A. C. (1993). Imitative learning of actions on objects by children, chimpanzees, and enculturated chimpanzees. *Child Development, 64,* 1688–705.

Tooby, J. and Cosmides, L. (1992). The psychological foundations of culture. In J. H. Barkow, L. Cosmides and J. Tooby (eds), *The adapted mind* (pp. 19–136). New York: Oxford University Press.

Tooby, J. and Cosmides, L. (1998). Evolutionizing the cognitive sciences: A reply to Shapiro and Epstein. *Mind and Language, 13,* 195–204.

Trivers, R. L. (1971). The evolution of reciprocal altruism. *The Quarterly Review of Biology, 46,* 35–57.

Tulving, E. (1985). Memory and consciousness. *Canadian Psychology, 26,* 1–12.

Tulving, E. (2005). Episodic memory and autonoesis: Uniquely human? In H. S. Terrace and J. Metcalfe (eds), *The missing link in cognition: Origins of self-reflective consciousness* (pp. 3–56). New York: Oxford University Press.

Tversky, A. and Kahneman, D. (1974). Judgment under uncertainty: Heuristics and biases. *Science, 185,* 1124–31.

Visalberghi, L., Boysen, S. and Visalberghi, E. (1995). Comprehension of cause–effect relations in tool-using task by chimpanzees (*Pan troglodytes*). *Journal of Comparative Psychology, 109,* 18–26.

Visalberghi, E. and Limongelli, L. (1996). Acting and understanding: Tool use revisited through the minds of capuchin monkeys. In A. Russon, K. Bard and S. Parker (eds), *Reaching into thought: The minds of the great apes* (pp. 57–79). Cambridge: Cambridge University Press.

Vogt, B. A. (1987). Cingulate cortex. In G. Adelman (ed.), *Encyclopedia of neuroscience* (Vol. 1, pp. 244–5). Boston: Birkhauser.

Vonnegut, K. (1973). *Breakfast of champions.* London: Cape.

Want, S. C. and Harris, P. L. (2002). How do children ape? Applying concepts from the study of non-human primates to the developmental study of 'imitation' in children. *Developmental Science, 5,* 1–13.

Wellman, H. M. (1990). *The child's theory of mind.* Cambridge, MA: MIT Press.

Wellman, H. M., Cross, D. and Watson, J. (2001). Meta-analysis of theory-of-mind development: The truth about false belief. *Child Development, 72,* 655–84.

Whiten, A. (1996). Imitation, pretence and mindreading: Secondary representation in comparative primatology and developmental psychology. In A. E. Russon, K. A. Bard and S. T. Parker (eds), *Reaching into thought: The minds of the great apes* (pp. 300–324). Cambridge: Cambridge University Press.

Whiten A. and Byrne, R. W. (1988). Tactical deception in primates. *Behavioral and Brain Sciences 11,* 233–73.

Whiten, A., Goodall, J., McGrew, W. C. *et al.* (1999). Cultures in chimpanzees. *Nature, 399,* 682–5.

Whiten, A., Homer, V., Litchfield, C. and Marshall-Peseini, S. (2004). How do apes ape? *Learning and Behaviour*, *32*, 36–52.

Wiebe, S. A., Espy, K. A. and Charak, D. (2008). Using confirmatory factor analysis to understand executive control in preschool children: I. Latent structure. *Developmental Psychology*, *44*, 575–87.

Wood, J. N., Glynn, D. D. Phillips, B. C. and Hauser, M. D. (2007). The perception of rational, goal-directed action in nonhuman primates. *Science*, *317*, 1402–5.

Zelazo, P. D., Carlson, S. M. and Kesek, A. (2008). The development of executive function in childhood. In C. A. Nelson and M. Luciana (eds), *Handbook of cognitive developmental neuroscience*, (second edition) (pp. 553–74). Cambridge, MA: MIT Press.

Zelazo, P. D., Sommerville, J. A. and Nichols, S. (1999). Age-related changes in children's use of external representation. *Developmental Psychology*, *35*, 1059–71.

Zilles, K., Dabringhaus, A., Geyer, S. *et al.* (1996). Structural asymmetries in the human forebrain and the forebrain of non-human primates and rats. *Neuroscience Behavioral Review*, *20*, 593–605.

3 Cooperation as a classic problem in behavioural biology

MICHAEL E. PRICE

CHAPTER OUTLINE

WHY HAS COOPERATION BEEN SUCH A BIOLOGICAL PUZZLE? 74

INDIVIDUAL-LEVEL SOLUTIONS TO THE PUZZLE: SELFISH REPLICATORS, COOPERATIVE VEHICLES 76

COOPERATION VIA GENIC SELF-FAVOURITISM (KIN SELECTION AND GREENBEARD ALTRUISM) 77

COOPERATION VIA RETURN BENEFITS (RECIPROCAL ALTRUISM, INDIRECT RECIPROCITY AND COSTLY SIGNALLING) 82

SUMMARY OF INDIVIDUAL-LEVEL THEORIES OF COOPERATION 86

GROUP SELECTION 87

COMPLEX HUMAN COOPERATION: COLLECTIVE ACTION 91

CONCLUSION 98

ACKNOWLEDGEMENTS 100

REFERENCES 100

Cooperative behaviour is, and has always been, a centrally important aspect of human sociality: cooperation in economic exchange, and in teams, groups and organisations of all kinds (religious, political, foraging, military and so on) is a defining characteristic of our species. Cooperative behaviour has also been a centrally important problem in behavioural biology for decades, both as a challenge that has stimulated major scientific advances and as a puzzle that has generated great confusion. Because of the importance of cooperation both in human social life and as a scientific puzzle, the evolution of human cooperation has received decades of intense attention from scholars representing diverse fields, including biology, psychology and all of the social sciences. In this chapter, I will review the history of the most important attempts that have been made to explain cooperation, examine the current state of our ability to explain it and make some suggestions about which future roads we should take in order to continue to enhance our understanding of this important topic.

WHY HAS COOPERATION BEEN SUCH A BIOLOGICAL PUZZLE?

Cooperation has been a puzzle for biologists primarily because it often involves altruism. The traditional definition of altruism in biology has been an action that lowers the actor's fitness while enhancing the fitness of some other individual (Hamilton, 1964; Maynard Smith, 1964; Williams and Williams, 1957). As Tooby and Cosmides (1996) note, this definition is problematic in that it does not give sufficient consideration of altruism's adaptive functionality, that is of the extent to which the altruistic behaviour was designed by natural selection for the purpose of delivering benefits to another individual. For example, a moth that has flown into a spider's web will benefit the spider's fitness at the expense of its own, but this 'altruism' will have been due to successful predation by the spider, rather than to some functional mechanism in moths that evolved in order to deliver benefits to spiders. Therefore, a more appropriate definition of altruism would be behaviour that has been designed by selection to benefit someone else's fitness at the expense of one's own (Tooby and Cosmides, 1996).

Cooperation can be broadly defined as two or more biological entities acting together to accomplish some common goal. The biological world is rife with cooperative behaviour. For example, a mother and the offspring she is nursing both have an interest in making sure the offspring gets fed. When you buy a pack of gum at a corner store, both you and the shopkeeper have the goal of carrying out an exchange transaction. In multicellular species, different specialised cellular types act in concert to help each other, because they all serve the larger goal of promoting the survival and reproduction of the whole organism. The members of a honeybee colony all strive to benefit the colony in which they live, and will sacrifice their own lives in defence of it. Wolves hunt in groups in order to kill a deer that they will consume together. Note that all of these examples involve altruism, because they all involve actors that incur some kind of fitness cost – for instance an expenditure of time and energy, an exhibition of restraint in the pursuit of one's own selfish interests or suicidal self-sacrifice – in the course of acting in a way that enhances the fitness of beneficiaries.

Besides being central to cooperation, altruism is also one of the most historically problematic issues in evolutionary biology. Altruism has achieved this status because it seems to challenge the idea that the primary engine of adaptation by natural selection, as specified by Darwin (1859/1958), is reproductive competition among individuals. Shouldn't all genes governing behaviour focus on enabling their individual carrier to out-compete rivals in the struggle to survive and reproduce, as opposed to altruistically benefiting these rivals? Shouldn't any gene that benefited these rivals, at the expense of the carrier, be promptly eliminated by selection? These are the basic questions that have driven biologists' intense efforts to understand altruistic co-operation over the past several decades. Darwin (1859/1958, p. 190) himself regarded such cooperation as a potential threat to his theory: 'If it could be proved that any part of the structure of any one species had been formed for the exclusive good of another species, it would annihilate my theory, for such could not have been produced through natural selection.' Over a century later, E. O. Wilson (1975, p. 3) still regarded altruism as 'the central theoretical problem of sociobiology'.

Table 3.1 helps define altruism in the context of other kinds of social action. In this table, 'social action' refers to any behaviour that has a negative or positive impact on the fitness of another individual (the 'recipient'). Two of these behaviours, selfishness and spite, are non-cooperative. As selfishness involves a fitness gain for the actor, it does not present any special challenge for Darwin's theory; spite, on the other hand, presents more of a challenge (Hamilton, 1970). Spite, as a costly action that harms a recipient but that provides no benefit to the actor, should not usually be favoured by selection; accordingly, spite appears to be rare in nature (Foster, Wenseleers and Ratnieks, 2001). The other two behaviours in Table 3.1, altruism and mutualism, can be considered kinds of cooperation. Altruism, as an action that harms the actor while benefiting the recipient, presents the puzzle that is the main subject of this chapter. Mutualism, as a mutually beneficial action, is much less puzzling. However, in reality, mutualism and altruism may be more difficult to distinguish than Table 3.1 suggests. For example, 'reciprocal altruism' (Trivers, 1971) can involve a protracted process of mutually beneficial exchange. A reciprocally altruistic actor may deliver a benefit to a recipient, and then much later receive a benefit from that recipient in return. In the long term, this interaction will look like 'mutualism' according to Table 3.1, but in the short term – before the actor has received the return benefit – it will resemble 'altruism'. The differences between reciprocal altruism and mutualism will be discussed in more detail later in the chapter, but this topic is raised here simply to make the point that Table 3.1 to some extent oversimplifies a more complex reality.

Table 3.1. *Social action classified by effects on fitness of actor and recipient.*

		Effect on Recipient	
		+	−
Effect on Actor	+	Mutualism	Selfishness
	−	Altruism	Spite

Each of the four social actions described in this table can have effects that are positive (+) or negative (−) for the respective fitnesses of actor and recipient.

Source: Based on Pizzari and Foster (2008).

INDIVIDUAL-LEVEL SOLUTIONS TO THE PUZZLE: SELFISH REPLICATORS, COOPERATIVE VEHICLES

As will be discussed later in this chapter, there are still important unresolved issues related to the topic of how altruistic cooperation evolves. Still, we can safely say that a great deal of progress towards solving this problem has been made since Darwin's era. Most of this progress occurred after biologists began switching their focus from the reproducing individual to the replicating gene. No theorist was more influential than Hamilton (1963, 1964) in promoting the realisation that the gene should be regarded as fundamental, both as the unit of selection and as the ultimate unit of analysis in evolutionary and behavioural biology. From a post-Hamiltonian perspective, a general solution to the puzzle of cooperation suggests itself: genes promote cooperation as a means of promoting their own replication. But how, exactly, can genes enable their own replication by building cooperative individuals?

Genes replicate by building individuals who are strongly motivated to help the genes make copies of themselves, that is individuals who act to promote their own inclusive fitness (or, technically, who act in ways that were inclusive fitness-promoting in the ancestral past). In other words, genes are 'replicators', and individual bodies are 'vehicles' they build in order to enable themselves to replicate (Dawkins, 1976). As fundamental vehicles of selection, individuals are endowed by genes with many adaptations which enable them to behave in fitness-promoting ways. Therefore, when researchers attempt to understand how cooperation evolved, they typically examine the ways in which individuals are adapted for cooperation. This focus on individual-level adaptation has always been a prominent feature of modern evolutionary biology; Darwin's theory of adaptation by natural selection, for example, was primarily a theory about individual adaptation.

However, research on cooperation also sometimes focuses on vehicles of selection other than the individual, especially the social group. In many species, individuals cooperate in groups, and groups can be considered important vehicles of selection because they are organisations that genes produce as a means of promoting their own replication. If individuals and groups are both important vehicles of selection, however, at which level of selection should we be searching for evidence of adaptation? This issue often comes up in the context of discussions about group selection and multilevel selection, and these will be discussed later in the chapter. First, however, we will review theories that focus on the individual as the primary vehicle of selection. These theories address the puzzle of cooperation in two general ways: by suggesting either that cooperative genes benefit replicas of themselves that are located in other individuals or else that cooperative individuals somehow reap benefits in return for their cooperation.

COOPERATION VIA GENIC SELF-FAVOURITISM (KIN SELECTION AND GREENBEARD ALTRUISM)

Kin selection

The essential insight that Hamilton (1963, 1964) developed is that a gene can succeed in replicative competition not only by promoting the reproduction of its carrier but also by promoting the reproduction of individuals who carry exact copies of itself. For example, if exact copies of Gene A are carried by Individual 1 and Individual 2, then the copy of Gene A located in Individual 1 can create exact replicas of itself by promoting the reproduction of either Individual 1 or Individual 2. The main problem that the gene must overcome in order to engage in such self-favouritism is that of how it can 'know' whether a replica of itself is likely to reside in another individual. One basic and relatively reliable route to such knowledge is to determine the likelihood that the individual is a genetic relative, because the closer two individuals are related genetically, the more likely they will be to share genes that are identical by descent. If Individual 1 and Individual 2 are full siblings, for instance, then the probability that they will share two alleles by virtue of common descent is ½ (because they each must have inherited the allele from one parent or the other). This probability is known as the 'coefficient of relatedness', and it decreases rapidly as genetic distance grows. For example, this coefficient is ¼ for half-siblings, for aunts/uncles and nieces/nephews, and for grandparents and grandchildren, and it drops off to 1/8 for first cousins and to 1/32 for second cousins.

Hamilton incorporated this coefficient into a simple inequality, now known as 'Hamilton's rule', which states that altruism will be likely to evolve when $rB > C$, where r is the coefficient of relatedness, B is the benefit to the recipient, and C is the cost to the altruist. For example, for an act of altruism between two full siblings ($r = \frac{1}{2}$) to be favoured by selection, it must benefit the recipient more than twice as much as it costs the altruist. Hamilton's rule predicts that altruism will be more likely to evolve when the two actors are more closely related, and when the benefits to the recipient are great and the costs to the altruist are low. Several new terms entered the biologist's lexicon following the publication of Hamilton's theory. If a gene causes an act of altruism to benefit a copy of itself that is located in another body, then the altruist was now said to have acted to increase his or her 'inclusive fitness'. Thus, an act which was detrimental to fitness in the sense that Darwin used the term (i.e. 'classical fitness') could be enhancing to inclusive fitness. The process that governs the evolution of inclusive fitness-enhancing behaviours among genetic relatives became known as 'kin selection'.

Hamilton was not the first to appreciate the link between genetic kinship and altruism (e.g. see Williams and Williams, 1957). However, his generalisation and formalisation of this idea led to him becoming regarded as the father of kin selection. As a theory that is very simple but which nonetheless explains a large portion of behaviour in a huge range of species, kin selection has been a major scientific triumph. It provides a fundamental explanation for the high levels of altruism that are routinely observed between close kin in a vast variety of species, including humans and other primates (e.g. Chagnon, 1979; Lieberman, Tooby and Cosmides, 2007; Silk, 2005). Further, kin selection helps resolve some long-standing puzzles about cooperative behaviour, in particular that of eusocial species – extraordinarily cooperative species characterised by features such as division of labour and cooperative care of young. The insect order Hymenoptera, which includes ants, bees and wasps, includes many eusocial species. Hymenoptera colonies include sterile worker and soldier castes, which perplexed Darwin (1859/1958), since the existence of sterile castes seemed to undermine his theory of adaptation by natural selection: how could sterile individuals pass on adaptations to offspring? As it turns out, the Hymenoptera order is characterised by a breeding system known as 'haplodiploidy', whereby females are more related to their sisters ($r = \frac{3}{4}$) than to their own offspring ($r = \frac{1}{2}$); thus, these females' genes can replicate more effectively via altruism towards sisters than via altruism towards offspring. Although haplodiploidy cannot be the whole explanation for eusociality (Wilson and Wilson, 2007), it does help resolve the sterility problem which so puzzled Darwin.

Although kin selection is one of the most important elements of modern evolutionary theory, important aspects of it are often misunderstood or underappreciated. First, although the theory is powerful, one should appreciate its limitations. It is especially important to note that coefficient r refers specifically to the likelihood of genes for altruism that are identical by descent, and cannot be regarded as an abstract measure of overall 'genetic similarity'. Kin selection theory does not predict, for instance, that individuals from the same ethnic group should be more altruistic to one another than should ethnically different individuals (for related debates, see Rushton, 1989 and associated commentaries, e.g. Tooby and Cosmides, 1989). In fact, kin selection should act only weakly on all but the very closest genetic relationships. For example, for kin altruism to evolve between first cousins (who by many standards would be considered close genetic relatives), the required B/C ratio (at least eight to one) will often be prohibitively high.

Another important yet sometimes unappreciated feature of kin selection is that related genes in different bodies cannot directly 'sense' each other's presence. Instead, kin altruism occurs as the result of some environmental regularity that enables altruistic behaviour to correlate positively with genetic kinship. For species with nervous systems, this regularity often comes in the form of some kind of information that can be cognitively processed and that reliably indicates the probability that another individual is a close relative. Such a kin detection mechanism may enable one to recognise kin based on, for instance, familiarity (as in ground squirrels and guppies), or on phenotypic matching via odour (as in paper wasps and wood frogs) (Hain and Neff, 2007; Sherman, Reeve and Pfennig, 1997). In humans, kin recognition cues include perinatal association with one's own mother and enduring co-residence in the same household (Lieberman, Tooby and Cosmides, 2007; Westermarck 1891/1921). As Lieberman *et al.* note, such mechanisms are important not just for directing kin altruism but also for enabling incest avoidance. Because these mechanisms require highly specific kinds of informational inputs in order to operate effectively, as opposed to being 'general purpose' kin detectors, they fail in the absence of such inputs. Thus, siblings who are not exposed to kinship cues (e.g. if they are raised in different households) should be less likely to perceive each other as siblings: they should feel less altruism and more sexual attraction towards one another, even if they consciously 'know' (i.e. they are verbally informed) that they are siblings. By the same token, non-siblings who are raised in the same household should regard each other with more altruism and less sexual attraction.

The broadening of r: Greenbeard altruism

The general principle underlying kin selection is one of genic self-favouritism: a gene can promote its own replication by benefiting replicas of itself that are located in other individuals. Note that there is nothing in this principle that stipulates that these other individuals must be close genetic kin in general. Any gene that enabled its carrier to recognise other carriers of the same gene, and to direct altruism towards them, could in principle evolve, regardless of whether the carriers were closely related at other loci. So while r in Hamilton's rule was initially regarded mainly as the probability of individuals sharing genes via common descent, its definition eventually broadened into the probability of individuals sharing the same genes for altruism, irrespective of general kinship (Hamilton, 1975).

In the absence of kinship, the problem of recognising other carriers of the same specific gene generally becomes more formidable. Kinship provides a relatively convenient solution to this problem, because kin relationships tend to be characterised by environmental regularities (e.g. spatial proximity of siblings) to which mechanisms for delivering benefits to kin can become adapted. This correlation between genetic kinship and environmental structure is a major reason for why kin altruism is by far the most commonly observed type of genic self-favouritism. Nevertheless, genic self-favouritism in the absence of general kinship may occur. This type of cooperation is often called 'greenbeard altruism', because of a colourful thought experiment proposed by Dawkins (1976) in his widely read popularisation of Hamilton's theories. Dawkins asks readers to imagine a gene which endows carriers with a green beard (any conspicuous phenotypic label of carrierhood would do; Dawkins just happened to choose this one) and caused them to direct altruism towards other greenbeards. Because carriers would be so recognisable, it would be relatively easy to direct altruism towards them, and altruism among greenbeards could therefore evolve.

However, although greenbeard altruism seems plausible in theory, in reality it is much less common than kin altruism. A likely reason this is true (in addition to the reason mentioned above, i.e. the fact that genetic kinship is relatively likely to be correlated with aspects of environmental structure) is that labels of altruistic disposition are generally easier to fake than are indicators of genetic kinship. (However, even kinship can be faked, for example cuckoo chicks pass themselves off as kin to their hosts.) In a system of greenbeard altruism, the biggest winners will be those who deceptively display the green beard without actually engaging in altruism towards other greenbeards. Mutations that cause their carriers to display the green beard but to engage in a reduced level of altruism towards other carriers would come to dominate the population; these selfish greenbeards would gain all the benefits of the system while paying reduced costs, and would eventually exploit the altruistic greenbeards to extinction (Figure 3.1 illustrates that just as altruistic greenbeards are advantaged over non-greenbeards, selfish greenbeards are advantaged over altruistic greenbeards). However, despite the fact that greenbeard systems will often be vulnerable to deception problems, such systems have been reported in species such as fire ants (Keller and Ross, 1998), slime mould (Queller *et al.*, 2003), side-blotched lizards (Sinervo *et al.*, 2006) and yeast (Smukalla *et al.*, 2008), as well as in human maternal–foetal interactions (Summers and Crespi, 2005).

The further broadening of r

Genic self-favouritism enables cooperation to evolve because it allows genes for cooperation to assist copies of themselves. However, these genes cannot interact directly, but only via the behaviour they encode. Thus, genic self-favouritism is possible only because cooperative genotypes encode cooperative phenotypes, and ultimately it is the individual's cooperative behaviour itself that delivers fitness benefits to other cooperative individuals. Therefore, in order for cooperation to evolve, it is not necessary

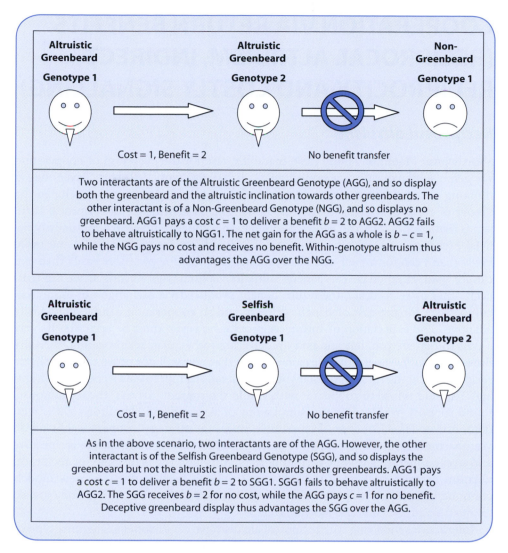

Figure 3.1. *Altruistic greenbeards beat non-greenbeards, but selfish greenbeards beat altruistic greenbeards.*

that interacting individuals be of the same cooperative genotype. Cooperative genotypes can proliferate by interacting preferentially with cooperative phenotypes, and r can be further broadened to represent the probability that an altruism beneficiary has a cooperative phenotype (Fletcher and Doebeli, 2006; Queller, 1985). In other words, a general rule for adaptive cooperation is 'cooperate with other cooperators', regardless of whether you share the exact same genes for cooperation with these others. If this general rule is followed, then cooperation can potentially evolve between genetic non-kin, indeed even between members of different species. In the next section, we will look first at the best-known example of how cooperation can evolve between cooperative phenotypes, irrespective of genotype: reciprocal altruism.

COOPERATION VIA RETURN BENEFITS (RECIPROCAL ALTRUISM, INDIRECT RECIPROCITY AND COSTLY SIGNALLING)

Reciprocal altruism

Shortly after Hamilton (1963, 1964) made the case for the evolution of cooperation via genic self-favouritism, a postgraduate in biology named Robert Trivers began thinking about other ways in which cooperation could evolve, and developed the theory of reciprocal altruism (Trivers, 1971). The basic principle of reciprocal altruism is that cooperation can evolve if interaction partners engage in a mutually beneficial exchange of costly altruistic acts. If you can produce a benefit for me more easily than I can for myself, and I can produce a benefit for you more easily than you can for yourself, then we can benefit mutually via exchange. As long as we can trust each other to reciprocate, the return benefit produced via exchange can more than compensate for the cost of benefit delivery, and so cooperation can be individually adaptive. The expectation of future reciprocity, however, must be accurate. If I pay a cost to benefit you, but you end up defecting rather than reciprocating, then my fitness will suffer. So if I have reason to think that you will not prove to be a reliable reciprocator in the future, and that you will instead attempt to gain a cheater's advantage, I should refuse to cooperate with you in the present. Trivers' theory famously found support in the computer simulations of Axelrod and Hamilton (1981), who demonstrated the adaptiveness of a simple 'tit-for-tat' strategy: cooperate at first with your partner, continue to cooperate as long as your partner continues to reciprocate and stop cooperating if your partner defects. Although the plausibility of reciprocal altruism became established in early formal models such as this one, new models continue to examine reciprocal altruism from novel angles (e.g. Imhof and Nowak, in press; Rand, Ohtsuki and Nowak, 2009).

Interactions involving true reciprocal altruism have a Prisoner's Dilemma type of pay-off structure. In a two-player Prisoner's Dilemma, each player gains more from mutual cooperation than from mutual defection, but can gain the biggest pay-off of all by defecting when the partner cooperates. Note that reciprocal altruism should not be confused with mutualism (sometimes referred to as 'by-product mutualism'; Brown, 1983), which occurs when an organism delivers a benefit to another organism in a cost-free manner, in the process of pursuing its own interests. Because this altruism is cost-free, defection ceases to be advantageous. For example, hummingbirds provide valuable pollinator services for flowering plants, but it costs them nothing to do so; this service occurs as a beneficial by-product of the hummingbird's efforts to consume plant nectar. Since the hummingbird's service is cost-free, it cannot gain a cheater's advantage by defecting. There are some costs involved for the plant, which must produce flowers in order to attract and feed hummingbirds, but these costs are just a fee that the plant must pay in order to ensure delivery of the hummingbird's positive externalities. Such mutually beneficial relationships are common in nature, both within species and between them. For instance, by huddling together for warmth, puppies utilise each others' excess body heat; when cleaner shrimp eat parasites off of fish, they get fed and the fish get rid of pests; and when gut flora reside in the human digestive tract, they gain a place to live and humans acquire a host of beneficial services (Guarner and Malagelada, 2003).

Because both partners can gain from defection in reciprocal altruism, unlike in mutualism, reciprocally altruistic relationships tend to be less stable than mutualistic ones. Reciprocal altruism is also relatively cognitively demanding, since it requires that interactants remember past interactions with potential reciprocal partners and that they detect and avoid cheaters. For these reasons, reciprocal altruism appears to occur relatively rarely across species as compared to mutualism. Nevertheless, researchers have claimed to observe true reciprocal altruism between, for example, wrasse cleaner fish and their hosts (Bshary and Grutter, 2002; Bshary and Schäffer, 2002), predator-inspecting stickleback fish (Milinski, 1987, 1990), blood-exchanging vampire bats (Wilkinson, 1984, 1988) and grooming, alliance and sharing partners of various primate species (for a review of the mixed evidence on reciprocity in primates, see Silk, 2005).

However, identifying reciprocal altruism in non-human species is often a difficult and controversial undertaking, in part because the lines between mutualism and reciprocal altruism tend to blur easily. As a result, interactions identified as reciprocal altruism by some researchers have been considered mutualism by others. For example, mobbing of predators by flycatcher birds is considered reciprocal altruism by Krams *et al.* (2008) and mutualism by Russell and Wright (2008), and researchers disagree about whether predator inspection in fish constitutes reciprocal altruism or mutualism (Connor, 1996; Dugatkin, 1996). Another problem with identifying reciprocal altruism is that it is often surprisingly difficult to judge whether an act of altruism from A to B should be regarded as having been contingent on a previous act of altruism from B to A (Silk, 2005). So, despite the very compelling theoretical plausibility of reciprocal altruism, biologists have identified relatively few uncontroversial examples of its occurrence in nature. This dearth, however, in no way diminishes the truth of the observation that reciprocity is massively important in human social life. Human social interactions are universally saturated with the logic of reciprocity (Brown, 1991; Gouldner, 1960; Trivers, 1971), and humans are generally considered the clearest and best example of a truly reciprocally altruistic species. Indeed, the theory of reciprocal altruism has served as the foundation for some of the best-known research in evolutionary psychology, that on cheater detection in the Wason Selection Task (e.g. Cosmides and Tooby, 1992, 2005); this research suggests that the human mind contains a mechanism which is specifically devoted to detecting violators of reciprocal social contracts.

Reciprocal altruism is not always necessarily distinct from genic self-favouritism

Note that there is no necessary reason why reciprocal altruism must involve genic self-favouritism. All reciprocal altruism requires is reciprocating phenotypes, and it could even involve partners of different species. Even if interactants are of the same species, reciprocal altruism need not involve genic self-favouritism. For instance, a variety of converging evidence suggests that, in chimpanzees, females provide sex to males in exchange for meat (Galdikas and Teleki, 1981; Stanford *et al.*, 1994; Teleki, 1973; Tutin, 1979); however, the genes enabling males to share meat are not necessarily the same as those enabling females to provide sex in exchange. On the other hand, although reciprocal altruism does not necessarily depend on genic self-favouritism, it may potentially involve it. If members of the same species engage in the exchange of the same kind of resource (e.g. if they groom one another), or in a relatively generalised type of exchange in which any type of resource can be traded (as with humans), then it is reasonable to expect that the same adaptations and hence genes are enabling this cooperativeness in each interactant (Price, 2006). If the genes encoding cooperative behaviour were the same in the interactants, then it would be reciprocal altruism *and* genic self-favouritism; if the genes were different, then it would just be reciprocal altruism. This example shows how reciprocal altruism and genic self-favouritism are often not as distinct as is typically assumed, and how they can easily shade into one another (Humphrey, 1997; Rothstein, 1980).

Indirect reciprocity

With reciprocal altruism, the assumption is that Individual A will learn about Individual B's history of cooperation and defection based on A's own interactions with B. With indirect reciprocity (Alexander, 1979, 1987), the assumption is that A could learn this history based on information about B's interactions with other partners. A could obtain this information, for example, by observing B's interactions with others, or via reputational information about B that was reported by others. If A makes a decision about whether to cooperate with B based on such second-hand experience – for example if A chooses to act cooperatively with B because A believes that B acted cooperatively with C in the past – then indirect reciprocity will have occurred. Indirect reciprocity is fundamentally similar to reciprocal altruism in several major ways. First, as with reciprocal altruism, verbal models of indirect reciprocity have been extensively supplemented and supported with more formal models (Leimar and Hammerstein, 2001; Nowak and Sigmund, 1998, 2005; Ohtsuki, Iwasa and Nowak, 2009; Panchanathan and Boyd, 2004). Second, while indirect reciprocity has been well-documented in humans (Rockenbach and Milinski, 2006; Semmann, Krambeck and Milinski, 2004, 2005; Simpson and Willer, 2008; Stanca, 2009; Wedekind and Milinski, 2000), its importance to other species is significantly less clear. And finally, indirect reciprocity may or may not involve genic self-favouritism. In order to evolve, indirect reciprocity must at a minimum enable interactants with cooperative phenotypes to have a better-than-random chance of interacting with one another. If these phenotypes are encoded by the same genotypes, then the indirect reciprocity will also constitute genic self-favouritism; if not, it will qualify as indirect reciprocity only.

Costly signalling

The costly signalling theoretical framework was developed in biology by theorists such as Zahavi (1975, 1977) and Grafen (1990) and more recently has been used to explain human cooperation (Bird, Smith and Bird, 2001; Gintis, Smith and Bowles, 2001; Gurven *et al.*, 2000; Hardy and van Vugt, 2006; Iredale, van Vugt and Dunbar, 2008; Nelissen, 2008; Smith and Bird, 2000). The basic idea of costly signalling theory is that a costly trait, such as engagement in altruistic behaviour, can bring reputational benefits to the signaller and thus make him or her seem more attractive to others as a social partner. The return benefits proposed by costly signalling theory, then, come from the increased social opportunities that one can acquire via engagement in conspicuous cooperation.

What types of desirable qualities might one be advertising through cooperative acts? An obvious answer would be cooperative disposition itself: what better way to signal your cooperativeness, and facilitate positive assortment with other cooperators than by broadcasting your cooperative deeds (Gurven *et al.*, 2000; Hardy and van Vugt, 2006; Nelissen, 2008)? However, it is also possible that a cooperative act could be used to advertise qualities that are only incidentally related to cooperative disposition itself. Smith and Bird (2000), for instance, suggest that among the Meriam of Australia, men make a great effort to hunt turtles, and share the meat widely, so that they can advertise qualities such as hunting ability, health and vigour. These qualities may make them more attractive as allies and mates, but this attractiveness is not due to them being perceived as particularly good cooperators.

So one version of costly signalling theory proposes that cooperators advertise cooperativeness itself (let's call this the 'auto-signal' theory), and another version suggests that they advertise qualities that are only incidentally related to cooperativeness (let's call this the 'other-signal' theory). While both versions have appeared in the literature on altruism and costly signalling in humans, the other-signal theory has been more prevalent in literature on non-human animal behaviour. The other-signal explanation, for example, has commonly been used to explain food sharing in birds. It has been suggested that males share with females in order to advertise their mate quality (Helfenstein *et al.*, 2003; Wiggins and Morris, 1986), and that males may share with other males in order to display their dominance (Kalishov, Zahavi and Zahavi, 2005), but it is not usually suggested that sharing serves as a signal of general cooperative disposition.

The distinction between the auto-signal and other-signal versions is important, because it affects how costly signalling theory relates to the other theories of cooperation that we have discussed so far. The auto-signalling theory is in fact difficult to distinguish from theories of reciprocal altruism and indirect reciprocity (both of which, as we have seen, could potentially involve greenbeard effects), because the signaller is seen as cooperating in order to attract cooperative partners for reciprocal relationships. In contrast, the other-signalling theory is qualitatively different from any other theory we have discussed. For example, if sharing meat attracts mates because it signals hunting ability, health and vigour, then reciprocal altruism and indirect reciprocity should not be important (since the signaller's value as a reciprocal partner is not what is being evaluated), and genic self-favouritism should also be irrelevant (because the genes that cause the signaller to share meat should be different from those which cause females to be attracted to him).

If the auto-signal theory is correct, then it may (ironically) be unnecessary, because it seems redundant with the two reciprocity theories. However, the other-signal theory is sometimes cast explicitly as an alternative to reciprocity theories (Bird, Smith and Bird, 2001; Gintis, Smith and Bowles, 2001; Smith and Bird, 2000), and could very well capture some dynamics of cooperation that are overlooked by reciprocity theories. Price (2003) tested between the other-signal and reciprocity theories in order to see which theory would better predict behaviour in a small-scale society; he found better support for reciprocity, but additional studies are needed.

SUMMARY OF INDIVIDUAL-LEVEL THEORIES OF COOPERATION

Table 3.2 summarises the six individual-level theories of cooperation that are discussed above, and notes where each one falls on the spectrum from genic self-favouritism to return benefits. On one end of the spectrum, we have kin and greenbeard altruism, two kinds of genic self-favouritism which can evolve without return benefits for cooperative individuals; the only required beneficiary is the shared gene for cooperation. (However, even though genic self-favouritism does not require return benefits, it will nonetheless often involve them, since there will often be a positive correlation

Table 3.2. *Comparing individual-level evolutionary theories of cooperation.*

	Necessarily involves genic self-favouritism?	*Potentially involves genic self-favouritism?*	*Necessarily involves return benefits for cooperator?*	*Potentially involves return benefits for cooperator?*
Kin altruism	Yes	—	No	Yes
Greenbeard altruism	Yes	—	No	Yes
Reciprocal altruism	No	Yes	Yes	—
Indirect reciprocity	No	Yes	Yes	—
Costly signalling ('auto-signal')	No	Yes	Yes	—
Costly signalling ('other-signal')	No	No	Yes	—

between receiving aid from an individual who shares one's cooperative genes and delivering aid to that individual. For instance, if A and B are siblings, then just as A will be inclined to aid B, B will be inclined to aid A.)

In the middle of the spectrum we have the reciprocity theories: reciprocal altruism and indirect reciprocity, and the auto-signal version of costly signalling theory (as we have seen, this last theory is largely redundant with the reciprocity theories). The reciprocity theories do require return benefits, but do not require genic self-favouritism and can even account for cooperation between members of different species. However, reciprocity can potentially involve genic self-favouritism, and would be likely to if carriers of the same gene(s) for reciprocity had some means of interacting preferentially with one another. On the far return benefits end of the spectrum we have the other-signal version of costly signalling theory, in which cooperative behaviour signals some attractive quality that is only incidentally related to cooperation itself. The other-signal theory must involve some sort of return benefit for the signaller (usually in the form of social partners such as mates or allies), but it does not involve genic self-favouritism.

GROUP SELECTION

Up to now our discussion has focused on individual-level theories of cooperation, that is theories which focus on the individual cooperator as a vehicle for replicating genes. However, as mentioned above, in many species social groups can also be considered as relevant vehicles of selection. When individuals assort into groups, and selection operates among groups (i.e. if the members of some groups have higher average fitnesses than the members of other groups), then the search for cooperative adaptations potentially becomes more complicated. For example, an adaptation at one level may conflict with the functioning of an adaptation at another level, if it is good for the group but bad for the individual or vice versa.

The issue of how evolution may favour traits that benefit a whole group is known, in general, as 'group selection'. (The term 'group selection' has held various more specific meanings to different researchers, and the issue has been complicated by semantic confusion, as discussed below.) The idea that group selection may be relevant to the evolution of altruism has a long history in behavioural biology. For most of the twentieth century it was common for biologists to engage in what is now considered 'naive group selectionism' (Wilson and Wilson, 2007). In this type of thinking, apparently altruistic individual behaviour is explained in terms of the benefits that it brings for the individual's group, without adequate consideration of how the behaviour could have avoided being selected against at the individual level. The classic example of naive group selectionism is Wynne-Edwards (1962), who proposed that animals refrain from reproducing too much at the individual level so that they can avoid overexploiting their resources at the population level.

The publication that was most instrumental in ending the era of naive group selectionism was George Williams' (1966) influential critique of evolutionary thought,

Adaptation and Natural Selection. Williams believed that selection at the individual level would, under normal circumstances, be much more intense than selection at the group level, and so he agreed with Darwin's (1859/1958) usual view that adaptations evolve to benefit not the success of groups or species but rather the fitness of individuals. In most species, most of the time, successful gene replication will depend much more on the fitness of the individual carrier, as opposed to the average fitness of the carrier's group. Therefore, when there is a conflict between individual-level and group-level fitness, the individual level will prevail. Williams thus emphasised that when an individual-level explanation for the evolution of altruism is sufficient, one should not invoke a group-selectionist explanation: 'When recognized, adaptation should be attributed to no higher a level of organization than is demanded by the evidence' (Williams, 1966, p. v). In the wake of Williams' critique, the term 'group selection' acquired a pejorative meaning to most biologists. A group selectionist was considered someone who believed that in a conflict between individual and group fitness, the group level would prevail. Most biologists became highly sceptical about this kind of group selectionism, and individual-level adaptation became the focus of most studies in behavioural biology and evolutionary psychology.

However, despite all the scepticism, group selection has been seriously considered by many influential theorists. Darwin himself, deviating from his normal emphasis on individual fitness, entertains group selectionist ideas in the *Descent of Man* (1871/1981). (However, he also considers problems with these ideas. For more discussion of Darwin's views on group selection, see Box 3.1.) And while Williams' critique did discourage naive group selectionist theories, it also encouraged more rigorous thinking about group selection. Shortly after Williams' critique, for example, G. R. Price (1970, 1972) published his eponymous equation showing how gene frequency changes in a population are the joint product of within-group and between-group selection. Interest in group selection is probably as strong now as it has been at any time over the past few decades, with theorists continuing to develop new models of how group selection could permit cooperation to evolve, and to argue that its semi-banishment from mainstream evolutionary theory was hasty and unwarranted (e.g. Gintis, 2000; Wilson and Sober, 1994; Wilson and Wilson, 2007). Like the Price equations, recent models have tended to emphasise multilevel selection, that is the joint effects of selection operating at both the individual and group levels, and sometimes at other levels (e.g. intragenomic, species) as well (Wilson and Wilson, 2007).

If group selectionism seems inconsistent with the fundamental focus in evolutionary biology of individual-level fitness and adaptation, then why has it made something of a comeback in recent years? There are several reasons, the first and least substantive of which is recent semantic confusion about what constitutes 'group selection'. Some arguments in favour of 'group selection' seem to actually be attempts to broaden its definition, in order to subsume processes that had previously been considered cases of individual selection. For instance, Wilson and Wilson (2007) suggest that the evolution of reciprocal altruism in a population of defectors could be considered a case of group selection, because the reciprocators and the defectors can each be considered a separate group, and the reciprocators have a higher average fitness than the defectors. Similarly, Wilson and Dugatkin (1997) suggest that assortative interactions among

BOX 3.1.   DARWIN'S SPECULATIONS ABOUT GROUP SELECTION IN THE *DESCENT OF MAN*

When advocates of group selection or multi-level selection want to demonstrate that Darwin seemed open to these ideas, they often (e.g. Sober and Wilson, 1998; Wilson, 2002) quote the following passage from Chapter 5 of the *Descent of Man, and Selection in Relation to Sex*:

> There can be no doubt that a tribe including many members who, from possessing in a high degree the spirit of patriotism, fidelity, obedience, courage and sympathy, were always ready to give aid to each other and to sacrifice themselves for the common good, would be victorious over most other tribes; and this would be natural selection.
>
> (Darwin, 1871/1981, p. 166)

It seems clear from this passage that Darwin is entertaining group selectionist ideas. However, broader consideration of Darwin's speculations in this chapter reveals that he was not simply engaging in 'naive group selectionism', and on the contrary, that he was well aware of the problems for group selection that would be caused by individual selection (Wilson, 2007; Wilson and Wilson, 2007). For example, consider Darwin's (1871/1981, p. 163) musings from earlier in the chapter:

> But it may be asked, how within the limits of the same tribe did a large number of members first become endowed with these social and moral qualities, and how was the standard of excellence raised? It is extremely doubtful whether the offspring of the more sympathetic and benevolent parents, or of those which were the most faithful to their comrades, would be reared in greater number than the children of selfish and treacherous parents of the same tribe. He who was ready to sacrifice his life, as many a savage has been, rather than betray his comrades, would often leave no offspring to inherit his noble nature. The bravest men, who were always willing to come to the front in war, and who freely risked their lives for others, would on an average perish in larger number than other men. Therefore it seems scarcely possible (bearing in mind that we are not here speaking of one tribe being victorious over another) that the number of men gifted with such virtues, or that the standard of their excellence, could be increased through natural selection, that is, by the survival of the fittest.

These passages reveal that in the case of human morality, Darwin perceived a conflict between the individual and group levels of selection: while adaptations for moral behaviour would have advantaged everyone in a group, they would not have advantaged the individuals who bore them. Darwin seems perplexed by this puzzle, and realises that a complete solution is beyond the scope of his work. However, he does suggest how the puzzle may begin to get solved, when he proposes some psychological mechanisms by which morality may satisfy individual interests. Interestingly, these mechanisms are reminiscent of two types of individually adaptive cooperative behaviours: reciprocal altruism and indirect reciprocity, which we have already discussed:

> Although the circumstances which lead to an increase in the number of men thus [morally] endowed within the

same tribe are too complex to be clearly followed out, we can trace some of the probable steps. In the first place, as the reasoning powers and foresight of the members became improved, each man would soon learn from experience that if he aided his fellow-men, he would commonly receive aid in return . . . But there is another and much more powerful stimulus to the development of the social virtues, namely, the praise and blame of our fellow men.

(Darwin, 1871/1981, p. 163–4)

In these allusions to reciprocal altruism ('receive aid in return') and indirect reciprocity (reputational effects associated with 'praise and blame'), Darwin is anticipating the kinds of individual-level solutions to the puzzle of cooperation that continue to be discussed and explored today.

altruists (e.g. greenbeard altruism) could be considered group selection, since the altruists would constitute a group in which members had relatively high average fitness. These re-labelling attempts are confusing to those who are used to thinking of group selection as an *alternative* to individual selection. As mentioned above, group selectionism has traditionally implied preference for a group-level explanation when there is a conflict between the individual and group levels. However, in the cases of reciprocal and greenbeard altruism, there is no conflict between the individual and group levels.

A second reason for renewed interest in group selection has been a proliferation of formal models showing how a kind of altruism known as 'strong reciprocity' could evolve by biological and/or cultural group selection (e.g. Boyd *et al.*, 2003; Gintis, 2000; Gintis *et al.*, 2003). A strong reciprocator is someone who acts cooperatively and punishes non-cooperators, even when doing so produces no direct return benefit for one's self. These formal models have been supplemented with a large body of cross-cultural data from experimental economic games that is presented as empirical evidence of strong reciprocity (e.g. Fehr, Fischbacher and Gächter, 2002; Henrich *et al.*, 2005). The interpretation of these results, however, has been questioned, mainly on the grounds of ecological validity: psychological mechanisms for cooperation which did produce return benefits in ancestral environments should not necessarily be expected to do so in the highly artificial environments of experimental economic games (Burnham and Johnson, 2005; Hagen and Hammerstein, 2006; Price, 2008; Trivers, 2004; West, Griffin and Gardner, 2007).

Finally, group selection continues to attract interest for the fundamental reason that it is an important biological phenomenon that does occur in nature. For example, in a strain of *Pseudomonas fluorescens* bacteria known as the 'wrinkly spreader', some individuals help produce a cellulosic polymer that enables the group to survive in the absence of oxygen. Polymer production is costly, and non-producers have higher relative within-group fitness; nevertheless, genes for producing the polymer are maintained via group selection (Rainey and Rainey, 2003). Group selection also helps explain why parasites often evolve to be less virulent to their hosts than they could be: parasites which reproduce relatively rapidly will increase in frequency within their host, but will risk killing their host and thus reducing their own chances of spreading to another host. Their 'cheating' (reproducing too quickly) damages their own long-term fitness, as well as that of other parasites who reside within the same host (Frank, 1996). However, probably the most fascinating example of group selection is the individual organism itself. According to the most widely accepted framework for explaining the major transitions in the history of life (Margulis, 1970; Maynard Smith and Szathmáry, 1995), the evolution of increased biological complexity has progressed via group selection. The first genes were lone replicating chemicals, which eventually began to join forces and surround themselves with the earliest prokaryotic cells; these simple cells began to cooperate with one another to form more complex eukaryotic cells, and groups of cells were eventually selected to compose the first multicellular organisms. At every major transition, lone biological agents found they could solve adaptive problems by forming cooperative groups, and these groups were ultimately selected to become the highly integrated packages that today we perceive as individuals.

As the driving force in the major transitions in life, group selection cannot be ignored as a fundamental and important biological process. Still, it is important to remember that in most cases of group selection, such as those referenced above, conflicts between the individual and group levels are minimal. For example, the various cellular types in a multicellular organism will generally all have an interest in working together to promote organismal fitness, since each type's own fate depends highly upon this fitness. If one cellular type acted to selfishly promote its own representation in the organism at the expense of another cellular type, and the result were organismal death, then this selfishness would be self-destructive. In other words, the best way that each type can promote its own long-term reproductive interests is to cooperate with other types, and this confluence of interest minimises the need to distinguish between the fitness interests of the 'group' (which in this case happens to be the organism) and the 'individuals' (the cell types). However, even this extremely high degree of alignment in fitness interests is not sufficient to completely preclude conflict. Various kinds of intragenomic conflict can cause within-organism cooperation to break down, sometimes with devastating consequences for organismal fitness (Burt and Trivers, 2006). For example, segregation distorter genes promote their own replication by increasing their representation in the organism's gametes, and damaged DNA may cause one cellular type to reproduce at the expense of other types (e.g. cancer).

COMPLEX HUMAN COOPERATION: COLLECTIVE ACTION

We have now covered the major individual-level adaptationist theories of cooperative behaviour, in addition to the theory of group selection. While these theories apply to a huge range of species, and not just to humans, each one has been used at one time or another to explain some aspects of human cooperative behaviour. However, with regard to one kind of human cooperative behaviour in particular, there is still a major lack of consensus about which kind of evolutionary explanation is correct.

Collective action: The remaining puzzle of human cooperation

Humans are a highly cooperative species, distinguished among other species by their remarkable ability to cooperate in huge groups of individuals who are not close genetic relatives (Boyd *et al.*, 2003). As mentioned at the outset of this chapter, this ability to cooperate in large groups is a fundamental feature of human sociality. However, it is also the aspect of human cooperation that is most difficult to explain. In order to understand the difficulty of explaining it, let's consider the nature of these groups in more detail. These groups typically take the form of collective actions in which any number of individuals engage in the joint production of a shared resource such as a public good (a public good is a resource that all group members will be able to access equally). For example, joint efforts to protect a whole group from attack from human or non-human predators, or to increase a whole group's access to food or water, would be considered public good-producing collective actions. In such collective actions, the extent of an individual group member's net benefit from the public good is determined by the extent to which he or she contributed to its production. Since all members have equal access to the good, those who sacrifice the most to produce it will end up reaping the lowest net benefit; therefore, each member should strive to contribute as little as possible (i.e. to free ride as much as possible on the efforts of other members), and collective actions should generally tend to unravel and fail (Olson, 1965). This classic quandary is variously known as the 'free rider problem', 'collective action problem', 'social dilemma' or 'tragedy of the commons' (Hardin, 1968). The free rider problem is not quite ubiquitous because it should be absent if the benefits of cooperation are high enough (see Box 3.2 for a discussion about the conditions under which free rider problems should arise in collective actions). But in most collective actions, sustained cooperation will depend on successful resolution of the free rider problem.

Research suggests that various types of solutions to the free rider problem do, thankfully, exist. Studies of collective actions often take the form of experimental economic public goods games. These studies suggest several ways in which group members strive to solve the collective action problem, that is how they attempt to contribute to the public good while minimising the extent to which they are exploited by free riders. First, they engage in conditional cooperation, which is a kind of reciprocal altruism in which they contribute more highly if they observe or expect high contributions from co-members (Fischbacher, Gächter and Fehr, 2001; Kurzban and Houser, 2005; Ledyard, 1995). Second, they engage in the punishment of free riding co-members, even when it is costly to the individual to engage in such punishment (Fehr and Gächter, 2002; Ostrom, Walker and Gardner, 1992; Price, 2005; Price, Cosmides and Tooby, 2002; Yamagishi, 1986). Third, they engage in partner choice: if they have some ability to choose their co-members, then higher contributors tend to choose to form groups with each other and to thus exclude free riders from the public

BOX 3.2. WHY THE FREE RIDER PROBLEM DISAPPEARS IN EXTREMELY PRODUCTIVE COLLECTIVE ACTIONS

To really understand why the free rider problem should in theory disappear when the benefits of cooperation become very high, it helps to understand the simple maths which describe the situations in which the free rider problem should and should not arise.

First, consider a collective action in which the value of the benefit produced is *not* extremely high. In this kind of interaction, free riding will be individually beneficial. Imagine that four villagers ($n = 4$) each have an equal amount of food growing in a shared garden. It has been raining for several days and three of the villagers decide to construct a wall to protect their garden from a flood; they cannot convince the fourth villager to help. Every one unit of contribution effort ($c = 1$) will produce two units of benefit ($b = 2$) in the form of protected food. Each of the three workers contributes $c = 1$, so they collectively produce $3 \times 2 = 6$ units of benefit. This benefit is shared equally by all four villagers, for a per capita benefit of $6 / 4 = 1.5$. Each worker receives a net gain of $1.5 - 1 = 0.5$, while the free rider receives 1.5 at no cost. If the free rider had contributed at the same level as the others ($c = 1$), then the group would have collectively produced $4 \times 2 = 8$ units of benefit, for a per capita benefit of $8 / 4 = 2$, and a per capita net gain of $2 - 1 = 1$. So had the free rider contributed like the others, he would have done worse (his profit would have been 1 instead of 1.5), and each other member would have done better (each one's profit would have been 1 instead of 0.5).

Next, consider a collective action in which the value of the benefit produced *is* extremely high. In this kind of interaction, free riding will be individually costly. Imagine that all of the above details are the same, except that the four villagers have been enduring serious food shortages, and so their garden food has become more valuable to them. Now, every one unit of contribution effort ($c = 1$) will produce not 2 but 5 units of benefit ($b = 5$) in terms of protected food. Again, three of the villagers contribute to building a flood wall while the fourth free rides. Each of the three workers contributes $c = 1$, so they collectively produce $3 \times 5 = 15$ units of benefit, for a per capita benefit of $15 / 4 = 3.75$. Each worker receives a net gain of $3.75 - 1 = 2.75$, while the free rider receives 3.75 at no cost. If the free rider *had* contributed at the same level of the others ($c = 1$), then the group would have collectively produced $4 \times 5 = 20$ units of benefit, for a per capita benefit of $20 / 4 = 5$, and a per capita net gain of $5 - 1 = 4$. So had the free rider contributed like the others, he would have done better (his profit would have been 4 instead of 3.75), and so would each of the other members (each one's profit would have been 4 instead of 2.75). Instead of benefiting from his free riding, the free rider suffered for it, because in this collective action the benefits of cooperation were very high.

The individual incentive to free ride, then, falls off in highly productive collective actions. Specifically, when the cost of an individual contribution is set at 1, free riding will be individually costly when the benefit produced by each contribution is greater than the number of collective action beneficiaries (i.e. when $c = 1$ and $b > n$).

good (Barclay and Willer, 2007; Ehrhart and Keser, 1999; Page, Putterman and Unel, 2005; Sheldon, Sheldon and Osbaldiston, 2000).

How well do the previously reviewed theories of cooperation explain behaviour in collective actions? Kin selection seems insufficient, because collective actions are often composed of non-kin. Other-signal costly signalling theory has been proposed as an explanation of some forms of public good provisioning (Bird, Smith and Bird, 2001; Gintis, Smith and Bowles, 2001; Smith and Bird, 2000), but it does not seem to predict key behaviours that have been observed in collective actions such as conditional cooperation and punishment of free riders. Because kin selection and other-signal costly signalling both seem to offer largely incomplete explanations of collective action, they will not be considered further here. Auto-signal costly signalling will also not be considered further as a distinct theory, since, as noted above, it is largely redundant with reciprocal altruism and indirect reciprocity. That leaves the following theories available for consideration: reciprocal altruism, indirect reciprocity, greenbeard altruism and group selection.

The reciprocity theories as explanations for collective action

Traditionally, reciprocal altruism has been represented as simple dyadic exchange, a model which is obviously inadequate for explaining collective actions involving many members. However, efforts have been made to adapt reciprocal altruism to n-person collective actions (Tooby, Cosmides and Price, 2006). The first formal model of n-person reciprocity (Boyd and Richerson, 1988) modelled the reciprocity strategy as a discrete one which could contribute either fully or not at all (i.e. contribute either zero or one), depending on how many of its co-members contributed. The conclusion of this model was that this kind of reciprocity was not sufficient to overcome the free rider problem and could therefore not account for the evolution of 'sizeable' collective actions; discrete reciprocity performs reasonably well in very small groups (e.g. three to five members) but starts doing badly if groups get much larger than this. However, this conclusion seems incompatible with the observation that reciprocal altruism (conditional cooperation) is commonly observed in collective actions. A later model represented reciprocal altruism in a more realistic form, not as a discrete all-or-nothing strategy but rather as a continuous strategy which matches the average co-member contribution and can contribute any amount between zero and one. This strategy, which mimics the way in which conditional cooperators in public goods games have been observed to behave, in some respects performs significantly better in collective action contexts than the discrete strategy does (Johnson, Price and Takezawa, 2008). However, even continuous reciprocity has difficulty evolving (i.e. invading a population of unconditional defectors) in sizeable collective actions (e.g. 100 members), except for in those which are extraordinarily productive.

Further studies and more formal models are needed to investigate whether and how reciprocal altruism could evolve in collective actions. While the models described above suggest that reciprocity has difficulty evolving in large groups, it is possible that human adaptations for reciprocity evolved in small groups, and that these adaptations are nevertheless routinely deployed in the larger groups that frequently characterise modern societies. Indeed, in human ancestral environments, small groups would have been the norm (e.g. Kelly, 1995; this issue, and the vital importance in evolutionary psychology of considering the nature of human ancestral environments in general, will be discussed in more detail in the conclusion to this chapter). Further, it may be the case that adaptations for reciprocity evolved simultaneously and synergistically with other cooperative behaviours, such as indirect reciprocity, positive assortation and punishment of free riders. For example, reciprocity and positive assortation interact synergistically in collective actions (Boyd and Richerson, 1988; Johnson, Price and Takezawa, 2008). If synergistic interactions between reciprocity and other behaviours occur, then models which examine the evolution of reciprocity in isolation, unaffected by these other behaviours, may underestimate its adaptiveness. Whatever the true story about the evolution of reciprocity in groups turns out to be, the ubiquity of reciprocity in collective actions lends credibility to the view that reciprocal altruism has indeed played a role in enabling the evolution of collective action.

It also seems plausible that indirect reciprocity has played a role in the evolution of collective action. In contrast to the case of reciprocal altruism, relatively little controversy has been associated with formal models showing how indirect reciprocity could evolve in collective action contexts (Nowak and Sigmund, 2005; Panchanathan and Boyd, 2004). Evidence from experimental economic games supports these formal theories: when contributors to collective actions engage in partner choice as a way of engaging other contributors and avoiding free riders, they tend to base their decisions on the information they have about potential partners' histories of cooperative interactions with other people (Barclay and Willer, 2007; Ehrhart and Keser, 1999; Page, Putterman and Unel, 2005; Sheldon, Sheldon and Osbaldiston, 2000).

Greenbeard altruism as an explanation for collective action

Greenbeard altruism's role in enabling the evolution of collective action remains a largely unexplored issue. If human cooperation has evolved significantly by greenbeard dynamics, then the conspicuous label of cooperative disposition required by these dynamics has likely been relatively non-arbitrary. Greenbeard systems become more unstable when they rely on a label of cooperative disposition that has a more arbitrary relationship with actual cooperative disposition. An arbitrary label like a green beard can easily be displayed by someone who does not truly possess a cooperative disposition, but it is more difficult to fake a label that can only be produced via actual engagement in cooperative behaviour. If greenbeard dynamics have been important in the evolution of human cooperation, therefore, then actual engagement in cooperative behaviour may have been the most common type of phenotypic label (Price, 2006; Wilson and Dugatkin, 1997). This system would evolve via mutations that caused people to engage in cooperative behaviour and to direct this behaviour towards people who displayed a similar tendency to engage in cooperative behaviour; as long as these behaviours were encoded by the same gene(s) in all of these interactants, it would be true genic self-favouritism. Thus, when high contributors to collective actions cooperate more with other high contributors, via either reciprocal

altruism (conditional cooperation) or indirect reciprocity (partner choice), an underlying process of greenbeard dynamics could potentially be involved.

Group selection as an explanation for collective action

Finally, could the evolution of collective action have been facilitated via a process of
group selection? It is possible, even if the individual-level reciprocity processes (with
or without greenbeard dynamics) have also been important. In a process of multilevel selection (Wilson and Wilson, 2007), collective action could have evolved via
both group- and individual-level selection. The group-selection component of this
process could retain genes for behaviour that was fitness-damaging to individuals
but fitness-enhancing for groups, provided that selection among groups was sufficiently intense and that migration among groups was sufficiently limited. However,
it has not proven easy to generate evidence for group-selected human cooperative
behaviour. One problem is that researchers of this topic often look for negative as
opposed to positive evidence: in controlled laboratory conditions, experimenters
attempt to eliminate the possibility that public goods games players could be striving
to gain individual-level benefits by cooperating (e.g. the experimenters impose strict
anonymity on all players, and make the games one-shot, in order to preclude reputation effects and reciprocity), and if players still continue to behave cooperatively, this
residual cooperativeness is considered evidence of group selection (Fehr, Fischbacher
and Gächter, 2002; Henrich *et al.*, 2005). Critics of this approach point out that behaviour which appears selfless in environmentally novel laboratory conditions may not
have been so in ancestral environments (Burnham and Johnson, 2005; Hagen and
Hammerstein, 2006; Price, 2008; Trivers, 2004; West, Griffin and Gardner, 2007).
If positive rather than negative evidence for group selection could be produced,
and if this evidence were predicted by group-selection theory alone, then the relevance of group selection would be easier to demonstrate.

Despite the lack of unequivocal evidence, some evidence is interpreted by some
researchers as indicating that group selection has been important in the evolution of
collective action. For example, as noted above, many contributors in public goods games
will engage in the costly punishment of free riding co-members. This punishment may
seem to provide a selfish incentive for would-be free riders to cooperate, since cooperation allows them to avoid punishment. However, punishment does not provide a good
general individual-level solution to the problem of collective action, since punishment
itself seems to constitute a second-order public good: it is costly to provide, and it benefits the group by eliciting contributions from would-be free riders. Punishment simply
creates a new, second-order problem of collective action (Boyd and Richerson, 1992;
Yamagishi, 1986). Some modellers have suggested that a process of biological and/or
cultural group selection is necessary to resolve this second-order problem (Boyd *et al.*,
2003; Gintis, 2000; Gintis *et al.*, 2003). On the other hand, some researchers maintain
that the second-order free rider problem would not have prevented free rider punishment from evolving by standard individual-level selection (Gardner and Grafen, 2009;
Price, 2003, 2005; Price, Cosmides and Tooby, 2002). For more in-depth discussion on
the topic of free riders and the second-order problem, see Box 3.3.

BOX 3.3.   FREE RIDER PUNISHMENT AND THE SECOND-ORDER PROBLEM

As noted in the main text, punishment can help solve the free rider problem in collective actions: when the costs of being punished outweigh the advantages of free riding, cooperation becomes more profitable than free riding. Evidence from both experimental and real-life collective actions suggests that groups cooperate more productively when free riders can be punished, and that group members will willingly accept the costs associated with punishing free riders (e.g. Fehr and Gächter, 2002; Ostrom, 2000; Price, 2005; Yamagishi, 1986). These costs may include not just the expenses of inflicting punishment (e.g. energy expenditure, monetary costs) but also those that may result from retaliation: after being punished, many free riders will attempt to retaliate against their punishers (Cinyabuguma, Page and Putterman, 2005; Nikiforakis, 2008).

However, while punishment at first glance seems to provide a solution to the free rider problem, a closer look suggests that it may simply replace this problem with a new problem of second-order free riding. When a collective action participant punishes a free rider, he or she produces resources for other participants because he or she coerces a contribution to the public good from the would-be free rider. But while all participants benefit from this contribution, only the punisher pays for it. Therefore, punishers should be disadvantaged relative to 'second-order free riders', that is participants who accept the benefits produced by free rider punishment but who do not help pay for these benefits by punishing free riders themselves (Boyd and Richerson, 1992; Yamagishi, 1986). For this reason, punishment of free riders is sometimes referred to as 'altruistic punishment' (Boyd et al., 2003; Johnson et al., 2009).

How can this second-order problem be solved? As noted, some theorists believe that the solution requires group selection (e.g. Boyd et al.,

2003; Gintis, 2000; Gintis et al., 2003). However, other theorists assume that there must be some individual-level explanation for the evolution of free rider punishment and the punitive sentiment which motivates it (e.g. Gardner and Grafen, 2009; Hauert et al., 2007; Price, Cosmides and Tooby, 2002). Given the problems associated with resorting to group selection when individual selection may in fact be sufficient, one should carefully consider all of the ways in which punishing free riders may have benefited ancestral punishers.

One individual-level explanation for how free rider punishment evolved is second-order punishment; this view assumes that punishments are directed not just at free riders but also at those who fail to punish free riders. (This may seem to lead to an infinitely recursive problem of third- and higher-order free riding – participants who fail to punish participants who fail to punish free riders, and so on – but the recursion problem seems to become trivial beyond the second order; for a discussion, see Kiyonari and Barclay, 2008.) However, the same sorts of experimental methods which have produced strong evidence for free rider punishment have not provided much evidence for punishment of non-punishers (Kiyonari and Barclay, 2008; Kiyonari, van Veelen and Yamagishi, 2008).

Fortunately, there are several more plausible individual-level explanations for free rider punishment. For instance, it may be that free riders are punished because they are shunned in private transactions outside of the context of collective actions, a process of indirect reciprocity that avoids the second-order problem (Panchanathan and Boyd, 2004). Alternatively, in collective actions where certain kinds of conditions apply (e.g. the collective good must be excludable), free rider punishment can evolve without the second-order problem if members of the population can opt out of collective action participation and instead pursue productive solitary pursuits (Hauert *et al.*, 2007).

Finally, and perhaps most promisingly, punishers may receive some kind of private reputational benefit as the result of others observing their behaviour. Support for this view is provided by experiments suggesting that participants who are being observed by an audience punish cheaters more than do those whose actions are anonymous (Kurzban, DeScioli and O'Brien, 2007; Piazza and Bering, 2008). What might be the nature of these reputational benefits? They could make the punisher seem like a relatively good choice as a cooperative partner; studies suggest that punishers are viewed as more trustworthy and are preferred as partners (Nelissen, 2008). Or they could make the punisher seem like a relatively bad choice as someone to cheat (Price, 2003): a willingness to punish free riders may send a message to the general public along the lines of 'mess with me and this is what you get'. This reputation could provide private benefits for the punisher in social contexts besides collective actions (e.g. dyadic exchanges), which could more than compensate for the punisher's disadvantage relative to second-order free riders in collective actions. For a discussion of some other possible individual-level solutions to the second-order free rider problem, see Price (2003).

Perhaps the best evidence in favour of group selection in humans is that people occasionally exhibit extremely altruistic behaviours in collective actions – for instance the deliberate sacrifice of one's own life during coalitional conflict – that seem particularly hard to explain in terms of individual-level theories (Sosis and Alcorta, 2008). These behaviours can be challenging to study, especially because it is often difficult or unethical to elicit them in the laboratory. Nevertheless, if efforts are made to better understand extremely self-sacrificial human behaviour, group selection may turn out to be a necessary part of the explanation. On the other hand, people who agree to kill themselves for their coalition – for example suicide bombers – often receive extraordinarily high status for doing so, before they are actually dead (Axell and Kase, 2002; Moghadam, 2003). It could be that in ancestral environments, attaining such high status was so highly positively correlated with fitness benefits – especially for males (Daly and Wilson, 1988) – that selection designed people to regard the attainment of such status as a deeply desirable end in itself. In modern societies characterised by environmental novelties (e.g. high explosives), status-striving (e.g. by suicide bombers) may lead relatively frequently to maladaptive, premature death; however, in ancestral environments, such striving may have on average been adaptive.

CONCLUSION

Cooperation and the evolution of altruism have been centrally important topics in behavioural biology since the days of Darwin, and will continue to be for the foreseeable future. A great deal of progress has been made in understanding these topics, especially since the shift in the mid-1960s in perspective which saw the gene take centre stage as the fundamental unit of selection. However, despite this progress, much important work remains to be done, especially for evolutionary psychologists interested in the evolution of collective action. Because collective action is so centrally important in human sociality, and because it still presents some of the greatest challenges facing behavioural biology, I will focus in this conclusion on emphasising two ways in which evolutionary investigations of collective action could most profitably proceed.

First, for reasons emphasised throughout this chapter, before we resort to higher-level explanations for the evolution of collective action, we should first focus on thoroughly applying existing individual-level theories, such as reciprocity theories and positive assortation theories like greenbeard altruism (Price, 2006). Moreover, as noted above, we should analyse these individual-level cooperative behaviours not just in isolation from one another but as strategies which can exist simultaneously and potentially interact synergistically. While this kind of 'bottom-up' approach would start by looking for individual-level solutions, it would not preclude an investigation into the effects of group selection. However if we start with an exhaustive investigation at the individual level, then by the time we work our way up to the group level we will be in a good position to understand how group-beneficial behaviours could have escaped being selected against at the individual level. Cutting-edge modelling work on the individual-level evolution of collective action is currently being carried out by theorists such as Martin Nowak, Christoph Hauert and colleagues (e.g. Hauert *et al.*, 2007, 2008; Wakano, Nowak and Hauert, 2009). In addition, particularly interesting new experimental tests of individual-level theories of collective action are being carried out by researchers like Louis Putterman and colleagues (e.g. Bochet and Putterman, 2009; Ertan, Page and Putterman, 2009), Pat Barclay and colleagues (e.g. Barclay and Willer, 2007; Kiyonari and Barclay, 2008) and Mark van Vugt and colleagues (e.g. O'Gorman, Henrich and van Vugt, 2008; van Vugt and Spisak, 2008).

Second, in attempting to identify human adaptations for collective action participation, we should always remember that these adaptations were designed by environments that were in important ways different from those of modern societies (Tooby, Cosmides and Price, 2006). These adaptations have specific environments of evolutionary adaptedness (EEA), and while they must have functioned adaptively in these ancestral environments, we should not always expect them to function adaptively in modern environments (Symons, 1990; Tooby and Cosmides, 1992). Nevertheless, as noted, some evolutionary analyses do make the mistake of assuming that if an adaptation promoted individual fitness in past environments then it should also do so in present environments – even when these present environments are radically different from those of the past, for example when they are the experimental laboratories of modern universities.

It would also be good to keep ancestral conditions in mind when we consider the adaptiveness of cooperative behaviour in large groups. For example, the influential model of the evolution of reciprocity in collective actions discussed above (Boyd and Richerson, 1988), which suggested that reciprocity would be unlikely to evolve in large collective actions, has led some to believe that when humans participate in large collective actions in modern environments, their behaviour cannot be explained in terms of adaptations for reciprocity (e.g. Fehr, 2004; Henrich, 2004). The problem with this conclusion is that an adaptation that was designed by small-group conditions in ancestral environments could nevertheless still function in large groups. For example, a decision rule for contributing in a collective action like 'match the mean co-member contribution' may scale up to a group of any size, even if it functioned adaptively in small groups and maladaptively in large groups. If humans do possess adaptations for reciprocity in collective actions, then it is likely that these did evolve in small groups. An average hunter-gatherer band contains only about seven or eight male and female full-time foragers (Kelly, 1995), which suggests that a typical same-sex collective action (e.g. a male hunting party) in ancestral environments may have consisted of only about four members. Human adaptations for reciprocity may have evolved in such small groups, and could govern human behaviour in the large groups of modern societies, regardless of whether they lead to adaptive outcomes in large groups.

In conclusion, our understanding of collective action is certainly challenged by levels-of-selection considerations, by the need to thoroughly apply individual-level theories of cooperation and by the requirement that we must always remember that adaptations for cooperation were designed by ancestral environments that were significantly different from those of today. Nevertheless, these challenges are currently being faced by many researchers, and there is no doubt that our understanding of the evolution of cooperation will improve as a result. If this understanding continues to progress as steadily as it has for the past several decades, then in the coming decades the puzzle of cooperation may no longer be regarded as a puzzle at all.

ACKNOWLEDGEMENTS

Thanks to Oliver Curry for drawing my attention to the depth of Darwin's thinking about levels of selection, and to Jade Price for suggesting revisions to the manuscript draft.

REFERENCES

Alexander, R. D. (1979). *Darwinism and human affairs*. Seattle: University of Washington Press.

Alexander, R. D. (1987). *The biology of moral systems*. Hawthorne, NY: Aldine de Gruyter.

Axell, A. and Kase, H. (2002). *Kamikaze: Japan's suicide gods*. New York: Longman.

Axelrod, R. and Hamilton, W. D. (1981). The evolution of cooperation. *Science, 211*, 1390–1396. New York.

Barclay, P. and Willer, R. (2007). Partner choice creates competitive altruism in humans. *Proceedings of the Royal Society B, 274*, 749–53.

Bird, R. L. B., Smith, E. A. and Bird, D. W. (2001). The hunting handicap: Costly signaling in human foraging strategies. *Behavioral Ecology and Sociobiology, 50*, 9–19.

Bochet, O. and Putterman, L. (2009). Not just babble: Opening the black box of communication in a voluntary contribution experiment. *European Economic Review*, 53, 309–26.

Boyd, R. and Richerson, P. J. (1988). The evolution of reciprocity in sizable groups. *Journal of Theoretical Biology*, 132, 337–56.

Boyd, R. and Richerson, P. J. (1992). Punishment allows the evolution of cooperation (or anything else) in sizable groups. *Ethology and Sociobiology*, 13, 171–95.

Boyd, R., Gintis, H., Bowles, S. and Richerson, P. J. (2003). The evolution of altruistic punishment. *Proceedings of the National Academy of Sciences USA*, 100, 3531–5.

Brown, D. E. (1991). *Human universals*. New York: McGraw-Hill.

Brown, J. L. (1983). Cooperation: A biologist's dilemma. *Advances in the Study of Behavior*, 13, 1–37.

Bshary, R. and Grutter, A. S. (2002). Asymmetric cheating opportunities and partner control in a cleaner fish mutualism. *Animal Behaviour*, 63, 547–55.

Bshary, R. and Schäffer, D. (2002). Choosy reef fish select cleaner fish that provide high-quality service. *Animal Behaviour*, 63, 557–64.

Burnham, T. and Johnson, D. D. P. (2005). The evolutionary and biological logic of human cooperation. *Analyse and Kritik*, 27, 113–135.

Burt, A. and Trivers, R. (2006). *Genes in conflict: The biology of selfish genetic elements*. Cambridge, MA: Belknap Press.

Chagnon, N. A. (1979). Mate competition, favoring close kin, and village fissioning among the Yanomamö Indians. In N. A. Chagnon and W. Irons (eds), *Evolutionary biology and human social behavior* (pp. 86–132). North Scituate, MA: Duxbury Press.

Cinyabuguma, M., Page, T. and Putterman, L. (2005). Cooperation under the threat of expulsion in a public goods experiment. *Journal of Public Economics*, 89, 1421–35.

Connor, R. C. (1996). Partner preferences in by-product mutualisms and the case of predator inspection in fish. *Animal Behavior*, 51, 451–4.

Cosmides, L. and Tooby, J. (1992). Cognitive adaptations for social exchange. In J. H. Barkow, L. Cosmides and J. Tooby (eds), *The adapted mind: Evolutionary psychology and the generation of culture* (pp. 163–228). New York: Oxford University Press.

Cosmides, L. and Tooby, J. (2005). Neurocognitive adaptations designed for social exchange. In D. M. Buss (ed.), *The handbook of evolutionary psychology* (pp. 584–627). Hoboken, NJ: John Wiley & Sons, Ltd.

Daly, M. and Wilson, M. (1988). *Homicide*. Hawthorne, NY: Aldine de Gruyter.

Darwin, C. (1859/1958). *The origin of species*. New York: Mentor.

Darwin, C. (1871/1981). *The descent of man, and selection in relation to sex*. Princeton, NJ: Princeton University Press.

Dawkins, R. (1976). *The selfish gene*. Oxford: Oxford University Press.

Dugatkin, L. A. (1996). Tit for tat: By-product mutualism and predator inspection: A reply to Connor. *Animal Behavior*, 51, 455–7.

Ehrhart, K. and Keser, C. (1999). *Mobility and cooperation: On the run. Working Paper 99s-24*. Montreal: CIRANO.

Ertan, A., Page, T. and Putterman, L. (2009). Who to punish? Individual decisions and majority rule in mitigating the free rider problem. *European Economic Review*, 53, 495–511.

Fehr, E. (2004). Don't lose your reputation. *Nature*, 432, 449–50.

Fehr E., Fischbacher, U. and Gächter, S. (2002). Strong reciprocity, human cooperation and the enforcement of social norms. *Human Nature*, 13, 1–25.

Fehr, E. and Gächter, S. (2002). Altruistic punishment in humans. *Nature*, 415, 137–40.

Fischbacher, U., Gächter, S. and Fehr, E. (2001). Are people conditionally cooperative? Evidence from a public good experiment. *Economic Letters*, 31, 397–404.

Fletcher, J. A. and Doebeli, M. (2006). How altruism evolves: Assortment and synergy. *Journal of Evolutionary Biology, 19*, 1389–93.

Foster, K. R., Wenseleers, T. and Ratnieks, F. L. W. (2001). Spite: Hamilton's unproven theory. *Annales Zoologici Fennica, 38*, 229–38.

Frank, S. A. (1996). Models of parasite virulence. *Quarterly Review of Biology, 71*, 37–78.

Galdikas, B. M. F. and Teleki, G. (1981). Variations in subsistence activities of male and female pongids: New perspectives on the origins of human labor divisions. *Current Anthropology, 22*, 241–56.

Gardner, A. and Grafen, A. (2009). Capturing the superorganism: A formal theory of group adaptation. *Journal of Evolutionary Biology, 22*, 659–71.

Gintis, H. (2000). Strong reciprocity and human sociality. *Journal of Theoretical Biology, 206*, 169–79.

Gintis, H., Smith, E. A. and Bowles, S. (2001). Cooperation and costly signaling. *Journal of Theoretical Biology, 213*, 103–19.

Gintis, H., Bowles, S., Boyd, R. and Fehr, E. (2003). Explaining altruistic behavior in humans. *Evolution and Human Behavior, 24*, 153–72.

Gouldner, A. W. (1960). The norm of reciprocity: A preliminary statement. *American Sociological Review, 25*, 161–78.

Grafen, A. (1990). Biological signals as handicaps. *Journal of Theoretical Biology, 144*, 517–46.

Guarner, F. and Malagelada, J. R. (2003). Gut flora in health and disease. *Lancet, 361*, 512–519.

Gurven, M. D, Allen-Arave, W., Hill, K. and Hurtado, A. M. (2000). It's a wonderful life: Signaling generosity among the Aché of Paraguay. *Evolution and Human Behavior, 21*, 263–82.

Hagen, E. H. and Hammerstein, P. (2006). Game theory and human evolution: A critique of some recent interpretations of experimental games. *Theoretical Population Biology, 69*, 339–48.

Hain, T. J. A. and Neff, B. D. (2007). Multiple paternity and kin recognition mechanisms in a guppy population. *Molecular Ecology, 16*, 3938–46.

Hamilton, W. D. (1963). The evolution of altruistic behavior. *American Naturalist, 97*, 354–6.

Hamilton, W. D. (1964). The genetical evolution of social behavior, I–II. *Journal of Theoretical Biology, 7*, 1–52.

Hamilton, W. D. (1970). Selfish and spiteful behaviour in an evolutionary model. *Nature, 228*, 1218–1220.

Hamilton, W. D. (1975). Innate social aptitudes in man: An approach from evolutionary genetics. In R. Fox (ed.), *Biosocial anthropology* (pp. 133–55). London: Malaby Press.

Hardin, G. J. (1968). The tragedy of the commons. *Science, 162*, 1243–8.

Hardy, C. and van Vugt, M. (2006). Nice guys finish first: The competitive altruism hypothesis. *Personality and Social Psychology Bulletin, 32*, 1402–13.

Hauert, C., Traulsen, A., Brandt, H. *et al.* (2007). Via freedom to coercion: The emergence of costly punishment. *Science, 316*, 1905–7.

Hauert, C., Traulsen, A., Brandt, H. *et al.* (2008). Public goods with punishment and abstaining in finite and infinite populations. *Biological Theory, 3*, 114–122.

Helfenstein, F., Wagner, R. H., Danchin, E. and Rossi, J. M. (2003). Functions of courtship feeding in black-legged kittiwakes: Natural and sexual selection. *Animal Behaviour, 65*, 1027–33.

Henrich, J. (2004). Cultural group selection, coevolutionary processes and large-scale cooperation. *Journal of Economic Behavior and Organization, 53*, 3–35.

Henrich, J., Boyd, R., Bowles, S. *et al.* (2005). 'Economic Man' in cross-cultural perspective: Ethnography and experiments from 15 small-scale societies. *Behavioral and Brain Sciences, 28*, 795–816, 838–55.

Humphrey, N. (1997). Varieties of altruism and the common ground between them. *Social Research, 64*, 199–209.

Imhof, L. A. and Nowak, M. A. (in press). Stochastic evolutionary dynamics of direct reciprocity. *Proceedings of the Royal Society B*.

Iredale, W., van Vugt, M. and Dunbar, R. (2008). Showing off in humans: Male generosity as a mating signal. *Evolutionary Psychology, 6*, 386–92.

Johnson, D. D. P., Price, M. E. and Takezawa, M. (2008). Renaissance of the individual: Reciprocity, positive assortment, and the puzzle of human cooperation. In C. Crawford and D. Krebs (eds.), *Foundations of evolutionary psychology* (pp. 331–52). New York: Lawrence Erlbaum Associates.

Johnson, T., Dawes, C. T., Fowler, J. H. *et al.* (2009). The role of egalitarian motives in altruistic punishment. *Economics Letters, 102*, 192–4.

Kalishov, A., Zahavi, A. and Zahavi, A. (2005). Allofeeding in Arabian babblers (*Turdoides squamiceps*). *Journal of Ornithology, 146*, 141–50.

Keller, L. and Ross, K. G. (1998). Selfish genes: A green beard in the red fire ant. *Nature, 394*, 573–5.

Kelly, R. (1995). *The foraging spectrum: Diversity in hunter-gatherer lifeways.* Washington: Smithsonian Institution Press.

Kiyonari, T. and Barclay, P. (2008). Free-riding may be thwarted by second-order rewards rather than punishment. *Journal of Personality and Social Psychology, 95*, 826–42.

Kiyonari, T., van Veelen, M. and Yamagishi, T. (2008). *Can second-order punishment solve the puzzle of human cooperation in one-shot games?* Manuscript submitted for publication.

Krams, I., Krama, T., Igaune, K. and Mänd, R. (2008). Experimental evidence of reciprocal altruism in the pied flycatcher. *Behavioral Ecology and Sociobiology, 62*, 599–605.

Kurzban, R., DeScioli, P. and O'Brien, E. (2007). Audience effects on moralistic punishment. *Evolution and Human Behavior, 28*, 75–84.

Kurzban, R. and Houser, D. (2005). An experimental investigation of cooperative types in human groups: A complement to evolutionary theory and simulations. *Proceedings of the National Academy of Sciences, 102*, 1803–7.

Ledyard, J. O. (1995). Public goods: A survey of experimental research. In J. H. Kagel and A. E. Roth (eds), *The handbook of experimental economics* (pp. 111–194). Princeton, MA: Princeton University Press.

Leimar, O. and Hammerstein, P. (2001). Evolution of cooperation through indirect reciprocity. *Proceedings of the Royal Society B, 268*, 2495–2501.

Lieberman, D., Tooby, J. and Cosmides, L. (2007). The architecture of human kin detection. *Nature, 445*, 727–31.

Margulis, L. (1970). *Origin of eukaryotic cells: Evidence and research implications for a theory of the origin and evolution of microbial, plant, and animal cells on the Precambrian Earth.* New Haven, CT: Yale University Press.

Maynard Smith, J. (1964). Group selection and kin selection. *Nature, 201*, 1145–7.

Maynard Smith, J. and Szathmáry, E. (1995). *The major transitions in evolution.* New York: W. H. Freeman/Spektrum.

Milinski, M. (1987). Tit for tat and the evolution of cooperation in sticklebacks. *Nature, 325*, 433–5.

Milinski, M. (1990). No alternative to tit-for-tat cooperation in sticklebacks. *Animal Behavior, 39*, 989–91.

Moghadam, A. (2003). Palestinian suicide terrorism in the Second Intifada: Motivations and organizational aspects. *Studies in Conflict and Terrorism, 26*, 65–92.

Nelissen, R. M. A. (2008). The price you pay: Cost-dependent reputation effects of altruistic punishment. *Evolution and Human Behavior, 29*, 242–8.

Nikiforakis, N. (2008). Punishment and counter-punishment in public good games: Can we really govern ourselves? *Journal of Public Economics, 92*, 91–112.

Nowak, M. A. and Sigmund, K. (1998). The dynamics of indirect reciprocity. *Journal of Theoretical Biology, 194*, 561–74.

Nowak, M. A. and Sigmund, K. (2005). Evolution of indirect reciprocity. *Nature, 437*, 1291–8.

O'Gorman, R. O., Henrich, J. and van Vugt, M. (2008). Constraining free-riding in public goods games: Designated solitary punishers can sustain human cooperation. *Proceedings of the Royal Society B, 276*, 323–9.

Ohtsuki, H., Iwasa, Y. and Nowak, M. A. (2009). Indirect reciprocity provides only a narrow margin for efficiency for costly punishment. *Nature, 457*, 79–82.

Olson, M. (1965). *The logic of collective action: Public goods and the theory of groups.* Cambridge, MA: Harvard University Press.

Ostrom, E. (2000). Collective action and the evolution of social norms. *Journal of Economic Perspectives, 14*, 137–58.

Ostrom, E., Walker, J. and Gardner, R. (1992). Covenants with and without a sword: Self governance is possible. *American Political Science Review, 86*, 404–17.

Page, T., Putterman, L. and Unel, B. (2005). Voluntary association in public goods experiments: Reciprocity, mimicry and efficiency. *The Economic Journal, 115*, 1032–53.

Panchanathan, K. and Boyd, R. (2004). Indirect reciprocity can stabilize cooperation without the second-order free rider problem. *Nature, 432*, 499–502.

Piazza, J. and Bering, J. M. (2008). The effects of perceived anonymity on altruistic punishment. *Evolutionary Psychology, 6*, 487–501.

Pizzari, T and Foster, K. R. (2008). Sperm sociality: Cooperation, altruism, and spite. *PLoS Biology, 6*, e130.

Price, G. R. (1970). Selection and covariance. *Nature, 227*, 520–521.

Price, G. R. (1972). Extension of covariance selection mathematics. *Annals of Human Genetics, 35*, 485–90.

Price, M. E. (2003). Pro-community altruism and social status in a Shuar village. *Human Nature, 14*, 191–208.

Price, M. E. (2005). Punitive sentiment among the Shuar and in industrialized societies: Cross-cultural similarities. *Evolution and Human Behavior, 26*, 279–87.

Price, M. E. (2006). Monitoring, reputation and 'greenbeard' reciprocity in a Shuar work team. *Journal of Organizational Behavior, 27*, 201–19.

Price, M. E. (2008). The resurrection of group selection as a theory of human cooperation. *Social Justice Research, 21*, 228–40.

Price, M. E., Cosmides, L. and Tooby, J. (2002). Punitive sentiment as an anti-free rider psychological device. *Evolution and Human Behavior, 23*, 203–31.

Queller, D. C. (1985). Kinship, reciprocity, and synergism in the evolution of social behavior. *Nature, 318*, 366–7.

Queller, D. C., Ponte, E., Bozzaro, S. and Strassmann, J. E. (2003). Single-gene greenbeard effects in the social amoeba *Dictyostelium discoideum. Science, 299*, 105–6.

Rainey, P. B. and Rainey, K. (2003). Evolution of cooperation and conflict in experimental bacterial populations. *Nature, 425*, 72–4.

Rand, D. G., Ohtsuki, H. and Nowak, M. A. (2009). Direct reciprocity with costly punishment: Generous tit-for-tat prevails. *Journal of Theoretical Biology, 256*, 45–57.

Rockenbach, B. and Milinski, M. (2006). The efficient interaction of indirect reciprocity and costly punishment. *Nature, 444,* 718–723.

Rothstein, S. I. (1980). Reciprocal altruism and kin selection are not clearly separable phenomena. *Journal of Theoretical Biology, 87,* 255–61.

Rushton, J. P. (1989). Genetic similarity, mate choice, and group selection. *Behavioral and Brain Sciences, 12,* 503–18.

Russell, A. F. and Wright, J. (2008). Avian mobbing: Byproduct mutualism not reciprocal altruism. *Trends in Ecology and Evolution, 24,* 3–5.

Semmann, D., Krambeck, H. J. and Milinski, M. (2004). Strategic investment in reputation. *Behavioral Ecology and Sociobiology, 56,* 248–52.

Semmann, D., Krambeck, H. J. and Milinski, M. (2005). Reputation is valuable within and outside one's own social group. *Behavioral Ecology and Sociobiology, 57,* 611–616.

Sheldon, K. M., Sheldon, M. S. and Osbaldiston, R. (2000). Prosocial values and group-assortation within an N-person prisoner's dilemma. *Human Nature, 11,* 387–404.

Sherman, P. W., Reeve, H. K. and Pfennig, D. W. (1997). Recognition systems. In J. R. Krebs and N. B. Davies (eds), *Behavioural ecology: An evolutionary approach* (pp. 69–96). Oxford: Oxford University Press.

Silk, J. B. (2005). The evolution of cooperation in primate groups. In H. Gintis, S. Bowles, R. Boyd and E. Fehr (eds), *Moral sentiments and material interests* (pp. 43–73). Cambridge, MA: MIT Press.

Simpson, B. and Willer, R. (2008). Altruism and indirect reciprocity: The interaction of person and situation in prosocial behavior. *Social Psychology Quarterly, 71,* 37–52.

Sinervo, B., Chaine, A., Clobert, J. *et al.* (2006). Self-recognition, color signals, and cycles of green-beard mutualism and altruism. *Proceedings of the National Academy of Science USA, 103,* 7372–7.

Smith, E. A. and Bird, R. L. B. (2000). Turtle hunting and tombstone opening: Public generosity as costly signaling. *Evolution and Human Behavior, 21,* 245–61.

Smukalla, S., Caldara, M., Pochet, N. *et al.* (2008). FLO1 is a variable green beard gene that drives biofilm-like cooperation in budding yeast. *Cell, 135,* 726–37.

Sober, E. and Wilson, D. S. (1998). *Unto others: The evolution and psychology of unselfish behavior.* Cambridge, MA: Harvard University Press.

Sosis, R. and Alcorta, C. S. (2008). Militants and martyrs: Evolutionary perspective on religion and terrorism. In R. D. Sagarin and T. Taylor (eds), *Natural security* (pp. 105–25). Berkeley, CA: University of California Press.

Stanca, L. (2009). Measuring indirect reciprocity: Whose back do we scratch? *Journal of Economic Psychology, 30,* 190–202.

Stanford, C. B., Wallis, J., Mpongo, E. and Goodall, J. (1994). Hunting decisions in wild chimpanzees. *Behaviour, 131,* 1–18.

Summers, K. and Crespi, B. (2005). Cadherins in maternal-foetal interactions: Red queen with a green beard? *Proceedings of the Royal Society B, 272,* 643–9.

Symons, D. (1990). Adaptiveness and adaptation. *Ethology and Sociobiology, 11,* 427–44.

Teleki, G. (1973). *The predatory behavior of wild chimpanzees.* Lewisburg, PA: Bucknell University Press.

Tooby, J. and Cosmides, L. (1989). Kin selection, genic selection, and information-dependent strategies. *Behavioral and Brain Sciences, 12,* 542–4.

Tooby, J. and Cosmides, L. (1992). The psychological foundations of culture. In J. H. Barkow, L. Cosmides and J. Tooby (eds), *The adapted mind: Evolutionary psychology and the generation of culture* (pp. 19–136). New York: Oxford University Press.

Tooby, J. and Cosmides, L. (1996). Friendship and the Banker's Paradox: Other pathways to the evolution of adaptations for altruism. In W. G. Runciman, J. Maynard Smith and R. I. M. Dunbar (eds), *Evolution of social behaviour patterns in primates and man. Proceedings of the British Academy, 88*, 119–143.

Tooby, J., Cosmides, L. and Price, M. E. (2006). Cognitive adaptations for *n*-person exchange: The evolutionary roots of organizational behavior. *Managerial and Decision Economics, 27*, 103–29.

Trivers, R. (1971). The evolution of reciprocal altruism. *Quarterly Review of Biology, 46*, 35–57.

Trivers, R. (2004). Mutual benefits at all levels of life. *Science, 304*, 964–5.

Tutin, C. E. G. (1979). Mating patterns and reproductive strategies in a community of wild chimpanzees (*Pan troglodytes schweinfurthii*). *Behavioral Ecology and Sociobiology, 6*, 29–38.

van Vugt, M. and Spisak, B. R. (2008). Sex differences in leadership emergence during competitions within and between groups. *Psychological Science, 19*, 854–8.

Wakano, J. Y., Nowak, M. A. and Hauert, C. (2009). Spatial dynamics of ecological public goods. *Proceedings of the National Academy of Sciences, USA, 106*, 7810–914.

Wedekind, C. and Milinski, M. (2000). Cooperation through image scoring in humans. *Science, 288*, 850–852.

West, S. A., Griffin, A. S. and Gardner, A. (2007). Social semantics: Altruism, cooperation, mutualism, strong reciprocity, and group selection. *Journal of Evolutionary Biology, 20*, 415–432.

Westermarck, E. A. (1891/1921). *The history of human marriage*, (fifth edition). London: Macmillan.

Wiggins, D. A. and Morris, R. D. (1986). Criteria for female choice of mates: Courtship feeding and parental care in the common tern. *American Naturalist, 128*, 126–9.

Wilkinson, G. S. (1984). Reciprocal food sharing in the vampire bat. *Nature, 308*, 181–4.

Wilkinson, G. S. (1988). Reciprocal altruism in bats and other mammals. *Ethology and Sociobiology, 9*, 85–100.

Williams, G. C. (1966). *Adaptation and natural selection: A critique of some current evolutionary thought*. Princeton, NJ: Princeton University Press.

Williams, G. C. and Williams, D. C. (1957). Natural selection of individually harmful social adaptations among sibs with special reference to social insects. *Evolution, 11*, 32–9.

Wilson, D. S. (2002). *Darwin's cathedral*. Chicago: University of Chicago Press.

Wilson, D. S. (2007). Social semantics: Toward a genuine pluralism in the study of social behaviour. *Journal of Evolutionary Biology, 21*, 368–73.

Wilson, D. S. and Dugatkin, L. A. (1997). Group selection and assortative interactions. *American Naturalist, 149*, 336–51.

Wilson, D. S. and Sober, E. (1994). Reintroducing group selection to the human behavioral sciences. *Behavioral and Brain Sciences, 17*, 585–654.

Wilson, D. S. and Wilson, E. O. (2007). Rethinking the theoretical foundation of sociobiology. *The Quarterly Review of Biology, 82*, 327–48.

Wilson, E. O. (1975). *Sociobiology: The new synthesis*. Cambridge, MA: Belknap Press.

Wynne-Edwards, V. C. (1962). *Animal dispersion in relation to social behaviour*. Edinburgh: Oliver and Boyd.

Yamagishi, T. (1986). The provision of a sanctioning system as a public good. *Journal of Personality and Social Psychology, 51*, 110–116.

Zahavi, A. (1975). Mate selection: A selection for a handicap. *Journal of Theoretical Biology, 53*, 205–14.

Zahavi, A. (1977). The cost of honesty (Further remarks on the handicap principle). *Journal of Theoretical Biology, 67*, 603–5.

selection

DAVID WAYNFORTH

CHAPTER OUTLINE

SEXUAL SELECTION 108
   Which sex should have evolved sexually selected
      displays in humans? 112
   Mate choice copying in humans 115

**WHICH HUMAN TRAITS ARE SEXUALLY SELECTED
SIGNALS?** 115

**SEXUAL SELECTION AND WITHIN-SEX
DIFFERENCES** 116
   Alternative mating tactics 117

   Do humans have alternative mating tactics, and if
      so, what are they? 118

TIME ALLOCATION 122

CONCLUSION 125

REFERENCES 126

Darwinian sexual selection provides a powerful theoretical basis for understanding a wide variety of human behaviours that are connected to sex, as well as some anatomical and hormonal differences between men and women. Although sexual selection theory is 150 years old, new implications of sexual selection continue to emerge. For example, one growth area in understanding is in sexual selection and female mating strategies and display. In this chapter, sexual selection theory is laid out in detail as a framework for understanding sex differences in physiology and behaviour related to sex. Armed with some of the most recent studies on sexual selection, I address sex differences in human mating, particularly in light of what is now known about sexual selection in females.

Another goal of this chapter is to examine evolutionary approaches to within-sex differences in mating-related behaviour. Two areas of within-sex variation are addressed: mating tactics, which includes behaviours used to attract the opposite sex, such as humour, and mating strategies, which is how much time and effort individuals devote to maintaining a long-term relationship versus seeking short-term sexual relationships. I approach the evolution of alternative mating tactics by presenting research on the evolution of alternative mating tactics in non-humans, and then address how human mating may be understood in light of theories of alternative mating tactics in non-humans. I use an optimality approach to differences between individuals in mating strategies, including a discussion of constraints on optimal behaviour. Optimality modelling is useful for clarifying thinking about adaptive problems faced by humans, but has been an underutilised tool in evolutionary psychology (see Gangestad and Simpson, 2000).

SEXUAL SELECTION

In *The Origin of Species*, Charles Darwin (1859) introduced the idea of sexual selection to explain the evolution of traits found only in males that appeared not to have evolved via survival advantage, but instead as displays to females in the hopes of being chosen as a mating partner, or to be used in competition between males for access to females. Fisher (1915) suggested a series of events that sexual selection could follow: first, a male produces an exaggerated form of a trait, such as a longer tail. Second, longer-tailed males have slightly higher survival. Third, some females show a preference for mating with long-tailed males. Given these conditions, the trait and preference for it become linked and are passed down through the generations together: individuals with the alleles that produce the trait will be chosen as mates by individuals with alleles that produce preference for the trait. Fisher envisaged this process as potentially a runaway process: in subsequent generations, long-tailed males would both have better survival *and* be preferred by females. The result would be the ever-increasing expression of the trait with each generation, only coming to a halt when the exaggerated trait becomes a significant enough survival disadvantage.

Research into sexual selection gained momentum with the introduction of the theory of costly signals as honest displays of high mate quality (Grafen, 1990;

Hamilton and Zuk, 1982; Zahavi, 1975). This model of the sexual selection process offered a second explanation for the evolution of sexually selected traits in addition to the Fisher process. In handicap models, the costs of the signal are of key importance: sexually selected signals must be costly for survival, and the ability of the bearer to express the signal acts as a guide to the overall quality of the mate. If all individuals were equally capable of taking on the physiological cost of producing high-quality signals, then the signals have no utility for members of the opposite sex attempting to select the highest-quality mate, or in the context of same-sex rivalry. Thus, sexually selected handicap signals can be considered honest indications of the genetic quality of an individual. Table 4.1 shows some features of traits that would be expected if they evolved via sexual selection by either the Fisherian process or costly signalling.

Darwinian sexual selection appears to have produced some of the most remarkable of all physical and behavioural displays in animals: the peacock's tail, the capercaille's dance and the walrus's tusks are just a few very well-known traits that are almost certainly products of sexual selection. In some species, sexually selected traits can be extreme, such as bright colouration in eclectus parrots, which led early naturalists to believe that they were observing different species rather than males and females of a single species. By contrast, humans do not possess any extraordinary sexually selected physical traits: no blue rear-end like a mandrill or antlers like deer. However, there is evidence for more subtle influences of sexual selection: I will continue this chapter with an outline of some implications of sexual selection, and discuss its role in human mate choice.

Sexual selection results in sex differences in signalling, or mating displays that tend to be sex-specific. As a general rule, males tend to have more physical ornamentation and behavioural displays of phenotypic quality than females do (e.g. Darwin, 1871; Williams, 1966). Bateman (1948) concluded that the underlying cause is that minimal

Table 4.1. *Common features of sexually selected traits.*

Feature of sexually selected trait	Explanation
Sex differences	One sex lacks trait or both sexes possess it but it is exaggerated in one sex.
Universality	The same sexually selected traits will typically be found in all cultures, except where local conditions do not favour display of the trait, or the trait has only very recently been undergoing sexual selection.
Mating preferences	One sex shows preference for sex partners with the trait.
Reproductive success	Individuals with exaggerated display of the trait should have higher mating and reproductive success.
Costs	Trait is physiologically costly to the bearer.
Phenotypic correlations	Bearers of the trait display high overall phenotypic quality.

investment in offspring differs for males and females: eggs are much larger and more energetically costly to produce than sperm (anisogamy). The result is that males compete for access to the limited commodity of female reproductive capacity, and that females discriminate between males to choose high-quality mates (see Figure 4.1).

Trivers (1972) emphasised the importance of sex differences in parental investment for the evolution of sexually selected traits: sexual selection should be greater in the sex that provides less investment in offspring overall. In mammals, the costs of pregnancy and lactation mean that, again, males will be subject to greater sexual selection. The signalling of mate quality via sexually selected traits, therefore, tends to be more extensive in males across a very wide variety of species (for a fuller explanation see, e.g., Clutton-Brock and Parker, 1992). A further reason why sexually selected display is often greater in males is that females have the option of directly investing in offspring: female reproductive success will likely be maximised if energy that could be allocated to display is allocated directly to reproductive functioning instead (Fitzpatrick, Berglund and Rosenqvist, 1995).

Despite the influence of anisogamy and benefits of direct investment in reproduction instead of display by females, sexual selection sometimes operates on female signals just as it does in males (e.g. see Clutton-Brock, 2009; LeBas, 2006). Competition between females for resources required for reproduction can potentially drive the evolution of sexually selected traits in females (LeBas, 2006). Competition between females could occur when resources (such as territory) are controlled by males, and when males provide substantial amounts of care for offspring (Burley, 1977; Fitzpatrick, Berglund and Rosenqvist, 1995). When this is the case, females can achieve higher reproductive success by being more attractive to males who control

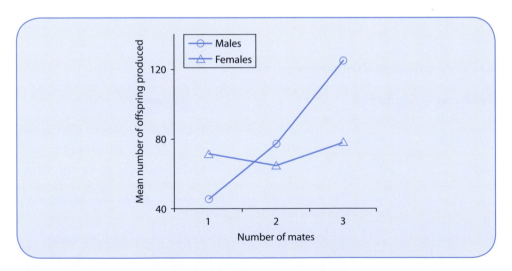

Figure 4.1. *Bateman's (1948) experiments on reproductive success as a function of number of matings suggested that, owing to higher reproductive payoffs to mating effort, sexual selection should be stronger in males.*

Source: Adapted from Table 8 in Bateman (1948).

more resources and can provide more paternal investment, and may compete with other females for access to the best potential providers.

Female display to attract mates may additionally occur if mating with several males increases female reproductive success. This situation was not seen in Bateman's experiments on fruit flies, which led to the prediction that competition and display for mating opportunities will lead to sexual selection being stronger in males: only male reproductive success was strongly influenced by number of matings in Bateman's fruit fly experiments (see Figure 4.1). However, subsequent research has highlighted the existence and importance of female multiple mating for female reproductive success in a number of species.

Table 4.2 provides a summary of some key conditions under which male and female sexual signals are theoretically predicted to evolve. There clearly are reasons for the evolution of mating display affecting both sexes, and the presence and relative strength of each of the conditions specified in Table 4.2 will determine whether mating displays will tend to be found in males, females or both sexes. One of the conditions included in Table 4.2, mate choice copying, can strengthen sexual selection in either sex. Mate choice copying is when, instead of directly assessing an opposite sex

Table 4.2. *Summary of explanations for the evolution of sexually selected mating displays and sex differences in choosiness that are likely to be applicable to humans.*

Condition underlying evolution of mating display	Displaying sex	Choosy sex
Lower investment in sex cells (anisogamy)	Males	Females
Lower overall male parental investment	Males	Females
Competition between males for mating access to females	Males	Females
Male-biased operational sex ratio	Males	Females
Assuming equal energy budgets, females who allocate energy to both display and fecundity will have lower reproductive success than females who allocate energy only to fecundity	Not Females	
Competition between females for resources required for reproduction	Females	Males
Significant costs of paternal care	Females	Males
High variation between females in fecundity	Females	Males
Multiple mating by females increases female reproductive success	Females	Males
Female biased operational sex ratio	Females	Males
Mate choice copying	Either sex	

individual for suitability for mating, some individuals copy others' choices. Copying strengthens sexual selection if individuals copy the choice of another who has chosen on the basis of a physical or behavioural display, because mating success will become more skewed towards those with the display (see Alonzo, 2008). Mate choice copying should be more likely to occur in the choosier sex in species where one sex is selective and the other has sexually selected displays, and is hypothesised to have evolved to decrease the time and energetic costs of mate choice (Dugatkin and Godin, 1992). In most mammals, copying would be expected in females, as sexually selected display is usually more common in males.

Which sex should have evolved sexually selected displays in humans?

Readers already familiar with the human mate choice literature in evolutionary psychology will no doubt be aware at this point that, in our own species, female sexual signals, such as waist-to-hip ratio and facial attractiveness have received a great deal of attention from researchers, and are clearly important in mate choice (e.g. Buss and Schmitt, 1993; Singh, 1993; Symons, 1979; see Chapter 5 in this volume). Therefore, evolutionary psychologists have worked under the assumption that humans are among the few species that show some reversal of the predominant pattern of male display expected from anisogamy and lower male parental investment.

The reasoning often given in support of the argument that human females have evolved sexually selected displays is that human males face the adaptive problem of identifying women with high fecundity, and consequently women have evolved signals of fecundity (e.g. Buss, 2004; Gaulin and McBurney, 2004). High variability in fecundity between individuals usually occurs between males: males show greater variance in reproductive success as a consequence of anisogamy and female-biased parental care, but factors creating high variability in female fecundity can drive the evolution of female sexual signals that indicate fecundity and increase male selectivity in mate choice (Arnold and Duvall, 1994; Cunningham and Birkhead, 1998).

Human societies clearly show the typical mammalian pattern of higher variance in male reproductive success (e.g. Borgerhoff Mulder, 1988; Hill and Hurtado, 1995), and so simply looking at the variance in reproduction in human societies would not lead to the expectation of the evolution of female sexual signals owing to high variance in female fecundity, especially when compared with males. However, given that humans often breed monogamously in long-term sexual relationships with biparental care, females will vary in the number of offspring that they can potentially produce in a long-term relationship as a function of their age at the start of the relationship. Average number of offspring expected in the future as a function of age is known as 'reproductive value', which declines more rapidly beginning from around the early twenties in women than it does in men. Numerous studies of age preferences in mate choice show that men prefer women who are close to the age of maximum reproductive value (e.g. Kenrick and Keefe, 1992; Waynforth and Dunbar, 1995). In addition, men focus on other signals of youth, such as youthful facial features (e.g. Jones and Hill, 1993). The importance to males of selecting a long-term mate with high reproductive value could explain the evolution of human female sexual signalling of youthful traits and male choosiness for these traits.

Female reproductive value peaks before age 20 (e.g. Hill and Hurtado, 1995), but age-specific fertility is maximised at older ages. In some traditional human societies, the years of peak fertility are substantially later than age 20. For example, Ache hunter-gatherer women are most likely to give birth from age 30 to 35 (Hill and Hurtado, 1995). Research on age at peak fecundity in women (the physiological ability to have children) has shown that rates of early foetal loss are key to age-related decline in female fecundity (Holman, Wood and Campbell, 2000), and that foetal loss is lowest after age 20, remaining very low until the early 30s in women living in industrialised societies (e.g. Nybo Andersen et al., 2000).

Collectively, research on female fecundity and on reproductive value implies that male preference for young women (close to peak reproductive value) must exist because men are adapted to seeking out a young woman and then monopolising her reproductive career. For shorter-term sexual relationships, men should be fairly unselective about the age of potential sex partners as long as they are between about 20- and 35 years old. This should weaken sexual selection for increased youthful appearance in women, and would lead to the prediction that in groups with a high prevalence of marital dissolution, there will be decreased male preference for youth. Men should also not prefer youth when looking for short-term partners, although the evidence so far does not suggest that this is the case when people are asked to state their age preferences for different lengths of sexual relationship (Buunk et al., 2001).

It appears that men's selectiveness about the physical appearance of mates is not yet very well understood: anisogamy and higher subsequent female investment in offspring in humans would predict female choosiness for male physical attractiveness, not the pattern of male choosiness that has been documented. If males are using attractiveness as a cue to the reproductive age of women, then we might expect to see divergent preferences for maximum reproductive value for long-term relationships, and peak fecundity for short-term relationships, but this has not been verified.

Reversals of the typical pattern of male display and female choosiness are found in species with higher levels of male parental care than female care (e.g. see Simmons, 1992). Although humans do not show this pattern, it is possible that male parental investment is high enough in humans to produce sexual selection and choosiness in both sexes. Human males take on parental care duties in long-term relationships, and the costs of male care may have driven the evolution of male choosiness and female display to attract parentally investing men. Human male parental care occurs both directly through infant and child care, and indirectly via provisioning of the family. If direct childcare by men has played a role in sexual selection, a pattern of shared direct care of infants by mothers and fathers should be evident across human societies.

In societies for which detailed time allocation data have been published, males appear to be responsible for roughly 5% of direct care of infants and young children (Flinn, 1992; Griffin and Griffin, 1992; Hames, 1988; Ivey, 2000). Males play a more significant role in indirect care of offspring via provisioning. Some of the clearest evidence that male provisioning is important can be found in studies of the effects of father absence owing to death or divorce. In human populations without good access to medical care, father absence during rearing raises infant and child mortality by at least twofold (Alam *et al.*, 2001; Hill and Hurtado, 1995). Divorce decreases paternal financial investment in offspring (Anderson, Kaplan and Lancaster, 1999; Anderson *et al.*, 1999), although a mother can replace some of the paternal investment lost owing to divorce by remarrying.

Variation between males in ability to provision offspring could create competition between females to mate with the best potential providers (see Table 4.2). In humans, men tend to control resources and advertise them to attract mates, while women place emphasis on economic indicators or male resource-holding potential (e.g. Borgerhoff Mulder, 1990; Buss, 1989; Waynforth and Dunbar, 1995). Hence, the evidence from studies of mate choice preferences has not highlighted female–female competition, but instead the conventional pattern of male competition and display of resources with female choosiness. Studies of competitive behaviour have also tended to be focused on male–male competition, again because men show lower parental investment and benefit more than women do from competition to secure mating access. Although men should be more willing to suffer injury as a result of intrasexual competition, competition can also involve non-aggressive tactics, and there is evidence that women show higher levels of non-aggressive competitive behaviour than men do (Campbell, 2004).

For example, Benenson *et al.* (2008) used an experimental study design to look at the use of exclusionary alliances in children. Exclusionary alliances are social alliances in which two or more individuals cooperate to exclude another individual. In Benenson *et al.*'s study, experimentally increasing the scarcity of a commodity led to far greater use of exclusionary alliances to gain access to the commodity in girls than in boys. These results and others on non-aggressive competition suggest that competition between females over resources is important in humans, and thus sexual selection operates on female display just as it does on male display, taking on sex-specific features as is common in the evolution of sexually selected traits (see Table 4.1).

Some of the strongest evidence suggesting that female display is likely to be under the influence of sexual selection comes from the study of short-term and extra-pair mating. Bateman's (1948) fruit fly experiments (see Figure 4.1) showed almost no benefit to females of mating with more than one male. However, if females can increase their reproductive success by mating with more than one male, then competition for mates and sexual selection will increase. There are several ways that multiple mating by females (mating with more than one male) can increase reproductive success: if multiple mating increases likelihood of conception in a menstrual cycle, then birth spacing could be decreased and offspring number increased. Second, multiple mating could increase offspring quality if a woman can attract a short-term mate with higher genetic quality than her long-term partner, or can fertilise her egg with a higher-quality male's sperm through sperm competition in the reproductive tract.

Some of the evidence supporting the idea that sperm competition and female multiple mating are important in humans comes from Baker and Bellis's (1993) study showing that controlling for sperm depletion from masturbation, men ejaculate greater numbers of sperm during sex with their partner when the couple have spent time apart. Thus sperm number appears to be manipulated according to an indicator of risk of female infidelity (time spent apart). The shape of the human penis also makes it an effective tool for displacing sperm already in the female reproductive tract (Gallup *et al.*, 2003).

Women's mate choice preferences also suggest that female multiple mating has been commonplace in our evolutionary past. Women show different mate choice preferences for long- versus short-term sexual relationships, and when in the fertile phase of the menstrual cycle, which implies that psychological mechanisms have evolved to maximise the fitness benefits from short-term mating. Preferences for a number of male physical traits vary according to whether a short-term sexual relationship is being sought, including facial masculinity and muscularity (Frederick and Haselton, 2007; Gangestad and Simpson, 2000; Johnston *et al.*, 2001; Waynforth, Delwadia and Camm, 2005).

Mate choice copying in humans

If mate choice copying occurs in only one sex in humans, then the copying sex is likely to be the choosier sex, and the non-copying sex should be the sex that has evolved sexually selected displays. The first studies of mate choice copying and very similar processes in humans addressed female mate choice copying, where the desirability of males with a female consort or signs of commitment was assessed (Eva and Wood, 2006; Jones *et al.*, 2007; Uller and Johansson, 2003; Waynforth, 2007). These studies showed that women do indeed use other women's preferences when making attractiveness judgements about men. Evidence that men show mate choice copying is less clear: Little *et al.* (2008) found evidence for it, but a larger study by Hill and Buss (2008) did not, and suggests that men will not show mate choice copying because depicting women with other men is a cue to the onlooker that paternity certainty of any offspring produced would be low.

WHICH HUMAN TRAITS ARE SEXUALLY SELECTED SIGNALS?

While neither human males nor females have dramatic sexually selected anatomical traits, a number of traits that are possibly sexually selected have been studied in the last few decades. These include the waist-to-hip ratio, bilateral symmetry in face and bodies, and indicators of sex hormones such as the ratio of second to fourth digits (e.g. Gangestad, Thornhill and Yeo, 1994; Manning *et al.*, 1998; Singh, 1993). Human behavioural sexually selected signals could include displays of physical prowess, risk-taking and bravery (Diamond, 1991; Kelly and Dunbar, 2001). Chapter 5 provides a detailed description of human traits that may have evolved by sexual selection, but at this point I will discuss a few physical, hormonal and behavioural traits to illustrate the range of human traits that appear to have been influenced by sexual selection.

One of the more obvious sex differences in human appearance is that men are taller than women on average. Mean sex differences in stature are universal across human groups, despite likely influence of natural selection resulting in large between-group differences in stature. Even just within Africa, there are fairly dramatic differences between human populations in stature, from the very short Aka and Baka to the very tall Nuer and Masai. Research by Nettle (2002) shows that women living in industrialised conditions have a preference for taller men as mates: tall men on average have more sexual relationships. Male stature shows the first four common features of sexually selected traits shown in Table 4.1: sex differences, universality across groups, mating preference by the opposite sex and higher reproductive success for those with the trait. There is also some evidence that being taller has physiological costs: in women height does not appear to be sexually selected, and the tallest women in Britain have lower reproductive success than women of average height (Nettle, 2002).

Another male trait that is likely to be sexually selected is display of the sex hormone testosterone. Having high levels of testosterone is physiologically costly owing to its immunosuppressant effects (e.g. Al-Afaleq and Homeida, 1998; Kanda, Tsuchida and Tamaki, 1996). Given this, its production above and beyond what is required to promote sex drive and reproductive functioning requires explanation (see Bribiescas, 2001). Folstad and Karter (1992) propose that male display of testosterone-induced characteristics represents a Zahavian signal of phenotypic quality: males who display testosterone are showing that they are able to offset its high physiological costs. Women can evaluate the long-term presence of testosterone in men because testosterone also stimulates craniofacial development. Among its effects is the square masculine jaw, which is the result of growth and flaring of the vertical ramus.

Research on human mate choice is generally consistent with the view that women use facial testosterone cues to evaluate male quality: women perceive masculine male faces as healthier (Rhodes *et al.*, 2003) and more attractive than feminine male faces when in the fertile phase of the menstrual cycle. Women who claim to be oriented towards short-term sexual relationships with men also rate male faces with a squarer, deeper jaw as more physically attractive (Waynforth, Delwadia and Camm, 2005). In the past few decades, a significant number of young men have begun to use anabolic steroids including testosterone to enhance their physical attractiveness rather than to build muscle mass for sporting competition (see Wroblewska, 1997, and references therein).

SEXUAL SELECTION AND WITHIN-SEX DIFFERENCES

The previous sections addressed how evolution shapes aspects of mating display that result in differences between the sexes and between species. Individuals of the same sex and species can also differ from each other in their mating behaviour and physiology, and sexual selection underlies these within-sex differences as well as differences between the sexes. I mentioned near the beginning of this chapter that, in some species, sexual selection has resulted in such large anatomical differences between males and females that early naturalists originally mistakenly assigned males and females as belonging to different species. Sexual selection can also result in large anatomical differences between individuals of one sex, although, again, we humans never evolved dramatic anatomical within-sex differences: all males and all females appear broadly similar to each other. This section addresses sexual selection and differences between individuals in mate acquisition tactics, decisions to remain with a mate or leave the relationship and whether an individual should pursue long- versus short-term sexual relationships.

Alternative mating tactics

All adult peacocks have elaborate tail feathers, but in many species there is diversity in mate acquisition display and tactics. For example, like a number of fish species, Pacific Coho salmon males are found in two distinct physical forms representing alternative life history trajectories. Some male Coho develop large hooked jaws and enlarged teeth that are used in combat over access to females. Other males remain very small, develop no secondary sexual characteristics and attempt to fertilise nests of eggs by sneaking unnoticed from behind rocks or other sheltered places (e.g. Gross, 1984). The two male morphs seem to have roughly equal reproductive success, and possibly represent genetic alternatives (Gross, 1985).

Male scorpion flies appear to have three different mating tactics: defending a dead insect to attract a female, producing a salivary nuptial gift for the female and forcible rape (Thornhill, 1979). These tactics do not have equal reproductive returns, and use of the most successful tactic (food presentation) tends to be restricted to larger males (Thornhill, 1981). Alternative mating tactics have also been identified in non-human primates. *Papio* baboon males opt for either a competitive, dominance-based tactic, or form 'special friendships' with females (Packer, 1979). Choice of tactic seems to be associated with age and physical prowess, with special friendships representing a relatively low mating success tactic adopted by older, less dominant males (Altmann, Altmann and Hausfater, 1986; Smuts, 1985).

Mating tactics are often separated into distinct categories in behavioural ecology. They are generally called 'conditional' if they are not simply a result of genetic differences between individuals. Conditional tactics often result from differences in competitive ability, where individuals with high competitive ability gain the highest fitness (genetic representation in future generations) via a specific tactic and those with low competitive ability adopt an alternative tactic, which often avoids direct male–male competition for mating opportunities. Such tactics are called 'status-dependent tactics' (Gross, 1996). Not all conditional tactics are based on differences in ability to successfully compete for mates, as evolution should favour the adoption of tactics that fit best with the particular traits or strengths that an individual has, as well as what potential mates are seeking in a particular context. This flexibility is likely to evolve as long as the costs to having alternative mating tactics and being able to assess when to apply each tactic do not outweigh the advantages.

Do humans have alternative mating tactics, and if so, what are they?

There are relatively few published studies on human mating tactics following approaches from behavioural ecology, with rape and sexual coercion being an exception (see Box 4.1). Thornhill and Thornhill (1983) propose that rape in humans is a status-dependent conditional tactic employed by men without the traits preferred by women in mate choice. Consistent with this, rape is more common in men of low socioeconomic status (see Thornhill and Palmer, 2000). However, other research indicates that sexually coercive men have more lifetime sex partners, which does not suggest status dependence (Malamuth, Huppin and Paul, 2005). Another possibility is that sexual coercion occurs as a genetically determined trait or via gene by environment interaction. If this is the case, human rape could be more similar to the jack mating tactic in Coho salmon, in which the proportion of males adopting the tactic stabilises at a particular level depending on the reproductive returns and proportions of males adopting each alternative tactic. Studies addressing the evolution of rape and sexual coercion as human male mating tactics are continuing to be carried out, but, as yet, none has provided conclusive evidence as to the underlying evolutionary processes that are involved (see Gladden, Sisco and Figueredo, 2008).

Focusing on male mating tactics, successful mating tactics other than rape or sexual coercion should appeal to some facet of female mate choice, and can evolve if fitness is maximised in some males who specialise in offering or display of a particular ability. Given that the tactical option set is likely to be limited by what females require for successful reproduction, two things that women can obtain from men other than 'good genes' are material resources to support their children and direct paternal care for infants and children. These are likely to be consistently necessary over a long period, and so women should also be looking for cues that a man will remain invested in the relationship.

Possibly the most obvious alternative human male mating tactic would be to offer higher levels of paternal commitment than other males in the population. Since offering higher paternal commitment entails costs, men offering higher levels of paternal commitment could be most likely to be those who are less attractive to females (i.e. offering higher paternal commitment may be status-dependent). Simpson et al. (1999) found that men display 'nice guy' behaviours in the presence of potential mates, but found no direct evidence for status dependence: in their study fluctuating asymmetry was used as a measure of male genetic quality. Men who deployed nice guy tactics in their verbal interactions with women in the study were not less symmetric than men who did not show nice guy behaviour.

It is possible that nice guy tactics in mating display bear little relation to actual male parental and marital investment behaviour, that is it could be deceptive tactics aimed at achieving mating access only. I carried out one test of this possibility using a sample of men in rural Belize (Waynforth, 2002). Men completed a verbal

BOX 4.1. THE APPLICATION OF EVOLUTIONARY THEORY TO UNDERSTAND WHY MEN RAPE

This theory has proved controversial: the prevailing view in the social sciences has been that rape is not primarily a crime of sex, but is instead practised to assert male dominance (e.g. Brownmiller, 1975). One of the problems with this view is that rape occurs in a wide variety of species without social systems including male power or social dominance comparable to human societies. In addition, males of some species have evolved structures only used in rape (see Thornhill, 1979). In others there appears to have been an evolutionary 'arms race' in which male penis morphology has evolved to allow sex without female consent and females have evolved counter-strategies. These include complex vaginas in which sperm from unpreferred males can be diverted to dead-end sacs (Brennan *et al.*, 2007).

Some (non-mutually-exclusive) evolutionary theories of human rape:

- Rape is a status-dependent tactic used by men lacking key traits that women find attractive (Thornhill and Thornhill, 1983).
- Rape is an environmentally dependent strategy that may potentially be triggered when encountering a female in a vulnerable situation (e.g. Thornhill and Palmer, 2000).
- Rape is a by-product of evolutionary processes that resulted in the evolution of higher male aggression and body size combined with high sexual desire compared to women (Symons, 1979).
- Rape within a marriage or relationship is an evolved sperm-competition tactic used when the man suspects his partner of sexual infidelity and is sexually unreceptive (Thornhill and Palmer, 2000).

questionnaire in which they answered questions about their willingness to provide direct paternal care and effort allocated to diligently caring for their wife or girlfriend. Men with high scores for these self-assessed measures of nice guy tactics reported fewer lifetime sex partners, and spent more time with family in time allocation surveys (see Figure 4.2). Therefore, in this sample, self-reported use of nice guy behaviours appeared to be honest. Like Simpson *et al.* (1999), I found that nice guys did not have higher fluctuating asymmetry, and they were not rated as less facially attractive. The trends for symmetry and facial attractiveness and self-reported nice guy tactics were in the opposite direction to the expectation for status dependence. These findings would not be surprising if instead of being an alternative mating tactic offered by less attractive men, nice guy behaviour is an honest signal of the very opposite: high genetic quality. Miller (2007) argues that morally virtuous behaviour including nice guy tactics of the type discussed in this chapter shows a number of features of sexually selected behaviour, for example it is costly to the actor, thus only individuals with high underlying genetic quality may be able to display virtuous behaviour. In addition, there is growing evidence that women prefer nice guys when seeking long-term relationships (e.g. see Urbaniak and Kilmann 2003), which suggests the involvement of sexual selection via female choice in shaping the display of nice guy behaviour.

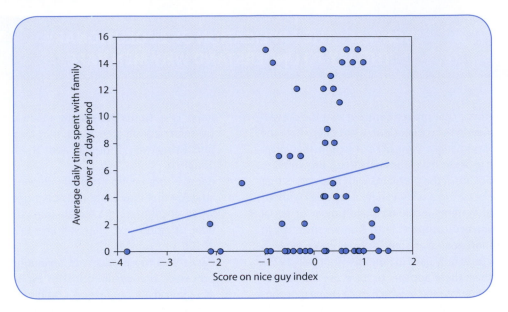

Figure 4.2. *Are self-reported nice guys genuinely men who invest more time in their partner and family?*

Analysis of data on a sample of men in rural Belize showed that men who self-reported a variety of nice guy behaviours in questionnaire form, including attentiveness to their partner's needs and commitment to childcare duties, spent more of their spare time with their wife and immediate family (including their parents, siblings, wife and children), although almost half of the men sampled spent no time with family at all by choice. Time allocation data were collected for one-hour blocks of time over two days in which the men did little or no work (n = 56 men, Poisson regression, R^2 = 13.98, p = 0.0002). The line shown on the plot is a least-squares regression line. For detailed methods, see Waynforth (1999, 2002).

If being a nice guy is a Zahavian sexually selected trait, then from a female perspective the benefits of higher genetic quality of offspring produced in the relationship must on average exceed any costs of being in a relationship with a nice guy. The costs may include lost resources if the man is a nice guy more generally in the community. My Belizean data suggest that self-reported nice guys in a mating and parenting context are also nice guys in other contexts: men with high scores on the mating and paternal care inventory gave significantly more money away in financial aid to needy members in their community (see Figure 4.3). In addition to there being a trade-off for women between any genetic benefits of mating with a nice guy and lost resources through any generosity that is not reciprocated, it is likely that sexual selection alone will not explain the evolution of nice guy behaviour, as the reproductive returns to being a nice guy are potentially partly connected to cooperative behaviour.

Other behaviours that may be more common in males and show intrasexual variability include use of humour and risk-taking. Miller (1998) proposes that, since the ability to successfully be humorous requires a high level of cognitive functioning, humour acts as a signal of overall phenotypic quality. Humour tends to be used by men more than

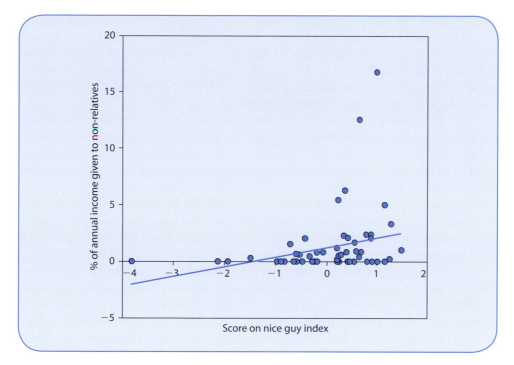

Figure 4.3. *Self-reported nice guys in the mating and parenting context appear to be generous men in other contexts.*

For the same sample of 56 Belizean men in Figure 4.2, scores on the index of nice guy behaviours were significantly associated with the percentage of their income that they reported to have given away in the year prior to data collection ($R^2 = 0.09$, $t = 2.22$, $p = 0.03$). The line shown on the plot is a least-squares regression line. Stated reasons for giving money away varied: some of the largest amounts were donated to one community member to repair his vehicle, while several of the smaller amounts were given to newly married couples forming new households. None of the money was given expressly as a loan.

women, and in social contexts in which men are likely to be engaging in mating effort (see Bressler and Balshine, 2006). Miller's hypothesis is that humour is a mating tactic that only high-quality males can use effectively, and should be attractive to women as a cue to underlying male genetic quality. Bressler and Balshine (2006) show that women do indeed rate male faces accompanied by a humorous autobiographical comment as more attractive than faces presented with less amusing statements, although it is still not clear that this effect on attractiveness judgements is limited to female preference for humour: in a similar study by McGee and Shevlin (2009), men showed a stronger preference for humour in women than women did for humorous men.

Owing to emphasis on sexual selection in males, alternative female mating tactics have not been directly addressed in the human mate choice literature, although female–female exclusionary alliance formation may fit into the category of alternative mating tactics (see Campbell, 2004). It is interesting to note that maternal and childcare skills appear neither to be rated as particularly important by men in mate choice nor are offered by women. Offering maternal orientation and mothering skills would be a likely candidate as a female mating tactic given the effects of variation in maternal care on child outcomes. It may be that women do not offer maternal skills as a mate acquisition tactic if men operate under the assumption that by selecting attractive mates they are selecting women with good genes and a higher energy budget for reproduction and maternal investment.

The vast majority of evolutionarily relevant research on mating tactics in humans has not been driven by behavioural ecology, but instead has come from differential, personality and social psychology. This work has the disadvantage of not being developed from first principles in evolutionary theory but is, nevertheless, very useful for evolutionary understanding of mating tactics. There is substantial evidence that personality traits are genetically influenced (for reviews, see Bouchard and Loehlin, 2001; Buss and Greiling, 1999; Chapter 8, in this volume), and psychologists have begun to look at the adaptive significance of individual personality traits, such as Extraversion and Openness to Experience (e.g. Egan and Angus, 2004; Linton and Wiener, 2001).

For example, extraverted individuals report higher numbers of lifetime sex partners (Nettle, 2005), suggesting that Extraversion is a personality trait linked to increased mating effort. Extraversion is in part defined by novelty-seeking and a desire for social stimulation, which may be the behavioural tactics that complement high mating effort. However, like nice guy tactics, extraversion contributes to individual fitness across a number of arenas simultaneously, and is unlikely to have a simple single function in mating (see Nettle, 2005).

Evolutionary understanding of human alternative mating tactics is not very well-developed. It may be the case that there has not been strong selection pressure on alternative mating tactics in our species owing to the evolution of choosiness and sexually selected traits in both rather than in only one sex. If only one sex is choosy (usually females) and the other sex has sexually selected displays (usually males), then an alternative mating tactic such as a 'jack' tactic that allows some mating success for males who would not be chosen as mates on the basis of their sexually selected characters would be strongly selected for. If both sexes are choosy about mating partners and possess sexually selected traits as indicators of genetic quality, then the possibility of assortative mating for quality is open to both sexes: unpreferred individuals can mate with other unpreferred individuals rather than failing to breed, thus weakening positive selection pressure on alternative mating tactics when mutations for alternative tactics arise.

TIME ALLOCATION

In the previous section I considered variation in mating tactics, but in addition to tactical specialisation, individuals vary the amount of time allocated to searching for new mating opportunities versus investing in a current mate. Evolutionary psychologists have often framed this decision as one of long- versus short-term mating strategies, with display and mate choice preferences being adjusted adaptively to suit the type of relationship being sought.

Evolution should result in optimal time allocation in the context of mating, for example individuals should begin to feel averse to continuing time investment to an existing sexual relationship when the fitness returns from that time allocation decline relative to the gains from pursuing another activity or relationship. This logic has been applied to within-sex variation in men's mating effort, where men who have higher returns to mating effort because they are more attractive to women have been shown to spend more time and effort seeking sexual access to new partners (Apicella and Marlowe, 2007; Marlowe, 1999; Waynforth, 1999). Although in these studies attractive men engaged in more mating effort, the prediction did not take into account the very likely possibility that attractive men get higher returns not only to mating effort but also to other activities. For example, attractive men (with high genetic quality) may experience higher returns to foraging or producing income, and to paternal investment. If this is the case, then it is not clear that attractive men should spend more time in mating effort. Using a very simple foraging patch choice model, it is possible to get more insight into why attractive men should spend more time in mating effort and have shorter relationships. Originally developed to address when foragers should switch to a new area to forage, patch choice models based on the marginal value theorem (Charnov, 1976) can be applied to thinking about time allocation to many activities that influence reproductive fitness. Box 4.2 displays a model to predict optimal relationship length for men. The model suggests that low search times to access new sex partners may be the key to understanding why attractive men are observed to spend more time in mating effort. This is because the model predicts shorter relationship times for attractive men.

The model shown in Box 4.2 is too simplistic to capture all of the variables at play in mating strategy decisions, for example the real shape of the returns to investing effort into a relationship is not known, and the model assumes that men have sequential sexual relationships rather than several simultaneously. Women's mating strategies require a different model, as search time to begin a new sexual relationship is not likely to be an adaptive problem for females. Bateman's principle would lead to the prediction that female returns to relationship investment might often decline less steeply than male returns after conception has occurred. One female tactic to avoid desertion at this point in the relationship would be to manipulate male search time by lengthening the time between first meeting and sex.

Optimality is often governed by constraints or trade-offs that individuals must make. Following from the law of conservation of energy in physics, the principle of allocation states that the body cannot allocate energy to one task, and then subsequently utilise the energy for a different purpose. One result of this for all forms of life is trade-offs between potential areas of energy allocation, for example between growth and reproduction, and number of offspring produced in a pregnancy or clutch versus the size of each of the offspring (see Stearns, 1992). Such trade-offs are central to life history theory, which predicts that selection pressure will favour optimal allocation of energy between competing demands or fitness-enhancing activities.

Life history theory has been applied to optimal mating strategy decisions in humans. A trade-off that appears to be important for mating strategy decisions is the trade-off between current and future reproduction: energy put directly into reproductive effort in the present is energy taken away from increasing future reproduction. In environments with high and unpredictable mortality, investment in current

BOX 4.2.   A GRAPHICAL OPTIMAL FORAGING PATCH EXPLOITATION-BASED APPROACH TO ADDRESS HOW LONG INDIVIDUALS SHOULD SPEND IN A SEXUAL RELATIONSHIP BEFORE MOVING ON TO A NEW PARTNER

Search time is the time it takes to find a new sex partner and initiate a sexual relationship. Time invested in the relationship is shown with diminishing fitness returns: the assumption is that once conception has occurred and offspring have received parental care potential fitness gains from staying with the partner will gradually decline. Fitness is maximised by maximising the slope of the returns curve. For a given search time, the slope is maximised at the point where the slope of the coloured gains curve is equal to the slope of the black line showing expected search time to accessing a new sexual relationship. Optimal time investment for different search times are shown using dashed lines.

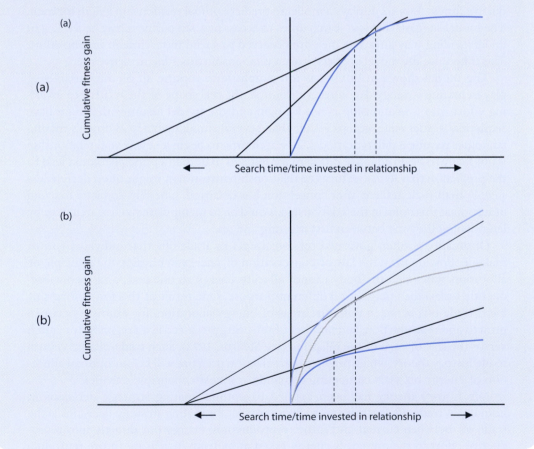

In (a) the model suggests that if an individual's search time to find a new mate is high, then they should stay longer with a partner. Variation in the shape of returns to time invested in a relationship is shown in (b), and will result in different optimal relationship lengths, from very short optimal relationship durations (which could occur, for example, with low returns to parental investment), to monogamy (grey line) where the returns to investing do not diminish enough to warrant switching to a new partner.

Search time will be influenced by factors such as the physical attractiveness of the searcher, and the sex ratio of breeding-age individuals in the population. Fitness gain from a relationship is likely to be influenced by the physical attractiveness of the mate, their parental capabilities, paternity certainty of offspring produced in the relationship (for males), costs of mate guarding and effects of parental investment on offspring survival and quality.

reproduction tends to be favoured over putting energy into creating a larger energy budget or better conditions for reproduction at a later date. Unpredictable mortality can reduce the returns to high parental effort, as fitness will be lower in individuals who invest a large amount of energy into each offspring if the offspring is at significant risk of dying anyway. Under conditions of environmental risk, it is optimal to reproduce early and often, with less investment or parental care given to each offspring.

There is experimental evidence that animals have evolved the flexibility to adjust their reproduction in ways consistent with this prediction. For example, in *Daphnia*, when the scent of predators is introduced into the water, age at first reproduction declines, and a larger number of smaller offspring are produced (Stibor, 1992). Chisholm (1993; Chisholm *et al.*, 2005) argues that life history trade-offs between current and future reproduction and offspring quality versus quantity explain patterns of sexual maturity and reproduction observed in humans. Unpredictable environments for humans include those with high levels of family stress, marital problems and divorce, and segments of society that experience increased risk or mortality rates. Under any of these conditions humans often show early sexual maturity and sexual activity, and tend to have short-term sexual relationships (e.g. see Chisholm *et al.*, 2005). Put into the terms of the optimality model for male reproductive strategies in Box 4.2, unpredictable mortality reduces the returns to long-term investment in a sexual relationship, and individuals should consequentially have a greater number of shorter relationships.

CONCLUSION

Researchers studying human mating psychology have used sexual selection theory to predict a number of sex differences in human mating. Bateman's principle provided the basis for several predictions about male display and female choosiness in mate choice. However, subsequent work, particularly in non-humans, uncovered theoretical reasons and evidence for reversal of sex differences, or display and choosiness evolving in both sexes. One implication is that the study of sex differences in human mating may provide less insight into sexual selection in humans than evolutionary psychologists would have hoped, as there is often no clear theoretical prediction: both sexes in humans should be choosy and both have reasons to have evolved sexually selected traits.

By no means have all studies of sexual selection in humans been focused on sex differences. Sexual selection theory has been drawn on to provide predictions about variability in the conditions that drive display and selectivity in mate choice. For example, Gangestad and Buss (1993) predict and show evidence that pathogen prevalence in the environment should influence sexual selection such that physical attractiveness, acting as a cue to genetic quality and immunocompetence, is more important in pathogen-prevalent regions of the world. Moore *et al.* (2006) studied variation in female resource control on women's mate choice preferences, as resource control is known to be important in the evolution of sexually selected display in females. Analyses of variability between and within populations in the conditions that drive sexual selection will no doubt continue to contribute greatly to understanding sexual selection in humans.

The evolution of differences between individuals in mating tactics remains relatively unexplored when compared with the study of between-sex differences and of sex-specific traits, as does the evolution of intrasex differences in mating strategies or time-use. Existing research unequivocally shows the existence of short- and long-term mating psychology and associated traits, but predicting an individual's strategy decisions requires explicit evolutionary models detailing the benefits and costs of pursuing different mating strategies. Optimality and life history theory-based models are very appropriate for understanding mating strategies, and progress in understanding mating tactics and strategies has probably been hampered by these methods not being a part of training or tradition in evolutionary psychology.

REFERENCES

Al-Afaleq, A. and Homeida, A. (1998). Effects of low doses of oestradiol, testosterone, and dihydrotestosterone on the immune response of broiler chicks. *Immunopharmacology and Immunotoxicology, 20*, 315–27.

Alam, N., Saha, S., Razzaque, A. and van Ginneken, J. (2001). The effect of divorce on infant mortality in a remote area of Bangladesh. *Journal of Biosocial Science, 33*, 271–8.

Alonzo, S. (2008). Mate choice copying affects sexual selection in wild populations of the oselated wrasse. *Animal Behaviour, 75*, 1715–23.

Altmann, J., Altmann, S. and Hausfater, G. (1986). Determinants of reproductive success in savannah baboons (*Papio cynocephalus*). In T. Clutton-Brock (ed.), *Reproductive success* (pp. 403–18). Chicago: Chicago University Press.

Anderson, K. G., Kaplan, H. and Lancaster, J. (1999). Paternal care by genetic fathers and step-fathers I: Reports from Albuquerque men. *Evolution and Human Behavior, 20*, 405–31.

Anderson, K. G., Kaplan, H., Lam, D. and Lancaster, J. (1999). Paternal care by genetic fathers and step-fathers II: Reports by Xhosa high school students. *Evolution and Human Behavior, 20*, 433–51.

Apicella, C. and Marlowe, F. (2007). Men's reproductive investment decisions: Mating, parenting and self-perceived mate value. *Human Nature, 18*, 22–34.

Arnold, S. and Duvall, D. (1994). Animal mating systems: A synthesis based on selection theory. *The American Naturalist, 143*, 317–48.

Baker, R. and Bellis, M. (1993). Human sperm competition: Ejaculate adjustment by males and the function of masturbation. *Animal Behaviour, 41*, 861–85.

Bateman, A. J. (1948). Intrasexual selection on *Drosophila. Heredity, 2*, 349–68.

Benenson, J., Antonellis, T., Cotton, B. *et al.* (2008). Sex differences in children's formation of exclusionary alliances under scarce resource conditions. *Animal Behaviour, 76*, 497–505.

Borgerhoff Mulder, M. (1988). Kipsigis bridewealth payments. In L. Betzig, M. Borgerhoff Mulder and P. Turke (eds), *Human reproductive behavior* (pp. 65–82). New York: Cambridge University Press.

Borgerhoff Mulder, M. (1990). Kipsigis women's preferences for wealthy men: Evidence for female choice in mammals. *Behavioural Ecology and Sociobiology, 27*, 255–64.

Bouchard, T. and Loehlin, J. (2001). Genes, evolution, and personality. *Behavior Genetics, 31*, 243–73.

Brennan, P., Prum, R., McCracken, K. *et al.* (2007). Coevolution of male and female genital morphology in waterfowl. *PLoS One, 2*, e418. doi: 10.1371/journal.pone.0000418.

Bressler, E. and Balshine, S. (2006). The influence of humor on desirability. *Evolution and Human Behavior, 27*, 29–39.

Bribiescas, R. (2001). Reproductive ecology and life history of the human male. *Yearbook of Physical Anthropology, 44*, 148–76.

Brownmiller, S. (1975). *Against our will: Men, women and rape.* New York: Simon & Schuster.

Burley, N. (1977). Parental investment, mate choice, and mate quality. *Proceedings of the National Academy of Sciences, USA, 74*, 3476–9.

Buss, D. M. (1989). Sex differences in human mate preferences: Evolutionary hypotheses tested in 37 cultures. *Behavioral and Brain Sciences, 12*, 1–49.

Buss, D. M. (2004). *Evolutionary psychology: The new science of the mind.* Upper Saddle River, NJ: Pearson.

Buss, D. M. and Greiling, H. (1999). Adaptive individual differences. *Journal of Personality, 67*, 209–43.

Buss, D. M. and Schmitt, D. P. (1993). Sexual strategies theory: An evolutionary perspective on human mating. *Psychological Review, 100*, 204–32.

Buunk, B., Dijkstra, P., Kenrick, D. and Warntjes, A. (2001). Age preferences for mates as related to gender, own age and involvement level. *Evolution and Human Behavior, 22*, 241–50.

Campbell, A. (2004). Female competition: Causes, constraints, content and contexts. *Journal of Sex Research, 41*, 16–26.

Charnov, E. (1976). Optimal foraging: The marginal value theorem. *Theoretical Population Biology, 9*, 129–36.

Chisholm, J. (1993). Death, hope and sex: Life history theory and the development of reproductive strategies. *Current Anthropology, 34*, 1–24.

Chisholm, J., Quinlivan, J., Peterson, R. and Coall, D. (2005). Early stress predicts age at menarche and first birth, adult attachment and expected lifespan. *Human Nature, 16*, 233–65.

Clutton-Brock, T. (2009). Sexual selection in females. *Animal Behaviour, 77*, 3–11.

Clutton-Brock, T. and Parker, G. A. (1992). Potential reproductive rates and the operation of sexual selection. *Quarterly Review of Biology, 67*, 437–56.

Cunningham, E. and Birkhead, T. (1998). Sex roles and sexual selection. *Animal Behaviour, 56*, 1311–21.

Darwin, C. (1859). *On the origin of species.* London: Murray.

Darwin, C. (1871). *The descent of man and selection in relation to sex.* London: Murray.

Diamond, J. (1991). *The third chimpanzee: The evolution and future of the human animal*. London: Hutchinson Radius.

Dugatkin, L. and Godin, J. (1992). Reversal of female mate choice by copying in the guppy. *Proceedings of the Royal Society B, 249*, 179–84.

Egan, V. and Angus, S. (2004). Is social dominance a sex specific strategy for infidelity? *Personality and Individual Differences, 36*, 575–86.

Eva, K. and Wood, T. (2006). Are all the taken men good? An indirect examination of mate-choice copying in humans. *Canadian Medical Association Journal, 175*, 1573–4.

Fisher, R. A. (1915). The evolution of sexual preferences. *Eugenics Review, 7*, 184–92.

Fitzpatrick, S., Berglund, A. and Rosenqvist, G. (1995). Ornaments or offspring: Costs to reproductive success restrict sexual selection processes. *Biology Journal of the Linnaean Society, London, 55*, 251–60.

Flinn, M. V. (1992). Paternal care in a Caribbean village. In B. S. Hewlett (ed.), *Father–child relations: Cultural and biosocial contexts* (pp. 57–84). New York: Aldine de Gruyter.

Folstad, I. and Karter, A. (1992). Parasites, bright males and the immunocompetence handicap. *American Naturalist, 139*, 603–22.

Frederick, D. L. and Haselton, M. G. (2007). Why is muscularity sexy? Tests of the fitness indicator hypothesis. *Personality and Social Psychology Bulletin, 33*, 1167–83.

Gallup, G., Burch, R., Zappieri, M. *et al.* (2003). The human penis as a semen displacement device. *Evolution and Human Behavior, 24*, 277–89.

Gangestad, S. W. and Buss, D. (1993). Pathogen prevalence and human mate preferences. *Ethology and Sociobiology, 14*, 89–96.

Gangestad, S. W. and Simpson, J. A. (2000). The evolution of human mating: Trade-offs and strategic pluralism. *Behavioral and Brain Sciences, 23*, 573–87.

Gangestad, S. W., Thornhill, R. and Yeo, R. A. (1994). Facial attractiveness, developmental stability, and fluctuating asymmetry. *Ethology and Sociobiology, 15*, 73–85.

Gaulin, S. and McBurney, D. (2004). *Evolutionary psychology*. Upper Saddle River, NJ: Pearson.

Gladden, P., Sisco, M. and Figueredo, J. (2008). Sexual coercion and life-history strategy. *Evolution and Human Behaviour, 29*, 319–26.

Grafen, A. (1990). Sexual selection unhandicapped by the Fisher process. *Journal of Theoretical Biology, 144*, 473–516.

Griffin, P. and Griffin, M. (1992). Fathers and childcare among the Cagayan Agta. In B. S. Hewlett (ed.), *Father–child relations: Cultural and biosocial contexts* (pp. 297–320). New York: Aldine de Gruyter.

Gross, M. (1984). Sunfish, salmon and the evolution of alternative reproductive strategies and tactics in fishes. In G. Potts and R. Wooton (eds), *Fish reproduction: Strategies and tactics* (pp. 55–75). London: Academic Press.

Gross, M. (1985). Disruptive selection for alternative life histories in salmon. *Nature, 313*, 47–8.

Gross, M. (1996). Alternative reproductive strategies and tactics: Diversity within sexes. *Trends in Ecology and Evolution, 11*, 92–8.

Hames, R. (1988). The allocation of parental care among the Ye'kwana. In L. Betzig, M. Borgerhoff Mulder and P. Turke (eds), *Human reproductive behaviour: A Darwinian perspective* (pp. 237–51). Cambridge: Cambridge University Press.

Hamilton, W. D. and Zuk, M. (1982). Heritable true fitness and bright birds: A role for parasites? *Science, 21*, 384–7.

Hill, S. and Buss, D. (2008). The mere presence of opposite-sex others on judgements of sexual and romantic desirability: Opposite effects for men and women. *Personality and Social Psychology Bulletin, 34*, 635–47.

Hill, K. and Hurtado, A. M. (1995). *Aché life history: The ecology and demography of a foraging people*. New York: Aldine de Gruyter.

Holman, D., Wood, J. and Campbell, K. (2000). Age-dependent decline of female fecundity is caused by early fetal loss. In E. TeVelde, P. Pearson and F. Broekmans (eds), *Female reproductive aging* (pp. 123–43). New York: Informa Healthcare Books.

Ivey, P. (2000). Cooperative reproduction in Ituri forest hunter-gatherers: Who cares for Efe infants? *Current Anthropology, 41*, 856–66.

Johnston, V. S., Hagel, R., Franklin, M. *et al.* (2001). Male facial attractiveness: Evidence for hormone-mediated adaptive design. *Evolution and Human Behavior, 22*, 251–67.

Jones, B., DeBruine, L., Little, A. *et al.* (2007). Social transmission of face preferences among humans. *Proceedings of the Royal Society B, 274*, 899–903.

Jones, D. and Hill, K. (1993). Criteria of facial attractiveness in five populations. *Human Nature, 4*, 271–96.

Kanda, N., Tsuchida, T. and Tamaki, K. (1996). Testosterone inhibits immunoglobulin production by human peripheral blood mononuclear cells. *Clinical and Experimental Immunology, 106*, 410–415.

Kelly, S. and Dunbar, R. I. M. (2001). Who dares wins: Heroism versus altruism in female mate choice. *Human Nature, 12*, 89–105.

Kenrick, D. and Keefe, R. (1992). Age preferences in mates reflect sex differences in reproductive strategies. *Behavioral and Brain Sciences, 15*, 75–118.

LeBas, N. (2006). Female finery is not for males. *Trends in Ecology and Evolution, 21*, 170–173.

Linton, D. and Wiener, N. (2001). Personality and potential conceptions: Mating success in a modern Western male sample. *Personality and Individual Differences, 31*, 675–88.

Little, A., Burriss, R., Jones, B. *et al.* (2008). Social influence in human face preference: Men and women are influenced more for long-term than short-term attractiveness decisions. *Evolution and Human Behavior, 29*, 140–146.

McGee, E. and Shevlin, M. (2009). Effect of humor on interpersonal attraction and mate selection. *Journal of Psychology, 143*, 67–77.

Malamuth, N., Huppin, M. and Paul, B. (2005). Sexual coercion. In D. Buss (ed.), *The handbook of evolutionary psychology* (pp. 394–418). Hoboken, NJ: John Wiley & Sons, Ltd.

Manning, J. T., Scutt, D., Wilson, J. and Lewis-Jones, D. (1998). The ratio of 2nd to 4th digit length: A predictor of sperm numbers and concentrations of testosterone, luteinizing hormone and oestrogen. *Human Reproduction, 13*, 3000–3004.

Marlowe, F. (1999). Male care and mating effort among Hadza foragers. *Behavioral Ecology and Sociobiology, 46*, 57–64.

Miller, G. (1998). How mate choice shaped human nature: A review of sexual selection and human evolution. In C. Crawford and D. Krebs (eds), *Handbook of evolutionary psychology: Ideas, issues, and applications* (pp. 87–129). Hoboken, NJ: Lawrence Erlbaum Associates.

Miller, G. (2007). Sexual selection for moral virtues. *Quarterly Review of Biology, 82*, 97–125.

Moore, F., Cassidy, C., Smith, M. and Perrett, D. (2006). The effects of female control of resources on sex-differentiated mate preferences. *Evolution and Human Behavior, 27*, 193–205.

Nettle, D. (2002). Height and reproductive success in a cohort of British men. *Human Nature, 13*, 473–91.

Nettle, D. (2005). An evolutionary approach to the extraversion continuum. *Evolution and Human Behavior, 26*, 363–73.

Nybo Andersen, A., Wohlfahrt, J., Christens, P. *et al.* (2000). Maternal age and fetal loss: Population-based register linkage study. *British Medical Journal, 320*, 1708–12.

Packer, C. (1979). Male dominance and reproductive activity in *Papio anubis*. *Animal Behaviour, 27*, 37–45.

Rhodes, G., Chan, J., Zebrowitz, L. and Simmons, L. (2003). Does sexual dimorphism in human faces signal health? *Proceedings of the Royal Society B, 270*, S93–S95.

Simmons, L. W. (1992). Quantification of role reversal in relative parental investment in a bushcricket. *Nature, 358*, 61–3.

Simpson, J. A., Gangestad, S., Christensen, P. and Leck, K. (1999). Fluctuating asymmetry, sociosexuality, and intrasexual competitive tactics. *Journal of Personality and Social Psychology, 76*, 159–72.

Singh, D. (1993). Adaptive significance of waist-to-hip ratio and female physical attractiveness. *Journal of Personality and Social Psychology, 65*, 293–307.

Smuts, B. (1985). *Sex and friendship in baboons*. New York: Aldine de Gruyter.

Stearns, S. (1992). *The evolution of life histories*. Oxford: Oxford University Press.

Stibor, H. (1992). Predator induced life-history shifts in a freshwater cladoceran. *Oecologia, 92*, 162–65.

Symons, D. (1979). *The evolution of human sexuality*. New York: Oxford University Press.

Thornhill, A. R. (1979). Male and female sexual selection and the evolution of mating systems in insects. In M. Blum and N. Blum (eds), *Sexual selection and reproductive competition in insects* (pp. 81–121). New York: Academic Press.

Thornhill, A. R. and Palmer, C. (2000). *A natural history of rape: Biological bases of sexual coercion*. Cambridge, MA: MIT Press.

Thornhill, A. R. and Thornhill, N. (1983). Human rape: An evolutionary analysis. *Ethology and Sociobiology, 4*, 137–73.

Thornhill, R. (1981). *Panorpa* (mecoptera: *Panorpidae*) scorpionflies: Systems for understanding resource-defense polygyny and alternative male reproductive efforts. *Annual Review of Ecology and Systematics, 12*, 355–86.

Trivers, R. L. (1972). Parental investment and sexual selection. In B. Campbell (ed.), *Sexual selection and the descent of man* (pp. 136–79). Chicago: Aldine.

Uller, T. and Johansson, L. (2003). Human mate choice and the wedding ring effect: Are married men more attractive? *Human Nature, 14*, 267–76.

Urbaniak, G. and Kilmann, P. (2003). Physical attractiveness and the nice guy paradox: Do nice guys really finish last? *Sex Roles, 49*, 413–426.

Waynforth, D. (1999). Differences in time-use for mating and nepotistic effort as a function of male attractiveness in rural Belize. *Evolution and Human Behavior, 20*, 19–28.

Waynforth, D. (2002). Fluctuating asymmetry and alternative mating tactics in men: Are nice guys simply losers in the competition for mates? In T. Akazawa and K. Aoki (eds), *Mate choice and marital patterns in modern and prehistoric societies* (pp. 126–40). Kyoto: Nichibunken Press.

Waynforth, D. (2007). Mate-choice copying in humans. *Human Nature, 18*, 264–71.

Waynforth, D., Delwadia, S. and Camm, M. (2005). The influence of women's mating strategies on preference for masculine facial architecture. *Evolution and Human Behavior, 26*, 409–16.

Waynforth, D. and Dunbar, R. I. M. (1995). Conditional mate choice strategies in humans: Evidence from 'lonely hearts' advertisements. *Behaviour, 132*, 755–79.

Williams, G. C. (1966). *Adaptation and natural selection*. Princeton, NJ: Princeton University Press.

Wroblewska, A. M. (1997). Androgenic-anabolic steroids and body dysmorphia in young men. *Journal of Psychosomatic Research, 42*, 225–34.

Zahavi, A. (1975). Mate selection: Selection for a handicap. *Journal of Theoretical Biology, 53*, 205–14.

5 The evolutionary psychology of human beauty

VIREN SWAMI AND NATALIE SALEM

CHAPTER OUTLINE

FACIAL ATTRACTIVENESS 134
Fluctuating asymmetry 134
Averageness 138
Facial sexual dimorphism 141
Summary 144

BODILY ATTRACTIVENESS 145
The waist-to-hip ratio hypothesis 145
Show me the module! 149
Critical tests 150

Temporal stability? 155
Cross-cultural and within-culture
preferences 158
Summary 161

**CONCLUSION AND FUTURE
DIRECTIONS** 162

REFERENCES 164

'What is wisest? Number.' Pythagoras of Samos, a Greek mathematician and philosopher of the sixth century BC, is perhaps best known for his contributions to mathematics and philosophy, but he and his followers are also often credited with the first exposition of an aesthetico-mathematical view of the universe. For Pythagoras, the origin of all things could be found in number; beauty, then, was a matter of having the right mathematical proportions, and the same principles that governed the attractiveness of human beings also dictated the splendour of architectural dimensions, the aural pleasure derived from music or the magnificence of a work of art (Armstrong, 2004; Gaut and Lopes, 2001; Swami, 2007a).

Although the Pythagorean view of beauty is much debated today, what it aspired to was an overarching framework for understanding the question of aesthetics. Attempting such a framework continues to dominate psychological approaches to aesthetics, particularly when applied to the topic of human beauty. In a sense, this preoccupation with scientific approaches to human beauty is not surprising: a person's physical attractiveness is known to have a significant impact on their social experiences, including interpersonal interactions, reproductive decision-making and self-perceptions (Dion, 1974; Eagly *et al.*, 1991; Langlois *et al.*, 1991; Swami and Furnham, 2008a).

As examples, compared with unattractive individuals, attractive individuals are judged to be more honest (Yarmouk, 2000), less maladjusted and disturbed (Cash *et al.*, 1977; Dion, 1972), happier, more successful, more sociable (Dion, Berscheid and Walster, 1972) and better at everything in general (Cash and Soloway, 1975; Patzer, 1985, 2002). In the courtroom, attractive defendants benefit from more lenient sentencing than less attractive defendants do (Mazella and Feingold, 1994; Stewart, 1984). Attractive individuals are also afforded higher grades in academic settings (Landy and Sigall, 1974; see also Hamermesh and Parker, 2005), are more likely to be hired (Dipboye, Fromkin and Wiback, 1975; Swami *et al.*, 2008a) and receive higher starting salaries in occupational settings (Hamermesh and Biddle, 1994; Hosoda, Stone-Romero and Coats, 2003; but see Tews, Stafford and Zhu, 2009) and are even more likely to be assisted following a traffic accident (Swami *et al.*, 2008a).

Indeed, in their meta-analysis of over 900 studies, Langlois and colleagues (2000) reported that individuals were treated differently based on the extent to which they were perceived as physically attractive. Specifically, attractive individuals were more likely than unattractive individuals to be judged as competent in their professions, to experience success in their occupations and to be treated more favourably by others. In the view of Langlois *et al.* (2000) and contrary to the received wisdom of maxims, such as 'beauty is only skin deep' and 'never judge a book by its cover', physical attractiveness *does* have an important influence on our everyday lives.

Perhaps the most developed attempt to explain these associations and one that has its roots in the Pythagorean worldview is provided by evolutionary psychological approaches to human beauty. Evolutionary psychology provides a distal framework for examining human mating behaviour (see Chapter 4, this volume): in very simple terms, an evolutionary approach to mate selection suggests that mate choice preferences are related to reproductive fitness-enhancing benefits (Miller, 2000), which may either be direct (those that increase the individual's reproductive success by benefiting the individual and any offspring) or indirect (those that increase the individual's inclusive fitness). These criteria are perceived and used by individuals to assess the quality and desirability of potential mates in order to enhance their chances of reproductive success (Buss, 1994, 1999; Symons, 1979).

Based on this framework, evolutionary psychologists have focused on a number of specific physical attributes that are said to be fitness indicators and that are used when forming judgements of attractiveness. In practice, this has included many different component parts of the human body, as well as adornments and non-physical traits. In this chapter, we review some of the most widely researched characteristics that have fallen under the purview of evolutionary psychology. This review is not exhaustive (see Swami and Furnham, 2008a, for a more extensive review); rather, our aim in this chapter is to provide a number of prominent examples of research inspired by evolutionary psychology. These examples, initially at least, focus on the human face, which is perhaps not surprising given the preponderance of evolutionary psychological research on facial attractiveness (see Rhodes, 2006), the differential role played by the body and face in conveying signals of mate quality (see Peters, Rhodes and Simmons, 2007) and the role that facial cues play in social interactions (Ferrario *et al.*, 1995).

A second, but no less important, aim of this chapter is to provide a counter-argument to the standard evolutionary psychological approach to human beauty. By focusing on one specific feature of human morphology, namely the waist-to-hip ratio, we aim to show how evolutionary psychological explanations of human beauty can sometimes be misleading and based on faulty theoretical and empirical data. That is to say, inventing evolutionary hypotheses can often be a 'seductively easy exercise' (Laland and Brown, 2002, p. 100) and an honest evolutionary psychological approach to human beauty will need to exercise greater caution in attempting to understand the multifaceted construct that is human beauty (see also Box 5.1).

BOX 5.1.   ARE BEAUTIFUL PEOPLE MORE INTELLIGENT?

Kanazawa and Kovar (2004, p. 229) argue that, given the tendency for humans to mate assortatively, 'more beautiful people are more intelligent than less beautiful people'. This 'theorem' is based on four specific assumptions:

1. Men who are more intelligent are more likely to attain high status than men who are less intelligent;
2. Higher-status men are more likely to mate with attractive women than lower-status men are;

3. Intelligence is heritable, and;
4. Physical attractiveness is heritable.

In Kanazawa and Kovar's view, it follows that beautiful individuals are more intelligent. While this theory has gained a great deal of coverage, it has also proven highly controversial, with some authors arguing that the purported relationship between intelligence and beauty is, at best, misleading and, at worst, not based on fact. Denny (2008), for example, highlights the fact that Kanazawa and Kovar (2004) relied on a selected reading of the available evidence, and that not all studies have reported positive correlations between intelligence and beauty (e.g. Feingold, 1992). Moreover, by gathering new sources of data, Denny (2008, p. 618) was able to conclude that, 'if anything . . . it is primarily low intelligence that is associated with lack of beauty'. Overall, he argues, there are any number of counter-arguments to the suggested association between beauty and intelligence, including:

'High status' is not a static component: what constitutes high status (either in terms of intelligence or attractiveness) changes over time as a function of the environment;

The correlation of genes associated with beauty and intelligence may be complicated if the individual genes affect multiple phenotypic traits (i.e. if they are pleiotropic);

Attractiveness itself may be heritable, but it is certainly not immutable, and changes as a function of the environment and subjective perceptions.

All in all, the available evidence does not lend itself to the conclusion that beautiful people are more intelligent.

FACIAL ATTRACTIVENESS

Fluctuating asymmetry

During foetal growth, a wide range of stressors or perturbations, such as reduced nutrition, disease and parasitic infections, can cause disturbances to the developmental process, giving rise to what are known as 'fluctuating asymmetries' (FAs). Put simply, FAs are small, non-directional (random) deviations from perfect symmetry in bilateral traits that are, on average, symmetric at the population level (Simmons, Rhodes, Peters and Koehler, 2004). FA increases with exposure to both environmental perturbations, including parasites (Møller, 1992a), radiation (Møller, 1998) and extreme environmental conditions (Parsons, 1992), as well as genetic perturbations, such as deleterious recessives (Lerner, 1954) and inbreeding (Polak, 2003; Roldan *et al.*, 1998).

Within populations, there is often a high degree of variability in FA, which leads to the suggestion that FA reflects the degree to which individuals are able to resist perturbations and so maintain developmental stability in the face of environmental and genetic stressors. Consistent with this notion, poor physiological function (Shackelford and Larsen, 1997), schizophrenia (Mellor, 1992) and chromosomal abnormalities such as Down's syndrome and Trisomy 14 (Fujimoto *et al.*, 1992; Malina and Buschang, 1984) have all been found to be associated with increased levels of FA. Since developmental stability may be heritable (see Møller and Thornhill, 1997), selection for potential mates on the basis of low FA or high symmetry may be adaptive; that is, a mate selection strategy informed by cues of FA can be expected to increase reproductive success.

Preferences for symmetrical male ornaments have been widely documented in a variety of species (e.g. Markow and Ricker, 1992; Schlüter, Parzefall and Schlupp, 1998;

Swaddle and Cuthill, 1994; Waitt and Little, 2006). For example, studies of female choice in barn swallows (*Hirundo rustica*) have shown that male swallows with symmetrical tails are preferred as mates and acquire mates more rapidly than males with asymmetrical tails (Møller, 1992b, 1993). Although there has been a relative paucity of research examining similar preferences in male mate choice, the few studies that have been conducted suggest that male preference also increases with increasing female trait symmetry (e.g. Hansen, Amundsen and Forsgren, 1999). For instance, when male cerambycid beetles (*Stenurella melanura*) are released onto a flower together with one female with symmetric antennae and one female with asymmetric antennae, males mate more often with the symmetrically ornamented female (Møller and Zamora-Muñoz, 1997).

Selection for symmetrical traits appears to occur in animals, but humans have not evolved conspicuous sexually selected ornaments or structures, such as the barn swallow tail. Even so, there is evidence to suggest that symmetry is preferred in human mate choice decisions. For one thing, a common feature in both early and contemporary forms of human art is the use of symmetrical designs (e.g. Boas, 1955; McManus, 2002; Washburn and Crowe, 1988; Weyl, 1952). Moreover, symmetric designs tend to elicit greater aesthetic appeal than asymmetric designs (Cárdenas and Harris, 2006; Jacobsen and Höfel, 2001; Rentschler *et al.*, 1999; Swami, in press – a; Washburn and Humphrey, 2001; see also Box 5.2 and Figure 5.1), although this may not extend to complex works of art (e.g. Swami and Furnham, 2009a).

BOX 5.2.   THE EFFECT OF SHAPE AND COLOUR SYMMETRY ON THE AESTHETIC VALUE OF DAYAK MASKS

One way of examining the preference for symmetry is to look at the aesthetic value of symmetric and asymmetric works of art (e.g. Cárdenas and Harris, 2006; Swami and Furnham, 2009a). In one study, Swami (in press – a) examined preferences for symmetric Dayak tribal masks. The Dayak are the indigenous population of the island of Borneo, and a distinguishing feature of this population is the making and use of tribal masks (Revel-MacDonald and Leyenaar, 1982). Masks are typically painted in bright colours with exaggerated features (e.g. long noses, curled ears and animal fangs) often depicting a morphing of hornbills (messengers of the upperworld) and dragons or wild boars (representatives of the underworld).

In his study, Swami (in press – a) created a series of images of shape-symmetric and colour-symmetric Dayak masks (see Figure 5.1). When participants rated these images, there was a significantly greater preference for symmetrically shaped over asymmetrically shaped masks, but not for symmetrically coloured masks. However, in a two-alternative forced-choice experiment, the symmetric mask was significantly preferred for both shape and colour manipulations. Overall, these results support the notion that symmetric shapes and possibly colour patterns are more appealing than asymmetric ones are (Cárdenas and Harris, 2006; Jacobsen and Höfel, 2001; Rentschler *et al.*, 1999; Washburn and Humphrey, 2001).

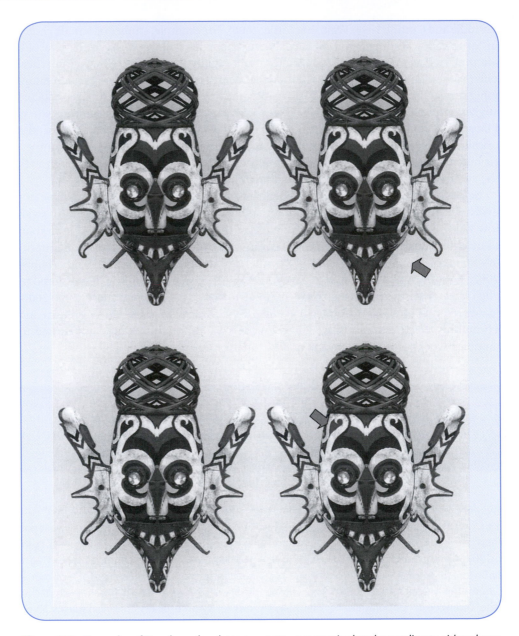

Figure 5.1. *Examples of Dayak masks whose symmetry was manipulated according to either shape (top row) or colour (bottom row).*

Images in the left column are bilaterally symmetrical (arrows indicate manipulated portions of the images for asymmetrical versions).

Source: Adapted from Swami (in press – a)

Moreover, there is evidence that the degree of FA is associated with mate choice in humans. For instance, the degree of bilateral symmetry is positively related to the number of lifetime and extra-pair sexual partners among men (Thornhill and Gangestad, 1994), while women partnered with men of low FA report a higher frequency of copulatory orgasms than those partnered with men of high FA (Thornhill, Gangestad and Comer, 1995). But these studies still leave open the question of whether symmetric human faces are perceived as more physically attractive than asymmetric faces. A number of early studies suggested that they were not, with slightly asymmetric faces preferred over perfectly symmetrical versions (e.g. Kowner, 1996; Samuels *et al.*, 1994; Swaddle and Cuthill, 1995).

One such study is that of Langlois, Roggman and Musselman (1994), in which headshot photographs of women were used to produce a set of perfectly symmetrical faces or 'chimeras'. For each photograph, two perfectly symmetric chimeras were created: in the first, the left half of the original face was aligned with its mirror image and in the second, the right half of the original face was aligned with its mirror image. Using this set of stimuli, Langlois *et al.* found that the original (slightly asymmetrical) faces were rated as more attractive than both the left symmetric and right symmetric chimeras. Only the extremely unattractive faces were judged as less attractive than their symmetric chimeras.

Subsequent work, however, has overturned these results, reporting that symmetric faces are more attractive than slightly asymmetric faces (e.g. Fink *et al.*, 2006; Little, Apicella and Marlowe, 2007; Little and Jones, 2006; Perrett *et al.*, 1999; Rhodes *et al.*, 1998; Rhodes, Roberts and Simmons, 1999; Rhodes, Sumich and Byatt, 1999; see also Little *et al.*, 2008). This discrepancy in the results appears to reflect the manner in which stimuli were created (Rhodes *et al.*, 1999b). Early studies, such as that by Langlois, Roggman and Musselman (1994), relied on reflections of the hemiface about the vertical midline, but these stimuli often display structural abnormalities and distortions of the face that are likely to be perceived as unattractive (Rhodes, 2006). For example, if the photograph is taken from a slight side angle or if one side of the face is naturally wider or narrower than the other half, this can result in atypically wide or narrow chimeras.

To address this issue, Rhodes *et al.* (1998) developed a novel set of faces that varied in symmetry (low, normal, high, perfect) by 'blending' the original and mirror images of photographic headshots. Using this new set of stimuli, Rhodes *et al.* (1998) found that ratings of attractiveness for both male and female faces increased with increasing symmetry. The same pattern of results has been replicated by other studies (Koehler *et al.*, 2002; Penton-Voak *et al.*, 2001; Perrett *et al.*, 1999; Rhodes, Roberts and Simmons, 1999; Rhodes, Sumich and Byatt, 1999) and remains stable when the effects of 'averageness' (Rhodes, Sumich and Byatt, 1999) and change in skin texture (Perrett *et al.*, 1999; Rhodes, Roberts and Simmons, 1999) are controlled. All in all, Rhodes *et al.* (1998) argue that the limited appeal of symmetric faces in earlier research could be attributed to the poor ecological validity of the images.

It should be noted, however, that in her review of the available literature, Rhodes (2006) points out that the effect sizes of symmetry were small-to-medium. Likewise, Gangestad and Scheyd (2005) argue that it is possible that symmetry matters very little in comparison with other facial characteristics such as sexually dimorphic traits (see below). Moreover, Scheib, Gangestad and Thornhill (1999) suggest that the apparent appeal of symmetric faces may not be driven by perceptions of symmetry. They found that facial symmetry predicted ratings of men's attractiveness just as well as the attractiveness of half-faces, which possess minimal cues of symmetry. Jaw size, prominent cheekbones and healthier-looking skin have all been shown to covary with symmetry and may account for its association with attractiveness (Gangestad and Thornhill, 2003; Jones *et al.*, 2004; see also Box 5.3 and Figure 5.2).

Averageness

A different cue to facial attractiveness is 'averageness', which is typically defined as the extent to which a face possesses mathematically average features and configurations for a given population (Rhodes, 2006). Averageness has been proposed as a candidate for a biologically rooted preference based on the notion that it maximises heritable fitness benefits, since average traits are thought to signal developmental stability

BOX 5.3. FLUCTUATING SYMMETRY AND THE ATTRACTIVENESS OF BODIES

Although a number of studies have established that symmetric faces are perceived as more attractive than slightly asymmetric faces, fewer studies have examined the effects of fluctuating asymmetry (FA) on bodily attractiveness. In one early study, Singh (1995a) used line drawings of the female figure that varied in body shape and breast asymmetry, and reported evidence that both variables mattered for attractiveness judgements. However, the effects for breast asymmetry were small and probably covaried with perceived age of the figures. In his study, Singh (1995a) created breast asymmetry by having one breast sag noticeably, and this may have resulted in raters judging the drawn figure to be significantly older, a suggestion corroborated by other studies (Furnham, Swami and Shah, 2006).

Recent research has used more ecologically valid sets of stimuli. Tovée, Tasker and Benson (2000) conducted a computer-enhanced symmetry study comparing the photographs of women's bodies with manipulated images of those photographs to produce perfect symmetry (see Figure 5.2). When observers were asked to rate these images for attractiveness, there was no statistically significant difference in their ratings of normal images (varying in symmetry) and morphed (completely symmetric) versions. However, when observers were presented with the unaltered image and its symmetric version simultaneously, and were forced to choose the more attractive of the two, they tended to choose the symmetric version. The effect size of this difference, however, was small and suggests that, although symmetry may matter for judgements of women's bodily attractiveness, it probably matters very little.

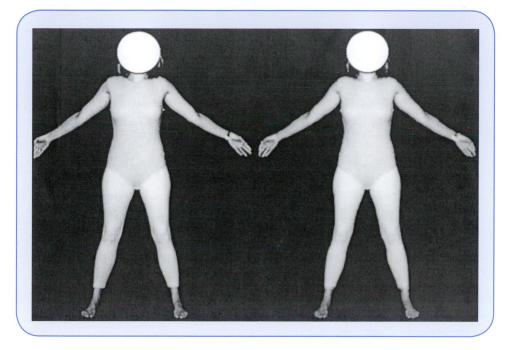

Figure 5.2. *Examples of stimuli used in the study by Tovée, Tasker and Benson (2000).*

The figure on the left is an example of an asymmetric image, whereas the figure on the right is an example of morphed (symmetric) image.

Source: Images reproduced here with permission from Martin Tovée.

(Møller and Swaddle, 1997; Thornhill and Møller, 1997). Gangestad and colleagues (Gangestad and Buss, 1993; Thornhill and Gangestad, 1993; see also Rhodes *et al.*, 2001) have further suggested that averageness may be a reliable cue for genetic heterozygosity, which is thought to be associated with enhanced immune system function (heterozygous individuals often carry a higher frequency of rare alleles, which pathogens are likely to have had limited opportunity to adapt to; Hamilton and Zuk, 1982).

Consistent with these theories, studies have found that individuals prefer male and female faces with average facial configurations (e.g. Baudouin and Tiberghien, 2004; Rhodes and Tremewan, 1996). In one of the earliest studies in the field, Galton (1878) used a photographic superposition technique to create facial composites by superimposing the photographic negatives of faces onto one another. He found that the composites created using this technique were considered more attractive than almost all of the constituent faces, a finding that hampered Galton's efforts to construct the prototypical 'criminal' face.

Subsequent work has attempted to investigate the effect of facial averageness using improved computer-averaging techniques. One widely cited study is that of Langlois and Roggman (1990), which digitised the facial photographs of male and

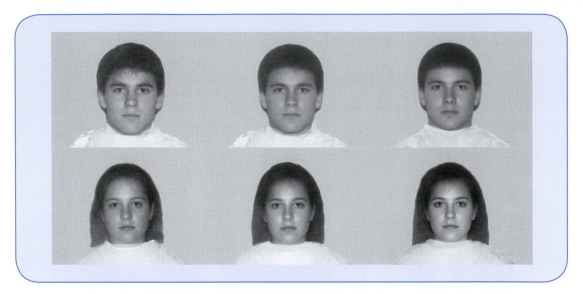

Figure 5.3. *Examples of stimuli used in the study by Langlois and Roggman (1990). Ranging from left to right, the images represent the geometric average of 8, 16 and 32 individual faces.*
Source: Used with permission of Judith Langlois.

female undergraduates. These images were then geometrically averaged (separately for each sex) to generate average composites for each face (see Figure 5.3). When each of the individual faces and their corresponding computer-averaged faces were rated for attractiveness, the composites were generally judged as more attractive than the set of individual faces that comprised them. This seems to tie in with research showing that typical, less recognisable faces are deemed more attractive than distinctive, more recognisable faces (Light, Hollander and Kayra-Stuart, 1981).

However, the study by Langlois and Roggman (1990) has been criticised on the grounds that the composites were not truly average (Alley and Cunningham, 1991; Benson and Perrett, 1992; Pittenger, 1991). For example, the combination of multiple images may lead to a decrease in the degree of bilateral asymmetry or blemishing in the resulting composite (Little and Hancock, 2002). Thus, more recent work has shown that averaged-composites remain attractive when controlling for feature alignment and complexion (Little and Hancock, 2002; O'Toole *et al.*, 1999; Rhodes, Sumich and Byatt, 1999).

Rhodes and Tremewan (1996), for example, used a computerised caricature generator to produce one undistorted line drawing, one caricature (a drawing low in facial averageness) and one anti-caricature (a drawing high in facial averageness) for each individual photograph in a set of male and female faces. Their results showed that the anti-caricature faces (high in averageness) were rated as more attractive than the undistorted faces which, in turn, were rated as more attractive than the caricature faces (low in averageness). Since the study used line-drawn images, any natural blemishes that could be found in photographic images would have been eliminated. Of course, line-drawn images have their own limitations (see Bateson, Cornelissen and Tovée, 2007; Swami, in press – b; Swami *et al.*, 2008b), but taken together these findings converge on the notion that averageness is beautiful. Moreover, averageness remains attractive when faces are seen in profile (Valentine, Darling and Donnelly, 2004), when cross-cultural samples are recruited (e.g. Apicella, Little and Marlowe, 2007) and when controlling for the effects of symmetry (Jones, DeBruine and Little, 2007; Rhodes, Sumich and Byatt, 1999), youthfulness (O'Toole *et al.*, 1999) and expression (O'Toole *et al.*, 1999; Rhodes, Sumich and Byatt, 1999).

One study has found that genetic heterozygosity within the major histocompatibility complex (MHC; a cluster of genes that encode cell surface proteins integral to immune system function) predicted both male facial attractiveness and facial averageness (Lie, Rhodes and Simmons, 2008). Moreover, when the effect of facial averageness was controlled, the relationship between MHC heterozygosity and attractiveness became non-significant, suggesting that this relationship was mediated by facial averageness. However, evidence for a similar relationship in female faces was not found, which runs counter to the evidence that averageness is attractive for both male and female faces (Rhodes, 2006).

Overall, then, the available evidence suggests that average faces are attractive, but it is also important to ask whether the most attractive face is average (put differently, are average faces optimally attractive; see DeBruine *et al.*, 2007)? It is worth briefly referring back to the study by Langlois and Roggman (1990) here. Although these authors found that composite faces were more attractive than their individual faces, this was not true of all faces. Rather, some of the original male and female faces were rated as even more attractive than their averaged composites. Since the individual faces possessed fewer average features than their corresponding composites, one possibility is that certain deviations from averageness are even more attractive than average facial configurations.

This speculation was supported by Perrett, May and Yoshikawa (1994), who found preferences for certain exaggerated or extreme facial features. Perrett *et al.* showed that a composite derived from the average of a set of 60 female faces was less attractive than a composite derived from the average of the 15 most attractive female faces from the same set. Moreover, the attractiveness of the 15-face composite was enhanced by exaggerating its shape differences from the average composite by 50%. Indeed, research indicates that highly attractive female faces differ systematically from an average face: they have, for example, larger eyes and smaller mouths than the average face (e.g. Johnston and Franklin, 1993). This has led some researchers to examine the effects of sexually dimorphic traits on facial attractiveness.

Facial sexual dimorphism

Sexually dimorphic facial traits are secondary sexual characteristics that differ between males and females of a species and that generally emerge during puberty (Farkas, 1988). Examples include male deer antlers, the elaborate tails of peacocks and the horns of the Rhinoceros beetle. Likewise, among men, testosterone stimulates the development of masculine facial traits (characterised by a pronounced jaw, chin, cheekbones and brow ridges; Tanner, 1978). This is paralleled by the development of feminine facial shapes, as a function of oestrogen, in women (typified by large eyes and lips and a small nose and chin; Enlow, 1990). Sexual dimorphism may signal sexual maturity, as it emerges during puberty (Johnston and Franklin, 1993; Symons, 1979, 1992, 1995) and may be an indicator of differences in mate quality.

For instance, among males, the high titre of testosterone required for the growth and maintenance of secondary sexual traits is physiologically costly: testosterone suppresses immune system function and so increases susceptibility to disease and parasitic infection (Kanda, Tsuchida and Tamaki, 1996; see Grossman, 1985, for a review). Therefore, only the highest-quality males can support the costs associated with these traits (Møller, Christe and Lux, 1999; Peters, 2000; Zahavi, 1975), which serve as reliable cues to heritable immunocompetence (Fölstad and Karter, 1992; for applications to human facial masculinity, see Little, Jones and DeBruine, 2008; Little *et al.*, 2008; Thornhill and Gangestad, 1993, 1999, 2006). The same may be true of feminine facial traits, if high titres of oestrogen similarly stress immune system function (see Rhodes *et al.*, 2003; Seli and Arici, 2002), although facial femininity may be a more direct index of a woman's history of energy balance appropriate for reproduction (Gangestad and Scheyd, 2005). Masculine traits may also be reliably associated with perceptions of dominance and status, which are generally desirable and valued (Buss, 1989; Mazur, Mazur and Keating, 1984).

If these hypotheses are correct, then we should expect to see feminine female faces and masculine male faces rated as highly physically attractive. Indeed, the available evidence does appear to support these predictions. Numerous studies have shown that feminine female traits are perceived as attractive on female faces (e.g. Cunningham, 1986; Cunningham *et al.*, 1995; Johnston and Franklin, 1993; Johnston *et al.*, 2001; Jones and Hill, 1993; Koehler *et al.*, 2004; Little *et al.*, 2002; O'Toole *et al.*, 1998; Penton-Voak, Jacobson and Trivers, 2004; Perrett *et al.*, 1998; Rhodes, Hickford and Jeffery, 2000; Rhodes *et al.*, 2003; Scott *et al.*, 2008) and that averaged composites with feminine features are preferred over average composites (Perrett, May and Yoshikawa, 1994). Moreover, using computer-averaging and morphing techniques, several studies have shown that exaggerating femininity increases attractiveness (Johnston *et al.*, 2001; Perrett *et al.*, 1998; Rhodes, Hickford and Jeffery, 2000; Russell, 2003).

Various studies have also reported associations between male facial masculinity and higher ratings of attractiveness, although the associations are weaker than for femininity (Cunningham, Barbee and Pike, 1990; Koehler *et al.*, 2004; Neave *et al.*, 2003; O'Toole *et al.*, 1998; Rhodes *et al.*, 2003; Scheib, Gangestad and Thornhill, 1999). Some studies have further suggested that exaggerated masculine traits can be attractive in male faces (e.g. Grammer and Thornhill, 1994; Penton-Voak *et al.*, 2001). However, other studies report a female preference for feminised male faces (e.g. Little *et al.*, 2001; Penton-Voak, Jacobson and Trivers, 2004; Perrett *et al.*, 1998; Rhodes, 2006; Rhodes, Hickford and Jeffery, 2000), although there is some debate as to whether averaged male composites used in these studies adequately capture masculine traits (Little and Hancock, 2002; Meyer and Quong, 1999; Swaddle and Reierson, 2002). Similarly, several studies have shown that women prefer men with a smaller than average jaw (Berry and McArthur, 1985; Little *et al.*, 2001) and yet others have found that a combination of both masculine and feminine features is maximally attractive (Cunningham, Barbee and Pike, 1990).

What explains the equivocal findings in relation to preferences for facial masculinity? One suggestion is that women seek a 'trade-off' between good mates and good fathers and that testosterone mediates men's behavioural allocation between mating effort and paternal investment (Little and Mannion, 2006; Little *et al.*, 2001, 2007; Penton-Voak *et al.*, 2003; Perrett *et al.*, 1998; Scott *et al.*, 2008; Waynforth, Delwadia and Camm, 2005). For example, high levels of testosterone are linked to having a high number of sexual partners (Dabbs and Morris, 1990) and to an increase in the likelihood of engaging in extramarital sex (Booth and Dabbs, 1993). Similarly, masculinity in men is associated with lower spousal investment and poor father–child relationships (Fleming *et al.*, 2002; Julian and McKenry, 1989; Roney *et al.*, 2006). Therefore, a mate-selection strategy based on facial dimorphism may be costly to women: by selecting mates on the basis of good genes, women may have to sacrifice the potential benefits of spousal and paternal investment (see Bellis and Baker, 1990). This is consistent with the finding that facial masculinity is associated with decreased attributions of honesty, parental quality and suitability as a partner (Boothroyd *et al.*, 2007; Perrett *et al.*, 1998; see also Box 5.4).

BOX 5.4. PREFERENCES FOR FACIAL DIMORPHISM AMONG THE MATSIGENKA OF AMAZONIAN PERU

While studies conducted among Western populations suggest that female preferences for male facial dimorphism is bidirectional (the desired degree of masculinity in a mate varies depending on whether the male is chosen for a long-term relationship or extra-pair matings), fewer studies have examined the same preferences among non-Western populations. This is important because, in many traditional societies, cultural rules help shape an individual's preferences, particularly in terms of parental decisions over the choice of spouse (Beckerman, 2000). Thus, any study of variation in preferences for long-term versus short-term partners must take into account kinship and marriage rules (and other similar sociocultural factors) that may influence mate choice decisions.

In one study, Yu, Proulx and Shepard (2007) examined preferences for facial dimorphism among the Matsigenka of Peru, also including in their study parental preferences. Among the Matsigenka, parents have a strong influence over the daughter's choice of marital partner, and emphasise food provision through hunting and swidden agriculture. The results of their study showed that women generally preferred more feminine male faces, in line with previous work (e.g. Perrett *et al.*, 1998). However, when asked to rate the male faces for a son-in-law, women were found to prefer masculine faces (or, at least, they did not show a preference for feminine faces for that role). Yu, Proulx and Shepard (2007) suggest that this result can be explained as a function of the association between facial masculinity and perceived resource provision, such that son-in-laws with more masculine faces were considered better providers of resources. Overall, it was suggested that 'Matsigenka mothers and daughters might disagree over the desirability of a particular suitor' (Yu, Proulx and Shepard, 2007, p. 102).

Additional support comes from the finding that women's preferences for facial masculinity vary across the menstrual cycle. Women demonstrate a stronger preference for masculine faces during the fertile (follicular) phase of the menstrual cycle than during the infertile (luteal) phase of the cycle (Danel and Pawłowski, 2006; Jones, DeBruine and Little, 2008; Jones *et al.*, 2008; Little, Jones and Burriss, 2007; Little, Jones and DeBruine, 2008; Penton-Voak and Perrett, 2000; Penton-Voak *et al.*, 1999). Recent evidence has also highlighted a direct relationship between specific hormones (primarily oestrogen and testosterone) and women's preferences for masculine traits (Roney and Simmons, 2008; Welling *et al.*, 2007; see also Rupp *et al.*, 2009). Corresponding evidence is provided by studies showing that, when women are close to ovulation, they are also attracted to the scent of symmetrical men (Gangestad and Thornhill, 1998; Garver-Apgar, Gangestad and Thornhill, 2008), deep, masculine male voices (Puts, 2005), masculine walking gaits (Provost, Troje and Quinsey, 2008) and more confident, intersexually competitive male behavioural displays (Gangestad *et al.*, 2004). These preference shifts suggest that cues to masculinity are most highly valued when women are fertile and are, therefore, able to maximise the benefits of heritable immunocompetence. That is, these changes in preferences across the menstrual cycle may reflect female decisions to weigh signals of heritable condition (good genes) more heavily when they are fertile (Perrett *et al.*, 1998).

Summary

Overall, the available evidence suggests that symmetry, averageness and sexually dimorphic traits are attractive for both men and women, possibly because they act as indicators of underlying quality (primarily, but not limited to, health; see Fink and Penton-Voak, 2002; Rhodes, 2006). Recent work, still in its infancy, has begun to extend these findings by investigating the social transmission of face preferences (e.g. Jones *et al.*, 2007a; see also Jones, DeBruine, Little, 2007; Jones *et al.*, 2007b), gaze and facial expressions (e.g. Jones *et al.*, 2006; Penton-Voak and Chang, 2008) and individual differences in mate choice preferences (e.g. Conway *et al.*, 2008; Little and Perrett, 2002). In terms of the latter, for example, Perrett *et al.* (2002) report that individuals born to old parents responded more positively to age cues in opposite-sex faces than did individuals with young parents. Other work has suggested that facial resemblance increases the attractiveness of some faces (e.g. Buston and Emlen, 2003; DeBruine, 2004) and that viewing faces results in a stronger preference for characteristics that are common to more attractive faces (Jones, DeBruine and Little, 2008).

One particularly fruitful avenue for research on facial attractiveness has been an examination of the effects of condition-dependent preferences, mirroring findings from the animal kingdom (e.g. Bakker, Künzler and Mazzi, 1999). For instance, some studies have shown that women who perceive themselves to be particularly attractive exhibit a stronger preference for masculinity and symmetry in men's faces (Little and Mannion, 2006; Little *et al.*, 2001). Other work has shown that women with attractive bodies show a greater preference for masculinity in men's faces (Jones *et al.*, 2005; Penton-Voak *et al.*, 2003). Finally, of course, averageness, symmetry and sexual dimorphism are not the only cues when making judgements of facial attractiveness. Recent work has stressed the importance of such cues as skin texture (Fink, Grammer and Thornhill, 2001; Jones *et al.*, 2004) and skin colour distribution (Fink, Grammer and Matts, 2006; Fink and Matts, 2008; Fink *et al.*, 2008).

BODILY ATTRACTIVENESS

The literature on facial attractiveness demonstrates some of the more developed applications of evolutionary psychology to the topic of human beauty. In contrast, the available research on bodily attractiveness, until recently at least, lacked the same degree of rigour and exactitude. Few other theories derived from evolutionary psychology so exemplifies the latter as the waist-to-hip ratio hypothesis of women's attractiveness. In this section, we unpack this hypothesis in detail, showing how it fails to stand up to scrutiny as an evidence-based application of evolutionary psychology. Our aim is not to provide a comprehensive account of theories of bodily attractiveness but rather to show how one particular theory that has come to dominate the literature evidences all the hallmarks of 'just-so stories' (Gould, 1997).

The waist-to-hip ratio hypothesis

According to some evolutionary psychologists, one of the main problems facing our hunter-gatherer ancestors living during the Late Stone Age was the identification of mate value. To overcome this problem, 'perceptual mechanisms' or mental modules evolved among human beings to detect and use information conveyed by phenotypic traits in determining an individual's underlying quality as a potential mate. As noted above, such indicators could include deviations from bilateral symmetry, averageness and sexually dimorphic traits. In terms of bodily attractiveness, a series of important papers published in the early 1990s highlighted one particular sexually dimorphic trait as being the primary cue used when making judgements of physical attractiveness: the waist-to-hip ratio (Singh, 1993a, 1993b, 1994a, 1994b, 1994c, 1995a, 1995b; Singh and Luis, 1995; Singh and Young, 1995).

While the body shape of boys and girls is more or less similar before puberty, the sex hormones (primarily oestrogen and testosterone) regulate the deposit and utilisation of fat from various anatomical areas during pubertal onset (LaVelle, 1995; Leong, 2006). For most women, fat (or adipose tissue) deposit is inhibited in the abdominal region and stimulated in the gluteofemoral region (buttocks and thighs) more than in any other region of the body. For most men, on the other hand, fat deposit is stimulated in the abdominal region and inhibited in the gluteofemoral region (Björntorp,

1991, 1997; Rebuffé-Scrive, 1988, 1991). It is this sexually dimorphic body fat distribution that underscores body shape differences between women and men, with women typically maintaining a lower WHR than men through adulthood (Jones *et al.*, 1986; Lanska *et al.*, 1985; Marti *et al.*, 1991).

In short, then, there are sex-typical differences in the pattern of fat distribution as a function of the sex hormones, which will influence perceptions of attractiveness. More than this, however, Singh (1993a) argues that the WHR is reliably associated with health and fertility outcomes in women and, so, over evolutionary time, men will have evolved to use the WHR as a direct assessment of women's underlying fitness. Specifically, Singh (1993a) amassed a great deal of evidence to show that low female WHRs are associated with improved life outcomes (e.g. lower incidence of cardio-vascular disorders and ovarian and breast cancer) and higher fertility (e.g. regular menstrual cycles and higher probability of successful conception and pregnancy). This allowed Singh (1993a) to conclude that low female WHRs were associated with lower susceptibility to various major physical diseases and improved fertility.

In evolutionary history, therefore, by paying close attention to the WHR and by mating with low-WHR (and, hence, healthier or more fertile) women, men likely enhanced their own reproductive success. Contemporary men are said to also use this method for assessing a woman's attractiveness, either because they possess the same mental modules governing behaviour as their ancestors (e.g. Buss, 1999) or because the association between low female WHRs and health or fertility continues to hold (but see Box 5.5). Accordingly, Singh (1993a) believes it would be possible to system-atically change men's evaluations of women's attractiveness by manipulating the size of the WHR.

To test this idea, Singh (1993a, 1993b) developed a set of 12 line drawings of the female figure, which were systematically varied with respect to overall body weight and the WHR (see Figure 5.4). In a series of experiments using these drawings, Singh (1993a, 1993b, 1994c; Singh and Luis, 1995) described a negative correlation between the WHR and ratings of women's attractiveness. That is, line drawings with low WHRs (typically 0.70) were judged as the most attractive and ratings decreased with increasing WHR. Although the body weight categories also had an effect, within each weight category, figures with the lower WHRs were judged more attractive than other figures in those groups.

Using Singh's original set of line drawings, the preference for low WHRs has been replicated with participants in the United States (Singh, 1994c), Britain (Furnham, Tan and McManus, 1997) and Germany (Henss, 1995). Supporting evidence was provided by Singh's (1995b) analysis of the WHRs of *Playboy* centrefolds and Miss America pageant winners across time. Specifically, Singh (1995b) argues that there was a degree of consistency in their (low) WHRs, which was taken as prima facie evidence of an evolved basis for a preference for a low WHR (Buss, 1999). That is, *Playboy* centrefolds and Miss America winners tended to have WHRs in the 'attract-ive range' because it is exactly this that men have evolved to find attractive.

In sum, Singh (1993a) argues that, to be considered attractive, a woman has to have a low WHR and fall within the normal body weight range. Importantly, Singh (1993a, p. 304) views the WHR as a 'wide first-pass filter, which would automatically

BOX 5.5.   ARE LOW FEMALE WAIST-TO-HIP RATIOS ASSOCIATED WITH IMPROVED HEALTH AND FERTILITY?

The lynchpin of the waist-to-hip ratio (WHR) hypothesis of women's attractiveness is the purported association between low female WHRs and improved health and fertility outcomes (Singh, 1993a). In terms of health outcomes, for instance, Singh (1993a, 2006) gathered a number of studies showing that a low female WHR was associated with increased mortality rates (Björntorp, 1987) and lower incidence of cardiovascular disorders, adult-onset diabetes, hypertension, endometrial, ovarian and breast cancer and gall bladder disease (Folsom *et al.*, 1993; Huang, Willet and Colditz, 1999; Misra and Vikram, 2003). The available evidence, however, is much more equivocal than has traditionally been acknowledged.

For one thing, studies showing an association between low female WHRs and improved health typically rely on post-menopausal women, who would not share the same disease patterns as women living during the Late Stone Age (Eaton, Eaton and Konner, 1997). Other work highlights the complex nature of interpreting the relationship between WHRs and health outcomes. For instance, two independent studies (Bigaard *et al.*, 2004; Seidell *et al.*, 2001) observe that waist and hip circumference are independently related in opposite directions to risk factors such as high insulin levels, suggesting that the independent effects of these two girth measures are confounded in the WHR. Yet others have shown that waist circumference alone is a better indicator of cardiovascular disease risk than the WHR (Lean, Han and Morrison, 1995).

Similarly, in terms of the relationship between the WHR and fertility, Singh (1993a, 2006) reports that (among other things) women with higher WHRs have more irregular menstrual cycles (Moran *et al.*, 1999) and lower probability of conception when the WHR is greater than 0.80 (Kaye *et al.*, 1990; Wass *et al.*, 1997; Zaadstra *et al.*, 1993). Importantly, however, some authors have questioned the validity of relying on these studies to substantiate adaptationist claims. Wetsman (1998), for example, points out that the difference in WHR between the women who did and did not have difficulty becoming pregnant in the Kaye *et al.* (1990) study was 0.838 versus 0.840. This difference was statistically significant because the study included over 40 000 women, but as Freese (2000, p. 329) points out, 'their substantive significance for shaping mate preference mechanisms is doubtful, especially since the mean differences would seem smaller than what men can actually perceive.'

Just as important, not all studies support the association between low WHRs and improved fertility. Thus, some studies report no significant associations between WHRs and ovulatory cycles (e.g. van Hooff *et al.*, 1999, 2000a, 2000b) or between WHRs and the likelihood of conception (Eijkemans *et al.*, 2003). Lassek and Gaulin (2008) further point out that, to date, there has been little discussion of the manner in which low WHRs might enhance fertility. Instead, Lassek and Gaulin (2008) argue that WHRs may be associated with the availability of critical fat reserves needed to sustain foetal and infant brain development, leading to improved cognitive ability.

Our point here is not to entirely dismiss the data suggesting associations between low WHRs and fertility or health. Rather, it is important to bear in mind that the available medical literature remains equivocal, making it difficult to establish a directional or causational link between WHRs and life outcomes. Of course, if researchers selectively choose which studies to present, it is easy to present a simple picture of improving health and fertility with low WHRs. In reality, however, the evidence is much more contradictory and difficult to interpret (Swami, 2005, 2008).

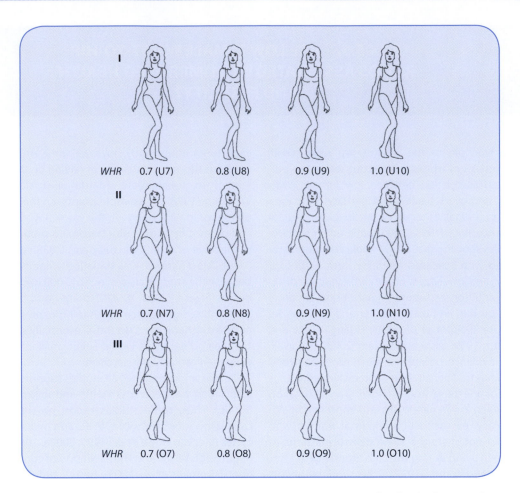

Figure 5.4. *Singh's (1993a, 1993b) original set of line drawings varying in four levels of waist-to-hip ratio (columns: 0.7, 0.8, 0.9, and 1.0) and three levels of body weight (rows: underweight, normal weight and overweight).*

Source: Used with permission of Devendra Singh.

exclude women who are unhealthy or who have low reproductive capacity'. It is only after this 'culturally invariant' filter is passed that other features such as facial attractiveness, skin tone or body weight become utilised in final mate selection. All in all, it is possible to summarise the WHR hypothesis as consisting of four related tenets:

1. That there is a mental module or perceptual mechanism in the male brain governing preferences for low WHRs;
2. That the preference for low WHRs first evolved among ancestral men and was passed on to subsequent generations of men (presumably through some form of genetic inheritance);

3. That the WHR acts as a 'first-pass filter', being the initial or primary cue on which judgements of women's attractiveness are based;

4. That the preference for low WHRs is universal, leading to both temporal and cross-cultural stability in preferences.

In the next several sections of this chapter, we consider each of the above tenets in greater detail (though in no particular order), showing that they remain controversial or that they have little basis in empirical fact.

Show me the module!

A first important limitation of the WHR hypothesis of women's attractiveness stems from the notion that there is (or are) a mental module in the male brain governing preferences for low WHRs. To date, there is no credible evidence that such a mental module exists and the existence of such a WHR module is based almost entirely on speculation about mental modularity (see Cosmides and Tooby, 1995; for critiques, see Buller, 2005; Swami, 2007b). Moreover, it appears to be normal practice to infer the existence of a WHR module a posteriori based on evidence demonstrating a preference for low WHRs.

To be sure, some evidence has suggested that there may be dedicated brain regions for face perception (e.g. Farah, 1996), biological motion perception (e.g. Blake and Shiffrar, 2006; Puce and Perrett, 2003) and the processing of body-specific information (e.g. Peelen and Downing, 2005). In terms of the latter, functional magnetic resonance imaging (fMRI) studies have shown that the extrastriate body area (EBA, located bilaterally in the posterior inferior temporal sulcus or middle temporal gyrus) and the fusiform body area (FBA, located in the fusiform gyrus) respond strongly and selectively to static images of human bodies and body parts, but only weakly to faces and objects (Peelen and Downing, 2005; Schwarzlose, Baker and Kanwisher, 2005; for a review, see Peelen and Downing, 2007).

For example, these brain regions have been shown to respond selectively to body silhouettes, stick figures and line drawings of the human form, suggesting some abstraction in visual processing (Downing *et al.*, 2001; Peelen and Downing, 2005; Peelen, Wiggett and Downing, 2006). Moreover, the EBA and FBA are activated in response to point-light displays of human motion (Peelen *et al.*, 2006) and the response of these regions is higher for non-human animals than it is for objects, suggesting that they may be partly activated by stimuli with similar body plans to humans (Downing *et al.*, 2006).

Given such evidence of brain regions involved in processing body-specific information, it may be suggested that the purported WHR mental module exists in the EBA or FBA. In our view, however, such conjecture would be premature. For one thing, it seems unlikely that either the FBA or EBA would respond selectively to a body region such as the WHR, which is difficult to disambiguate from neighbouring body regions, such as the abdomen. It seems more likely that activation of these brain regions would be strongest for clearly defined body regions (such as the hands or feet) or for overall depictions of the human body.

Just as important, the WHR hypothesis requires that the mental module governing WHR-related preferences should exist only in the male brain. However, at present, there is no suggestion that the selective responsivity of the EBA or FBA is specific to the male brain. In other words, there is no evidence to support the conjecture that there are sex differences in brain-region responsivity to static images of human bodies or body parts. Overall, then, there is (at present, at least) no credible evidence that there exists a mental module in the male brain governing preferences for low WHRs. Until real evidence can be presented for the existence of such a module, an important tenet of the WHR hypothesis remains on shaky ground.

Critical tests

Ever since the WHR hypothesis was first postulated in the early 1990s, there have been numerous tests of its validity. Several studies have provided support for the notion that there is a male preference for low WHRs, relying either on line-drawn stimuli (e.g. Forestell, Humphrey and Stewart, 2004; Freedman et al., 2004; Furnham, Dias and McClelland, 1998; Furnham, Lavancy and McClelland, 2001; Furnham, Moutafi and Baguma, 2002; Furnham, Petrides and Constantinides, 2005; Furnham, Swami and Shah, 2006; Gray, Heaney and Fairhall, 2003; Markey et al., 2002) or artificially generated manipulations of images of real individuals (e.g. Henss, 2000; Streeter and McBurney, 2003). In terms of the latter, for example, Henss (2000) designed a study using full frontal photographs that included the face and breasts of different women with computer-altered WHRs. For each photograph, two versions of the WHR were created using morphing techniques: in one picture the waist was tightened (lower WHR) and in the other it was widened (higher WHR). Using this new set of stimuli, Henss (2000) found support for Singh's argument that low female WHRs were perceived as more attractive than high WHRs.

The obvious benefit of the above techniques is that they allow researchers to manipulate the WHR with some precision, thus ensuring that the resultant variation is sufficient to affect judgements of attractiveness. Moreover, it is assumed in these studies that any variation in judgements of attractiveness must be caused by the manipulation of the WHR, as no other variation in physical cues is evident (McBurney and Streeter, 2007). However, there are important problems relying on such assumptions, primarily because of the lack of ecological validity associated with extant stimulus sets and because of the manner in which WHR is measured in these studies.

In the first instance, line drawings and similar stimuli have been criticised for lacking ecological validity (Tassinary and Hansen, 1998), that is they do not fully capture the range of bodily variation that can be perceived in real-life figures and may overly simplify the way in which judgements of attractiveness are made. Indeed, a number of studies have suggested that line drawings are only crude approximations of reality and that such 'paper people' do not adequately mirror reality (Swami, 2007a; Swami and Furnham, 2006; Tassinary and Hansen, 1998). The results of research on facial cues, for instance, suggests that line drawings of faces yield very different judgements than the facial photographs from which they were derived do (Leder, 1996) and body image research suggests that participants have difficulty relating line drawings to corresponding real-life body shapes (Parkinson, Tovée and Cohen-Tovée, 1998). Even where photographic images of real people are used (e.g. Streeter and McBurney, 2003), extreme variation in a manipulated attribute can lead to the stimulus person being perceived as unrealistic or implausible (Bateson, Cornelissen and Tovée, 2007).

In a similar vein, most studies of the WHR hypothesis mistakenly assume that variance in two-dimensional images accurately captures the range of visual cues available in three dimensions (Bateson, Cornelissen and Tovée, 2007). Specifically, the WHR of two-dimensional stimuli can only be quantified as the direct path across the waist and hips, not their actual circumference. However, only the latter measurement has been correlated with improved health and fertility outcomes. In other words, actual WHR is the index that has been linked with better fitness, whereas the WHR as measured across the front is just one possible visual cue to this (Swami, 2005). The assumption inherent in many studies that the two measures are equivalent or identical is erroneous. Indeed, Tovée and Cornelissen (2001) have shown that the two measures of WHR are correlated, but only poorly so ($r = 0.60$). Moreover, it is not entirely clear that measurements of the WHR across the front of the body are sufficiently accurate. Furnham and Reeves (2006), for instance, suggest that Singh (1993a) miscalculated the WHRs of his line drawings, perhaps because of the difficulty of assessing what is inherently a three-dimensional trait in only two dimensions. In this sense, the confusion between the two possible ways of measuring the WHR may have led to an overestimation of the role played by the WHR in physical attraction.

This leads on to a related methodological concern with studies of the WHR hypothesis, namely the issue of covariance in human morphology. As noted above, the assumption in most studies that have singled out the WHR to be manipulated is that, when such manipulations are made, all other physical characteristics are held constant (see Box 5.6). This, however, is erroneous: converging evidence suggests that line drawings and photographic stimuli that have manipulated the WHR have also inadvertently varied perceived body weight (Tovée and Cornelissen, 2001). In other words, when figures are modified by altering the width of the torso, this alters not only the WHR but also apparent body weight, thus making it impossible to say whether changes in attractiveness ratings are made on the basis of WHR, body weight or both (Tovée and Cornelissen, 2001; Tovée et al., 1997, 1998, 1999). Almost all early studies of the WHR hypothesis made this error, suggesting that the importance attributed to WHR was an artefact of covarying WHR with body weight (see Bateson, Cornelissen and Tovée, 2007; Cornelissen, Tovée and Bateson, 2008).

To investigate the relative importance of body weight and WHR in the perception of women's attractiveness, Tovée and colleagues designed a new set of stimuli consisting of real images of women, for whom BMI and WHR were known precisely (see Figure 5.5). In their analyses, both BMI and WHR emerged as significant predictors of ratings of women's attractiveness, but BMI was by far the more important predictor (Tovée and Cornelissen, 2001; Tovée et al., 1998, 1999). Indeed, across studies, BMI generally accounted for more than 70% of the variance in attractiveness ratings, whereas WHR accounted for little more than 2% (Tovée and Cornelissen, 2001; Tovée et al., 1998, 1999, 2002; see also Smith et al., 2007).

Importantly, these results cannot be explained as an artefact of the stimulus set, as cues of body shape emerge as more important predictors of men's attractiveness

BOX 5.6.   THE LESSONS OF WAIST-TO-HIP RATIO APPLIED TO OTHER RESEARCH

The problem of covariation between manipulated phenotypic traits is not limited to waist-to-hip ratio (WHR) stimuli. For example, Swami, Einon and Furnham (2006) suggest that the leg-to-body ratio (LBR) – measured as the ratio of leg length relative to the torso including the head – may play a role in judgements of attractiveness because of the possibility that the trait is a cue to health status in women and men. To test this idea, Swami, Einon and Furnham (2006) presented participants with five line drawings of men and women, respectively, varying in LBR. They found that women with relatively longer legs were judged more attractive than were women with shorter legs. In contrast, men with relatively shorter legs were judged more attractive than were men with longer legs (but see Swami, Einon and Furnham, 2007).

An important limitation of this study, however, was that manipulations of the LBR resulted in confounding perceptual variation in characteristics such as upper-body muscularity, arm length and crotch size (Swami, in press – b). In a more recent study, Sorokowski and Pawłowski (2008) used silhouettes of male and female figures, reporting a preference for male and female LBRs in the mid- to upper-middle ranges of their stimuli. Unfortunately, the stimuli used by Sorokowski and Pawłowski (2008) also represent a compromise on ecological validity, because their hand-drawn stimuli showed intrastimuli variation (e.g. differences in head posture). The latest research has begun to use computer-graphics programs to design better sets of stimuli (e.g. Swami *et al.*, 2009d), but the message to researchers is clear: the above methodological problems limit the inferences that can be drawn about the attraction process, and, at the very least, suggest that some previous conclusions need to be attenuated.

than body weight when similar images of men are rated by women (Maisey *et al.*, 1999). Moreover, the results pertaining to women's attractiveness remain stable when women were presented in profile, as opposed to a frontal view (Tovée and Cornelissen, 2001) and when different methodological designs and stimuli are used (Puhl and Boland, 2001; Wilson, Tripp and Boland, 2005). Studies using three-dimensional images of women, for example, have found evidence consistent with the hypothesis that body weight is the dominant predictor of women's attractiveness (Fan, 2007; Fan *et al.*, 2004; Smith, Cornelissen and Tovée, 2007). Nor are these results unique to Western cultures: cross-cultural studies using the same or similar methodologies have shown that body weight 'trumps' WHR in explaining variance in attractiveness ratings (indeed, in many traditional societies, WHR does not emerge as a significant predictor of women's attractiveness; e.g. Scott *et al.*, 2007; Swami and Tovée, 2005a, 2007a, 2007b, 2007c; Swami *et al.*, 2006a, 2007a, 2007b, 2009a; Tovée, Furnham and Swami, 2007; Tovée *et al.*, 2006; see also Box 5.7).

In sum, then, this research serves to question the suggestion that the WHR acts as a first-pass filter of women's attractiveness. Indeed, corroborating research has shown

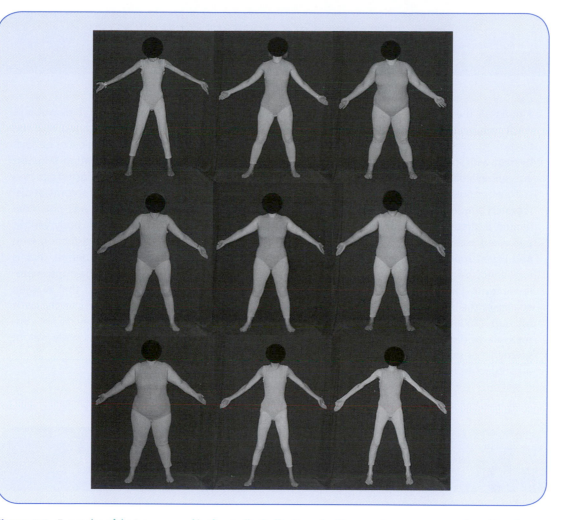

Figure 5.5. *Examples of the images used in the studies by Tovée and colleagues. Images are reproduced here in no particular order.*

Source: Images used with permission of Martin Tovée.

that breast size (Furnham and Swami, 2007), perceived ethnicity (Swami *et al.*, 2009b), waist circumference alone (Rilling *et al.*, 2009; Rozmus-Wrzesinska and Pawłowski, 2005) and abdominal depth (Rilling *et al.*, 2009) all account for greater variance in attractiveness ratings than the WHR does. More generally, there are important (and, as yet, unresolved) questions about the extent to which perceptions of human beauty are guided by filters (as in the WHR model) and the role of the contextualised relationship between elemental (e.g. physical) precepts and other attitudes (e.g. non-physical attraction; see Box 5.8) that ultimately form a Gestalt impression (for discussion, see Johnson and Tassinary, 2007; Swami and Furnham, 2008a, Chapters 4 and 10).

BOX 5.7.   DOES THE WAIST-TO-HIP RATIO MATTER TO WOMEN?

Almost all the data on the importance of the waist-to-hip ratio (WHR) to judgements of attractiveness have focused on opposite-sex ratings by men, with scant attention being paid to women's self-evaluations of the relevance of WHR to self-perception. Certainly, the preponderance of research suggests that women's body dissatisfaction is predominantly related to actual and perceived body weight (e.g. Frederick, Peplau and Lever, 2006), although part of this may be explained as a dissatisfaction with the size of the lower trunk (Bailey *et al.*, 1990). To assess the relevance of the WHR to women's self-perceptions, Mussap (2006) had participants complete a measure of disordered eating as well as measurements of subjective (or self-perceived), ideal and objective (or actual) WHR and body weight.

Results of this study showed that measures of WHR were not significantly associated with the presence or severity of psychological or behavioural symptoms of disordered eating (Mussap, 2006). Moreover, although self-reported concern with WHR was correlated with symptoms of disordered eating, this association was not independent of level of concern with body weight (suggesting that it may be dissatisfaction with body weight, rather then WHR per se, that is most relevant to disordered eating symptomatology). Overall, it does not appear that women engage in body change behaviours on the basis of their WHR, possibly because they do not consider it as amenable to change as body weight (Mussap, 2006).

BOX 5.8.   BEAUTY IS MORE THAN SKIN-DEEP

Much of the extant literature on physical attractiveness has been based, tacitly at least, on the notion that beauty is 'but skin-deep', that is the idea that human beauty is best understood at the level of physical traits. In contrast, however, a growing body of empirical research has suggested that beauty is a multifaceted feature that should include variables of dynamic attractiveness, such as an individual's conversational skills, body language and sense of humour (e.g. Jensen-Campbell, Graziano and West, 1995; Li, Bailey and Kenrick, 2002; Lundy, Tan and Cunningham, 1998; for a review, see Swami and Furnham, 2008a, Chapter 9).

One important psychological variable that has caught the attention of researchers is the influence of personality information on the perceptions of physical attractiveness. For example, early research showed that certain personality dimensions, primarily extraversion and exhibition, are positively correlated with attraction ratings in initial encounters (e.g. Riggio, Friedman and DiMatteo, 1981). More recently, Kniffin and Wilson (2004) showed how the perception of physical attractiveness, based on evaluations of known individuals in high school yearbooks, was highly influenced by both familiarity and what is known about individuals in terms of their non-physical traits. In further studies, the authors showed that, in task-oriented groups, the 'perception of physical attractiveness is based largely on traits that cannot be detected from physical appearance alone' (Kniffin and Wilson, 2004, p. 98).

Other studies have examined the effect of presenting personality information concurrently with stimuli of target individuals. Gross and Crofton (1977) had participants rate the physical attractiveness of targets based on a profile containing personality and physical information. They showed that both the attractiveness of the target as well as the favourability of the personality profile had an influence on ratings of physical attractiveness. Another study employed a within-subjects design, where participants rated the attractiveness of opposite-sex facial photographs, participated in a distraction task, and then rated the same photographs again, but paired with desirable, undesirable or no personality information (Lewandowski, Aron and Gee, 2007). Results showed that positive personality information produced significant changes in ratings of physical attractiveness, such that targets were perceived as more desirable as friends and dating partners.

Three recent studies have utilised a similar design for examining the influence of personality information on body size perceptions. Swami, Greven and Furnham (2007) presented participants with line-drawn stimuli that varied in body shape and weight, as well as two levels of personality information (Extraversion versus Introversion). They report that, while there was an independent effect of each of the three variables, the variables also interacted to determine a figure's physical attractiveness. Similarly, based on ratings of the Contour Drawing Figure Rating Scale (CDFRS), Fisak, Tantleff-Dunn and Peterson (2007) show that participants chose a wider range of body sizes as being attractive for female figures described with a positive personality, compared with figures described with a negative personality or no personality information.

Finally, one study examined the influence of the personality information on perceptions of the physical attractiveness of a range of female body sizes (Swami et al., in press). A sample of over 2000 men were randomly assigned to one of 10 groups in which they received personality information (polar opposites of the 'Big Five' personality factors) about women they were rating, or a control group in which they received no personality information. Controlling for participants' age and body weight, the authors found no significant between-group differences in the body size that participants found most attractive. However, participants provided with positive personality information perceived a wider range of body sizes as physically attractive compared with the control group, whereas participants provided with negative personality information perceived a narrower range of body sizes as attractive. Taken together, the available evidence suggests that beauty is indeed more than skin-deep.

Temporal stability?

A third limitation of the WHR hypothesis is the notion of temporal stability in the preference for low WHRs, beginning with ancestral populations. For a start, it is highly unlikely that the ancestral male preference would have been for low WHRs. Ancestral human populations inhabited environmental contexts characterised by food shortages and, in such situations, individuals who were able to quickly increase their body mass (including truncal obesity, or higher WHRs) would have had an advantage in terms of health and, possibly, fertility (Wood, 2006). 'Thrifty genes' that promote rapid abdominal obesity may also have increased rates of survival during periods of severe nutritional stress (Groop, 2000). Indeed, the tendency towards higher WHRs with changing dietary patterns is shared by all hunter-gatherer populations in existence today (e.g. Clastres, 1972; Junshi *et al.*, 1990; O'Keefe and Cordain, 2004; Salzano and Callegari-Jacques, 1988).

This line of thinking is corroborated by the archaeological record of 'Venus figurines' from the Late Stone Age (Swami, 2007a). These are small figurines and representations depicting obese women with extreme WHRs (Passemard, 1938), characteristically with robust hips and buttocks and with arms and legs that are often reduced (Jelínek, 1975). In general, the figurines – like the Venus of Laussel or the Venus of Willendorf – are extremely fat-bodied and resemble a spherical ellipsoid. Given that the living conditions of the Late Stone Age were extremely difficult, characterised by nutritional stress and resource scarcity, it seems unlikely that these figures depicted the normal state of women during the period (Graziosi, 1960). Rather, it seems more likely that these obese figures were images with sexual and economic implications (Jelínek, 1975; Leroi-Gourhan, 1968; Ucko, 1962).

For instance, some research suggests that the Venus figurines may not be fertility goddesses but depictions of actual women idolised for their obesity (Sandars, 1968). This is further indicated by the fact that any likeness is noticed only in the torso; otherwise, the Venus figurines have no faces, unnaturally thin arms and no feet (Rice, 1982). Moreover, the fact that numerous examples of this type of female figure, all generally exhibiting the same essential characteristics, have been found over a broad geographical area ranging from France to Siberia suggests that some system of shared perception of a particular type of woman existed during this period in evolutionary history (Jelínek, 1975).

Whatever their ultimate attribution, these figurines are important because they suggest that our ancestors living during the Late Stone Age are unlikely to have idealised low female WHRs. Of course, like other statuettes and artistic representations, it is difficult to be entirely certain about what purpose they served in ancestral human populations (Swami, 2007a). But given that they are unlikely to have been aberrations and originate from the period during which some evolutionary psychologists claim the architecture of the human mind was 'built', their existence certainly raises very difficult questions for the WHR hypothesis of women's attractiveness.

In a similar vein, the evidence that there is temporal stability in the WHRs of *Playboy* centrefolds and Miss America pageant winners does not stand up to scrutiny (Voracek and Fisher, 2002). For instance, Freese and Meland (2002) show that the actual range of WHR values of Miss America pageant winners and *Playboy* centrefolds is much wider than what was claimed and, at the very least, the narrow ranges reported by Singh (1995b) do not encompass most of the members of either sample. Freese and Meland (2002) show, for example, that winners of the Miss America pageant had WHRs ranging from 0.61 to 0.78, whereas the overall range for *Playboy* centrefolds was even wider (0.53 to 0.79). Furthermore, correlations between WHR and a linear measure of the time of pageant victory or magazine appearance showed that the WHRs of Miss America contestants and *Playboy* centrefolds have changed over time (Freese and Meland, 2002).

This also fits with the available data showing that the idealised figures of women's bodily beauty, at least in the West, have not remained static over time (for discussions, see Calogero, Boroughs and Thompson, 2007; Fallon, 1990; Swami, 2007a). As a simple example of this, Swami, Gray and Furnham (2007) made measurements of nearly 30 female nudes depicted in paintings by the Flemish painter Pieter Pauwel Rubens, considered one of the most important artists of the seventeenth century and whose stylised plump figures became the definition of exuberant sensuality in Baroque painting (giving rise to the term 'Rubenesque'). By taking such measurements, they showed that the range of WHRs of Rubens' women were highly variable, but in general were much higher than what is considered attractive in the evolutionary psychological scheme. Nor was Rubens' taste idiosyncratic: the available evidence suggests that the 'ideal' woman in seventeenth and eighteenth century Europe was plump, even overweight, by today's standards (Swami, 2007a). Overall, such studies suggest that the preferred body shape for women has changed markedly over time (see also Box 5.9).

BOX 5.9.   MANIPULATING THE WAIST-TO-HIP RATIOS OF FAMOUS PAINTINGS AND SCULPTURES

Another way of examining preferences for waist-to-hip ratios (WHRs) is to look at the effect of manipulating the body shape of non-living representations of the human form, such as in paintings and sculptures. For example, it has been suggested that, despite local aesthetic canons, artists cross-culturally and cross-generationally have represented female WHRs in the healthy and fertile range (Singh, Davis and Randall, 2000). That is, despite differences in local taste, cultural conditions and economic factors, almost all cultures and generations share a particular notion of a low WHR as healthy and, therefore, attractive. Thus, Singh *et al.* measured the WHRs of some 300 ancient sculptures from India, Egypt, Greece and some African tribes, and found a high degree of similarity in depictions of the WHR in all four cultural groups.

One concern with this study, as Swami (2007a) points out, is that different cultural groups and historical epochs have used figurines and sculptures for very different reasons, some of which may have little to do with aesthetic tastes and canons. Swami (2007a) uses the example of the *Vénus de Milo*, perhaps one of the most famous statues in art history and one with an 'attractive' WHR in the evolutionary psychological sense, to show that there were a range of historical, religious and socio-cultural meanings associated with the statue, which make it impossible to say whether it truly was held up as an example of ideal beauty in ancient times. In short, ancient statues and sculptures may have served very different functions than those attributed to them by modern-day evolutionary psychologists.

In a different study, Swami and colleagues (2008f) digitally altered the WHRs of women in famous paintings and sculptures, creating three images for each stimulus (the original, one displaying a lower WHR and one displaying a higher WHR) (see Figure 5.6). If the WHR hypothesis of women's attractiveness were correct, one would expect that the paintings and sculptures with the lowest WHRs should be rated as most aesthetically appealing (see Henss, 2000). In their study,

Figure 5.6. *Examples of images used in the study by Swami et al. (2008f). The image in the centre is the original (Bouguereau's The Bather), the image on the left is the digitally altered version with a low WHR ratio, and the image on the right is the digitally altered version with a high WHR.*

however, Swami *et al.* (2008f) found that both men and women considered the original and, in some cases, the image with the higher WHR as the most aesthetically pleasing. Overall, the authors suggest that there was no discernible preference for low WHRs; rather, they argue that the original paintings and sculptures used in their study demonstrated an 'optimal aesthetic configuration' (see Locher, 2003) that increases aesthetic appeal.

Cross-cultural and within-culture preferences

Given that a central claim of the WHR hypothesis is that it first evolved among ancestral populations, evolutionary psychologists have been keen to test WHR preferences among contemporary hunter-gatherer and forager groups that most closely approximate the living conditions of our ancestors. *Pace* the limitations of line drawings discussed above, most studies conducted among hunter-gatherer populations have found a preference for high, rather than low, female WHRs. Using Singh's original line drawings, for instance, Yu and Shepard (1998) report that the Matsigenka of Peru ranked the figures first by weight (heavyweight preferred over underweight) and only then ranked high WHR over low WHR. These authors were also able to show that the preference for low WHRs varied as a function of exposure to Westernisation, there being no significant difference in attractiveness preferences between a Westernised group of Matsigenka and men in the United States.

Similarly, Wetsman and Marlowe (1999) show that, among the Hadza of Tanzania, the size of the WHR did not affect men's judgements of attractiveness when using line drawings. Instead, the Hadza preferred heavy- over medium- and medium- over lightweight line drawings when selecting for attractiveness, health and desirability as a wife, regardless of WHR. In a more recent study, also with line drawings in which only the WHR was varied, Marlowe and Wetsman (2001) report that Hadza men still preferred high over low WHRs, which may be explained as a function of their preference for heavier body weights (given that WHR and body weight were likely covaried in their stimuli).

One recent explanation for these cross-cultural differences in preferred WHR was put forward by Marlowe, Apicella and Reed (2005), who point out that most previous studies of the WHR hypothesis have tended to use line drawings of women seen in frontal view, but that this obscures potentially important cues to the WHR provided by buttocks protrusion. Using images of women in profile, they found that the Hadza actually preferred a lower profile WHR (i.e. more protruding buttocks) than American men, which contrasts with their preference for a higher frontal WHR (Marlowe and Wetsman, 2001; Wetsman and Marlowe, 1999). As a result, there may be less disparity in their theoretical preferences for actual WHR, which they considered similar across cultures.

This conclusion, however, should be interpreted with caution. First, as some authors have noted (e.g. Swami and Tovée 2007c; Swami et al., 2009b), the stimuli developed by Marlowe, Apicella and Reed (2005) confound buttocks protrusion with perceived body weight (i.e. as buttocks protrusion increases, so does apparent body weight). Moreover, the available evidence concerning judgements of profile WHR is equivocal: other studies using photographic stimuli of women in profile have found that the WHR is a negligible predictor of attractiveness ratings, in contexts of both high (Tovée and Cornelissen, 2001; see also Furnham and Swami, 2007) and low socioeconomic status (Swami and Tovée, 2007c). Thus, an alternative explanation for the findings of Marlowe, Apicella and Reed (2005) are that the Hadza prefer heavier women, which in their study manifested itself as a preference for lower profile WHRs.

A different explanation for cross-cultural differences in WHR preferences relies on the notion of calibration to local conditions. In one contribution to the literature, Sugiyama (2004) notes that forager women have high fecundity, parasite loads and caloric dependence on fibrous foods, all of which increase their WHRs. If mate selection calibrates for local conditions, then WHR-preference modules should assess the local distribution of female WHR and recalibrate as conditions change. Instead of expecting uniform cross-cultural preference for low WHRs, researchers should anticipate only that WHR values lower than the local average will be attractive.

Thus, taking into account the local distribution of Ecuadorian Shiwiar WHRs, Sugiyama (2004) found that Shiwiar men use female WHRs in a way that is consistent with the hypothesis that WHR assessment is sensitively calibrated to local parameters. The average female WHR of the Shiwiar is not as low as typically found in Western societies, although the average female WHR was still lower than the average male WHR. When Shiwiar men were asked to judge a set of photographic images of women, Sugiyama (2004) found that they judged overweight figures with a low WHR as physically attractive. When differences in body weight were minimised, Shiwiar men preferred lower-than-locally-average female WHRs.

The concept of facultative adjustments in WHRs is currently the only plausible way of reconciling the WHR hypothesis with evidence of cross-cultural differences in WHR preferences (Sugiyama, 2005; see also Box 5.10). Even setting aside concerns with the ultimate existence of mental modules that calibrate WHR preferences (see above), it should be noted that not all studies have reached similar conclusions to that of Sugiyama (2004). For instance, using photographic stimuli, Swami and Tovée (2005a) show that, controlling for body weight, high WHRs were preferred over low WHRs among rural villagers in Malaysia (these authors, however, did not measure the local distribution of WHRs). Similar results have been reported using different stimulus sets (e.g. Swami and Tovée, 2007c) and among other tribal, rural and forager

BOX 5.10.   DO WAIST-TO-HIP RATIOS PREDICT CHILD SEX?

One early, but now seemingly obsolete, explanation of cross-cultural differences in waist-to-hip ratio (WHR) preferences rested on the WHR acting as a predictor of child sex. A high pre-conceptual WHR was said to be a good predictor of having a male child, and so in cultures that 'value' male children, an androgynous (or high) WHR should be judged as more attractive. This predictive value of WHR is based on studies measuring women who already have children and correlating their WHRs with the proportion of existing male children. Thus, three studies suggested that women with high WHRs tended to have more sons, and that the preference for women with a high WHR may, therefore, result in selection for increased testosterone levels in children (Manning, Anderton and Washington, 1996; Manning *et al.*, 1999; Singh and Zambarano, 1997).

However, an important limitation of these studies is that carrying a male child may alter the WHR in a different way to carrying a female child. If this is correct, then a high WHR may be an effect, rather than a cause, of a child's sex. To test the predictive power of pre-conceptual WHR and offspring gender, Tovée, Brown and Jacobs (2001) took WHR measures from almost 500 women who intended to become pregnant and correlated this with the sex of the subsequent child. They found no significant correlation, suggesting that WHR does not act as a predictor of child sex. In recent years, support for the child-sex-predictor hypothesis of the WHR has consequently waned.

groups (e.g. Swami and Tovée, 2007a, 2007b; Swami *et al.*, 2007a; Tovée, Furnham and Swami, 2007; Tovée *et al.*, 2006).

Even accepting evidence of cross-cultural differences in WHR preferences, most supporters of the WHR hypothesis maintain that there will be no major differences in preferences within cultures. This prediction, too, has been proved incorrect. For one thing, a small body of work has shown that there are individual differences in WHR preferences: differences in the strength of preference for low WHRs have been found as a function of 'power motive' (a predisposition to strive for status and power; Schmalt, 2006), ethnic identity (Freedman *et al.*, 2004; see also Swami *et al.*, 2009b) and sociosexuality (see Brase and Walker, 2004). In terms of the latter, for instance, one study showed that men with a restricted sociosexual style (i.e. requiring high emotional investment and prolonged courtship before engaging in sexual relations) preferred a higher female WHR than unrestricted men (i.e. men who were more willing to engage in sexual relations in the absence of commitment) (Swami *et al.*, 2008c).

Other work has shown that men involved in particular subcultures may idealise significantly heavier WHRs. For instance, Swami and colleagues (Swami and Furnham, 2009b; Swami and Tovée, 2009) have examined the WHR preferences of male 'fat admirers', that is men who are sexually attracted to heavier female partners. Although the preferences of fat admirers can be wide-ranging, a consistent thread appears to be their preferences for heavier (often overweight or even morbidly obese) bodies and, in conjunction, higher female WHRs. Using line drawings, for example, Swami and Furnham (2009b) report that fat admirers rated figures first by weight (overweight preferred over underweight) and then by WHR (high WHRs over low WHRs). These studies with fat admirers appear to be the first to document marked within-culture differences in WHR preferences and show how involvement with particular subgroups can lead to different aesthetic preferences.

Summary

It seems to us that the WHR hypothesis of women's attractiveness exemplifies some of the worst recesses of evolutionary psychological thinking: a misleading adaptive story coupled with poor theoretical exactitude and insufficiently grounded empirical data. But if we accept that the WHR plays a negligible role in perceptions of women's attractiveness, then a necessary question that arises is: what role *does* the WHR play in attractiveness judgements? The most likely answer, given that the WHR is sexually dimorphic post-puberty, is that the WHR plays a role in distinguishing broad categories of individuals, particularly between women and men (other examples may include distinguishing pregnant from non-pregnant women) (Johnson and Tassinary, 2007; Tovée *et al.*, 2002; see also Voracek and Fisher, 2006).

In an interesting study of this possibility, Johnson and Tassinary (2007) had participants judge the sex and gender of humanoid animations that depicted a person walking in place. These 'walkers' varied in their WHR as well as their walk motion (there were five types of gait, from a masculine shoulder 'swagger' to a feminine hip 'sway'). Their results showed that sex judgements were tightly coupled to WHR, but only moderately coupled to body motion. Gender judgements, on the other hand, were strongly related to body motion, but were also moderately related to WHR. In short, although related both to sex and gender judgements, the WHR appeared to be the primary cue used to make sex category judgements.

In a second experiment, Johnson and Tassinary (2007) presented participants with the same set of walkers but in which the sex of the figure was either specified or unspecified. Using an eye-tracking design, they were able to measure the distribution of visual scanning within four critical areas of the body in both tasks (the head, the chest, the waist and hips, and the legs). The results of their study showed that, when the sex of the figure was unspecified, participants spent more time scanning the waist and hips. But when the sex of the walker was specified, visual scanning of the waist and hip region dropped to chance levels and was significantly lower than scanning of the region when sex was unspecified. In other words, participants appeared to be scanning the waist and hip region only when doing so was necessary to learn the target's sex.

Johnson and Tassinary (2007) go on to explain their results under the rubric of 'social metaperception'. They argue that the waist and hips are primarily involved in judgements of sex, for both women and men, and that such judgements can be understood as a cognitive process of social categorisation. Once this process of social categorisation is completed, attractiveness judgements are formed on the basis of additional bodily cues. Specifically, individuals are considered 'attractive' if they have a body motion that is consistent with their sex (i.e. women are judged as attractive when they have a feminine body motion, whereas men are judged as attractive when they are masculine in body motion) and if they fall within socioculturally defined ideal body size ranges. Importantly, their model does not specify whether preferences for specific body motions and sizes are the result of mate choice adaptations or sociocultural influences, but it does specify a common cognitive mechanism that can result in culture-specific preferences. In other words, judgements of both women and men arise from a common psychological mechanism, rather than a psychological adaptation that is unique to male psychology, and more generally the model requires no adaptationist theorising.

CONCLUSION AND FUTURE DIRECTIONS

In this chapter, we have seen how an evolutionary perspective has helped shape discussions of human physical attractiveness. In our view, this body of research exemplifies both the best and worst examples of scientific research based on an evolutionary framework. While the large body of work on facial attractiveness typifies the best research that evolutionary psychology has to offer, work on bodily attractiveness has been mired in seemingly endless permutations of the WHR hypothesis. Indeed, the debates around the utility of the WHR hypothesis contain important lessons for researchers working within an evolutionary psychological framework, particularly that of accepting diversity and the need for theoretical certainty and empirical fortitude.

Moreover, there are several ways in which an evolutionary approach to human beauty can become more rounded and appealing. First, it will need to take into account a multitude of factors in the shaping of attractiveness preferences. For example, recent work has highlighted the combined effects of individual difference factors (e.g. Swami *et al.*, 2008d; see also Swami *et al.*, 2008c), proprioceptive physiology (e.g. Nelson and Morrison, 2005; Swami and Tovée, 2006; Swami, Poulogianni and Furnham, 2006) and sociocultural factors (eating habits: Swami *et al.*, 2007b; gender role stereotyping: Furnham and Nordling, 1998; Swami *et al.*, 2006a, 2006b; media exposure: Swami *et al.*, 2009a; national differences: Furnham and Nordling, 1998; Swami *et al.*, 2007d, 2008e; socioeconomic status: Swami and Tovée, 2005a, 2005b, 2007a, 2007b, 2007c; Swami *et al.*, 2006a, 2006b, 2007a, 2007b, 2009a; Tovée, Furnham and Swami, 2007; Tovée *et al.*, 2006) in shaping body size preferences. Such work has the potential to provide an overarching framework for understanding attractiveness judgements, but researchers have generally not sought to combine perspectives in their work.

Much of the current literature also retains a focus on objective criteria of attractiveness, a throwback it would seem to the Pythagorean view of beauty as a matter of having the right mathematical proportions. However, by definition and in part at least, beauty remains in the eye of the beholder and requires greater attention on individual difference correlates of attractiveness judgements. Such work would also do well to examine the relationship between perceptions of the self and others. Recent work, for instance, has documented a positive illusion in romantic partner perceptions, such that partners are typically perceived as more physically attractive than the self on a range of body components – what Swami and colleagues have termed the 'love-is-blind bias' (Swami, 2009; Swami and Furnham, 2008b; Swami *et al.*, 2007e, 2009c). The time is also ripe for different methodological paradigms other than rating studies, including observational techniques (e.g. Gueguen, 2007).

Finally, contemporary discussions of physical attractiveness from an evolutionary psychological perspective have tended not to consider practical applications of this research. Given the large number of individuals who report body dissatisfaction and symptoms of negative body image, there is a need to better understand the relationship between perceptions of attractiveness and psychological functioning. More generally, it is our view that psychologists have a role to play in challenging the notion of ideal beauty and showing how and when beauty ideals can be challenged and changed.

REFERENCES

Alley, T. R. and Cunningham, M. R. (1991). Averaged faces are attractive but very attractive faces are not average. *Psychological Science, 2*, 123–5.

Apicella, C., Little, A. C. and Marlowe, F. (2007). Facial averageness and attractiveness in an isolated population of hunter-gatherers. *Perception, 36*, 1813–1820.

Armstrong, J. (2004). *The secret power of beauty*. London: Penguin.

Bailey, S. M., Goldberg, J. P., Swap, W. C. *et al.* (1990). Relationships between body dissatisfaction and physical measurements. *International Journal of Eating Disorders, 9*, 457–61.

Bakker, T. C. M., Künzler, R. and Mazzi, D. (1999). Condition-related mate choice in sticklebacks. *Nature, 401*, 234.

Baudouin, J. Y. and Tiberghien, G. (2004). Symmetry, averageness and feature size in the facial attractiveness of women. *Acta Psychologica, 117*, 313–332.

Bateson, M., Cornelissen, P. L. and Tovée, M. J. (2007). Methodological issues in studies of female attractiveness. In V. Swami and A. Furnham (eds), *The body beautiful: Evolutionary and sociocultural perspectives* (pp. 46–62). Basingstoke: Palgrave Macmillan.

Beckerman, S. (2000). Mating and marriage, husbands and lovers: Commentary on Gangestad and Simpson (2000). *Behavioral and Brain Sciences, 23*, 590–591.

Bellis, M. A. and Baker, R. R. (1990). Do females promote sperm competition? Data for humans. *Animal Behaviour, 40*, 997–9.

Benson, P. and Perrett, D. (1992). Face to face with the perfect image. *New Scientist, 1809*, 32–5.

Berry, D. S. and McArthur, L. Z. (1985). Some components and consequences of a baby face. *Journal of Personality and Social Psychology, 48*, 312–323.

Bigaard, J., Frederiksen, K., Tjonneland, A. *et al.* (2004). Waist and hip circumferences and all-cause mortality: Usefulness of the waist-to-hip ratio? *International Journal of Obesity, 28*, 741–7.

Björntorp, P. (1987). Fat cell distribution and metabolism. In R. J. Wurtman and J. J. Wurtman (eds), *Human Obesity* (pp. 66–72). New York: New York Academy of Sciences.

Björntorp, P. (1991). Adipose tissue distribution and function. *International Journal of Obesity, 15*, 67–81.

Björntorp, P. (1997). Body fat distribution, insulin resistance and metabolic disease. *Nutrition, 13*, 795–803.

Blake, R. and Shiffrar, M. (2006). Perception of human motion. *Annual Review of Psychology, 58*, 47–73.

Boas, F. (1955). *Primitive art*. New York: Dover Publications.

Booth, A. and Dabbs, J. M. (1993). Testosterone and men's marriages. *Social Forces, 72*, 463–77.

Boothroyd, L. G., Jones, B. C., Burt, D. M. and Perrett, D. I. (2007). Partner characteristics associated with masculinity, health and maturity in faces. *Personality and Individual Differences, 43*, 1161–73.

Brase, G. L. and Walker, G. (2004). Male sexual strategies modify ratings of female models with specific waist-to-hip ratios. *Human Nature, 15*, 209–24.

Buller, D. J. (2005). *Adapting minds: Evolutionary psychology and the persistent quest for human nature*. Cambridge, MA: MIT Press.

Buss, D. (1989). Sex differences in human mate preferences: Evolutionary hypotheses tested in 37 cultures. *Behavioural and Brain Sciences, 12*, 1–49.

Buss, D. (1994). *The evolution of desire*. New York: Basic Books.

Buss, D. (1999). *Evolutionary psychology: The new science of the mind*. Boston: Allyn & Bacon.

Buston, P. M. and Emlen, S. T. (2003). Cognitive processes underlying mate choice: The relationship between self perception and mate preference in Western society. *Proceedings of the National Academy of Science, USA, 110*, 8805–8810.

Calogero, R. M., Boroughs, M. and Thompson, J. K. (2007). The impact of Western beauty ideals on the lives of women: A sociocultural perspective. In V. Swami and A. Furnham (eds), *The body beautiful: Evolutionary and sociocultural perspectives* (pp. 259–98). Basingstoke: Palgrave Macmillan.

Cárdenas, R. A. and Harris, L. J. (2006). Symmetrical decorations enhance the attractiveness of faces and abstract designs. *Evolution and Human Behavior, 27*, 1–18.

Cash, T. F. and Soloway, D. (1975). Self-disclosure and correlates of physical attractiveness: An exploratory study. *Psychological Reports, 36*, 579–86.

Cash, T. F., Kerr, J. A., Polyson, J. and Freeman, V. (1977). Role of physical attractiveness in peer attribution of psychological disturbance. *Journal of Consulting and Clinical Psychology, 45*, 987–93.

Clastres, P. (1972). The Guayaki. In M. Biccheri (ed.), *Hunters and gatherers today* (pp. 138–74). New York: Holt, Rinehart and Winston.

Conway, C. A., Jones, B. C., DeBruine, L. M. *et al.* (2008). Integrating physical and social cues when forming face preferences: Differences among low and high anxiety individuals. *Social Neuroscience, 1*, 89–95.

Cornelissen, P. L., Tovée, M. J. and Bateson, M. (2008). Patterns of subcutaneous fat deposition and the relationship between body mass index and waist-to-hip ratio: Implications for models of physical attractiveness. *Journal of Theoretical Biology, 256*, 343–50.

Cosmides, L. and Tooby, J. (1995). From function to structure: The role of evolutionary biology and computational theories in cognitive neuroscience. In M. Gazzaniga (ed.), *The cognitive neurosciences* (pp. 1199–210). Cambridge, MA: MIT Press.

Cunningham, M. R. (1986). Measuring the physical in physical attractiveness: Quasi-experiments on the socio-biology of female facial beauty. *Journal of Personality and Social Psychology, 50*, 925–35.

Cunningham, M. R., Barbee, A. P. and Pike, C. L. (1990). What do women want? Facialmetric assessment of multiple motives in the perception of male facial physical attractiveness. *Journal of Personality and Social Psychology, 59*, 61–72.

Cunningham, M. R., Roberts, A. R., Barbee, A. P. *et al.* (1995). 'Their ideas of beauty are, on the whole, the same as ours': consistency and variability in the crosscultural perception of female physical attractiveness. *Journal of Personality and Social Psychology, 68*, 261–79.

Dabbs, J. M. and Morris, R. (1990). Testosterone, social class and anti-social behaviour in a sample of 4,462 men. *Psychological Science, 1*, 209–11.

Danel, D. and Pawłowski, B. (2006). Attractiveness of men's faces in relation to women's phase of menstrual cycle. *Collegium Anthropologicum, 30*, 285–9.

DeBruine, L. (2004). Facial resemblance increases the attractiveness of same-sex faces more than other-sex faces. *Proceedings of the Royal Society B, 271*, 2085–90.

DeBruine, L. M., Jones, B. C., Unger, L. *et al.* (2007). Dissociating averageness and attractiveness: Attractive faces are not always average. *Journal of Experimental Psychology: Human Perception and Performance, 33*, 1420–1430.

Denny, K. (2008). Beauty and intelligence may – or may not – be related. *Intelligence, 36*, 616–618.

Dion, K. K. (1972). Physical attractiveness and evaluation of children's transgressions. *Journal of Personality and Social Psychology, 24*, 285–90.

Dion, K. K. (1974). Children's physical attractiveness and sex as determinants of adult punitiveness. *Developmental Psychology, 10*, 772–8.

Dion, K. K., Berscheid, E. and Walster, E. (1972). What is beautiful is good. *Journal of Personality and Social Psychology, 24*, 285–90.

Dipboye, R. L., Fromkin, H. L. and Wiback, K. (1975). Relative importance of applicant sex, attractiveness and scholastic standing in evaluation of job applicant resumes. *Journal of Applied Psychology, 60*, 39–43.

Downing, P. E., Chan, A. W., Peelen, M. V. *et al.* (2006). Domain specificity in visual cortex. *Cerebral Cortex, 16*, 1453–61.

Downing, P. E., Jiang, Y., Shuman, M. and Kanwisher, N. (2001). A cortical area selective for visual processing of the human body. *Science, 293*, 2470–2473.

Eagly, E. H., Ashmore, R. D., Makhijani, M. G. and Longo, L. C. (1991). What is beautiful is good, but . . . A meta-analytic review of research on the physical attractiveness stereotype. *Psychological Bulletin, 110*, 109–28.

Eaton, S. B., Eaton, S. B., III and Konner, M. J. (1997). Paleolithic nutrition revisited: A twelve-year retrospective on its nature and implications. *European Journal of Clinical Nutrition, 51*, 207–16.

Eijkemans, M. J. C., Imani, B. A., Mulders, A. G. M. *et al.* (2003). High singleton live birth rate following classical ovulation induction in normogonadotrophic anovulatory infertility. *Human Reproduction, 18*, 2357–62.

Enlow, D. H. (1990). *Facial growth*. Philadelphia: W. B. Saunders.

Fan, J., Liu, F., Wu, J. and Dai, W. (2004). Visual perception of female physical attractiveness. *Proceedings of the Royal Society B, 271*, 347–52.

Fan, J. T. (2007). The volume-height index as a body attractiveness index. In. V. Swami and A. Furnham (eds), *The body beautiful: Evolutionary and socio-cultural perspectives* (pp. 29–45). Basingstoke: Palgrave Macmillan.

Farah, M. J. (1996). Is face recognition 'special'? Evidence from neuropsychology. *Behavior and Brain Research, 76*, 181–9.

Farkas, L. G. (1988). Age- and sex-related changes in facial proportions. In L. G. Farkas and I. R. Munro (eds), *Anthropometric proportions in medicine* (pp. 29–56). Springfield, IL: Charles C. Thomas.

Feingold, A. (1992). Good-looking people are not what we think. *Psychological Bulletin, 111*, 304–41.

Ferrario, V. F., Sforza, C., Poggio, C. E. and Tartaglia, G. (1995). Facial morphology of television actresses compared with normal women. *Journal of Oral and Maxillofacial Surgery, 53*, 1008–14.

Fink, B., Grammer, K. and Matts, P. J. (2006). Visual skin color distribution plays a role in the perception of age, attractiveness, and health of female faces. *Evolution and Human Behavior, 27*, 433–42.

Fink, B., Grammer, K. and Thornhill, R. (2001). Human (*Homo sapiens*) facial attractiveness in relation to skin texture and color. *Journal of Comparative Psychology, 115*, 92–9.

Fink, B. and Matts, P. J. (2008). The effects of skin colour distribution and topography cues on the perception of female facial age and health. *Journal of the European Academy of Dermatology and Venerology, 22*, 493–8.

Fink, B., Matts, P. J., Klingenberg, H. *et al.* (2008). Visual attention to variation in female facial skin colour distribution. *Journal of Cosmetic Dermatology, 7*, 155–61.

Fink, B. and Penton-Voak, I. S. (2002). Evolutionary psychology of facial attractiveness. *Current Directions in Psychological Science, 11*, 154–8.

Fink, B., Neave, N., Manning, J. T. and Grammer, K. (2006). Facial symmetry and judgements of attractiveness, health and personality. *Personality and Individual Differences, 41*, 491–9.

Fisak, B., Jr., Tantleff-Dunn, S. and Peterson, R. D. (2007). Personality information: Does it influence attractiveness ratings of various body sizes? *Body Image, 4*, 213–217.

Fleming, A. S., Corter, C., Stallings, J. and Steiner, M. (2002). Testosterone and prolactin are associated with emotional responses to infant cries in new fathers. *Hormones and Behavior, 42*, 399–413.

Folsom, A. R., Kaye, S. A., Sellers, T. A. *et al.* (1993). Body fat distribution and 5-year risk of death in older women. *Journal of the American Medical Association, 269*, 483–7.

Fölstad, I. and Karter, A. J. (1992). Parasites, bright males, and the immunocompetence handicap. *American Naturalist, 139*, 603–22.

Forestell, C. A., Humphrey, T. M. and Stewart, S. H. (2004). Involvement of body weight and shape factors in ratings of attractiveness by women: A replication and extension of Tassinary and Hansen (1998). *Personality and Individual Differences, 36*, 295–305.

Frederick, D. A., Peplau, L. A. and Lever, J. (2006). The swimsuit issue: Correlates of body image in a sample of 52,677 heterosexual adults. *Body Image, 4*, 413–419.

Freedman, R. E. K., Carter, M. M., Sbrocco, T. and Gray, J. J. (2004). Ethnic differences in preferences for female weight and waist-to-hip ratio: A comparison of African-American and White American college and community samples. *Eating Behaviors, 5*, 191–8.

Freese, J. (2000). *What should sociobiology do about Darwin? Evaluating some potential contributions of sociobiology and evolutionary psychology to sociology.* Doctoral dissertation, Indiana University, Indiana.

Freese, J. and Meland, S. (2002). Seven-tenths incorrect: Heterogeneity and change in the waist-to-hip ratios of *Playboy* centrefold models and Miss America pageant winners. *Journal of Sex Research, 39*, 133–8.

Fujimoto, A., Allanson, J., Crowe, C. A. *et al.* (1992). Natural history of mosaic trisomy 14 syndrome. *American Journal of Medical Genetics, 44*, 189–96.

Furnham, A., Dias, M. and McClelland, A. (1998). The role of body weight, waist-to-hip ratio, and breast size in judgments of female attractiveness. *Sex Roles, 34*, 311–326.

Furnham, A., Lavancy, M. and McClelland, A. (2001). Waist-to-hip ratio and facial attractiveness. *Personality and Individual Differences, 30*, 491–502.

Furnham, A., Moutafi, J. and Baguma, P. (2002). A cross-cultural study on the role of weight and waist-to-hip ratio on judgements of women's attractiveness. *Personality and Individual Differences, 32*, 729–45.

Furnham, A. and Nordling, R. (1998). Cross-cultural differences in preferences for specific male and female body shapes. *Personality and Individual Differences, 25*, 635–48.

Furnham, A., Petrides, K. V. and Constantinides, A. (2005). The effects of body mass index and waist-to-hip ratio on ratings of female attractiveness, fecundity and health. *Personality & Individual Differences, 38*, 1823–34.

Furnham, A. and Reeves, E. (2006). The relative influence of facial neoteny and waist-to-hip ratio on judgements of female attractiveness and fecundity. *Psychology, Health and Medicine, 11*, 129–41.

Furnham, A. and Swami, V. (2007). Perceptions of female buttocks and breast size in profile. *Social Behavior and Personality*, *35*, 1–8.

Furnham, A., Swami, V. and Shah, K. (2006). Female body correlates of attractiveness and other ratings. *Personality and Individual Differences*, *41*, 443–54.

Furnham, A., Tan, T. and McManus, C. (1997). Waist-to-hip ratio and preferences for body shape: A replication and extension. *Personal and Individual Differences*, *22*, 539–49.

Galton, F. (1878). Composite portraits. *Journal of the Anthropological Institute of Great Britain and Ireland*, *8*, 132–44.

Gangestad, S. W. and Buss, D. M. (1993). Pathogen prevalence and human mate preferences. *Ethology and Sociobiology*, *14*, 89–96.

Gangestad, S. W. and Scheyd, G. J. (2005). The evolution of human physical attractiveness. *Annual Review of Anthropology*, *34*, 523–48.

Gangestad, S. W. and Thornhill, R. (1998). Menstrual cycle variation in women's preferences for the scent of symmetrical men. *Proceedings of the Royal Society B*, *265*, 727–33.

Gangestad, S. W. and Thornhill, R. (2003). Facial masculinity and fluctuating asymmetry. *Evolution and Human Behavior*, *24*, 231–41.

Gangestad, S. W., Simpson, J. A., Cousins, A. J. *et al.* (2004). Women's preferences for male behavioural displays change across the menstrual cycle. *Psychological Science*, *15*, 203–7.

Garver-Apgar, C. E., Gangestad, S. W. and Thornhill, R. (2008). Hormonal correlates of women's mid-cycle preference for the scent of symmetry. *Evolution and Human Behavior*, *49*, 509–18.

Gaut, B. and Lopes, D. M. (2001). *The Routledge companion to aesthetics*. London: Routledge.

Gould, S. J. (1997). Evolution: The pleasures of pluralism. *New York Review of Books*, 47–52.

Grammer, K. and Thornhill, R. (1994). Human (*Homo sapiens*) facial attractiveness and sexual selection: The role of symmetry and averageness. *Journal of Comparative Psychology*, *108*, 233–42.

Gray, R. D., Heaney, M. and Fairhall, S. (2003). Evolutionary Psychology and the challenge of adaptive explanation. In K. Sterelny and J. Fitness (eds), *From mating to mentality: Evaluating evolutionary psychology* (pp. 247–68). London: Psychology Press.

Graziosi, P. (1960). *Palaeolithic art*. New York: McGraw-Hill.

Groop, L. (2000). Genetics of the metabolic syndrome. *British Journal of Nutrition*, *83*, S39–S48.

Gross, A. E. and Crofton, C. (1977). What is good is beautiful. *Sociometry*, *40*, 85–90.

Grossman, C. J. (1985). Interactions between the gonadal steroids and the immune system. *Science*, *227*, 257–61.

Gueguen, N. (2007). Women's bust size and men's courtship solicitation. *Body Image*, *4*, 386–90.

Hamermesh, D. and Biddle, J. E. (1994). Beauty and the labor market. *American Economic Review*, *84*, 1174–994.

Hamermesh, D. and Parker, A. M. (2005). Beauty in the classroom: Professor's pulchritude and putative pedagogial productivity. *Economics of Education Review*, *24*, 369–76.

Hamilton, W. D. and Zuk, M. (1982). Heritable true fitness and bright birds: A role for parasites? *Science*, *218*, 384–7.

Hansen, L. T. T., Amundsen, T. and Forsgren, E. (1999). Symmetry: Attractive not only to females. *Proceedings of the Royal Society B*, *266*, 1235–40.

Henss, R. (1995). Waist-to-hip ratio and attractiveness: Replication and extension. *Personality and Individual Differences*, *19*, 479–88.

Henss, R. (2000). Waist-to-hip ratio and female attractiveness: Evidence from photographic stimuli and methodological considerations. *Personality and Individual Differences*, *28*, 501–13.

van Hooff, M. H. A., Voorhorst, F. J., Kaptein, M. B. H. and Hirasing, R. A. (1999). Endocrine features of polycystic ovary syndrome in a random population sample of 14–16 year old adolescents. *Human Reproduction*, *14*, 2223–9.

van Hooff, M. H. A., Voorhorst, F. J., Kaptein, M. B. H. *et al.* (2000a). Insulin, androgen, and gonadotropin concentrations, body mass index, and waist to hip ratio in the first years after menarche in girls with regular menstrual cycles, irregular menstrual cycles, or oligomenorrhea. *Journal of Clinical Endocrinology and Metabolism*, *85*, 1394–400.

van Hooff, M. H. A., Voorhorst, F. J., Kaptein, M. B. H. *et al.* (2000b). Polycystic ovaries in adolescents and the relationship with menstrual cycle patterns, luteinizing hormone, androgens, and insulin. *Fertility and Sterility*, *74*, 49–58.

Hosoda, M., Stone-Romero, E. F. and Coats, G. (2003). The effects of physical attractiveness on job-related outcomes: A meta-analysis of experimental studies. *Personnel Psychology*, *56*, 431–62.

Huang, Z., Willet, W. C. and Colditz, G. A. (1999). Waist circumference, waist:hip ratio, and risk of breast cancer in the Nurses' Health Study. *American Journal of Epidemiology*, *150*, 1316–1324.

Jacobsen, T. and Höfel, L. (2001). Aesthetic electrified: An analysis of descriptive symmetry and evaluative aesthetic judgement processes using event-related brain potentials. *Empirical Studies of the Arts*, *19*, 177–90.

Jelínek, J. (1975). *The pictorial encyclopedia of the evolution of man*. London: Hamlyn.

Johnson, K. L. and Tassinary, L. G. (2007). Interpersonal metaperception: The importance of compatability in the aesthetic appreciation of bodily cues. In V. Swami and A. Furnham (eds), *The body beautiful: Evolutionary and sociocultural perspectives* (pp. 159–84). Basingstoke: Palgrave Macmillan.

Johnston, V. S. and Franklin, M. (1993). Is beauty in the eye of the beholder? *Ethology and Sociobiology*, *14*, 183–99.

Johnston, V. S., Hagel, R., Franklin, M. *et al.* (2001). Male facial attractiveness: Evidence for a hormone-mediated adaptive design. *Evolution and Human Behaviour*, *22*, 251–67.

Jones, B. C., DeBruine, L. M. and Little, A. C. (2007). The role of symmetry in attraction to average faces. *Perception and Psychophysics*, *69*, 1273–7.

Jones, B. C., DeBruine, L. M. and Little, A. C. (2008). Adaptation reinforces preferences for attractive faces. *Visual Cognition*, *16*, 849–58.

Jones, B. C., DeBruine, L. M., Little, A. C. and Feinberg, D. R. (2006). Integrating gaze direction and expression in preferences for attractive faces. *Psychological Science*, *17*, 588–91.

Jones, B. C., DeBruine, L. M., Little, A. C. *et al.* (2007a). Social transmission of face preferences influences judgments of attractiveness in humans. *Proceedings of the Royal Society B*, *274*, 899–903.

Jones, B. C., DeBruine, L. M., Little, A. C. and Feinberg, D. R. (2007b). The valence of experiences with faces influences generalized preferences. *Journal of Evolutionary Psychology*, *1–4*, 119–130.

Jones, B. C., DeBruine, L. M., Perrett, D. I. *et al.* (2008). Effects of menstrual cycle phase on face preferences. *Archives of Sexual Behaviour*, *37*, 78–84.

Jones, B. C., Little, A. C., Boothroyd, L. *et al.* (2005). Women's physical and psychological condition independently predict their preference for apparent health in faces. *Evolution and Human Behavior*, *26*, 451–7.

Jones, B. C., Little, A. C., Feinberg, D. L. *et al.* (2004). The relationship between shape symmetry and perceived skin condition in male facial attractiveness. *Evolution and Human Behavior, 25*, 24–30.

Jones, D. and Hill, K. (1993). Criteria of facial attractiveness in five populations. *Human Nature, 4*, 271–96.

Jones, P. R. M., Hunt, M. J., Brown, T. P. and Norgan, N. G. (1986). Waist-hip circumference ratio and its relation to age and overweight in British men. *Human Nutrition: Clinical Nutrition, 40*, 239–47.

Julian, T. and McKenry, P. C. (1989). Relationship of testosterone to men's family functioning at mid-life: A research note. *Aggressive Behaviour, 15*, 281–9.

Junshi, C., Campbell, T. C., Junyao, L. and Peto, R. (1990). *Diet, life-style and mortality in China.* Oxford: Oxford University Press.

Kanazawa, S. and Kovar, J. L. (2004). Why beautiful people are more intelligent. *Intelligence, 32*, 227–43.

Kanda, N., Tsuchida, T. and Tamaki, K. (1996). Testosterone inhibits immunoglobulin production by human peripheral blood mononuclear cells. *Clinical and Experimental Immunology, 106*, 410–415.

Kaye, S. A., Folsom, A. R., Prineas, R. J. and Gapstur, S. M. (1990). The association of body fat distribution with lifestyle and reproductive factors in a population study of postmenopausal women. *International Journal of Obesity, 14*, 583–91.

Kniffin, K. M. and Wilson, D. S. (2004). The effect of non-physical traits on the perception of physical attractiveness: Three naturalistic studies. *Evolution and Human Behavior, 25*, 88–101.

Koehler, N., Simmons, L. W., Rhodes, G. and Peters, M. (2004). The relationship between sexual dimorphism in human faces and fluctuating asymmetry. *Proceedings of the Royal Society B, 271*, S223–6.

Kowner, R. (1996). Facial asymmetry and attractiveness judgment in developmental perspective. *Journal of Experimental Psychology: Human Perception and Performance, 22*, 662–75.

Laland, K. N. and Brown, G. R. (2002). *Sense and nonsense: Evolutionary perspectives on human behaviour.* Oxford: Oxford University Press.

Landy, D. and Sigall, H. (1974). Beauty is talent: Task evaluation as a function of the performer's physical attractiveness. *Journal of Personality and Social Psychology, 29*, 299–304.

Langlois, J. H. and Roggman, L. A. (1990). Attractive faces are only average. *Psychological Science, 1*, 115–121.

Langlois, J. H., Ritter, J. M., Roggman, L. A. and Vaughn, L. S. (1991). Facial diversity and infant preferences for attractive faces. *Developmental Psychology, 27*, 79–84.

Langlois, J. H., Roggman, L. A. and Musselman, L. (1994). What is average and what is not average about attractive faces? *Psychological Science, 5*, 214–220.

Langlois, J. H., Kalakanis, L. E., Rubenstein, A. J. *et al.* (2000). Maxims and myths of beauty: A meta-analytic and theoretical review. *Psychological Bulletin, 126*, 390–423.

Lanska, D. J., Lanska, M. J., Hartz, A. J. and Rimm, A. A. (1985). Factors influencing anatomical location of fat tissue in 52,953 women. *International Journal of Obesity, 9*, 29–38.

Lassek, W. D. and Gaulin, S. J. C. (2008). Waist-hip ratio and cognitive ability: Is gluteofemoral fat a privileged store of neurodevelopmental resources? *Evolution and Human Behavior, 29*, 26–34.

LaVelle, M. (1995). Natural selection and developmental sexual variation in the human pelvis. *American Journal of Physical Anthropology, 98*, 59–72.

Lean, M. E., Han, T. S. and Morrison, C. E. (1995). Waist circumference as a measure for indicating need for weight management. *British Medical Journal*, *311*, 158–61.

Leder, H. (1996). Line drawings of faces reduce configural processing. *Perception*, *25*, 355–66.

Leong, A. (2006). Sexual dimorphism of the pelvic architecture: A struggling response to destructive and parsimonious forces by natural and mate selection. *McGill Journal of Medicine*, *9*, 61–6.

Lerner, I. M. (1954). *Genetic homeostasis*. Edinburgh: Oliver & Boyd.

Leroi-Gourhan, A. (1968). *The art of prehistoric man in Western Europe*. London: Thames & Hudson.

Li, N., Bailey, J. and Kenrick, D. T. (2002). The necessities and luxuries of mate preferences: Testing the tradeoffs. *Journal of Personality and Social Psychology*, *82*, 947–55.

Lie, H. C., Rhodes, G. and Simmons, L. W. (2008). Genetic diversity revealed in human faces. *Evolution*, *62*, 2473–86.

Light, L. L., Hollander, S. and Kayra-Stuart, F. (1981). Why attractive people are harder to remember. *Personality and Social Psychology, Bulletin*, *7*, 269–76.

Little, A. C., Apicella, C. L. and Marlowe, F. W. (2007). Preferences for symmetry in human faces in two cultures: Data from the UK and the Hadza, an isolated group of hunter-gatherers. *Proceedings of the Royal Society B*, *274*, 3113–3117.

Little, A. C. and Hancock, P. J. (2002). The role of masculinity and distinctiveness on the perception of attractiveness in human male faces. *British Journal of Psychology*, *93*, 451–64.

Little, A. C. and Jones, B. C. (2006). Attraction independent of detection suggests special mechanisms for symmetry preferences in human face perception. *Proceedings of the Royal Society B*, *273*, 3093–9.

Little, A. C., Jones, B. C. and Burriss, R. P. (2007). Preferences for masculinity in male bodies change across the menstrual cycle. *Hormones and Behaviour*, *51*, 633–9.

Little, A. C., Jones, B. C. and DeBruine, L. M. (2008). Preferences for variation in masculinity in real male faces change across the menstrual cycle. *Personality and Individual Differences*, *45*, 478–82.

Little, A. C. and Mannion, H. (2006). Viewing attractive or unattractive same-sex individuals changes self-rated attractiveness and face preferences in women. *Animal Behaviour*, *72*, 981–7.

Little, A. C. and Perrett, D. I. (2002). Putting beauty back in the eye of the beholder: Evolution and individual differences in face preference. *Psychologist*, *15*, 28–32.

Little, A. C., Burt, D. M., Penton-Voak, I. S. and Perrett, D. I. (2001). Self-perceived attractiveness influences human female preferences for sexual dimorphism and symmetry in male faces. *Proceedings of the Royal Society B*, *268*, 39–44.

Little, A. C., Cohen, D. L., Jones, B. C. and Belsky, J. (2007). Human preferences for facial masculinity change with relationship type and environmental harshness. *Behavioral Ecology and Sociobiology*, *61*, 967–73.

Little, A. C., DeBruine, L. M., Jones, B. C. and Feinberg, D. R. (2008). Symmetry and sexual-dimorphism in human faces: Interrelationships in preference suggest both signal quality. *Behavioural Ecology*, *19*, 902–8.

Little, A. C., Jones, B. C., Penton-Voak, I. S. *et al.* (2002). Partnership status and the temporal context of relationships influence human female preferences for sexual dimorphism in male face shape. *Proceedings of the Royal Society B*, *269*, 1095–100.

Locher, P. J. (2003). An empirical investigation of the visual rightness theory of picture perception. *Acta Psychologica*, *114*, 147–64.

Lundy, D. E., Tan, J. and Cunningham, M. R. (1998). Heterosexual romantic preferences: The importance of humor and physical attractiveness for different types of relationships. *Personal Relationships, 5*, 311–325.

McBurney, D. H. and Streeter, S. A. (2007). Waist-to-hip ratios and female attractiveness: Comparing apples, oranges, and pears. In V. Swami and A. Furnham (eds), *The body beautiful: Evolutionary and sociocultural perspectives* (pp. 15–28). Basingstoke: Palgrave Macmillan.

McManus, C. (2002). *Right hand, left hand: The origin of asymmetry in brains, bodies, atoms and cultures.* London: Phoenix.

Maisey, D. M., Vale, E. L. E., Cornelissen, P. L. and Tovée, M. J. (1999). Characteristics of male attractiveness for women. *Lancet, 353*, 1500.

Malina, R. M. and Buschang, P. H. (1984). Anthropometric asymmetry in normal and mentally retarded males. *Annals of Human Biology, 11*, 515–531.

Manning, J. T., Anderton, K. and Washington, S. M. (1996). Women's waist and the sex ratio of their progeny: Evolutionary aspects of the ideal female body shape. *Journal of Human Evolution, 31*, 41–7.

Manning, J. T., Trivers, R. L., Singh, D. and Thornhill, A. (1999). The mystery of female beauty. *Nature, 399*, 214–215.

Markey, C. N., Tinsley, B., Ericksen, A. J. *et al.* (2002). Preadolescent's perception of female's body size and shape: Evolutionary and social learning perspective. *Journal of Youth and Adolescence, 31*, 137–47.

Markow, T. A. and Ricker, J. P. (1992). Male size, developmental stability, and mating success in natural populations of three *Drosophila* species. *Heredity, 69*, 122–7.

Marlowe, F. and Wetsman, A. (2001). Preferred waist-to-hip ratio and ecology. *Personality and Individual Differences, 30*, 481–9.

Marlowe, F. W., Apicella, C. L. and Reed, D. (2005). Men's preferences for women's profile waist-hip-ratio in two societies. *Evolution and Human Behavior, 26*, 458–68.

Marti, B., Tuomilehto, J., Saloman, V. *et al.* (1991). Body fat distribution in the Finnish population: Environmental determinants and predictive power for cardiovascular risk factor level. *Journal of Epidemiological Community Health, 45*, 131–7.

Mazella, R. and Feingold, A. (1994). The effect of physical attractiveness, race, socioeconomic status, and gender of defendants and victims on judgements of mock jurors: A meta-analysis. *Journal of Applied Social Psychology, 24*, 1315–1344.

Mazur, A., Mazur, J. and Keating, C. F. (1984). Military rank attainment of a West Point class effects of cadets' physical features. *American Journal of Sociology, 90*, 125–50.

Mellor, C. S. (1992). Dermatoglyphic evidence of fluctuating asymmetry in schizophrenia. *British Journal of Psychiatry, 160*, 467–72.

Meyer, D. A. and Quong, M. W. (1999). The bio-logic of facial geometry. *Nature, 397*, 661–2.

Miller, G. F. (2000). *The mating mind: How sexual choice shaped the evolution of human nature.* New York: Doubleday.

Misra, A. and Vikram, N. (2003). Clinical and pathophysiological consequences of abdominal adiposity and abdominal adipose tissue depots. *Nutrition, 19*, 456–7.

Møller, A. P. (1992a). Parasites differentially increase the degree of fluctuating asymmetry in secondary sexual characters. *Journal of Evolutionary Biology, 5*, 691–9.

Møller, A. P. (1992b). Females prefer large and symmetrical ornaments. *Nature, 357*, 238–40.

Møller, A. P. (1993). Female preference for apparently symmetrical male sexual ornaments in the barn swallow *Hirundo rustica. Behavioural Ecology and Sociobiology, 32*, 371–6.

Møller, A. P. (1998). Developmental instability of plants and radiation from Chernobyl. *Oikos*, *81*, 444–8.

Møller, A. P., Christe, P. and Lux, E. (1999). Parasitism, host immune function, and sexual selection. *Quarterly Review of Biology*, *74*, 3–74.

Møller, A. P. and Swaddle, J. P. (1997). *Asymmetry, developmental stability, and evolution*. New York: Oxford University Press.

Møller, A. P. and Thornhill, R. (1997). A meta-analysis of the heritability of developmental stability. *Journal of Evolutionary Biology*, *10*, 1–16.

Møller, A. P. and Zamora-Muñoz, C. (1997). Antennal asymmetry and sexual selection in a cerambycid beetle. *Animal Behaviour*, *54*, 1509–15.

Moran, C., Hernandez, E., Ruiz, J. E. *et al.* (1999). Upper body obesity and hyperinsulinemia are associated with anovulation. *Gynecologic and Obstetric Investigation*, *47*, 1–5.

Mussap, A. (2006). Waist-to-hip ratio and unhealthy body change in women. *Sex Roles*, *56*, 33–43.

Neave, N., Laing, S., Fink, B. and Manning, J. T. (2003). Second to fourth digit ratio, testosterone and perceived male dominance. *Proceedings of the Royal Society B*, *270*, 2167–72.

Nelson, L. D. and Morrison, E. L. (2005). The symptoms of resource scarcity: Judgements of food and finances influence preference for potential partners. *Psychological Science*, *16*, 167–73.

O'Keefe, J. H. and Cordain, L. (2004). Cardiovascular disease resulting from a diet and lifestyle at odds with our Paleolithic genome: How to become a 21st-century hunter-gatherer. *Mayo Clinic Proceedings*, *79*, 101–8.

O'Toole, A. J., Deffenbacher, K. A., Valentine, D. *et al.* (1998). The perception of face gender: The role of stimulus structure in recognition and classification. *Memory and Cognition*, *26*, 146–60.

O'Toole, A. J., Price, T., Vetter, T. *et al.* (1999). 3D shape and 2D surface texture of human faces: The role of 'averages' in attractiveness and age. *Image and Visual Computing*, *18*, 9–19.

Parkinson, K. N., Tovée, M. J. and Cohen-Tovée, E. M. (1998). Body shape perceptions of preadolescent and young adolescent children. *European Eating Disorders Review*, *6*, 126–35.

Parsons, P. A. (1992). Fluctuating asymmetry: A biological monitor of environmental and genomic stress. *Heredity*, *68*, 361–4.

Passemard, L. (1938). *Les statuettes féminines Paléolithiques dites Vénus stéatopyges*. Nîmes: Teissier.

Patzer, G. L. (1985). *Physical attractiveness phenomena*. New York: Plenum Press.

Patzer, G. L. (2002). *The power and paradox of physical attractiveness*. Boca Raton, FL: BrownWalker Press.

Peelen, M. V. and Downing, P. E. (2005). Selectivity for the human body in the fusiform gyrus. *Journal of Neurophysiology*, *93*, 803–8.

Peelen, M. V. and Downing, P. E. (2007). The neural basis of visual body perception. *Nature Reviews: Neuroscience*, *8*, 636–48.

Peelen, M. V., Wiggett, A. J. and Downing, P. E. (2006). Patterns of fMRI activity dissociate overlapping functional brain areas that respond to biological motion. *Neuron*, *49*, 815–822.

Penton-Voak, I. S. and Chang, H. Y. (2008). Attractiveness judgements of individuals vary across emotional expression and movement conditions. *Journal of Evolutionary Psychology*, *6*, 89–100.

Penton-Voak, I. S., Jacobson, A. and Trivers, R. (2004). Populational differences in attractiveness judgments of male and female faces: Comparing British and Jamaican samples. *Evolution and Human Behavior*, *25*, 355–70.

Penton-Voak, I. S. and Perrett, D. I. (2000). Female preference for male faces changes cyclically: Further evidence. *Evolution and Human Behavior, 21*, 39–48.

Penton-Voak, I. S., Jones, B. C., Little, A. C. *et al.* (2001). Symmetry, sexual dimorphism in facial proportions and male facial attractiveness. *Proceedings of the Royal Society B, 268*, 1617–1623.

Penton-Voak, I. S., Little, A. C., Jones, B. C. *et al.* (2003). Female condition influences preferences for sexual dimorphism in faces of male humans (*Homo sapiens*). *Journal of Computational Psychology, 117*, 264–71.

Penton-Voak, I. S., Perrett, D. I., Castles, D. L. *et al.* (1999). Menstrual cycle alters face preference. *Nature, 399.* 741–2.

Perrett, D. I., May, K. A. and Yoshikawa, S. (1994). Facial shape and judgments of female attractiveness. *Nature, 368*, 239–42.

Perrett, D. I., Burt, D. M., Penton-Voak, I. S. *et al.* (1999). Symmetry and human facial attractiveness. *Evolution and Human Behaviour, 20*, 295–307.

Perrett, D. I., Lee, K. J., Penton-Voak, I. *et al.* (1998). Effects of sexual dimorphism on facial attractiveness. *Nature, 394*, 884–7.

Perrett, D. I., Penton-Voak, I., Little, A. C. *et al.* (2002). Facial attractiveness judgments reflect learning of parental age characteristics. *Proceedings of the Royal Society B, 269*, 873–80.

Peters, A. (2000). Testosterone treatment is immunosuppressant in superb fairy wrens, yet free-living males with high testosterone are more immunocompetent. *Proceedings of the Royal Society B, 267*, 883–9.

Peters, M., Rhodes, G. and Simmons, L. W. (2007). Contributions of the face and body to overall attractiveness. *Animal Behavior, 73*, 937–42.

Pittenger, J. B. (1991). On the difficulty of averaging faces: Comments on Langlois and Roggman. *Psychological Science, 2*, 351–3.

Polak, M. (2003). *Developmental instability: Causes and consequences.* New York: Oxford University Press.

Provost, M. P., Troje, N. F. and Quinsey, V. L. (2008). Short-term mating strategies and attraction to masculinity in point-light walkers. *Evolution and Human Behavior, 29*, 65–9.

Puce, A. and Perrett, D. (2003). Electrophysiology and brain imaging of biological motion. *Philosophical Transaction of the Royal Society B, 358*, 435–45.

Puhl, R. M. and Boland, F. J. (2001). Predicting female physical attractiveness: Waist-to-hip ratio versus thinness. *Psychology, Evolution and Gender, 3*, 27–46.

Puts, D. A. (2005). Menstrual phase and mating context affects women's preferences for male voice pitch. *Evolution and Human Behavior, 26*, 388–97.

Rebuffé-Scrive, M (1988). Metabolic differences in deposits. In C. Bouchhard and F. E. Johnston (eds), *Fat distribution during growth and later health outcomes* (pp. 163–73). New York: Alan R. Liss.

Rebuffé-Scrive, M. (1991). Neuroregulation of adipose tissue: Molecular and hormonal mechanisms. *International Journal of Obesity, 15*, 83–6.

Rentschler, I., Jüttner, M., Unzicker, A. and Landis, T. (1999). Innate and learned components of human visual preference. *Current Biology, 9*, 665–71.

Revel-MacDonald, N. and Leyenaar, M. (1982). Dayak and Kalimantan masks. *Drama Review: TDR, 26*, 70–72.

Rhodes, G. (2006). The evolutionary psychology of facial beauty. *Annual Review of Psychology, 57*, 199–226.

Rhodes, G., Hickford, C. and Jeffery, L. (2000). Sex-typicality and attractiveness: Are super-male and superfemale faces super-attractive? *British Journal of Psychology, 91*, 125–40.

Rhodes, G. and Tremewan, T. (1996). Averageness, exaggeration, and facial attractiveness. *Psychological Science, 7*, 105–10.

Rhodes, G., Roberts, J. and Simmons, L. (1999). Reflections on symmetry and attractiveness. *Psychology of Evolution and Gender, 1*, 279–95.

Rhodes, G., Sumich, A. and Byatt, G. (1999). Are average facial configurations attractive only because of their symmetry. *Psychological Science, 10*, 52–8.

Rhodes, G., Chan, J., Zebrowitz, L. A. and Simmons, L. W. (2003). Does sexual dimorphism in human faces signal health? *Proceedings of the Royal Society B, 270*, S93–S95.

Rhodes, G., Proffitt, F., Grady, J. M. and Sumich, A. (1998). Facial symmetry and the perception of beauty. *Psychonomic Bulletin and Review, 5*, 659–69.

Rhodes, G., Zebrowitz, L. A., Clark, A. *et al.* (2001). Do facial averageness and symmetry signal health? *Evolution and Human Behaviour, 22*, 31–46.

Rice, P. C. (1982). Prehistoric Venuses: Symbols of motherhood or womanhood? *Journal of Anthropological Research, 37*, 402–14.

Riggio, R. E., Friedman, H. S. and DiMatteo, M. R. (1981). Nonverbal greetings: Effects of the situation and personality. *Personality and Social Psychology Bulletin, 7*, 682–9.

Rilling, J. K., Kaufman, T. L., Smith, E. O. *et al.* (2009). Abdominal depth and waist circumference as influential determinants of human female attractiveness. *Evolution and Human Behavior, 30*, 21–31.

Roldan, E. R. S., Cassinello, J., Abaigar, T. and Gomendio, M. (1998). Inbreeding, fluctuating asymmetry and ejaculate quality in an endangered ungulate. *Proceedings of the Royal Society B, 265*, 243–8.

Roney, J. R. and Simmons, Z. L. (2008). Women's estradiol predicts preference for facial cues of men's testosterone. *Hormones and Behavior, 53*, 14–19.

Roney, J. R., Hanson, K. N., Durante, K. M. and Maestripieri, D. (2006). Reading men's faces: Women's mate attractiveness judgments track men's testosterone and interest in infants. *Proceedings of the Royal Society B, 273*, 2169–75.

Rozmus-Wrzesinska, M. and Pawłowski, B. (2005). Men's ratings of female attractiveness are influenced more by changes in female waist size compared with changes in hip size. *Biological Psychology, 68*, 299–308.

Rupp, H. A., James, T. W., Ketterson, E. D. *et al.* (2009). Neural activation in women in response to masculinized male faces: Mediation by hormones and psychosexual factors. *Evolution and Human Behavior, 30*, 1–10.

Russell, R. (2003). Sex, beauty, and the relative luminance of facial features. *Perception, 32*, 1093–107.

Salzano, F. M. and Callegari-Jacques, S. M. (1988). *South American Indians: A case study in evolution.* Oxford: Clarendon Press.

Samuels, C. A., Butterworth, G., Roberts, T. *et al.* (1994). Facial aesthetics: Babies prefer attractiveness to symmetry. *Perception, 23*, 823–31.

Sandars, N. K. (1968). *Prehistoric art in Europe.* Baltimore: Penguin Books.

Scheib, J. E., Gangestad, S. W. and Thornhill, R. (1999). Facial attractiveness, symmetry and cues of good genes. *Proceedings of the Royal Society B, 266*, 1913–1917.

Schlüter, A., Parzefall, J. and Schlupp, I. (1998). Female preference for symmetrical vertical bars in male sailfin mollies. *Animal Behaviour, 56*, 147–53.

Schmalt, H.-D. (2006). Waist-to-hip ratio and female physical attractiveness: The moderating role of power motivation and the mating context. *Personality and Individual Differences, 41,* 455–65.

Schwarzlose, R., Baker, C. and Kanwisher, N. (2005). Separate face and body selectivity on the fusiform gyrus. *Journal of Neuroscience, 25,* 11055–9.

Scott, I., Bentley, G. R., Tovée, M. J. *et al.* (2007). An evolutionary perspective on male preferences for female body shape. In V. Swami and A. Furnham (eds), *The body beautiful: Evolutionary and sociocultural perspectives* (pp. 65–87). Basingstoke: Palgrave Macmillan.

Scott, I., Swami, V., Josephson, S. C. and Penton-Voak, I. (2008). Quality and choice: Context-dependent preferences for facial dimorphism in a rural Malaysian population. *Evolution and Human Behavior,* 289–96.

Seidell, J. C., Perusse, L., Despres, J. P. and Bouchard, C. (2001). Waist and hip circumferences have independent and opposite effects on cardiovascular disease risk factors: The Quebec Family Study. *American Journal of Clinical Nutrition, 74,* 315–321.

Seli, E. and Arici, A. (2002). Sex steroids and the immune system. *Immunology and Allergy Clinics of North America, 22,* 407–33.

Shackelford, T. K. and Larsen, R. J. (1997). Facial asymmetry as an indicator of psychological, emotional, and physiological distress. *Journal of Personality and Social Psychology, 72,* 456–66.

Schwarzlose, R. F., Baker, C. I. and Kanwisher, N. (2005). Separate face and body selectivity on the fusiform gyrus. *Journal of Neuroscience, 25,* 11055–9.

Simmons, L. W., Rhodes, G., Peters, M. and Koehler, N. (2004). Are human preferences for facial symmetry focussed on signals of developmental instability? *Behavioral Ecology, 15,* 864–71.

Singh, D. (1993a). Adaptive significance of female physical attractiveness: Role of waist-to-hip ratio. *Journal of Personality and Social Psychology, 65,* 292–307.

Singh, D. (1993b). Body shape and women's attractiveness. The critical role of waist-to-hip ratio. *Human Nature, 4,* 297–321.

Singh, D. (1994a). Is thin really beautiful and good? Relationship between waist-to-hip ratio (WHR) and female attractiveness. *Personality and Individual Differences, 16,* 123–32.

Singh, D. (1994b). Waist-to-hip ratio and judgements of attractiveness and healthiness of females' figures by male and female physicians. *International Journal of Obesity, 18,* 731–7.

Singh, D. (1994c). Body fat distribution and perception of desirable female body shape by young black men and women. *International Journal of Eating Disorders, 16,* 289–94.

Singh, D. (1995a). Female health, attractiveness and desirability for relationships: Role of breast asymmetry and WHR. *Ethology and Sociobiology, 16,* 465–81.

Singh, D. (1995b). Female judgement of male attractiveness and desirability for relationships: Role of waist-to-hip ratio and financial status. *Journal of Personality and Social Psychology, 69,* 1089–101.

Singh, D. (2006). Universal allure of the hourglass figure: An evolutionary theory of female physical attractiveness. *Clinics in Plastic Surgery, 33,* 359–70.

Singh, D., Davis, M. and Randall, P. (2000). Fluctuating ovulation: Lower WHR, enhanced self-perceived attractiveness, and increased sexual desire. Paper presented at Human Evolution and Behaviour Society meeting, London, 13–17th June.

Singh, D. and Luis, S. (1995). Ethnic and gender consensus for the effect of waist-to-hip ratio on judgements of women's attractiveness. *Human Nature, 6,* 51–65.

Singh, D. and Young, R. K. (1995). Body weight, waist-to-hip ratio, breasts, and hips: Role in judgements of female attractiveness and desirability for relationships. *Ethology and Sociobiology*, *16*, 483–507.

Singh, D. and Zambarano, R. J. (1997). Offspring sex ratio in women with android body fat distribution. *Journal of Human Biology*, *69*, 545–56.

Smith, K. L., Cornelissen, P. L. and Tovée, M. J. (2007). Color 3D bodies and judgements of human female attractiveness. *Evolution and Human Behavior*, *28*, 48–54.

Smith, K. L., Tovée, M. J., Hancock, P. J. B. *et al.* (2007). An analysis of body shape attractiveness based on image statistics: Evidence for a dissociation between expressions of preference and shape discrimination. *Visual Cognition*, *15*, 1–27.

Sorokowski, P. and Pawłowski, B. (2008). Adaptive preferences for leg length in a potential partner. *Evolution and Human Behavior*, *29*, 86–91.

Stewart, J. E. (1984), Appearance and punishment: The attraction-leniency effect in the courtroom. *Journal of Social Psychology*, *125*, 373–78.

Streeter, S. A. and McBurney, D. (2003). Waist-hip ratio and attractiveness: New evidence and a critique for a 'critical test'. *Evolution and Human Behaviour*, *24*, 88–98.

Sugiyama, L. S. (2004). Is beauty in the context-sensitive adaptations of the beholder? Shiwiar use of waist-to-hip ratio in assessments of female mate value. *Evolution and Human Behaviour*, *25*, 51–62.

Sugiyama, L. S. (2005). Physical attractiveness in adaptationist perspective. In D. M. Buss (ed.), *The handbook of evolutionary psychology* (pp. 293–343). New York: John Wiley & Sons, Ltd.

Swaddle, J. P. and Cuthill, I. C. (1994). Female zebra finches prefer males with symmetric chest plumage. *Proceedings of the Royal Society B*, *258*, 267–71.

Swaddle, J. P. and Cuthill, I. C. (1995). Asymmetry and human facial attractiveness: Symmetry may not always be beautiful. *Proceedings of the Royal Society B*, *261*, 111–116.

Swaddle, J. P. and Reierson, G. W. (2002). Testosterone increases perceived dominance but not attractiveness in human males. *Proceedings of the Royal Society B*, *269*, 2285–9.

Swami, V. (2005). *Evolutionary psychology and the study of human physical attractiveness: The influence of body weight and shape across cultures.* PhD Thesis, University College London.

Swami, V. (2007a). *The missing arms of Vénus de Milo: Reflections on the science of physical attractiveness.* Brighton: The Book Guild.

Swami, V. (2007b). Evolutionary psychology: 'New science of the mind' or 'Darwinian fundamentalism'? *Historical Materialism*, *15*, 105–36.

Swami, V. (2008). The waist-to-hip ratio hypothesis of women's attractiveness: Time to let go? Plenary talk, European Human Behaviour and Evolution conference, Montpellier, 5th April.

Swami, V. (2009). An examination of the love-is-blind bias among gay men and lesbians. *Body Image: An International Journal of Research*, *6*, 149–51.

Swami, V. (in press – a). The effect of shape and colour symmetry on the aesthetic value of Dayak masks from Borneo. *Imagination, Cognition, and Personality*.

Swami, V. (in press – b). Methodological and conceptual issues in the science of physical attraction. In F. Columbus (ed.), *Visual perception: New research*. New York: Nova Science Publishers.

Swami, V., Einon, D. and Furnham, A. (2006). An investigation of the leg-to-body ratio as a human aesthetic criterion. *Body Image: An International Journal of Research*, *3*, 317–323.

Swami, V., Einon, D. and Furnham, A. (2007). The cultural significance of leg-to-body ratio preferences? Evidence from Britain and rural Malaysia. *Asian Journal of Social Psychology*, *10*, 265–9.

Swami, V. and Furnham, A. (2006). The science of attraction. *Psychologist, 19*, 362–5.

Swami, V. and Furnham, A. (2008a). *The psychology of physical attraction*. London: Routledge.

Swami, V. and Furnham, A. (2008b). Is love really so blind? *Psychologist, 21*, 108–11.

Swami, V. and Furnham, A. (2009a). The rhythm of straight lines and colour planes: The effect of introducing symmetry into Piet Mondrian's neo-plastic paintings and individual difference antecedents of aesthetic preferences. Manuscript under review.

Swami, V. and Furnham, A. (2009b). Big and beautiful: The body weight and shape preferences of 'fat admirers'. *Archives of Sexual Behavior, 38*, 201–8.

Swami, V., Gray, M. and Furnham, A. (2007). The female nude in Rubens: Disconfirmatory evidence of the waist-to-hip ratio hypothesis of female physical attractiveness. *Imagination, Cognition and Personality, 26*, 139–47.

Swami, V., Greven, C. and Furnham, A. (2007). More than just skin-deep? A pilot study integrating physical and non-physical factors in the perception of physical attractiveness. *Personality and Individual Differences, 42*, 563–72.

Swami, V., Poulogianni, K. and Furnham, A. (2006). The influence of resource availability on preferences for human body weight and non-human objects. *Journal of Articles in Support of the Null Hypothesis, 4*, 17–28.

Swami, V. and Tovée, M. J. (2005a). Female physical attractiveness in Britain and Malaysia: A cross-cultural study. *Body Image, 2*, 115–28.

Swami, V. and Tovée, M. J. (2005b). Male physical attractiveness in Britain and Malaysia: A cross-cultural study. *Body Image, 2*, 383–93.

Swami, V. and Tovée, M. J. (2006). Does hunger influence judgements of female physical attractiveness? *British Journal of Psychology, 97*, 353–63.

Swami, V. and Tovée, M. J. (2007a). Differences in attractiveness preferences between observers in low and high resource environments in Thailand. *Journal of Evolutionary Psychology, 5*, 149–60.

Swami, V. and Tovée, M. J. (2007b). Perceptions of female body weight and shape among indigenous and urban Europeans. *Scandinavian Journal of Psychology, 48*, 43–50.

Swami, V. and Tovée, M. J. (2007c). The relative contribution of profile body shape and weight to judgements of women's physical attractiveness in Britain and Malaysia. *Body Image: An International Journal of Research, 4*, 391–6.

Swami, V. and Tovée, M. J. (2009). Big beautiful women: The body size preferences of male fat admirers. *Journal of Sex Research, 46*, 89–96.

Swami, V., Antonakopoulos, N., Tovée, M. J. and Furnham, A. (2006a). A critical test of the waist-to-hip ratio hypothesis of female physical attractiveness in Britain and Greece. *Sex Roles, 54*, 201–11.

Swami, V., Buchanan, T., Furnham, A. and Tovée, M. J. (2008d). Five-factor personality correlates of perceptions of women's body sizes. *Personality and Individual Differences, 45*, 697–9.

Swami, V., Caprario, C., Tovée, M. J. and Furnham, A. (2006b). Female physical attractiveness in Britain and Japan: A cross-cultural study. *European Journal of Personality, 20*, 69–81.

Swami, V., Chan, F., Wong, V. *et al.* (2008a). Weight-based discrimination in occupational hiring and helping behaviour. *Journal of Applied Social Psychology, 38*, 968–81.

Swami, V., Frederick, D. A., Hadji-Michael, M. and Furnham, A. (2009d). The influence of leg-to-body ratio on judgements of attractiveness. Manuscript under review.

Swami, V., Furnham, A., Chamorro-Premuzic, T. *et al.* (in press). More than skin deep? Personality information influences men's ratings of the attractiveness of women's body sizes. *Journal of Social Psychology*.

Swami, V., Furnham, A., Georgiades, C. and Pang, L. (2007d). Evaluating self and partner physical attractiveness. *Body Image: An International Journal of Research, 4,* 97–101.

Swami, V., Grant, N., Furnham, A. and McManus, I. C. (2008f). Perfectly formed? The effect of manipulating the waist-to-hip ratios of famous paintings and sculptures. *Imagination, Cognition and Personality, 27,* 47–62.

Swami, V., Henderson, G., Custance, D. and Tovée, M. J. (2009a). A cross-cultural investigation of men's judgments of female body weight in Britain and Indonesia. Manuscript under review.

Swami, V., Jones, J., Einon, D. and Furnham, A. (2009b). Men's preferences for women's profile waist-to-hip ratio, breast size and ethnic group in Britain and South Africa. *British Journal of Psychology, 100,* 313–325.

Swami, V., Knight, D., Tovée, M. J. *et al.* (2007a). Perceptions of female body size in Britain and the South Pacific. *Body Image: An International Journal of Research, 4,* 219–23.

Swami, V., Miller, R., Furnham, A. *et al.* (2008c). The influence of men's sexual strategies on perceptions of women's bodily attractiveness, health and fertility. *Personality and Individual Differences, 44,* 98–107.

Swami, V., Neto, F., Tovée, M. J. and Furnham, A. (2007b). Preference for female body weight and shape in three European countries. *European Psychologist, 12,* 220–227.

Swami, V., Rozmus-Wrzesinska, M., Voracek, M. *et al.* (2008e). The influence of skin tone, body weight and hair colour on perceptions of women's attractiveness, health and fertility: A cross-cultural investigation. *Journal of Evolutionary Psychology, 6,* 321–41.

Swami, V., Salem, N., Furnham, A. and Tovée, M. J. (2008b). Initial examination of the validity and reliability of the female photographic figure rating scale for body image assessment. *Personality and Individual Differences, 44,* 1752–61.

Swami, V., Smith, J., Tsiokris, A. *et al.* (2007c). Male physical attractiveness in Britain and Greece: A cross-cultural study. *Journal of Social Psychology, 147,* 15–26.

Swami, V., Stieger, S., Haubner, T. *et al.* (2009c). Evaluating the physical attractiveness and oneself and one's romantic partner: Individual and relationship correlates of the love-is-blind bias. *Journal of Individual Differences, 30,* 35.

Symons, D. (1979). *The evolution of human sexuality.* New York: Oxford University Press.

Symons, D. (1992). On the use and misuse of Darwinism in the study of human behaviour. In J. H. Barkow, L. Cosmides and J. Tooby (eds), *The adapted mind: Evolutionary psychology and the generation of culture* (pp. 137–59). New York: Oxford University Press.

Symons, D. (1995). Beauty is the adaptations of the beholder: The evolutionary psychology of human female sexual attractiveness. In P. R. Abramhamson and S. D. Pinker (eds), *Sexual nature/Sexual culture* (pp. 80–118). Chicago: Chicago University Press.

Tanner, J. M. (1978). *Foetus into man: Physical growth from conception to maturity.* London: Open Books.

Tassinary, L. G. and Hansen, K. A. (1998). A critical test of the waist-to-hip ratio hypothesis of female physical attractiveness. *Psychological Science, 9,* 150–155.

Tews, M. J., Stafford, K. and Zhu, J. (2009). Beauty revisited: The impact of attractiveness, ability, and personality in the assessment of employment suitability. *International Journal of Selection and Assessment, 17,* 92–100.

Thornhill, R. and Gangestad, S. W. (1993). Human facial beauty: Averageness, symmetry and parasite resistance. *Human Nature, 4,* 237–69.

Thornhill, R. and Gangestad, S. W. (1994). The evolutionary psychology of extrapair sex: The role of fluctuating asymmetry. *Evolution and Human Behaviour, 18,* 69–88.

Thornhill, R. and Gangestad, S. W. (1999). Facial attractiveness. *Trends in Cognitive Science*, *3*, 452–60.

Thornhill, R. and Gangestad, S. W. (2006). Facial sexual dimorphism, developmental stability and susceptibility to disease in men and women. *Evolution and Human Behavior*, *27*, 131–44.

Thornhill, R., Gangestad, S. W. and Comer, R. (1995). Human female orgasm and mate fluctuating asymmetry. *Animal Behaviour*, *50*, 1601–15.

Thornhill, R. and Møller, A. P. (1997). Developmental stability, disease and medicine. *Biological Reviews*, *72*, 497–548.

Tovée, M. J., Brown, J. E. and Jacobs, D. (2001). Maternal waist-hip ratio does not predict child gender. *Proceedings of the Royal Society London B*, *268*, 1007–10.

Tovée, M. J. and Cornelissen, P. L. (2001). Female and male perceptions of female physical attractiveness in front-view and profile. *British Journal of Psychology*, *92*, 391–402.

Tovée, M. J., Furnham, A. and Swami, V. (2007). Healthy body equals beautiful body? Changing perceptions of health and attractiveness with shifting socioeconomic status. In V. Swami and A. Furnham (eds), *The body beautiful: Evolutionary and sociocultural perspectives* (pp. 108–29). Basingstoke: Palgrave Macmillan.

Tovée, M. J., Tasker, K. and Benson, P. J. (2000). Is symmetry a visual cue to attractiveness in the human female body? *Evolution and Human Behavior*, *21*, 191–200.

Tovée, M. J., Hancock, P., Mahmoodi, S. *et al.* (2002). Human female attractiveness: Waveform analysis of body shape. *Proceedings of the Royal Society B*, *269*, 2205–13.

Tovée, M. J., Maisey, D. S., Emery, J. L. and Cornelissen, P. L. (1999). Visual cues to female physical attractiveness. *Proceedings of the Royal Society B*, *266*, 211–218.

Tovée, M. J., Mason, S., Emery, J. *et al.* (1997). Supermodels: Stick insects or hourglasses? *Lancet*, *350*, 1474–5.

Tovée, M. J., Reinhardt, S., Emery, J. and Cornelissen, P. (1998). Optimum body-mass index and maximum sexual attractiveness. *Lancet*, *352*, 548.

Tovée, M. J., Swami, V., Furnham, A. and Mangalparsad, R. (2006). Changing perceptions of attractiveness as observers are exposed to a different culture. *Evolution and Human Behavior*, *27*, 443–56.

Ucko, P. J. (1962). The interpretation of prehistoric anthropomorphic figurines. *Journal of the Royal Anthropological Institute of Great Britain and Ireland*, *92*, 38–54.

Valentine, T., Darling, S. and Donnelly, M. (2004). Why are average faces attractive? The effect of view and averageness on the attractiveness of female faces. *Psychonomic Bulletin and Review*, *11*, 482–7.

Voracek, M. and Fisher, M. L. (2002). Shapely centrefolds? Temporal change in body measures: Trend analysis. *British Medical Journal*, *325*, 1447–8.

Voracek, M. and Fisher, M. L. (2006). Success is all in the measures: Androgenousness, curvaceousness and starring frequencies in adult media actresses. *Archives of Sexual Behavior*, *35*, 297–304.

Waitt, C. and Little, A. C. (2006). Preferences for symmetry in conspecific facial shape among rhesus macaques (*Macaca mulatta*). *International Journal of Primatology*, *27*, 133–45.

Washburn, D. and Crowe, D. (1988). *Symmetries of culture: Theory and practise of plane pattern analysis*. Seattle: University of Washington Press.

Washburn, D. and Humphrey, D. (2001). Symmetries in the mind: Production, perception and preference for seven one-dimensional patterns. *Visual Arts Research*, *70*, 57–68.

Wass, P., Waldenstrom, U., Rossner, S. and Hellberg, D. (1997). An android body fat distribution in females impairs the pregnancy rate of in-vitro fertilisation-embryo transfer. *Human Reproduction, 12*, 2057–60.

Waynforth, D., Delwadia, S. and Camm, M. (2005). The influence of women's mating strategies on preference for masculine facial architecture. *Evolution and Human Behavior, 26*, 409–16.

Welling, L. L. M., Jones, B. C., DeBruine, L. M. *et al.* (2007). Raised salivary testosterone in women is associated with increased attraction to masculine faces. *Hormones and Behavior, 52*, 156–61.

Wetsman, A. and Marlowe, F. (1999). How universal are preferences for female waist-to-hip ratios? Evidence from the Hadza of Tanzania. *Evolution and Human Behaviour, 20*, 219–228.

Wetsman, A. F. (1998). *Within- and between-sex variation in human mate choice: An evolutionary perspective.* Unpublished doctoral dissertation, University of California, Los Angeles.

Weyl, H. (1952). *Symmetry.* Princeton, NJ: Princeton University Press.

Wilson, J. M. B., Tripp, D. A. and Boland, F. J. (2005). The relative contributions of waist-to-hip ratio and body mass index to judgements of attractiveness. *Sexualities, Evolution and Gender, 7*, 245–67.

Wood, L. E. P. (2006). Obesity, waist-hip ratio and hunter-gatherers. *BJOG: An International Journal of Obstetrics and Gynaecology, 113*, 1110–1116.

Yarmouk, U. (2000). The effect of presentation modality on judgements of honesty and attractiveness. *Social Behavior and Personality, 28*, 269–78.

Yu, D. W., Proulx, S. R. and Shepard, G. H. (2007). Masculinity, culture and the paradox of the lek. In V. Swami and A. Furnham (eds), *The body beautiful: Evolutionary and sociocultural perspectives* (pp. 88–107). Basingstoke: Palgrave Macmillan.

Yu, D. W. and Shepard, G. H. (1998). Is beauty in the eye of the beholder? *Nature, 396*, 321–2.

Zaadstra, B. M., Seidell, J. C., van Noord, P. A. H. *et al.* (1993). Fat and female fecundity: Prospective study of effect of body fat distribution on conception rates. *British Medical Journal, 306*, 484–7.

Zahavi, A. (1975). Mate selection: A selection for a handicap. *Journal of Theoretical Biology, 53*, 205–14.

6 Life history theory and human reproductive behaviour

DAVID W. LAWSON

CHAPTER OUTLINE

TRADE-OFFS IN HUMAN LIFE HISTORY 185

Methodological issues 185

Trade-offs between growth and reproduction 186

Trade-offs between current reproduction and
future success 187

Trade-offs between quantity and quality of
offspring 189

**THE OPTIMISATION OF FAMILY SIZE IN
TRADITIONAL SOCIETIES** 193

Mechanisms of fertility optimisation 193

Predicted optima and observed fertility 194

Wealth and reproductive success 195

**THE OPTIMISATION OF FAMILY SIZE IN MODERN
SOCIETIES** 196

The demographic transition 196

Maladaption to novel contraceptive
technologies 198

Cultural evolution of fertility decline 198

Parental investment models of modern
fertility 199

CONCLUSIONS AND FUTURE DIRECTIONS 204

ACKNOWLEDGEMENTS 205

REFERENCES 206

The marvel of the natural world lies in its diversity. Variation in *life histories*, which, by clear Darwinian logic, will be subject to strong forces of natural selection, hold particular captivation for evolutionary biologists. For example, the number of offspring produced during a single reproductive bout (referred to as 'clutch size') ranges between a few relatively large offspring (most birds and mammals) to tens or hundreds of intermediate size (most insects and plants) to the thousands of miniscule offspring produced by some marine invertebrates. Many species are iteroparous, spreading reproduction over sequential breeding periods, while, more rarely, species such as salmon and 'annual plants' likes watermelon and cauliflower, structure their life-cycle around a single act of reproduction, closely followed by death. Reproductive maturity is reached relatively soon after birth in many species, while in others, including our own, offspring spend an extended period in immature or juvenile states, often heavily reliant on extensive parental care. Within the phenotypic constraints of a species, such life history parameters also demonstrate considerable plasticity across local ecological and demographic conditions. Life history theory is the principle analytical framework concerned with the study of this variation and since its inception has fuelled an extensive research programme in evolutionary and behavioural ecology (Lessells, 1991; Roff, 2002; Stearns, 1992).

The fundamental concept of life history theory is that observed life histories are constrained by a combination of finite resource budgets and the 'Principle of Allocation', that is resources (time, energy, effort) allocated to one function cannot be allocated to another (Cody, 1966). Thus, natural selection cannot simultaneously optimise individual life history traits in isolation, but instead must optimise realisable trade-offs between competing dimensions of an organism's life history. At the macro level, these competing functions are normally recognised as survival, growth and reproduction, but are more commonly analysed within finer subdivisions, most notably the trade-off between investment in current versus future reproduction, and between quantity of offspring and levels of parental care (Gadgil and Bossert, 1970; Stearns, 1992).

As a branch of evolutionary ecology, life history theory takes an optimality approach (see Parker and Smith, 1990) to understanding variation in observed life histories, recognising that the maximisation of inclusive fitness will be served by distinct phenotypic optima across varying ecological and demographic niches, and in relation to individual condition and resource access. Life history studies are thus principally concerned with deriving and testing predictions about the particular optima populations, and individuals can be expected to evolve under natural selection of various alternative strategies. In recent years, increasing research attention has also been devoted to the mechanisms of life history adaptation and the developmental, physiological and cognitive constraints which may prevent observed life histories reaching predicted optima (Partridge and Sibly, 1991).

In this chapter, I concentrate on the application of life history theory to the diversity of reproductive strategies observed in human populations. This area of research has traditionally been dominated by anthropologists and demographers adopting the theory and methods of evolutionary ecology (Hill, 1993; Hill and Kaplan, 1999;

Kaplan *et al.*, 2000; Low, 2001; Lummaa, 2007; Mace, 2000, 2007; Voland, 1998). Evolutionary psychologists and researchers of cultural evolution have also become active players in life history research, particularly in the context of 'culturally modern' populations, incorporating new hypotheses and research methodologies into the field (Borgerhoff Mulder, 1998a; Kaplan and Gangestad, 2005). I first overview the main trade-offs faced in human life history and the key socioecological factors that may shift the costs and benefits associated with their resolution. I focus this section on contemporary and historical hunter-gatherer and agriculturalist societies. Using the example of human family size (offspring number), I then focus in more detail on the issue of individual optimisation of life history in both traditional high fertility populations and those which have undergone a demographic transition to modern low fertility. The chapter is rounded off with some thoughts on the key future directions for human life history research.

TRADE-OFFS IN HUMAN LIFE HISTORY

Methodological issues

The first step in any life history study is to identify and measure the underlying trade-offs that constrain the option set of reproductive strategies available to an organism. Quantifying trade-offs is, however, complicated by the problem of phenotypic correlations: individuals with access to a large pool of resources may be able to divert investments into multiple traits simultaneously, while individuals with relatively poor resource access will invest little effort in the same traits. Such variation can obscure a trade-off, leading to positive correlation between two competing functions, rather than the negative correlation predicted by the Principle of Allocation (van Noordwijk and de Jong, 1986).

Experimental methods which manipulate single factors in isolation are often used to get around this problem in animal studies. For example, in birds, the consequences of clutch size strategy have been explored by artificially manipulating the number of eggs per nest and measuring chick survival and recruitment rates against a control group (e.g. Gustafsson and Sutherland, 1988; Pettifor, Perrins and McCleery, 2001). Researchers interested in human life history must rely on observational methods, measuring covariation between life history traits and fitness-related outcomes from unmanipulated conditions, while statistically controlling for differences in individual resource base. This alternative method is widely acknowledged as problematic, as results will be 'unreliable unless a strong case can be made that all relevant variables have been included in the analysis' (Roff, 2002, p. 149). Relevant heterogeneity between individuals is often difficult to measure, particularly in cases when intrinsic factors are important (including genetic differences). Thus, methodological concerns are a recurrent issue in discussions of human life history (e.g. Gagnon *et al.*, 2009; Lawson and Mace, 2009; Sear, 2007).

Trade-offs between growth and reproduction

Humans exaggerate the extension of juvenility which characterises primate taxa relative to other mammals (Pereira and Fairbanks, 2002). Unlike our primate cousins, feeding dependency also extends far beyond weaning, so that one or more elder offspring may require provisioning while the mother simultaneously nurses a young infant (Bogin, 1997; Gurven and Walker, 2006; Lancaster and Lancaster, 1987). From a life history perspective, this relatively long period of juvenile dependence can be understood in terms of trade-off between investments in growth-related benefits on the one hand and immediate sexual maturity and reproduction on the other. Delayed maturity has the potential to improve adult reproductive potential, because of physical benefits such as large body size (which also reduces offspring mortality; e.g. Allal et al., 2004; Sear et al., 2004) and, perhaps particularly fundamental to human resource and mate competition, because it facilitates brain development and increased investment in learning-based knowledge (Bogin, 1997; Kaplan et al., 2000). Yet, in the face of extrinsic mortality hazards, such as predation, food shortages or con-specific violence, delayed maturity can also increase chances of reproductive failure. A reduction in extrinsic mortality over the course of human evolutionary history is, therefore, considered a necessary precursor for the evolution of our relatively 'slow' life histories (Charnov, 1993). Comparison of chimpanzee to hunter-gatherer mortality rates suggests this reduction has been significant, with, for example, the probability of survival to age 15 for contemporary hunter-gatherer populations almost twice as high as that recorded for wild chimpanzees (Kaplan et al., 2000).

Differences in extrinsic mortality rates may also explain differences in growth between human populations. Human height is normally considered a product of differences in nutrition and environmental stress (leading many studies to use growth as a general biomarker for physical health and related aspects of the early rearing environment; e.g. Lawson and Mace, 2008). However, while such factors are robust predictors of growth patterns within populations, they correspond relatively weakly to cross-population variation in adult heights, suggesting important genetic differences remain (Deaton, 2007). For example, pygmy populations found in regions of Africa, Southeast Asia, and South America have notably small adult heights, defined as population mean male stature of less than 155 cm (around five feet), in comparison to related populations with similarly poor levels of childhood nutrition (Migliano, Vinicius and Lahr, 2007; Perry and Dominy, 2009). Migliano, Vinicius and Lahr (2007) argue that the unique growth pattern of pygmy populations is a direct consequence of their exceptionally high levels of childhood and adult mortality (driven by the high parasite and pathogen load of their local ecology). Consistent with this hypothesis, modal age at first reproduction in pygmy populations is also exceptionally early, and women who reproduce at these earlier ages have higher predicted fitness than comparative late starters (Migliano, Vinicius and Lahr, 2007; see also Walker et al., 2006).

Trade-offs between current reproduction and future success

Once mature, investment in current reproduction must also be traded off against the allocation of resources to future survival and reproduction. A simple formulation of life history theory therefore predicts, all else being equal, negative effects of early fertility on later survival and reproduction (Gadgil and Bossert, 1970; Kirkwood, 1977; Williams, 1966). An early test of this hypothesis using historical data on the British aristocracy provided apparent strong evidence that current versus future trade-offs constrain human life history, demonstrating a positive association between age at first birth and longevity and a reduction in number of offspring produced for women living beyond 80 years (Westendorp and Kirkwood, 1998). This study has, however, drawn serious methodological criticism, regarding analysis design and incomplete genealogies (Le Bourg, 2001), and related investigations have found it difficult to replicate the results, with now perhaps almost as many studies finding the predicted negative relationships between early fertility and later success as those finding null or positive relationships (Le Bourg, 2007).

Some of this variation may reflect context-dependency: Lycett, Dunbar and Voland (2000), for example, in an analysis of a historical dataset of the German Krummhörn population, report that fertility had a negative impact on maternal longevity, but only amongst landless peasants (with wealthier families apparently able to simultaneously invest in high fertility and survival-related maintenance). Methodological problems in controlling for such heterogeneity in resource base between families, often particularly difficult in historical samples, may account for null findings in some cases (Gagnon *et al.*, 2009; Lummaa, 2007; Sear, 2007). The most recent research suggests the trade-off is detectable, providing fertility is relatively high and the sufficient adjustments are made for differences in socioeconomic and maternal health status, with a sophisticated comparative analysis of two historical datasets from Quebec and one from Utah demonstrating a negative effect of parity and a positive effect of age at last birth on post-reproductive survival in all three populations (Gagnon *et al.*, 2009).

The consequences of high investment in current reproduction can also be measured in comparison of mothers who produce singletons and twins. These studies are less susceptible to the problem of phenotypic correlations, because twinning rates can effectively be treated as random with respect to many sociodemographic factors which may otherwise confound associations between fertility and later outcomes (Lummaa, 2007). Accordingly, a number of studies have documented increased likelihood of maternal death at childbirth in twin deliveries (Gabler and Voland, 1994; Haukioja, Lemmetyinen and Pikkola, 1989; McDermott, Steketee and Wirima, 1995). There is also evidence that women bearing twins have increased post-reproductive mortality, and are more likely to fail to raise their next offspring, or to terminate reproduction altogether, as compared to mothers producing singletons (Helle, Lummaa and Jokela, 2004; Lummaa, 2001; Sear, 2007).

Just as twins are more costly than a single birth, male foetuses also receive higher energy allocations during pregnancy. They have a faster rate of growth (Marsal *et al.*, 1996), are heavier at birth (Anderson and Brown, 1943; Loos *et al.*, 2001) and pregnant women carrying a male foetus have been shown to have a higher energy intake than those carrying a female (Tamimi *et al.*, 2003). Some studies have also reported relatively long birth intervals following male births, suggesting increases in early post-natal investment practices such as breastfeeding (e.g. Mace and Sear, 1997). In light of these inequalities, higher reproductive costs of son relative to daughter production on future reproduction or survival may be anticipated. Support for a negative impact of sons on maternal longevity has been gathered from a number of studies, including historical populations in Finland (Helle, Lummaa and Jokela, 2002), Belgium (van de Putte, Matthijs and Vlietinck, 2004), Bangladesh (Hurt, Ronsmans and Quigley, 2006) and possibly Germany (Beise and Voland, 2002). The magnitude of effects and relative impact of the sexes is, however, far from uniform across studies, and in some cases differences are only apparent in particular subgroups. This suggests the increased physiological expense of male births may interact to varying degrees with the wider costs and benefits of rearing offspring of each sex, for example owing to differing contributions to household tasks and later patterns of resource transfer at marriage. Future studies are required to disentangle these effects.

Humans are remarkable among other primates, and animals in general, because females experience menopause – the fixed and irreversible cessation of reproductive potential at around 50 years of age, several decades before the end of the lifespan. Thus, human females have evolved to selectively invest resources into longevity at a cost to any chance of further reproduction, which at face value seems difficult to reconcile with an optimisation of life history. Why would natural selection not favour continued reproduction and earlier death? The 'grandmother hypothesis' provides one possible explanation, which has generated much debate in the literature (Hawkes, 2003; Mace, 2000; Marlowe, 2000; Peccei, 2001; Williams, 1957). According to this hypothesis, post-menopausal women are better able to enhance their lifetime reproductive success by assisting their current children to reproduce successfully than they would by having additional children of their own, which may be more costly at older ages owing to increased difficulties in childbirth (which may also endanger current offspring) and less chance of surviving long enough to provide adequate post-natal care.

Because all women experience menopause, we cannot directly examine the costs and benefits of alternative strategies. However, studies from a range of populations confirm the existence of significant grandmaternal effects on offspring fertility and the health and survival of grandchildren (Gibson and Mace, 2005; Hawkes, O'Connell and Blurton Jones, 1997; Lahdenpera *et al.*, 2004; Sear and Mace, 2008). In fact, it has been suggested that it is this help from grandmothers, along with other extended kin, which has enabled humans to simultaneously maintain relatively high reproductive rate and extended juvenile dependency relative to other primates of similar body size (Hawkes, 2003). Modelling work based on observed life histories and grandmother effects in rural Gambia suggests that these effects may be sufficient to explain the evolution of human menopause (Shanley *et al.*, 2007).

Trade-offs between quantity and quality of offspring

Resources invested in increasing reproductive rate cannot simultaneously be invested in advancing the development and competitive prospects of offspring. Life history theory therefore predicts a further trade-off between fertility and offspring survival and reproductive success (Lack, 1954; Smith and Fretwell, 1974; Williams, 1966; see also Box 6.1).

BOX 6.1.   THE EVOLUTION OF SIBLING RIVALRY

The importance of resource competition between siblings in the natural world is also revealed by the evolution of sibling rivalry (Hudson and Trillmich, 2008; Mock and Parker, 1997). In extreme cases, facultative and obligate systems of siblicide have evolved (occasionally referred to as 'cainism' following the Biblical account of Cain's murder of Abel). In many avian species, older siblings routinely kill younger hatchlings, a strategy which enables them to monopolise parental feeds (Mock, Drummond and Stinson, 1990; Simmons, 2002). Siblicide has also been documented at notable frequencies in several mammals, particularly when critical resources are scarce, including spotted hyenas (Wahaj *et al.*, 2007) and vampire bats (Leippet, Goymann, and Hofer, 2000). In my favourite example of sibling rivalry, Fraser and Thompson (1991) argue that domestic pigs have evolved early erupting canines as specialised 'sibling weaponry' to shift weaker sibling rivals off prime teats. The abstract of their manuscript (entitled 'Armed sibling rivalry among suckling piglets') has such unusual charm it deserves a full quotation:

A piglet's most precious possession
Is the teat that he fattens his flesh on.
He fights for his teat with tenacity
Against any sibling's audacity.
The piglet, to arm for this mission,
Is born with a warlike dentition
Of eight tiny tusks, sharp as sabres,
Which help in impressing the neighbors;

But to render these weapons less harrowing,
Most farmers remove them at farrowing.
We studied pig sisters and brothers
When some had their teeth, but not others,
We found that when siblings aren't many.
The weapons help little if any,
But when there are many per litter,
The teeth help their owners grow fitter,
But how did selection begin
To make weapons to use against kin?
(Fraser and Thompson, 1991, p. 9)

Anecdotal evidence suggests the rare occurrence of siblicide in humans also corresponds with cases of intense resource competition. Human history is full of examples of intrafamily conflict in the succession to inheritance. For example, in the fifteenth, sixteenth and seventeenth centuries, it was judicial law that all surviving brothers were murdered at the appointment of a new ruling Sultan of the Ottoman Empire, with the most famous case being when Mehmet III ordered the execution of 19 brothers. This grisly practice, later replaced by a more formalised system of primogeniture, was explicitly intended to minimise disputes to the throne and associated political instability (Quataert, 2000). Whether more modest forms of sibling rivalry in humans, such as the common quarrels and physical fights between children and adolescents (see Kettrey and Emery, 2007), can be explained from a strategic resource competition perspective remains an open question for research.

This simple concept of a 'quantity/quality trade-off', albeit without specific reference to Darwinian fitness, is also central to economic models of the human family (Becker, 1981; Blake, 1989; Downey, 2001). Studies of child mortality provide strong support of quantity/quality trade-off models when spacing between births is narrow, with most populations demonstrating negative effects of short birth intervals on child survival (Gibson and Mace, 2006; Hobcraft, McDonald and Rutstein, 1985; Rutstein, 1984). These costs are probably best explained by poor recovery of maternal somatic resources between births and by dilution of the particularly intense care required in the first years of infant life. Accordingly, excessively short birth intervals are rare in human populations. Chances of early survival are also substantially reduced in children from multiple births (Gabler and Voland, 1994; Rutstein, 1984; Sear *et al.*, 2001).

Considering associations between total family size and offspring outcomes across the full range of observed birth intervals presents a more complex picture. Studies of hunter-gatherer communities have not found strong evidence of quantity/quality trade-off effects. Among the !Kung, an African hunter-gatherer group on which the earliest studies of human life history were carried out (Blurton-Jones, 1986), researchers have failed to demonstrate higher mortality in children with many siblings (Draper and Hames, 2000; Pennington and Harpending, 1988). Among the South American Aché, number of siblings depressed likelihood of survival between the ages of 5 and 9 years. However, infant mortality below these ages was uninfluenced by parental fertility (Hill and Hurtado, 1996). Furthermore, in both populations, large sibships failed to depress female reproductive success and were actually associated with higher fertility for males (Draper and Hames, 2000; Hill and Hurtado, 1996).

Negative relationships between family size and child survival have been more effectively demonstrated in a number of contemporary African agriculturalist societies (Meij *et al.*, 2009; Strassmann and Gillespie, 2002; see also Figure 6.1, but see Borgerhoff Mulder 1998b) and historical European and American populations (Gillespie, Russell and Lummaa, 2008; Penn and Smith, 2007; Voland and Dunbar, 1995). There is also evidence of an association between family size and child anthropometric status among surviving children. Negative effects have been suggested in the South American Yanomamö (Hagen *et al.*, 2001) and Shuar (Hagen, Barrett and Price, 2006), while in a cross-national analysis of 15 developing populations, Desai (1995) found height-for-age in children less than 3 years old is significantly reduced by the presence of siblings close in age in almost all cases. However, despite using the same set of covariates for each country, effect magnitude was highly variable.

Studies of marital and reproductive success, focusing on the division of inherited capital such as land or cattle, also show clear costs of resource division between siblings which survive childhood. As inheritance usually goes to males, these effects are particularly visible on sons. For example, Mace (1996) found a negative effect of older brothers on male reproductive success in the Kenyan Gabbra. This resulted from smaller initial bridewealth herds and later age at marriage in comparison with their elder brothers. Number of sisters, however, had a moderately positive effect on male reproductive success. Similar effects have been demonstrated on the Kenyan Kipsigis (Borgerhoff Mulder, 1998b). Gillespie, Russell and Lummaa (2008) found that

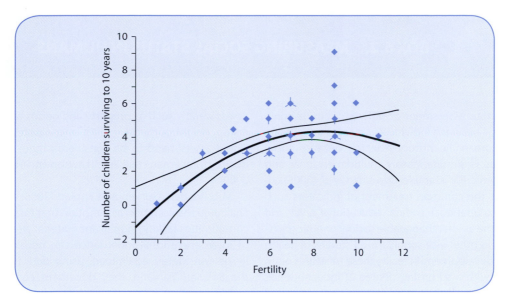

Figure 6.1. *The relationship between female fertility and number of offspring surviving to age 10 years in the Dogon of Mali, plus 95% confidence limits.*

Each petal represents an additional data point. High fertility is associated with increased child mortality, with intermediate fertility maximising number of surviving children.

Source: Adapted from Strassmann and Gillespie (2002).

large sibships reduced survival, but not fertility among survivors in eighteenth- and nineteenth-century Finland. However, this analysis did not test for sex-specific effects. In analysis of nineteenth-century Swedish data, Low (1991) found that both men's and women's reported reproductive success decreased as number of siblings increased, but particularly for men, and particularly with respect to number of brothers. Voland and Dunbar (1995) show that in Germany in the eighteenth and nineteenth centuries, number of same-sex siblings reduced likelihood of marriage, which likely further reduces reproductive success for both sexes.

In summary, a number of lines of evidence confirm that the human family is characterised by trade-off effects in the quantity and quality of children. However, for each outcome considered, be it survival, health or reproductive success, the effects of large family size appear somewhat variable and in a significant number of studies trade-offs are absent or positive effects are reported. Methodological issues may account for much of this variance. In particular, trade-offs may go undetected in the absence of sufficient controls of family level resources (van Noordwijk and de Jong, 1986). This may be a particular issue for studies of relatively egalitarian hunter-gathers who, unlike agriculturalist or wage-labour communities, lack obvious measures of relevant resource variation between families (Draper and Hames, 2000; Hill and Kaplan, 1999; see also Box 6.2).

But should we anticipate a uniform pattern of trade-off functions across cultures? Children often contribute significantly to economic pursuits in traditional societies,

BOX 6.2.   MEASURING SOCIAL STATUS IN HUMANS

Accurate assessment of differences in resource access between individuals presents a challenge to human life history research because social status is simultaneously multidimensional and dynamic. For example, Braveman *et al.* (2005) critique the common treatment of indicators such as occupational coding, educational level and income as interchangeable socioeconomic measures in otherwise sophisticated studies of health and development. In reality these measures often vary with a surprising degree of independence, signifying distinct domains which have varied influence on the phenotype. They also note the inadequacy of income as the most commonly used measure of material wealth in affluent societies (e.g. see Nettle and Pollet, 2008). This is partly because income data are volunteered with weak reliability in survey research, but more crucially because they assess current resource generation rather than total accumulated resources, which is largely determined by past economic activities and family inheritance (e.g. Keister, 2003). Income measures may be particularly inappropriate for older age individuals who may be retired or younger age individuals who are often enrolled in education and are rarely financially independent (the dominant sample population for many evolutionary psychologists). Thus, alternative measures of social status, which more directly assess wealth, such as property and goods ownership, neighbourhood quality or measures of 'liquid assets' need to be considered more frequently (Braveman *et al.*, 2005; Lawson and Mace, 2009).

Von Rueden, Gurven and Kaplan (2008) also challenge the common assumption that forager communities lacking significant material wealth or intergenerational inheritance can necessarily be considered 'egalitarian'. Using data from the Bolivian Tsimane, they document considerable variation along dimensions of physical condition, skill in resource accumulation, social support and level of acculturation – each with unique relationships to multiple photo-ranked assessments of social status, including recognised respect, community influence and the likelihood of winning dyadic fights. Reiches *et al.* (2009) further note that conceptualising and measuring resource access at the individual level presents problems because resources in all societies occupy 'pooled energy budgets', shared between kin and non-kin. In light of these non-trivial points, researchers should experiment with multiple approaches to measuring social status in their own analyses and retain a critical eye in the face of frequent claims that relevant resource variation has been reliably 'controlled' by statistical adjustment.

such as foraging, and may play important roles as 'alloparents' (Kramer, 2005; Sear and Mace, 2008). While the benefits of these behaviours may rarely offset the net drain on family resources, engagement in these activities may modify the local costs of sibling resource competition. Wider patterns of cooperative breeding, whereby relatives share the burden of childcare, may also alleviate trade-offs to varying degrees (Desai, 1992, 1995; Sear and Mace, 2008). In many contexts, siblings may serve as valuable political allies, such as in providing an advantage in community disputes or access to neighbouring hunting or foraging territories (Draper and Hames, 2000). Environmental risk factors associated with local socioecology and levels of economic development will also influence relationships between parental care and offspring development, establishing different trade-off functions (Lawson and Mace, 2010; Quinlan, 2007; Winterhalder and Leslie, 2002). I discuss this point further in the context of modernisation later in the chapter. Finally, cross-culturally variable patterns of biased parental investment by offspring sex and birth order will alter the costs and benefits of siblings (considered in more depth by Sear, in Chapter 7 of this volume).

THE OPTIMISATION OF FAMILY SIZE IN TRADITIONAL SOCIETIES

Mechanisms of fertility optimisation

The evolutionary ecology approach predicts that observed life histories represent ecologically dependent individual optima of fitness maximisation (sometimes referred to as the 'individual optimisation hypothesis': Pettifor, Perrins and McCleery, 2001). A number of mechanisms by which the human organism responds to local socioecology to optimise the quantity/quality trade-off have been proposed. At the physiological level, for example, automatic suppression of ovulation through lactation amenorrhea while nursing a young infant, or owing to intense physical stress or nutritional deficit, prevents conception and subsequent dilution of parental investment at a time when current offspring are highly vulnerable (Bentley, 1999; Ellison, 1990, 2003; see also Bribiescas, 2001).

At the psychological level, we can expect reproductive decision-making to be regulated by equivalent cognitive mechanisms utilising environmental information on observed or expected relationships between parental investment and offspring development (Kaplan, 1996; Kaplan and Gangestad, 2005; but see Box 6.3). Experimental studies show that such cognitive mechanisms are important regulators of fertility behaviour in many animal taxa. For example, Eggers *et al.* (2006) demonstrate that Siberian jays exposed to playbacks of predator calls seek out nests offering more protective covering and adjust current clutch size, even when predation itself is not increased. In humans, behavioural pathways of fertility regulation may often be institutionalised in cultural practices, such as rules regulating marriage, inheritance, celibacy, contraception and in extreme cases infanticide and abandonment (Hrdy, 1999; Kaplan, 1996). In modern societies, it has also been argued that we can add individual use of novel reproductive technologies including abortion and artificial fertility treatments to the list of strategic tools available to optimise reproductive timing and achieved family size (e.g. Lycett and Dunbar, 1999).

BOX 6.3. REPRODUCTIVE SUPPRESSION AND FEMALE EATING DISORDERS

A number of evolutionary psychologists have argued that female eating disorders, such as anorexia and bulimia, may have origins in an evolved mechanism of fertility regulation which was in fact adaptive in ancestral environments (e.g. Anderson and Crawford, 1992; Juda, Campbell and Crawford, 2004; Salmon and Crawford, 2008; Salmon et al., 2008). The theoretical foundation for this hypothesis is based on two observations. First, in the face of poor ecological conditions, lifetime reproductive success may be improved by a postponement of reproduction until circumstances become more favourable (Wasser and Barash, 1983; Williams, 1966). Second, according to the 'critical-fat hypothesis' a reduction of body fat under a certain threshold leads to a termination of ovulation (Frisch and McArthur, 1974). As such, it is argued that voluntary weight reduction evolved as a strategy to delay reproduction when social or ecological cues predict poor reproductive outcomes and that this mechanism is activated at pathological levels by equivalent, but somehow amplified, cues in the contemporary West.

In my view, this 'reproductive suppression hypothesis' (RSH) is weakened by a number of fundamental problems poorly addressed by its supporting literature. Most importantly, while reproductive ecologists have indeed demonstrated that harsh environmental conditions are associated with temporary suppression of ovulation, this is ecologically enforced (e.g. owing to local food shortages), occurring entirely through automatic physiological pathways (Bentley, 1999; Ellison, 1990, 2003). In no case has the voluntary denial of available food been recorded in response to environmental hardship. It is also contentious that a simple regulation of body fat would provide sufficiently reliable grounds for fertility regulation, as the associated critical-fat hypothesis has been criticised as overly simplistic (see references in Mircea, Lujan and Pierson, 2007). Proponents of the RSH have also failed to conduct a formal cost-benefit model of the proposed ancestral strategy, yet clearly voluntary starvation in poor conditions, even over short periods, would elevate risks of mortality. Instead, the main evidence presented for the RSH has been repeated demonstrations of positive associations between disordered attitudes to dieting and various indicators of social stress and 'parental unreadiness' in Western women (usually North American college students). Such associations are consistent with, but hardly uniquely attributable to, the RSH. Consequently, the RSH fits an unfortunate stereotype of evolutionary psychology as 'adaptive storytelling'; out of sync with current anthropological literature and advocated without adequate theoretical or empirical rigour.

Predicted optima and observed fertility

Animal behavioural ecologists have tested the individual optimisation hypothesis with the prediction that neither the experimental addition nor the experimental removal of young will result in increased parental fitness relative to control broods (e.g. Gustafsson and Sutherland, 1988; Humphries and Boutin, 2000; Pettifor, Perrins and McCleery, 2001; Tinbergen and Daan, 1990). Anthropologists have had to make do with alternative methods. One approach has been to first determine the fertility level that leads to the highest fitness returns in some measurable currency (while control-ling for differences in parental resources) and then to compare this to the population mode. If fertility is optimised, then optimal and modal fertility should converge.

Studies of the !Kung (Draper and Hames, 2000; Pennington and Harpending, 1988) and Aché (Hill and Hurtado, 1996) reveal positive linear relationships between number of children, and the lifetime reproductive success of the mother, with a substantial slope. This implies that both groups of hunter-gatherers failed to optimise family size, as higher fitness could have been achieved by increasing fertility beyond observed levels. Borgerhoff Mulder's (2000) study of the Kipsigis identified a quantity/quality trade-off in family size, with intermediate numbers of children maximising grandchildren for women, but not for men. For women, the calculated optima corresponded with the population mode. In the Dogon, Strassmann and Gillespie (2002) found family size had a clear negative effect on child survival rates, so that an intermediate level of fertil-ity (eight offspring) optimised this measure of reproductive success (see Figure 6.1). A large majority of women had a completed fertility within the confidence limits of this estimate, leading the authors to conclude that observed family size optimised paren-tal fitness. However, subsequent studies of child survival attempting to replicate the results of Strassmann and Gillespie (2002) have found little evidence that intermediate levels of fertility maximise the number of surviving children (e.g. Meij et al., 2009).

The mixed success of these studies may largely rest on the difficulty involved in calculating precise fertility optima with available data (Hill and Hurtado, 1996). Lifetime reproductive success, as measured by the number of surviving children or grandchildren, is probably an effective proxy for fitness in many ecologies, provided mortality rates are relatively high (Jones, 2009). However, studies focusing on child survival alone will not detect negative effects of large family size, which become apparent in later life, such as through early death of the mother (Meij et al., 2009) or in future generations caused by the division of inherited resources (McNamara and Houston, 2006). Hence, such studies are likely to systematically overestimate the optimum family size. This line of reasoning is consistent with the fact that all studies that have failed to demonstrate a convergence between modal and optimal fertility have suggested that observed levels lie below the optimum.

Wealth and reproductive success

A more generalised approach, that does not require the calculation of precise optima, is to consider covariation in the strength of trade-off effects and observed fertility. Life history studies typically operate under the assumption that negative effects of competition between offspring are at their strongest when resources are scarce (van Noordwijk and de Jong, 1986; Tuomi, Hakala and Haukioja, 2010). Economic mod-els of the family have also assumed that, since quantity/quality trade-offs are driven by 'credit constraint', increases in personal or societal wealth will reduce negative effects of high fertility on offspring (Becker and Lewis, 1973; Grawe, 2010). Empirical support for this position has been demonstrated in a number of animal studies (e.g. Boyce and Perrins, 1987; Risch, Dobson and Murie, 1995).

In humans, costs of high parental fertility in individual offspring have been shown to be less pronounced in relatively wealthy strata in both contemporary African (Borgerhoff Mulder, 2000; Meij *et al.*, 2009) and eighteenth- and nineteenth-century European agriculturalists (Gillespie, Russell and Lummaa, 2008; Lummaa *et al.*, 1998). Therefore, positive relationships between individual wealth and fertility are anticipated, as when sibling competition is relaxed there are fewer costs to outweigh the benefits of large family size. Consistent with widespread fertility optimisation, anthropologists and historical demographers have demonstrated strong positive relationships between socioeconomic status and fertility in practically all traditional societies where such relationships have been considered (Borgerhoff Mulder, 1987; Cronk, 1991; for a review, see Hopcroft, 2006).

THE OPTIMISATION OF FAMILY SIZE IN MODERN SOCIETIES

The demographic transition

Demographic transition refers to the population shift from high mortality and fertility to low mortality and fertility, which typically occurs in the economic development of a population from a pre-industrial to an industrialised economy. In classic models, this is a multistage process starting with a fall in death rates, followed in time by reduced birth rates, leading to an interval of first increased and then decreased population growth (Coale and Watkins, 1986; Lee, 2003). The first demographic transitions occurred in northwest Europe, where mortality began a secular decline around 1800. It has now 'spread' to all areas of the world, with most developing populations in at least the early stages of transition, and the completion of a 'global demographic transition' projected by 2100 (Lee, 2003).

Initial mortality declines in modernising countries were largely driven by innovations in healthcare along with advancements in food storage and transportation, which reduced rates of and susceptibility to infectious disease and famine. Changes in mortality were mostly focused on infants and children, with death becoming increasingly concentrated in a relatively narrow band of older age. Following these advancements, fertility began to decline in most European countries between 1890 and 1920 (Coale and Treadway, 1986). However, there are notable cases where fertility decline has commenced without prior shifts in mortality, presenting a challenge to transition theories that envisage fertility decline as a direct response to mortality shifts. Less developed countries began to reduce fertility from around the 1960s, with fertility decline typically occurring more rapidly than for those in current developed countries (Lee, 2003). The total fertility rate has now fallen to below replacement level in practically all industrialised populations and many countries in East Asia.

Modern post-demographic-transition societies immediately appear at odds with adaptive models of fertility optimisation (Borgerhoff Mulder, 1998a; Vining, 1986). First, despite substantial increases in personal wealth and the establishment of the welfare state, which aims to guarantee basic levels of well-being independent of parental care, fertility has fallen in recent decades to the lowest levels in recorded human history. Current levels of resource abundance appear to buffer out any evolutionarily relevant costs of high fertility on offspring survival or reproduction. This is demonstrated by a number of studies applying traditional life history models to modern fertility. In all cases, researchers have failed to detect any trade-off between number of children and grandchildren, even in very large families, suggesting observed family sizes fall considerably below any fitness maximising optimum (Kaplan *et al.*, 1995; Mueller, 2001; see also Figure 6.2).

Second, although there is wide variation in timing, speed and magnitude across societies, fertility decline within societies is generally characterised by markedly larger reductions of fertility in wealthy families compared to the rest of the population (Clark and Cummins, 2009; Livi-Bacci, 1986). As a consequence, modern fertility is not only dramatically reduced in comparison to traditional populations but is also typified by relative socioeconomic levelling (Nettle and Pollet, 2008). Thus,

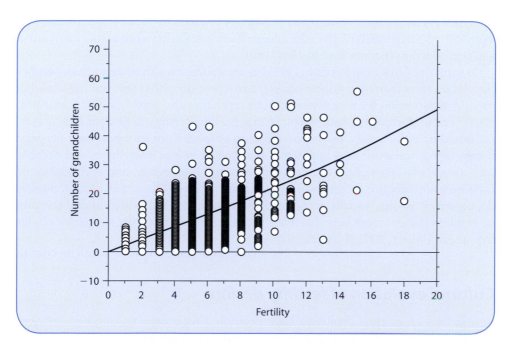

Figure 6.2. *The relationship between male fertility and number of grandchildren in Albuquerque, New Mexico.*

There is no indication of a trade-off between fertility and fitness as measured by number of grandchildren. Modal fertility is two, but number of grandchildren is maximised at the highest observed fertility.

Source: From Kaplan *et al.* (1995).

contrary to adaptive predictions, relationships between wealth and fertility are typically recorded as null or negative in demographic surveys (Kaplan *et al.*, 1995, 2002; Lawson and Mace, 2010). Some studies have suggested that when education is held constant positive correlations between income and fertility persist, at least for males (Fieder and Huber, 2007; Hopcroft, 2006; Nettle and Pollet, 2008). However, these relationships appear to operate on mating success, rather than reproductive success per se (i.e. influencing levels of childlessness, rather than family size amongst reproducing individuals) and remain considerably weaker than relationships observed in traditional societies (Nettle and Pollet, 2008). Alternative evolutionary models, emphasising inherent limitations in evolved mechanisms of adaptation, have consequently gathered popularity as explanations of modern fertility decline.

Maladaption to novel contraceptive technologies

Adaptive behaviour should not always be anticipated when current environments differ from the ancestral conditions under which our physiological and cognitive mechanisms of fertility regulation evolved (Irons, 1998). Modern fertility patterns may, therefore, be explained by the interaction of ancestrally formed adaptations and novel socioecological factors. Taking this perspective, many evolutionary psychologists have argued that the widespread availability of efficient birth control technology in modern environments negates the ancestral association between sexual intercourse and reproduction (Barkow and Burley, 1980).

In support of this view, Perusse (1993) has shown that wealthier men achieve higher copulation rates than their poorer counterparts, proposing that without the availability of contraception the wealthy would out-reproduce the poor (see also Kanazawa, 2003). The importance of contraception in regulating fertility behaviour is, however, contested by evolutionary and economic demographers, not least because European demographic transition was apparently initiated by coitus interruptus and because such models fail to explain the demand driving the invention and accessibility of modern contraceptive technology (Borgerhoff Mulder, 1998a; Lee, 2003). Studies documenting strong, socially recognised motivations for reproduction and the care of children distinct from sexual activity further dissuade from the simplicity of this hypothesis (Foster, 2000; Rotkirch, 2007).

Cultural evolution of fertility decline

Researchers of cultural evolution have promoted their own accounts of modern fertility behaviour. These models have much in common with a rising number of social demographers who reject the individual-level rational choice perspective of economic demography in favour of models of cultural diffusion and social influence (see Bongaarts and Watkins, 1996; Kohler, 2001; Montgomery and Casterline, 1996). Boyd and Richerson (1985), for example, suggest that throughout our history imitating behaviour associated with social prestige offered an efficient mechanism to enhance individual fitness. In traditional societies, imitation of esteemed patriarchs and matriarchs would thus cause individuals to strive to attain similar high fertility. Modernisation offers novel social roles of high prestige, such as teachers and heads of organised workforces. Competition for such positions is advanced by increased investments in education and production away from the family, at the cost of limited fertility. Thus, imitation of prestigious individuals could consequently lead fertility levels to diverge from individual optima, sparking fertility decline. This hypothesis, however, fails to provide an effective explanation for why the first individuals decided to limit fertility in the early stages of demographic transition (Borgerhoff Mulder, 1998a), nor does it take into account that social prestige is itself constructed by societal norms and values (Newson et al., 2005).

An alternative perspective, combining models of social learning and the importance of extended kin in human life history, has been offered by Newson et al. (2005). Here it is suggested that kin can be expected to place social pressure and rewards upon reproduction, at least when conditions are favourable, as this would lead to inclusive fitness benefits. Thus, traditional societies, which are characterised by frequent and sustained interaction with kin, lead to high fertility norms consistent with fitness maximisation. However, cultural modernisation dramatically changes the nature of social networks through the fragmentation of the extended family. Non-kin have less inclination to support our reproductive interests and, therefore, high fertility strategies are less likely to become socially favoured, encouraging low and potentially maladaptive fertility norms.

In support of this model, Newson et al. (2007) report that in role-playing experiments individuals adopting the role of friends, in contrast to relatives, are less likely to offer favourable advice about reproduction. The validity of the 'kin-influence hypothesis' ultimately rests on demonstrating the role of kin networks in actual rather than imagined reproductive decisions and in demonstrating influence above and beyond a response to the economic benefits of kin presence or absence. Few existing studies currently speak directly to this point. In one recent study, Mace and Colleran (2009) report that contraception use (normally considered a precursor to fertility decline) was uninfluenced by whether individuals in the wider kin network had previously used contraception, once individual level economic factors had been taken into account.

Parental investment models of modern fertility

While it seems obvious that fertility limitation has no meaningful influence on offspring survival or reproductive success in modern families, research from across the social sciences confirms that high fertility carries a number of important costs to both offspring and parents (see Figure 6.3). For this reason, evolutionary ecologists, along with many economic demographers, have remained resistant to the view that modernisation leads to an 'uncoupling' of reproductive decision-making from the real or perceived costs and benefits of rearing children (Kaplan et al., 2002; Lawson and Mace, 2010; Mace, 2007).

Lawson and Mace (2010), for example, demonstrate that high fertility in contemporary Britain is associated with increased maternal perceptions of economic hardship, even when controlling for a range of household level socioeconomic measures. Family

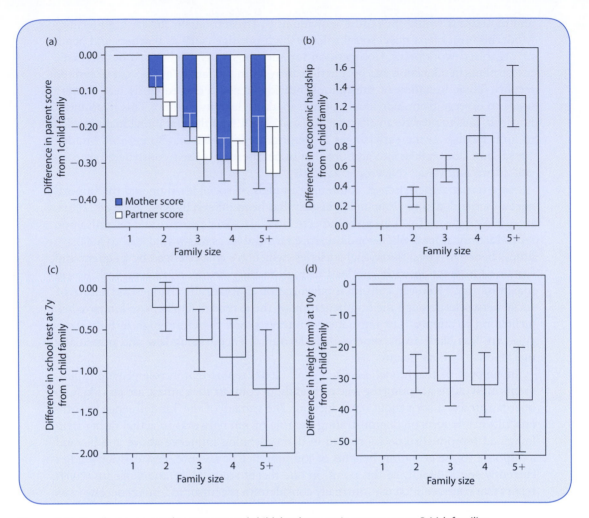

Figure 6.3. *Family size, parental investment and child development in contemporary British families.*

The relationship between family size and (a) maternal and paternal allocations of care time between 1 and 9 years (from Lawson and Mace, 2009); (b) maternal perception of economic hardship from 0 to 7 years (from Lawson and Mace, 2010); (c) school test results at 7 years (from Lawson, 2009); (d) height at age 10 years (from Lawson, 2009; Lawson and Mace, 2008). Children with more siblings receive less time from parents, grow up in more economically stressed households and exhibit relatively poor physical and cognitive/educational development. Confidence intervals are set at 95%.

Source: Data are from the Avon Longitudinal Study of Parents and Children, a large cohort study (*n* = 14 000 +) of children born in 1991/1992.

size also has a strong negative influence on allocations of care time to individual children from both mothers and fathers; with family size having a larger influence on parental time investment over the first decade of life than any other covariate considered, including socioeconomic indicators and parental age (Lawson and Mace, 2009). Studies throughout the developed world show that children in larger families perform significantly worse on IQ tests and on formal educational assessments throughout life, a pattern recognised as one of the most stable relationships in the study of education

(Blake, 1989; Downey, 1995, 2001; Lawson, 2009; Steelman *et al.*, 2002). There is also evidence that the presence of siblings is associated with deficits in childhood growth, which may stem from reduced parental attention to healthcare or nutrition in early life (Lawson and Mace, 2008). Finally, number of siblings has an important negative effect on achieved socioeconomic status in adulthood, particularly on wealth owner-ship (Kaplan *et al.*, 1995; Keister, 2003, 2004). Keister (2003), for instance, demonstrates that number of siblings is a strong determinant of the likelihood of receiving a trust fund or an inheritance (see also Cooney and Uhlenberg, 1992).

In the presence of these quantity/quality trade-off effects, it is possible that mod-ern low fertility remains adaptive in the long-run if we take into account that imme-diate deficits in reproductive success may eventually be offset by acquired benefits to wealth inheritance or other predictors of lineage survival. Such a scenario has been formally modelled as theoretically plausible by a number of researchers (Boone and Kessler, 1999; Hill and Reeve, 2005; Mace, 1998; McNamara and Houston, 2006). Alternatively, Kaplan (1996) argues that modern low fertility is indeed maladaptive, but nevertheless the product of an evolved psychology which regulates reproduction in balance with the local effects of parental investment on offspring status. This psy-chology fails to function adaptively in modern contexts because novel factors, such as the establishment of skill-based wage economies, offer radically extended scope for status competition between individuals at levels which now fail to translate into significant survival or reproductive benefits (Kaplan, 1996; Kaplan *et al.*, 2002).

Both perspectives share a key prediction which challenges the standard model of life history trade-offs: in order to favour low fertility in a time of economic prosperity and furthermore negative or null intrapopulation relationships between socioeco-nomic status and fertility, cultural modernisation must establish unusually intense resource competition between offspring *when resources are relatively abundant rather than scarce*. Evidence for this reversal is accumulating, albeit sketchy, as until recently few studies have directly considered variation in trade-off functions in association with modernisation or between socioeconomic strata within modern populations.

High levels of extrinsic risk in offspring survival and development character-ises traditional populations, leading to substantial diminishing returns to parental investment, with a low saturation point beyond which 'chance' becomes the prin-cipal determinant of offspring success (Pennington and Harpending, 1988; Quinlan, 2007). As the traditional life history model assumes, this pattern is associated with reduced levels of resource competition between offspring when resources are relat-ively abundant, favouring high fertility norms. Cultural modernisation through the abolishment of extrinsic risks (i.e. reductions in the incidence of famine, infectious disease, warfare, crime and environmental catastrophes) buffers populations from environmental instability and may therefore create a higher degree of reliability in investment returns (Winterhalder and Leslie, 2002). As such, it is possible that higher levels of wealth may lead to a closer association between parental investment and offspring quality, and subsequently increased costs to resource competition between offspring, favouring family limitation (Kaplan, 1996; Kaplan *et al.*, 2002). Gibson and Lawson (in press) consider this model in the context of a development initiative in rural Ethiopia that in some villages has radically reduced early childhood mortality: the installation of water taps (Gibson and Mace, 2006; see also Figure 6.4). In villages

Figure 6.4. *An Oromo woman collecting water from a newly installed tap stand in Southern Ethiopia.*

Development projects are radically changing local mortality patterns in many parts of the world, and life histories are shifting in response (Gibson and Lawson, in press; Gibson and Mace, 2006).

Source: Photo courtesy of Mhairi Gibson and Lucie Clech.

where tap stands have been installed, parents are more likely to invest in child educa-tion, indicating increased investment per offspring, and the likelihood of receiving education is more determined by position in the family, suggesting elevated costs to investment division. In further support, Desai's (1995) cross-cultural study of child-hood growth demonstrates that improved access to safe drinking water and health-care facilities is associated with larger negative effects of sibship size on height.

Modern skill-based wage economies and the welfare state may place additional rewards on fertility limitation when parental resources are in good supply (Kaplan *et al.*, 2002; Lawson and Mace, 2010). This is because investments in skill-acquisition or direct transfers of wealth now also radically increase an offspring's ability to gen-erate new wealth over the life course and further invest in their own status. Strong welfare states may also selectively reduce investment competition in the poorest families through guaranteed provisioning of basic schooling, healthcare and social opportunity; consequently, families with potential to invest above this 'base' level (e.g. in private schooling and healthcare) may experience more substantial costs to investment division (Downey, 2001; Lawson and Mace, 2010). In support of these proposed mechanisms, Keister (2004) and Grawe (2010) both demonstrate that large family size is associated with negative consequences on the income generation and wealth ownership of offspring in middle and high socioeconomic families in the United States, but of relatively little consequence to children from impoverished backgrounds. Lawson and Mace (2010) also report that relatively high social class British mothers record larger increases in economic hardship associated with reproducing above the two-child norm, suggesting that the perceived costs of high fertility are magnified in high socioeconomic strata.

It is currently impossible to determine whether small family sizes are adaptive in the long-term; we lack sufficient multigenerational data to test this model (see also Box 6.4). Nevertheless, in contrast to the popular hypotheses proposed by many

BOX 6.4. MODERN REPRODUCTIVE BEHAVIOUR AND ADAPTIVE REASONING

A number of researchers have modelled reproductive differentials in contemporary Western populations to deduce selection pressures currently acting on modern humans (e.g. Jokela, 2009; Nettle and Pollet, 2008) or alternatively to deduce the ancestral selection pressures which have shaped the extant human phenotype (e.g. Nettle, 2002). A life history perspective on reproductive behaviour suggests scepticism should be exercised in both cases. For example, Jokela (2009) finds that physical attractiveness is associated with high fertility in a modern population, while Nettle and Pollet (2008) find that male (but not female) income is positively correlated with fertility once negative effects of education have been taken into account. Thus, it has been argued that natural selection is currently acting positively on female and male attractiveness and male 'wealth' (see also Box 6.2). However, as we have discussed, under conditions of low mortality and high intergenerational transmission of resources, it remains quite possible that small or intermediate family size will maximise long-term genetic fitness. This point is particularly pertinent to Nettle and Pollet (2008) because any reproductive gains to above-average wealth will fail to be transmitted to offspring when a high-fertility strategy is followed, owing to the sharp division of inherited wealth between siblings

(Keister, 2003; Lawson and Mace, 2010; Mace, 1998).

The deduction of past selection pressures from current fertility patterns is also problematic when it is acknowledged that behavioural optima necessarily vary between populations, particularly when socioecological differences are dramatic (clearly the case in the comparison of modern urban to ancestral hunter-gatherer demography). The potential for modern populations to suffer 'adaptive lag' in the face of environmental novelty also suggests that reproductive patterns are unlikely to be analogous (Irons, 1998). As an illustration, Nettle (2002) suggests that sexual selection has acted in opposing directions on male and female height, explaining current levels of sexual dimorphism in stature. This conjecture is based on analyses of contemporary Western populations, which have indicated relatively tall men are rated as more attractive and achieve higher fertility, while the reverse is true for women. However, Sear (2006) critiques this hypothesis because available data from traditional populations show male height is not significantly associated to number of children and that female height is actually positively associated with reproductive success, largely because of the improved survival of their children (see also Monden and Smits, 2009; Sear, 2009).

evolutionary psychologists and cultural evolutionists (Barkow and Burley, 1980; Boyd and Richerson, 1985; Kanazawa, 2003; Newson *et al.*, 2005; Perusse, 1993), these effects suggest that modern low fertility may be best understood as a directed reproductive strategy of extended parental investment in sync with the local costs and benefits of raising socially and economically competitive offspring.

CONCLUSIONS AND FUTURE DIRECTIONS

Four billion years of evolution by natural selection, from the earliest prokaryotes (single-celled life forms) to the collection of successful organisms currently inhabiting our planet, has laid witness to a radical variety in reproductive strategies. Life history theory argues that this diversity, from the bird that always lays two eggs only for the first chick to murder the second (Mock, Drummond and Stinson, 1990; Simmons, 2002), to the chameleon that lives most of its life as an egg (Karsten *et al.*, 2008), or the 'matriphagous' spider whose first meal is always its mother (Kim, Roland and Horel, 2000), can be understood as competitive resource allocation tactics 'designed' to maximise Darwinian inclusive fitness.

Each species has a unique life history because each species is adapted to its own unique ecological and demographic niche. Populations vary within species, and individuals vary within populations, because natural selection rarely favours organisms 'inert' to local environment contingencies; instead it supplements genetic variation with high levels of phenotypic plasticity – reaction norms that shift developmental trajectories and behavioural responses favouring life history optimisation at the individual level (West-Eberhard, 2007). Studies of human life history aim to elucidate both the ultimate origins of variation in human growth, mortality and reproduction, and the evolved proximate mechanisms regulating observed phenotypes. Emphasis is placed simultaneously on broad comparative study, including both cross-cultural and cross-species generalisations, and on detailed anthropological and sociological surveys at the local and individual level. It is acknowledged that not only will life history optima vary between environments but also that adaptive responses will necessarily be limited by the imperfect design of both our physiology and psychology, which are perhaps particularly sensitive to patterns of adaptive lag in the face of rapidly changing environments (Irons, 1998; but see Laland and Brown, 2006).

In this chapter, I have reviewed the main trade-offs in human life history and the evidence for fertility optimisation across both traditional and modern societies. It should be clear from the research summarised that life history studies are inherently interdisciplinary; while most of its practitioners are trained as biologists or anthropologists, a shared concern with differences in health, social status and schedules of fertility and mortality ensure significant empirical overlap with neighbouring sciences. Theoretical overlap is also often substantial, with, for example, many evolutionary anthropologists and demographers adapting existing frameworks from economic models of fertility and family resource dilution (e.g. Kaplan, 1994; Lawson and Mace, 2009).

In contrast, explicitly evolutionary models of human behaviour do not always find much favour with the mainstream social sciences (Segerstråle, 2000). There are multiple reasons for this, including the fact that the evolutionary approaches remain a young and partially fragmented field (Sear, Lawson and Dickins, 2007), that few researchers in the neighbouring sciences have the formal training in biology required to understand, critique and incorporate Darwinian hypotheses, and regrettably the persistence of less rigorous forms of evolutionary psychology that capitalise on the popular appeal and controversy of some hypotheses, rather than adherence to the scientific method (for recent critiques, see Dickins, Sear and Wells 2007; Gelman, 2007; Lawson, Jordan and Magid, 2008).

Overcoming such difficulties is an important aim for future research. A dedicated focus on topics of social and public relevance represents one sure pathway to encourage greater interchange. Here, I have discussed a life history perspective on demographic transition and the effects of modernisation on family life (Bock, 1999, provides a more detailed discussion of how evolutionary models may be used to strengthen and unify outlooks across demography). Other researchers have emphasised the potential for life history theory to advance our current understanding of health inequalities, providing an overarching theoretical framework to study both inherent disease susceptibility and the motivations behind disease-causing behaviours (Hill, 1993; Strassmann and Mace, 2008). Tucker and Rende Taylor (2007) provide a thoughtful discussion of how life history models, as a foundation of human evolutionary ecology, may also be used to critique (and ultimately improve) the implementation of government and non-governmental organisation projects and policies aimed at improving public health and social welfare (see also Gibson and Mace, 2006). All of these research developments represent exciting and vital steps forward in establishing the value of a considered and integrative evolutionary perspective on human behaviour.

ACKNOWLEDGEMENTS

This review was supported by a UK Economic and Social Research Council (ESRC) Research Fellowship. The author would like to thank Gillian Bentley, Mhairi Gibson, Shakti Lamba, Rebecca Sear and Ruth Mace for valuable discussion and criticism.

REFERENCES

Allal, N., Sear, R., Prentice, A. M. and Mace, R. (2004). An evolutionary model of stature, age at first birth and reproductive success in Gambian women. *Proceedings of the Royal Society B*, *271*, 465–70.

Anderson, J. and Crawford, C. (1992). Modelling costs and benefits of adolescent weight control as a mechanism for reproductive suppression. *Human Nature*, *3*, 299–334.

Anderson, N. A. and Brown, E. W. (1943). Causes of prematurity, III. Influence of race and sex on duration of gestation and weight at birth. *American Journal of the Diseases of Children*, *65*, 523–34.

Barkow, J. H. and Burley, N. (1980). Human fertility, evolutionary biology, and the demographic transition. *Ethology and Sociobiology*, *1*, 163–80.

Becker, G. S. (1981). *A treatise on the family*. Cambridge, MA: Harvard University Press.

Becker, G. S. and Lewis, H. G. (1973). Interaction between quantity and quality of children. In T. W. Schultz (ed.), *Economics of the family: Marriage, children and human capital* (pp. 81–90). Chicago: University of Chicago Press.

Beise, J. and Voland, E. (2002). Effect of producing sons on maternal longevity in premodern populations. *Science*, *298*, 317.

Bentley, G. (1999). Aping our ancestors: Comparative aspects of reproductive ecology. *Evolutionary Anthropology*, *7*, 175–85.

Blake, J. (1989). *Family size and achievement*. Los Angeles: University of California.

Blurton Jones, N. (1986). Bushman birth spacing: A test of optimal interbirth intervals. *Ethology and Sociobiology*, *7*, 91–105.

Bock, J. (1999). Evolutionary approaches to population: Implications for research and policy. *Population and Environment*, *21*, 193–222.

Bogin, B. (1997). Evolutionary hypotheses for human childhood. *American Journal of Physical Anthropology*, *104*, 63–89.

Bongaarts, J. and Watkins, S. C. (1996). Social interactions and contemporary fertility transitions. *Population and Development Review*, *22*, 639–82.

Boone, J. L. and Kessler, K. L. (1999). More status or more children? Social status, fertility reduction, and long-term fitness. *Evolution and Human Behavior*, *20*, 257–77.

Borgerhoff Mulder, M. (1987). On cultural and reproductive success: Kipsigis evidence. *American Anthropologist*, *88*, 617–634.

Borgerhoff Mulder, M. (1998a). The demographic transition: Are we any closer to an evolutionary explanation? *Trends in Ecology and Evolution*, *13*, 266–70.

Borgerhoff Mulder, M. (1998b). Brothers and sisters. How sibling interactions affect optimal parental allocations. *Human Nature*, *9*, 119–162.

Borgerhoff Mulder, M. (2000). Optimizing offspring: The quantity–quality tradeoff in agropastoral Kipsigis. *Evolution and Human Behaviour*, *21*, 391–410.

Boyce, M. S. and Perrins, C. M. (1987). Optimizing great tit clutch size in a fluctuating environment. *Ecology*, *68*, 142–53.

Boyd, R. and Richerson, P. J. (1985). *Culture and the evolutionary process*. Chicago: University of Chicago Press.

Braveman, P. A., Cubbin, C., Susan, E. *et al.* (2005). Socioeconomic status in health research: One size does not fit all. *Journal of the American Medical Association*, *294*, 2879–88.

Bribiescas, R. G. (2001). Reproductive ecology and life history of the human male. *American Journal of Physical Anthropology*, *116*, 148–76.

Charnov, E. L. (1993). *Life history invariants*. Oxford: Oxford University Press.

Clark, G. and Cummins, N. (2009). Urbanization, mortality, and fertility in Malthusian *England*. *American Economic Review*, *99*, 242–7.

Coale, A. and Treadway, R. (1986). A summary of the changing distribution of overall fertility, marital fertility, and the proportion married in the provinces of Europe. In A. Coale and S. C. Watkins (eds), *The decline of fertility in Europe* (pp. 31–181). Princeton, NJ: Princeton University Press.

Coale, A. and Watkins, S. (1986). *The decline of fertility in Europe*. Princeton, NJ: Princeton University Press.

Cody, M. L. (1966). A general theory of clutch size. *Evolution*, *20*, 174–84.

Cooney, T. M. and Uhlenberg, P. (1992). Support from parents over the life course: The adult child's perspective. *Social Forces*, *71*, 63–84.

Cronk, L. (1991). Wealth, status and reproductive success among the Mukogodo. *American Anthropologist*, *93*, 345–60.

Deaton, A. (2007). Height, health, and development. *Proceedings of the National Academy of Sciences of the USA*, *104*, 13232–7.

Desai, S. (1992). Children at risk: The role of family structure in Latin America and West Africa. *Population and Development Review*, *18*, 689–717.

Desai, S. (1995). When are children from large families disadvantaged? Evidence from cross-national analyses. *Population Studies*, *49*, 195–210.

Dickins, T. E., Sear, R. and Wells, A. J. (2007). Mind the gap(s) . . . in theory, method and data: Re-examining Kanazawa (2006). *British Journal of Health Psychology*, *12*, 167–78.

Downey, D. B. (1995). When bigger is not better: Family size, parental resources and children's educational performance. *American Sociological Review*, *60*, 746–61.

Downey, D. B. (2001). Number of siblings and intellectual development: The resource dilution explanation. *American Psychologist*, *56*, 497–504.

Draper, P. and Hames, R. (2000). Birth order, sibling investment, and fertility among Ju/'Hoansi (!Kung). *Human Nature*, *11*, 116–156.

Eggers, S., Griesser, M., Nystrand, M. and Ekman, J. (2006). Predation risk induces changes in nest-site selection and clutch size in the Siberian jay. *Proceedings of the Royal Society B*, *273*, 701–6.

Ellison, P. T. (1990). Human ovarian function and reproductive ecology: New hypotheses. *American Anthropologist*, *92*, 933–52.

Ellison, P. T. (2003). Energetics and reproductive effort. *American Journal of Human Biology*, *15*, 342–51.

Fieder, M. and Huber, S. (2007). The effects of sex and childlessness on the association between status and reproductive output in modern society. *Evolution and Human Behavior*, *28*, 392–8.

Foster, C. (2000). The limits to low fertility: A biosocial approach. *Population and Development Review*, *26*, 209–34.

Fraser, D. and Thompson, B. K. (1991). Armed sibling rivalry among suckling piglets. *Behavioral Ecology and Sociobiology*, *29*, 9–15.

Frisch, R. E. and McArthur, J. W. (1974). Menstrual cycles: Fatness as a determinant of minimum weight for height necessary for their maintenance or onset. *Science*, *185*, 949–51.

Gabler, S. and Voland, E. (1994). Fitness of twinning. *Human Biology*, *66*, 699–713.

Gadgil, M. and Bossert, W. H. (1970). Life historical consequences of natural selection. *American Naturalist*, *104*, 1–24.

Gagnon, A., Smith, K. R., Tremblay, M. *et al.* (2009). Is there a trade-off between fertility and longevity? A comparative study of women from three large historical databases accounting for mortality selection. *American Journal of Human Biology*, *21*, 533–40.

Gelman, A. (2007). Letter to the editors regarding some papers of Dr. Satoshi Kanazawa. *Journal of Theoretical Biology*, *245*, 597–9.

Gibson, M. and Lawson, D. W. (in press). 'Modernization' increases parental investment and sibling resource competition: Evidence from a rural development initiative in Ethiopia. *Evolution and Human Behavior*.

Gibson, M. A. and Mace, R. (2005). Helpful grandmothers in rural Ethiopia: A study of the effect of kin on child survival and growth. *Evolution and Human Behavior*, *26*, 469–82.

Gibson, M. A. and Mace, R. (2006). An energy-saving development initiative increases birth rate and childhood malnutrition in rural Ethiopia. *PLoS Medicine*, *3*, 476–84.

Gillespie, D., Russell, A. and Lummaa, V. (2008). When fecundity does not equal fitness: Effects of an offspring quantity versus quality trade-off in pre-industrial humans. *Proceedings of the Royal Society B*, *275*, 713–22.

Grawe, N. (2010). Bequest receipt and family size effects. *Economic Inquiry*, *48*, 156–162.

Gurven, M. and Walker, R. (2006). Energetic demand of multiple dependents and the evolution of slow human growth. *Proceedings of the Royal Society B*, *279*, 835–41.

Gustafsson, L. and Sutherland, W. J. (1988). The costs of reproduction in the collared flycatcher *Ficedula-Albicollis*. *Nature*, *335*, 813–815.

Hagen, E. H., Barrett, C. and Price, M. E. (2006). Do human parents face a quantity-quality tradeoff? Evidence from a Shuar community. *American Journal of Physical Anthropology*, *130*, 405–18.

Hagen, E. H., Hames, R. B., Craig, N. M. *et al.* (2001). Parental investment and child health in a Yanomamö village suffering short-term food stress. *Journal of Biosocial Science*, *33*, 503–28.

Haukioja, E., Lemmetyinen, R. and Pikkola, M. (1989). Why are twins so rare in *Homo sapiens*? *American Naturalist*, *133*, 572–77.

Hawkes, K. (2003). Grandmothers and the evolution of human longevity. *American Journal of Human Biology*, *15*, 380–400.

Hawkes, K., O'Connell, J. F. and Blurton Jones, N. G. (1997). Hadza women's time allocation, offspring provisioning, and the evolution of long postmenopausal life spans. *Current Anthropology*, *38*, 551–77.

Helle, S., Lummaa, V. and Jokela, J. (2002). Sons reduced maternal longevity in preindustrial humans. *Science*, *298*, 1085.

Helle, S., Lummaa, V. and Jokela, J. (2004). Accelerated immunosenescence in preindustrial twin mothers. *Proceedings of the National Academy of Sciences of the USA*, *101*, 12391–6.

Hill, K. (1993). Life history theory and evolutionary anthropology. *Evolutionary Anthropology*, *2*, 78–88.

Hill, K. and Hurtado, A. M. (1996). *Aché life history: The ecology and demography of a foraging people*. New York: Aldine de Gruyter.

Hill, K. and Kaplan, H. (1999). Life history traits in humans: Theory and empirical studies. *Annual Review of Anthropology*, *28*, 397–430.

Hill, S. E. and Reeve, H. K. (2005). Low fertility in humans as the evolutionary outcome of snowballing resource games. *Behavioural Ecology*, *16*, 398–402.

Hobcraft, J. N., McDonald, J. W. and Rutstein, S. O. (1985). Demographic determinants of infant and early child mortality: A comparative analysis. *Population Studies, 39*, 363–85.

Hopcroft, R. L. (2006). Sex status and reproductive success in the contemporary United States. *Evolution and Human Behavior, 27*, 104–20.

Hrdy, S. B. (1999). *Mother Nature: A history of mothers, infants and natural selection.* New York: Pantheon.

Hudson, R. and Trillmich, F. (2008). Sibling competition and cooperation in mammals: Challenges, developments and prospects. *Behavioral Ecology and Sociobiology, 62*, 299–307.

Humphries, M. H. and Boutin, S. (2000). The determinants of optimal litter size in free-ranging red squirrels. *Ecology, 81*, 2867–77.

Hurt, L. S., Ronsmans, C. and Quigley, M. (2006). Does the number of sons born affect long-term mortality of parents? A cohort study in rural Bangladesh. *Proceedings of the Royal Society B, 273*, 149–55.

Irons, W. (1998). Adaptively relevant environments versus the environment of evolutionary adaptedness. *Evolutionary Anthropology, 6*, 194–204.

Jokela, M. (2009). Physical attractiveness and reproductive success in humans: Evidence from the late 20th century United States. *Evolution and Human Behavior, 30*, 342–50.

Jones, J. H. (2009). The force of selection on the human life cycle. *Evolution and Human Behavior, 30*, 305–14.

Juda, M. N., Campbell, L. and Crawford, C. B. (2004). Dieting symptomatology in women and perceptions of social support: An evolutionary approach. *Evolution and Human Behavior, 25*, 200–208.

Kanazawa, S. (2003). Can evolutionary psychology explain reproductive behaviour in the contemporary United States? *Sociological Quarterly, 44*, 291–302.

Kaplan, H. (1994). Evolutionary and wealth flow theories of fertility: Empirical tests and new models. *Population and Development Review, 20*, 753–91.

Kaplan, H. (1996). A theory of fertility and parental investment in traditional and modern human societies. *Yearbook of Physical Anthropology, 39*, 91–135.

Kaplan, H. and Gangestad, S. (2005). Life history theory and evolutionary psychology. In D. M. Buss (ed.), *The handbook of evolutionary psychology* (pp. 68–95). Hoboken, NJ: John Wiley & Sons, Ltd.

Kaplan, H., Hill, K., Lancaster, J. and Hurtado, A. M. (2000). A theory of human life history evolution: Diet, intelligence, and longevity. *Evolutionary Anthropology, 9*, 156–85.

Kaplan, H., Lancaster, J. B., Bock, J. and Johnson, S. (1995). Fertility and fitness among Albuquerque men: A competitive labour market theory. In R. I. M. Dunbar (ed.), *Human reproductive decisions: Biological and social perspectives* (pp. 96–136). London: Macmillan.

Kaplan, H., Lancaster, J. B., Tucker, W. T. and Anderson, K. G. (2002). Evolutionary approach to below replacement fertility. *American Journal of Human Biology, 14*, 233–56.

Karsten, K. B, Andriamandimbiarisoa, L. N., Fox, S. F. and Raxworthy, C. J. (2008). A unique life history among tetrapods: An annual chameleon living mostly as an egg. *Proceedings of the National Academy of Sciences of the USA, 105*, 8980–4.

Keister, L. A. (2003). Sharing the wealth: The effect of siblings on adults' wealth ownership. *Demography, 40*, 521–42.

Keister, L. A. (2004). Race, family structure, and wealth: The effect of childhood family on adult asset ownership. *Sociological Perspectives, 47*, 161–87.

Kettrey, H. and Emery, B. (2007). The discourse of sibling violence. *Journal of Family Violence, 22*, 769.

Kim, K. W., Roland, C. and Horel, A. (2000). Functional value of matriphagy in the spider *Amaurobius ferox*. *Ethology*, *106*, 729–42.

Kirkwood, T. B. L. (1977). Evolution of ageing. *Nature*, *270*, 301–4.

Kohler, H. P. (2001). *Fertility and social interaction*. Oxford: Oxford University Press.

Kramer, K. L. (2005). Children's help and the pace of reproduction: Cooperative breeding in humans. *Evolutionary Anthropology*, *14*, 224–37.

Lack, D. (1954). *The natural regulation of animal numbers*. Oxford: Clarendon Press.

Lahdenpera, M., Lummaa, V., Helle, S. *et al.* (2004). Fitness benefits of prolonged post-reproductive lifespan in women. *Nature*, *428*, 178–81.

Laland, K. N. and Brown, G. R. (2006). Niche construction, human behaviour, and the adaptive-lag hypothesis. *Evolutionary Anthropology*, *15*, 95–104.

Lancaster, J. B. and Lancaster, C. (1987). The watershed: Change in parental-investment and family formation strategies in the course of human evolution. In J. B. Lancaster, J. Altmann, A. Rossi and R. Sherrod (eds), *Parenting across the human lifespan: Biosocial dimensions* (pp. 187–205). Hawthorne, NY: Aldine de Gruyter.

Lawson, D. W. (2009). *The behavioural ecology of modern families: A longitudinal study of parental investment and child development*. Unpublished PhD thesis. London: University College London.

Lawson, D. W., Jordan, F. M. and Magid, K. (2008). On sex and suicide bombing: An evaluation of Kanazawa's 'Evolutionary Psychological Imagination'. *Journal of Evolutionary Psychology*, *6*, 73–84.

Lawson, D. W. and Mace, R. (2008). Sibling configuration and childhood growth in contemporary British Families. *International Journal of Epidemiology*, *37*, 1408–21.

Lawson, D. W. and Mace R. (2009). Trade-offs in modern parenting: A longitudinal study of sibling competition for parental care. *Evolution and Human Behavior*, *30*, 170–183.

Lawson, D. W. and Mace, R. (2010). Optimizing modern family size: Trade-offs between fertility and the economic costs of reproduction. *Human Nature*, *21*, 39–61.

Le Bourg, E. (2001). A mini-review of the evolutionary theories of aging: Is it time to accept them? *Demography Research*, *4*, 1–29.

Le Bourg, E. (2007). Does reproduction decrease longevity in human beings? *Ageing Research Reviews*, *6*, 141–9.

Lee, R. (2003). The demographic transition: Three centuries of fundamental change. *Journal of Economic Perspectives*, *17*, 167–90.

Leippet, D., Goymann, W. and Hofer, H. (2000). Between-litter siblicide in captive Indian false vampire bats (*Megaderma lyra*). *Journal of Zoological Society of London*, *251*, 537–40.

Lessells, C. M. (1991). The evolution of life histories. In J. R. Krebs and N. B. Davies (eds), *Behavioural ecology* (3rd edition, pp. 32–68). Oxford: Blackwell.

Livi-Bacci, M. (1986). Social-group forerunners of fertility control in Europe. In A. Coale and S. C. Watkins (eds), *The decline of fertility in Europe* (pp. 182–200). Princeton, NJ: Princeton University Press.

Loos, R. J. F., Derom, C., Eeckels, R. *et al.* (2001). Length of gestation and birthweight in dizygotic twins. *Lancet*, *358*, 560–561.

Low, B. (2001). *Why sex matters: A Darwinian look at human behaviour*. Princeton, NJ: Princeton University Press.

Low, B. S. (1991). Reproductive life in 19th-century Sweden: An evolutionary perspective on demographic phenomena. *Ethology and Sociobiology*, *12*, 411–448.

Lummaa, V. (2001). Reproductive investment in preindustrial humans: The consequences of offspring number, gender and survival. *Proceedings of the Royal Society B*, *268*, 1977–1983.

Lummaa, V. (2007). Life history theory, longevity and reproduction in humans. In R. I. M. Dunbar and L. Barrett (eds), *Oxford handbook of evolutionary psychology* (pp. 397–413). Oxford: Oxford University Press.

Lummaa, V., Haukioja, E., Lemmetyinen, R. and Pikkola, M. (1998). Natural selection on human twinning. *Nature*, *394*, 533–4.

Lycett, J. and Dunbar, R. I. M. (1999). Abortion rates reflect the optimization of parental investment strategies. *Proceedings of the Royal Society B*, *266*, 2355–8.

Lycett, J., Dunbar, R. I. M. and Voland, E. (2000). Longevity and the costs of reproduction in a historical human population. *Proceedings of the Royal Society B*, *267*, 31–5.

McDermott, J., Steketee, R. and Wirima, J. (1995). Mortality associated with multiple gestation in Malawi. *International Journal of Epidemiology*, *24*, 413–419.

McNamara, J. M. and Houston, A. I. (2006). State and value: A perspective from behavioural ecology. In J. C. K. Wells, S. S. Strickland and K. N. Laland (eds), *Social information transmission and human biology* (pp. 59–88). London: CRC Press.

Mace, R. (1996). Biased parental investment and reproductive success in Gabbra pastoralists. *Behavioural Ecology and Sociobiology*, *38*, 75–81.

Mace, R. (1998). The coevolution of human wealth and inheritance strategies. *Philosophical Transactions of the Royal Society B*, *353*, 389–97.

Mace, R. (2000). Evolutionary ecology of human life history. *Animal Behaviour*, *59*, 1–10.

Mace, R. (2007). The evolutionary ecology of human family size. In R. I. M. Dunbar and L. Barrett (eds), *The Oxford handbook of evolutionary psychology* (pp. 383–96). Oxford: Oxford University Press.

Mace, R. and Colleran, H. (2009). Kin influence on the decision to start using modern contraception: A longitudinal study from rural Gambia. *American Journal of Human Biology*, *21*, 472–7.

Mace, R. and Sear, R. (1997). Birth interval and the sex of children in a traditional African population: An evolutionary analysis. *Journal of Biosocial Science*, *29*, 499–507.

Marlowe, F. (2000). The patriarch hypothesis. *Human Nature*, *11*, 27–42.

Marsal, K., Persson, P., Larsen, T. H. L. *et al.* (1996). Intrauterine growth curves based on ultrasonically estimated foetal weights. *Acta Paedoatrica*, *85*, 843–8.

Meij, J. J., van Bodegom, D., Ziem, J. B. *et al.* (2009). Quality-quantity tradeoff of human offspring under adverse environmental conditions. *Journal of Evolutionary Biology*, *22*, 1014–1023.

Migliano, A. B., Vinicius, L. and Lahr, M. M. (2007). Life history trade-offs explain the evolution of human pygmies. *Proceedings of the National Academy of Sciences of the USA*, *104*, 20216–20219.

Mircea, C. N., Lujan, M. E. and Pierson, R. A. (2007). Metabolic fuel and clinical implications for female reproduction. *Journal of Obstetrics and Gynaecology Canada*, *29*, 887–902.

Mock, D., Drummond, H. and Stinson, C. (1990). Avian siblicide. *American Scientist*, *78*, 438–49.

Mock, D. and Parker, G. A. (1997). *The evolution of sibling rivalry*. New York: Oxford University Press.

Monden, C. W. S. and Smits, J. (2009). Maternal height and child mortality in 42 developing countries. *American Journal of Human Biology*, *21*, 305–11.

Montgomery, M. R. and Casterline, J. B. (1996). Social learning, social influences, and new models of fertility. *Population and Development Review, 22*, 151–75.

Mueller, U. (2001). Is there a stabilizing selection around average fertility in modern human populations? *Population and Development Review, 27*, 469–98.

Nettle, D. (2002). Women's height, reproductive success and the evolution of sexual dimorphism in modern humans. *Proceedings of the Royal Society B, 269*, 1919–1923.

Nettle, D. and Pollet, T. V. (2008). Natural selection on male wealth in humans. *American Naturalist, 172*, 658–66.

Newson, L., Postmes, T., Lea, S. E. G. and Webley, P. (2005). Why are modern families small? Toward an evolutionary and cultural explanation for the demographic transition. *Personality and Social Psychology Review, 9*, 360–375.

Newson, L., Postmes, T., Lea, S. E. G. *et al.* (2007). Influences on communication about reproduction: The cultural evolution of low fertility. *Evolution and Human Behavior, 23*, 199–210.

van Noordwijk, A. J. and de Jong, G. (1986). Acquisition and allocation of resources: Their influence on variation in life history tactics. *American Naturalist, 128*, 137–42.

Parker, G. A. and Smith, J. M. (1990). Optimality theory in evolutionary biology. *Nature, 348*, 27–33.

Partridge, L. and Sibly, R. (1991). Constraints on the evolution of life histories. *Philosophical Transactions of the Royal Society B, 332*, 3–13.

Peccei, J. S. (2001). A critique of the grandmother hypotheses: Old and new. *American Journal of Human Biology, 13*, 434–52.

Penn, D. J. and Smith, K. R. (2007). Differential fitness costs of reproduction between the sexes. *Proceedings of the National Academy of Sciences of the USA, 104*, 553–8.

Pennington, R. and Harpending, H. (1988). Fitness and fertility among Kalahari !Kung. *American Journal of Physical Anthropology, 77*, 303–19.

Pereira, M. E. and Fairbanks, L. A. (2002). *Juvenile primates: Life history, development, and behaviour.* Oxford: Oxford University Press.

Perusse, D. (1993). Cultural and reproductive success in industrial societies: Testing the relationship at the proximate and ultimate levels. *Behavioral and Brain Sciences, 16*, 267–323.

Perry, G. H. and Dominy, N. J. (2009). Evolution of the human pygmy phenotype. *Trends in Ecology and Evolution, 24*, 218–225.

Pettifor, R. A., Perrins, C. M. and McCleery, R. H. (2001). The individual optimization of fitness: Variation in reproductive output, including clutch size, mean nestling mass and offspring recruitment, in manipulated broods of Great Tits *Parus major. Journal of Animal Ecology, 70*, 62–9.

van de Putte, B., Matthijs, K. and Vlietinck, R. (2004). A social component in the negative effect of sons on maternal longevity in pre-industrial humans. *Journal of Biosocial Science, 36*, 289–97.

Quataert, D. (2000). *The Ottoman Empire, 1700–1922.* Cambridge: Cambridge University Press.

Quinlan, R. J. (2007). Human parental effort and environmental risk. *Proceedings of the Royal Society B, 247*, 121–5.

Reiches, M. W., Ellison, P. T., Lipson, S. F. *et al.* (2009). Pooled energy budget and human life history. *American Journal of Human Biology, 21*, 421–9.

Risch, T. S., Dobson, F. S. and Murie, J. O. (1995). Is mean litter size the most productive? A test in Columbian ground squirrels. *Ecology, 76*, 1643–54.

Roff, D. A. (2002). *Life history evolution.* Sunderland, MA: Sinauer Associates.

Rotkirch, A. (2007). All that she wants is a(nother) baby? Longing for children as a fertility incentive of growing importance. *Journal of Evolutionary Psychology*, *5*, 89–104.

von Rueden, C., Gurven, M. and Kaplan, H. (2008). The multiple dimensions of male social status in an Amazonian society. *Evolution and Human Behavior*, *29*, 402–15.

Rutstein, S. O. (1984). *Infant and child mortality: Levels, trends and demographic differentials, (revised edition). World fertility survey, comparative studies, no. 43*. Voorburg: International Statistical Institute.

Salmon, C. and Crawford, C. (2008). Anorexic behaviour, female competition and stress: Developing the female competition stress test. *Evolutionary Psychology*, *6*, 96–112.

Salmon, C., Crawford, C., Dane, L. and Zuberbier, O. (2008). Ancestral mechanisms in modern environments. *Human Nature*, *19*, 103–17.

Sear, R. (2006). Height and reproductive success: How a Gambian population compares to the West. *Human Nature*, *17*, 405–18.

Sear, R. (2007). The impact of reproduction on Gambian women: Does controlling for phenotypic quality reveal costs of reproduction? *American Journal of Physical Anthropology*, *132*, 632–41.

Sear, R. (2009). How universal are human mate choices? Size does not matter when Hadza foragers are choosing a mate. *Biology Letters 5*, 606–9.

Sear, R., Lawson, D. and Dickins, T. (2007). Synthesis in the human evolutionary behavioural sciences. *Journal of Evolutionary Psychology*, *5*, 3–28.

Sear, R. and Mace, R. (2008). Who keeps children alive: A review of the effects of kin on child survival. *Evolution and Human Behavior*, *29*, 1–18.

Sear, R., Allal, N., Mace, R. and Michael, A. (2004). Height, marriage and reproductive success in Gambian women. *Research in Economic Anthropology*, *23*, 203–24.

Sear, R., Shanley, D., McGregor, I. A. and Mace, R. (2001). The fitness of twin mothers: Evidence from rural Gambia. *Journal of Evolutionary Biology*, *14*, 433–43.

Segerstråle, U. (2000). *Defenders of the truth: The sociobiology debate*. Oxford: Oxford University Press.

Shanley, D. P., Sear, R., Mace, R. and Kirkwood, T. B. L. (2007). Testing evolutionary theories of menopause. *Proceedings of the Royal Society B*, *274*, 2943–9.

Simmons, R. (2002). Siblicide provides food benefits for raptor chicks: Re-evaluating brood manipulation studies. *Animal Behaviour*, *64*, F19–F24.

Smith, C. C. and Fretwell, S. D. (1974). The optimal balance between size and number of offspring. *American Naturalist*, *108*, 499–506.

Stearns, S. C. (1992). *The evolution of life history*. Oxford: Oxford University Press.

Steelman, L., Powell, B., Werum, R. and Carter, S. (2002). Reconsidering the effects of sibling configuration: Recent advances and challenges. *Annual Review of Sociology*, *28*, 243–69.

Strassmann, B. I. and Gillespie, B. (2002). Life-history theory, fertility and reproductive success in humans. *Proceedings of the Royal Society B*, *269*, 553–62.

Strassmann, B. and Mace, R. (2008). Perspectives on human health and disease from evolutionary and behavioral ecology. In S. Stearns and J. Koella (eds), *Evolution in health and disease* (pp. 109–21). Oxford: Oxford University Press.

Tamimi, R. M., Lagiou, P., Mucci, L. A. *et al.* (2003). Average energy intake among pregnant women carrying a boy compared with a girl. *British Medical Journal*, *326*, 1245–6.

Tinbergen, J. M. and Daan, S. (1990). Family-planning in the Great Tit (*Parus-Major*): Optimal clutch size as integration of parent and offspring fitness. *Behaviour*, *114*, 161–90.

Tucker, B. and Rende Taylor, L. (2007). The human behavioral ecology of contemporary world issues. *Human Nature*, *18*, 181–9.

Tuomi, J., Hakala, T. and Haukioja, E. (1983). Alternative concepts of reproductive effort, costs of reproduction, and selection in life-history evolution. *American Zoologist*, *23*, 25–34.

Vining, D. R. J. (1986). Social versus reproductive success: The central theoretical problem of human sociobiology. *Behaviour and Brain Sciences*, *9*, 167–216.

Voland, E. (1998). Evolutionary ecology of human reproduction. *Annual Review of Anthropology*, *27*, 347–74.

Voland, E. and Dunbar, R. I. M. (1995). Resource competition and reproduction. *Human Nature*, *6*, 33–49.

Wahaj, S. A., Place, N. J., Weldele, M. L. *et al.* (2007). Siblicide in the spotted hyena: Analysis with ultrasonic examination of wild and captive individuals. *Behavioural Ecology*, *18*, 976–84.

Walker, R., Gurven, M., Hill, K. *et al.* (2006). Growth rates and life histories in twenty-two small-scale societies. *American Journal of Human Biology*, *18*, 95–311.

Wasser, S. K. and Barash, D. P. (1983). Reproductive suppression among female mammals: Implications for biomedicine and sexual selection theory. *Quarterly Review of Biology*, *58*, 513–538.

West-Eberhard, M. J. (2007). *Developmental plasticity and evolution.* Oxford: Oxford University Press.

Westendorp, R. and Kirkwood, T. (1998). Human longevity at the cost of reproductive success. *Nature*, *396*, 746.

Williams, G. C. (1957). Pleiotrophy, natural selection and the evolution of senescence. *Evolution*, *11*, 398–411.

Williams, G. C. (1966). Natural selection, the costs of reproduction, and a refinement of Lack's principle. *American Naturalist*, *100*, 687–90.

Winterhalder, B. and Leslie, P. (2002). Risk-sensitive fertility: The variance compensation hypothesis. *Evolution and Human Behavior*, *23*, 59–82.

7 Parenting and families

REBECCA SEAR

CHAPTER OUTLINE

WHAT IS PARENTAL INVESTMENT? 216

WHO INVESTS IN OFFSPRING? 217

Who invests in human children? 219

How extensive is paternal investment in humans? 219

What affects paternal investment: Paternity certainty 221

What affects paternal investment: Costs and benefits of parenting versus mating 223

Proximate mechanisms of paternal care 225

Who else invests? 226

FAMILIAL CONFLICT 227

WHAT IS INVESTED? 228

WHO IS INVESTED IN? 230

Birth order 230

Sex biases in investment 234

Interactions between birth order and sex biases 239

How parental condition affects who is invested in 240

The role of environmental quality and risk 241

CONCLUSION 242

ACKNOWLEDGEMENTS 243

REFERENCES 243

Parenting in *Homo sapiens* is rather different from parenting in most other primates. Our long developmental period and relatively short birth intervals mean that offspring are 'stacked', with mothers having to simultaneously look after several dependent children at different developmental stages. This creates a high burden of care for mothers, which mothers appear to alleviate by co-opting other relatives into helping out. This cooperative breeding strategy introduces complexity into 'parental' investment: various individuals may be investing in children, not just parents, but also grandparents, older siblings of the child and potentially step-parents. The stacking of human offspring also introduces complexity into the allocation of parental investment across children within the same family, given that a number of children of different ages will be competing with one another for parental resources.

This chapter surveys the relevant literature on human parental investment. It first introduces parental investment theory, and then discusses the issue of who invests in human children. Mothers clearly invest, but who else helps out? This section ends with a brief discussion of familial conflict, since family relationships may be competitive, as well as cooperative. The second half of the chapter starts by considering what is invested in children, and then moves on to a detailed examination of who is invested in, with particular reference to parental investment biases according to sex and birth order. Throughout, ecological variation in parenting and parental investment patterns is considered.

WHAT IS PARENTAL INVESTMENT?

Parental investment is defined as any action by a parent which benefits an offspring at some cost to the parent. The concept was originally formulated by Trivers, who defined parental investment rather precisely as investment in an offspring which results in some cost to the parent's ability to invest in other offspring (Trivers, 1972). Subsequently, Clutton-Brock (1991) broadened the definition to include investment in offspring which has a cost to *any* component of a parent's fitness, including mating success or somatic maintenance.

Parental investment is a key concept in life history theory (see Chapter 6 in this volume). Given a limited energy budget, life history theory predicts that parents have a number of decisions, or trade-offs, to make, in order to allocate energy appropriately to maximise their fitness (Roff, 1992; Stearns, 1992).

The three most fundamental trade-offs of life history theory concern parental investment. First, any energy devoted towards parenting cannot also be used for other functions, such as mating or maintaining body condition. So parents must trade-off parenting effort with mating effort and with somatic maintenance. Second, since there is a trade-off between current and future reproduction, parents must decide how much to invest in a current offspring (or litter), in order to conserve energy for future reproductive bouts. Finally, parenting effort must be traded off between quality and quantity of offspring. Parents may either produce many offspring but invest relatively little in each one (the quantity strategy) or produce few offspring but invest considerably in each (the quality strategy). Parents engaged in the quality strategy must then decide how to allocate investment between their offspring, since equal investment in each may not be the optimal strategy.

Our own species is one in which parents adopt the quality strategy, by investing substantially in a relatively small number of offspring. Human children are relatively altricial at birth (i.e. helpless, in contrast to many species which have precocial young, who are relatively independent of parental care from birth), and have an unusually extended period of childhood during which they are reliant on carers for provisioning and protection (Bogin, 1997). Children are not able to fully provision themselves until well into their teens or later: delayed maturity means they do not reach full adult size or strength until this age, and our ecological niche, which relies on difficult-to-acquire foodstuffs, means that children must engage in a long period of learning before becoming proficient producers of calories (Hill, 1993; Kaplan *et al.*, 2000). Even after maturity, the social and group-living nature of our species results in lifelong bonds between parents and offspring, so that parents may continue to invest in offspring by transferring resources, providing grandparenting services and social support well beyond reproductive maturity. Before discussing in more detail exactly what is invested in children, and how this investment is shared out between children within the same family, we will start with a consideration of who invests in children.

WHO INVESTS IN OFFSPRING?

Parental investment may come from mothers, fathers or both, but maternal investment is rather more common than paternal investment (Clutton-Brock, 1991). Explanations for this biased investment pattern have tended in the past to hinge on anisogamy (the difference in size between male and female gametes): it seems to make intuitive sense that females should invest more heavily than males throughout the period of parental investment, since the larger size of eggs compared to sperm means that females are committed to investing relatively heavily at the outset (Trivers, 1972). However, Kokko and Jennions (2008) caution that such arguments, while superficially appealing, have logical flaws and that the full explanation for sex differences in parental investment may be relatively complex. The anisogamy argument for female-biased parental investment makes the Concorde fallacy, for example (Dawkins and Carlisle, 1976). Decisions about whether to continue investing in an offspring should depend only on the future costs and benefits of investing or ceasing to invest in that offspring, and should disregard how much has already been invested (a strategy not adopted by the French and British governments, who continued to invest in Concorde long after it become obvious the aircraft was a poor economic bet because they did not want to be seen to have wasted the considerable amounts they had already invested).

Anisogamy, and the relative cheapness of sperm to produce, also provides a superficially appealing explanation for why males would do better to invest effort in attracting additional mates rather than investing in parenting – since each additional female fertilised may result in a greater increase in reproductive success compared to any incremental benefit obtained through improving the survival and reproductive prospects of existing offspring. But again, this argument needs some refinement. Although such a strategy of pursuing mates rather than investing in offspring may benefit males who are particularly successful at acquiring mates, every offspring has one mother and one father so that the average male will not succeed in fertilising large numbers of females. It is also not necessarily clear that investing effort in finding additional matings always increases reproductive success more than investing in parental care.

Kokko and Jennions (2008) suggest that a more cautious and subtle approach is taken to understanding why maternal care tends to be more common than paternal care, taking into account a number of factors. These include: the importance of sexual selection, which will determine whether some males can lucratively adopt a mating-focused strategy; both adult and operational sex ratios (the former refers to the ratio of adult males to females, the latter to the ratio of sexually receptive males to females), which again affects the costs and benefits of searching for mates rather than caring for offspring; the effects of caring or competing on mortality rates, which will in turn affect sex ratios; and the probability of paternity.

The considerable variation in this list of factors across species means that, though maternal care is numerically more common than paternal care, there are numerous species in which paternal care, either alone or alongside maternal care, is seen (Clutton-Brock, 1991). Male-only care is in fact the predominant mode of parental care in fish, though it is rare in other classes of animal and not seen in mammals. Biparental care is by far the most common mode of care in birds, seen in 90% of species (note, however, that biparental care does not necessarily mean that males and females contribute equally to parental care, just that both contribute; Cockburn, 2006). Female-only care is the most common mammalian pattern, where any kind of male care is relatively rare: direct care from males is seen in less than 5% of species and 9–10% of genera. Primate fathers seem to be at the caring end of the mammalian spectrum. Though female-only care is still seen in the majority of species, direct male care has been observed in 40% of primate genera (Kleiman and Malcolm, 1981).

One problem with quantifying paternal investment is that what fathers do for offspring can be difficult to identify. The statistics above refer to direct forms of parental care. This includes care directed towards an offspring which has an immediate effect on the survival or well-being of the young, such as feeding, carrying or grooming. Indirect care is care performed in the absence of the offspring but which may also have an effect on its health or survival, such as territorial defence. The problem with counting indirect care as paternal investment is that its primary purpose may not be parental investment. Territorial defence will also prevent other males from gaining access to females residing within the territory, so that it may be mating effort which fortuitously happens also to improve offspring reproductive success. In fact, this problem applies more generally to male care, even direct forms of care: is male care always parental investment, or is it mating effort? If females prefer males who provide useful services to their offspring, then males may use caring for offspring to attract females, rather than solely for the purposes of improving the reproductive prospects of their offspring (Smuts and Gubernick, 1992).

A final complication with identifying paternal investment is that it can be diffi-cult to determine whether the objects of male care are in fact his offspring, which is why the literature on this topic often refers to 'male care' rather than 'paternal investment'. Maternal care, at least in species with internal fertilisation, such as birds and mammals, is more difficult to mistake. The biparental care which characterises most bird species was initially thought to be a clear-cut case of paternal investment, but the advent of DNA fingerprinting demonstrated that a surprisingly high pro-portion of chicks in the nests of some species were the result of extra-pair copula-tions and were not the offspring of the male caring for them (Petrie and Kempenaers, 1998). Male care which is consistently directed towards unrelated offspring may well be a form of mating effort, though it is also possible that it results from misdirected parental effort.

This brief zoological summary of who cares for offspring suggests that the subject is complicated. Observations suggest that where post-natal investment occurs it is most common from mothers alone, sometimes from both mothers and fathers and sometimes just fathers, but that the reasons for this variation are numerous and not yet fully understood. The next section covers the question of who cares for children in our own species.

Who invests in human children?

Clearly, mothers invest substantially. As with all mammals, human females are com-mitted to gestation and a lengthy period of lactation, which typically lasts at least two years, often longer, in traditional societies (those without access to modern medical care or contraception, where both fertility and mortality tend to be high). A review of child mortality in such societies suggested that children who lose their mothers in the first year or two of life have very much higher risks of dying than those whose moth-ers are still alive, demonstrating the almost exclusive reliance of infants on maternal care (Sear and Mace, 2008; see also Figure 7.1). The reliance of children on maternal care once they are weaned appears to be surprisingly low, however: the survival of slightly older children (more than two years) who lose their mothers is often remark-ably high. Two-year-old children are clearly not able to feed and care for themselves, so some other individual(s) must be stepping in to invest in these children. The father of the child may appear to be the obvious candidate for this alternative carer, but is that what the evidence shows?

How extensive is paternal investment in humans?

Much of the evolutionary psychological literature gives the impression that pater-nal investment is universal and substantial in *Homo sapiens*. It is not uncommon for evolutionary psychologists to base arguments about our evolved mental architecture around assumptions that men invest heavily in children, and that women universally seek men who are willing and able to invest in children (Buss, 1989; Geary, 2000; Geary, Vigil and Byrd-Craven, 2004). These assumptions build on a long-standing

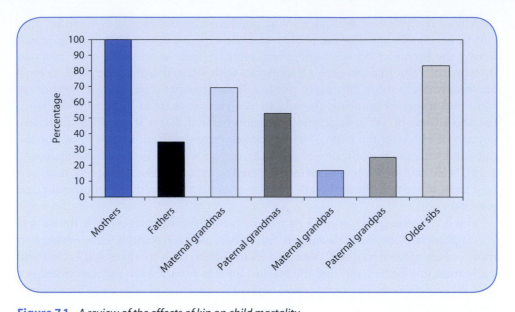

Figure 7.1. *A review of the effects of kin on child mortality.*

Bars represent the percentage of studies in which the presence of that relative improved child survival.

Source: From a review of all studies which investigated the impact of particular relatives on child survival; Sear and Mace (2008).

belief amongst students of human origins that the provisioning of women and children by men has been of vital importance in human evolution, and led to many distinctly human characteristics.

This idea perhaps reached its apotheosis in a 1981 *Science* article by Owen Lovejoy on how the origin of man [sic] depended on behavioural shifts towards the nuclear family and extensive male provisioning of women and children (Lovejoy, 1981). This view has proved remarkably hard to shift (see e.g. Lawrence and Nohria, 2002) despite a concerted assault on this hypothesis over the last few decades by researchers attempting, and failing, to find evidence that heavy paternal investment is universal in our species. The alternative perspective, now accepted by some of the behavioural ecology community, is that the role of human fathers is very variable, and may be surprisingly inconsequential. Surprisingly, because children need substantial investment in order to reach adulthood as healthy, competitive adults (Hrdy, 2009).

Whether you consider human fathers to be paragons of paternal investment or somewhat paternally delinquent depends to some extent on your frame of reference. Geary (2000), for example, argues that, compared to the average mammal, human fathers do seem to be unusually closely involved in their offspring: many men do maintain relationships and invest substantially in their offspring throughout childhood and beyond, in contrast to the majority of mammalian fathers who have no contact with offspring after conception. On the other hand, Hrdy (2008) points out that human paternal investment appears somewhat less impressive when only primates are considered, since primate fathers are rather more likely than the average mammal to engage in care of offspring. In some species, such as siamang (a South East Asian ape), titi monkeys, owl monkeys and some callitrichids (marmosets and tamarins), male care is intensive and essential for offspring survival. For example, the father is often responsible for carrying infants, which incurs substantial energetic costs.

Yet in our own species, at least some fathers invest little or nothing at all. In post-industrial societies, a high proportion of divorced and never-married fathers lose contact with their children and invest little or nothing after the dissolution of the parental relationship (Seltzer, 1991). Hrdy (2008) even quotes a study which found that Americans are 16 times more likely to pay used-car loans than their child support payments. A similar picture of variable paternal investment is found in traditional societies: the same review of child mortality which found much higher mortality for young children without mothers found that when the effects of fathers on child mortality are investigated, in only one-third of studies (seven of 22) did the absence of fathers result in higher child mortality (Sear and Mace, 2008; see Figure 7.1). These results are not expected if fathers are always vital to the provisioning and care of women and children.

Despite their different perspectives, however, both Hrdy and Geary agree on the fact that paternal investment, unlike maternal investment, is facultative in our species: some fathers invest in their offspring and some do not, though they may disagree on the extent to which fathers invest. Given that there is agreement that paternal investment can vary both between and within populations, the next question becomes: what determines the extent to which a particular father will invest? A pre-condition of paternal investment is a social system in which fathers and offspring maintain bonds and can recognise one another (Chapais, 2008). Human societies fit this condition: in most, women and men form reasonably long-term unions, and even in the absence of such long-term bonds, men's role in generating children is often understood so that biological paternity can be recognised (see Box 7.1 for a brief overview of the form of the human family). Given a set-up in which paternal investment is at least possible, how much individual fathers then choose to invest will be determined by some combination of the following factors: paternity certainty, and the costs and benefits of investing in offspring versus investing in additional mating effort (Kempenaers and Sheldon, 1997; Kleiman and Malcolm, 1981).

What affects paternal investment: Paternity certainty

Paternity certainty refers to the probability that a man's putative children (often operationalised as his wife's children) are his own genetic offspring. Cross-cultural studies suggest paternity certainty rates are rather high in most human populations, but are not 100%. There is something of an urban myth that paternity uncertainty is widespread in humans, based on an unpublished study using blood group data which apparently estimated that 20–30% of children in one Liverpool tower block were not the offspring of their putative fathers (sometimes known as the 'Liverpool flats' study, cited in Cohen, 1977). While paternity uncertainty may be this high under

BOX 7.1.   THE FORM OF THE HUMAN FAMILY

The human family is a diverse entity. Humans cluster with their kin and their mate(s), who cooperate to varying degrees in the raising of children and productive work, but exactly how such families organise varies between populations. Some form of socially recognised union between a man and woman is pretty much universal across human societies, though the stability and the length of these unions differ. Most cultures worldwide allow polygynous marriage (one man married to several wives) (Murdock and White, 1969). A marital system of polyandry, one woman married to several husbands, is rare but has been observed in a handful of populations, and a polyandrous mating system may be much more common than a polyandrous marital system (Hrdy, 2000a). Numerically, the most common form of marriage which currently exists is monogamy, since the rise of socially imposed monogamy in some of the dominant global cultures (MacDonald, 1995). Socially imposed monogamy is a form of marriage maintained by social pressures and rules, even where other marriage forms may be ecologically viable. Usually, these marriage systems will involve co-residence between husbands and wives, but may in some societies involve visiting unions or living-apart-together relationships.

The nuclear family household, containing just a wife, husband and children residing in isolation from other kin, though the dominant family form in modern Western societies, is a rather rare family form. Instead, most couples will live with, or near, to either the wife's or the husband's relatives or both (the former is known as 'matrilocality' or 'female-philopatry – females stay in the natal home; the latter known as 'patrilocality' or 'male-philopatry'). There is some debate in the literature about what 'ancestral' patterns of residence may be, since this may have an impact on the evolution of human social structure and other traits. There has been a long-standing view that residence patterns throughout most of our species' history have been patrilocal (Chapais, 2008; Ember, 1978). Early analysis of cross-cultural ethnographic data suggested most forager populations were patrilocal (Ember, 1978), but a careful reanalysis of these data found instead that not only was matrilocality much more common than had been believed but also forager residence patterns were very flexible (Alvarez, 2004). Foragers are mobile and can potentially move to reside with whichever kin are needed at any one time. In the early years of a marriage, at least, this residence often seems to be matrilocal, perhaps so that women have their own kin around to support them through the early, and difficult, years of childbearing (Blurton Jones, Hawkes and O'Connell, 2005).

The advent of accumulated resources associated with the emergence of agriculture does seem to have resulted in a shift towards higher levels of patrilocality (Hrdy, 2000). Where men need to defend resources, this may be easier if they cooperate with their male kin. Genetic evidence confirms that, in our recent past, females seem to have dispersed more widely than males (Wilkins and Marlowe, 2006). Even in patrilocal societies, however, women may still have access to their natal kin during a marriage, since dispersal tends to be neither very long-distance nor irreversible. So the distinction between patrilocality and matrilocality may not be quite as stark as it seems. The overall picture of the human family is one of flexibility, both between and within populations.

a particular set of circumstances, most human fathers appear to have a considerably higher confidence of paternity.

Anderson reviewed the cross-cultural evidence and suggested the range of paternity uncertainty was 1.9–3.9% (Anderson, 2006). Such low figures suggest either that women rarely conceive children through extra-pair matings and/or that men are good at detecting any such children so that paternity is generally not mistaken. Low paternity uncertainty, therefore, does not necessarily imply the existence of lifelong and faithful pair-bonds. It simply means that, on the whole, paternity of children is usually correctly attributed. In 'partible paternity' societies, for example, such as some forager communities in South America, women form relationships with several men, often simultaneously (Beckerman *et al.*, 2002; Hill and Hurtado, 1996). Children have multiple 'fathers' in these societies, since a 'father' is defined as any man who had sex with the mother during or around the time of pregnancy. But there is a hierarchy of such fathers, with 'primary' fathers being more likely to be the biological father, than 'secondary' fathers are.

The study by Anderson (2006) did not include any partible paternity studies, and has been criticised for relying heavily on agricultural and industrialised societies (Hrdy, 2009), and including too few forager societies, as unfortunately do the majority of such cross-cultural studies given that relatively few foraging communities exist today. The advent of agriculture allowed the accumulation of wealth to a much greater extent than is possible in forager societies, which is likely to have changed relationships between men and women (Kaplan and Lancaster, 2003). When resources can feasibly be acquired and accumulated, men tend to do so, in order to attract mates (Holden and Mace, 2003). In situations where men control resources, women become more dependent on men, and men's bargaining power within relationships increases. This allows them to demand exclusive sexual access to their wives, resulting in relatively high rates of paternity confidence. Whether men demand exclusive sexual access primarily because they do not want the paternal investment they intend to bestow on their children to be wasted on another man's child, or because they want to monopolise their wives' reproductive capacity and exclude other males from the mating pool is a question which is difficult to answer, given that both benefits are likely to accrue from mate-guarding.

Regardless of the exact level of paternity uncertainty, there is clearly at least some room for doubt in a man's relationship with his putative offspring. If he is considering whether to invest substantial resources in an offspring, he should take the risk of paternity uncertainty into account.

What affects paternal investment: Costs and benefits of parenting versus mating

The costs and benefits of investing in further mating effort rather than parenting effort will depend both on the availability of other mating opportunities and on the sensitivity of offspring to male care. In our own species, whether children are heavily dependent on paternal investment for their health and well-being is often not empirically tested; instead, it is simply assumed to be the case. It is worthwhile, therefore, to consider the evidence available on what it is that men do for their children, and what impact this has on the children. The forager literature has tended to focus on male provisioning of children, since this has long been assumed to be the father's main role in the human family. Cross-cultural analysis suggests that men do contribute substantially to production in hunter-gatherer societies, but so do women. On average, men bring back just over half the calories consumed by a group, women just under half (Marlowe, 2005). Similar results have been obtained when cross-cultural analysis is broadened to other subsistence strategies (Hewlett, 2000).

Some anthropologists working on African hunter-gatherers have questioned, however, whether the main purpose of the hunting that men do in such societies is the provisioning of children (Hawkes, 2004; Hawkes and Bird, 2002). Meat, particularly large game, tends to be shared fairly widely among the whole camp, rather than directed at the hunter's own children. The 'show-off hypothesis' for hunting, then, suggests that men's hunting efforts are at least partially directed towards attracting additional mates, rather than solely providing for children (Hawkes, 1991). The higher mating success of successful hunters attests to the success of this strategy (Kaplan and Hill, 1985).

Anthropologists working on South American foragers, in contrast, present evidence that most hunted game does end up with the hunter's own family, and argue more strongly for hunting as parental effort (Gurven and Hill, 2009). This group has recently tried to devise tests which tease apart mating from parenting effort in the Tsimane (Bolivian forager-farmers) by investigating the patterning of direct male care, and concluded that their evidence shows more support for parenting rather than mating effort (Winking *et al.*, 2009). Such research only highlights the difficulty of distinguishing the mating and parenting hypotheses, however, since the services men provide to children could serve both purposes simultaneously. Perhaps the only conclusion to be drawn is that hunting and other male efforts may serve as both mating and parenting effort, though the relative balance between the two may differ between societies.

There is similar confusion in the literature on non-forager populations about what constitutes paternal investment. In stratified societies, well-known links between higher paternal socioeconomic status or education and positive child outcomes have been cited as evidence for paternal investment (Geary, 2000). In the post-industrial world, fathers are of great interest to policy-makers, where they are assumed to be vital to a child's functioning and success in this particular environment. A large body of research has suggested that children without fathers have poorer outcomes than those who grow up in intact nuclear families (see Sigle-Rushton and McLanahan, 2004, for a review). However, such patterns do not necessarily provide clear-cut evidence of paternal investment.

As stated earlier, in non-forager societies, most resources tend to be owned by males. Such societies involve the exploitation of subsistence niches which allow the accumulation of resources (including land in agricultural populations, animals in pastoralist communities and money and other assets in market economies), which men take control of in order to attract mates. These resources are then used to provide for children, but whether this is primarily mating or parenting effort is open to question. The positive relationship between paternal resources and beneficial child outcomes may be a side effect of male monopolisation of resources resulting in female preferences for male resources: in other words, men may accumulate resources in order to attract women; women then use these resources to raise children successfully. Disentangling mating from parenting effort may again be impossible, given that other forms of resource transfer can serve both mating and parenting purposes simultaneously, just as does the transfer of meat.

But fathers are not simply providers of resources; they can perform other services for children, such as protecting them from other males, direct care, teaching subsistence skills and support in social interactions or conflicts. All these activities are likely to be beneficial for children (though this is rarely quantified), but again it is difficult to determine whether such behaviours can entirely be considered paternal investment, or whether mating effort may also be involved. The existence and extent of such behaviours certainly varies between societies, suggesting that they may be at least partially dependent on whether there are alternative mating opportunities available. The few tests which have attempted to determine whether this is a factor in paternal behaviour suggest that the relative ease with which men can find other mates is indeed important. Blurton Jones and colleagues (2000) investigated divorce in four forager populations, and concluded that the availability of alternative mating partners was a better predictor of divorce than the benefits that children gained from the presence of fathers. Again, we return to the conclusion that paternal investment is facultative. What fathers do for children may well benefit them (intentionally or not), but there are at least some occasions when men will cut short such benefits if alternative reproductive options are available.

Proximate mechanisms of paternal care

One final piece of evidence on paternal investment relates to the proximate determinants of male care. Hormonal changes during and after pregnancy may promote maternal care in women (Ellison and Gray, 2009). Recent research suggests men also undergo hormonal changes in relation to their marital and paternal status, which may promote shifts in strategy between mating and parenting effort. In some populations, including modern Western populations, testosterone is lower in married than in single men, and lower in fathers compared to in non-fathers (Burnham et al., 2003; Gray, Yang and Pope, 2006; Gray et al., 2004). This may be correlated with the relative amounts of effort devoted towards attracting a mate compared to investing in children – the former may require competitive behaviour facilitated by high levels of testosterone, the latter more affiliative behaviours which require lower levels of this hormone.

Research emerging from non-Western populations suggests there may be some variation in these hormonal shifts between populations. In a polygynous Kenyan sample, for example, testosterone was not lower in married compared to single men, possibly because in polygynous societies even married men continue to invest relatively heavily in mating effort (Gray, 2003). A Tanzanian study compared a high paternal care population, Hadza hunter-gatherers, with a low paternal care population, Datoga pastoralists, and confirmed the authors' prediction that testosterone would be lower in fathers in the high paternal care group than in fathers in the low paternal care group (Muller *et al.*, 2009). Such proximate, hormonal correlates of paternal status and paternal care suggest that men do have adaptations which allow them to shift into a parenting mode (or at least allocate a certain proportion of resources to parenting, rather than mating, effort) but that these adaptations are flexible and sensitive to environmental conditions.

In summary, paternal investment is facultative in our species. There is both inter- and intrapopulation variation in how much men invest in children, and exactly what they do for children. Male (not necessarily paternal) care and provisioning does seem important, however, given that the male contribution to the diet is often substantial. Whether this is primarily mating or parenting effort may be difficult to assess: it probably serves both functions. Rather than assuming that any act on the part of a male which improves child outcomes is paternal investment, it may be better to consider carefully exactly what men are doing and why.

Who else invests?

So fathers are contributing to child well-being, but these contributions vary quite substantially between and within populations, and are sometimes negligible. Does this mean that women who can rely on relatively little paternal support must absorb the full burden of raising children? It appears not, since raising human children is a very energetically intensive exercise, probably too expensive for mothers to manage alone. Women instead rely on help from other quarters. The question of whether humans are cooperative breeders has been raised in recent years, given this very heavy burden of parenting (Hrdy, 2005, 2009). Cooperative breeders are those species where non-parental care of young is common. Cooperative breeding is a relatively rare strategy, commonest in birds, where it is estimated that 9% of species breed cooperatively (Clutton-Brock, 1991; Cockburn, 2006). The strategy is less common in mammals, but a handful of species, including some canids, meerkats, naked mole rats and callitrichids, do it.

Recent research suggests that humans can be added to that list (Foster and Ratnieks, 2005). In our species it seems that relatives, particularly older women and pre-reproductive children, are the 'helpers-at-the-nest' who allow women to raise many dependent children simultaneously. It has been known for some time that children contribute considerably to the household economy, thereby effectively underwriting their parents' subsequent fertility (Kramer, 2005; Lee and Kramer, 2002). Older individuals also may continue to be productive long after they have any dependent children of their own, suggesting grandparental, particularly grandmaternal, effort is important in our species (Bock and Johnson, 2008; Hawkes, O'Connell and Blurton Jones, 1989).

Grandmothers and older children are ideal 'helpers-at-the-nest' since they are not occupied with children of their own. Pre- and post-reproductive individuals do not, in fact, have the option of producing their own offspring. A hypothesis gaining ground is that the unusual feature of human menopause may have evolved precisely because of such beneficial grandmaternal effects (Hawkes, O'Connell and Blurton Jones, 1997; Shanley *et al.*, 2007). It is certainly becoming clear that grandmothers are often very important to child well-being. Several evolutionary anthropologists have now tested the hypothesis that children with grandmothers present will have better outcomes, including survival rates, than those without grandmothers. A review of this literature found that maternal grandmothers were particularly beneficial, their presence improving child survival in just under 70% of cases (Sear and Mace, 2008; see Figure 7.1). Paternal grandmothers were also often beneficial, though less commonly than maternal grandmothers, improving child survival in about half of the populations studied.

It is difficult to assess the contributions of older children within the household, since sibling relationships are characterised by competition as well as cooperation, but there was evidence that the presence of siblings old enough to act as helpers-at-the-nest was also frequently beneficial to children (Sear and Mace, 2008; see Figure 7.1). An additional strategy which women can use to help raise children is to seek investment from men other than the child's father. Polyandrous mating, found in partible paternity societies, may be one such strategy which women use to confuse issues of paternity, and convince other men to invest in their children (Hrdy, 2000b). Children with more than one father in such populations have been found to have higher survival rates than those with only one father (Beckerman *et al.*, 1998; Hill and Hurtado, 1996). This may be brought about by the provisioning of breeding couples by other adult males, which has been demonstrated in one partible paternity society (Hill and Hurtado, 2009). Overall, this review provides empirical evidence that humans are indeed cooperative breeders, but that we adopt a relatively flexible cooperative breeding strategy, with help coming from many different potential sources, varying both between and within societies. 'Parental' investment may not just come from parents, but several other individuals too.

FAMILIAL CONFLICT

The preceding section should not give the impression that family relations are always entirely harmonious. Within the family, there is also considerable conflict. Trivers (1972) was the first to develop the concept of parent–offspring conflict. Parents and offspring will disagree about the optimal amount of investment given to each offspring. Parents in iteroparous species like our own must allocate their effort carefully between all their offspring to maximise fitness. But each offspring wants parents to invest more in itself than its siblings, since each offspring can gain greater fitness from its own reproduction than from that of its siblings.

This conflict between parents and offspring over investment has been well studied in the context of pre-natal investment. Haig (1993, 1996a) suggests that the desire of offspring to extract more investment than the mother wants to give leads to an arms race during pregnancy. The foetus develops adaptations which try and extract as many nutrients as possible from the mother; the mother develops adaptations to protect herself from the foetus's demands. The foetus is at an advantage in placental mammals, since it has direct access to the mother's bloodstream through the placenta. Haig proposes that obstetric problems such as gestational diabetes and pre-eclampsia in our own species may result directly from the foetus's attempts to manipulate maternal energy supplies through placental hormones and the mother's attempts to resist the foetus's manipulations.

Such conflicts during pregnancy may be exacerbated by conflicts between not just the mother and foetus but also the maternal and paternal genes within the foetus (Haig, 1996). During a pregnancy, the mother may be trying to keep resources in reserve for future reproduction, but the father of the child may not be related to any of the mother's future children. Paternal genes within the foetus may, therefore, be interested in extracting more nutrients from the mother for the current offspring than maternal genes. Such conflict may be implicated not just in disorders of pregnancy but also in behavioural disorders of children. Prader-Willi syndrome, for example, may be a disorder accidentally resulting from this conflict between maternal and paternal genes, as it is associated with behaviours which reduce the mother's costs of childrearing (and therefore represents a 'win' for maternal genes: Haig and Wharton, 2003).

Siblings will also compete among themselves for parental resources. Sibling competition reaches its most extreme form in siblicidal bird species (see Chapter 6 in this volume). Such within-family homicide is relatively unusual in humans, but is sometimes seen where very valuable resources are at stake. Historical accounts of the relatively homicide-prone Vikings have been analysed to demonstrate that the probability of an individual killing a close relative depended on the value of the resources at stake: high rewards were necessary before the murder of a relative became likely (Dunbar, Clark and Hurst, 1995). Usually, however, sibling competition takes a more subtle form, involving variations in how much investment children can acquire from parents, observed as apparent biases in parental investment (discussed below).

WHAT IS INVESTED?

Who invests in human children is relatively complex, but so too is the question of what is invested. Parental investment can be both pre-natal (for mothers only) and post-natal (all other investors). Pre-natal care involves investing somatic resources in offspring: mothers sustain pregnancy by directly transferring reserves of energy to the foetus. Mothers continue to invest somatically after birth, during breastfeeding. Mothers and other individuals have important roles in provisioning children after birth with food, and protecting and cleaning them, activities which take time and therefore involve opportunity costs. Human children also need considerable investment beyond simply ensuring they survive to reproductive maturity in order to ensure they become productive and competitive adults.

All human societies, whatever mode of subsistence they use, involve skills which need to be taught to children. Such training takes more time, and may involve the transfer of extra-somatic resources (those stored outside the body). Parents may continue to invest after offspring reach reproductive maturity. In societies which accumulate extra-somatic resources, parents commonly transfer such resources directly to children in order to launch them onto the marriage market, including bridewealth and dowry payments (the former involve transfers from groom's to bride's family, the latter from bride's to groom's). The final transfer which occurs from parents to children occurs after death, when parents pass on any accumulated resources to their offspring. Such transfers are still likely to be costly to the parent and therefore fit the definition of parental investment, though they occur after death, since resources may be accumulated with the express purpose of donating to children, and not used during the parent's own lifetime.

It is worth noting that parental investment is often measured indirectly. Determining exactly how much energy parents are transferring to children, how much time they spend on them and what extra-somatic resources are being transferred is not always easy. Instead, parental investment is frequently measured by determining its result: the effects on the child (Borgerhoff Mulder, 1998). The following is a by no means complete list of variables which have been used as indicators of parental investment: child survival rates, nutritional status, immunisation rates, attendance at medical clinics, length of birth intervals, educational attainment, age at marriage and inheritance bequests. Measuring child outcomes rather than parental investment itself is problematic since such outcomes are likely to correlate with, but may not match exactly, parental investment itself.

An additional problem with measuring parental investment in our species is that not all forms of investment are equal, so that different parental investment patterns may be seen if different measures of parental investment are examined. Social scientists have made a distinction between base and surplus resources (Downey, 2001). The former are those required for basic survival and adequate health; the latter those that enhance child well-being and social competitiveness over and above that which is necessary to ensure survival alone. All children need base resources, but parents can choose to allocate surplus resources differentially between children. Such a distinction may be of lesser value in the evolutionary literature, since a child that survives but is not sufficiently competitive to reproduce successfully is not particularly useful in terms of Darwinian fitness, but still may have some heuristic worth. For example, a study in rural Ethiopia found that biases in parental investment became stronger for 'surplus' resources (education) under conditions of reduced environmental risk, but not for 'base' resources (breastfeeding and immunisation: Gibson and Lawson, 2009), suggesting that parents do allocate varying types of investment differently.

Distinctions should also be made between shareable and non-shareable resources (Downey, 2001). Certain forms of parental investment, such as parental energy reserves or extra-somatic capital, are non-shareable – any unit of energy or wealth given to one child cannot be given to another. But other forms of investment, perhaps certain types of teaching or, in modern societies, the presence of a computer in the household, can more easily be shared between siblings. Again, different patterns of parental investment may be seen for shareable and non-shareable resources.

WHO IS INVESTED IN?

Perhaps the most commonly asked question in the parental investment literature focuses on who parents invest in. Parents do not necessarily invest equally in all their offspring, but will bias their investment towards those offspring likely to provide the greatest fitness return. As Hrdy (2000b) points out, 'mother love', and therefore investment, is not automatic and unconditional, but will be contingent on the characteristics of both child and mother, just as paternal investment is facultative (the same applies to any other relative who may potentially invest in a child). Humans are relatively unusual among primates in that they will sometimes retrench entirely on post-natal parental investment, by abandoning or killing children (Daly and Wilson, 1984). This practice is likely to be related to the intense investment needed in human children after birth to raise them successfully to adulthood. While both infanticide and abandonment are relatively rare, they are known to occur at least occasionally in the majority of human cultures, and to occur in situations where the prospects of raising that particular child successfully are low. More common are more subtle manipulations of parental investment: all children may be invested in, but some are more invested in than others. This bias in parental investment has been investigated most intensively for two characteristics of the child: birth order and sex.

Birth order

At the simplest level, birth order is likely to affect the amount of parental investment children receive because of the trade-off between the quantity and quality of offspring, known in the social sciences as the 'resource dilution' effect (Downey, 2001): higher birth order children (i.e. children with many older siblings) will receive less investment than lower birth order children since the former only exist in large families, and parental resources are spread more thinly in large, compared to small, families. In fact, all else being equal, the parental investment that each child receives will take the form of $y = 1/x$, where x is the number of children in the family. But all else is not equal. Children of different birth orders will differ systematically in other ways, so that much ink has been spilt trying to determine whether birth order in and of itself affects parental investment.

Both the social science and evolutionary literature is filled with studies investigating the effects of birth order on traits from personality (Sulloway, 1996), intelligence (Kristensen and Bjerkedal, 2007) and educational achievement (Bock, 2002; Travis and Kohli, 1995), to status (Davis, 1997) and career achievement (Lindert, 1977), to mortality (Lynch and Greenhouse, 1994; Manda, 1999) and anthropometric status (Floyd, 2005; Lawson and Mace, 2008), to sexual orientation (Bogaert, 2006) and familial sentiment (Salmon and Daly, 1998), all the way up to reproductive success (Borgerhoff Mulder, 1998; Draper and Hames, 2000; Mace, 1996). The problem with this literature is that many studies fail to adequately control for the many factors which could cause spurious correlations between birth order and these outcomes, such as family size, socioeconomic status and parental resources and the differing ages and needs of children (see Box 7.2).

BOX 7.2.   ARE LATER-BORNS 'BORN TO REBEL'?
BIRTH ORDER AND PERSONALITY DIFFERENCES

One of the more influential ideas in the birth order literature is that birth order affects personality, a thesis given an evolutionary framework by Sulloway (1996) in his book *Born to Rebel: Birth Order, Family Dynamics and Creative Lives.* Evidence has steadily accumulated that birth order affects career achievement since Galton first observed in the nineteenth century that eminent scientists were more likely to be first-borns (Galton, 1874). Subsequent sociological research has suggested a mechanism for this differential, which is that it is driven by personality differences between birth orders (Ernst and Angst, 1983). Sulloway's thorough survey of historical revolutions and the men who were responsible for them concluded that these differences could be boiled down to the conservative nature of firstborns compared to their more rebellious younger siblings. He argued that scientific breakthroughs, for example, had largely been driven by later-borns, such as Charles Darwin, since they were more capable of 'thinking outside the box'.

The evolutionary twist which Sulloway added was that these differences arise from sibling competition for parental investment. Children within the family all compete for parental resources, but because humans give birth to single children typically at several-year intervals, the playing field is not level for sibling competition. Sulloway argued that children of different birth orders would therefore have to adopt different tactics for attracting parental attention. Early-born children, with the advantage of being older, larger and more cognitively advanced, could adopt a conservative niche within the family, emulating parental attitudes, while later-borns would of necessity be forced to adopt a different niche, involving more flexible and more

risky behaviours, seizing opportunities for investment where they could. Salmon (2003; Salmon and Daly, 1998) has extended this research to examine variation in familial sentiment by birth order, arguing that middle-borns in particular should be less family-oriented than first or last-borns, since middle-borns suffer the most sibling competition and the least parental investment.

Such research, while well-received within much of the evolutionary community, has been criticised for methodological flaws (e.g. see Townsend, 2000, and response: Sulloway, 2000). Sulloway's work, for example, has been criticised for focusing on a rather biased sample of individuals (his survey of historically important figures is largely a survey of rich, white men) and also for not systematically taking into account differences between biological and 'functional' birth order (the latter describing children, for example, whose elder siblings died young so that they were effectively raised as the first-born child, even if they were not in reality the first child to be born to their parents; Freese, Powell and Steelman, 1999). What will matter for sibling competition is not the actual birth placement of each child but the number and order of the siblings each child had during the period of parental investment.

The subsequent work by evolutionary psychologists such as Salmon similarly has methodological flaws. As with Sulloway's work, it extrapolates a supposedly human universal from a very biased sample: like much evolutionary psychology, it depends entirely on a non-random sample of college undergraduates. It also fails to control for potentially confounding factors, such as the age and residence of other siblings. Such methodological problems should not, however, be used to conclude that birth order has no effect on personality, or other traits for that matter. As described in the main text, there are sound evolutionary reasons why children of different birth orders should receive different levels of investment from parents. Instead, the reader should approach birth order research with appropriate caution, and judge each study on its own merits, including assessing whether it has satisfactorily dealt with potentially confounding factors.

This has led to something of a backlash against birth order studies in the social science literature, and calls for much greater methodological rigour (Somit, Arwine and Peterson, 1996; Steelman *et al.*, 2002; Wichman, Rodgers and MacCallum, 2006). Birth order research tends to be accepted somewhat less critically in the evolutionary literature, perhaps because there are good evolutionary reasons why parents should invest differently in children of different birth orders, regardless of resource dilution effects: children of different birth orders will differ in both age and the level and type of investment they require (which does not mean, of course, that such studies should not also be carefully assessed for methodological rigour).

Child's age will affect predicted investment patterns because age is correlated with reproductive value. Reproductive value is defined as the expected future reproductive output of an individual, at a given age (Fisher, 1930). It is the product of both surviving and successfully reproducing, both of which vary strongly by age. In our species, mortality is highest immediately after birth, declines to a low point in late childhood, then begins a more or less continuous rise at adolescence before increasing rapidly among elderly adults (Gurven and Kaplan, 2006). Reproductive value follows a similar path: newborn children have a relatively low reproductive value; it increases as children age, before peaking at the average age at first birth, when individuals have a high expectation of future reproductive output (see Figure 7.2; reproductive value curves may also differ for sons and daughters).

All else being equal, then, older children have higher reproductive value than younger children do, so that older children may be expected to be favoured over younger. This leads to the prediction that older children will always receive higher parental investment than younger, at least up to the point of sexual maturity. This may explain why early-born children do frequently seem to be advantaged in a variety of outcomes. When infanticide occurs, for example, it is very commonly the younger child in which investment is terminated, not older children. Among Aché hunter-gatherers in Paraguay, a group in which rather remarkably high rates of child homicide are seen, 5% of all children born were killed in their first year of life, compared to about 2% of children killed per year between the ages of 5 and 9 (Hill and Hurtado, 1996). This conforms with findings from a cross-cultural survey that younger children, as well as those of low reproductive value for reasons of deformity or ill-health, were much more vulnerable to infanticide (Daly and Wilson, 1984).

Counteracting the trend for older children to get higher parental investment because of their greater reproductive value is that parents also invest according to

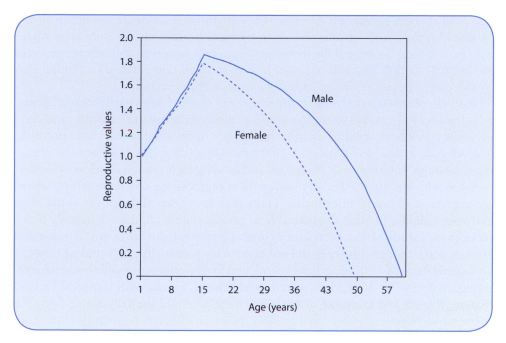

Figure 7.2. *Reproductive value for women and men based on data from South Africa.*
Source: From Bowles and Posel (2005); reproduced by permission of Nature Publishing Group.

the child's need or, more technically, the marginal value of that parental investment to each child (Clutton-Brock, 1991). A unit of parental care given to a 10-year-old child may improve its survival chances slightly, but the same unit of parental care given to a newborn may increase the newborn's chances of survival much more dramatically. Newborns may, therefore, get more investment from mothers, in terms of both nutrition and time, because the marginal value of that investment is greater for younger children. Jeon (2008) attempted to theoretically model the solutions to this dilemma for parents – should they invest more in older children because they have higher reproductive value or younger children because they derive greater marginal returns to investment? – and concluded that in the majority of cases parents should resolve this dilemma in favour of older children.

Perhaps the most extreme form of this favouring of oldest children is primogeniture: when the oldest child (usually in fact the eldest son) inherits all or most parental resources. While almost every pattern of bequeathing wealth from parents to offspring is seen in human societies – eldest son or daughter inherits (primogeniture), youngest son or daughter inherits (ultimogeniture), all children or all children of favoured sex inherit equally – primogeniture is the most common pattern, certainly where parents differentiate between children in their inheritance (Hrdy and Judge, 1993; Murdock, 1967). Such a pattern may stem from a couple of other advantages of investing in first-borns: first, that this gives parents more time to contribute to this child's reproductive success and, second, that investing heavily in the eldest child may well shorten generation times, which will ultimately increase the fitness of the parental lineage. Such extreme biases in parental investment are only seen where resource-holding is essential for reproductive success, however, and where resources are limited, so that bequeathing wealth to more than one child risks diluting that wealth until it becomes almost useless for reproductive success.

Patterns of investment by birth order may not always favour early-born offspring, or at least may not always result in a linear relationship between birth order and child outcomes. Firstborn children tend to have lower birth weights than later-borns do (e.g. Magadi, Madise and Diamond, 2001), though it is not clear whether this results from maternal investment decisions or confounding factors such as selection effects (women who are not particularly successful at reproducing will be overrepresented among the mothers of first births). Hints that later-born children do better than early-born children in that they are able to produce more children than early-borns come from a study of southern African hunter-gatherers, the Ju/'hoansi (Draper and Hames, 2000: though this study did not control for potentially confounding factors). U-shaped effects of birth order have been found for the number of children produced, though not number of children reared to adulthood, for males in historical Finland (Faurie, Russell and Lummaa, 2009). Such patterns could partially result from the cooperative effects of elder siblings, and therefore children benefiting from non-parental investment. But Hertwig, Davis and Sulloway (2002) caution that unequal outcomes can arise from an 'equity heuristic', a decision rule stating that parents should invest equally in all their children. They argue that, even if at any one time parents invest equally across all offspring, middle-borns will always receive less cumulative investment than first- or last-borns because they never benefit from an exclusive period of parental investment (see Figure 7.3).

Thus, a 'middle-born disadvantage' can arise even if parents show no bias towards any of their offspring. This is based on the assumption, however, that parents only invest while children are resident in the parental household, which is likely not to hold across all measures of parental investment in our species, since parents continue to invest in children throughout their lives. One final complication is that, where parents invest unequally in sons and daughters (see next section), the equity heuristic will not hold. In this case, what may be relevant to the child is same-sex birth order, so a modification of the middle-born disadvantage may be that it will only hold when same-sex siblings are considered, as in historical Finland, where a middle-born disadvantage in fertility was seen only for male offspring (Faurie, Russell and Lummaa, 2009).

Sex biases in investment

One of the richest veins of literature on parental investment is on sex biases in parental investment. In a population with an even sex ratio, the average number of grandoffspring produced by a son and a daughter will be the same but, given that the variance in reproductive success differs between the sexes (usually, but not always, higher in males), the riskiness of producing sons rather than daughters will differ, sons being the higher-risk sex in populations where male variance in reproductive

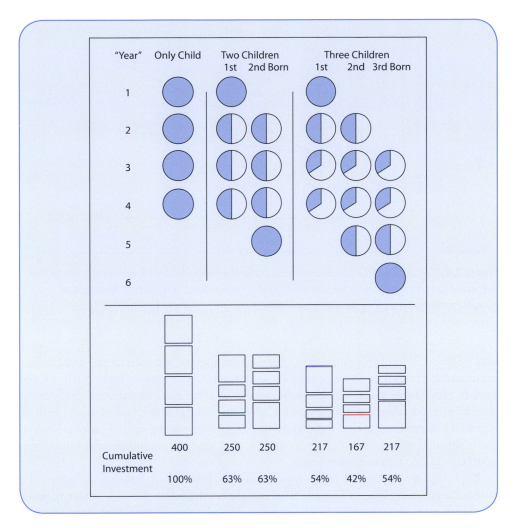

Figure 7.3. *Unequal investment in children arising from an equity heuristic.*

Spheres in the upper part of the figure represent resource allocation according to the equity heuristic as a function of birth rank in families with one, two and three children. The bars in the lower part show the absolute and relative (i.e. calculated as a proportion of that for an only child) cumulative investments across four growth periods, or 'years').

Source: From Hertwig, Davis and Sulloway (2002); reproduced by permission of American Psychological Association.

success is higher than female variance. More importantly, parental investment may have differential impacts on sons versus daughters. Under certain circumstances, a unit of parental investment may be more valuable to a son than to a daughter, if it can increase his reproductive output relatively more than the same unit of parental investment given to his sister.

This is the principle behind what is perhaps the most common framework for investigating sex biases in investment: the 'Trivers–Willard hypothesis' (TWH; Trivers

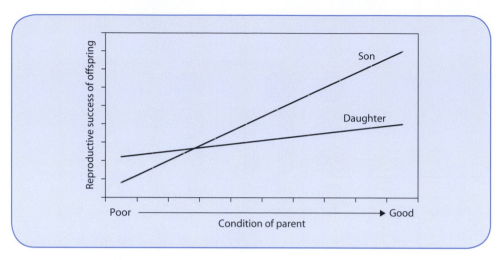

Figure 7.4. *Schematic of the conditions necessary for the Trivers–Willard hypothesis: reproductive success of sons must be greater for parents in good condition but the reproductive success of daughters must be higher for parents in poor condition.*

and Willard, 1973). As formulated for non-human species, it concerns pre-natal investment and states that, if three conditions hold, then the sex ratio at birth (SRB) should vary in predictable ways. These conditions are: (1) that the condition of the mother (investor) is correlated with the condition of the young at the end of the period of parental investment; (2) that the condition of the young at the end of parental investment should endure into adulthood; and (3) that one sex should benefit more from good condition than the other does.

Typically, males benefit more from good condition than females do: given the generally greater variance in male than female reproductive success, males in good condition can out-compete poor-condition males and achieve high reproductive success. Females in good condition may also out-compete females in poor condition, but the discrepancy between females in good and poor condition will be much less than the discrepancy between males in good and poor condition (see Figure 7.4). So the TWH predicts that mothers in good condition will produce relatively more sons and mothers in poor condition will produce relatively more daughters.

Numerous attempts have been made to find evidence of the TWH in SRBs in our species, with varying degrees of success (see Box 7.3 for the typical SRB of our species). Most of these have measured parental condition as 'status' (including wealth, education and social class): Lazarus (2002) reports that of 54 analyses in the literature testing the TWH in humans, 26 (48%) supported the hypothesis. Fewer studies have attempted to test the TWH using measures of physiological condition, but with similarly mixed results. A strong effect of lower nutritional status resulting in more female births was found in a poorly nourished Ethiopian population (Gibson and Mace, 2003; see also Figure 7.5). Lower pre-pregnancy energy intake was also found to correlate with fewer male births in a British sample (Mathews, Johnson and Neil,

BOX 7.3.   WHY ARE SEX RATIOS AT BIRTH MALE-BIASED IN *HOMO SAPIENS*?

On average, human sex ratios at birth (SRBs) are around 105 males to every 100 females. This male bias has traditionally been ascribed to Fisher's original idea that on average parental investment in sons and daughters must be equal, given that on average the reproductive value of a male and a female must be equal (Fisher, 1930). The typically higher male mortality throughout childhood means that the average son will receive lower investment than the average daughter will, since he will be more likely to die before the end of parental investment. The slight male bias at birth adjusts for this shorter period of parental care for males so that overall investment in males and females is equal. This hypothesis assumes that the marginal value of investment to each sex is the same, however, which the Trivers–Willard hypothesis (TWH) states may not always be the case (though the TWH attempts to explain within-species biases in sex ratios at birth, not a species level phenomenon). Despite long-standing interest in evolutionary biology, then, the male-biased SRB in our species is not yet fully understood (Lazarus, 2002). This problem with predicting population-level sex ratios in other vertebrate species (Frank, 1990) has led some to argue that predicting individual variation in SRBs is likely to be a much more productive approach (West, Reece and Sheldon, 2002; West and Sheldon, 2002).

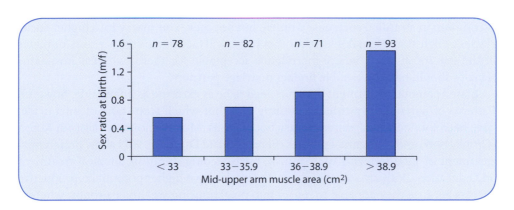

Figure 7.5. *Higher sex ratio at birth in better-nourished women in rural Ethiopia.*
Source: From Gibson and Mace (2003); reproduced by permission of the Royal Society.

2008), but Stein and colleagues (2004) found no effect of acute undernutrition on SRB during the Dutch famine. The British study rather unfortunately also reported that women who ate breakfast cereals were more likely to produce boys, a somewhat unlikely finding which was widely reported across the media and raised doubts in the minds of other scientists as to the quality of the study (Young, Bang and Oktay, 2009). Such a finding, which could easily be interpreted as a statistical quirk, highlights one of the potential problems with finding a Trivers and Willard effect: any effect sizes are likely to be small, which makes identifying such biases in the SRB statistically challenging (Gelman and Weakliem, 2009).

A wider problem with identifying the Trivers and Willard effect is that many studies do not demonstrate the three conditions necessary for the TWH to hold in their study populations (Brown, 2001), nor do they give much thought to the mechanism by which biased sex ratios could be brought about. Some authors do attempt to test the pre-conditions (e.g. Cameron and Dalerum, 2009), and some are attempting to tackle the latter problem (e.g. Grant, 1998) but, as with birth order studies, research investigating the TWH in human populations should be judged on its individual merits.

In addition to SRB studies, there is plentiful research investigating whether the TWH holds for post-natal investment. In some respects, patterns of biased post-natal investment should be easier to investigate, since the mechanisms of biased post-natal investment can potentially be investigated directly (Cronk, 2007). At least some such studies have also attempted to determine whether the pre-conditions for the TWH hold, in particular whether the reproductive success of sons and daughters differs by parental status. Even if manipulating sex ratios before birth is mechanistically tricky, infanticide may be used as a means of post-natally adjusting the sex ratios of children. Dickemann's (1979) classic study of historical literature in Asia and Europe observes that female infanticide was much more common among upper social strata: she cites one high-caste Indian group which claimed never to have let a female child born within the caste live. This fits with the TWH, since high-status males are more likely to find wives than low-status males are, given that hypergyny is common in stratified societies (women, but not men, can marry into higher social classes). High-status females, on the other hand, will face fierce competition for mates in the few social strata where marriage is acceptable for them, whereas low-status females should have no trouble finding marriage partners.

Biased parental investment does not need to be as extreme as infanticide, however. Patterns of parental investment favouring girls, but which stop short of infanticide, have been found in two contemporary populations. Mukogodo pastoralists in Kenya (Cronk, 1989) and Hungarian gypsies (Bereczkei and Dunbar, 1997) show preferential treatment of girls in terms of, variously, breastfeeding duration, medical treatment and education. Both are societies in which females have higher potential reproductive success because they are able to marry into neighbouring wealthier groups, whereas males face competition between men from both within and outside the community for mates. At a much later stage in development, Mace (1996) interprets a bias in inheritance patterns towards males in Gabbra pastoralists in Kenya as adaptive within a society where males benefit much more from inherited wealth (by becoming polygynous) than females do. This particular parental bias cannot be ascribed to the TWH, since all parents give wealth to sons in this society, but fits in with the principle, which can be generalised from the TWH, that parents will invest their resources strategically in order to gain the greatest fitness return.

The TWH is not the only candidate for explaining sex-biased parental investment, just the most tested. Other possible explanations are local resource enhancement

(Emlen, Emlen and Levin, 1986) or local resource competition (Clark, 1978; Silk, 1983). In the former case, children who enhance their parents' reproductive success, for example, by helping out with childcare, may be favoured. In the latter case, children that compete with parents or other siblings for local resources may be disfavoured. Biased breastfeeding patterns in favour of daughters have been suggested to result from local resource enhancement effects in two populations where daughters are known to provide childcare: Hutterites (a north American Anabaptist sect: Margulis, Altmann and Ober, 1993) and a Caribbean community (Quinlan, Quinlan and Flinn, 2005). As previously noted, daughters frequently provide childcare and other services to mothers, but daughter-biased investment tends to be relatively uncommon. Instead, such explanations will only apply if daughters are particularly helpful compared to sons, which appears to be the case at least in the Caribbean example: a matrifocal society where girls are more productive than boys within the household (Quinlan, Quinlan and Flinn, 2005).

Local resource enhancement/competition explanations are sometimes explicitly given by parents as the reason why sons are favoured in patrilocal societies, where sons stay in the family home and contribute to the household economy, but daughters marry out ('daughters are like crows, you feed them then they fly away'). That more contemporary societies are patrilocal rather than matrilocal may explain why stated preferences for male offspring tend to be much more common than for female offspring (Arnold, 1992), though we should perhaps interpret such statements with caution, since what people say and what they do are not necessarily the same thing. Pennington and Harpending (1993) documented what appeared to be daughter preference in the Herero, cattle pastoralists in Botswana: girls were much more likely to survive childhood than boys were. The authors attributed these effects to local resource enhancement: daughters brought in cattle at marriage, which could be used to marry off sons. But the Herero themselves did not attribute the higher survival of girls to daughter preference (at least in conversations with anthropologists). Instead, they claimed this was the result of witchcraft directed at women with many sons, stemming from jealousy of such fortunate women. The authors' own observations, along with those of nearby ethnic groups, however, attributed this discrepancy squarely to biased parental investment, in particular noting that the Herero simply did not feed their sons as well as their daughters.

Interactions between birth order and sex biases

The complicated nature of both birth order effects and sex biases in parental investment means that neither should be examined in isolation. The combination of the differential costs of raising boys and girls, the differential reproductive returns of each, plus local resource competition and enhancement effects often mean that a simple preference for boys or girls, or children of a particular birth order, is not seen. Even in societies with a clearly expressed preference for sons, certain sons may be more favoured than others, just as some daughters may be less discriminated against than others. Discrimination against girls may be particularly harsh against girls with many older sisters, showing up as increased mortality rates for such girls (Das Gupta, 1987; Muhuri and Preston, 1991). Similarly, boys with many older brothers may be discriminated against even in societies which apparently bias investment towards sons: in Gabbra pastoralists, later-born boys receive relatively little inherited wealth and marry at a later age than their elder brothers (Mace, 1996).

Borgerhoff Mulder (1998) investigated parental biases by both birth order and sex in an attempt to distinguish between the TWH and local resource enhancement/competition models in Kipsigis agropastoralists in Kenya. She found that the results varied according to measure of parental investment. A TWH effect was evident in education, for example, with richer parents favouring sons and poorer parents favouring daughters, which was consistent with stronger effects of wealth on the reproductive success of males than of females in this population. There was also evidence of both local competition and enhancement between siblings, however. Brothers seemed to compete reproductively with one another, but gain benefits from sisters, so that parents invested more in sons with few brothers and in sons with many sisters. Girls were less affected by their siblings and, predictably, experienced less biased parental investment according to their number of brothers or sisters. Borgerhoff Mulder's (1998) conclusion was that studies of parental investment biases should consider a broad range of socioecological factors constraining parental options and payoffs, the value of children and the costs of parental investment, as well as which measures of investment are appropriate for comparing investment patterns between the sexes and between classes, an appropriately holistic conclusion with which to leave the subject of parental biases between children.

How parental condition affects who is invested in

One further factor to consider when investigating parental investment is the characteristics of the parent. Just as the child's reproductive value varies with age, so does the parent's; more precisely, parental reproductive value will decline throughout the reproductive period. This may influence parental decisions about whether to invest in children. Abortion and infanticide rates are higher among younger than older women, since older women have fewer opportunities to replace such children (Daly and Wilson, 1984; Lycett and Dunbar, 1999). It will also influence how much to invest. A well-known hypothesis, but one which has so far received relatively little support, is the 'terminal investment hypothesis' (Williams, 1966). This states that parental investment should increase in later, and particularly last-born, offspring, since there will be no need to conserve resources for future children.

There is some support for this hypothesis in our species in that rates of twinning and children born with genetic abnormalities increase with maternal age (Forbes, 1997). This has been suggested to result from a relaxation of the screening process which screens out less than optimal conceptuses in younger women. Since such screening mechanisms may result in false positives, where healthy foetuses are terminated in error, a relaxation of such mechanisms may result in at least some chance of a healthy birth for older women (Forbes, 1997). Otherwise, the evidence for terminal investment in humans is not strong, perhaps because other aspects of parental condition may also change with parental age (Fessler *et al.*, 2005).

Other parental characteristics which change with age, and which may result in higher investment towards the end of a parent's reproductive life, are experience and accumulated resources. Increasing experience may explain why first births are at particular risk of dying (Hobcraft, McDonald and Rutstein, 1985). In societies with inherited wealth, resources tend to accumulate with age, and in wage economies, salaries may increase with age and experience. Food production in subsistence societies may follow a more curvilinear pattern, with younger and older adults relatively less efficient than adults in middle age, as it is often related to changes in physical condition and strength (Bock and Johnson, 2008; Hill and Hurtado, 1996). This decline in physiological condition with age may prove the nail in the coffin of the terminal investment hypothesis. A theoretical investigation by McNamara *et al.* (2009) found that if both changes in parental reproductive value and parental condition with age are factored into the model then parental investment is predicted to decline, and not increase, with age, suggesting that constraints on behaviour need to be carefully considered as well as the behaviour's potential adaptive benefits.

The role of environmental quality and risk

To finish this section on parental investment, we should consider the effects of environmental quality and risk – both of which will affect parental condition, ability to invest and the potential payoffs to investment. Environmental risk may affect both overall parental effort and how biased parental effort is. High risk may result in reduced effort overall: if parents cannot predictably ameliorate environmental risks to their offspring, there may be little point wasting effort trying to do so (Quinlan, 2007). High environmental risk may also result in a 'bet-hedging' strategy whereby parents discriminate little between children in investment, since they are unable to determine with confidence which children will survive and prosper. Such a strategy has been observed among educational investment in South African children (Liddell, Barrett and Henzi, 2003).

Similarly, chronic conditions of resource scarcity may result in relatively low investment and limited discrimination between children, since under such conditions parents are unable to fully control their children's survival and reproductive chances. As resources become more abundant, parents become more biased in their investment, as heavy investment in few children becomes a safer bet. Evidence for this can again be seen in educational investment in two African populations, in rural Ethiopia and Malawi. In both societies, birth order biases in educational outcomes are stronger in wealthy compared to poor families (Gibson and Sear, 2010). This increase in biased parental investment, and shift towards investing heavily in few, rather than little in many, offspring, has been proposed as an explanation for the fertility decline which is now universal across human societies (Mace, 2007).

CONCLUSION

The human species is one characterised by intensive parental investment, but also one where 'parental' investment may come from individuals other than the child's parents. The evolution of the human family, as well as some of our physiological traits, may in fact have been guided by the need for parents to involve other relatives in the raising of several expensive children, at different developmental stages. Our long period of dependence, requiring a transfer of skills as well as resources, introduces further complexity into 'parental' investment: what is invested also takes many different forms, both somatic and extra-somatic, and different patterns of investment may be seen for different types of investment. Measuring parental investment therefore requires a careful consideration of who invests, what is invested, who is being invested in and in what kind of environment the investment is taking place, as well as carefully controlling for the many potentially confounding factors which could influence the measurement of such investment.

The existing literature does not always take such a careful approach to the analysis of parental investment, so that it is important to carefully assess each study on its own merits. Such problems of measurement and methodology particularly beset the literature on birth order and sex biases in parental investment, but are not absent from any section of the literature. Current research is rightly beginning to focus on getting the methods right in order to properly understand parental investment strategies (e.g. using advanced statistical techniques to control for confounding factors when investigating parental biases in investment: Lawson and Mace, 2008), and also beginning to test between alternative hypotheses for parental behaviour (essential if progress is to be made in interpreting parenting patterns: e.g. Winking *et al.*, 2009).

This chapter has taken a broad-brush approach to evolutionary psychology: much of the research described in this chapter has been done by evolutionary anthropologists and behavioural ecologists, who have been traditionally more interested in questions surrounding family relationships and parental investment than on evolutionary psychology (in the most narrow sense), where focus tends to be on sexual selection. The emphasis of the former disciplines on traditional, high-fertility societies has led to a growing understanding of parental investment in small-scale, subsistence economies, but a dearth of evidence of parenting strategies in industrialised, low-fertility societies. These disciplines also tend to ignore the mechanisms by which particular behaviours are brought about. In order to fully understand parental investment strategies, evidence needs to be gathered from a range of environments in order to assess commonalities and variation in parenting, and an obvious way to fill the gap would be to expand parental investment research in modern societies (an exception is perhaps grandparental investment, which is not entirely neglected in industrialised societies: see e.g. Coall *et al.*, 2009; Euler and Weitzel, 1996). Social scientists have collated a large body of research on parenting in modern societies, but since they do not work within an evolutionary framework they do not always ask the questions that have relevance to evolutionary debates about parental investment. More evidence could also be gathered on the proximate determinants of parental care and the mechanisms by which biases in investment are brought about, perhaps investigating in more detail how parental 'solicitude' (Daly and Wilson, 1980) varies as a function of sex and birth order.

Future research therefore needs to continue to develop good data collection and statistical techniques in order to fully control for confounding factors; to explicitly set up tests to distinguish between rival hypotheses for investment strategies; to focus more on identifying parental investment itself, rather than relying on child outcomes; to consider the mechanisms by which patterns of investment are brought about; and to do all this across a range of different environments and economies, in order to develop a full understanding of human parenting and family relationships.

ACKNOWLEDGEMENTS

Thanks to David Lawson, Gillian Brown and Mhairi Gibson for helpful comments and discussion that improved the chapter.

REFERENCES

Alvarez, H. (2004). Residence groups among hunter-gatherers: A view of the claims and evidence for patrilocal bands. In B. Chapais and C. M. Berman (eds), *Kinship and behaviour in primates* (pp. 420–42). Oxford: Oxford University Press.

Anderson, K. G. (2006). How well does paternity confidence match actual paternity? Evidence from worldwide nonpaternity rates. *Current Anthropology, 47,* 513–520.

Arnold, F. (1992). Sex preference and its demographic and health implications. *International Family Planning Perspectives, 18,* 93–101.

Beckerman, S., Lizarralde, R., Ballew, C. *et al.* (1998). The Barí partible paternity project: Preliminary results. *Current Anthropology, 39,* 164–7.

Beckerman, S., Lizarralde, R., Lizarralde, M. *et al.* (2002). The Barí partible paternity project: Phase One. In S. Beckerman and P. Valentine (eds), Cultures of multiple fathers: The theory and practice of partible paternity in lowland South America (pp. 27–41). Gainsville, FL: University Press of Florida.

Bereczkei, T. and Dunbar, R. I. M. (1997). Female-biased reproductive strategies in a Hungarian Gypsy population. *Proceedings of the Royal Society B, 264,* 26417–26422.

Blurton Jones, N., Hawkes, K. and O'Connell, J. (2005). Hadza grandmothers as helpers: Residence data. In E. Voland, A. Chasiotis and W. Schiefenhoevel (eds), *Grandmotherhood: The evolutionary significance of the second half of female life* (pp. 160–176). New Brunswick, NJ: Rutgers University Press.

Blurton Jones, N. G., Marlowe, F., Hawkes, K. and O'Connell, J. F. (2000). Paternal investment and hunter-gatherer divorce rates. In L. Cronk, N. Chagnon and W. Irons (eds), *Adaptation and human behaviour: An anthropological perspective.* New York: Aldine de Gruyter.

Bock, J. (2002). Evolutionary demography and intrahousehold time allocation: School attendance and child labor among the Okavango Delta Peoples of Botswana. *American Journal of Human Biology, 14*, 206–21.

Bock, J. and Johnson, S. (2008). Grandmothers' productivity and the HIV/AIDS pandemic in sub-Saharan Africa. *Journal of Cross-Cultural Gerontology, 23*, 131–45.

Bogaert, A. F. (2006). Biological versus nonbiological older brothers and men's sexual orientation. *Proceedings of the National Academy of Science USA, 103*, 10771–4.

Bogin, B. (1997). Evolutionary hypotheses for human childhood. *Yearbook of Physical Anthropology, 40*, 63–89.

Borgerhoff Mulder, M. (1998). Brothers and sisters: How sibling interactions affect optimal parental allocations. *Human Nature, 9*, 119–161.

Bowles, S. and Posel, D. (2005). Genetic relatedness predicts South African migrant workers' remittances to their families. *Nature, 434*, 380–383.

Brown, G. R. (2001). Sex-biased investment in nonhuman primates: Can Trivers and Willard's theory be tested? *Animal Behaviour, 61*, 683–94.

Burnham, T. C., Chapman, J. F., Gray, P. B. *et al.* (2003). Men in committed, romantic relationships have lower testosterone. *Hormones and Behavior, 44*, 119–122.

Buss, D. M. (1989). Sex differences in human mate preferences: Evolutionary hypotheses tested in 37 countries. *Behavioral and Brain Sciences, 12*, 1–49.

Cameron, E. Z. and Dalerum, F. (2009). A Trivers-Willard effect in contemporary humans: Male-biased sex ratios among billionaires. *PLoS One, 4*, e4195.

Chapais, B. (2008). *Primeval kinship: How pair bonding gave birth to human society.* Cambridge, MA: Harvard University Press.

Clark, A. B. (1978). Sex ratio and local resource competition in a prosimian primate. *Science, 201*, 163–5.

Clutton-Brock, T. H. (1991). *The evolution of parental care.* Princeton, NJ: Princeton University Press.

Coall, D. A., Meier, R. Hertwig, M. *et al.* (2009). Grandparental investment: The influence of reproductive timing and family size. *American Journal of Human Biology, 21*, 455–63.

Cockburn, A. (2006). Prevalence of different modes of parental care in birds. *Proceedings of the Royal Society B, 273*, 1375–83.

Cohen, J. (1977). *Reproduction.* London: Butterworths.

Cronk, L. (1989). Low socioeconomic status and female-biased parental investment: The Mukogodo example. *American Anthropologist, 91*, 414–429.

Cronk, L. (2007). Boy or girl: Gender preferences from a Darwinian point of view. *Reproductive Biomedicine Online, 15*, 23–32.

Daly, M. and Wilson, M. (1980). Discriminative parental solicitude: A biological perspective. *Journal of Marriage and Family, 42*, 277–88.

Daly, M. and Wilson, M. (1984). A sociobiological analysis of human infanticide. In G. Hausfater, S. B. Hrdy (eds), *Infanticide: Comparative and evolutionary perspectives* (pp. 487–502). New York: Aldine de Gruyter.

Das Gupta, M. (1987). Selective discrimination against female children in India. *Population and Development Review, 13*, 77–101.

Davis, J. N. (1997). Birth order, sibship size, and status in modern Canada. *Human Nature, 8*, 205–30.

Dawkins, R. and Carlisle, T. R. (1976). Parental investment, mate desertion and a fallacy. *Nature, 262*, 131–3.

Dickemann, M. (1979). Female infanticide, reproductive strategies and social stratification: A preliminary model. In N. A. Chagnon and W. Irons (eds), *Evolutionary biology and human social behaviour* (pp. 321–67). North Scituate, RI: Duxbury Press.

Downey, D. B. (2001). Number of siblings and intellectual development: The resource dilution explanation. *American Psychologist, 56*, 497–504.

Draper, P. and Hames, R. (2000). Birth order, sibling investment, and fertility among Ju/'hoansi (!Kung). *Human Nature, 11*, 117–156.

Dunbar, R. I. M., Clark, A. and Hurst, N. L. (1995). Conflict and cooperation among the Vikings: Contingent behavioral decisions. *Ethology and Sociobiology, 16*, 233–46.

Ellison, P. T. and Gray, P. B. (2009). *Endocrinology of social relationships*. Cambridge, MA: Harvard University Press.

Ember, C. R. (1978). Myths about hunter-gatherers. *Ethnology, 17*, 439–48.

Emlen, S. T., Emlen, J. M. and Levin, S. A. (1986). Sex-ratio selection in species with helpers-at-the-nest. *American Naturalist, 127*, 1–8.

Ernst, C. and Angst, J. (1983). *Birth order: Its influence on personality*. Berlin: Springer.

Euler, H. A. and Weitzel, B. (1996). Discriminative grandparental solicitude as reproductive strategy. *Human Nature, 7*, 39–60.

Faurie, C., Russell, A. F. and Lummaa, V. (2009). Middleborns disadvantaged? Testing birth-order effects on fitness in pre-industrial Finns. *PLoS One, 4*, e5680.

Fessler, D. M. T., Navarrete, C. D., Hopkins, W. and Izard, M. K. (2005). Examining the terminal investment hypothesis in humans and chimpanzees: Associations among maternal age, parity, and birth weight. *American Journal of Physical Anthropology, 127*, 95–104.

Fisher, R. A. (1930). *The genetical theory of natural selection*. Oxford: Oxford University Press.

Floyd, B. (2005). Heights and weights of Da-an boys: Did sisters really make a difference? *Journal of Biosocial Science, 37*, 287–300.

Forbes, L. S. (1997). The evolutionary biology of spontaneous abortion in humans. *Trends in Ecology and Evolution, 12*, 446–50.

Foster, K. R. and Ratnieks, F. L. W. (2005). A new eusocial vertebrate? *Trends in Ecology and Evolution, 20*, 363–4.

Frank, S. A. (1990). Sex allocation theory for birds and mammals. *Annual Review of Ecology and Systematics, 21*, 13–55.

Freese, J., Powell, B. and Steelman, L. C. (1999). Rebel without a cause or effect: Birth order and social attitudes. *American Sociological Review, 64*, 207–31.

Galton, F. (1874). *English men of science: Their nature and nurture*. London: Macmillan.

Geary, D. C. (2000). Evolution and proximate expression of human paternal investment. *Psychological Bulletin, 126*, 55–77.

Geary, D. C., Vigil, J. and Byrd-Craven, J. (2004). Evolution of human mate choice. *Journal of Sex Research, 41*, 27–42.

Gelman, A. and Weakliem, D. (2009). Of beauty, sex and power. *American Scientist, 97*, 310–316.

Gibson, M. A. and Lawson, D. W. (2009). *'Modernization' increases parental investment and sibling resource competition: Evidence from a rural development initiative in Ethiopia*. Manuscript under review.

Gibson, M. A. and Mace, R. (2003). Strong mothers bear more sons in rural Ethiopia. *Proceedings of the Royal Society B, 270*, S108–S109.

Gibson, M. A. and Sear, R. (2010). *Does wealth increase parental investment biases in child education? Evidence from two African populations on the cusp of the fertility transition*. Current Anthropology, 51, 693–701.

Grant, V. J. (1998). *Maternal personality, evolution and the sex ratio*. London: Routledge.

Gray, P., Chapman, J., Burnham, T. *et al.* (2004). Human male pair bonding and testosterone. *Human Nature, 15*, 119–131.

Gray, P. B. (2003). Marriage, parenting, and testosterone variation among Kenyan Swahili men. *American Journal of Physical Anthropology, 122*, 279–86.

Gray, P. B., Yang, J. C.-F. and Pope, H. G. (2006). Fathers have lower salivary testosterone levels than unmarried men and married non-fathers in Beijing, China. *Proceedings of the Royal Society B, 273*, 333–9.

Gurven, M. and Hill, K. (2009). Why do men hunt? A reevaluation of 'Man the Hunter' and the sexual division of labor. *Current Anthropology, 50*, 51–74.

Gurven, M. and Kaplan, H. (2006). Longevity among hunter-gatherers: A cross-cultural examination. *Population and Development Review, 33*, 321–65.

Haig, D. (1993). Genetic conflicts in human pregnancy. *Quarterly Review of Biology, 68*, 495–532.

Haig, D. (1996). Altercation of generations: Genetic conflicts of pregnancy. *American Journal of Reproductive Immunology, 35*, 226–32.

Haig, D. and Wharton, R. (2003). Prader-Willi syndrome and the evolution of human childhood. *American Journal of Human Biology, 15*, 320–329.

Hawkes, K. (1991). Showing off: Tests of an hypothesis about men's foraging goals. *Ethology and Sociobiology, 12*, 29–54.

Hawkes, K. (2004). Mating, parenting and the evolution of human pair bonds. In B. Chapais and C. M. Berman (eds), *Kinship and behaviour in primates* (pp. 443–73). Oxford: Oxford University Press.

Hawkes, K. and Bird, R. B. (2002). Showing off, handicap signaling, and the evolution of men's work. *Evolutionary Anthropology, 11*, 58–67.

Hawkes, K., O'Connell, J. F. and Blurton Jones, N. G. (1989). Hardworking Hadza grandmothers. In V. Standen and R. A. Foley (eds), *Comparative socioecology: The behavioural ecology of humans and other mammals* (pp. 341–66). Oxford: Blackwell.

Hawkes, K., O'Connell, J. F. and Blurton Jones, N. G. (1997). Hadza women's time allocation, offspring provisioning and the evolution of long postmenopausal life spans. *Current Anthropology, 38*, 551–78.

Hertwig, R., Davis, J. N. and Sulloway, F. J. (2002). Parental investment: How an equity motive can produce inequality. *Psychological Bulletin, 128*, 728–45.

Hewlett, B. S. (2000). Culture, history and sex: Anthropological contributions to conceptualizing father involvement. *Marriage and Family Review, 29*, 59–73.

Hill, K. (1993). Life history theory and evolutionary anthropology. *Evolutionary Anthropology, 2*, 78–88.

Hill, K. and Hurtado, A. M. (1996). *Aché life history: The ecology and demography of a foraging people*. New York: Aldine de Gruyter.

Hill, K. and Hurtado, A. M. (2009). Cooperative breeding in South American hunter-gatherers. *Proceedings of the Royal Society B, 276*, 3863–70.

Hobcraft, J. N., McDonald, J. W. and Rutstein, S. O. (1985). Demographic determinants of infant and early child mortality: A comparative analysis. *Population Studies, 39*, 363–85.

Holden, C. J. and Mace, R. (2003). Spread of cattle led to the loss of matrilineal descent in Africa: A coevolutionary analysis. *Proceedings of the Royal Society B, 270*, 2425–33.

Hrdy, S. B. (2000a). The optimal number of fathers: Evolution, demography, and history in the shaping of female mate preferences. *Annals of the New York Academy of Sciences, 90*, 775–96.

Hrdy, S. B. (2000b). *Mother Nature: Maternal instincts and the shaping of the species*. London: Vintage.

Hrdy, S. B. (2005). Cooperative breeders with an ace in the hole. In E. Voland, A. Chasiotis and W. Schiefenhoevel (eds), *Grandmotherhood: The evolutionary significance of the second half of female life* (pp. 295–317). New Brunswick, NJ: Rutgers University Press.

Hrdy, S. B. (2008). Cooperative breeding and the paradox of facultative fathering. In R. S. Bridges (ed.), *Neurobiology of the parental brain* (pp. 407–16). New York: Academic Press.

Hrdy, S. B. (2009). *Mothers and others: The evolutionary origins of mutual understanding*. Cambridge, MA: Belknap Press.

Hrdy, S. B. and Judge, D. S. (1993). Darwin and the puzzle of primogeniture: An essay on biases in parental investment after death. *Human Nature, 4*, 1–45.

Jeon, J. (2008). Evolution of parental favoritism among different-aged offspring. *Behavioral Ecology, 19*, 344–52.

Kaplan, H. and Hill, K. (1985). Hunting ability and reproductive success among male Aché foragers: Preliminary results. *Current Anthropology, 26*, 131–3.

Kaplan, H. and Lancaster, J. (2003). An evolutionary and ecological analysis of human fertility, mating patterns and parental investment. In K. W. Wachter and. R. A. Bulatao (eds), *Offspring: Human fertility in biodemographic perspective* (pp. 170–223). Washington: National Academies Press.

Kaplan, H., Hill, K., Lancaster, J. and Hurtado, A. M. (2000). A theory of human life history evolution: Diet, intelligence, and longevity. *Evolutionary Anthropology, 9*, 156–85.

Kempenaers, B. and Sheldon, B. C. (1997). Studying paternity and paternal care: Pitfalls and problems. *Animal Behaviour, 53*, 423–7.

Kleiman, D. G. and Malcolm, J. R. (1981). The evolution of male parental investment in mammals. In D. G. Gubernick and P. H. Klopfer (eds), *Parental care in mammals* (pp. 347–87). New York: Plenum Press.

Kokko, H. and Jennions, M. D. (2008). Parental investment, sexual selection and sex ratios. *Journal of Evolutionary Biology, 21*, 919–948.

Kramer, K. L. (2005). Children's help and the pace of reproduction: Cooperative breeding in humans. *Evolutionary Anthropology, 14*, 224–37.

Kristensen, P. and Bjerkedal, T. (2007). Explaining the relation between birth order and intelligence. *Science, 316*, 1717.

Lawrence, P. R. and Nohria, N. (2002). *Drive: How human nature shapes our choices*. Boston: Harvard Business School Press.

Lawson, D. W. and Mace, R. (2008). Sibling configuration and childhood growth in contemporary British families. *International Journal of Epidemiology, 37*, 1408–21.

Lazarus, J. (2002). Human sex ratios: Adaptations and mechanisms, problems and prospects. In I. C. W. Hardy (ed.), *Sex ratios: Concepts and research methods* (pp. 287–311). Cambridge: Cambridge University Press.

Lee, R. D. and Kramer, K. L. (2002). Children's economic roles in the Maya family life cycle: Cain, Caldwell, and Chayanov revisited. *Population and Development Review, 28*, 475–99.

Liddell, C., Barrett, L. and Henzi, P. (2003). Parental investment in schooling: Evidence from a subsistence farming community in South Africa. *International Journal of Psychology, 38*, 54–63.

Lindert, P. H. (1977). Sibling position and achievement. *Journal of Human Resources, 12*, 198–219.

Lovejoy, C. O. (1981). The origin of man. *Science, 211*, 341–50.

Lycett, J. E. and Dunbar, R. I. M. (1999). Abortion rates reflect the optimization of parental investment strategies. *Proceedings of the Royal Society B, 266,* 2355–8.

Lynch, K. A. and Greenhouse, J. B. (1994). Risk factors for infant mortality in nineteenth century Sweden. *Population Studies, 48,* 117–134.

MacDonald, K. (1995). The establishment and maintenance of socially imposed monogamy in Western Europe. *Politics and the Life Sciences, 14,* 3–23.

Mace, R. (1996). Biased parental investment and reproductive success in Gabbra pastoralists. *Behavioural Ecology and Sociobiology, 38,* 75–81.

Mace, R. (2007). The evolutionary ecology of human family size. In R. I. M. Dunbar and L. Barrett (eds), *The Oxford handbook of evolutionary psychology* (pp. 383–96). Oxford: Oxford University Press.

McNamara, J. M., Houston, A. I., Barta, Z. *et al.* (2009). Deterioration, death and the evolution of reproductive restraint in late life. *Proceedings of the Royal Society B, 276,* 4061–6.

Magadi, M., Madise, N. and Diamond, I. (2001). Factors associated with unfavourable birth outcomes in Kenya. *Journal of Biosocial Science, 33,* 199–225.

Manda, S. O. M. (1999). Birth intervals, breastfeeding and determinants of childhood mortality in Malawi. *Social Science and Medicine, 48,* 301–312.

Margulis, S. W., Altmann, J. and Ober, C. (1993). Sex-biased lactational duration in a human population and its reproductive costs. *Behavioural Ecology and Sociobiology, 32,* 41–5.

Marlowe, F. W. (2005). Hunter-gatherers and human evolution. *Evolutionary Anthropology, 14,* 54–67.

Mathews, F., Johnson, P. J. and Neil, A. (2008). You are what your mother eats: Evidence for maternal preconception diet influencing foetal sex in humans. *Proceedings of the Royal Society B, 275,* 1661–8.

Muhuri, P. K. and Preston, S. H. (1991). Effects of family composition on mortality differentials by sex among children in Matlab, Bangladesh. *Population Development Review, 17,* 415–34.

Muller, M. N., Marlowe, F. W., Bugumba, R. and Ellison, P. T. (2009). Testosterone and paternal care in East African foragers and pastoralists. *Proceedings of the Royal Society B, 276,* 347–54.

Murdock, G. P. (1967). Ethnographic atlas. Pittsburgh: University of Pittsburgh Press.

Murdock, G. P. and White, D. R. (1969). Standard cross-cultural sample. *Ethnology, 8,* 329–69.

Pennington, R. and Harpending, H. (1993). *The structure of an African pastoralist community: Demography, history and ecology of the Ngamiland Herero.* Oxford: Clarendon Press.

Petrie, M. and Kempenaers, B. (1998). Extra-pair paternity in birds: Explaining variation between species and populations. *Trends in Ecology and Evolution, 13,* 52–8.

Quinlan, R. J. (2007). Human parental effort and environmental risk. *Proceedings of the Royal Society B, 274,* 121–5.

Quinlan, R. J., Quinlan, M. B. and Flinn, M. V. (2005). Local resource enhancement and sex-biased breastfeeding in a Caribbean community. *Current Anthropology, 46,* 471–80.

Roff, D. A. (1992). *The evolution of life histories.* New York: Chapman and Hall.

Salmon, C. (2003). Birth order and relationships: Family, friends, and sexual partners. *Human Nature, 14,* 73–88.

Salmon, C. A. and Daly, M. (1998). Birth order and familial sentiment: Middleborns are different. *Evolution and Human Behaviour, 19,* 299–312.

Sear, R. and Mace, R. (2008). Who keeps children alive? A review of the effects of kin on child survival. *Evolution and Human Behavior, 29,* 1–18.

Seltzer, J. A. (1991). Relationships between fathers and children who live apart: The father's role after separation. *Journal of Marriage and Family, 53*, 79–101.

Shanley, D. P., Sear, R., Mace, R. and Kirkwood, T. B. L. (2007). Testing evolutionary theories of menopause. *Proceedings of the Royal Society B, 274*, 2943–9.

Sigle-Rushton, W. and McLanahan, S. (2004). Father absence and child well-being: A critical review. In D. P. Moynihan, T. Smeeding and L. Rainwater (eds), *The future of the family* (pp. 116–58). New York: Russell Sage Foundation.

Silk, J. B. (1983). Local resource competition and facultative adjustment of sex ratios in relation to competitive abilities. *American Naturalist, 121*, 56–66.

Smuts, B. and Gubernick, D. J. (1992). Male-infant relationships in nonhuman primates: Paternal investment or mating effort? In B. S. Hewlett (ed.), *Father-child relations: Cultural and biosocial contexts* (pp. 1–30). New York: Aldine de Gruyter.

Somit, A., Arwine, A. and Peterson, S. A. (1996). *Birth order and political behavior*. Lanham, MD: University Press of America.

Stearns, S. C. (1992). *The evolution of life histories*. Oxford: Oxford University Press.

Steelman, L. C., Powell, B., Werum, R. and Carter, S. (2002). Reconsidering the effects of sibling configuration: Recent advances and challenges. *Annual Review of Sociology, 28*, 243–69.

Stein, A. D., Zybert, P. A. and Lumey, L. H. (2004). Acute undernutrition is not associated with excess of females at birth in humans: The Dutch Hunger Winter. *Proceedings of the Royal Society B, 271*, S138–S141.

Sulloway, F. J. (1996). *Born to rebel: Birth order, family dynamics and creative lives*. London: Little, Brown and Company.

Sulloway, F. J. (2000). 'Born to Rebel' and its critics. *Politics and the Life Sciences, 19*, 181–202.

Townsend, F. (2000). Birth order and rebelliousness: Reconstructing the research in 'Born to Rebel'. *Politics and the Life Sciences, 19*, 135–156.

Travis, R. and Kohli, V. (1995). The birth order factor: Ordinal position, social strata, and educational achievement. *Journal of Social Psychology, 135*, 499–507.

Trivers, R. (1972). Parental investment and sexual selection. In B. Campbell (ed.), *Sexual selection and the descent of man, 1871–1971* (pp. 136–79). New York: Aldine de Gruyter.

Trivers, R. L. and Willard, D. E. (1973). Natural selection of parental ability to vary the sex ratio of offspring. *Science, 17*, 990–992.

West, S. A., Reece, S. E. and Sheldon, B. C. (2002). Sex ratios. *Heredity, 88*, 117–124.

West, S. A. and Sheldon, B. C. (2002). Constraints in the evolution of sex ratio adjustment. *Science, 295*, 1685–8.

Wichman, A. L., Rodgers, J. L. and MacCallum, R. C. (2006). A multilevel approach to the relationship between birth order and intelligence. *Personality and Social Psychology Bulletin, 32*, 117–127.

Wilkins, J. F. and Marlowe, F. W. (2006). Sex-biased migration in humans: What should we expect from genetic data? *BioEssays, 28*, 290–300.

Williams, G. C. (1966). *Adaptation and natural selection*. Princeton, NJ: Princeton University Press.

Winking, J., Gurven, M., Kaplan, H. and Stieglitz, J. (2009). The goals of direct paternal care among a South Amerindian population. *American Journal of Physical Anthropology, 139*, 295–304.

Young, S. S., Bang, H. and Oktay, K. (2009). Cereal-induced gender selection? Most likely a multiple testing false positive. *Proceedings of the Royal Society B, 276*, 1211–1212.

differences

ADRIAN FURNHAM

CHAPTER OUTLINE

THE CURRENT STATE OF DIFFERENTIAL PSYCHOLOGY 254

PERSONALITY AND THE EVOLUTIONARY IMPERATIVE 257

  Fecundity, sexual behaviour, mate choice and relationships 257

  Personality, health and longevity 260

  Personality, career success and the acquisition of resources 261

A COST-BENEFIT ANALYSIS OF THE BIG FIVE 262

  Extraversion 263

  Neuroticism 264

  Openness to Experience 264

  Agreeableness 264

  Conscientiousness 265

AUTHORITARIANISM 267

ABILITY AND INTELLIGENCE 268

'DARK-SIDE' DISORDERS 271

CONCLUSION 276

REFERENCES 276

There are clearly both similarities and differences between differential and evolutionary psychology. Both, though perhaps the latter more than the former, look back to great nineteenth-century thinkers, such as Darwin, as key figures. In addition, it could be argued that both are universalist in the sense that they specify that short-term, cultural or situational factors have less of an impact on long-term social behaviour than intrapersonal factors do. Third, both are (at least, now) committed to explanations of behavioural processes that go beyond early descriptive and taxonomic work. Finally, both fields of research are currently flourishing and beginning to forge fruitful links with one another (Buss, 1991; Nettle, 2006).

There are, however, three important caveats worth mentioning right at the beginning. In both evolutionary and differential psychology, there are multiple theories, systems and models that have been relied upon in terms of empirical research. Partly because personality theory has so much longer a history in academic psychology (over a hundred years), there is considerable variability in theories of the aetiology, structure and functioning of personality (Furnham, 2008). So, for example, there are orthodox and neopsychoanalytic theories of personality; there are also self-theorists, as well as those interested in temperaments and traits. Indeed, Webster (2007) makes the interesting point that the evolution of scientific theories may indeed mimic Darwinian selection processes, as they compete, merge and disappear over time.

It is probably the case that by far the most 'successful' and dominant approach to differential psychology at the moment is trait theory, especially the Five Factor Model of personality (Costa and McCrae, 1992). This chapter will focus on this model, with a more general evaluation of the 'biopsychosocial' perspective, which accepts certain biological foundations of individual differences. That is, it is asserted in this perspective that individual differences are heritable and explicable primarily in terms of biological, hormonal and physiological processes.

Second, while evolutionary psychologists have sought out distal explanations for myriad behaviours, much of personality research has been taxonomic in nature. Great debates between the orthogonal parsimonious, three-factor model of Eysenck and the oblique comprehensive 16-factor model of Cattell continued for over 30 years (Furnham, 2008). Whilst most trait researchers accept the Big Five model, there remain powerful voices that argue for a six-, seven- or eight-dimensional model. There have also been attempts to derive a two-factor model (labelled 'plasticity and stability') and even a general single-factor model, which has been of particular interest to evolutionary personality theorists (Rushton, Bons and Hur, 2008). Description precedes explanation and much more effort has gone into the latter, partly because it is assumed that this needs to be fully established (and agreed) before a parsimonious explanation is possible. Third, personality theorists have been more 'experimental' than evolutionary psychology, though there are increasingly experimental studies that specifically test hypotheses derived from evolutionary psychology.

This chapter will consider an evolutionary psychological perspective on differential psychology. It will document and evaluate the evidence concerning evolutionary explanations for the origin and function of both personality and intelligence. Social and cross-cultural psychologists have never resisted an evolutionary perspective.

Thus, Whiting (1961) proposed an 'adaptive ecological model', in which different systems of variables were considered:

1. The *ecology*: The physical environment, resources, geography.
2. The *subsistence system*: Methods of exploitation of the ecology to survive, such as agriculture, fishing, gathering and industrial work.
3. The *sociocultural system*: Institutions, norms, roles and values as they exist outside the individual.
4. The *individual system*: Perception, learning, motivation and subjective culture (the last includes the perception of the elements of the cultural system).
5. The *interindividual system*: Patterns of social behaviour, including child-rearing methods.

These different systems are interrelated but have led to numerous well-established studies which have shown how ecological (i.e. geographical) conditions lead to various different subsistence systems (i.e. agricultural versus hunter-gatherer), which in turn lead to different socialisation (and possibly selection) strategies that influence inter- and intrapersonal differences (Berry and Annis, 1974). However, it is equally likely that the reverse causal pattern is possible, in that the individual can modify both the culture and the ecology. Social psychologists have preferred to consider mainly inter- rather than intra-individual differences, which is the chief interest of differential psychologists.

Social psychologists have also concentrated on specific behaviours (e.g. altruism and aggression), as well as mate choice and relationships. Many have been happy to compare and consider humans with other social animals and accept evolutionary concepts like inclusive fitness, differential parental involvement and sexual selection (Kenrick, 2004). Many accept that patterns and regulations in social behaviour (within and between cultures) reflect specific adaptive mechanisms designed to aid survival and reproduction. However, most tend not to prefer trait or stable intra-individual difference explanations and theories, preferring to assert the influence of social and interpersonal factors regulating behaviour.

A number of papers have been published, both theoretical as well as empirical, that spell out an evolutionary perspective on personality (e.g. Buss, 1991). Shackelford (2006, p. 1553), for example, offers a simple and clear conception of personality from an evolutionary perspective:

A key message of evolutionary psychology is that the complex architecture of species-typical, domain-specific psychological mechanisms allows for the tremendous context-dependant flexibility of human behaviour. Modern evolutionary approaches aspire to understand – in addition to our species-typical, culturally differentiated, and sex-specific human nature – the ways that individuals differ within species, within cultures, and within sex. Thus, the architectural unit of personality is the evolved psychological mechanism. But these mechanisms cannot and do not operate in a vacuum. The mechanisms are dependant for their activation on the contextual input to which they have evolved a sensitivity. Thus, personality is relatively stable in the sense of being comprised of a finite set of species-typical psychological mechanisms. At the level of cognitive, affective, and behavioural output of these mechanisms, however, personality is better described as variable. The most accurate depiction of personality is that it is both consistent and variable – that it is comprised of a finite set of species-typical and domain-specific psychological mechanisms that are activated by relevant contextual input. And because no two individual psychologies will receive and process identical input in an identical manner, individual differences are an important domain of inquiry for evolutionary psychologists.

Evolutionary personality psychology was pioneered by Buss (1985, 1987, 1988, 1991) and subsequently reviewed by Figueredo *et al.* (2005), who divide current theories of evolutionary psychology into three groups. First, there are theories of *selective neutrality* that specify various processes (e.g. reactive heritability, frequency-dependent strategies and non-adaptive developmental amplification of traits). Second, there are theories of *adaptive significance*, which argue that personality differences reflect specific adaptive strategies. Third are theories of *frequency dependence*, which specify conditions under which polymorphism occurs and the mechanisms from which it can arise. This approach attempts to 'explain how different and fragmented personality dimensions provide a balance for individuals adopting alternative or conditional adaptive strategies' (Figueredo *et al.*, 2005, p. 855).

THE CURRENT STATE OF DIFFERENTIAL PSYCHOLOGY

Differential psychology has two distinct branches. One concerns the study of abilities and uses power tests; it seeks to describe and explain the range of human abilities at the most detailed, specific level (e.g. riding a bicycle, reading a map) to abstract thinking. The central interest is in cognitive abilities, more commonly known as 'intelligence'. Group differences, specifically age, race and sex, in intelligence have been reported since the early twentieth century (see below), but it is really only since towards the end of the last century that some psychologists have invoked evolutionary explanations for these differences (Rushton, 1985, 2000). This section will look at the ideas of three of these researchers and evaluate them accordingly.

Intelligence researchers appear to split between those who assert that there is a general intelligence (*g*) and those who believe in multiple intelligences, though the evidence clearly supports the former group. The evolutionary advantages of high intelligence seem so obvious that there are few studies on the topic. However, there is interesting speculation as to explanations for such findings as the link between intelligence and longevity. Thus, Deary (2008) offers four possible explanations for the data from various sources that show that intelligent people live longer. These were:

- Intelligent people have better, safer, less stressful and less dangerous jobs, because of their higher educational attainment.
- Intelligent people engage in healthier behaviours.
- Low intelligence is associated with other physical problems in youth.
- Intelligence is an index of well-wired or integrated body systems that predict mortality.

The second branch of differential psychology is the study of preferences, often called 'personality theory'. Here, tests involve choice, tend not to be timed and scores are bidirectional. Preference tests have been used to measure temperaments, traits and types as well as attitudes, beliefs and values. Even when measuring traits, which is the focus of the chapter, there are different tests depending on whether the focus is on 'abnormal' versus 'normal' traits. The adaptive significance of 'abnormal traits', and specifically personality disorders, will be considered below. Attention will also be paid to the personality disorders that are linked to normal personality traits. This section will examine both parts of differential psychology, specifically the nature of evolutionary explanations for both personality and cognitive ability.

Current studies of personality theory are problematic, partly because of long-standing arguments between 'lumpers', who advocate a very parsimonious response to personality description, and 'splitters', who advocate comprehensiveness. Hence, there remains a fairly large number of competing theories, models and tests of personality. Some advocate typological categorisation, which often prefers continuous trait measures. There are also many instruments measuring 'styles' (e.g. attribution, cognitive, coping, learning) and it is not clear how these differ from traits (Furnham, 2008).

Nevertheless, over the past 30 years or so there has been something of a rapprochement between the various personality theorists, who have come to realise both that their internal arguments were perhaps bad for their discipline and that there was considerable overlap between their various models. Hence, the current dominance of the Five Factor Model (FFM). Many researchers have been able to show that various models are in fact relatively similar, despite the use of very different terminology. So, for example, Extraversion has also been labelled 'ambition', 'ascendancy', 'sociability' and 'surgency', while Conscientiousness has also been labelled 'dependability', 'prudence', 'self-control' and 'will-to-succeed'.

Trait theorists came together in the 1990s to assert their axioms. They argued that trait theories were explicit and testable with replicable evidence. McCrae and Costa (1995, p. 248) argue that:

1. Personality traits are not descriptive summaries of behaviour but rather dispositions that are inferred from and can predict and account for patterns of thoughts, feelings and actions.

2. Scientific evidence for the existence of traits is provided, in part, by studies that show patterns of covariation across time, twin pairs and cultures – covariation that cannot be readily explained by such alternatives as transient influences, learned responses and cultural norms.

3. Patterns of covariation provide non-circular explanations, because observation of some behaviours allows the prediction of other, non-observed behaviours.

4. Psychological constructs give conceptual coherence to the covarying patterns of thoughts, feelings and actions; good constructs have surplus meaning that points beyond the known correlates of trait.

5. Trait explanations are not themselves mechanistic; the mechanisms through which they operate may or may not be specified in a psychological theory.

6. When trait standing in an individual is assessed using a validated method, knowledge of the trait's manifestations can legitimately, albeit fallibly, be invoked to explain that individual's behaviour.

7. Personality traits are hypothetical psychological constructs, but they are presumed to have a biological basis.

8. Over time, traits interact with the environment to produce culturally conditioned and meaning-laden characteristic adaptations (such as attitudes, motives and relationships).

9. Specific behaviours occur when these characteristic adaptations interact with the immediate situation; traits are thus best construed as indirect or distal causes of behaviour.

Deary and Matthews (1993) argue that the trait approach is not only 'alive and well' but flourishing. They highlight various 'bright spots' in current trait theory. First, growing agreement concerning the number, character and stability of personality dimensions. Second, greater understanding of the heritability of personality traits, and hence a greater appreciation of the role of the environment. Third, a growing sophistication of research, which aims to elucidate the biological and social bases of trait differences. Fourth, an appreciation of the extent to which personality differences predict outcomes, or act as moderators, in cognitive and health settings. They assert, as many others have done before them, two fundamental points:

1. The Primary Causality of Traits: The idea that causality flows from traits to behaviour and that, although there is a feedback loop, it is less important.

2. The Inner Locus of Traits: The idea that traits describe the fundamental core qualities of a person that are latent rather than manifest.

Whilst there inevitably remain dissenters from the FFM perspective, it has galvanised personality research since the 1990s. Furthermore, more confident researchers and renewers have asserted that well-constructed measures of personality predict most of the most important life events, including physical health and mortality, job performance, social relationships, educational outcomes and mental health. All of these 'life events' have adaptive significance. Thus, if personality traits can be shown to systematically, logically and consistently predict these, then evolutionary psychology may be able to offer a succinct and parsimonious distal explanation for why they may have evolved. Given the adaptive advantage of all of the above, therefore, it is not surprising that there has been an interest in evolutionary personality theory.

PERSONALITY AND THE EVOLUTIONARY IMPERATIVE

One way of ordering the diverse literature on evolutionary personality theory is to look for evidence for the natural selection of personality traits in very specific areas. Figueredo *et al.* (2005) identify two main components of fitness: survivorship and fecundity, while Hogan adds the concept of adapting to and leading groups (van Vugt, Hogan and Kaiser, 2008). The latter is associated with the accumulation of resources (wealth), which has obvious adaptive significance. These factors, longevity, health and resource accumulation, could be considered fundamental to adaptation and survival. Thus, if these are consistent and explicable personality correlates of these factors, this may be taken as good evidence for an evolutionary personality psychology.

Fecundity, sexual behaviour, mate choice and relationships

There is an extensive social psychological literature on personal relationships, which pays passing attention to individual differences. Personality psychologists, on the other hand, have looked at such issues as trait correlates of sexual experience, marital satisfaction and relationship stability, all of which relate to the number and health of an individual's offspring. More recently, they have switched their attention to mate or partner choice. However, having a healthy and stable relationship may not be in itself a powerful predictor of fecundity, though it must have moderating and mediating effects. Social class, religion and psychopathology may also be predictors of fecundity over and above personality traits.

Figueredo *et al.* (2005) reviewed several studies of 'completed' fertility that looked at both fertility and infertility using very different measures of personality. The results seemed unclear, as the most obvious hypothesis that 'negative' traits associated with Neuroticism (i.e. anxiousness, depression, hypochondriasis) were not always associated with low fertility or infertility. They also noted several studies that looked at personality correlates of fertility, with results seeming to point to 'super-traits' such as Extraversion and Psychoticism being associated with frequency of sex and promiscuity, which may be taken as a marker of fertility.

Figueredo, Sefcek and Jones (2006, p. 432) argue that there 'are two dominant approaches to the study of personality and mate choice: (1) the study of *absolute* preferences for one personality trait over another, also called *consensual* preferences because they are observed to be similar across all individuals; and (2) that of *relative* preferences for a sexual romantic partner's personality in relation to one's own personality. This second type of preference presumes assortative mating according to personality, and this type comes in two possible varieties: (1) *positive* assortative mating, based on the presumed attraction to similarity in personality with one's sexual romantic partner (similarity theory), and (2) *negative* assortative mating, or *dis*assortative mating, based on the presumed attraction to dissimilarity in personality with one's sexual romantic partner (complementarity theory)'. In studies using the FFM, they found two things: first, evidence of aspirational positive assortative mating, which was that, to some degree, people sought out people like themselves in terms of personality and, second, tended to seek people higher in Conscientiousness, Extraversion and Agreeableness, but lower in Neuroticism than themselves.

There continues to be studies on trait correlates of sexual activity. Since the publication of Eysenck's (1976) book, many researchers have been able to replicate his findings. Thus, Heaven *et al.* (2000) found Neuroticism and Extraversion most clearly related to such things as sexual curiosity, excitement, nervousness and satisfaction. Later, Heaven *et al.* (2003) found sexual attitudes, beliefs and behaviours factored into two distinct categories, namely sexual anxiety or fear of sex and sexual motivation or preoccupation. They found that Emotional Stability (low Neuroticism), Openness to Experience, and Extraversion were most associated with low sexual anxiety and fear of sex. Thus, personality traits predict interest in, as well experience of, sexual activity, which should be related to fecundity.

Added to this, there is a highly relevant literature on assortative mating and general mate selection. The assortative mating literature has attempted to test three models: similarity, dissimilarity and complementarity. It is a scattered literature, with many equivocal findings partly explained by Glicksohn and Golan (2001), who found no evidence of assortative mating for the Eysenckian three factors. They note: 'Presumably, similarity (and dissimilarity) may be assessed along key personality dimensions, though it is far from clear: (1) how similarity should be defined (e.g. as a proximity [distance] measure between profiles, or as the degree of correlation of key traits); and (2) at what level in the hierarchy of personality should this be assessed (e.g. at the [supertrait] level of Extraversion. Psychoticism and Neuroticism, or at the [trait] level of sociability, impulsivity, sensation seeking etc)' (Glicksohn and Golan, 2001, p. 1200).

Research on mate selection suggests that there are differences in what men and women look for in a (long- and short-term) mate and that a number of factors, other than personality, appear to be important (e.g. health, wealth, ability). Barrett, Dunbar and Lycett (2002) suggest that heterosexual women place emphasis on wealth and status as well as the man's willingness to invest time and effort in the relationship. Women also consistently specify physical fitness and social skills; men tend to emphasise physical attractiveness above all other features. Todosijevic, Ljubinkovic and Arancil (2003) found for both men and women, the top five most desirable traits were: sincerity, faithfulness, tenderness, reliability and communicative. This suggests Conscientiousness and Agreeableness are the most desirable traits in a mate.

More recently, Furnham (2009) had participants describe themselves and their ideal partner in their own words, rate 14 desirable characteristics classified under five headings (ability, personality, physical, social and values) and complete a short measure of the Big Five personality traits. Women rated intelligence, stability, Conscientiousness, height, education, social skills and political/religious compatibility significantly higher than men did, who rated good looks higher than women did. There was clear evidence of the 'birds of a feather' or 'personality-likeness' hypothesis: the trait score of participants on each of the Big Five factors was predictive of the desired trait in a mate. This was strongest for Extraversion and Conscientiousness and throws in dispute Jungian ideas of 'opposites' attracting one another.

However, Furnham (2009) did note a limitation in these mate selection studies. Research using photographs and 'live models' suggest that small visual cues have a powerful effect below consciousness on the ratings of attractiveness. 'Thus, it may be that results in this area are very methodologically dependent because people actually respond more powerfully to physical cues they rarely mention and maybe are even unaware of. It may be possible to test the relative power of different factors experimentally by varying body-cues and verbal descriptions to see whether mate selection is based more on subtle physical markers of health, than sociological markers of status or wealth. It may also mean that ultimately the self-report methodology of questionnaires may lead to findings that are misleading in the sense that they do not represent how people behave when faced with visual cues' (Furnham, 2009, p. 266).

Whilst personality traits may predict the sort of person one is attracted to and the likelihood of establishing a satisfactory sexual relationship, an equally important question is whether personality predicts the stability of relationships, which is relevant to the reproduction of offspring. There is also long-standing literature on personality and relationship satisfaction (Robins, Caspi and Moffitt, 2000, 2002) that dates back to Terman's (1938) early work on marital happiness. This work shows that, of the personality factors implicated in relationship satisfaction, it is clearly Neuroticism (negative emotionality) that is most predictive. There is also some work on personality and marital interaction and satisfaction (Gottman, 1994, 1998). This literature tends to 'implicate' Neuroticism, Agreeableness and Conscientiousness in marital interaction and stability.

In an example of this literature, Donnellan, Conger and Bryant (2004) looked at the Big Five personality traits and enduring marriages using both self-report and observational data in 400 couples. The results showed Neuroticism was positively correlated with everyday negative interaction and negatively correlated with global evaluations of marriage, whilst for Agreeableness it was precisely the opposite pattern. Interestingly, Openness was correlated negatively with observer reports of negative interaction. Conscientiousness was a less powerful correlate, though the authors do suggest a mechanism to explain their findings: it is possible that conscientious individuals create fewer areas of disagreement because they are generally responsible, dependable and hardworking. The link between Conscientiousness and marital outcomes may also be mediated by processes such as a more equitable household division of labour or a reduction in problem behaviour involvement such as drug or alcohol abuse.

In short, the literature on trait correlates of sexual behaviour, mate selection and relationship stability and satisfaction shows Neuroticism consistently related to these factors. Extraverts and Agreeable people are most sought after as mates and have better long-term relationships.

Personality, health and longevity

Personality psychologists' interest in health dates back over a hundred years. The central questions have always been threefold: (1) which personality traits predict or correlate with health beliefs and behaviours? (2) how does the process work (i.e. what are the mechanism dynamics)? (3) what other moderator or mediator factors are important? The 'dependent variable' of health has included physical health (chronic and acute), mental health and health-reporting. Apart from the relationship between personality and general health, research has tended to concentrate on relationships between personality and cancer, coronary heart disease, longevity and stress. The central theme has been that personality is related to health because it is systematically and predictably related to the lifestyle (diet, personal habits), risk-taking, illness vulnerability, causal attributions, reaction to stress and the seeking of source support.

However, there are at least four rather different models in the literature. The first is the most simple: traits that are based on biological differences cause different health outcomes. The second is that the same biological determinants and processes (genes, hormones) underlie both trait and biological health outcomes. The third is that traits determine health behaviours like substance abuse, exercise and so on, which lead to very specific health outcomes. The fourth reserves the causality and suggests that various illnesses can induce changes in personality. Friedman (2008, p. 668) notes that, whilst there are numerous well-documented studies on the link between personality and illness, 'the causal interconnections are often much more complex than originally anticipated. Multiple causal patternship may operate simultaneously as the individual travels an idiosyncratic route across the life-span'.

Furnham and Heaven (1998) reviewed the literature on the relationship between personality and health. They note rather different approaches: the specific approach where certain traits are seen to be related to various illnesses (hypertension, asthma) and the more general approach where personality factors are seen to facilitate, inhibit or mediate the influence of causal factors on health. Reviews of specific areas like the relationship between personality and coronary heart disease and cancer include many studies with non-Big Five traits, such as Type A or B distinctions, as well as the 'disease-prone' personality, which are linked to very specific illnesses. There are also many studies on social-cognitive individual difference variables like attribution style, locus of control and coping preferences, which link these factors with specific health outcomes. However, Furnham and Heaven do note that the evidence then did logically implicate the Big Five with health: Neuroticism with anxiety and depressive illness; Extraversion with social illnesses; Openness with risk-taking activities; and Conscientiousness with many forms of wellness behaviour.

Since the millennium there have been numerous large- and small-scale studies linking personality variables with various health outcomes. Thus, Korotkov and Hannah (2004) examined the extent to which the Big Five personality traits could predict health status, sick-role and illness behaviour. They found that the five factors were independently (rather than interactively) related to health states and the relationship was strongest with subjective health measures. Hong and Paunonen (in press) looked at Big Five predictors of alcohol and tobacco consumption as well as speeding in over a thousand university students. They found that low Conscientiousness and low Agreeableness were associated with these potentially health-damaging behaviours, while Extraversion was associated with alcohol use.

It follows that if personality predicts both chronic and acute health and illness it should be related to longevity. Despite the difficulty in this sort of research, there have been several studies that have examined this possibility. For example, Friedman *et al.* (1993) used seven-decade longitudinal data to trace the impact of personality on longevity in over a thousand American adults. They found both data to confirm and disconfirm their hypotheses. There was clear evidence that Conscientiousness in childhood predicted later life survival, but that cheerfulness or optimism did not. Thus, while Conscientiousness is less associated with mate choice and relationships, it does seem, along with Neuroticism, to be the most powerful Big Five trait correlates of physical healthy and longevity.

Personality, career success and the acquisition of resources

Survival is in part related to the acquisition of resources. Indeed studies on mate selection have noted that the wealth of a male is among the most powerful attractants to women. While the study on personality and career success has flourished since the end of the last century (Boudreau, Boswell and Judge, 2001), it was not until the first decade of the next that occupational and business psychologists took an evolutionary perspective. For instance, Saad and Gill (2000) looked at the evolutionary psychology of marketing, while van Vugt, Hogan and Kaiser (2008) examined the evolutionary psychology of leadership.

Gelissen and Graaf (2006) looked at personality correlates of income attainment and occupational career transitions in some four thousand Dutch adults. They found that Extraversion related positively to remuneration, but only for men; Emotional Stability was positively related to remuneration for both sexes; Agreeableness was not associated with career outcomes; Conscientiousness was negatively related to women's upward-status mobility; and Openness to Experience negatively related to earning, but only for men. These results were in accordance with previous findings, but the relationships were weak. In a smaller Singaporean sample (Wu, Foo and Turban, 2008), all five factors correlated with career satisfaction, with Extraversion and Neuroticism being the strongest correlates. Neuroticism was negatively correlated with the number of promotions, but for Agreeableness the correlation was positive.

There have been various studies of the link between personality and career success. Seibert and Kraimer (2001) found that Extraversion was positively related to salary level, promotions and career satisfaction; Neuroticism and Agreeableness was negatively related to career satisfaction; and Openness was negatively related to salary level. Conscientiousness was surprisingly not closely linked to many factors

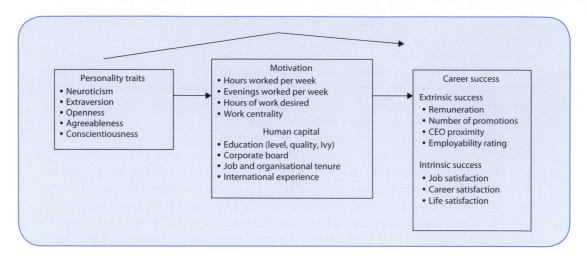

Figure 8.1. *The associations between personality traits and career success.*

except career satisfaction. They attributed the importance of Extraversion to the people-orientation and skills associated with extraverts. They also note: 'Although the amount of variance explained by the personality variables was small, they could be considered meaningful to the individuals involved. For example, a one standard deviation increase on the extraversion scale was associated with a \$5,706 increase in yearly salary and a one standard deviation increase on the openness to experience scale was associated with a \$5,256 decrease in yearly salary, after controlling for the other variables included in the model' (Seibert and Kraimer, 2001, p. 15).

Boudreau, Boswell and Judge (2001) also examined the effects of personality traits on executives' career success in both America and Europe. Some previous findings were supported: Extraversion was positively and Neuroticism negatively associated with intrinsic career success. However, Agreeableness was negatively related to extrinsic success and Conscientiousness unrelated to extrinsic success, but negatively related to intrinsic success. Their work tended to support the model they proposed (see Figure 8.1). In short, organisational psychologists have demonstrated personality trait correlates of job success, career path leadership and consequently salary. This suggests that certain traits are related to the acquisition and retention of material sources, which relate both to success and mate value.

A COST-BENEFIT ANALYSIS OF THE BIG FIVE

It should be pointed out that some influential evolutionary psychologists have argued that evolution should leave little systemic variation in personality traits. Tooby and Cosmides (1990) argue that natural selection is essentially a winnowing procedure that removes all but the most fit individuals. Nettle (2006) notes that the evidence from genetics attests to the high heritability of both traits and abilities that are demonstrably related to reproductive success. The high heritability coefficient means, by definition, abundant genetic variation in the population. The evolutionary task, therefore, is to attempt to provide a convincing account of the adaptiveness of specific traits, particularly when at extremes.

Research trying to 'marry' differential and evolutionary psychology goes back to Buss's (1991) work on the functional importance of individual difference. Other well-known personality theorists like Hogan (1996) have always acknowledged and incorporated evolutionary ideas like his 'striving to get along' and 'striving to get ahead' concepts. He argues that the primary task of social animals is both being accepted by the group as well as getting to lead the group. Furthermore, he has always stressed replications or the 'observer's perspective', which implies the importance of personality information in signalling to others how 'fit' one is.

Buss (1991, 1996) argues that natural selection has resulted in different detection mechanisms that allow us to evaluate crucial individual differences in others. These include finding a mate or a leader, how and who to cooperate with and who to compete with. Thus, those high in Agreeableness and Conscientiousness should be good allies, while those low on those traits are more likely to be adversaries. Buss also argues that self-knowledge about traits and preferences inevitably leads to one making better decisions. Thus, extraverts succeed in groups by their sociability, while conscientious people do so by being dependable and reliable.

Further, MacDonald (1991, p. 449) pursues the idea that 'individual differences in human psychological characteristics are evolutionary, meaningful and are linked to mechanisms which assess the resource value of intraspecific genetic and phenotypic diversity'. He argues that a strong evolutionary theory posits that individual differences occur to solve specific adaptive processes. The theory posits universality in the neurophysiological mechanisms underlying variation. Further, traits at the extreme ends of the normal range may be maladaptive and indicate the use of high-risk strategies (this is the 'spectrum hypothesis' discussed below). MacDonald (1998) set out to illustrate his ideas by looking at traits associated with Extraversion/Sensation Seeking/Dominance or Sensitivity to Reward. Interestingly, this already signals a problem as these concepts may be related, but are clearly not the same. Some may argue that Sensation Seeking is really only a dimension of Extraversion, while Gray's 'sensitivity to reward' idea incorporates important features of Emotional Stability. However, it was probably Nettle (2006) who attempted a full and parsimonious description of the benefits and costs of increasing levels of the Big Five. His argument is thus:

Extraversion

Extraverts are more sociable, sensation-seeking and have more social support. Their attitude to, interest in and experience of sex means they tend to have greater sexual partners, 'mating success' and offspring. However, it also means they are more prone to infidelity (Nettle, 2005), which suggests that their children are more likely to be later exposed to step-parents, which is an established risk factor in their development. They tend also to be more active and exploratory and, therefore, more likely to be involved in accidents. Their sensation-seeking and risk-taking, particularly if it is combined with other traits like Neuroticism and Psychoticism, mean they are highly likely to get involved in antisocial and general criminal behaviour. Introverts are less sociable but safer; they run the risk of a lower likelihood of finding mates and social support networks, but leading a more secure lifestyle, which is better for child rearing.

Neuroticism

Neurotics are more likely to be anxious, depressed, guilt-ridden, phobic and sick. They are less likely to have good long-standing and satisfying personal relationships and jobs. It remains problematic, then, trying to find any benefits of being less adjusted (Claridge and Davis, 2001). One such, noted by Nettle (2006), is vigilance, wariness and risk aversion. Neurotics are very aware of subtle (and possibly threatening) social changes, which can be a strong survival mechanism in certain environments. Further, combined with other factors like intelligence and Conscientiousness, Neuroticism (at optimal levels) can act as a very efficient source of achievement and competitiveness (Furnham, 2008). On the other hand, those very low in Neuroticism, who could be labelled 'stable' or 'highly adjusted', may have some disadvantages. They may be too trusting and eager to avoid social and physical hazards; they may underperform and strive less hard because they are afraid of failure. They may also be socially insensitive to the anxieties and worries of those around them and, therefore, have a small social support network.

Openness to Experience

Openness to Experience is marked by creativity and cognitive complexity. It is also associated with intelligence and a 'life of the mind': open individuals are attracted to the unusual and the unconventional. Openness is a good predictor of artistic and scientific achievement and innovation (Furnham, 2008). However, it is also associated with schizophrenia and schizotypy, with mental breakdown and (very) poor personal relationships. The flipside of novel thinking is delusions and supernatural and paranormal ideas. Creative individuals, when emotionally stable and particularly in the arts, are highly attractive to others and, therefore, have many different mates and a wide relationship network. However, those with 'unusual' beliefs can easily be described as 'mad' and rejected by society. With all these traits, it is social situational variables that really determine the adaptiveness of the trait, but this is probably more the case with Openness than with any of the other Big Five trait factors.

Agreeableness

Agreeable people are empathic, trusting and kind. They are well-liked, respected and valued as friends. They are conflict-averse, always seeking and attempting to create harmony and concord. The trait is highly valued and being sensitive (emotionally intelligent) to others' moods is clearly advantageous. However, being too trusting, particularly of antisocial individuals, could be counter-productive. Being excessively attentive to the needs of others rather than self may also be less adaptive. Agreeable people may be easy to exploit and unable or unwilling to assert their rights. Paradoxically, it appears that people who are called tough-minded, critical and sceptical often do better in the professions and business than those with high Agreeableness scores.

Conscientiousness

Conscientious individuals are hardworking, dutiful and orderly. They show self-control and tend to be moral. They seek out and follow good advice – such as that of health practitioners – and therefore live longer. They may be achievement-oriented and highly diligent. It is no surprise than this trait is one of the clearest markers of success in educational and occupational life. If matched with cognitive ability and social intelligence, it is a very important marker of adaptive success. Conscientious people plan for the future and are happy to work constantly for desirable long-term payoffs. An antipathy to all sorts of opportunities, however, may mean that they fail to exploit certain opportunities which come their way. The major downside of high conscientiousness is associated with perfectionism, rigidity and social dogmatism. Conscientiousness may also be thought of as a reaction to low ability in competitive settings. That is, students learn to be competitive to compensate or 'make up' for ability. Thus, Conscientiousness is associated not with what in business circles is described as 'doing the right thing' but with 'doing the right thing right'. This trait is rarely associated with creativity. However, bright, Open, Conscientious people can and do become very successful entrepreneurs.

Nettle (2006) summarised his ideas in a table: Table 8.1 here is an adaptation and extension of one of his. Nettle (2006) notes that his 'trade off' evolutionary account of traits may be useful partly because it is hypothesis-generating. Thus, for instance, Neuroticism may facilitate performance on particular perceptual motor tasks; highly Open people may be either particularly culturally embraced or marginalised; Conscientious people are slow to respond to affordances in the local environment; or Agreeable people are often regarded as 'suckers' or victims of exploitative individuals. He is eager to suggest the framework is not a *post hoc* explanation of the past' but rather an engine for 'predictors about the consequences of dispositional variation in the present' (Nettle, 2006, p. 629).

Over the last decades, various researchers have proposed that it may be meaningful to consider not a five-factor model but a two-factor model, or even a general factor of personality. Rushton (1985) argues from an evolutionary perspective that a suite of traits evolved essentially to meet the trials of life (growth, reproduction and survival). He argues that diverse traits co-varied with altruism, attachment styles, fecundity, growth, intelligence and reproductive qualities. Rushton, Bons and Hur (2008) relate their *r-k* evolutionary theory to Musek's (2007) claim for the single-factor of personality. Thus, they argue that this single, fundamental, general factor of personality is logically related to everything from longevity and sex guilt to self-reported

Table 8.1. *Examples of adjectives, Q-sort items and cost benefits defining the five factors of personality.*

Factor	Factor Definers		Positive benefits	Negative costs
	Adjectives	Q-sort items		
Extraversion	Active Assertive Energetic Enthusiastic Outgoing Talkative	Talkative Skilled in play, humour Rapid personal tempo Facially, gesturally expressive Behave assertively Gregarious	Big social networks Relationship and mating success Explorer of opportunities Happiness	Accidents and risk-taking Impulsivity and poor decision-making Relationship instability
Neuroticism	Anxious Self-pitying Tense Touchy Unstable Worrying	Thin-skinned Brittle ego defences Self-defeating Basically anxious Concerned with adequacy Fluctuating moods	Hyper vigilance Achievement-striving Emotional sensitivity Competitiveness	Poor mental health Stress sensitivity Poor physical health
Openness	Artistic Curious Imaginative Insightful Original Wide interests	Wide range of interests Introspective Unusual thought processes Values intellectual matters Judges in unconventional terms Aesthetically reactive	Social attractiveness Creativity Flexibility Change-oriented	Mental illness Social exclusion Bizarre belief-system and lifestyle
Agreeableness	Appreciative Forgiving Generous Kind Sympathetic Trusting	Not critical, sceptical Behaves in giving way Sympathetic, considerate Arouses liking Warm, compassionate Basically trustful	Psychological mindedness Social networks Strong relationships Valued group member	Vulnerable to exploitation Failure to maximise personal advantages Too conflict-avoidant Low assertiveness
Conscientiousness	Efficient Organised Planning ability Reliable Responsible Thorough	Dependable, responsible Productive Able to delay gratification Not self-indulgent Behave ethically Has high aspirational level	Long-term planning Longer life expectancy Good citizenship Dependable and dutiful team member	Obsessionality and perfectionism Rigidity with poor flexibility Slow to respond

delinquency. Personality, they argue, is embedded in our evolutionary and neuro-logical endowment: personality arose from the necessity to confer fitness across the physical and social environment.

This general factor has positive and negative poles: the advantaged and the chal-lenged. Rushton *et al.* (2008) posit that the positive pole is associated with emotional intelligence and the negative end with the personality disorders. However, while they are cautious in suggesting their single factor may be useful to understand social behaviour, they do argue strongly that this (and all) personality traits result from social competition and reproductive dynamics that direct human evolution. 'In a competitive world, there are always rewards (personal and professional) for more effi-cient persons – those who are more level headed, agreeable, friendly, dependable and open' (Rushton, Bons and Hur, 2008, p. 1183).

What is perhaps most interesting from an evolutionary perspective is to under-stand how neurotics or disagreeable people attract mates or succeed at work. Nettle (2006, p. 626) notes that 'a much more challenging issue, then, is finding any compens-atory benefit to Neuroticism', given that it is a good predictor of relationship failure and social isolation. What about an analysis at the facet level? Neurotics may be prone to anxiety, depression, phobias and hypochondria. Indeed, the diagnostic category has been challenged because it is too vague and all-encompassing. What are the benefits of passive-aggressiveness or borderline or schizoid personality disorder? This will be considered below.

It may be possible that there is a reproductive niche for highly introverted or neurotic people. Equally, it may be that the highly Open, low Conscientious, cre-ative person serves a very useful evolutionary function for the group even though they may have rather unhappy lives. However, it may be too early to judge. The mar-riage of dispositional and evolutionary psychology is young. It may well be that the latter approach is able to generate interesting and important hypotheses, which the latter can test empirically.

AUTHORITARIANISM

Along with the Big Five, there are numerous other individual difference variables, some more 'social' or 'cognitive' than others. One well-established factor, namely authoritarianism, has attracted evolutionary explanations. It has been described as a trait or syndrome marked by conservative beliefs, attitudinal and social intolerance, rigid cognitive functioning and repressed anxiety and hostility. Authoritarianism is linked to a range of the other psychological concepts, such as conservatism, dogmat-ism and social distancing.

Authoritarians – low on Agreeableness and Openness, but high on Conscientious-ness – are supposedly ethnocentric and xenophobic because they see the world as a particularly dangerous place. Hastings and Shaffer (2008) propose an interesting evolutionary explanation for authoritarianism. Authoritarians are highly sensitive to interpersonal threat, which can be highly adaptive. All three core components of the trait – submission to authority, conventionalism to norms and aggression to outgroup members – could be seen as adaptive, as it may improve kin selection and improve coalition formation:

> When a person is threatened, the level of intensity of an authoritarian individual's group identification increases. Thus, during time of threat, the authoritarian individual utilises the group as a 'safe haven' from outside threat wherein resources are pooled in a collective effort against the dangers posed by others. They turn to their 'kin' in times of need. Social cohesion within the group facilitates mutual cooperation and therefore increases the chances that the goals and objectives of the individual will be met.
>
> *(Hastings and Shaffer, 2008, p. 429)*

Further, they argue that authoritarianism is adaptive in relation to social exchange and reciprocal altruism. That is, authoritarians strongly align themselves with others who can assist them in times of need: they seek out others with similar belief systems and help them. They are in turn helped by others, particularly those in religious groups. Thus, authoritarians are good at maintaining and sustaining group relations, which gives 'the appearance of positive return with minimal investment' (Hastings and Shaffer, 2008, p. 430). Authoritarians, particularly when under threat, sacrifice energy, time and money to 'fellow believers' in the hope and belief that they will be rewarded and protected during threatening times. Within their group, they are cooperative, seeking harmony and concord.

It has also been argued that status hierarchy facilitates cooperative effort when working towards a common goal. Status hierarchies, fundamental to authoritarian beliefs, could be seen to be healthy and adaptive because they ensure better coordination in groups. Hence, Hastings and Shaffer (2008, p. 436) note that there is a positive and negative side to authoritarianism, which results from a fundamental perception of threat: authoritarians who are threatened process this information using evolved psychological mechanisms like social exchange, group coalition-building or one of the other various utilities. Moreover, authoritarians are more likely to submit to authority, adhere to conventional norms and promote group cohesion. These characteristic tendencies of the authoritarian individual, in turn, promote survival by encouraging the use of collective action and the pooling of resources.

ABILITY AND INTELLIGENCE

A number of psychologists have enthusiastically embraced evolutionary explanations that try to account for group, particularly sex and race, differences in intelligence. Their accounts are similar, though their focus has been slightly different and their evolutionary explanations reasonably orthodox and robust. But it has come at some personal cost: Rushton from the University of Western Ontario received death threats and had armed guards while at the university; Brand from the University of Edinburgh was sacked, a very rare event in any university; Lynn from the University of Ulster has avoided trouble by doing his most controversial work after he retired. They have been called 'scientific racists', realists and fascists. The issue has not been with their studies or their data: all psychologists accept sex and race differences in intelligence as an objective fact. The issue is *how* they have explained these differences, specifically whether they allocate most of the variance to biological race or cultural learning.

Whilst Lynn (2006) concentrated on sex differences, Brand (1996) and Rushton (2000) concentrated more on race. Indeed, the evolutionary explanations for sex differences in overall intelligence, as opposed to specific abilities, are not particularly persuasive. Debates and data on race differences in cognitive ability go back over a hundred years, but it was Jensen's (1969) now infamous paper that provoked current interest in the field. It tentatively suggested a sizeable genetic component to intelligence at the high-point of extreme environmentalism.

The acrimonious ideological arguments have persisted even since Rushton and Jensen (2005) provided a review of 30 years of this research, in which they argue for a distinction between the culture-only (0% genetic, 100% environmental) and hereditarian (50% genetic, 50% environmental) models of the causes of Black/White differences in behaviour. They note that, in all, the hereditarian model is supported: 'The new evidence reviewed here points to *some* genetic component in black–white differences in mean IQ' (Rushton and Jensen, 2005, p. 235, italics added). They believe, however, that the genetic component of the model of evidence was unable to identify the environmental 'on the basis of the present evidence, perhaps the genetic component must be given greater weight and the environmental component correspondingly reduced'. In fact, Jensen's (1998, p. 279) latest statement of the hereditarian model, termed the 'default hypothesis', is that 'genetic and cultural factors carry the exact same weight in causing the mean Black–White difference in IQ as they do in causing individual differences in IQ, about 80% genetic–20% environmental by adulthood'.

Richard Lynn has published nearly 50 papers looking at race and sex differences in intelligence. Much of this is summarised in his 2006 book, which has a chapter looking at the evolutionary explanation in intelligence in 11 groups from Arctic peoples and Bushmen, through East Asians and Europeans to Southeast Asians. The argument is relatively simple, namely that the IQs of the races can be explained as having arisen from the different environments in which they evolved. The Ice Ages in the northern hemisphere exerted selection pressures for greater intelligence for survival during particularly cold winters. Further, mutations for high intelligence appeared in the races with the larger populations and under the greatest cold stress:

> The IQ differences between the races explain the differences in achievement in making the Neolithic transition from hunter-gatherer to settled agriculture, the building of early civilisations and the development of mature civilisations during the last two thousand years. The position of environmentalists that over the course of some 100,000 years peoples separated by geographical barriers in different parts of the world evolved into ten different races with pronounced genetic differences in morphology, blood groups, and the incidence

of genetic differences, and yet have identical genotypes for intelligence, is so improbable that those who advance it must either be totally ignorant of the basic principles of evolutionary biology or else have a political agenda to deny the importance of race. Or both.

(Lynn, 2006, pp. 243–4)

Rushton's extensive 20-year research into race differences appears to be underpinned by *r-k* theory first set out by the biologist E. O. Wilson. The letters stand for $r =$ Natural Rate of Reproduction and $k =$ Amount of care parents give to their surviving offspring. The *r*-strategists have many offspring, which have to fend for themselves, while *k*-strategists have fewer offspring in which they invest energy, time and care. Rushton (2000, p. 35) notes: 'This basic law of evolution links reproductive strategy to intelligence and brain development.' Further, 'Orientals are the most *k*, Blacks are the most *r*, and Whites fall in between.' Being more *r* means, among other things:

- shorter gestation periods
- earlier physical maturation (muscular control, bone and dental development)
- smaller brains
- earlier puberty (age at first menstruation, first intercourse, first pregnancy)
- more biological than social control of behaviour (length of menstrual cycle, periodicity of sexual response, predictability of life history from start of puberty)
- more permissive sexual attitudes
- higher intercourse frequencies (premarital, marital, extramarital)
- weaker pair bonds
- more siblings
- higher rates of child neglect and abandonment
- greater frequency of disease
- shorter life expectancy.

He hypothesises that race differences may be due to testosterone and the 'out of Africa hypothesis'. The idea is that Blacks have higher testosterone levels than Orientals or Whites and put greater energy into having offspring, while Asians and Whites have fewer offspring but put more effort into looking after them. The out of Africa hypothesis is that those who left Africa (becoming Asians and Whites) had more environmental and climatic challenges to adapt to, which required making tools and learning agriculture. This called for 'higher intelligence' and moving into more *k*-type life history strategies. Rushton (2000), in his chart 6, gives the average IQ scores for four groups: Africans (70), US Blacks (85), Whites (100) and Orientals (106). He also notes that intelligence is modestly related to brain size and that there are significant and predictable differences in brain and skull size across race groups.

Rushton's work then is very strictly an evolutionary explanation for race difference in intelligence. He argues that the data are robust and that the explanation for the difference can be explained in terms of evolutionary theory. He concludes that the races differ, on average, in brain size, intelligence, sexual behaviour, fertility, personality, maturation, lifespan, crime and in family stability. Orientals fall at one end of the three-way pattern of differences, Blacks fall at the other end and Whites usually fall in between: 'Only a theory that looks at both genes and environment in terms of Darwin's theory of evolution can explain why the races differ so consistently throughout the world and over the course of time' (Rushton, 2000, p. 49).

The issue of race differences in intelligence inevitably excites tremendous passions. It is clear that all researchers in intelligence accept that there are clear racial differences, but that they tend to disagree as to why they exist. There are, it seems, three explanations. First, there is evidence of genetic differences between the races. Second, there is evidence of sociocultural, economic and political forces that are quite distinct from racial characteristics though confounded with them. Third, race differences are essentially artefacts of test design, administration or measurement. In other words, there are no real differences.

Brody (1992, p. 310) argues that those who reject race differences as a function of test measurement are wrong. He asserts that research on Black–White differences in intelligence fails to provide answers to three critical questions: (1) What are the reasons for the difference? (2) Can we eliminate it? (3) Can we design an environment in which the effects of individual differences in intelligence are mitigated, such that they are not determinative to the extent they are now of racial differences in performance in schools and in other socially relevant contexts? Note that evolutionary ability theory seems to take it as axiomatic that high intelligence is adaptive and beneficial in all areas of life. There is no suggestion that low intelligence can ever have evolutionary advantages.

'DARK-SIDE' DISORDERS

One of the most problematic issues for evolutionary personality is to explain the advantages and adaptiveness of Neuroticism and other traits associated with mental illness. While it has been possible to offer some evolutionary explanations for the Big Five, it must seem possible to go further and consider traits associated with mental illnesses. It is for evolutionary psychologists much more problematic to try to explain the continuity of particularly devastating and maladaptive conditions, such as schizophrenia.

However, of late there have been many studies that have attempted to conceptualise the personality disorders from a general model of personality functioning. Thus, Gudonis *et al.* (2008) used the 240-item NEO Five Factor personality questionnaire to derive a Personality Disorder Score. They took 18 of the 30 facets, reversed a number (mainly from Agreeableness and Conscientiousness) and combined them into a single scale. This they rotated to a whole range of behaviours from delinquency, risky sexual behaviour and substance use and abuse. They concluded that the personality disorders 'can be understood as collections of traits from a general model of personality functioning like the FFM' (Gudonis *et al.*, 2008, p. 260). They also note: 'we . . . believe that the FFM helps tie applied clinical research on the [personality disorders] to a corpus of knowledge derived from basic research on personality. Much is known about the structure, genetics, neurobiology and development of basic personality. This knowledge can be applied to research on the Personality Disorders to extend our understanding of mechanisms and treatment and to generate theory' (p. 261).

However, there have been attempts to assess a cost-benefit analysis of the personality disorders. Hogan (1996) has always been sympathetic to evolutionary explanations, especially for such things as leadership. He has also developed a 'dark-side' personality measure that has some of its intellectual origin in the personality disorders. He has always argued that those dark-side dimensions can be seen as both strengths and weaknesses. Indeed, he has done very much what Nettle (2006) has done in his cost-benefit analysis of the Big Five.

Nelson and Hogan (2009) list the dark-side facets and their costs and benefits. Their argument is that of optimalisation, that is that there are clear psychological advantages to having 'some' of the characteristics of the dark-side traits. They argue that dimensions have distinctive positive features that are initially attractive in business settings and actually positively related to performance in terms of evolutionary psychology. This is once again an example of the spectrum hypothesis which sees all mental illnesses on a series of dimensions which are extreme scores on 'normal traits'. Hence, the term 'schizotypy' rather than 'psychophrenia': the former tends to be a dimensional conception, the latter a categorical one. Related to this is the idea that the more extreme the score, the more problematic and intransigent the individual and the less adaptive and flexible his or her behavioural predispositions. It has long been recognised that people with certain mental illnesses, such as bipolar disorders, have been able to explore and exploit those talents if first they are not too extreme; they are accompanied by very real abilities and talents; and thirdly they get professional help and social support in dealing with those illnesses.

It is suggested that one can interpret all the personality disorders in terms of the Big Five. Thus, narcissistic personality disorder is associated with very low Agreeableness and Neuroticism; obsessive compulsive disorder with high Conscientiousness and Neuroticism and low Agreeableness; and schizotypal personality disorder with very low Extraversion and high Neuroticism (Furnham and Crump, 2005). Indeed, Decuyper *et al.* (2009) in an extensive meta-analysis showed how antisocial personality disorder and psychopathy were systematically related to the Big Five at domain and facet levels. Most consistently, these mental disorders were associated with low Conscientiousness and Agreeableness.

Given the cost-benefit analysis offered earlier it may, therefore, be possible to see certain advantages of the personality disorders. Table 8.2 offers a cost-benefit analysis of the personality disorders much as Table 8.1 does for personality traits. The argument is that if these disorders have no advantages they would over time disappear: being associated with evolutionary unfitness, they would disappear. However, we still get between 0.5 and 3% of the population experiencing these disorders in some degree because at certain times and in certain situations they confer an evolutionary advantage. Because psychiatrists prefer categorical distinctions of people

Table 8.2. *The structure of the dark-side personality.*

DSM-IV Personality Disorder	HDS themes		Dark-side dimension		Benefits	Costs
Borderline	Inappropriate anger; unstable and intense relationships alternating between idealisation and devaluation	Excitable	Moody and hard to please; intense but short-lived enthusiasm for people, projects or things	Excitable	Mood swings, emotional outbursts and inability to persist on projects	Empathy and concern	Emotional explosiveness
Paranoid	Distrustful and suspicious of others; motives are interpreted as malevolent	Sceptical	Cynical, distrustful and doubting others' true intensions	Sceptical	Mistrusting others, questioning their motives and challenging their integrity	Social and political insight	Excessive suspicion
Avoidant	Social inhibition; feelings of inadequacy and hypersensitivity to criticism or rejection	Cautious	Reluctant to take risks for fear of being rejected or negatively evaluated	Cautious	Fearful of making mistakes, avoid making decisions	Evaluates risks appropriately	Indecisiveness and risk aversions
Schizoid	Emotional coldness and detachment from social relationships; indifferent to praise and criticism	Reserved	Aloof, detached and uncommunicative; lacking interest in or awareness of the feelings of others	Reserved	Remaining aloof, communicating poorly and ignoring the welfare of their staff	Emotionally unflappable	Insensitive and poor communicator
Passive-Aggressive	Passive resistance to adequate social and occupational performance; irritated when asked to do something he/she does not want to	Leisurely	Independent; ignoring people's requests and becoming irritated or argumentative if they persist	Leisurely	Procrastinating, pursuing their own agendas and failing to set clear expectations for, or following through with commitments to, their staff	Good social skills	Passive-aggressive

(continued)

Table 8.2. *(continued)*

DSM-IV Personality Disorder		HDS themes		Dark-side dimension		Benefits	Costs
Narcissistic	Arrogant and haughty behaviours or attitudes, grandiose sense of self-importance and entitlement	Bold	Unusually self-confident; feelings of grandiosity and entitlement; overvaluation of one's capabilities	Bold	Feeling entitled, not sharing credit for success, blaming their mistakes on others and not learning from experience, but are fearless about pursuing grand goals	Courage and energy	Overbearing and manipulative
Antisocial	Disregard for the truth; impulsivity and failure to plan ahead; failure to conform	Mischievous	Enjoying risk-taking and testing the limits; needing excitement; manipulative, deceitful, cunning and exploitative	Mischievous	Lying and breaking rules to test the limits, ignoring commitments and thinking they can talk their way out of any problem	Unafraid of risk	Reckless and deceitful
Histrionic	Excessive emotionality and attention-seeking; self-dramatising, theatrical and exaggerated emotional expression	Colourful	Expressive, animated and dramatic; wanting to be noticed and needing to be the centre of attention	Colourful	Needing to be the centre of attention, so that others can admire them, preoccupied with being noticed, unable to maintain focus and resist sharing credit	Celebrations and entertainment	Impulsive and distractible

(continued)

Table 8.2. (continued)

DSM-IV Personality Disorder	HDS themes	Dark-side dimension	Benefits	Costs
Schizotypal — Odd beliefs or magical thinking; behaviour or speech that is odd, eccentric or peculiar	Imaginative — Acting and thinking in creative and sometimes odd or unusual ways	Imaginative — Thinking in eccentric ways, often changing their minds and making strange decisions	Creativity and vision	Bad ideas
Obsessive-Compulsive — Preoccupations with orderliness; rules, perfectionism and control; over-conscientiousness and inflexible	Diligent — Meticulous, precise and perfectionistic, inflexible about rules and procedures; critical of others' performance	Diligent — Frustrating and disempowering their staff with micro-management, poor prioritisation and an inability to delegate	Hard work and high standards	Micro-management
Dependent — Difficulty making everyday decisions without excessive advice and reassurance; difficulty expressing disagreement out of fear of loss of support or approval	Dutiful — Eager to please and reliant on others for support and guidance; reluctant to take independent action or to go against popular opinion	Dutiful — Sucking up to supervisors, unable to deny unrealistic requests, won't stand up for their staff and burn them out as a result	Corporate citizenship	Indecisiveness

at the extreme of continua, it appears initially as if there can be few disadvantages of being, say, schizoid, paranoid or narcissistic. Clearly, this remains highly speculative. However, it does signal the potential usefulness of evolutionary psychiatry that attempts to describe and explain the adaptive significance and origin of many mental disorders, though always to be undesirable for individuals.

CONCLUSION

The rise in popularity and perceived explanatory power of evolutionary psychology over the past 20 to 30 years has meant that some personality psychologists have been interested to see to what extent it can inform their science. There is no doubt that the established links between personality traits and such things as health, social relationships and occupational success can be explained in evolutionary terms.

Evolutionary explanations are simultaneously beguiling and difficult to test. As Figueredo *et al.* (2005, p. 873) recognise, evolutionary personality psychology is 'ahead of the data'. It is, however, possible to derive hypotheses which are, and have been, testable, even though not necessarily originally informed by psychological theory. The question is essentially whether the hypothesis tested is strictly that derived from evolutionary theory. This is an interesting time to be alive both for personality and evolutionary psychologists. Progress in behaviour genetics influence them both and it seems likely that the rapprochement between personality trait psychologists and personality disorder psychiatrists will both be informed by evolutionary hypotheses as to the origin and functioning of stable individual differences.

REFERENCES

Barrett, L., Dunbar, R. and Lycett, J. (2002). *Human evolutionary psychology*. Basingstoke: Palgrave.

Berry, J. and Annis, R. (1974). Ecology, culture and psychological differentiation. *International Journal of Psychology*, 9, 173–93.

Boudreau, J., Boswell, W. R. and Judge, T. A. (2001). Effects of personality on executive career success in the United States and Europe. *Journal of Vocational Behaviour*, 58, 53–81.

Brand, C. (1996). *The g factor: General intelligence and its implications*. Chichester: John Wiley & Sons, Ltd.

Brody, N. (1992). *Intelligence*. New York: Academic Press.

Buss, D. M. (1985). Human mate selection. *American Scientist*, 73, 47–51.

Buss, D. M. (1987). Sex differences in human mate selection criteria: An evolutionary perspective. In C. Crawford, M. Smith and D. Kerbs (eds). *Sociobiology and psychology: Issues, goals and findings* (pp. 335–54). Hillsdale, NJ: Lawrence Erlbaum Associates.

Buss, D. M. (1988). The evolution of human intrasexual competition: Tactics of mate attraction. *Journal of Personality and Social Psychology, 54,* 616–28.

Buss, D. (1991). Evolutionary personality psychology. *Annual Review of Psychology, 42,* 459–91.

Buss, D. (1996). Social adaptation and five major factors of personality. In J. Wiggins, (ed.). *The five-factor model of personality* (pp. 180–207). New York: Guilford.

Claridge, G. and Davis, C. (2001). What's the use of neuroticism? *Personality and Individual Differences, 31,* 383–400.

Costa, P. and McCrae, R. (1992). *Revised NEO Personality Inventory and NEO Five Factor Inventory Professional Model.* Odessa, FL: Psychological Assessment Resource.

Deary, I. (2008). Why do intelligent people live longer? *Nature, 456,* 175–6.

Deary, I. and Matthews, G. (1993). Personality traits are alive and well. *Psychologist, 6,* 299–300.

Decuyper, M., de Pauw, S., De Fruyt, F. *et al.* (2009). A meta-analysis of pychopathy-, Antisocial PD- and FFM associations. *European Journal of Personality, 23,* 531–65.

Donnellan, M. B., Conger, R. D. and Bryant, C. M. (2004). The Big Five and enduring marriages. *Journal of Research in Personality, 38,* 481–504.

Eysenck, H. J. (1976). *Sex and personality.* London: Open Books.

Figueredo, A. J., Sefcek, J. A. and Jones, D. N. (2006). The ideal romantic partner personality. *Personality and Individual Differences, 41,* 431–41.

Figueredo, A., Sefcek, J., Vasquez, G. *et al.* (2005). Evolutionary psychology. In D. M. Buss (ed.), *Handbook of evolutionary psychology* (pp. 851–77). Hoboken, NJ: John Wiley & Sons, Ltd.

Friedman, H. S. (2008). The multiple linkages of personality and disease. *Brain, Behavior, and Immunity, 22,* 668–75.

Friedman, H. S., Tucker, J. S., Tomlinson-Keasey, C. *et al.* (1993). Does childhood personality predict longevity? *Journal of Personality and Social Psychology, 65,* 176–85.

Furnham, A. (2008). *Personality and intelligence at work.* London: Routledge.

Furnham, A. (2009). Sex differences in mate selection preferences. *Personality and Individual Differences, 47,* 262–7.

Furnham, A. and Crump, J. (2005). Personality traits, types and disorders: An examination of the relationship between three self-report measures. *European Journal of Personality, 19,* 167–84.

Furnham, A. and Heaven, P. (1998). *Personality and social behaviour.* London: Arnold.

Gelissen, J. and de Graaf, P. M. (2006). Personality, social background, and occupational career success. *Social Science Research, 35,* 702–26.

Glicksohn, J. and Golan, H. (2001). Personality, cognitive style and assortative mating. *Personality and Individual Differences, 30,* 1199–209.

Gottman, J. M. (1994). *What predicts divorce? The relationship between marital processes and marital outcomes.* Hillsdale, NJ: Lawrence Erlbaum Associates.

Gottman, J. M. (1998). Psychology and the study of the marital processes. *Annual Review of Psychology, 49,* 169–97.

Gudonis, L., Miller, D., Miller, J. and Lynam, D. (2008). Conceptualising personality disorders from a general model of personality functioning. *Personality and Mental Health, 2,* 249–64.

Hastings, B. and Shaffer, B. (2008). Authoritarianism: The role of threat, evolutionary psychology and the will to power. *Theory and Psychology, 18,* 423–40.

Heaven, P. C., Crocker, D., Edwards, B. *et al.* (2003). Personality and sex. *Personality and Individual Differences, 35,* 411–419.

Heaven, P. C., Fitzpatrick, J., Craig, F. L. *et al.* (2000). Five personality factors and sex: Preliminary findings. *Personality and Individual Differences, 28,* 1133–41.

Hogan, R. (1996). A socioanalytic perspective on the five-factor model. In J. Wiggins (ed.), *The five factor model of personality* (pp. 163–79). New York: Guilford.

Hong, R. and Paunonen, S. (in press). Personality traits and health-risk behaviours in university students. *European Journal of Personality.*

Jensen, A. R. (1969). How much can we boost IQ and scholastic achievement? *Harvard Educational Review, 39,* 1–123.

Jensen, A. R. (1998). *The g factor.* Westport, CT: Praeger.

Kenrick, D. T. (2004). Evolutionary social psychology. *International Encyclopedia of the Social & Behavioural Sciences,* 5022–4.

Korotkov, D. and Hannah, T. E. (2004). The five-factor model of personality: Strengths and limitations in predicting health status, sick-role and illness behaviour. *Personality and Individual Differences, 36,* 187–99.

Lynn, R. (2006). *Race differences in intelligence: An evolutionary analysis.* Augusta, GA: Washington Summit Publishers.

McCrae, R. and Costa, P. (1995). Trait explanation in personality psychology. *European Journal of Personality, 9,* 211–52.

MacDonald, K. (1991). A perspective on Darwinian psychology. *Ethology and Sociobiology, 12,* 449–80.

MacDonald, K. (1998). Evolution, culture and the five factor model. *Journal of Cross-Cultural Psychology, 29,* 119–45.

Musek, J. (2007). A general factor of personality. *Journal of Research in Personality, 41,* 1213–1233.

Nelson, E. and Hogan, R. (2009). Coaching the dark side. *International Coaching Psychology Review, 4,* 7–19.

Nettle, D. (2005). An evolutionary approach to the extraversion continuum. *Evolution and Human Behaviour, 26,* 363–73.

Nettle, D. (2006). The evolution of personality variation in humans and other animals. *American Psychologist, 61,* 622–31.

Robins, R. W., Caspi, A. and Moffitt, T. E. (2000). Two personalities, one relationship: Both partners' personality traits shape the quality of their relationship. *Journal of Personality and Social Psychology, 79,* 251–9.

Robins, R. W., Caspi, A. and Moffitt, T. E. (2002). It's not just who you're with, it's who you are: Personality and relationship experiences across multiple relationships. *Journal of Personality, 70,* 925–64.

Rushton, J. (1985). Differential k theory. *Personality and Individual differences, 6,* 441–52.

Rushton, J. (2000). *Race, evolution and behaviour: A life history perspective.* Port Huron, MI: CDRI.

Rushton, J., Bons, T. and Hur, Y-M. (2008). The genetics and evolution of a general factor of personality. *Journal of Research in Personality, 42,* 1173–85.

Rushton, J. and Jensen, A. (2005). Thirty years of research on race differences in cognitive ability. *Psychology, Public Policy and Law,* 235–94.

Saad, G. and Gill, T. (2000). Application of evolutionary psychology in marketing. *Psychology and Marketing, 17,* 1005–34.

Seibert, S. E. and Kraimer, M. L. (2001). The five-factor model of personality and career success. *Journal of Vocational Behaviour, 58,* 1–21.

Shackelford, T. K. (2006). Recycling, evolution and the structure of human personality. *Personality and Individual Differences, 41*, 1551–6.

Terman, L. M. (1938). *Psychological factors in marital happiness*. New York: McGraw-Hill.

Todosijevic, B., Ljubinkovic, S. and Arancil, A. (2003). Mate selection criteria: A trait desirability assessment of sex differences in Serbia. *Evolutionary Psychology, 1*, 116–126.

Tooby, J. and Cosmides, L. (1990). On the universality of human nature and the uniqueness of the individual. *Journal of Personality, 58*, 17–67.

van Vugt, M., Hogan, R. and Kaiser, R. B. (2008). Leadership, followership, and evolution: Some lessons from the past. *American Psychologist, 63*, 182–96.

Webster, G. (2007). Evolutionary theory's increasing role in personality and social psychology. *Evolutionary Psychology, 5*, 84–91.

Whiting, J. (1961). Socialisation process and personality. In F. Hsu (ed.), *Psychological anthropology*. Homewood, IL: Dorsey.

Wu, P., Foo, M. and Turban, D. B. (2008). The role of personality in relationship closeness, developer assistance, and career success. *Journal of Vocational behaviour, 73*, 440–448.

9 Evolution, cognition and mental illness: The imprinted brain theory

CHRISTOPHER BADCOCK

CHAPTER OUTLINE

THE ILLNESSES THAT MADE US HUMAN 282

ANTITHESES OF MENTALISM IN AUTISM
AND PSYCHOSIS 288

THE IMPRINTED BRAIN 294

IMPLICATIONS FOR EVOLUTIONARY
PSYCHOLOGY 303

ACKNOWLEDGEMENTS 305

REFERENCES 305

Up to the present, the primary focus of evolutionary psychology has been on problems of psychological adaptation. However, explaining mental illnesses like autism and schizophrenia from an adaptive view point has been a particular challenge thanks to the obviously maladaptive nature of mental illness – at least from the individual's point of view, not to mention society's! Furthermore, the known causes of both disorders seem to defy any single theory or unitary perspective. We have long known that both tend to run in families and that if one of two identical twins has such a disorder, there is a much higher-than-average probability that the other will too. Autism is sometimes associated with genetic syndromes, such as Rett, Down and Turner's, phenylketonuria and tuberous sclerosis. The clearest single-gene cause of autism spectrum disorder (ASD) is Fragile X syndrome, with a wide range of severity in symptoms and between a quarter and a half of affected males meeting the criteria for autism. The strongest link between a psychotic illness and genetics is found in cases of Prader-Willi syndrome caused by duplication of the individual's maternal copy of chromosome 15 who are invariably diagnosed psychotic in adulthood. But neither autism nor schizophrenia obeys classical Mendelian laws of inheritance in the way that cystic fibrosis or colour blindness does.

There is also good evidence for social and environmental causes of mental illnesses. Studies of the Dutch wartime famine and of the Chinese famine of 1959–61 reported increased incidence of schizophrenia among children born just after the events (St Clair, 2005; Susser, St Clair and He, 2008). And a study of two million Swedish children born between 1963 and 1983 revealed a significant link between schizophrenia and poverty in childhood. Those with four out of five measured indicators of hardship had an almost three-fold greater risk of schizophrenia than those with none (Wicks, 2005). Where ASD is concerned, the exponential increase in diagnoses since the 1980s has prompted some to suggest environmental or social causes: most controversially, childhood vaccines like MMR. Autism can certainly result from ethanol or valproic acid poisoning during the mother's pregnancy, and in the 1964 rubella epidemic in the United States, the rate of incidence of autism exceeded 7% at a time when the normal rate of diagnosis was not much more than a tenth of 1%. Autism can also be caused by thalidomide, where it affects about 5% of those with birth defects attributable to this cause.

In this chapter, I present a new theory that attempts to explain these seemingly contradictory findings. As I shall now try to show, both ASD and psychoses like schizophrenia can be considered from an adaptive point of view, which gives remarkable new insights not only into psychopathology but also into social cognition, normality and even genius. Indeed, in my concluding remarks I shall argue that it has profound implications for both evolutionary psychology and the future of society as a whole.

THE ILLNESSES THAT MADE US HUMAN

In the past, both autism and psychosis were seen mainly in terms of the obvious deficits that characterise the diagnosed conditions. Nevertheless, recent research has begun to reveal a more positive and complex picture, with symptomatic compensations found in both cases. For example, the founding father of modern psychiatry, Eugen Bleuler, who coined the term 'schizophrenia', noted that schizophrenics who seem totally withdrawn and uninterested in their environment nevertheless 'pick up an astounding amount of information from snatches of conversation about the personal lives of their doctors and care personnel, and about tensions among them' (Sass, 1992, p. 415). The evolutionary psychiatrist, Randolph Nesse notes that 'those who have worked with schizophrenics know the eerie feeling of being with someone whose intuitions are acutely tuned to the subtlest unintentional cues, even while the person is incapable of accurate empathic understanding' (Nesse, 2004, p. 62). Other authorities comment regarding the case histories of psychotics that, 'Reported experience of "telepathic" contact with another person close by . . . may well indicate a genuine hyper-awareness of "leaked" social signals which are then interpreted, rightly or wrongly, as having psychological meaning . . . Anyone who has interacted with psychotics will know of their uncanny capacity to respond to subtle social cues, believed to have been concealed from them' (Claridge, Pryor and Watkins, 1990, p. 221). The same writer concludes that 'the underlying quality of schizophrenia is not a defect at all, but an exquisite sensitivity of the nervous system, which . . . gets translated into an *appearance* of deficit . . .' (Claridge, 1987, p. 40, emphasis in original).

Experimental studies suggest that such impressions are by no means subjective. For example, one carefully controlled study found that paranoid patients even when on medication are demonstrably better than normal controls in interpreting non-verbal cues – at least where the resulting expressions are genuine and where the situation is one of expectation of an electric shock. With simulated expressions, normal subjects performed better than paranoid ones, but as the experimenter herself points out, this is just what you would expect if you thought that paranoiacs have a special sensitivity to non-verbal cues (LaRusso, 1978). Children diagnosed with a rare form of childhood-onset schizophrenia showed enhanced performance by comparison to autistic children and normal controls in a task involving deception of others (Pilowsky *et al.*, 2000). Positive associations have also been reported between measures of empathy and milder so-called schizotypy (Dinn *et al.*, 2002; Rim, 1994). Again, a test of divergent thinking in which subjects had to invent uses for a range of conventional and ambiguous objects showed that the schizotypical group performed particularly well in comparison with schizophrenics and normal controls, activating much more of the right prefrontal cortex in doing so (Folley and Park, 2005). Indeed, such mildly psychotic tendencies have been associated with enhanced social-emotional creativity and imagination in general (Claridge, Pryor and Watkins, 1990; Nettle, 2001).

Crespi, Summers and Dorus (2007) screened human and primate genes for evidence of positive selection. They found statistically significant evidence for positive selection on 26 of 80 genes mediating liability to schizophrenia, including some which exhibit some of the best-supported functional and genetic links to this disorder. Previous studies indicated that recent positive selection in humans has driven the evolution of a suite of additional genes linked with schizophrenia risk, and variants of three genes associated with schizophrenia have recently been linked with measures of creativity. Taken together, the authors conclude that these findings provide evolutionary and genetic support for the hypothesis that schizophrenia represents 'the illness that made us human' (Horrobin, 1998).

Similar findings relate to autism. Asperger's syndrome describes a so-called high-functioning form of ASD in which speech and intelligence are intact, but in which there are qualitative impairments in social interaction and communication, and restrictive interests. Specific deficits in social skills include failure to develop friendships, impaired non-verbal behaviour relating to gaze, body language and facial expression and deficits in identifying and interpreting social cues and conventions. Where verbal communication is concerned, there is usually fluent speech but difficulty with conversation skills, a tendency to be pedantic and to interpret things literally. Finally, there is usually a special interest of unusual intensity and single-mindedness and a preference for routine and consistency (Attwood, 2006).

Nevertheless, as early as 1960 (and well before diagnoses of Asperger's syndrome were being made), writers on autism were pointing out that the autistic child is 'not mentally retarded in the ordinary sense of the word, but rather is a child with an inadequate form of mentation which manifests itself in the inability to handle symbolic forms and assume an abstract attitude' (Kaplan, 2006, p. 44). Today, some leading authorities argue that the perceived association between ASD and mental retardation is not based on the fact that they usually have common causes but is more likely to be because the presence of both greatly increases the probability of a clinical diagnosis (Skuse, 2007). Indeed, according to the latest research, intelligence in autistics has generally been underestimated, and they are not as impaired in fluid intelligence as many theories predict. On the contrary, autistic intelligence is revealed by the most complex single test of general intelligence in the literature: Raven's Progressive Matrices (Dawson et al., 2007). Such findings have been interpreted to suggest that Asperger's syndrome in fact involves superior abstract reasoning ability or higher general fluid intelligence (Hayashi et al., 2008).

High-functioning autistics often have a remarkable eye for detail, and notice things that may escape the attention of others. That such impressions are not without an objective basis was recently demonstrated when the vision of a group of people with ASD was compared with that of non-autistic controls. Astonishingly, all 15 of the ASD subjects tested had superior eyesight, which was 2.79 times better than average (giving a score of 20:7, meaning that they could see details from 20 feet that an average person could only see at seven feet). As the researchers remark, this approximately two-to-three-fold superiority in vision is comparable to that of birds of prey, and their results suggest that increased visual acuity applies to individuals across the autistic spectrum, making this yet another respect in which autistics outperform the normal population (Ashwin et al., 2008).

Indeed, there is now evidence that autistics may have heightened sensitivities in all senses. For example, despite sometimes giving the impression of being deaf, people with ASD often have superior hearing, as a number of studies have confirmed where discrimination of pitch is concerned (Bonnel et al., 2003; O'Riordan and Passetti, 2006). A study which explored sensitivity to touch found that people with ASD had a lower threshold for tactile stimulations than normal controls do (Blakemore et al., 2006). Another which investigated both touch and hearing in 20 adults with and 20 without ASD matched for sex, age and IQ found that the autistic subjects were hypersensitive in both hearing and touch (Tavassoli et al., 2011). A study which compared

17 ASD subjects with 17 normal controls in a standard test of sensitivity to smell found a quantitative relationship between level of enhanced sensory processing and the number of autistic traits, with greater severity of autistic behaviour related to higher sensory perception than normal. However, there was no correlation between sensory thresholds and age or level of cognitive functioning, suggesting that hyper-sensitivity to smell may be a core feature in ASD (Ashwin *et al.*, in press).

In his original paper on autism, Hans Asperger (1906–1980), the co-discoverer of autism, remarked that:

> To our own amazement, we have seen that autistic individuals, as long as they are intellec-tually intact, can almost always achieve professional success, usually in highly specialized academic professions, with a preference for abstract content. We found a large number of people whose mathematical ability determines their professions: mathematicians, technologists, industrial chemists, and high ranking civil servants . . . A good professional attitude involves single-mindedness as well as a decision to give up a large number of other interests . . . It seems that for success in science or art, a dash of autism is essential . . . Indeed we find numerous autistic individuals among distinguished scientists.
>
> *(Asperger, 1991, pp. 89, 74)*

Perhaps appropriately, Asperger himself has been put forward as an example of his own syndrome (Lyons and Fitzgerald, 2007), and autistic tendencies allied with outstanding skills and even genius have been detected in other famous scientists and mathematicians. Examples are Sir Isaac Newton, Albert Einstein, Paul Dirac (James, 2006), Alan Turing (O'Connell and Fitzgerald, 2003) and Charles Richter, the seismologist who gave his name to the Richter Scale of earthquake intensity (Hough, 2007). Another is Michael Ventris, the cryptographer who deciphered the ancient Mycenaean script known as *Linear B* (Baron-Cohen, 2003). Others who have been retrospectively diagnosed as being somewhere on the autistic spectrum include the poet, artist, sculptor and architect Michelangelo Buonarroti, the philosopher Ludwig Wittgenstein and the mathematician, Srinivasa Ramanujan (Arshad and Fitzgerald, 2004; Fitzgerald, 2004). Writers and poets include Hans Christian Andersen, Herman Melville, Jonathan Swift, William Butler Yeats and Lewis Carroll (Fitzgerald, 2005). Politicians and statesmen too have been added to the list of those suspected of hav-ing been Asperger's cases: specifically Thomas Jefferson (Ledgin, 1998), Eamon de Valera and perhaps most interestingly of all Adolf Hitler (Fitzgerald, 2004).

Michael Fitzgerald published a book about what he terms 'Asperger's savants', that is 'persons with high functioning autism or Asperger's syndrome who produce works of genius' (Fitzgerald, 2005, p. 20). Despite the fact that, as Fitzgerald himself notes, persons with Asperger's syndrome are often 'anti-theory' and have problems with abstraction, he includes the philosophers Spinoza, Immanuel Kant and A. J. Ayer (1910–1989). Less surprising perhaps is his inclusion of several famous musicians, such as Wolfgang Amadeus Mozart, Ludwig van Beethoven, Eric Satie and Béla Bartók, and along with van Gogh, the painters L. S. Lowry and Andy Warhol (Fitzgerald, 2005).

According to some authorities, up to 10% of autistics, but only 1% with other developmental deficits, show some kind of so-called savant skills, in other words remarkable cognitive and/or memory ability found among more prevalent disability (Treffert, 2006). Such talents are usually limited to music, art, maths and calendar calculation, mechanical and spatial skills, often featuring astonishing memorisation feats; while the combination of blindness, autism and musical genius is unusually frequent (Treffert, 2001). For example, the late Kim Peek, the inspiration for the film *Rain Man*, walked with a sideways gait, needed help buttoning his clothes and managing many of the practical chores of daily life, had great difficulty understanding abstraction and had an overall IQ of 87. Yet he had an encyclopaedic knowledge of history, political leaders, roads and highways in the United States and Canada, professional sports, the space programme, movies, actors and actresses, Shakespeare, the Bible, Mormon doctrine and history, calendar calculations, literature, telephone area codes, major postcodes, television stations, classical music, along with the detailed content of 9000 individual books (Treffert, 2000; Treffert and Christensen, 2005).

So-called acquired savant syndrome can occasionally emerge after brain injury or disease in a previously normal person. For example, a 9-year-old who was deaf-mute and paralysed by a gunshot wound to the left hemisphere developed outstanding mechanical skills after the injury (Treffert, 2006). Another remarkable case is that of Daniel Tammet. Diagnosed with Asperger's syndrome, Daniel developed an unusual combination of synaesthesia and savantism following a series of childhood epileptic seizures. Synaesthesia describes the mixing of senses so that in Daniel's case, for example, every number up to about 10 000 is seen as a uniquely coloured and textured shape, occasionally also associated with a specific emotional feeling. By means of manipulating numbers visualised in this way, Daniel can perform calculations with the speed and accuracy of a computer, and currently holds the British and European record for the rote recitation of the places of π from memory to 22 514 places – a feat achieved in just over five hours. His synaesthesia also extends to words, and following a challenge from a TV producer, Daniel learned one of the world's most difficult and distinct languages, Icelandic, in one week sufficiently well to be successfully interviewed live in the language on Icelandic television – so much so that one of the Icelanders described Daniel's linguistic skill as 'not human' (Tammet, 2006, p. 226). Certainly, the cognitive style of autistic savants seems more like that of a computer than a person, and you could accurately describe it as 'mechanistic', rather than mentalistic, in quality.

Folk physics is an intuitive ability to grasp physical principles involved in mechanical systems and machines, and as such an epitome of mechanistic cognition. When tests of folk physics were administered to them, Asperger's cases functioned significantly above their mental age by comparison with normal children, despite the fact that on comparable tests of folk psychology the autistic children performed predictably worse. Although the experiment could not determine whether such so-called folk physics and folk psychology are independent of one another or just inversely related, it did demonstrate a significant superiority in the Asperger's children where such skills was concerned. Indeed, the fascination with machines of all kinds that is so frequently found in autistics is almost certainly another manifestation of the same bias towards inanimate objects, as the researchers themselves point out (Baron-Cohen *et al.*, 2001).

According to a survey of 919 families of children with autism or Asperger's syndrome which listed occupations of parents, fathers of children with ASD were twice as often employed in engineering as were fathers in any of four control groups of children with Tourette's or Down syndrome. The Autism-Spectrum Quotient, or AQ, Test consists of 50 questions covering social skill, attention switching, attention to detail, communication and imagination. Fifty-eight adults with Asperger's syndrome, 174 randomly selected controls, 840 students at Cambridge University and the 16 winners of the UK Mathematics Olympiad were each sent a questionnaire by post. Results showed that the majority of people with Asperger's syndrome scored above 32 (out of a maximum of 50). But interestingly, among the students at Cambridge University, those in the sciences and technology had a higher AQ score compared to those in the arts and humanities. Mathematicians scored the highest of all – around 20 out of 50 – and were closely followed by engineers, computer scientists and physicists. Among the scientists, biologists and medics scored the lowest, around 14 out of 50 (Baron-Cohen and Else, 2001). These results strongly suggest that mentalising is independent of IQ, executive function (planning, prioritising and postponing) and reasoning about the physical world – or what you might call mechanistic cognition. The researchers conclude that there seems to be a small but statistically significant link between autism and engineering (Baron-Cohen *et al.*, 1999, pp. 475–83). Such findings as these

> might also help to explain why a condition like autism persists in the gene pool: the very same genes that lead an individual to have a child with autism can lead to superior functioning in the domain of folk physics. Engineering and related folk physics skills have transformed the way in which our species live [sic], without question for the better. Indeed, without such skills, Homo sapiens would still be pre-industrial.
>
> *(Baron-Cohen et al., 1997, pp. 106–7)*

If this is so, then schizophrenia was the illness that made us only *half* human. As this quotation suggests, a parallel case can be made for genes involved with ASD where what you might call mechanistic, rather than mentalistic, cognition is concerned. Part of the paradox of why severe mental illnesses like autism and schizophrenia have genetic causes may, therefore, lie in the fact that the very same genes that can produce these pathological conditions also underpin the twin cognitive systems on which human pre-eminence as a species relies: mentalistic and mechanistic cognition. One gave us our society, culture, language and ability to empathise and interact with other people's minds. The other gave us science, technology and all the manual, mechanical and technical skills on which our civilizations depend. If this view is correct, autism and psychoses like schizophrenia are indeed the price we pay for these critical cognitive adaptations (Badcock, 2002/4).

At the very least, such insights may certainly explain some of the apparent epidemic in ASD. In 1993, there were 4911 diagnosed cases of ASD in Silicon Valley (Santa Clara County, California). In 1999, the figure passed 10 000, and in 2001 there were 15 441 cases, with new ones added at seven per day, 85% of them children. Furthermore, such hotspots for autism are not limited to California: comparable findings are reported from the Cambridge area in England. Given that employment in Silicon Valley and around Cambridge is primarily in electronic engineering and computing, and that equal-opportunity employment means that many children born there will have both parents in these industries, so-called assortative mating has been suggested as the most likely explanation. This is the finding that likes attract, and that people tend to marry partners who have much in common with themselves. In other words, it looks as if mentalistic deficits in people with engineering, maths and computer skills are being compounded in their children by inheritance of these deficits from both parents (Constantino and Todd, 2005; Silberman, 2001). Studies to confirm this conclusion are currently under way, but the first results suggest that mothers of children with autism are indeed more likely to have a more technological turn of mind than normal (Baron-Cohen, 2005).

ANTITHESES OF MENTALISM IN AUTISM AND PSYCHOSIS

Insights like these may explain both why genes for ASD and psychoses like schizophrenia exist in the human gene pool, and why, in the case of the former, diagnosed autism may be increasing in certain places. But we still need to know how and why autistic or psychotic symptoms are produced in individuals, and how the strange, non-Mendelian pattern of their inheritance is to be explained. A start can be made by looking at the symptoms of the two types of disorder more closely.

The primate researcher Daniel Povinelli points out that appreciating the idea that others 'see' is fundamental to 'the entire question of theory of mind – at least with respect to our human understanding of the mind' – or, in other words, to what might be termed 'mentalism' (Badcock, 2002/4). He adds that 'most of our social interactions begin with determination of the attentional state of our communicative partners, and from that point forward we constantly monitor their attentional focus throughout the interaction. Nothing can disrupt a social interaction more quickly than realising that someone is no longer looking at you' (Povinelli, 2000, p. 20). Indeed, eyes are often called 'the windows of the soul', and detection of another person's direction of gaze and shifts of attention have been described as 'the linchpin of social cognition' (Langdon et al., 2006). It has been proposed that young children first experience the 'meeting of minds' which epitomises mentalism when they shift their attention to join that of someone else as indicated by the other person's direction of gaze (Baron-Cohen, 1995, pp. 38–58). In other words, where the eyes lead, the mind follows, and what may at first have seemed an after effect of social living, or a trivial detail in it – direction of gaze – now begins to take on the appearance of a central, fundamental and strategic adaptation. Indeed, direction of gaze turns out to be a better measure of mentalising ability than the standard verbal response in tests of false belief, and is even more discriminating between autistic and non-autistic mentally handicapped children (Frith, 2003, p. 105). However, the deficit is not simply a perceptual one: autistic children matched with controls show similar reflexive responses to shifts in direction of gaze in laboratory experiments. Like chimpanzees, autistic children can follow a shift in direction of another's gaze that indicates the location of an object. This rules out the possibility that autistic deficits in gaze-monitoring can be accounted for by a purely perceptual impairment in responding to eye movements in others. But also like chimps, autistic children do not appear to interpret or understand the meaning of such shifts in mental terms such as attention or emotion (Senju *et al.*, 2004; Swettenham *et al.*, 2004).

By contrast, feelings of being watched, stared at or spied on are common in paranoid schizophrenia. One schizophrenic objected to the 'eye-language' used by the judge who examined him and to the fact that 'before I entered my flat somebody always had to annoy me with some meaningless glance' (Jaspers, 1962, p. 101), while yet another described being continuously monitored by a 'Watcher-Machine' (Sass, 1992, p. 235). Indeed, delusions of being watched, stared at or spied on are so common in paranoid schizophrenia that Harry Stack Sullivan, a psychiatrist famed for treating schizophrenics, advised his colleagues to sit at the side of such a patient rather than facing them, never to look them in the eyes and to address them in the third person (Thompson, personal communication)! Recent laboratory experiments have provided the first direct scientific evidence that people with schizophrenia are indeed unusually sensitive to the direction of another person's gaze. Furthermore, the researchers point out that the social deficits seen in schizophrenia could be the outcome of such an oversensitivity – particularly in preventing them making accurate inferences about what another person is likely to be thinking (Langdon *et al.*, 2006). In other words, both excessive sensitivity and insensitivity can result in perceptual deficits. This clearly happens in the case of sensitivity to light or sound causing visual or auditory impairments, and it can just as easily occur in relation to social inferences: too much sensitivity can be as bad as too little.

Monitoring and interpreting other people's gaze leads naturally to interpretations of their intentions, for example when a person looks at something and thereby indicates an interest in it. As in the case of gaze-monitoring, autistics are symptomatically poor at this basic skill, and often misunderstand simple situations as a result. Autistic people often fail to pick up cues directed at them in otherwise obvious and unmistakable ways, and are poor at interpreting facial expressions, body language or judging the implications of others' statements and behaviour. Where language is concerned, this is because human beings normally do not use words completely literally, and expect communications to be relevant to the speaker, their state of mind, knowledge and beliefs. Consequently, people with ASD tend to use language more literally than normal and to misinterpret meanings which rely on understanding an expression relative to another person's intention or point of view. For example, a young autistic woman is said to have actually painted the flowers at an art class rather than make a painting of them, and another became alarmed when told that she would be 'sleeping on the train' rather than in a bed inside the train. Families with autistic children who have been taught to answer the telephone sometimes report that the child will reply to the enquiry of a caller 'Is so-and-so in?' with a simple 'Yes!' but then replace the receiver, evidently thinking that a correct factual response is all that is required in such a situation (Houston and Frith, 2000, p. 113). Another common example is provided in this reminiscence from an autistic's autobiography: 'During the third grade I remember a classmate telling me that he felt like a pizza. I couldn't figure out what made him feel like a pizza. Eventually I realized he meant that he felt like eating a pizza' (Shore, 2001, p. 53). Indeed, all failures to understand or respond to others' feelings and expressions, verbal or otherwise, are failures to correctly interpret intention, at least if we assume that the basic intention of any expressive communication is to be correctly understood. To this extent, mentalistic deficits in autistics' language and conversation skills could be seen as symptomatic of a fundamental shortcoming where interpretation of intention is concerned.

However, the exact opposite is found in psychotics, where a striking over-interpretation of intention is found. This can take two forms, depending on whether the intention detected is positive or negative. A schizophrenic patient illustrates both in his recollection that 'I was hardly out of the house when somebody prowled round me, stared at me and tried to put a cyclist in my way. A few steps on, a schoolgirl smiled at me encouragingly . . .' (Jaspers, 1962, p. 101). Positive over-interpretation of others' intentions underlies erotomania, otherwise known as 'de Clérambault's syndrome' or 'erotomanic type delusional disorder' (de Clérambault, 1942). The latter term describes how the subject delusionally believes that others are infatuated or are in love with them, and most sufferers are female (American Psychiatric Association, 2000, pp. 324–5). Nevertheless, negative overvaluation of intention is more common, particularly in men, and is seen in the delusions of persecution which are found in so many paranoid psychotics (sometimes along with erotomania).

Yet another autistic deficit is found in shared attention mechanism. Autistic people typically do not become involved in group conversations or activities, because they usually fail to understand the element of collective psychological activity that is inevitably involved (Leekam and Moore, 2001). Once again, paranoiacs are characteristically even more mentalistic and are given to imagining not mere telepathic communication but concerted group activity often expressed as conspiracies against them. Paranoid delusions of conspiracy can be seen as fantastic elaborations of the shared-attention mechanism that enables normal people to understand what goes on in groups, meetings and social gatherings of all kinds. Although autistics find appreciating what goes on in a group difficult, and often give it little serious thought or attention, paranoid psychotics pay far too much attention to groups, and tend to see conspiracies everywhere and imagine everyone intriguing behind their backs: a tendency that can easily reinforce feelings of persecution to produce severe and highly elaborated delusions.

By contrast, and thanks to their deficits in mentalism, people with autistic tendencies not only fail to understand mental terminology in full but are often remarkably immune to its intended effects, so that other people perceive them to be callous, self-centred and insensitive to the wishes and needs of other people. Indeed, far from hearing imagined voices as psychotics symptomatically do, a common complaint about autistics is that they often seem not to listen to real ones, with the result that they are often mistakenly thought to be deaf. According to one: 'Autism makes me hear other people's words but be unable to know what the words mean. Or autism lets me speak my own words without knowing what I am saying or even thinking' (Williams, 1994, p. 207).

Another manifestation of this tendency to mentalise to excess is what has been called 'magical ideation'. The Magical Ideation Scale developed at the University of Wisconsin presents a questionnaire asking the respondent to agree or disagree with a list of statements. These range from what you might call commonplace superstition (such as, 'Horoscopes are right too often for it to be a coincidence') to some with a distinctly delusional tone, themselves ranging from the erotomanic ('I sometimes have the passing thought that strangers are in love with me') to the more conventionally paranoid ('I have sometimes sensed an evil presence around me'). Also included are many sentiments endorsed by conventional religions ('I have wondered whether the spirits of the dead can influence the living'), belief in the paranormal ('I think I could learn to read other people's minds if I wanted to') or even extra-terrestrial life ('The government refuses to tell us the truth about flying saucers') (Eckblad and Chapman, 1983). Students who scored high on the scale also showed more psychotic symptoms than students with lower scores did, and in a study of psychiatric patients those with schizophrenia had a higher magical ideation score than non-schizophrenic patients or normal controls. A longitudinal study of 7800 students revealed that students who scored high on magical ideation in college showed more symptoms of schizotypy and other schizophrenia-related disorders a decade later, and reported more psychotic experiences than others. Ten years later, the number of people who had developed some form of psychosis was significantly greater in the group that had scored high on magical ideation (Chapman et al., 1994).

These findings make complete sense if you consider the fact that mentalistic thinking, although perfectly true and applicable in its own, proper psychological setting, inevitably becomes delusional if substituted for mechanistic, objective cognition of the physical world. However, intention can even more easily be extended beyond its proper, purely mental domain. Another of the statements from the Magical Ideation Questionnaire reads, 'I have felt that I might cause something to happen just by thinking about it too much.' An example is found in one famous paranoid psychotic's claim that 'the weather is now to a certain extent dependent on *my* actions and thoughts; as soon as I indulge in thinking nothing, or in other words stop an activity which proves the existence of the human mind such as playing chess in the garden, the wind arises at once'. The same individual concluded that *'everything that happens is in reference to me'* (Schreber, 2000, pp. 22, 233, emphasis in original). Other schizophrenics claim that 'When my eyes are bright blue, the sky gets blue' or that 'all the clocks of the world feel my pulse', while another recalls that 'I really thought the world was turning around me . . . I referred everything to myself as if it were made for me' (Jaspers, 1962, pp. 296, 101–2).

Such 'delusions of reference', as they are often called, can be seen as an exaggeration of the normal belief in yourself as the agent responsible for your own intentions. They result from an extension of the fundamental mentalistic sense of your own responsibility for your conscious acts outwards onto acts and events which in reality cannot be caused by your own mind, intention or behaviour. Indeed, such delusions of reference sometimes border on true megalomania, with schizophrenics claiming that 'everything from the largest to the smallest is contained in me' (Sass, 1992). Authorities comment that, 'The self is identified with the All. The patient is not just someone else (Christ, Napoleon, etc.) but simply the All. His own life is experienced as the life of the whole world, his strength is world-sustaining and world-vitalising' (Jaspers, 1962, p. 296, quoting Hilfiker).

Autistics, by contrast, often exhibit a diminished sense of self. For example, autistic children typically make pronoun-reversal errors, referring to themselves as 'you' and their mothers as 'I' or 'me'. However, language-impaired controls, such as sufferers from Down syndrome, do not make comparable errors, despite their poor speech competence (Baron-Cohen, 1989). Again, three autistic young men with normal IQ but varying degrees of mentalistic impairment were asked to record their thoughts at particular but unpredictable moments during a normal day (cued by a special device they carried with them). What struck the authors of this study about the boys' reports was that all three described inner experience which was literal and visual, and appeared to lack verbal or other imagery. There was little or nothing in the way of introspective commentary on the events described that reflected the subjects' own reactions. Such findings appear to be in line with other studies which suggest that when children are able to report their own mental states they are also able to report the psychological states of others, but that when they cannot report and understand the mental states of others, they do not report those states in themselves (Frith and Happé, 1999). In other words, 'It is impossible to build up a sense of oneself without a good theory of other people's minds' (Fitzgerald, 2005, p. 84).

You could sum up these findings by saying that, whereas ASD is characterised by deficits in mentalism (hypo-mentalism) psychotics represent the exact opposite and are symptomatically hyper-mentalistic. Furthermore, the concepts of hypo- and hyper-mentalism readily explain one last item: age of onset. Typically, this is early childhood for autism but late adolescence or adulthood for schizophrenia: a difference which up until now has lacked an obvious explanation. But the fact that you have to develop normal mentalistic skills before you can overdevelop them to the point of psychosis readily explains why the mentalistic deficits of autism are apparent in childhood and why the hyper-mentalism of psychosis can only become fully apparent much later (see Table 9.1 and Box 9.1).

Table 9.1. *Diametrically different characteristics of autism and psychosis.*

Autism/Asperger's syndrome	*Psychosis/Paranoid schizophrenia*
gaze-monitoring deficits	delusions of being watched/spied on
apparent deafness/insensitivity to voices	hallucination of and hyper-sensitivity to voices
shared-attention deficits	delusions of conspiracy
intentionality deficits	erotomania/delusions of persecution
theory of mind deficits	magical ideation/delusions of reference
deficit in sense of self/personal agency	megalomania/delusions of grandeur
infantile onset	adult onset

BOX 9.1.   WHAT ABOUT PSYCHOTHERAPY?

Some success can be obtained with autistic children by teaching them to mind-read, in other words to compensate for their mind-blindness by learning explicit mentalistic skills. If it is indeed true that psychotics are the exact opposite of this, and implicitly over-mentalise where autistics under-mentalise, it follows that it may be worth trying the exact opposite of psychoanalysis: to teach psychotics the contrary skills to those prescribed for autistics. There is evidence that even in normal individuals who have suffered bereavement, avoidance of mentalising their loss reduced grief symptoms after 14 months, and most certainly did not increase them, as conventional Freudian wisdom would have suggested. Avoiding unpleasant thoughts and emotions, in other words, may not be such a bad thing after all (Bonanno *et al.*, 1990). Indeed, according to a comparatively recent summary of the literature, despite assertions that lack of observable grief is pathological and frequent endorsement among clinicians of the existence of so-called delayed grief reactions, there is little evidence that expression of emotions has any beneficial effect following bereavement. On the contrary, there is evidence that it may impede successful coping (Seery *et al.*, 2008, p. 658).

The same could apply to other kinds of traumatic experience. In an online survey of a large national sample of Americans, researchers tested people's responses to the terrorist attacks of the 11th of September 2001, beginning immediately after the event and continuing for the following two years. The study did not support the common assumption that choosing not to express one's thoughts and feelings in the immediate aftermath of a collective trauma is harmful and indicative of vulnerability to future negative consequences. Instead, the opposite pattern emerged. The researchers found that people who chose not to express their feelings about the event had fewer negative physical and mental health symptoms than people who did choose to do so. Indeed, when the researchers tested the length of the responses of those who chose to express their thoughts and feelings they found a similar pattern: those who did had worse mental and physical health than those who expressed less, and no other factor could explain the effect. They conclude that 'Contrary to common assumption, this study demonstrates that individuals who choose not to express their thoughts and feelings in the immediate aftermath of a collective trauma are capable of coping successfully and in fact are more likely to do so than individuals who do express' (Seery *et al.*, 2008, p. 666).

Findings like these suggest that an obvious therapeutic strategy would be to try to induce hyper-mentalising psychotics to be less mentalistic – or more autistic, if you like – and consciously to try to avoid reading too much into each and every thing. Paranoid schizophrenics might be encouraged to reduce their sensitivity to gaze or to avoid over-interpreting other people's words, expressions and behaviour; to avoid ruminating about other people's intentions; to distrust magical and megalomaniac thinking, and so on. Indeed, some benefit may even be gained from computerised psychotherapy for such cases. Computer-based training helps schizophrenics when it involves mechanistic cognitive skills found in autism, such as pitch-discrimination (which is often perfect in autistics) (Fisher *et al.*, in press); and a review of the literature carried out in 2001 concluded that people receiving computer-aided treatments had as good or better outcomes as those in control groups treated by human psychotherapists alone (Jacobs *et al.*, 2001). One reason could have been that there is little danger that a computer could hyper-mentalise in the way in which human psychotherapists all too easily can. At the very least, interacting with a machine mind could be a salutary experience for people on the psychotic spectrum because it would be a constant reminder of the mechanistic aspect of reality that they so readily discount, and may even help their own thinking style to become more 'autistic' and thereby compensate for their hyper-mentalistic tendency.

Of course, a very similar strategy is already used in Cognitive Behavioural Therapy (CBT), and many psychotherapists using CBT or similar methods already routinely follow something like this approach – indeed, some patients discover it for themselves. But psychoanalysis has one huge advantage that CBT lacks, and that is the provocative persuasiveness of its seemingly profound view of the mind and of mental development. Modern therapies like CBT seem ad hoc and eclectic by comparison, and lacking in a unified theoretical foundation. But should the imprinted brain theory be fully, or even partially, vindicated by the facts, things would be very different, and CBT could be rebuilt on a theory with even deeper foundations and much greater credibility than psychoanalysis.

THE IMPRINTED BRAIN

How can the remarkable antithetical pattern set out in Table 9.1 be explained? According to the so-called imprinted brain theory, the paradoxes can be explained in terms of the expression of genes, and not simply their inheritance. 'Imprinted genes' are those which are only expressed when they are inherited from one parent rather than the other. The classic example is *IGF2*, a growth factor gene only normally expressed when inherited from the father, but silent when inherited from the mother. According to the most widely accepted theory, genes like *IGF2* are silenced by mammalian mothers because only the mother has to pay the costs associated with gestating and giving birth to a large offspring. The father, on the other hand, gets all the benefit of larger offspring, but pays none of the costs. Therefore, his copy is activated. If the mother's *IGF2* gene is also expressed, Beckwith-Wiedemann syndrome results. Beckwith-Wiedemann babies are one-and-a-half times normal birth weight and show excessive growth during adolescence along with other overgrowth symptoms, such as tumours. Normally, the mother's copy of the *IGF2* gene is silenced, or imprinted. But if both copies of this gene are silenced, the result is the opposite: the pre- and post-natal growth retardation of Silver-Russell syndrome.

Paternally active genes favour growth much more than maternally active ones and are particularly strongly expressed in the placenta, an organ primarily designed to extract resources from the mother. Indeed, an abnormal conceptus with a double set of paternal genes and without any genes whatsoever from the mother results in a massive proliferation of the placenta without any associated foetus (Newton, 2001). The human placenta is the most invasive of all mammalian placentas, and in some cases can be so invasive that it perforates the uterus, killing the mother. Cells originating in the placenta aggressively widen the mother's arteries that feed it by breaking down their walls and weakening them, so that they sag and distend, thereby increasing blood supply to the cavities that the placenta excavates to receive it. Paternally active genes in the foetus/placenta also drive up the mother's blood pressure and blood-sugar levels to the benefit of the foetus (Haig, 1999).

Conflict between maternal and paternal genes can continue after birth. Prader-Willi syndrome affects about 1 in 15 000 births, and is caused by the loss or silencing of genes inherited from the father on chromosome 15 through receiving both copies of this chromosome from the mother, or losing part of the paternal copy (Nicholls, Saitoh and Horsthemke, 1998). Symptoms listed include lack of appetite, poor suckling ability, a weak cry, inactivity and sleepiness, high pain threshold and reduced tendency to vomit (Franke, Kerns and Giacalone, 1995). By contrast to Prader-Willi, in its sister disorder, Angelman syndrome, only the paternal chromosome 15 is present in its entirety, and the critical maternal genes involved in Prader-Willi syndrome are missing (Nicholls, Saitoh and Horsthemke, 1998). Symptoms include prolonged suckling, hyperactivity and frequent waking.

Although both Prader-Willi and Angelman children are retarded, Angelman retardation is usually much more severe, and speech is absent. Whereas Prader-Willi patients have a high pain threshold (and often damage themselves as a result), Angelman patients have a low pleasure threshold to the extent that frequent paroxysms of laughter are listed as a major diagnostic feature and the condition is sometimes known as 'Happy Puppet Syndrome' (Angelman, 1965). Again, whereas Prader-Willi children with two copies of their mother's chromosome 15 are always diagnosed as psychotic, as I pointed out at the beginning, Angelman cases are much more likely to be diagnosed as autistic in their behaviour (Cook *et al.*, 1997). Indeed, there is a striking contrast where appetite is concerned: Prader-Willi children, although poor sucklers at first, become indiscriminate and uncontrollable foragers for food, and obese as a result (Haig and Wharton, 2003) (see Table 9.2).

You could see the prolonged suckling, hyperactivity and frequent waking of Angelman syndrome as embodying every mother's worst fear, and not coincidentally

Table 9.2. *Diametrically different symptoms of Angelman and Prader-Willi syndromes.*

Angelman syndrome	Prader-Willi syndrome
prolonged suckling	poor suckling
frequent crying	weak crying
hyperactive/sleepless	inactive/sleepy
low pleasure threshold	high pain threshold
tendency to autism	tendency to psychosis

associated with paternally expressed genes. The suppression of paternal and the enhancement of maternal genes in Prader-Willi children, on the other hand, could be seen as explaining why, despite being seriously retarded, these children make much less demand on the mother thanks to their lethargy, sleepiness, weak cry and poor suckling. Indeed, even the indiscriminate food foraging and obesity of older Prader-Willi children can be seen to conform to this interpretation. This is because, when these traits evolved in primal hunter-gather pre-history, they would have made children more independent of the mother's resources (principally breastmilk) and more likely to survive periods of prolonged neglect by her thanks to their fat reserves (Haig and Wharton, 2003).

We saw earlier that many of the most striking symptoms of psychotic illnesses like paranoid schizophrenia could be seen as the exact opposite of those found in autism. The clear implication is that, rather than being totally unconnected, ASD and psychosis now begin to look as if they could represent poles of a continuum of mentalism stretching from the extreme hypo-mentalism of autism to the bizarre hyper-mentalism of psychotics. But now we can begin to see a further remarkable similarity: this is that this pattern of diametrically opposed extremes of pathology can also be seen in Prader-Willi and Angelman syndromes. Furthermore, the fact that some Angelman cases are diagnosed autistic and some Prader-Willi ones psychotic suggests that a similar pattern of oppositely expressed parentally active genes may underlie autism and psychosis as a whole. However, because a large number of genes on many different chromosomes appear to be involved, and because gene expression related to parent of origin can vary from gene to gene and tissue to tissue in the same individual, the range of symptoms in autism and psychosis can be expected to be much greater than in Prader-Willi and Angelman syndromes, explaining why the antithetical features listed in Table 9.1, which is by no means exhaustive, are usually only found in some cases. Again, autism is common in Rett, Turner's and Fragile X syndromes, in tuberous sclerosis and more rarely in numerous other conditions (Aitken, 2008). Autistic disorders can also be environmentally induced by pre-natal thalidomide, or viral infection, and by ethanol or valproic acid poisoning in pregnancy. Valproic acid (sodium valproate) is an anticonvulsant and mood-stabilising drug which affects gene expression and when administered to pregnant mice or rats in early foetal development induces an equivalent of autism in these animals (Crespi, Summers and Dorus, 2009). Indeed, all of these factors could mediate genetic effects within the individuals concerned via the same kind of genomic imprinting that also accounts for Angelman and Prader-Willi syndromes.

Mammals as a whole show a notable sex difference in social behaviour to which human beings are no exception. In general, females have been found to be more sociable, cooperative and nurturing than males – particularly among primates (Keverne, 1992). This may explain why the mother's genes appear to promote mentalism in human beings and why the father's seem to motivate more self-interested behaviour. From an evolutionary point of view, every one of a mother's offspring carries an equal complement of her genes (half of them). But uncertainty of paternity, the bane of mammals thanks to internal, unseen fertilisation, means that the genes of a father have no necessary reason to find themselves in any of a woman's other children:

Mother's baby. Father's? Maybe! The result is that, from an evolutionary and genetic point of view, paternally active genes do not have the same self-interest in family cohesion and social cooperation that the mother's characteristically do. Why should the father's encourage his offspring to cooperate with those of the mother's other mates (Haig, 1997)?

According to this way of looking at things, development can be pushed to either extreme by any factors that affect gene expression either before or after birth. Where purely genetic factors are concerned, the theory proposes that increased expression of paternal genes like *IGF2* will predispose to autism – and expression of that gene is now known to be enhanced in individuals with ASD (Badcock and Crespi, 2006). This will result in the features listed in Figure 9.1: higher birth weight, an increased vulnerability to cancer (which is another expression of overgrowth) and a larger brain in childhood with more white matter (Crespi and Badcock, 2008). Further-more, increased nutrition would mimic the effect of genes like *IGF2* and predispose to growth, perhaps explaining part of the recent exponential increase in milder ASDs such as Asperger's syndrome. Indeed, the fact that birth weights of newborn babies in Vienna rose an unprecedented amount during the 1920s perhaps partly explains why Asperger was to discover the autistic syndrome named after him during the next couple of decades (Badcock, 2009). And because all fathers are male the new theory can also be reconciled with the extreme male brain theory of autism, which persuasively argues that ASDs can often be linked to increased testosterone exposure *in utero* and to the more lateralised brain characteristic of males (Crespi and Badcock, 2008).

Significantly then, what we might symmetrically term 'psychotic spectrum dis-orders' (PSDs), and schizophrenia, in particular, are associated with the features listed on the other side of the diagram: low birth weight, a reduced vulnerability to

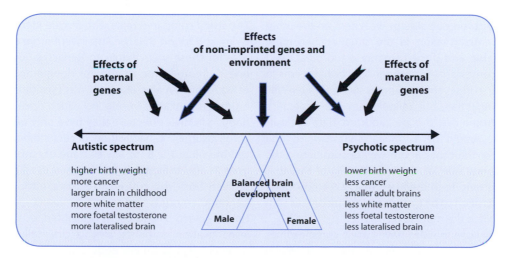

Figure 9.1. *The imprinted brain theory.*

Source: Redrawn and modified from Crespi, B. and Badcock, C. (2008). "Psychosis and autism as diametrical disorders of the social brain." *Behavioral and Brain Sciences, 31*, 241–320.

cancer (despite schizophrenics smoking much more!) and smaller adult brains with less white matter. Correspondingly, just as increased nutrition in pregnancy and/or early life may mimic paternally active genes like *IGF2* to predispose to ASD, the contrary conditions (starvation during pregnancy and/or early life) could be predicted to increase the risk of PSD, as we saw at the beginning that they indeed do, at least in the case of schizophrenia. And because all mothers are female, enhanced expression of maternal genes also goes with reduced foetal testosterone and the less lateralised brain typical of women. Indeed, the fact that mammalian females have two X sex chromosomes (XX) by contrast to the male's one (XY) means that X chromosome gene expression is also implicated. In cases where an extra X chromosome is present, X trisomy (XXX) and Klinefelter syndrome (XXY), the presence of the additional X results in brain features similar to those found in schizophrenia, along with a notably increased vulnerability to psychosis, just as the theory would predict (Badcock, 2009; Crespi and Badcock, 2008; Crespi, Summers and Dorus, 2009; see also Box 9.2).

BOX 9.2.   IS ASPERGER'S SYNDROME A RESULT OF A GENETIC TUG-OF-WAR?

Figure 9.1 suggests that a person's place on the autism–psychosis spectrum is the outcome of a conflict between maternal and paternal genes. However, it is important to understand that such conflicts are like a tug-of-war. The situation is stable if both sides are evenly matched, but strength on one side or weakness on the other can equally result in the situation becoming unstable, and if the disparity is too great, send the contestants sprawling! This is what seems to happen in severe syndromes such as Prader-Willi or Angelman, but milder ones like Asperger's syndrome can also be expected. Here the outcome would be a smaller shift towards one side or the other, and if we are considering the mother's side of the genetic tug-of-war, it is important to remember that X chromosome genes need to be included in the picture, as suggested in the main text.

Because females have two X chromosomes but males only one, selection will act on female-benefiting X genes twice as often as it will on

male-benefiting ones (Badcock, 2009, pp. 179–83). Verbal IQ is known to be X-linked, and a study of identical female twins revealed that pro-social behaviour, peer problems, and verbal ability – all factors critical to diagnosis of Asperger's syndrome – were also X-linked (Loat *et al.*, 2004). The study compared male with female identical twins, and found that the latter were more variable for these traits thanks to X-inactivation of one X chromosome to counter double-dosing of X genes in females (also known as 'Lyonization': a process similar to imprinting which does not happen in males because they have only one X chromosome). X-inactivation occurs randomly cell-by-cell at the 8- to 16-cell stage of embryogenesis and the outcome is retained in all cells derived from the critical precursors. Although genomic imprints are normally re-set every time a sperm or egg cell is generated, existing X-inactivation imprints may accidentally be retained in a woman's eggs cells (Green and Keverne, 2000), suggesting that maternally inactivated X genes may play a role in predisposing males to mild forms of autism such as Asperger's syndrome thanks to the one and only X chromosome they get coming from their mother. This is predicted by the theory to the extent that a failure by the mother's genes in the tug-of-war with the father's represents a victory for his side of the genetic conflict.

The same could apply to females because it is now known that X-inactivation can become highly skewed in some cases, with 35% of women having >70:30 skews in either direction, and 7% with extreme skews >90:10 (Loat *et al.*, 2008). If the skew favoured maternal X genes with residual maternal imprints affecting cognitive and social skills critical to Asperger's syndrome in a girl, and if those genes happened to be disproportionately expressed in the critical parts of the brain as they appear to be, then it may explain why some female cases of Asperger's syndrome are found. But of course, it would also explain even more easily why male cases seem greatly to outnumber them (by five to 25 times, according to different authorities).

Another counter-intuitive prediction of the theory is that if all this is true, then the so-called autism epidemic should go with a parallel decline in psychosis. At the very least, improving living conditions should make maternal starvation during pregnancy much less likely, and this alone ought to reduce the incidence of schizophrenia, albeit perhaps only marginally, and any other environmental or social factor should work the same way – especially if those factors are influential in increasing the incidence of ASD. Here it may be significant to note that a decline in schizophrenia has indeed been reported in many Western countries. Bleuler himself noticed that schizophrenia was becoming milder during the twentieth century, and other authorities were asking, 'Where have all the catatonics gone?' First-admission rates for schizophrenia show a considerable decrease in England beginning in about 1960, and those for Scotland a decline of 57%, with falls of 37% also reported in Denmark and New Zealand, and 9% in Australia (Der, Gupta and Murray, 1990). A study in Canada showed a 42% decrease in the number of first-admission schizophrenia cases over 20 years, and the same study found that annual inpatient prevalence rates decreased by 52% between 1986 and 1996, with no corresponding change in outpatient rates, regardless of sex (Woogh, 2001). Admittedly, part of this must be accounted for by the fact that ASD was often mistaken for schizophrenia in the past – perhaps particularly childhood-onset schizophrenia. But the decrease in adolescent and adult-onset schizophrenia seems too large to be accounted for by simply supposing that what was once called a psychosis is now more likely to be diagnosed as a form of autism. Indeed, the fact that any reduction at all has been noticed seems significant, and is certainly predicted by the theory outlined here.

Surprising as it may seem, the new theory can even encompass the finding that infectious agents can sometimes be implicated in causing schizophrenia. People infected with the protozoan parasite *Toxoplasma gondii* are three times more likely to suffer from schizophrenia than those not infected, and so too are cat-owners

(Webster *et al.*, 2006). The significance of the latter may lie in the fact that the parasite can only complete the reproductive phase of its life cycle inside a cat. It achieves this by causing its principal carriers, rats and mice, to lose their fear of cats, and so be much more likely to be eaten by one. Inside the rodent's brain, the parasite attacks the amygdalas, which play the same role in triggering fear reactions that they do in humans. But when infected rats are treated with antipsychotic drugs like those given to human schizophrenics the rats' fear of felines returns. Men with *Toxoplasma* infection tend to be more reckless than normal, and infected people of both sexes are almost three times more likely to be involved in car accidents, and have measurably slowed reaction times (Ginsburg, 2004; Randerson, 2002). In mice, only paternal genes are expressed in the amygdalas and there is good evidence suggesting that the same is true in humans. There is also evidence that reduced activity of the amygdalas may represent a general feature of schizophrenia-like conditions (Taylor *et al.*, 2007). This finding suggests the intriguing possibility that an explanation may lie in the parasite suppressing paternally controlled brain systems like the amygdalas to produce an overall preponderance of maternal brain function, which according to the new theory is the fundamental basis of psychosis in general and of schizophrenia in particular. *T. gondii*, in other words, could be another of those environmental effects portrayed in the figure, but one pushing development pathologically towards the psychotic end of the spectrum by sabotaging brain systems built by paternal genes. Indeed, given its known affinity for the limbic system, much the same might be said for the other suspected infectious cause of schizophrenia: *Cytomegalovirus* (Yolken and Torrey, 2008).

Finally, what of normal development? The implication is clear and is graphically represented in Figure 9.1: so-called normality represents a more-or-less balanced expression of genes and environmental developmental influences. However, the fact that all fathers are male and all mothers are female implies that the norms for the sexes are likely to be slightly offset, as Figure 9.1 suggests. This would fit with the finding that ASD afflicts more males than females and that men typically do worse on tests of mentalistic competence than do women. Women, on the other hand, would be symmetrically offset to the more mentalistic side of the spectrum, and this may explain why rates of incidence of schizophrenia among family members of women with the disorder are higher than those among family members of men with schizophrenia. And although there is a slightly higher incidence of schizophrenia overall in men, erotomania appears to be a predominantly female pathology, with women also suffering more paranoid delusions and hallucinations than men do, particularly in late-onset cases (see Figure 9.1).

The striking symmetry of Figure 9.1 suggests that if there are autistic savants with outstanding skills in mechanistic aspects of cognition, there ought also to be psychotic ones with the opposite, mentalistic skills. However, the very same excellence in mentalism would make such psychotic savants much less noticeable than their autistic counterparts, whose deficits immediately identify them as odd, socially isolated and eccentric. Psychotic savants, by contrast, can be expected to be deeply embedded in successful social networks and found at the centre of

Table 9.3. *Contrasting characteristics of mentalistic and mechanistic cognition.*

Mentalistic cognition	Mechanistic cognition
psychological interaction with self and others	physical interaction with nature and objects
uses social, psychological and political skills	uses mechanical, spatial and engineering skills
deficits in autism, augmented in women	accentuated in autism, augmented in men
voluntaristic, subjective, particularistic	deterministic, objective, universal
abstract, general, ambivalent	concrete, specific, single-minded
verbal, metaphoric, conformist	visual, literal, eccentric
top-down, holistic, centrally coherent	bottom-up, reductionistic, field-independent
epitomised in literature, politics and religion	epitomised in science, engineering and technology
'pseudo-science': astrology, alchemy, creationism	'hard science': astronomy, chemistry, Darwinism
nurtured: culturally and personally determined	natural: factually and genetically determined
belief-based therapies: placebos, faith-healing, psychotherapy etc.	physical effect-based therapies: drugs, surgery, physiotherapy, etc.

excellence in such things as religious and ideological evangelism, literary and theatrical culture, litigation and the law, hypnosis, faith-healing and psychotherapy, fashion and advertising, politics, public-relations and the media and commerce, confidence-trickery and fraud of all kinds (Badcock, 2009). Table 9.3 gives some idea of the inverted symmetry to be found between mentalistic and mechanistic cognition.

The model appears to rule out anyone suffering from an ASD and a PSD simultaneously, and such comorbidity does appear to be rare – but is not unknown. However, there are cases of individuals diagnosed with bipolar disorder who also show unmistakable signs of ASD during their non-manic phases. Indeed, there is one who suffers from severe gaze-aversion, autistic deficits in a sense of self and social anxiety most of the time, but who becomes comfortable with other people during manic episodes when his sense of self hypertrophies into megalomania with the feeling that he is the returned Jesus Christ (Badcock, 2009). Furthermore, there is evidence of both ASD and PSD in Newton and Beethoven, and incontrovertibly so in the Nobel-prize winning mathematician John Nash. Here the theory predicts that the ASD must come first (typically in childhood) and leave a permanent savant-like basis later built on by hyper-mentalistic tendencies to produce an unusually broadened and dynamically balanced cognitive configuration: that of true genius (Badcock, 2009; see also Box 9.3).

BOX 9.3.   FURTHER FINDINGS RELATING TO THE THEORY

Apart from those cited in the main text, a number of other facts and findings fit the new theory, often with surprising precision and unexpected logic. Among them are the following:

- Drugs which act as antagonists to cell-surface receptors critically involved in neurotransmission (the mGlur5 glutamate receptor and the nicotinic cholinergic CHRNA7 receptor) have been proposed as treatments for ASD. Other drugs are also being experimented with as agonists to these receptors in the treatment of schizophrenia (in other words, they enhance the same receptors in treating psychosis which are blocked in treating autism). If findings like these are confirmed, the symmetry between ASD and PSD proposed here would be shown to reach right down to the level of cell chemistry and could be exploited in pharmacology (Crespi, 2009a).

- FMR1 is a gene whose loss of function in humans is associated with Fragile X syndrome, itself one of the most common causes of ASD. FMR1-knockout mice mimic fragile X symptoms and have seizures in response to sound. Twenty-five to thirty per cent of autistics have seizures, and 50–70% noisy brain activity, so to this extent you could say that these mice mimic autism in man. RGS4 is a gene whose reduced effect is implicated in causing schizophrenia, but surprisingly FMR1/RGS4-double-knockout mice are cured of seizures (effectively by making them more 'schizophrenic'). Seizures induced by electric shock or insulin were found to be an effective therapy for schizophrenia and most antipsychotics in current use, including Clozapine, tend to lower the threshold for seizures to occur. Why should inducing seizure help psychotics, but reducing them benefit autistics? Could the answer be the inverted symmetry that the imprinted brain theory proposes between ASD and PSD (Crespi, 2009b)?

- Pre-frontal lobotomy/leucotomy (PFL) was widely used from the 1930s to the 1950s as surgery for psychotic illnesses. Indeed, Antonio Moniz won the Nobel Prize for medicine with it in 1949, and Freeman and Watts popularised it in the United States with their ice-pick method (which may explain much of the disrepute into which the procedure fell later). Today, the medial pre-frontal cortex is known to be active in relation to mentalism (especially thinking about interacting with others) but is hyperactive in schizophrenics. This is the very part of the brain that was disconnected or destroyed by PFL, perhaps explaining any real effect it had.

- Recent studies show that the mother's, but not necessarily their psychotic child's, HLA (human leukocyte antigen) genes are implicated in schizophrenia. HLA genes mediate immune responses to pathogens and other non-self tissues, as well as orchestrating aspects of neurodevelopment and neurological function. As such, they are exactly the kind of maternal genes that the theory predicts should play a role in causing psychosis (Crespi, 2009c).

IMPLICATIONS FOR EVOLUTIONARY PSYCHOLOGY

An article in the *New York Times* remarked that the new idea outlined here 'provides psychiatry with perhaps its grandest working theory since Freud, and one that is founded in work at the forefront of science' (Carey, 2008). But clearly, the imprinted brain theory also has some major implications for evolutionary psychology. First of all, and as I suggested in the opening section of this chapter, the theory builds on existing research to establish a credible evolutionary basis, not simply for illnesses like autism and schizophrenia but for human cognition in general. As I showed, the genes underlying autism appear to be linked to what I called mechanistic cognition, and those implicated in schizophrenia with mentalism. I also suggested that these were the two fundamental modes of human cognition: one adapted to the physical, non-human world of objective reality, the other to the phenomenological, human world of subjective experience. Excesses and/or deficits in one or the other underlie ASD and PSD, as I argued in the second section, with the clear implication that normality rests on a balance of both: not so much mentalism as to make you paranoid but enough to make you a competent player in the game of social interaction.

What I did not mention is that, as the symmetry of the theory may lead you to expect, there is good evidence of mechanistic deficits in hyper-mentalising psychotics. Indeed, even the enhanced visual acuity of autistics that I mentioned earlier finds a striking antithesis here. Comparable studies of the vision of psychotics reveals that they have characteristic deficits in vision that symmetrically balance the enhancements found in autism (Viertiö *et al.*, 2007). Some psychotic patients certainly report that they have deficits in 'sensory discrimination', along with 'poor neuromuscular coordination' and 'sensorimotor activity' thanks to domination by 'central-symbolic, particularly verbal activity' serving the 'ideological level', which 'is the most highly developed' in schizophrenics (Lang, 1940). Another psychotic remarks that 'I'd like a pack of cards with four suits – morals, phantasy, reality – I'd like to get rid of the reality suit' (Sass, 1992, p. 518). According to one psychiatric authority, 'the mentally sane person . . . is subjectively certain and not to be corrected when speaking about her own mental states', that is when speaking mentalistically. However, the 'patient with delusions differs . . . in so far as he speaks with subjective certainty and incorrigibly about facts which do not lie within the scope of his mentality: things, events, other persons, in short, the external world'. Psychotic delusions can, therefore, be defined as '*statements about external reality which are uttered like statements about a mental state, i.e., with subjective certainty and incorrigible by others*' (Spitzer, 1990, p. 391, emphasis added).

In other words, delusional thinking is hyper-mentalistic in the sense of not simply going beyond normal mentalism but encroaching on non-mental, mechanistic reality. Schizophrenics have been found to have impaired visuospatial and maths abilities relative to their verbal skills, and to be especially poor at solving practical and commonsensical problems (Cutting and Murphy, 1988). Again, one study found that carriers of a genetic tendency to psychosis in their near relatives showed impairments in verbal memory and in visual and spatial abilities. A separate study concluded that a relative superiority of verbal to spatial skills – or what I would call mentalistic to mechanistic cognition – represents a cognitive asymmetry characteristic of schizophrenia (Kravariti *et al.*, 2006; Toulopoulou *et al.*, 2006). Indeed, even depression has been linked to deficits in spatial memory to the extent that depressed patients have been found to perform significantly less well than healthy controls in video games demanding good spatial recall (*New Scientist*, 2007).

This insight has important implications for normality too, or at least what passes for it in modern societies. First, it suggests that the real problem with what Richard Dawkins calls in the title of his book *The God Delusion* is not religion as such, but hyper-mentalism. As I pointed out earlier, magical ideation is a prime measure of psychotic thinking, and hyper-mentalism is institutionalised in magic, religion and superstition in all human cultures. This in turn means that, whatever its level of social acceptability, religion and superstition should not be seen as evolved adaptations of the human mind but as socially sanctioned pathologies comparable to the delusions of psychotics. No wonder Darwinists have had such problems with them! The problem – if this approach is correct – is identical to that of explaining mental illness in general. But why should delusions seem adaptive merely because they are shared by many, and why should maladaptive behaviour be regarded as normal merely because it has reached pandemic levels of prevalence in the past?

The clear implication of the theory outlined here is that, contrary to what most have imagined up until now, human beings have not evolved a single, unitary cognitive system. On the contrary, the evidence outlined here suggests that we have evolved two parallel systems, and that contamination of one with thinking from the other is a common but major malfunction of the evolved mind (Badcock, 2002/4). In particular, the theory suggests that mentalism underwent a sudden primeval inflation when, having evolved to facilitate social interaction, it became applied to the physical, non-human world in the form of magic, religion and superstition thanks to the fact that mechanistic cognition could not at that stage of human development meet the challenge of explaining nature objectively. As we know, that development was a long time in coming and relied on cultural and technological developments like literacy, the invention of mathematics and of instruments like the telescope. But the clear and counter-intuitive implication for evolutionary psychology is that mechanistic cognition is only now beginning to achieve its implicit goal of adaptation to the physical world with the coming of modern, science- and technology-based industrial societies. In other words, far from modern society being some kind of paradox or contradiction to Darwinian evolution, it is in fact its ultimate and inevitable outcome, and only now is it beginning to appear for what it really is: the institutionalisation and embodiment of both mechanistic *and* mentalistic cognition in a much more balanced and stable configuration – at least by contrast to the psychotic hyper-mentalism which unbalanced traditional, pre-modern societies in this respect. No wonder psychosis is in decline and autism increasing! Our minds are not just adapted to the past: on the contrary, the future will be adapted to our minds, and those minds will be inevitably much more mechanistic – even autistic, if you like – than those of the past. To make the same point another way, you could say that we are still evolving towards the balanced but greatly extended cognitive configuration that constitutes the true genius of our species (Badcock, in press).

ACKNOWLEDGEMENTS

The author would like to record his thanks to Bernard Crespi and Robert Plomin.

REFERENCES

Aitken, K. J. (2008). Intersubjectivity, affective neuroscience, and the neurobiology of autistic spectrum disorders: A systematic review. *Keio Journal of Medicine, 57*, 15–36.

American Psychiatric Association. (2000). *Diagnostic and Statistical Manual of Mental Disorders* (4th edition). Washington: American Psychiatric Association.

Angelman, H. (1965). 'Puppet' children: A report on three cases. *Developmental Medicine and Child Neurology, 7*, 681–8.

Arshad, M. and Fitzgerald, M. (2004). Did Michelangelo (1475–1564) have high-functioning autism? *Journal of Medical Biography, 12*, 115–120.

Ashwin, E., Ashwin, C., Rhydderch, D. *et al.* (2008). Eagle-eyed visual acuity: An experimental investigation of enhanced perception in autism. *Biological Psychiatry, 65*, 17–21.

Ashwin, C., Ashwin, E., Tavassoli, T. *et al.* (in press). Olfactory hypersensitivity in autism spectrum conditions.

Asperger, H. (1991). Autistic psychopathy' in childhood (U. Frith, Trans.). In U. Frith (ed.), *Autism and Asperger syndrome* (pp. 37–92). Cambridge: Cambridge University Press.

Attwood, T. (2006). What is Asperger's Syndrome? In K. L. Simmons (ed.), *The official Autism 101 manual: Autism today* (pp. 6–7). Alberta, Canada: Autism Today.

Badcock, C. (2009). *The imprinted brain: How genes set the balance between autism and psychosis.* London: Jessica Kingsley.

Badcock, C. R. (2002/4). Mentalism and mechanism: The twin modes of human cognition. Pre-publication (2002) of Chapter 5 in C. Crawford and C. Salmon (eds), *Human nature and social values: Implications of evolutionary psychology for public policy* (pp. 99–116). London: Lawrence Erlbaum Associates.

Badcock, C. R. (in preparation). *The age of Asperger: Autism, society and history.*

Badcock, C. R. and Crespi, B. (2006). Imbalanced genomic imprinting in brain development: An evolutionary basis for the etiology of autism. *Journal of Evolutionary Biology, 19*, 1007–32.

Baron-Cohen, S. (1989). Are autistic children 'behaviourists'? An examination of their mental-physical and appearance-reality distinctions. *Journal of Autism and Developmental Disorders, 19*, 579–600.

Baron-Cohen, S. (1995). *Mindblindness: An essay on autism and theory of mind.* Cambridge, MA: MIT Press.

Baron-Cohen, S. (2003). *The essential difference: Men, women, and the extreme male brain.* London: Allen Lane.

Baron-Cohen, S. (2005). The assortative mating theory. *Edge, 158*. Retrieved April 6, 2005, from http://www.edge.org/documents/archive/edge158.html.

Baron-Cohen, S. and Else, L. (2001, April 14). In a different world. *New Scientist*.

Baron-Cohen, S., Wheelwright, S., Spong, A. *et al.* (2001). Are intuitive physics and intuitive psychology independent? A test with children with Asperger Syndrome. *Journal of Developmental and Learning Disorders, 5*, 47–78.

Baron-Cohen, S., Wheelwright, S., Stone, V. and Rutherford, M. (1999). A mathematician, a physicist and a computer scientist with Asperger Syndrome: Performance on folk psychology and folk physics tests. *Neurocase, 5*, 475–83.

Baron-Cohen, S., Wheelwright, S., Stott, C. *et al.* (1997). Is there a link between engineering and autism? *Autism, 1*, 101–9.

Blakemore, S.-J., Tavassoli, T., Calò, S. *et al.* (2006). Tactile sensitivity in Asperger syndrome. *Brain and Cognition, 61*, 5–13.

Bonanno, G., Holen, A., Keltner, D. and Horowitz, M. J. (1990). When avoiding unpleasant emotions might not be such a bad thing: Verbal-autonomic response dissociation and midlife conjugal bereavement. *Journal of Personality and Social Psychology, 69*, 975–89.

Bonnel, A., Mottron, L., Peretz, I. *et al.* (2003). Enhanced pitch sensitivity in individuals with autism: A signal detection analysis. *Journal of Cognitive Neuroscience, 15*, 226–35.

Carey, B. (2008, November 11). In a novel theory of mental disorders, parents' genes are in competition. *The New York Times*, D4 & 10.

Chapman, L. J., Chapman, J. P., Kwapil, T. R. *et al.* (1994). Putatively psychosis prone subjects ten years later. *Journal of Abnormal Psychology, 103*, 171–83.

Claridge, G. (1987). Schizophrenia and human individuality. In C. Blakemore and S. Greenfield (eds), *Mindwaves: Thoughts on intelligence, identity, and consciousness*. Oxford: Blackwell.

Claridge, G., Pryor, R. and Watkins, G. (1990). *Sounds from the bell jar: Ten psychotic authors*. London: Macmillan Press.

de Clérambault, G. G. (1942). Les psychoses passionelles. In J. Fretet (ed.), *Œuvre Psychiatrique* (Vol. 1, pp. 323–443). Paris: Presses Universitaires de France.

Constantino, J. N. and Todd, R. D. (2005). Intergenerational transmission of subthreshold autistic traits in the general population. *Biological Psychiatry, 57*, 655–60.

Cook, E. H. J., Lindgren, V., Leventhal, B. L. *et al.* (1997). Autism or atypical autism in maternally but not paternally derived proximal 15q duplication. *American Journal of Human Genetics, 60*, 928–34.

Crespi, B. (2009a). The dawn of Darwinian psychopharmacology. *The Evolution and Medicine Review*, http://evmedreview.com/.

Crespi, B. (2009b). Saving the autistic mouse – with schizophrenia. *The Evolution and Medicine Review*, http://evmedreview.com/.

Crespi, B. (2009c). Blaming your mother's genes. *The Evolution and Medicine Review*, http://evmedreview.com/.

Crespi, B. and Badcock, C. (2008). Psychosis and autism as diametrical disorders of the social brain. *Behavioral and Brain Sciences, 31*, 241–320.

Crespi, B., Summers, K. and Dorus, S. (2007). Adaptive evolution of genes underlying schizophrenia. *Proceedings of the Royal Society B, 274*, 2801–10.

Crespi, B. J., Summers, K. and Dorus, S. (2009). Genomic sister-disorders of neurodevelopment: An evolutionary approach. *Evolutionary Applications, 2*, 81–100.

Cutting, J. and Murphy, D. (1988). Schizophrenic thought disorder: A psychological and organic interpretation. *British Journal of Psychiatry*, *152*, 310–319.

Dawson, M., Soulières, I., Morton, A. G. and Mottron, L. (2007). The level and nature of autistic intelligence. *Psychological Science*, *18*, 657–62.

Der, G., Gupta, S. and Murray, R. M. (1990). Is schizophrenia disappearing? *Lancet*, *335*, 513–516.

Dinn, W. M., Harris, C. L., Aycicegi, A. *et al.* (2002). Positive and negative schizotypy in a student sample: Neurocognitive and clinical correlates. *Schizophrenia Research*, *56*, 171–85.

Eckblad, M. and Chapman, L. J. (1983). Magical ideation as an indicator of schizotypy. *Journal of Consulting and Clinical Psychology*, *51*, 215–225.

Fisher, M., Holland, C., Subramaniam, K. and Vinogradov, S. (in press). Neuroplasticity-based cognitive training in schizophrenia: An interim report on the effects 6 months later. *Schizophrenia Bulletin*.

Fitzgerald, M. (2004). *Autism and creativity*. Hove: Brunner-Routledge.

Fitzgerald, M. (2005). *The genesis of artistic creativity: Asperger's Syndrome and the arts*. London: Jessica Kingsley.

Folley, B. S. and Park, S. (2005). Verbal creativity and schizotypal personality in relation to prefrontal hemispheric laterality: A behavioral and near-infra-red optical imaging study. *Schizophrenia Research*, *80*, 271–82.

Franke, U., Kerns, J. A. and Giacalone, J. (1995). The SNRPN gene Prader-Willi syndrome. In R. Ohlsson, K. Hall and M. Ritzen (eds), *Genomic imprinting: Causes and consequences* (pp. 309–21). Cambridge: Cambridge University Press.

Frith, U. (2003). *Autism: Explaining the enigma* (2nd edition). Oxford: Blackwell.

Frith, U. and Happé, F. (1999). Theory of mind and self-consciousness: What is it like to be autistic? *Mind and Language*, *14*, 23–32.

Ginsburg, J. (2004, November 6). Coughs and sneezes spread mind diseases. *New Scientist*, 40.

Green, R. and Keverne, E. B. (2000). The disparate maternal aunt/uncle ratio in male transsexuals: An explanation invoking genomic imprinting. *Journal of Theoretical Biology*, *202*, 55–63.

Haig, D. (1997). Parental antagonism, relatedness asymmetries, and genomic imprinting. *Proceedings of the Royal Society B*, *264*, 1657–62.

Haig, D. (1999). Genetic conflicts of pregnancy and childhood. In S. C. Stearns (ed.), *Evolution in health and disease* (pp. 77–90). Oxford: Oxford University Press.

Haig, D. and Wharton, R. (2003). Prader-Willi syndrome and the evolution of human childhood. *American Journal of Human Biology*, *15*, 320–329.

Hayashi, M., Kato, M., Igarashi, K. and Kashima, H. (2008). Superior fluid intelligence in children with Asperger's disorder. *Brain and Cognition*, *66*, 306–10.

Horrobin, D. F. (1998). Schizophrenia: The illness that made us human. *Medical Hypotheses*, *50*, 269–88.

Hough, S. E. (2007). *Richter's Scale: Measure of an earthquake, measure of a man*. Princeton, NJ: Princeton University Press.

Houston, R. and Frith, U. (2000). *Autism in history: The case of Hugh Blair of Borgue*. Oxford: Blackwell.

Jacobs, M. K., Christensen, A., Snibbe, J. R. *et al.* (2001). A comparison of computer-based versus traditional individual psychotherapy. *Professional Psychology: Research and Practice*, *32*, 92–8.

James, I. (2006). *Asperger's Syndrome and high achievement: Some very remarkable people*. London: Jessica Kingsley.

Jaspers, K. (1962). *General psychopathology*. Manchester: Manchester University Press.

Kaplan, L. P. (2006). How autism has been understood. In K. L. Simmons (ed.), *The official Autism 101 manual: Autism today* (pp. 44–5). Alberta, Canada: Autism Today.

Keverne, E. B. (1992). Primate social relationships: Their determinants and consequences. *Advances in the Study of Behavior, 21*, 1–35.

Kravariti, E., Toulopoulou, T., Mapua-Filbey, F. *et al.* (2006). Intellectual asymmetry and genetic liability in first-degree relatives of probands with schizophrenia. *British Journal of Psychiatry, 188*, 186–7.

Lang, J. (1940). The other side of the ideological aspects of schizophrenia. *Psychiatry and Clinical Neurosciences, 3*, 389–92.

Langdon, R., Corner, T., McLarena, J. *et al.* (2006). Attentional orienting triggered by gaze in schizophrenia. *Neuropsychologia, 44*, 417–429.

LaRusso, L. (1978). Sensitivity of paranoid patients to nonverbal cues. *Journal of Abnormal Psychology, 87*, 463–71.

Ledgin, N. (1998). *Diagnosing Jefferson: Evidence of a condition that guided his beliefs, behavior, and personal associations*. Arlington, TX: Future Horizons.

Leekam, S. and Moore, C. (2001). The development of attention and joint attention in children with autism. In J. A. Burack, C. Charman, N. Yirmiya and P. R. Zelazo (eds), *The development of autism: Perspectives from theory and research* (pp. 105–129). Mahwah, NJ: Lawrence Erlbaum Associates.

Loat, C. S., Asbury, K., Galsworthy, M. J. *et al.* (2004). X inactivation as a source of behavioural differences in monozygotic female twins. *Twin Research, 7*, 54–61.

Loat, C. S., Haworth, C. M., Plomin, R. and Craig, I. W. (2008). A model incorporating potential skewed X-inactivation in MZ girls suggests that X-linked QTLs exist for several social behaviours including Autism Spectrum Disorder. *Annals of Human Genetics, 72*, 742–51.

Lyons, V. and Fitzgerald, M. (2007). Did Hans Asperger (1906–1980) have Asperger Syndrome? *Journal of Autism and Developmental Disorders, 37*, 2020–1.

Nesse, R. M. (2004). Cliff-edged fitness functions and the persistence of schizophrenia. *Behavioral and Brain Sciences, 27*, 862–3.

Nettle, D. (2001). *Strong imagination: Madness, creativity and human nature*. Oxford: Oxford University Press.

New Scientist (2007, March 10). Video game helps detect depression. *New Scientist*, 18.

Newton, G. (2001). The case of the biparental mole. *Wellcome News*, 18–19.

Nicholls, R. D., Saitoh, S. and Horsthemke, B. (1998). Imprinting in Prader-Willi and Angelman syndromes. *Trends in Genetics, 14*, 194–200.

O'Connell, H. and Fitzgerald, M. (2003). Did Alan Turing have Asperger's Syndrome? *Irish Journal of Psychological Medicine, 20*, 28–31.

O'Riordan, M. and Passetti, F. (2006). Discrimination in autism within different sensory modalities. *Journal of Autism and Developmental Disorders, 36*, 665–75.

Pilowsky, T., Yirmiya, N., Arbelle, S. and Mozes, T. (2000). Theory of mind abilities of children with schizophrenia, children with autism, and normally developing children. *Schizophrenia Research, 42*, 145–55.

Povinelli, D. J. (2000). *Folk physics for apes: The chimpanzee's theory of how the world works*. Oxford: Oxford University Press.

Randerson, J. (2002, October 26). All in the mind? Suspicion is growing that one of the most common human parasites in the world is messing with our minds. *New Scientist*, 10.

Rim, Y. (1994). Impulsivity, venturesomeness, empathy and schizotypy. *Personality and Individual Differences*, 17, 853–4.

St Clair, D. (2005). Rates of adult schizophrenia following prenatal exposure to the Chinese famine of 1959–1961. *Journal of the American Medical Association*, 294, 557–62.

Sass, L. A. (1992). *Madness and modernism*. New York: Basic Books.

Schreber, D. P. (2000). *Memoirs of my nervous illness* (I. Macalpine and R. A. Hunter, Trans.). New York: New York Review of Books.

Seery, M. D., Silver, R. C., Holman, E. A. *et al.* (2008). Expressing thoughts and feelings following a collective trauma: Immediate responses to 9/11 predict negative outcomes in a national sample. *Journal of Consulting and Clinical Psychology*, 76, 657–67.

Senju, A., Tojo, Y., Dairoku, H. and Hasegawa, T. (2004). Reflexive orienting in response to eye gaze and an arrow in children with and without autism. *Journal of Child Psychology and Psychiatry*, 45, 445–58.

Shore, S. (2001). *Beyond the wall: Personal experiences with autism and Asperger Syndrome*. Shawnee Mission, KS: Autism Asperger Publishing Co.

Silberman, S. (2001). The geek syndrome. *Wired*, 9.

Skuse, D. H. (2007). Rethinking the nature of genetic vulnerability to autistic spectrum disorders. *Trends in Genetics*, 23, 387–95.

Spitzer, M. (1990). On defining delusions. *Comprehensive Psychiatry*, 31, 377–97.

Susser, E., St Clair, D. and He, L. (2008). Latent effects of prenatal malnutrition on adult health: The example of schizophrenia. *Annals of the New York Academy of Sciences*, 1136, 185–92.

Swettenham, J., Condie, S., Campbell, R. *et al.* (2004). Does the perception of moving eyes trigger reflexive visual orienting in autism? In U. Frith and E. Hill (eds), *Autism: Mind and brain* (pp. 89–107). Oxford: Oxford University Press.

Tammet, D. (2006). *Born on a blue day: A memoir of Asperger's and an extraordinary mind*. London: Hodder & Stoughton.

Tavassoli, T., Ashwin, E., Ashwin, C. *et al.* (2011). *Tactile and auditory hypersensitivity in autism spectrum disorders* Manuscript under preparation.

Taylor, S. F., Welsh, R. C., Chen, A. C. *et al.* (2007). Medial frontal hyperactivity in reality distortion. *Biological Psychiatry*, 61, 1171–8.

Toulopoulou, T., Mapua-Filbey, F., Quraishi, S. *et al.* (2006). Cognitive performance in presumed obligate carriers for psychosis. *British Journal of Psychiatry*, 187, 284–5.

Treffert, D. A. (2000). *Extraordinary people: Understanding savant syndrome*. Lincoln, NE: iUniverse.

Treffert, D. A. (2001). Savant syndrome: 'Special faculties' extraordinaire. *Psychiatry Times*, 20–21.

Treffert, D. A. (2006). Savant syndrome. In K. L. Simmons (ed.), *The official Autism 101 manual: Autism today* (pp. 8–22). Alberta, Canada: Autism Today.

Treffert, D. A. and Christensen, D. D. (2005). Inside the mind of a savant. *Scientific American*, 293, 88–91.

Viertiö, S., Laitinen, A., Perälä, J. *et al.* (2007). Visual impairment in persons with psychotic disorder. *Social Psychiatry and Psychiatric Epidemiology*, 42, 902–8.

Webster, J. P., Lamberton, P. H. L., Donnelly, C. A. and Torrey, E. F. (2006). Parasites as causative agents of human affective disorders? The impact of anti-psychotic, mood-stabilizer and anti-parasite medication on *Toxoplasma gondii*'s ability to alter host behaviour. *Proceedings of the Royal Society B, 273*, 1023–30.

Wicks, S. (2005). Social adversity in childhood and the risk of developing psychosis: A national cohort study. *American Journal of Psychiatry, 162*, 1652–7.

Williams, D. (1994). *Somebody somewhere*. London: Jessica Kingsley.

Woogh, C. (2001). Is schizophrenia on the decline in Canada? *Canadian Journal of Psychiatry, 46*, 61–7.

Yolken, R. H. and Torrey, E. F. (2008). Are some cases of psychosis caused by microbial agents? A review of the evidence. *Molecular Psychiatry, 13*, 470–479.

cognition and culture

JEREMY KENDAL

CHAPTER OUTLINE

SOCIAL TRANSMISSION 315

Conditions favouring the evolution of social learning 315

Selection for social learning rules/strategies/ biases 316

The evolution of social learning biases: Context biases 317

The evolution of social learning biases: Content biases 319

Modes of social transmission 320

Social learning processes 322

GENE-CULTURE CO-EVOLUTION OF COGNITION AND CULTURE (MAINLY) IN THE HOMINID LINEAGE 325

Intelligence hypotheses 326

The evolution of cooperation and altruistic helping behaviour 330

Cumulative cultural evolution 331

CONCLUSION: A NICHE CONSTRUCTION FRAMEWORK OF MULTIMODAL INHERITANCE 333

REFERENCES 334

This chapter takes a broad and often comparative perspective to look at the interactions between cognition and culture. After a brief introduction of the methods used to study cultural evolution and gene-culture co-evolution (G-CC), there is a review of research on social transmission of information, including the conditions favouring the evolution of social learning, particular context or content-specific social learning biases, the influence of transmission mode on cultural evolution and the cognitive requirements for different social learning processes. The chapter then develops some of the key theories concerning the cognitive evolution of learning and intelligence in hominids, such as social, technical and cultural intelligence, the Baldwin effect, niche construction, the evolution of cooperative behaviour and cumulative cultural evolution. The chapter concludes in support of a multimodal niche-constructive framework to provide a full description of the interactions between cognition and culture.

The *Oxford Handbook of Evolutionary Psychology* takes an important move forward for the field of evolutionary psychology by acknowledging the role that cultural dynamics play in the evolution of psychology (Dunbar and Barrett, 2007). In the same spirit, this chapter considers the effects of psychology that have shaped human culture and the reciprocal effects that culture can have on psychology. To understand these processes, we start by introducing the fields of cultural evolution and G-CC, also known as 'dual-inheritance theory' (see Box 10.1).

G-CC theory stems from theoretical population genetics and incorporates a quantitative theory for the evolution of cultural traits – including behaviour, beliefs, attitudes and ideas – that could be analysed in conjunction with genetic traits. Cultural evolutionary theory assumes variation in cultural traits that evolve through social transmission, selection (including Darwinian selection and differential trait adoption/abandonment) and drift or stochastic sampling effects (Feldman, 2008). These processes may be affected by particular ecological and social environments, including environmental variation, non-random social structure and migration. The approach is not adaptationist as, while evolved cognition may affect the adoption or use of socially learned information in particular environments, the adoption of cultural traits is not assumed to be dependent on their fitness consequences (Feldman and Laland, 1996).

The science of cultural evolution is based on a rich theoretical framework following seminal works by Cavalli-Sforza and Feldman (1981) and Boyd and Richerson (1985), and is starting to flourish, using powerful quantitative techniques to generate causal explanations for historic and contemporary cultural diversity (McElreath *et al.*, 2008; Tehrani and Collard, 2009). The development of mathematical theory continues and has been complemented in recent years by techniques to test the theory developed by psychologists, biologists and anthropologists. What follows is a small sample of the range of empirical approaches used in the laboratory and the field to examine cultural evolution in humans and non-human animals.

The laboratory is an ideal environment to examine population-level cultural dynamics in a controlled environment. For instance, Laland and Williams (1998) employed a transmission chain design where members of a founding population of guppy fish (*Poecilia reticulata*) were trained to swim either a long or short route to a foraging patch. The founding members were gradually replaced by naive individuals

BOX 10.1.   GENE-CULTURE CO-EVOLUTION

A key assumption of gene-culture co-evolution (G-CC) is that there are two paths of information transmission: genetic inheritance and social learning (Aoki, 2001). G-CC deals with cases where the two transmission systems cannot be treated independently, first because 'what an individual learns may depend on its genotype' and, second, because 'the selection acting on the genetic system may be generated or modified by the spread of a cultural trait' (Feldman and Laland, 1996, p. 453). Feldman and Laland outline a number of important evolutionary dynamics that can be caused by G-CC, including modified selection pressures (see below for an example with dairy farming); new evolutionary mechanisms such as cultural group selection (discussed later); time lags or accelerated selection caused by homogenising behaviour and conformity; the evolution of non-random associations between genes and cultural traits (equivalent to linkage disequilibrium between genetic traits); and, finally, the cultural evolution of maladaptive behaviour .

The most well-known case of G-CC is the co-evolution of the tradition for dairy farming and a genotype for lactase persistence (for more examples, see Laland, Odling-Smee and Myles, 2010; Richerson, Boyd and Henrich, 2010). In the majority of the world, the capacity to digest lactose in (unprocessed) milk does not persist in adults. Most Northern European adults, however, have no problem digesting raw milk. The derived genetic capacity to digest lactose most likely evolved in, and was preceded by, dairy farming populations around 7500 years ago between the central Balkans and central Europe (Aoki, 1986; Feldman and Cavalli-Sforza, 1989; Holden and Mace, 1997; Hollox, 2005; Itan *et al.*, 2009). The estimated positive selection induced by dairy farming for the lactase persistence haplotype is particularly high (1.5–15%; Bersaglieri *et al.*, 2004). It is facilitated by the rate of change in the selective environment caused by the spread of the dairy farming tradition across Europe and may result from the nutritional advantage gained from energy-rich sugars and calcium. However, computational analysis by Itan *et al.* (2009) suggests that the lactase persistence allele was not favoured in northern latitudes as a result of increased vitamin D requirement.

over repeated trials. This design allowed the authors to investigate the transmissibility and longevity of traditions, in this case showing that maladaptive foraging information can be socially transmitted through animal populations, as the tradition for swimming the long route was maintained after all the founding population had been replaced.

Another example is work by Mesoudi and O'Brien (2008), who asked human subjects in a networked computer lab to design and test virtual projectile points (e.g. arrowheads) in a virtual hunting environment. This setup is flexible and yet controlled, allowing the influence of particular cultural evolutionary processes on the distribution of designs to be assessed. For instance, they showed that indirect cultural transmission of design (preferential adoption of traits exhibited by successful individuals) resulted in a higher correlation between traits than guided variation did (cultural transmission followed by individual trial-and-error learning) (Mesoudi and O'Brien, 2008). These results supported Bettinger and Eerkens' (1999) hypothesis explaining trait correlation differences between prehistoric Great Basin projectile designs found in Nevada and California.

Experiments can also be performed outside the laboratory, provided there can be sufficient control over the environment to make informative tests (Kendal, Galef and van Schaik, 2010). The main benefits are that a participant's behaviour is typically less affected by the experimental setup than in a laboratory setting, and it allows populations to be studied that cannot feasibly be brought into the laboratory. Biro *et al.* (2003) used the field experiment approach to examine the influence of social learning on how nut-cracking tool use (with stone anvils and hammers) becomes integrated into the behavioural repertoire of wild chimpanzees (*Pan troglodytes*) in Bossou, Guinea. They presented the chimpanzees with unfamiliar species of nuts and found that while juveniles were more likely to explore the novel nuts than adults were, the subjects were most likely to observe nut-cracking activities of individuals that were older or the same age. Thus, while highlighting the importance of social learning in wild nut-cracking behaviour, they showed that biased attention may restrict the spread of tool use upwards from offspring to parental generations.

Experimental studies in human populations have been carried out to study between-population cultural variation. Henrich *et al.* (2001, 2006, 2010) played the Ultimatum game in 15 small-scale societies to examine variation in altruistic behaviour and costly punishment. A player decides what proportion of a fixed sum of money to donate to an opponent, in the knowledge that the remaining sum will be lost if the opponent refuses to accept the donation. The results showed substantial between-population variation, where the degree of altruistic behaviour positively covaried across populations with the willingness to administer costly punishment of offers that were deemed too low. This finding supports the theory that costly punishment stabilises costly norms from invading defectors (Henrich *et al.*, 2006). Performing the experiment in natural populations also allowed the researchers to consider the effect of real-world explanatory variables, for instance finding that altruistic behaviour covaried with the extent of market integration (Henrich *et al.*, 2001).

Cultural evolutionary theory can be tested by exploiting natural variation in cultural traits across populations or over time, where model selection procedures are a powerful method to compare the relative fit of expectations from different theoretical assumptions against observed data. Randomisation can also be used to compare a bootstrapped distribution of the null hypothesis against observed data. Rogers and Ehrlich (2008) used this technique to help show that functional traits in Polynesian canoe design were more conserved than symbolic traits. A fantastic resource for a quantitative study of cultural evolutionary dynamics is found in the archaeological record. Shennan and Wilkinson (2001) considered ceramic style variation from Linearbandkeramik (LBK) Neolithic settlements of the Merzbachtal in western Germany. They provided evidence that a cultural evolution model including selection through a bias for novelty provides a better fit than a neutral model to frequency distributions of the ceramic styles. Historical inferences about cultural evolutionary dynamics across populations can be made using phylogenetic reconstructive techniques adapted from biology. For instance, Tehrani and Collard (2009) used the cladistic method to show that most of the variation among the studied Iranian tribes' craft assemblages can be explained by descent with modification.

The aforementioned techniques provide quantitative methods to study both cultural evolution and aspects of G-CC. Next we review the findings generated using these and similar methods on factors affecting social transmission, drawing on theory and empirical research relating to human and non-human animals. Social transmission is a central requirement of both cultural and gene-culture co-evolutionary systems and is heavily influenced by cognitive facilities or constraints.

SOCIAL TRANSMISSION

Social learning can be defined as 'any process through which one individual (the 'demonstrator') influences the behaviour of another individual (the 'observer') in a manner that increases the probability that the observer learns' (Hoppitt and Laland, 2008, p. 108). Typically, it is assumed that the demonstrator is in possession of information that the observer learns, although it is not always the case (an observer can learn from mistakes made by a demonstrator).

Conditions favouring the evolution of social learning

The evolution of the cognitive propensity for social learning hangs on the adaptive value of the socially learned information. Theoretical work has established that social learning most likely evolved under intermediate levels of environmental variation (Wakano, Aoki and Feldman, 2004). If the rate of environmental change is particularly slow, the rate of genetic mutation is sufficient for genetic selection to respond to new challenges set by changes in the environment. In environments that change more quickly, organisms require some phenotypic plasticity to make an appropriate response. If the environment changes within an organism's lifetime, there can be selection for learning, where the addition neuronal costs are paid for by the benefits accrued through learning appropriate responses to environmental challenges.

For social species, the opportunity to learn from conspecifics provides a mechanism of acquiring information that avoids costs associated with asocial learning, for instance learning asocially (e.g. by trial and error) can take time and energy, and may be associated with elevated risks of direct interaction with unfamiliar aspects of the environment, such as heightened predation risk. Information acquired socially may come cheap, but it runs the risk of being outdated and inaccurate in comparison to asocially derived information; the interval between the production of adaptive information through asocial learning by one individual and its implementation by social learning conspecifics may render the manifest behaviour redundant if exceeded by the rate of change in the environment. Furthermore, it is likely that social learning is imperfect, resulting in a reduction in fidelity of information transmission as it propagates through a chain of social learners.

Selection for asocial learning accurate information is highest when environmental change is particularly fast. At intermediate rates of environmental variation, however, the loss in accuracy paid by social learning is balanced by the unique asocial learning costs. The selection for social learning is typically frequency-dependent as asocial learning is required at a frequency that can update information in response to changes in the environment (Laland and Kendal, 2003; Wakano, Aoki and Feldman, 2004).

Selection for social learning rules/strategies/biases

The trade-off between asocial and social learning is encapsulated by Boyd and Richerson's (1985) 'costly information hypothesis', which purports that, in a variable or uncertain environment, adaptive information will be costly to evaluate. It follows that psychology will have evolved social learning rules (also referred to as 'biases' or 'strategies'; Boyd and Richerson, 1985; Laland, 2004) to acquire adaptive information through selective use of when to use social learning over asocial learning, and from whom to learn. A small number of plausible rules have been subject to theoretical analysis (e.g. Boyd and Richerson, 1985; Henrich and McElreath, 2003; Laland, 2004) and some have received experimental support (Coolen *et al.*, 2003; Galef and Whiskin, 2008; Kendal *et al.*, 2005). These rules require information to be adaptive most of the time, but inevitably any compromise on the expensive acquisition of accurate information will allow some maladaptive traditions to evolve (Richerson and Boyd, 2005). This possibility provides an alternative explanation to the traditional view from some evolutionary psychologists that maladaptive behaviour occurs when environments have changed too fast for selection to respond (Tooby and Cosmides, 1990).

Rogers (1988) shows that the fitness of social learners at the polymorphic equilibrium with asocial learners would be no greater than the average individual fitness in a population of asocial learners, assuming asocial learning fitness is constant (or independent of social learning frequency) and that social learners' only benefit over asocial learners is the cost-free acquisition of information. When rare, the fitness of social learners exceeds that of asocial learners, but declines with frequency as there are fewer asocial learners producing adaptive information in a changing environment. The population evolves to a mixed evolutionarily stable strategy (ESS) where, by definition, the fitness of social learners equates to that of asocial learners (Giraldeau, Valone and Templeton, 2002; Henrich and McElreath, 2003). Rogers (1988) assumed that social learners were unbiased in their choice of whom to copy and thus the probability of social learning of a behaviour was proportional to its frequency in the population. Boyd and Richerson (1995) suggest that Rogers' (1988) result was paradoxical in that it contrasts with a commonly held assertion that culture enhances fitness. Although Rogers' result is not inherently paradoxical, it appears to conflict with the observation that social learning underlies the effect of human culture on our ecological success and population growth.

In a variable environment, selection of social learning rules, biases or strategies can also resolve this conundrum. Compared to a population composed entirely of asocial learners, the average individual fitness at equilibrium is enhanced if individuals exhibit cognitive flexibility, switching between asocial and social learning in a noisy two-state environment (Boyd and Richerson, 1995; Kameda and Nakanishi, 2003). Similarly, Enquist, Eriksson and Ghirlanda (2007) show that a strategy of 'critical social learning', where individuals only adopt asocial learning if social learning is unsatisfactory, also enhances average fitness at equilibrium. Boyd and Richerson (1995) also show that average fitness is higher than that in a population of asocial learners if social learners can improve their learned behaviour so that there is cumulative cultural evolution. For instance, the adaptive filtering of information to remove maladaptive information may be critical for cumulative cultural evolution (Enquist and Ghirlanda, 2007). Overall, Kendal, Giraldeau and Laland (2009) predict that among competing social learning rules the dominant rule will be the one that can persist with the lowest frequency of asocial learning. This is a key characteristic of the winning strategy from a recent public 'social learning strategies tournament' carried out by Rendell *et al.* (2010).

The evolution of social learning biases: Context biases

Social learning rules, or biases, have been classified by some authors into 'context biases' and 'content biases' (Boyd and Richerson, 1985; Henrich and McElreath, 2003; Mesoudi and Whiten, 2001). Henrich and McElreath (2003) split context biases into 'frequency-dependent biases' and 'model-based biases', and both consider cases where the decision of whom to copy is *not* governed by the content of the learned information (Boyd and Richerson, 1985, refer to 'indirect bias'). 'Frequency-dependent bias' refers to a relationship between the frequency of a behaviour and its probability of adoption. In particular, conformist bias is a non-linear exaggerated tendency to copy the majority and anti-conformist bias (sometimes referred to as 'non-conformist bias') is the reverse.

Boyd and Richerson (1985) show that there can be a fitness advantage of conformity over unbiased social learning in a metapopulation across a spatially variable environment, where conformist migrants adopt locally adaptive and thus commonly held behavioural variants with a high probability. Henrich and Boyd (1998) used a simulation study where agents choose between two habitats in an uncertain environment and conclude that a conformist bias should be favoured under a very broad range of parameter values. They also emphasise that conformity bias can facilitate cultural group selection by enhancing within-population homogeneity of behaviour and maintaining between-population variation. I discuss later their suggestion that this process may facilitate the evolution of altruistic punishment (Boyd and Richerson, 1985; Henrich and Boyd, 1998, 2001; Richerson and Boyd, 2005).

However, the adaptive value of conformist bias may not be as clear as first thought. Since Henrich and Boyd's (1998) study, a number of mathematical models have found a negative relationship between the evolutionarily stable strength of conformist bias and environmental stability (Kendal, Giraldeau and Laland, 2009; Nakahashi, 2007; Wakano and Aoki, 2007). Furthermore, Eriksson, Eriksson and Ghirlanda (2007) relaxed the assumption employed by Henrich and Boyd (1998), that all cultural variants are known to every individual, and found that the genetic evolution of conformity is only likely if the rate of cultural evolution is particularly slow, whereupon it is polymorphic with unbiased social learning. They also note that conformist-bias may be maladaptive where culture evolves cumulatively as it constrains the adoption of new, rare but adaptive, cultural variants. Conformist transmission has also been predicted to have a strong adverse effect on the evolution of culturally inherited helping traits (Lehmann and Feldman, 2008).

There is evidence for conformity in animals across phylogenetically distant taxa. Day *et al.* (2001) provide evidence consistent with conformity bias in guppies that occurs as a function of shoaling behaviour. Using domestic strains, they found that large groups were faster than small groups to swim to a food patch through a transparent partition, but that the trend was reversed when the partition was opaque, where fish that swam to the food patch would lose visual contact with conspecifics. Here the strength of conformity is a function of group size, and in the opaque condition, conformity bias constrains the rate at which members of large groups swim to the food patch. Whiten, Horner and de Waal (2005) provide evidence for conformity in chimpanzees learning a two-action extractive foraging task from a trained demonstrator. Individuals that learned both methods continued to use the group normative action that was first introduced by the demonstrator, even though the alternative action was the more conducive in the absence of social influence. Nonetheless, the study did not rule out the possibility of prestige bias (see below) directed towards the trained demonstrator.

In humans, Efferson *et al.* (2008) found that people's self-assessment of whether they conformed was consistent with their behaviour in an experiment involving social learning of a preference between two arbitrarily labelled technologies that differed in expected payoff, where social learners observed the distribution of choices among asocial learners. Nonetheless, they also noted a wide variation in frequency-dependent bias. Indeed, Eriksson and Coultas (2009) provide evidence for anti-conformity in questionnaire-based responses to vignettes. The result, they suggest, is supported by 'social impact theory', developed in social psychology, which proposes that minority sources of influence have relatively greater impact than majority sources do (Latané and Wolf, 1981).

Next we consider model-based biases, which are thought to evolve if copying a type of model provides a low-cost shortcut to evaluating the content of the learned information (Henrich and McElreath, 2003). However, in a variable environment such strategies can be susceptible to the spread of maladaptive information. Strategies such as copy-familiar-individuals or copy-kin trade on the likely similarity of environment between model and copier, and may be maintained by reciprocity and kin selection, respectively (Hamilton, 1964; Trivers, 1971). Swaney *et al.* (2001) provide evidence that guppy fish more effectively acquire foraging information from familiar over non-familiar conspecifics.

Mesoudi (2008) provides experimental evidence for the model-based bias to copy successful individuals, particularly in multimodal fitness landscapes where asocial learning is difficult, and as part of an adaptive flexible strategy whereby subjects switch between asocial learning and social learning using success bias. Copying successful individuals is an indirect method of acquiring adaptive information, but natural selection may be expected to favour copying of a wide suite of cultural traits from successful individuals when direct assessment of the utility of the acquired information is costly. This bias may form the basis for cumulative cultural evolution, as learners' attention is skewed towards models that demonstrate adaptive behaviour over multiple generations. Nonetheless, the same strategy can allow fitness-neutral or maladaptive traits to spread, hitch-hiking as part of the collection of traits acquired from successful individuals.

Henrich and Gil-White (2001) postulate how copying successful individuals can also generate prestige hierarchies, whereby learners pay deference, such as gifts or helping behaviour, to those they assess to be successful. This allows a further shortcut in information-gathering costs to evolve as new learners can assess patterns of deference to determine whom they should copy. Again, these indirect methods of assessment are open to the spread of maladaptive behaviour and can lead to a Fisherian-like runaway process, where costly traits become markers of prestige and exaggerated by their association with the preference for the prestige marker. This process may explain, for example, the production of extremely large yams for feasts as markers of prestige amongst farmers on the Micronesian island of Ponapae (Boyd and Richerson, 1985).

The evolution of social learning biases: Content biases

Content biases (or 'direct biases') include payoff-biased transmission, which assumes that the probability of adoption is directly related to characteristics of the observed behaviour (Boyd and Richerson, 1985). Using an optimality approach to compare social learning rules in a multi-armed bandit setting, Schlag (1998) discovered that the most successful strategy was the 'proportional imitation rule', where an individual copies a demonstrator that received a higher payoff than their own with a probability that is proportional to the difference in payoffs (approximating the replicator dynamic). Payoff-related biases have clear fitness consequences so it is unsurprising if we find such biases across the animal kingdom, such as in sticklebacks (Kendal *et al.*, 2009).

Sperber (1996) suggests that the content of socially transmitted information may be influenced by pre-existing cognitive biases. Some cultural traits, such as masks and caricatures, appear to be aimed towards well-established cognitive modules, such as for facial recognition, where exaggerated traits act as super-stimuli (Sperber and Hirschfeld, 2004). The finding by Mesoudi, Whiten and Dunbar (2006), that information about third-party social interactions was transmitted with higher fidelity than information with non-social content, may reflect a cognitive bias towards cognition for social intelligence. Other biases include a preference for minimally counter-intuitive information, shown by Barrett and Nyhof (2001) using sample American students, to be recalled and transmitted better than either bizarre or common items. Also, there is evidence that the transmission of cultural stereotypical information can be more stable than that of stereotype-inconsistent information (Kashima, 2000).

Content biases are common in many non-human animals. Biases in diet preferences in Norwegian rats are reflected in the longevity of a socially learned tradition for diet choice (Galef and Allen, 1995). The guppy fish preference for the colour red can affect traditions for colour-cued escape routes (Reader, Kendal and Laland, 2003). Putative bowerbird traditions of nest decoration type are often biased to species-specific colour preference, which is a bias that is also reflected in their preferred food items (Madden, 2008).

Of course, there may be many reasons for content biases and they should not be presumed to be the direct result of natural selection for a cognitive bias or 'attractor' (Sperber and Hirschfeld, 2004). For instance, cognitive bias may be influenced by environmental effects during development, including enculturation to social norms that may bias the adoption of information. Also, there may be interactions between content and the aforementioned context biases (Claidiere and Sperber, 2007), where, depending on the environment, some context biases may be more likely than others to result in an apparent content bias for non-adaptive behaviour.

The content of a tradition can also affect its own transmissibility without direct recourse to a cognitive bias or an adaptationist stance. Tanaka, Kendal and Laland (2009) show that maladaptive self-medication can be expected, despite a tendency to revert from such a treatment, because its maladaptive quality prolongs the period of treatment and enhances the opportunity for social transmission. Another example is a bias towards compositionality in the evolution of languages that are infinitely expressive, and thus where it is impossible to memorise the entire system of mappings from symbols to meanings. Compositionality, or the rules of composition of symbols, is a form of content bias that enhances the learnability of the language through a 'learning bottleneck', where the number of learned mappings is naturally limited (Smith and Kirby, 2008). Compositionality could be adaptive by enhancing the communicated range of expression or meaning (e.g. Nowak, Plotkin and Jansen, 2000), and thus there is the potential selection for cognitive bias towards compositionality (Chomsky, 1980; Pinker and Bloom, 1990). However, Smith and Kirby's (2008) ESS analysis of Bayesian language learners suggests an alternative, that cultural evolution can shield cognitive machinery from selection if individuals always pick the most likely grammar based on their prior evidence. Consequently, compositionality bias is predicted to be minimised to reduce associated neural costs.

Modes of social transmission

There is commonly an association between the content of a tradition and the mode of its transmission. At the crude level, there are three modes of transmission: vertical, from parents to offspring; oblique, from parental to offspring generations (but not parents to offspring); and horizontal, within a generation or peer group. Cavalli-Sforza and Feldman (1981) provide a thorough mathematical analysis of these three modes of transmission. Population genetic-type models can be adapted to consider various forms of vertical transmission of cultural traits (akin to genetic traits), while epidemiological-like models can be modified to consider the horizontal transmission of cultural traits (akin to disease traits). Needless to say, the models are modified to incorporate the processes of transmission that are distinct from the biological analogues.

Theory suggests that vertically transmitted traits should be the most conserved of the three modes for a number of reasons. There may be a developmental effect, as parents have the opportunity to transmit information to their children, when the latter are particularly sensitive to acquiring preferences that may then be retained (Guglielmino *et al.*, 1995). There may also be an evolutionary timescale effect, as adaptive vertically transmitted traditions must remain useful over a generational timescale, and are unlikely to be effective if the environment (to which the tradition is applied) changes on a faster timescale (Laland, Richerson and Boyd, 1996; McElreath and Strimling, 2008). In contrast, horizontally transmitted information can be useful in a far more ephemeral environment (Laland and Kendal, 2003). Context biases are also likely to be non-randomly associated with the mode of transmission. For instance, it follows that kin-biased social learning of altruistic helping behaviour may be more likely through vertical transmission than through horizontal transmission (between non-related peers). However, social norms supporting large-scale cooperation may be transmitted through oblique or horizontal transmission, for instance, by homogenising behaviour within groups through copying the majority or one-to-many transmission (more on these types below) (Lehmann, Feldman and Foster, 2008; Richerson and Boyd, 2005).

Horizontal transmission is considered relatively common in non-human animals, while vertical transmission appears to be prevalent in humans (Laland, Richerson and Boyd, 1996; Shennan and Steele, 1999). In ephemeral environments, traditions concerning foraging locations or predator escape routes may only be adaptive over short periods (within-season, a few days or even minutes). A transition from predominantly horizontal to vertical transmission may result from, amongst other things, extension of the period of parental care and, more speculatively, a reduction in environmental variation through niche construction (Odling-Smee, Laland and Feldman, 2003). Vertical transmission may be particularly restricted if the period of parental care is short and if the information can only be learned following sufficient cognitive development by the offspring. Hominid pelvic adaptations for bipedalism constrain brain size at birth and thus are associated with secondary altriciality and delayed maturity, providing a prolonged time-window for enculturation and trans-generational social learning (Coward and Gamble, 2008).

A model by McElreath and Strimling (2008) also predicts that vertical transmission would be expected when the learned behaviour affects fertility rather than survival to adulthood, simply because selection on fertility affects the opportunity for vertical transmission. Guglielmino *et al.* (1995) fit 47 cultural traits from 277 African societies to three models (demic diffusion, environmental adaptation and cultural diffusion). They found that most traits, particularly those affecting family structure and kinship, were best fit to the demic model, and were thus most likely vertically transmitted (although the model may also be consistent with other conservative transmission biases such as conformity; Tehrani and Collard, 2009). Only a few fit traits such as house-related traditions (affected by local ecology) and fashions best fit to the cultural model of horizontal (or oblique) transmission. Hewlett, Silvestra and Guglielmino (2002) used a similar analysis and found vertical transmission of kinship, family and community and political stratification. In addition, they found evidence for horizontal or oblique transmission in house construction and postpartum sex taboo traditions.

A number of studies have examined how, in recent history and contemporary society, the typical reduction in preferred family size, accompanied by modernisation (the demographic transition), may be influenced by a transition of vertical transmission to horizontal or oblique transmission. Newson *et al.* (2005) suggest that, with modernisation and movement away from the family, there is an increase in the influence from non-kin (typically advising against large family size) over kin (who are more likely to encourage reproduction than non-kin are). Borenstein, Kendal and Feldman (2006) show how enhanced education that accompanies modernisation allows the construction of communication channels that facilitate horizontal transmission of information, through which fertility control preferences can percolate. Ihara and Feldman (2004) model Boyd and Richerson's (1985) suggestion that individuals that have fewer children than normal can invest to achieve high-status roles (e.g. leaders or teachers), where they can influence others through a one-to-many form of social transmission. This form of oblique or horizontal transmission can result in the spread of a preference for small family size throughout the population in accordance with the demographic transition. One-to-many transmission can also favour the cultural evolution of altruistic helping behaviour for which it may be a more effective mode of transmission than conformist bias (Lehmann and Feldman, 2008; see also below).

Social learning processes

Transmission modes and content biases may often be associated with particular social learning processes (or mechanisms). Most social learning processes are defined in terms of the role of the demonstrator in generating matching behaviour by the observer (Heyes, 1994). Hoppitt and Laland (2008) lay out a comprehensive classification scheme of social learning processes. Here we consider just a few processes to illustrate the range of cognitive capacity that social learning may require. The simplest forms of social learning are social enhancement effects, where a conspecific draws the attention of the social learner to a particular stimulus-type ('stimulus enhancement') or a locale ('local enhancement'). Following this modified state of attention, or single-stimulus learning (Heyes, 1994), the individual can learn about a new aspect of the environment, such as the association between a location and a food reward (a form of classical conditioning), or a new foraging technique focused on the stimulus (a form of instrumental conditioning). It is feasible that these simple forms of social learning existed in the common ancestor of vertebrates (untested), and many extant taxa have been shown to use stimulus (or local) enhancement (see Hoppitt and Laland, 2008).

The social learning process of 'emulation' typically requires a more complex cognitive process than the enhancement processes and evidence of the former has been found in birds, monkeys, and apes. 'Emulation learning', originally defined by Tomasello (1990), is when the observer learns about the change that occurs to the environment during the task manipulation rather than the demonstrator's behaviour itself, although this term has since been used in a variety of ways (Custance, Whiten and Fredman 1999; see Box 10.2). The social learning process of 'imitation' can be defined as 'a process whereby one individual copies some part of the form of an action from another' (Whiten *et al.*, 2004, p. 38). Despite such a simple definition, researchers have found it extremely difficult to test for imitation, as there are so many other social learning processes that must be controlled for. Imitation has been the focus of much research by psychologists, aware that imitation may require complex cognitive mechanisms (see Box 10.2).

BOX 10.2.   EMULATION AND IMITATION

Emulation learning can take a number of different forms (Whiten *et al.*, 2004). Upon observing a demonstrator that manipulates an object to receive a food reward, the observer may (i) learn to copy the movement of the object, called 'object movement re-enactment' (OMR); (ii) learn the properties of an object and how it can be manipulated, known as 'affordance learning'; or (iii) learn that food can be obtained by manipulating the object without necessarily using the demonstrated behaviour, known as 'goal emulation'. These versions of emulation may be used in combination. For example, an observer may learn about the affordances of an object to recreate the goal of the demonstrator's behaviour.

Imitation may require an individual to (i) execute visual-motor cross-modal processing to transform an observed action into a motor pattern; (ii) be capable of imitating a perceptually opaque action, where the imitator's perception associated with observing an action (performed by a demonstrator or model) is quite different from their perception associated with executing the action; and (iii) have some understanding of the intentional state underlying an action. In both birds and apes, there is evidence for the imitation of 'perceptually opaque' actions, although it is debatable whether this requires the imitator to take the perspective or understand the intention of the demonstrator of the action (Heyes, 1998; Tomasello, 1996). Some apes show a high proficiency for complex forms of imitation. In chimpanzees, there is evidence for 'programme level' imitation, where non-arbitrary sequences of behaviours are copied to extract food from a task (Horner and Whiten, 2005). Byrne and Byrne (1993) suggest that gorillas are likely to use programme-level imitation to manipulate plant leaves that are protected by stings, hooks and spines (but see Tennie *et al.*, 2008). Also, do-as-I-do imitation, exhibited only in apes and dolphins, may require some awareness of the concept of imitation (Whiten, 2000), although perhaps enculturation and reward-based associative learning to do-as-I-do may also be in effect without cause for the animal to reflect on its behaviour. It is plausible that New Caledonian crows may use programme-level imitation to create multistep leaf tools used to extract insects (Hunt and Gray, 2003). Passerine birds copy long sequences of song units, although the auditory stimulus and response is unimodal and thought not to involve the same cognitive acrobatics as visual-motor cross-modal matching, required to imitate a behaviour from its observation (Zentall, 2004).

Whiten *et al.* (2004) suggest that some instances of OMR, goal emulation and imitation may require a similar cognitive mechanism. For instance, both imitation and OMR may be used to copy perceptually opaque object manipulation. Furthermore, both the imitation of perceptually opaque tasks and goal emulation may require the observer to take the perspective of the demonstrator. Further consideration of issues concerning imitation (and emulation) can be found in a special edition introduced by Heyes (2009).

Horner and Whiten (2005) examined the tendency of young wild-born chimpanzees and 3- to 4-year-old children to use emulation or imitation to solve a tool-using task. The subjects observed a human demonstrating causally relevant and irrelevant actions with a tool to retrieve a reward from a puzzle-box. The chimpanzees, but not the children, ignored irrelevant actions when the effect of the action on the task was visible, indicating that the former used emulation, while the latter used imitation. The chimpanzees' focus on the 'results' of the demonstrated action is consistent with the work of Call, Carpenter and Tomasello (2005), who show that chimpanzees, who observed a demonstrator try but fail to retrieve a reward using one of two alternative methods, were able to selectively ignore the unsuccessful method in favour of the alternative, potentially successful technique, thus utilising the available causal information. The children were old enough to have the cognitive capacity to understand the causal mechanics of the task, but they may be more inclined than chimpanzees to view the actions of the demonstrator as intentional (Gergely, Bekkering and Kiraly, 2002).

Biologists and anthropologists have noted that imitation may hold an evolutionary significance within hominids as a prerequisite for 'cumulative cultural evolution', where information is acquired through social learning and then modified, resulting in an increase in complexity or efficiency of the transmitted information over cultural generations (Tomasello, 1999). Critically, imitation may be unique in allowing the direct transmission of information about how to solve a task with high fidelity and a low cost to the imitator (Jablonka and Lamb, 2006a, 2006b). Chimpanzees have been shown to have a sophisticated capacity for imitation that may include an understanding of the concept of what it means to imitate and the ability to copy sequences of actions (Nielson et al., 2005; Whiten, 2005; Whiten et al., 2004).

All the aforementioned processes can result in inadvertent social learning (i.e. inadvertent on the part of the demonstrator). However, it is also possible for these processes to be used in the active transfer of information through teaching (Hoppitt et al., 2008). Caro and Hauser (1992) propose that teaching requires the teacher to modify their behaviour in the presence of the pupil, at a cost to the teacher (or without immediate benefit), with the result of enhancing the rate (or efficiency) of learning in the pupil. There is evidence of teaching across a range of animals, including ants that guide naive workers to food by 'tandem running' (Franks and Richardson, 2006), as well as cheetahs and meerkats releasing caught prey for juveniles to hunt (Caro and Hauser, 1992; Thornton and McAuliffe, 2006). Teaching in animals can take the form of drawing attention to a stimulus, demonstrating the learned behaviour, altering the environment that the learned behaviour affects (e.g. presenting disabled prey) and even coaching by responding appropriately to the pupil's behaviour (e.g. meerkats will present first dead, then disabled, then intact scorpions as the pupil's hunting skill improves) (Hoppitt et al., 2008). Teaching in non-human animals incurs an immediate cost, and thus can be considered a form of altruistic behaviour that could evolve in small groups through kin selection or direct reciprocity (Hamilton, 1964; Hoppitt et al., 2008; Thornton and Raihani, 2008; Trivers, 1971).

An important means of active communication of information is through symbolism and language. Semantic traditional communication systems are found in some non-humans animals, including gestural communication in chimpanzees and vocal dialects in cetaceans and songbirds (Call and Tomasello, 2004; Catchpole and Slater,

1995; Rendell and Whitehead, 2001). Many forest primates and bird species are limited by small repertoires, and this may favour the evolution of combinatorial signals (e.g. free-ranging putty-nosed monkeys; Arnold and Zuberbuhler, 2006). Smith and Kirby (2008) argue that the unique syntax observed in human language results from a combination of language features (defined originally by Hockett, 1960, p. 6), including arbitrariness ('the ties between the meaningful message elements and their meanings can be arbitrary'); duality of patterning ('a few tens of phonemes that are combined to form tens of thousands of words'); recursion ('a signal of a given category can contain component parts that are of the same category'); and compositionality (defined earlier).

Human language allows the communication of functional information about the past or the future to predict environmental states, as well as describing imagined realities that may be important for the cultural evolution of religion. Tomasello (2008) suggests that, while communication in other apes is 'almost exclusively for the purpose of getting others to do what they want', humans are often willing to share information and have a heightened capacity for pedagogy. In comparison with non-human vocal communication systems, the human capacity for a recursive compositional system, in particular, facilitates the potential communication of infinite meanings. In conjunction with the co-evolution of anatomy, motor control, sound perception and grammatical competence, language evolution is likely to be a central aspect of major transition in human evolution, including its effect on teaching (Maynard Smith and Szathmary, 1995).

Premack (2007) suggests that both language and theory of mind (see below) are distinct features of human teaching. Csibra and Gergely (2006) also propose that teaching, or 'pedagogy', is a human adaptation, although for this they do not pre-suppose either language or high-level theory of mind. However, their requirements for ostensive communication of relevant and generalisable knowledge (i.e. to circumstances beyond the 'here and now') may be satisfied by (or be similar to) the case of meerkat teaching of hunting. Furthermore, in some traditional apprenticeships, such as Iranian rug-weavers, ostensive instruction can be rare, and learning appears to be largely through inadvertent demonstration with occasional active intervention (Tehrani and Riede, 2008). Thus, human teaching appears to be characterised by a continuum of processes, from those that require a unique cognitive capacity to others that use cognition that is homologous to that found in non-humans (Hoppitt *et al.*, 2008).

GENE-CULTURE CO-EVOLUTION OF COGNITION AND CULTURE (MAINLY) IN THE HOMINID LINEAGE

Human culture is characterised, in part, by complex technology and by complex sets of social norms. I examine the evolution of the cognitive capacities required to facilitate these aspects of human culture. The potential drivers of technical and social intelligence have been tested using comparative methods, regressing potential factors against some measure of brain size, as a proxy for intelligence. The analysis typically uses neocortex ratio (implicated in higher brain functions) and should correct for variation in research effort across species and for shared phylogenetic history as a source of non-independence between species.

Intelligence hypotheses

The 'social intelligence hypothesis' (also 'Machiavellian Intelligence Hypothesis' or 'social brain hypothesis') suggests that primates evolved a large brain principally in response to the selective social environment to manage volatile social alliances (Byrne and Whiten, 1988; Humphrey, 1976; Kummer *et al.*, 1997). Researchers examined both the possibility that the selective social environment could have influenced the evolution of a domain-general capacity or for evolution along particular dimensions or modules of intelligence, such as 'theory of mind'. Theory of mind 'represents level 2 in a hierarchically reflexive sequence of reflection on belief states known generically as "intentional states", so "I *believe* that you *suppose* (that something is the case)" identifies two distinct belief or intentional states' (Dunbar, 2003, p. 170). This capacity could be crucial for social learning about the social environment to service an effective set of alliances. It has also been implicated when perspective-taking is important for the social learning of tasks (e.g. found in some forms of teaching such as apprenticeships, or do-as-I-do procedures).

It is likely that chimpanzees display only theory of mind in a broad but not the narrow sense (Call and Tomasello, 2008). Evidence suggests that chimpanzees have perception-goal psychology, understanding goals and intentions of others (Whiten *et al.*, 2004). However, current evidence suggests they lack human-like belief-desire psychology, including an understanding of false-belief, where 'an observer predicts or explains the behavior of an actor based on a judgment of what that actor believes to be the case, not what really is the case as the observer knows it (e.g. the actor believes the food is in one place when the observer knows that it is really in another)' (Call and Tomasello, 2008, p. 189).

Dunbar and colleagues' analyses provide evidence that social clique size (group size) and tactical deception are good predictors of neocortex ratio in primates, carnivores and bats (Barton and Dunbar, 1997; Dunbar, 2003). Dunbar (2003) acknowledges that, at the end of the day, the driving force of selection derives from ecology, but suggests that the adaptive solution was more likely one of social-cognitive skills, rather than of individual technical intelligence. Large brains were required to pay the cost of social living (e.g. social group bonding) primed by a change in the environment, and ecological skills were a result but not a cause of this process. Dunbar and colleagues' analyses suggest that the relationship between brain size and group size is found particularly in anthropoid primates and may have its origins in selection induced by the demands of pair-bonding, which is positively related to brain size across vertebrates (Dunbar and Schultz, 2007).

In birds, the neopallium (equivalent to neocortex) appears to be larger in the relatively social corvids than other species (Emery and Clayton, 2004). Their work supports the social intelligence hypothesis on the basis that selection acts on the capacity to keep track on the status of a high number of individuals in large groups. Nonetheless, in terms of absolute brain size, clearly the relationship between big brains and cognitively complex social tasks is countered by cases such as the scrub-jay. Clayton, Dally and Emery (2007) suggest that these food-storing birds have undergone a cognitive arms race, where food-caching and food-stealing strategies become ever-more sophisticated to maximise resources. Another special small-brained case is the social complexity exhibited by 'cleaner'-fish species that remove ectoparasites, mucus and scales from 'client' fish (Cote, 2000). Bshary, Salwiczek and Wickler (2007, p. 86) has collected evidence in this system for 'nepotism, social prestige, reciprocity, alliance formation, tactical deception, punishment and reconciliation . . . individual recognition, and knowledge about the relationships between other individuals', as defined operationally without the underlying cognitive mechanism. The influence of selection for 'technical intelligence' (or 'ecological intelligence') is supported by evidence for ecological correlates of brain size. Birds show a positive association between brain size and ecological skills, for instance, between the size of the hyperstriatum ventrale and neostriatum (equivalent to the mammalian neocortex) and innovation rate. (Lefebvre, Reader and Sol, 1994) Also, in mammals and birds, hippocampus volume is positively correlated with spatial task performance (Bshary, Salwiczek and Wickler, 2007; Krebs *et al.*, 1996).

An analysis by Reader and Laland (2002) used a phylogenetic comparison across primates and provided evidence for the evolution of a general capacity for intelligence. They found that neocortex size was predicted by a suite of factors, including evidence of innovation, social learning and tool use. They suggest that 'individuals capable of inventing new solutions to ecological challenges, or exploiting the discoveries and inventions of others, may have had a selective advantage over less able conspecifics, which generated selection for those brain regions that facilitate complex technical and social behaviour' (Reader and Laland, 2002, p. 4440).

With some exceptions, encephalisation appears to be a good predictor of diverse and stable traditional behaviour within populations, such as in chimpanzees, orang-utans, dolphins and humans (Rendell and Whitehead, 2001; van Schaik *et al.*, 2003; Whiten *et al.*, 1999). Interestingly, these four species are able to learn the concept of imitation to perform 'do-as-I-do' routines (absent in monkeys) and have the ability for self-recognition in a mirror (of the monkeys, only found in cotton-top tamarins) (Herman, 2002; Reiss and Marino, 2001; Tomasello and Call, 1997). Evidence from autistic spectrum disorders suggests that some aspects of social intelligence may be modular, such as self-recognition and theory of mind, as well as the capacity for imitation (Williams, Whiten and Singh, 2004). Indeed, mirror neurons, which fire when both performing an action and observing it performed, have been proposed as important for both imitation and theory of mind, by linking the mental state of self with that of others (Gallese, 2007).

A complement of the social intelligence hypothesis is the 'cultural intelligence hypothesis' (Herrmann *et al.*, 2007; Whiten and van Schaik 2007). Whiten and van Schaik (2007, p. 614) envisage an 'adaptive complex' characterised by positive feedback between intelligence and cultural evolution such that 'social learning capacities, social learning opportunities, and encephalization suggest an evolutionarily spiraling process in which social learning may engender traditions, the emergence of multiple traditions selects for enhanced social learning, multiple traditions generate smarter individuals, smarter individuals innovate and learn better, and there is associated selection for encephalization'. Enquist *et al.* (2008) present a mathematical analysis to suggest that in human evolutionary history creativity is required, in addition to social transmission, to account for the observed exponential increase in the amount of culture. Consistent with Whiten and van Schaik's hypothesis, they predict G-CC between amount of culture and the capacity for creativity.

Herrmann *et al.* (2007, p. 1360) emphasise that the 'skills of social-cultural cognition early in ontogeny serve as a kind of "bootstrap" for the distinctively complex development of human cognition in general' and for the acquisition of skilled cultural practices. Whiten and van Schaik (2007) also emphasise the role of the developmental period, that in primates is characterised by particularly slow post-natal brain growth positively associated with brain size across mammals, in providing the opportunity for the development of cognitive ability as well as the social acquisition of information. The capuchin monkeys, although not particularly well encephalised, share apes' characteristic diversity of cultural traits in the wild and a particularly slow rate of development and exhibit high social tolerance (Perry *et al.*, 2003).

Evolutionary biologists have posited a number of related hypotheses where behaviour actively influences genetic evolutionary dynamics. The cultural intelligence hypothesis is a form of the 'behavioural drive' and 'cultural drive' hypotheses (Wilson, 1985; Wyles, Kunkel and Wilson 1983), which propose that innovation and social learning result in the invasion of new niche space resulting in exposure to novel selection pressures and accelerating the rate of anatomical evolution. Other related processes are the 'Baldwin effect' and 'cultural niche construction' (Baldwin, 1902; Odling-Smee, Laland and Feldman, 2003).

The Baldwin effect is a mechanism whereby there is genetic selection on the capacity for an organism to express an ontogenetic phenotype. In a variable environment, phenotypic plasticity is required to generate a suitable ontogenetic response to novel environments and can result in selection of general learning ability (Ancel, 2000; Bateson, 2004). Learning can generate adaptive complex sequences of behaviour that would have been highly unlikely to result from unlearned genetic selection, but by the Baldwin effect genetic variants that reduce cost or increase efficiency of the learned sequence of behaviour would be favoured by natural selection, resulting in genetic evolution of the developmental mechanism underlying the behaviour. For instance, elements of the sequence of behaviour could evolve to become unlearned (without compromising the organism's general capacity for plasticity in a variable environment). Bateson (2007) refers to this effect as the 'adaptability driver' because adaptability by the organism has driven a change in the evolutionary trajectory (maintaining a phenotype that otherwise would have been highly unlikely to have evolved as a result of genetic mutation alone). Bateson (2007) suggests that complex sequences of behaviour such as tool-using culture, as found in chimpanzees, could have been subject to the Baldwin effect (or the adaptability driver) to enhance cognitive capacity in the hominid lineage.

Cultural niche construction is the process whereby organisms modify or construct aspects of the selective environment as a result of socially transmitted behaviour or activity (Kendal, Tehrani and Odling-Smee, 2011; Odling-Smee, Laland and Feldman, 2003). Selection induced by the altered environment can be on either genetic or cultural variation, or both, depending on the evolvability of each form of heritable information. Typically, cultural evolution can occur at faster rates than genetic evolution, so the feedback between cultural niche construction and selection on genetic variation can accelerate the rate of genetic evolution. This dynamic may have occurred for evolving brain size in archaic *Homo sapiens* during the latter half of the Middle Pleistocene, where the invention of cooking partially externalised the digestive process. Selection in response to this cultural modification of the environment is encapsulated in part by the 'expensive tissue hypothesis', whereby cooking facilitates a reduction in gut size, requiring fewer energetic resources and paying for the extremely high mass-specific metabolic rate of a large brain (Aiello and Wheeler, 1995; Laland, Odling-Smee and Feldman, 2000).

Sterelney (2007) recognises that both the social and technical intelligence hypotheses are encapsulated by the niche construction of social and ecological environments that results in reciprocal feedback between selection for social and ecological competence. Sterelney focuses on the fitness benefits of generating resource through cooperative technological foraging, which, mediated by social transmission, would provide a selective advantage within the hominin lineage favouring both social and technical intelligence. Construction of the social environment and the concurrent accumulation of technical knowledge can feed back to affect both genetic and cultural selection. This view sits well with the 'Vygotskian intelligence hypothesis', that the evolution of hominin brain size was driven by sharing and directing focus on an ecological problem to generate a solution through cooperation and collaboration (Moll and Tomasello, 2007).

Technology can often be incorporated in a 'sociotechnology of assembly', where cooperation and social norms are intrinsic to function (Girard and Stark, 2007). For instance, in a modern context, a public hearing might require distinctive combinations of social networks between socially constructed agents, protocols prescribing who can speak when, and technologies including microphone and stopwatch (Girard and Stark, 2007, p. 151). Also, cooperative foraging technology often relies on the coordination of sets of skills and resources distributed across individuals within and sometimes between populations. Theory of mind may facilitate some forms of cooperation, allowing communicative intentions to be shared (Gallese, 2007; Tomasello *et al.*, 2005). The cultural evolution of normative behaviour and symbolic group markers provides a social environment that reduces the risk of being cheated in a cooperative game and enhances the efficiency of coordinated responses within a group to a cooperation problem.

The evolution of cooperation and altruistic helping behaviour

Richerson and Boyd (2005) describe how cooperative behaviour may evolve through group-level selection: cooperative behaviours may provide benefit to the group, and thus variation in cooperation between groups can result in group-level selection, while institutional norms, conformity and symbolic markers can reduce within-group variation in competition (Henrich and Boyd, 1998; McElreath, Boyd and Richerson, 2003). This can heighten the relative effect of between-group competition and result in the cultural evolution of cooperative or altruistic traits that are intrinsically costly to the individual yet enhance group survival, welfare and expansion (Henrich, 2004a; but see Lehmann, Feldman and Foster, 2008). The cultural evolution of cooperative group-beneficial traits may also co-evolve with social institutions such as food sharing and monogamy (Bowles, Choi and Hopfensitz, 2003).

The benefits of cooperative behaviour may have also favoured the genetic selection of pro-social emotions, such as a sense of justice, pride, guilt and honour, that facilitate strong reciprocity, that is 'a propensity to cooperate with others, and to punish those who violate the norms of cooperation, at personal cost, even when it is implausible to expect that these costs will be repaid either by others or at a later date' (Gintis *et al.*, 2007, p. 605). There has been much empirical and theoretical work to establish evidence for strong reciprocity in humans and to show how strong reciprocity can evolve and result in the evolution of cooperative behaviour (e.g. Bowles and Gintis, 2003; Fehr and Fischbacher, 2003; Lehmann *et al.*, 2007).

In contrast, there is very little support for strong reciprocity in non-human primates (Perry, 2009; Silk *et al.*, 2005; Tomasello, 2008). Hauser (1992) reports rhesus monkeys punishing non-callers to enforce food calling when food is found, but here the enforcers may have had a direct interest in enforcing the rule (Perry, 2009). Nonetheless, policing is found in primates, such as in pig-tailed macaques (Flack, de Waal and Krakauer, 2005) and the social transmission of an unusual tradition of pacificity has been observed in baboons (Sapolsky and Share, 2004). Also, shared intentionality has been observed in bonobos (*Pan paniscus*) when playing social games with humans (Pika and Zuberbuhler, 2007). Chimpanzees participate in collective activities including cooperative hunting and food sharing; however, experiments indicate that, like other non-human primates, they are not motivated by other-regarding preferences (as opposed to self-regarding) and there is little evidence for pro-social emotions (Silk *et al.*, 2005). Gintis (2006) notes that human sociopaths lack the pro-social emotions that may have been critical to the evolution of human society, yet there is still little consensus on how these emotions combine to influence cooperative behaviour. Many cognitive states closely related to social intelligence, such as pro-social emotions and theory of mind, are evident in much modern cultural rhetoric including arguments of religious belief and art-forms such as plays (Carrithers, 2005; Dunbar, 2003).

Using a relative measure of forebrain size as an indication of the cognitive capacity for intentionality, Dunbar (2003) predicts that complex forms of culture requiring four-level intentionality were unlikely prior to the evolution of anatomically modern humans. Dunbar suggests that four levels of intentionality are required to ensure coordinated agreement over social norms and an understanding that punishment follows infringement. For instance, 'For a supernatural-based religion to have any force in making us toe the social line, I have to *believe* that you *suppose* that there are supernatural beings who can be made to *understand* that you and I *desire* that things should happen in a particular way' (Dunbar 2003, p. 177). Although we may need four levels to reflect upon the complicated social reasoning, cultural transmission of a belief in the supernatural being and its propensity to punish norm-violators removes the requirement for the advanced cognition while deciding whether to cooperate or defect: 'I believe that the supernatural being will punish me if I violate a social norm.' The transmitted information effectively reinforces and contextualises the disposition for strong reciprocation and pro-social emotions. Indeed, it is possible that strong reciprocity evolved through a Baldwin-like process (see above).

Cumulative cultural evolution

Cumulative cultural evolution is both a likely causal factor and consequence of the evolution of intelligence in the hominin lineage. The efficiency or complexity of traits can increase through a process of descent with selective modification, such as through imitation followed by modification through individual learning (e.g. insight or trial-and-error learning), or through selective imitation or adaptive filtering of transmitted information (Boyd and Richerson, 1985; Enquist and Ghirlanda, 2007; Enquist *et al.*, 2008; Ghirlanda and Enquist, 2007). Cumulative cultural evolution is also typified by an acceleration in the accumulation of cultural traits (Enquist *et al.*, 2008).

Hunt and Gray (2003, p. 867) note that one should observe three characteristics of cumulative technological evolution: (i) 'diversification of tool design', where 'a new tool design is added to one or more existing, related designs' to form 'a branching sequence of tool evolution from a single ancestral design, and contrasts with the independent development of similar designs'; (ii) 'cumulative change to tool lineages' through a 'ratchet-like' process 'where design changes are retained at the population level until new improved designs arise' (Tomasello, 1999); and (iii) 'faithful transmission of tool design through social learning' such that individuals do not need to reinvent old designs.

Simple social learning processes, including some stimulus and emulation effects, have been referred to as 'socially influenced individual learning' in recognition that the learned information is not transmitted directly from demonstrator to pupil, but has to be reinvented by each learner. This imposes a huge constraint on the potential for socially transmitted information to accumulate through descent, between cultural generations, and modification (overall, the 'ratchet effect'). In contrast, imitation has been proposed as a prerequisite for cumulative cultural evolution, as information can be transmitted directly with high fidelity (Henrich and McElreath, 2003; Tomasello *et al.*, 1993).

The most obvious types of adaptive cumulative culture in the hominin lineage are tool use and language syntax. In both cases, evidence of natural cases in non-humans is extremely limited. An exception is tool use by New Caledonian crows. Hunt and Gray (2003) document, from 21 sites, the shapes of 5550 tools displaying a range of barbed edges of *Pandanus* species leaves, used to facilitate the capture of invertebrates in trees. They found three distinct pandanus tool designs: narrow tools, wide tools and stepped tools, which are likely to have gone through a process of cumulative change from a common historical origin, particularly as the designs lacked ecological correlates and exhibited different, continuous and overlapping geographical distributions. Taylor *et al.* (2009) show that the New Caledonian crows can solve complex physical problems by reasoning both causally and analogically about causal relations (see also Weir and Kacelnik, 2006). In contrast, Marshall-Pescini and Whiten (2008) performed an experiment that did not show cumulative cultural evolution of a tool used to probe for a food reward in chimpanzees. Instead, their results showed that the chimpanzees are inclined to stick with their initial solution to the foraging problem and that this could provide a constraint on the species' capacity for cumulative culture of technology. Whiten (2005) points out that, for cumulative cultural evolution of technical traits, there may be critical differences between humans and other apes in the content of the socially transmitted information. For instance, chimpanzees can "only fashion tools by "removing and modifying subcomponents" to create hammers, anvils, sponges, clubs, seats and probes. In contrast, humans can construct tools from complementary parts, including simple animal traps made by hunter-gatherers" (Whiten, 2005, p. 54).

Cumulative culture in animals may occur using simple forms of social learning for types of learned information that hitherto have been largely disregarded. For instance, van der Post and Hogeweg (2008) use an individual-based simulation to show that in a diverse, patchy environment there can be cumulative cultural evolution of diet choice across generations as a by-product of group living, where the social influence of the group is simply to affect an individual's foraging location. Diet quality increases over generations, particularly when naive individuals are highly selective of diet quality, pulling the group average closer to the optimum.

The rate of human cumulative cultural evolution is likely to interact with demographic factors. Ghirlanda and Enquist (2007) note a common positive association between the two, for example the invention of new stone tools accompanying the expansion of *Homo sapiens* out of Africa, as well as exponential cultural and population growth within the last millennium. They develop a mathematical model to show that if the transmission of adaptive culture is accurate enough, there can be a transition from stable state to a demo-cultural explosion as observed in recent history.

It is possible that population size and cumulative culture can also be positively associated if dispersal into new selective environments provokes adaptation through cumulative cultural evolution, although the isolation of small founder populations can have a contrasting effect (see below). Also, an increase in population density resulting from population expansion can potentially feed back on the rate of cumulative cultural evolution by increasing the rate of information exchange (Powell, Shennan and Thomas, 2009). Population expansion may also result in modification of the social environment, provoking change in social norms (Mellars, 2005). Under some conditions, this may result in the cultural evolution of cooperative, coordinated sets of skills (Sterelney, 2007).

Human cultural evolution does not always result in population expansion, as mechanisms already discussed can result in the spread of cultural traits that reduce Darwinian fitness, including those that explicitly constrain fertility or implement a carrying capacity, such as preferences or laws constraining family size. Also, human cultural evolution is not always characterised by an exponential trajectory. Striking examples include the loss of mathematical and scientific knowledge at the end of the classical Greek era (Russo, 2004) and the loss of skills and technologies in Tasmanian hunter-gatherers (Henrich, 2004b). In the latter case, mainland population expansion resulted in a small founder population of Palaeolithic foragers that were isolated approximately 12 000 to 10 000 years ago for 10 000 years. During this time (unlike mainland aboriginals), they lost or never developed technologies including the manufacture of bone tools, cold-weather clothing, fishing tools and boomerangs. Henrich (2004b) developed a mathematical model to show that, with imperfect social learning, a reduction in effective population size (the size of the interacting pool of social learners), consistent with the small founding population, may have prevented the increase in complex skills and encouraged the adoption of simple technologies that are easy to acquire with high fidelity (also see Powell, Shennan and Thomas, 2009 for a spatial analysis, based on Henrich 2004b, examining demographic effects on the rate of cumulative cultural evolution and behavioural modernity).

CONCLUSION: A NICHE CONSTRUCTION FRAMEWORK OF MULTIMODAL INHERITANCE

It is clear that interactions between cognition and culture are highly complex. The cognitive state can affect socially learned behaviour through transmission biases (contextual, modal and content) and by influencing social learning processes. Reciprocally, socially transmitted information, norms and material culture can alter the cognitive state by influencing social and ecological environments (niche construction).

Jablonka and Lamb (2006a, 2006b) recognise that, while natural selection takes place on the phenotype, the genotype-phenotype mapping needs to account for the impact of other forms of information transmission during development. They propose a four-dimensional multimodal inheritance evolutionary system, specifying genetic, epigenetic, behavioural and symbolic-based modes of information transmission. The epigenetic inheritance includes, for example, RNA-mediated inheritance and chromatin marking. Behavioural and symbolic inheritance account for the social transmission of information. They are separated in the scheme, in part, because symbolic systems are, by nature, referential, giving far greater potential range of expression (in conjunction with the language characteristics discussed above). Also, symbolic information, but not behaviour, can remain latent for generations (e.g. through writing). While there may be debate over the delineation of the types of social transmission, it is clear that the genotype-phenotype map for learning cognition can be strongly influenced by non-genetic modes of inheritance. An obvious case is the effect of education-related traditions on the capacity for learning. Furthermore, there may be interactions between the various transmission modes, for instance, if traditional practices of parental/maternal care have trans-generational epigenetic effects on cognitive development (Bjorklund, 2006).

The niche construction perspective is important not only because it naturally incorporates the interactions between these different modes of inheritance (e.g. the tradition of dairy farming, a social transmission mode, provides a selective environment affecting the evolution of lactase persistence, a genetic transmission mode – see Box 10.1) but also because it incorporates the ecological inheritance of aspects of our social and 'natural' environments that are not typically transmitted directly between individuals, such as the social structure of an institution (Brown and Feldman, 2009) or the physical infrastructure of a human settlement. This type of ecologically inherited information and physical resource can have important effects on the development of the cognitive state, for instance, affecting the spread of education-related traditions (Borenstein, Kendal and Feldman, 2006).

For the future, research into the interactions between cognition and culture is entering an exciting phase. Technological advances in genetics and neurobiology are being matched with novel theory and experimental techniques in behaviour and cognition, which can combine to forge a better understanding of the complex interactions relating cognition and culture. These findings will fit naturally within a niche constructive framework, accounting for multimodal inheritance and across multiple levels of analysis.

REFERENCES

Aiello, L. C. and Wheeler, P. (1995). The expensive-tissue hypothesis: The brain and the digestive system in human and primate evolution. *Current Anthropology, 36*, 199–221.

Ancel, L. W. (2000). Undermining the Baldwin expediting effect: Does phenotypic plasticity accelerate evolution? *Theoretical Population Biology, 58*, 307–19.

Aoki, K. (1986). A stochastic model of gene-culture coevolution suggested by the 'culture historical hypothesis' for the evolution of adult lactose absorption in humans. *Proceedings of the National Academy of Science USA, 83*, 2929–33.

Aoki, K. (2001). Theoretical and empirical aspects of gene-culture coevolution. *Theoretical Population Biology, 59*, 253–61.

Arnold, K. and Zuberbuhler, K. (2006). Semantic combinations in primate calls. *Nature, 441*, 303.

Baldwin, J. M. (1902). *Development and evolution*. New York: Macmillan.

Barrett, J. L. and Nyhof, M. A. (2001). Spreading non-natural concepts: The role of intuitive conceptual structures in memory and transmission of cultural materials. *Journal of Cognition and Culture, 1*, 69–100.

Barton, R. A. and Dunbar, R. I. M. (1997). Evolution of the social brain. In A. Whiten and R. W. Byrne (eds), *Machiavellian intelligence II: Extensions and evaluations* (pp. 240–263). Cambridge: Cambridge University Press.

Bateson, P. P. G. (2004). The active role of behaviour in evolution. *Biological Philosophy*, 19, 283–98.

Bateson, P. P. G. (2007). The adaptability driver: Links between behaviour and evolution. *Biological Theory*, 1, 342–5.

Bersaglieri, T., Sabeti, P. C., Patterson, N. *et al.* (2004). Genetic signatures of strong recent positive selection at the lactase gene. *American Journal of Human Genetics*, 74, 1111–1120.

Bettinger, R. L. and Eerkens, J. (1999). Point typologies, cultural transmission, and the spread of bow-and-arrow technology in the prehistoric Great Basin. *American Antiquity*, 64, 231–42.

Biro, D., Inoue-Nakamura, N., Tonooka, R. *et al.* (2003). Cultural innovation and transmission of tool use in wild chimpanzees: Evidence from field experiments. *Animal Cognition*, 6, 213–223.

Bjorklund, D. F. (2006). Mother knows best: Epigenetic inheritance, maternal effects, and the evolution of human intelligence. *Developmental Review*, 26, 213–242.

Borenstein, E., Kendal, J. R. and Feldman, M. W. (2006). Cultural niche construction in a meta-population. *Theoretical Population Biology*, 70, 92–104.

Bowles, S., Choi, J. and Hopfensitz, A. (2003). The co-evolution of individual behaviours and social institutions. *Journal of Theoretical Biology*, 223, 135–47.

Bowles, S. and Gintis, H. (2003). Origins of human cooperation. In P. Hammerstein (ed.), *Genetic and cultural evolution of cooperation* (pp. 429–43). Cambridge, MA: MIT Press.

Boyd, R. and Richerson, P J. (1985). *Culture and the evolutionary process*. Chicago: Chicago University Press.

Boyd, R. and Richerson, P. (1995). Why does culture increase human adaptability? *Ethology and Sociobiology*, 16, 125–43.

Brown, M. J. and Feldman, M. W. (2009). Sociocultural epistasis and cultural exaptation in foot-binding, marriage form, and religious practices in early 20th-century Taiwan. *Proceedings of the National Academy of Sciences USA*, 106, 22139–44.

Bshary, R., Salwiczek, L. and Wickler, W. (2007). Social cognition in non primates. In R. I. M. Dunbar and L. S. Barrett (eds), *Oxford handbook of evolutionary psychology* (pp. 83–101). Oxford: Oxford University Press.

Byrne, W. R. and Byrne, J. M. E. (1993). Complex leaf gathering skills of mountain gorillas (*Gorilla g. beringei*): Variability and standardization. *American Journal of Primatology*, 31, 241–61.

Byrne, W. R. and Whiten, A. (eds) (1988). *Machiavellian intelligence*. Oxford: Oxford University Press.

Call, J., Carpenter, M. and Tomasello, M. (2005). Copying results and copying actions in the process of social learning: Chimpanzees (*Pan troglodytes*) and human children (*Homo sapiens*). *Animal Cognition*, 8, 151–63.

Caro, T. M. and Hauser, M. D. (1992). Is there teaching in nonhuman animals? *Quarterly Review of Biology*, 67, 151–74.

Call, J. and Tomasello, M. (2008). Does the chimpanzee have a theory of mind? 30 years later. *Trends in Cognitive Science*, 12, 187–92.

Call, J. and Tomasello, M. (eds) (2004). *The gestural communication of apes and monkeys*. Hillsdale, NJ: Lawrence Erlbaum Associates.

Carrithers, M. B. (2005). Why anthropologists should study rhetoric. *Journal of the Royal Anthropological Institute*, 11, 577–83.

Catchpole, C. K. and Slater, P. J. B. (1995). *Bird song: Biological themes and variations*. Cambridge: Cambridge University Press.

Cavalli-Sforza, L. L. and Feldman, M. W. (1981). *Cultural transmission and evolution: A quantatitive approach*. Princeton, NJ: Princeton University Press.

Chomsky, N. (1980). *Rules and representations*. London: Basil Blackwell.

Claidiere, N. and Sperber, D. (2007). The role of attraction in cultural evolution. *Journal of Cognition and Culture, 7*, 89–111.

Clayton, N. S., Dally, J. M. and Emery, N. J. (2007). Social cognition by food-caching corvids: The western scrub-jay as a natural psychologist. *Philosophical Transactions of the Royal Society B, 362*, 507–22.

Coolen, I., Bergen, Y., Day, R. and Laland, K. (2003). Species difference in adaptive use of public information in sticklebacks. *Proceedings of the Royal Society B, 270*, 1413–1419.

Cote, I. M. (2000). Evolution and ecology of cleaning symbioses in the sea. *Oceanographic and Marine Biology, 38*, 311–55.

Coward, F. and Gamble, C. (2008). Big brains, small worlds: Material culture and the evolution of the mind. *Philosophical Transactions of the Royal Society B, 363*, 1969–79.

Csibra, G. and Gergely, G. (2006). Social learning and social cognition: The case for pedagogy. In Y. Munakata and M. H. Johnson (eds), *Processes of change in brain and cognitive development: Attention and performance, XXI* (pp. 249–74). Oxford: Oxford University Press.

Custance, D. M., Whiten, A. and Fredman, T. (1999). Social learning of artificial fruit processing in capuchin monkeys (*Cebus apella*). *Journal of Computational Psychology, 113*, 13–23.

Day, R., Macdonald, T., Brown, C. *et al.* (2001). Interactions between shoal size and conformity in guppy social foraging. *Animal Behaviour, 62*, 917–925.

Dunbar, R. I. M. (2003). The social brain: Mind, language and society in evolutionary perspective. *Annual Review of Anthropology, 32*, 163–81.

Dunbar, R. I. M. and Barrett, L. (2007). Evolutionary psychology in the round. In R. I. M. Dunbar and L. S. Barrett (eds), *The Oxford handbook of evolutionary psychology* (pp. 3–10). Oxford: Oxford University Press.

Dunbar, R. I. M. and Shultz, S. (2007). Evolution in the social brain. *Social Cognition, 317*, 1344–7.

Efferson, C., Lalive, R., Richerson, P. *et al.* (2008). Conformists and mavericks: The empirics of frequency-dependent cultural transmission. *Evolution and Human Behavior, 29*, 56–64.

Emery, N. J. and Clayton, N. S. (2004). The mentality of crows: Convergent evolution of intelligence in corvids and apes. *Science, 306*, 1903–7.

Enquist, M., Eriksson, K. and Ghirlanda, S. (2007). Critical points in current theory of conformist social learning. *Journal of Evolutionary Psychology, 5*, 67–87.

Enquist, M. and Ghirlanda, S. (2007). Evolution of social learning does not explain the origin of human cumulative culture. *Journal of Theoretical Biology, 246*, 129–35.

Enquist, M., Ghrirlanda, S., Jarrick, A. and Wachtmeister, C. A. (2008). Why does human culture increase exponentially? *Theoretical Population Biology, 74*, 46–55.

Eriksson, K. and Coultas, J. (2009). Are people really conformist-biased? An empirical test and a new mathematical model. *Journal of Evolutionary Psychology, 7*, 5–21.

Fehr, E. and Fischbacher, U. (2003). The nature of human altruism. *Nature, 425*, 785–91.

Feldman, M. W. (2008). Dissent with modification: Cultural evolution and social niche construction. In M. J. Brown (ed.), *Explaining culture scientifically*. Washington: University of Washington Press.

Feldman, M. W. and Cavalli-Sforza, L. L. (1989). On the theory of evolution under genetic and cultural transmission with application to the lactose absorption problem.

In M. W. Feldman (ed.), *Mathematical evolutionary theory* (pp. 145–73). Princeton, NJ: Princeton University Press.

Feldman, M. W. and Laland, K. N. (1996). Gene-culture coevolution theory. *Trends in Ecology and Evolution, 11*, 453–7.

Flack, J. C., de Waal, F. B. M. and Krakauer, D. C. (2005). Social structure, robustness and policing cost in a cognitively sophisticated species. *American Naturalist, 165*, 126–39.

Franks, N. R. and Richardson, T. (2006). Teaching in tandem-running ants. *Nature, 439*, 153.

Galef, B. and Whiskin, E. (2008). 'Conformity' in rats? *Animal Behavior, 75*, 2035–9.

Galef, B. G., Jr. and Allen, C. (1995). A new model system for studying animal tradition. *Animal Behavior, 50*, 705–17.

Gallese, V. (2007). Before and below 'theory of mind': Embodied simulation and the neural correlates of social cognition. *Philosophical Transaction of the Royal Society B, 362*, 659–69.

Gergely, G., Bekkering, H. and Kiraly, I. (2002). Rational imitation in preverbal infants. *Nature, 415*, 755.

Ghirlanda, S. and Enquist, M. (2007). Cumulative culture and explosive demographic transitions. *Quality and Quantity, 41*, 591–600.

Gintis, H. (2006). A framework for the unification of the behavioural sciences. *Behavioral and Brain Sciences, 30*, 1–61.

Gintis, H., Bowles, S., Boyd, R. and Fehr, E. (2007). Explaining altruistic behaviour in humans. In R. I. M. Dunbar and L. S. Barrett (eds), *The Oxford handbook of evolutionary psychology* (pp. 605–20). Oxford: Oxford University Press.

Giraldeau, L. A., Valone, T. and Templeton, J. (2002). Potential disadvantages of using socially acquired information. *Philosopical Transactions of the Royal Society B, 357*, 1559–66.

Girard, M. and Stark, D. (2007). Socio-technologies of assembly: Sense-making and demonstration in rebuilding Lower Manhattan. In D. Lazer and V. Mayer-Schoenberger (eds), *Governance and information: The rewiring of governing and deliberation in the 21st century* (pp. 145–176). New York, NY: Oxford University Press.

Guglielmino, C. R., Viganotti, C., Hewlett, B. and Cavalli-Sforza, L. L. (1995). Cultural variation in Africa: Role of mechanisms of transmission and adaptation. *Proceedings of the National Academy of Sciences USA, 92*, 7585–9.

Hamilton, W. D. (1964). The genetical evolution of social behaviour, I and II. *Journal of Theoretical Biology, 7*, 1–52.

Hauser, M. D. (1992). Costs of deception: Cheaters are punished in rhesus monkeys. *Proceedings of National Academy of Sciences USA, 89*, 12137–9.

Henrich, J. (2004a). Cultural group selection, coevolutionary processes and large-scale cooperation. *Journal of Economics and Behavioral Organization, 53*, 3–35.

Henrich, J. (2004b). Demography and cultural evolution: How adaptive cultural processes can produce maladaptive losses: The Tasmanian case. *American Antiquities, 69*, 197–214.

Henrich, J. and Boyd, R. (1998). The evolution of conformist transmission and the emergence of between-group differences. *Evolution and Human Behavior, 19*, 215–241.

Henrich, J. and Boyd, R. (2001). Why people punish defectors. *Journal of Theoretical Biology, 208*, 79–89.

Henrich, J. and Gil-White, F. J. (2001). The evolution of prestige freely conferred deference as a mechanism for enhancing the benefits of cultural transmission. *Evolution and Human Behavior, 22*, 165–96.

Henrich, J. and McElreath, R. (2003). The evolution of cultural evolution. *Evolutionary Anthropology, 12*, 123–35.

Henrich, J., Boyd, R., Bowles, S. *et al.* (2001). In search of Homo economicus: Behavioural experiments in 15 small-scale societies. *AEA Papers and Proceedings, May*, 73–8.

Henrich, J., Ensimger, J., McElreath, R. *et al.* (2010). Markets, religion, community size, and the evolution of fairness and punishment. *Science, 327*, 1480–1484.

Henrich, J., McElreath, R., Barr, A. *et al.* (2006). Costly punishment across human societies. *Science, 312*, 1767–70.

Herman, L. M. (2002). Vocal, social and self-imitation by bottlenosed dolphins. In K. Dautenhahn and C. L. Nehaniv (eds), *Imitation in animals and artifacts* (pp. 63–108). Cambridge, MA: MIT Press.

Herrmann, E., Call, J., Hernàndez-Lloreda, M. V. *et al.* (2007). Humans have evolved specialized skills of social cognition: The cultural intelligence hypothesis. *Science, 317*, 1360–1366.

Hewlett, B. S., Silvestra, A. and Guglielmino, C. R. (2002). Semes and genes in Africa. *Current Anthropology, 43*, 313–321.

Heyes, C. M. (1994). Social learning in animals: Categories and mechanisms. *Biological Review, 69*, 207–31.

Heyes, C. M. (1998). Theory of mind in non-human primates. *Behavioral and Brain Sciences, 21*, 101–48.

Heyes, C. M. (2009). Evolution, development and intentional control of imitation. *Philosophical Transactions of the Royal Society B, 364*, 2293–8.

Hockett, C. F. (1960). The origin of speech. *Scientific American, 203*, 88–96.

Holden, C. and Mace, R. (1997). Phylogenetic analysis of the evolution of lactose digestion in adults. *Human Biology, 69*, 605–28.

Hollox, E. (2005). Genetics of lactase persistence: Fresh lessons in the history of milk drinking. *European Journal of Human Genetics, 13*, 267–9.

Hoppitt, W. J. E. and Laland, K. N. (2008). Social processes influencing learning in animals: A review of the evidence. *Advances in the Study of Animal Behavior, 38*, 105–65.

Hoppitt W. J. E., Brown, G. R., Kendal, R. *et al.* (2008). Lessons from animal teaching. *Trends in Ecology and Evolution, 23*, 486–93.

Horner, V. and Whiten, A. (2005). Causal knowledge and imitation/emulation switching in chimpanzees (*Pan troglodytes*) and children (*Homo sapiens*). *Animal Behavior, 8*, 164–81.

Humphrey, N. K. (1976). The social function of intellect. In P. P. G. Bateson and R. A. Hinde (eds), *Growing points in ethology* (pp. 303–17). Cambridge: Cambridge University Press.

Hunt, G. R. and Gray, H. D. (2003). Diversification and cumulative culture in New Caledonian crow tool manufacture. *Proceedings of the Royal Society B, 270*, 867–74.

Ihara, Y. and Feldman, M. W. (2004). Cultural niche construction and the evolution of small family size. *Theoretical Population Biology, 65*, 105–11.

Itan, Y., Powell, A., Beaumont, M. A. *et al.* (2009). The origins of lactase persistence in Europe. *PLoS Computational Biology, 5*, e1000491.

Jablonka, E. and Lamb, M. J. (2006a). Precis of *Evolution in four dimensions. Behavioral and Brain Sciences, 30*, 353–92.

Jablonka, E. and Lamb, M. J. (2006b). *Evolution in four dimensions: Genetic, epigentic, behavioral, and symbolic variation in the history of life.* Princeton, NJ: MIT Press.

Kameda, T. and Nakanishi, D. (2003). Does social/cultural learning increase human adaptability? Rogers' question revisited. *Evolution and Human Behavior, 24*, 242–60.

Kashima, Y. (2000). Maintaining cultural stereotypes in the serial reproduction of narratives. *Personality and Social Psychology Bulletin, 26*, 594–604.

Kendal, R. L., Galef, B. G. and van Schaik, C. P. (2010). Social learning research outside the laboratory: How and why? *Learning and Behavior*, *38*,187–94.

Kendal, J. R., Giraldeau L-A. and Laland, K. N. (2009). The evolution of social learning rules: Payoff-biased and frequency dependent biased transmission. *Journal of Theoretical Biology*, *260*, 210–219.

Kendal, J. R., Tehrani, J. J. and Odling-Smee, J. (2011). Human niche construction in inter-disciplinary focus. *Philosophical Transactions of the Royal Society B* (in press).

Kendal, R. L., Coolen, I., van Bergen, Y. and Laland, K. N. (2005). Tradeoffs in the adaptive use of social and asocial learning. *Advances in the Study of Behavior*, *35*, 333–79.

Kendal, J. R., Rendell, L., Pike, T. W. and Laland, K. N. (2009). Nine-spined sticklebacks deploy a hill-climbing social learning strategy. *Behavioral Ecology*, *20*, 238–44.

Krebs, J. R., Clayton, N. S., Healy, S. D. *et al.* (1996). The ecology of the avian brain: Food-storing memory and the hippocampus. *Ibis*, *138*, 34–46.

Kummer, H., Daston, L., Gigerenzer, G. and Silk, J. (1997). The social intelligence hypothesis. In P. Weingart, P. Richerson, S. D. Mitchell and S. D. Maasen (eds), *Human by nature: Between biology and the social sciences* (pp. 157–79). Hillsdale, NJ: Lawrence Erlbaum Associates.

Laland, K. N. (2004). Social learning strategies. *Learning and Behavior*, *32*, 4–14.

Laland, K. N. and Kendal, J. R. (2003). What the models say about animal social learning. In D. M. Fragaszy and S. Perry (eds), *The biology of traditions: Models and evidence* (pp. 33–55). Chicago: Chicago University Press.

Laland, K. N., Odling-Smee, F. J. and Feldman, M. W. (2000). Niche construction, biological evolution, and cultural change. *Behavioral and Brain Science*, *23*, 131–75.

Laland, K. N., Odling-Smee, F. J. and Myles, S. (2010). How culture shaped the human genome: Bringing genetics and the human sciences together. *Nature Reviews Genetics*, *11*, 137–48.

Laland, K. N., Richerson, P. J. and Boyd, R. (1996). Developing a theory of animal social learn-ing. In C. M. Heyes and Galef, B. G., Jr. (eds), *Social learning in animals: The roots of culture* (pp. 129–54). London: Academic Press.

Laland, K. N. and Williams, K. (1998). Social transmission of maladaptive information in the guppy. *Behavioral Ecology*, *9*, 495–9.

Latané, B. and Wolf, S. (1981). The social impact of majorities and minorities. *Psychological Review*, *88*, 438–53.

Lefebvre, L., Reader, S. M. and Sol, D. (2004). Brains, innovations and evolution in birds and primates. *Brain, Behavior and Evolution*, *63*, 233–46.

Lehmann, L. and Feldman, M. W. (2008). The co-evolution of culturally inherited altruistic helping and cultural transmission under random group formation. *Theoretical Population Biology*, *73*, 506–16.

Lehmann, L., Feldman, M. W. and Foster, K. R. (2008). Cultural transmission can inhibit the evolution of altruistic helping. *American Naturalist*, *170*, 12–24.

Lehmann, L., Rousset, F., Roze, D. and Kellder, L. (2007). Strong reciprocity or strong ferocity? A population genetic view of the evolution of altruistic punishment. *American Naturalist*, *170*, 21–36.

Madden, J. R. (2008). Do bowerbirds exhibit cultures? *Animal Cognition*, *11*, 1–12.

Marshall-Pescini, S. and Whiten, A. (2008). Chimpanzees (*Pan troglodytes*) and the question of cumulative culture: An experimental approach. *Animal Cognition*, *11*, 449–56.

Maynard Smith, J. and Szathmary, E. (1995). *The major transitions in evolution*. London: Freeman.

McElreath, R., Boyd, R. and Richerson, P. J. (2003). Shared norms and the evolution of ethnic markers. *Current Anthropology*, *44*, 122–9.

McElreath, R. and Strimling, P. (2008). When natural selection favours imitation of parents. *Current Anthropology, 49*, 307–16.

McElreath, R., Bell A. V., Efferson, C. *et al.* (2008). Beyond existence and aiming outside the laboratory: Estimating frequency-dependent and pay-off-biased social learning strategies. *Philosophical Transactions of the Royal Society B, 363*, 3515–28.

Mellars, P. (2005). The impossible coincidence: A single species model for the origins of modern human behavior in Europe. *Evolutionary Anthropology, 14*, 12–27.

Mesoudi, A. (2008). An experimental simulation of the 'copy-successful-individuals' cultural learning strategy: Adaptive landscapes, producer-scrounger dynamics and informational access costs. *Evolution and Human Behavior, 29*, 350–363.

Mesoudi, A. and O'Brien, M. J. (2008). The cultural transmission of great basin projectile-point technology I: An experimental simulation. *American Antiquity, 73*, 3–28.

Mesoudi, A. and Whiten, A. (2008). The multiple roles of cultural transmission experiments in understanding human cultural evolution. *Philosophical Transactions of the Royal Society B, 363*, 3489–501.

Mesoudi, A., Whiten, A. and Dunbar, R. (2006). A bias for social information in human cultural transmission. *British Journal of Psychology, 97*, 405–23.

Moll, H. and Tomasello, M. (2007). Cooperation and human cognition: The Vygotskian intelligence hypothesis. *Philosophical Transactions of the Royal Society B, 362*, 639–49.

Nakahashi, W. (2007). The evolution of conformist transmission in social learning with the environment changes periodically. *Theoretical Population Biology, 72*, 52–66.

Newson, L., Postmes, T., Lea, E. G. and Webley, P. (2005). Why are modern families small? Toward an evolutionary and cultural explanation for the demographic transition. *Personality and Social Psychology Review, 9*, 360–75.

Nielsen, M., Collier-Baker, E., Davis, J. M. and Suddendorf, T. (2005). Imitation recognition in a captive chimpanzee (*Pan troglodytes*). *Animal Cognition, 8*, 31–6.

Nowak, M. A., Plotkin, J. B. and Jansen, V. A. A. (2000). The evolution of syntactic communication. *Nature, 404*, 495–8.

Odling-Smee, F. J., Laland, K. N. and Feldman, M. W. (2003). Niche construction: The neglected process in evolution. *Monographs in Population Biology, 37*. Princeton, NJ: Princeton University Press.

Perry, S. (2009). Are nonhuman primates likely to exhibit cultural capacities like those of humans? In K. N. Laland and B. G. Galef (eds), *A question of animal culture* (pp. 247–68). Cambridge, MA: Harvard University Press.

Perry, S., Panger, M., Rose, L. M. *et al.* (2003). Traditions in wild whitefaced capuchin monkeys. In D. M. Fragaszy and S. Perry (eds), *The biology of traditions: Models and evidence.* pp. 391–425. Cambridge: Cambridge University Press.

Pika, S. and Zuberbuhler, K. (2007). Social games between bonobos and humans: Evidence for shared intentionality? *American Journal of Primatology, 69*, 1–6.

Pinker, S. and Bloom, P. (1990). Natural language and natural selection. *Behavioral and Brain Sciences, 13*, 707–84.

van der Post, D. J. and Hogeweg, P. (2008). Diet traditions and cumulative cultural processes as side-effects of grouping. *Animal Behavior, 75*, 133–44.

Powell, A., Shennan, S. and Thomas, M. G. (2009). Late Pleistocene demography and the appearance of modern human behavior. *Science, 324*, 1298–301.

Premack, D. (2007). Human and animal cognition: Continuity and discontinuity. *Proceedings of the National Academy of Sciences USA, 104*, 13861–7.

Reader, S. M., Kendal, J. R. and Laland, K. N. (2003). Social learning through local enhancement in wild guppy fish in Trinidad. *Animal Behavior, 66*, 729–39.

Reader, S. M. and Laland, K. N. (2002). Social intelligence, innovation, and enhanced brain size in primates. *Proceedings of the National Academy of Sciences USA, 99*, 4436–41.

Reiss, D. and Marino, L. (2001). Mirror self-recognition in the bottlenose dolphin: A case of cognitive convergence. *Proceedings of the National Academy of Sciences USA, 98*, 5937–42.

Rendell, L. E. and Whitehead, H. (2001). Culture in whales and dolphins. *Behavioral and Brain Sciences, 24*, 309–82.

Rendell, L., Boyd, R., Cownden, D. *et al.* (2010). Why copy others? Insights from the Social Learning Strategies Tournament. *Science, 328*, 208–13.

Richerson, P. J. and Boyd, R. (2005). *Not by genes alone*. Chicago: University of Chicago Press.

Richerson, P. J., Boyd, R. and Henrich, J. (2010). Gene-culture coevolution in the age of genomics. *Proceedings of the National Academy of Sciences USA, 107*, 8985–92.

Rogers, A. (1988). Does biology constrain culture? *American Anthropology, 90*, 819–31.

Rogers, D. S. and Ehrlich, P. R. (2008). Natural selection and cultural rates of change. *Proceedings of the National Academy of Sciences USA, 105*, 3416–3420.

Russo, L. (2004). *The forgotten revolution*. Berlin: Springer Verlag.

Sapolsky, R. M. and Share, L. J. (2004). A pacific culture among wild baboons: Its emergence and transmission. *PloS Biology, 2*, e106.

van Schaik, C. P., Ancrenaz, M., Borgen, G. *et al.* (2003). Orangutan cultures and the evolution of material culture. *Science, 299*, 102–5.

Schlag, K. (1998). Why imitate, and if so, how? *Journal of Economic Theory, 78*, 130–156.

Shennan, S. and Steele, J. (1999). Cultural learning in hominids: A behavioural ecological approach. In H. Box and K. Gibson (eds), *Mammalian social learning* (pp. 367–88). Cambridge: Cambridge University Press.

Shennan, S. and Wilkinson, J. R. (2001). Ceramic style change and neutral evolution: A case study from Neolithic Europe. *American Antiquity, 66*, 577–93.

Silk, J. B., Brosnan, S. F., Vonk, J. *et al.* (2005). Chimpanzees are indifferent to the welfare of unrelated group members. *Nature, 437*, 1357–9.

Smith, K. and Kirby, S. (2008). Cultural evolution: Implications for understanding the human language faculty and its evolution. *Philosophical Transactions of the Royal Society B, 363*, 3591–603.

Sperber, D. (1996). *Explaining culture*. Oxford: Oxford University Press.

Sperber, D. and Hirschfeld, L. A. (2004). The cognitive foundations of cultural stability and diversity. *Trends in Cognitive Science, 8*, 40–46.

Sterelney, K. (2007). Social intelligence, human intelligence and niche construction. *Philosophical Transactions of the Royal Society B, 362*, 719–730.

Swaney, W., Kendal, J. R., Capon, H. *et al.* (2001). Familiarity facilitates social learning of foraging behaviour in the guppy. *Animal Behaviour, 62*, 591–8.

Tanaka, M. M., Kendal, J. R. and Laland, K. N. (2009). From traditional medicine to witchcraft: Why medical treatments are not always efficacious. *PloS ONE, 4*, 1–9.

Taylor, A. H., Hunt, G. R., Medina, F. S. and Gray, R. D. (2009). Do New Caledonian crows solve physical problems through causal reasoning? *Proceedings of the Royal Society B, 276*, 247–54.

Tehrani, J. J. and Collard, M. (2009). On the relationship between inter-individual cultural transmission and population-level cultural diversity: A case study of weaving in Iranian tribal populations. *Evolution and Human Behavior, 30*, 286–300.

Tehrani, J. and Riede, F. (2008). Towards an archaeology of pedagogy: Learning, teaching and the generation of material culture traditions. *World Archaeology, 40*, 316–331.

Tennie, C., Hedwig, D., Call, J. and Tomasello, M. (2008). An experimental study of nettle feeding in captive gorillas. *American Journal of Primatology*, *70*, 1–10.

Thornton, A. and McAuliffe, K. (2006). Teaching in wild meerkats. *Science*, *313*, 227–9.

Thornton, A. and Raihani, N. J. (2008). The evolution of teaching. *Animal Behavior*, *75*, 1823–36.

Tomasello, M. (1990). Cultural transmission in the tool use and communicatory signalling of chimpanzees? In S. Parker and K. Gibson (eds), *Language and intelligence in monkeys and apes: Comparative developmental perspectives* (pp. 274–311). Cambridge: Cambridge University Press.

Tomasello, M. (1996). Do apes ape? In C. M. Heyes and B. G. Galef, Jr. (eds), *Social learning in animals: The roots of culture* (pp. 319–46). London: Academic Press.

Tomasello, M. (1999). *The cultural origins of human cognition*. Cambridge, MA: Harvard University Press.

Tomasello, M. (2008, May 25). How are humans unique. *New York Times*.

Tomasello, M. and Call, J. (1997). *Primate cognition*. Oxford: Oxford University Press.

Tomasello, M., Carpenter, M., Call, J. *et al.* (2005). Understanding and sharing intentions: The origins of cultural cognition. *Behavioural and Brain Science*, *28*, 1–17.

Tomasello, M., Kruger, A. C. and Ratner, H. H. (1993). Cultural Learning. *Behavioral and Brain Science*, *16*, 495–552.

Tooby, J. and Cosmides, L. (1990). On the universality of human nature and the uniqueness of the individual: The role of genetics and adaptation. *Journal of Personality*, *58*, 17–67.

Trivers, R. L. (1971). The evolution of reciprocal altruism. *Quarterly Review of Biology*, *46*, 35–57.

Wakano, J. Y. and Aoki, K. (2007). Do social learning and conformist bias coevolve? Henrich and Boyd revisited. *Theoretical Population Biology*, *72*, 504–12.

Wakano, J. Y., Aoki, K. and Feldman, M. W. (2004). Evolution of social learning: A mathematical analysis. *Theoretical Population Biology*, *66*, 249–58.

Weir, A. S. and Kacelnik, A. (2006). A New Caledonian crow (*Corvus moneduloides*) creatively re-designs tools by bending or unbending aluminium strips. *Animal Cognition*, *9*, 317–334.

Whiten, A. (2000). Primate culture and social learning. *Cognitive Science*, *24*, 477–508.

Whiten, A. (2005). The second inheritance system of chimpanzees and humans. *Nature*, *437*, 52–5.

Whiten, A., Horner, V. and de Waal, F. B. M. (2005). Conformity to cultural norms of tool use in chimpanzees. *Nature*, *437*, 737–40.

Whiten, A. and van Schaik, C. P. (2007). The evolution of animal 'cultures' and social intelligence. *Philosophical Transactions of the Royal Society B*, *362*, 603–20.

Whiten, A., Goodall, J., McGrew, W. C. *et al.* (1999). Cultures in chimpanzees. *Nature*, *399*, 682–5.

Whiten, A., Horner, V., Litchfield, C. A. and Marshall-Pescini, S. (2004). How do apes ape? *Learning and Behavior*, *32*, 36–52.

Williams, J. H. G., Whiten, A. and Singh, T. (2004). A systematic review of action imitation in autistic spectrum disorder. *Journal of Autism and Developmental Disorders*, *34*, 285–99.

Wilson, A. C. (1985). The molecular basis of evolution. *Scientific American*, *253*, 148–57.

Wyles, J. S., Kunkel, J. G. and Wilson, A. C. (1983). Birds, behavior and anatomical evolution. *Proceedings of the National Academy of Sciences USA*, *80*, 4394–7.

Zentall, T. R. (2004). Action imitation in birds. *Learning and Behavior*, *32*, 15–23.

11 The future of evolutionary psychology

KEVIN N. LALAND AND GILLIAN R. BROWN

CHAPTER OUTLINE

A BRIEF HISTORICAL PERSPECTIVE 344

CAN THE EEA BE MADE WORKABLE? 347

UNIVERSALS AND THE CHALLENGE OF EXPLAINING VARIATION 351

HYPOTHESIS TESTING: ALTERNATIVE APPROACHES 354

A VISION OF THE FUTURE 359

ACKNOWLEDGEMENTS 361

REFERENCES 362

Before we can contemplate the future of evolutionary psychology, it is necessary to evaluate the past and the present. A consideration of the strengths and weaknesses of contemporary evolutionary psychology is a necessary precondition for understanding how the field is changing, or failing to change, and the issues that enhance or hinder its development. Given the long-standing history of controversy associated with applying evolutionary theory to human behaviour, it is essential that any such appraisal be an honest one. Although we are openly committed to the use of evolutionary ideas and methods within the behavioural sciences, we believe that a field must be self-critical if it is to progress. There is not space here for us to dwell greatly on this appraisal, but a more expansive analysis that more fully justifies our stance can be found elsewhere (Laland and Brown, 2002).

In the sections that follow, we first ask 'What is the current state of play within evolutionary psychology?' and 'How did we reach this position?' We then go on to consider two areas of controversy within the field, namely whether there is scientific utility in the 'environment of evolutionary adaptedness' concept, and whether the field of evolutionary psychology currently provides adequate explanations for human behavioural variation. We go on to reflect on the charge that evolutionary psychologists merely tell adaptive stories and consider additional means by which evolutionary psychologists could evaluate their hypotheses, drawing from developments in adjacent fields. Finally, we end by drawing out our vision for the future of evolutionary psychology, as a rich, pluralistic interdisciplinary field that employs a broad range of theoretical and empirical methods in a rigorous and disciplined manner.

A BRIEF HISTORICAL PERSPECTIVE

We begin with a short summary of how we perceive the theory of evolution to have been received and utilised by psychology and related disciplines during the past 100 years or so (for more extensive reviews, see Boakes, 1984; Laland and Brown, 2002; Plotkin, 2004). In our view, a historical perspective is key to understanding the current state of the field and the theoretical stance of its leaders.

Looking back over the last century, we see that, in the early 1900s, psychology, particularly in the United States, was dominated by the school of thought known as 'behaviourism'. Behaviourists typically dismissed evolutionary theory, particularly instincts, as providing any useful contribution to the understanding of behaviour and argued that learning and conditioning could override any natural, 'innate' behaviour. A key aspect of behaviourism was, therefore, the assumption that the brain could be viewed as a *tabula rasa*, with no centrally initiated processes other than a general ability to learn.

Behaviourism began to decline in the mid-twentieth century, partly as a result of events related to the Second World War, such as the rise of computers and cybernetics. During the war, research on perception, attention and signal detection came to the fore, and researchers began to theorise about different forms of cognitive processing.

For example, the argument, proposed by linguist Noam Chomsky (1965), that all human beings have an in-built 'language organ' in the brain that allows human beings to acquire a language helped bring to prominence the view that a single, general-purpose learning system could not account for all learning. That perspective gelled with research on animals revealing constraints on learning. For instance, Garcia and Koelling (1966) showed that, in rats, learning an association between a taste and nausea is easier than learning an association between a taste and an electric shock. Therefore, during the 1960s, the idea that the brain is not blank at birth, and that a history of natural selection has moulded the way that the brain works, was returning to psychology. This overthrowing of behaviourism within psychology has been called the 'cognitive revolution'.

At around the same time, a group of researchers known as the 'ethologists' were describing stereotyped, species-typical patterns of behaviour in animals, and the ideas of 'innate' or 'instinctive' behaviour were being re-energised. In response to the ethologists, the 'comparative psychologists', such as Theodore Schneirla and Daniel Lehrman, argued that 'innate' and 'acquired' aspects of behaviour could not easily be separated, as behavioural development is always a complex interaction between genetic information, the organism and the environment. Nonetheless, prominent ethologists, such as Niko Tinbergen and Konrad Lorenz, who received widespread recognition through being awarded Nobel Prizes, helped usher in a return to nativist thinking. This was reinforced in the 1970s and 1980s by the rise of sociobiology and behavioural ecology, the former with the publication of *Sociobiology: A new synthesis*, by E. O. Wilson (1975). In this book, Wilson describes how the groundbreaking, gene-centred research of William Hamilton and Robert Trivers could revolutionise our understanding of animal and, controversially, human behaviour. This view was popularised a year later by Richard Dawkins (1976) in *The Selfish Gene*. Wilson argued that the selfish-gene perspective could be used to understand human sexuality, parenting, ethics and morality, and he received a huge amount of criticism from social scientists for his (sometimes naive) stance. While learning and culture were still given a role in understanding human behaviour (e.g. Lumsden and Wilson, 1981), the emphasis of human sociobiology rested resoundingly on the idea of an evolved 'human nature'.

Wilson's human sociobiology also received harsh criticism from his Harvard colleagues, biologists Richard Lewontin and Steven Jay Gould. Controversies surrounding the application of evolutionary theory to human beings were not new to the Harvard campus. Louis Agassiz, an influential professor of zoology at Harvard from the 1840s to 1870s, was a leading proponent of 'polygeny', the idea that different human races should be considered as separate species (Gould, 1981). Although this theory was well and truly overthrown, the idea of differentially evaluating people of different races according to worth and ability would not disappear. In 1969, Arthur Jensen published a notorious paper from Harvard that argued for inherited and irreversible differences in intelligence between Whites and Blacks in America. The race and intelligence debate was itself merely the latest of a long line of controversies over the use of evolutionary ideas to interpret human behaviour. Into this arena, Wilson strode with the publication of *Sociobiology*. His colleagues in the Department of Anthropology at Harvard, including Irvin DeVore and Robert Trivers, who were teaching evolutionary approaches to human behaviour, were somewhat dismayed by Wilson's apparent naivety to the potential reception of his book (Segerstråle, 2000). The storm over human sociobiology illustrates how the evaluation of scientific theories in this domain is surrounded by history.

Moving forward to the 1980s, a graduate student in psychology at Harvard, called Leda Cosmides, began to explore experimentally whether natural selection has shaped how human beings reason (see Chapter 1, in this volume). Using an established experimental procedure from psychology, the Wason Selection Task, Cosmides argued that a history of past selection has fashioned human beings to be particularly good at detecting cheaters in social exchange situations, and less good at performing exactly the same task in other contexts (Cosmides, 1989). After teaming up with John Tooby, a Harvard anthropologist who had been working with DeVore, Cosmides and Tooby founded the first Centre for Research in Evolutionary Psychology, at the University of California, Santa Barbara. More so than any others, these researchers have had a profound impact upon the direction of recent evolutionary psychological research.

While the cognitive revolution had ousted behaviourism and its reliance on a *tabula rasa* notion of how the mind works, and while the work of Chomsky, Garcia and others had highlighted how selection might have produced predispositions that influence what is learned, the application of evolutionary theory within psychology really took off with the work of Cosmides and Tooby. These researchers not only provided exemplars of experimental practice but also provided a specific adaptationist theoretical framework for the field (Cosmides and Tooby, 1987, 1992). Other prominent evolutionary psychologists, such as Steven Pinker, David Buss, Martin Daly and Margo Wilson, identified with this explanatory framework, and the field of evolutionary psychology was born. Perhaps unsurprisingly, given the criticism directed towards Wilson, some proponents of evolutionary psychology view their field as not directly related to Wilson's version of human sociobiology that preceded it (Buss, 1995; Cosmides and Tooby, 1987; Pinker, 1997).

In this chapter, we focus on the style of evolutionary psychology that has grown out of the writings of Cosmides and Tooby, and other relatively like-minded researchers, and use capital letters to distinguish this particular version of 'Evolutionary Psychology' from more general applications of evolutionary theory to psychological questions. In the final section, we consider to what extent the writings of leading Evolutionary Psychologists are representative of the larger field of evolutionary psychology. The distinct theoretical concepts of Evolutionary Psychology are: (i) a focus on universal 'evolved psychological mechanisms' as adaptations that underlie human cognition and behaviour; (ii) the concept of the 'environment of evolutionary adaptedness' (EEA) as a means of constructing adaptive problems faced by our ancestors; and (iii) an emphasis on domain-specific modules within the brain (see Laland and Brown, 2002). Evolutionary Psychology has produced a wealth of practitioners throughout the world, and its researchers, journals and scientific meetings are growing in number and impact, supported by a number of societies; and it is the focus of unrivalled scientific and popular interest. There can be no doubt that the field has moved on dramatically in the last 20 years, and matured into a vibrant research programme. We welcome these developments and believe credit is owing to the pioneers of Evolutionary Psychology that have brought it thus far.

However, several criticisms of Evolutionary Psychology have been raised. In the following sections, we provide an evaluation of both the position of the Evolutionary Psychologists and their critics, dwelling on the concepts of the EEA and human universals. In addition to these topics, other psychologists have been critical of a lack of consideration of how the brain develops (Karmiloff-Smith, 2000; Lickliter and Honeycutt, 2003), an overemphasis on domain-specific modules rather than general processing (Chiappe and MacDonald, 2005) and a narrow view of how evolution can be applied to the field of psychology (Heyes, 2000). Yet others have argued that Evolutionary Psychology has been poor at tracking developments in evolutionary biology and, therefore, has overly relied on a simplistic or even outdated version of evolutionary theory (Brown, Laland and Borgerhoff-Mulder, 2009; Laland and Brown, 2002; Lloyd and Feldman, 2002). For instance, Evolutionary Psychology appears to retain a gradualistic notion of evolutionary change, despite findings by molecular and population geneticists to the contrary (Endler, 1986; Kingsolver *et al.*, 2001; Wang *et al.*, 2006) and to reject group-selectionist hypotheses, despite the fact that evolutionary biologists now regularly consider multilevel selection (Rose and Lauder, 1996; Sober and Wilson, 1998).

In the following sections, we focus on three specific questions. First, what does the concept of the EEA really contribute to our understanding of human beings? Second, does Evolutionary Psychology adequately explain variation in human behaviour? Third, without a reliance on the EEA and an assumption of universality, how can Evolutionary Psychology generate testable hypotheses, and how can it actually test these? We argue that the answers to these questions are key to the future of evolutionary psychology, and that some of the historical controversies surrounding the application of evolutionary theory to human beings need to be appreciated, and confronted once again, in order to make progress. We elaborate on these topics below.

CAN THE EEA BE MADE WORKABLE?

The concept of the environment of evolutionary adaptedness was initially developed by the psychiatrist John Bowlby (1969), influenced by ethologist Robert Hinde. Bowlby recognised that many human characteristics will not be of obvious survival value in contemporary environments, but could have been of value at the time and in the environment in which they evolved. He called this past selective environment the 'environment of evolutionary adaptedness' (EEA). This concept was later brought to prominence through the writings of Cosmides and Tooby. In what has become one of the most famous quotes of the field, Cosmides and Tooby (1987, p. 280) wrote:

> The recognition that adaptive specializations have been shaped by the statistical features of ancestral environments is especially important in the study of human behavior. Our

species spent over 99% of its evolutionary history as hunter-gatherers in Pleistocene environments. Human psychological mechanisms should be adapted to those environments, not necessarily to the twentieth-century industrialized world. The rapid technological and cultural changes of the last several thousand years have created many situations . . . that would have been uncommon (or nonexistent) in Pleistocene conditions. Evolutionary theorists ought not to be surprised when evolutionarily unprecedented environmental inputs yield maladaptive behavior.

Cosmides and Tooby reasoned that if researchers could establish the nature of the selective environment encountered by our ancestors, they might be able to guess the kind of psychological mechanisms that would be necessary to cope with such conditions, and hence make predictions about contemporary human's psychological capabilities. They and other early Evolutionary Psychologists asserted that the human mind was best understood as fashioned over the last two million years for a past world of hunting and gathering on the African savannah. However sophisticated and merited the initial conception (Daly and Wilson, 1999; Tooby and Cosmides, 1990), the EEA now pervades the Evolutionary Psychology literature as a Pleistocene-African-savannah stereotype. Here, we briefly outline some of the criticisms that have been directed towards the concept of the EEA and then go on to argue that the idea that human beings exhibit a particularly large 'adaptive lag', by which we mean a mismatch between current selection pressures and their environment, is likely to be misguided.

One immediate problem with the EEA is that comparatively little is known about the lifestyle of our ancestors throughout the Pleistocene, which leaves few facts that can constrain hypotheses (Foley, 1996; Richardson, 2007). Foley (1996) points out that our ancestors did not simply have one lifestyle in one geographical region, nor were their livelihoods unchanging over time. Stone Age people comprise several hominin species, who lived not only on the African savannah but also in deserts, next to rivers, by oceans, in forests and in the Arctic, experiencing highly varied environmental conditions, employing very different foraging methods and living off diverse diets (Boyd and Silk, 2009; Foley, 1996; Klein, 1999). Tooby and Cosmides (2005) defend the EEA concept, arguing that sufficient is known about our ancestors' lives, but the essential problems remain: there exists no single hominin model for re-constructing human selection pressures, and for the vast majority of characters current knowledge is too vague to specify adaptive problems with precision.

Moreover, every human descended from ancestors has collectively been subject to natural selection for three and a half billion years, since the beginning of life on Earth. The advent of our species, or the duration of the Pleistocene, are of no special significance when it comes to reconstructing selective environments. Some human psychological attributes will have a time depth that long precedes the appearance of *Homo sapiens* in East Africa (Boyd and Silk, 2009; Laland and Brown, 2002). This adds to the challenge facing Evolutionary Psychologists if they are to look to the past to derive hypotheses about the future. How far back should they look? No doubt the lifestyle of *Homo erectus* 1.7 million years ago (at the beginning of the Pleistocene) was very different from that of *Homo sapiens* 50 000 years ago (towards the end of the Pleistocene).

Neither is a description of our ancestors as 'hunter-gatherers' a sufficiently detailed account of their life history to greatly constrain putative selection pressures. Countless animals are hunter-gatherers, in the sense that they both hunt live prey and gather other foods. Of course, they do not exhibit the cooperative, coordinated, socially organised, linguistically guided hunting and gathering that modern human hunter-gatherers exhibit, but it is not known whether our ancestors during the Pleistocene did so either (Foley, 1996; Klein, 1999). To what extent early *Homo* species, or even *Homo sapiens* prior to 40 000 years ago, had sophisticated linguistic abilities, hunted large game, shared food and had home bases remains a matter of great contention within paleo-anthropological and archaeological circles (Boyd and Silk, 2009; Klein, 1999).

More recently, the EEA concept has witnessed a further challenge from molecular genetic analyses of data from the human genome, which reveal numerous genes subject to recent selective sweeps over the last 50 000 years (e.g. Laland *et al.*, 2010; Nielsen *et al.*, 2007; Sabeti *et al.*, 2006, 2007; Voight *et al.*, 2006; Wang *et al.*, 2006; Williamson *et al.*, 2007). Estimates for the number of human genes subject to recent rapid evolution range from a few hundred to two thousand; Williamson *et al.* (2007) conclude that as much as 10% of the genome is affected by linkage to a selective sweep. Many are very recent – Voight *et al.* (2006) estimate average ages of 6 000–11 000 years for these selective sweeps – which leads geneticists to the view that events in the Holocene, particularly the adoption of agriculture, domestication of animals and the increases in human densities these practices afforded, were a major source of selection on our species (Hawks *et al.*, 2007; Varki, Geschwind and Eichler, 2008; Voight *et al.*, 2006; Wang *et al.*, 2006). Note that such selective events are frequently population-specific rather than universal (Voight *et al.*, 2006; Wang *et al.*, 2006), a point to which we shall return later.

Genes expressed in the human nervous system and brain are well-represented in this recent selection (Laland *et al.*, 2010; Voight *et al.*, 2006; Wang *et al.*, 2006). The argument of leading Evolutionary Psychologists that minds are co-adapted gene complexes that are unable to respond quickly to selection (Buss, 2008; Cosmides and Tooby, 1987; Tooby and Cosmides, 1990, 2005) must be regarded as untenable in the face of these data. Molecular geneticists have now identified numerous brain-expressed genes in the human genome (or, indeed, no longer in the human genome) that have been subject to recent selection, they have estimated the time depth of these changes and they have mapped them onto gene-expression networks using molecular tools such as co-expression analysis (Varki, Geschwind and Eichler, 2008). The gradualism emphasised by Evolutionary Psychologists must now be rejected. Our lineage has clearly experienced a major acceleration in adaptive evolution over the last few millennia (Hawks *et al.*, 2007).

Tooby and Cosmides (1990, pp. 386–7) responded to some of the earlier criticism by arguing that the EEA concept was not a particular place or time, claiming that it was rather:

> a statistical composite of the adaptation relevant properties of the ancestral environments encountered by members of ancestral populations, weighted by their frequency and their fitness consequences.

This conceptualisation has the advantage that it is compatible with ancestral environments that varied in space and time, but the serious disadvantage that it seemingly cannot be implemented. Except in rare circumstances, researchers would struggle to compute a 'statistical composite' of all the relevant environments encountered by our ancestors, and weight them accordingly.

A further problem for the EEA argument is that, at best, it can only be true in part (Laland and Brown, 2002, 2006). Human beings cannot be exclusively adapted to a past world and not at all adapted to modern life; otherwise, we would not survive (to be fair, many, perhaps most, Evolutionary Psychologists would accept this). It is in the Holocene, the period since the Pleistocene, that we see the explosion in human numbers and human colonisation of the globe. Population growth corresponds to high absolute fitness, which implies that a significant fraction of human characteristics remain adaptive even in modern environments. Modern environments, for all their apparent differences with those of our Pleistocene ancestors, either share the truly critical features of past environments or have been rendered more benign than those of the past.

Leading Evolutionary Psychologists apparently believe that the adaptive lag for humans is atypically large, because human technology and innovation have changed human environments so extensively and so quickly. Yet this perspective is misleading because it portrays humans as passive victims of selection rather than as potent constructors of their niche (Odling-Smee, Laland and Feldman, 2003). In fact, there are strong reasons for anticipating that the adaptive lag associated with our species may be far less than casual appearance might imply (Laland and Brown, 2006). First, humans, like other animals, largely construct their world to suit their adaptations, generating hidden commonalities between ancestral and contemporary environmental states. Second, humans frequently respond to novel challenges through cultural niche-constructing processes, which restore the adaptive match between our genotypes and the modern world. For instance, we could survive outside the tropics because we manufactured clothes and shelters, controlled fire and so on. Third, when humans are unable to buffer an adaptive lag fully through further cultural niche construction, natural selection on genes ensues, and, as we have seen, selection on human genes does not inevitably take millions of years, but can be measured in a few thousand years.

These arguments describe events that are not instantaneous or unfailing, so naturally humans will still experience *some* adaptive lag. Our taste for salt, fat and sugar provides a likely example (Nesse and Williams, 1996). Plausibly valued as rare commodities by our ancestors, modern food production methods have solved the problem of scarce food for many of us, but we continue to crave these now abundant foods to such an extent that we consume quantities that are excessive and sometimes can lead to disease. Yet such examples are probably best regarded as exceptions. In spite of the massive changes humans have brought about in their worlds, we suspect that humans maintain a largely adaptive match between themselves and their environments.

EEA reasoning allows a posteriori hypotheses to be formulated; indeed, it is commonly deployed in this manner. To return to the aforementioned example, armed with the knowledge that contemporary humans suffer from several diseases affected by salt or sugar intake, researchers can make the reasonable guess that salts and sugars may not have been as abundant in the past as they are at present, without needing to know the precise conditions in which our ancestors evolved, leading to the hypothesis that some disease occurs today because the rarity of relevant foods in the past meant that regulatory processes operating against consuming excess were never required (Bateson and Martin, 1999; Nesse and Williams, 1996). But, of course, such reasoning, even formulated a posteriori, leads to a hypothesis, not an established explanation (Richardson, 2007).

In sum, the EEA concept is not predictive: it can rarely be specified with sufficient precision to allow researchers a priori to generate reliable predictions about human cognition based on detailed knowledge of ancestral selective environments. Deployed in the manner that Cosmides and Tooby (1987) originally envisaged, it can be a source of ideas that can be formulated into testable hypotheses, but ideas that are no more likely to be reliable than any other source. That does not mean the EEA concept is without virtue. One should not underestimate the value of a theoretical framework that has the capacity to generate realistic, empirically testable hypotheses in the domain of the human sciences. Any hypothesis-generating tool has some value, provided means exist for testing the ideas generated. We address the issue of how evolutionary psychologists can better evaluate their hypotheses below.

UNIVERSALS AND THE CHALLENGE OF EXPLAINING VARIATION

The behavioural sciences have long struggled to account satisfactorily for variation in human behaviour. At the heart of many recent scientific controversies, from the race and IQ dispute of the 1960s to the human sociobiology debate of the 1970s and 1980s, lies conflict over the existence and causes of differences between people. Particularly contentious is any suggestion of genetic differences between groups, such as between the sexes, socioeconomic classes, ethnic groups or cultures, or any kind of evolutionary explanation for such differences. In the past, evolutionary arguments have been put forward as pretexts to justify the eugenics movement, fascism, unfettered capitalism, racist immigration policies and enforced sterilisation, as well as to argue that some 'races' were more advanced than others (Oldroyd, 1980; Plotkin, 1997).

Is it coincidence that an Evolutionary Psychological framework that essentially ignores human genetic variation has become the most popular ideological stance? Did the founders of Evolutionary Psychology in the early 1980s recall the treatment that Jensen (1969) and Wilson (1975) received for suggesting that genetic variation might underlie differences between groups of people, and shy away from this political dynamite? We have no grounds for suspecting that the ideological stance of early Evolutionary Psychologists was formulated on anything other than a scientific basis. Yet there can be no doubt that Evolutionary Psychology is rendered all the more palatable because of its stress on *universal* psychological mechanisms. Evolution is not dangerous if it leaves us all the same, and genes are not threatening if we all have the same genome. As every modern Evolutionary Psychologist knows, behavioural variation can still be explained in the face of genetic uniformity if people respond flexibly to environmental variation, such that different conditions evoke different behavioural responses. Evolutionary Psychologists commonly argue that variation in behaviour can result from the expression of condition-dependent or situation-dependent strategies, which themselves are the product of our universal, evolved psychological mechanisms (e.g. Gangestad and Simpson, 2000).

We find this situation unsatisfactory. However, any such 'fear' of genes is entirely misplaced, and rests upon fundamental misunderstandings about what genes are and how they operate. Gene expression typically has subtle influences on the phenotype, for instance, by assembling a protein, increasing the circulating level of a hormone or signalling the release of a neurotransmitter. Genetic effects are always entirely mediated by environmental factors, and are commonly switched on and off by experience (Bateson and Martin, 1999; Gilbert, 2003; Ridley, 2003). Equally, every bout of learning, all forms of experience and every impact of culture is entirely dependent on gene expression. Genetic variation does explain a lot of differences between people, but so do developmental factors, early experience and culture. There are genetic differences between different groups of people from different countries or cultures, but these are swamped by genetic variation within populations, which accounts for 93–95% of human genetic variation (Rosenberg *et al.*, 2002). Genetic differences between populations are frequently small compared to learned differences between groups too. Genetic influences on the phenotype are far from fixed, and in most cases can be eradicated or reversed by particular experiences. A genetic influence on a trait does not prevent it from changing over the lifetime of an individual, and equally the observation that the distribution of a trait across a society changes over time does not mean that genes are not partly responsible for the trait.

In our view, by committing itself to universal psychological mechanisms and a large amount of innate structure in the mind from the outset, the dominant Evolutionary Psychological paradigm has undermined its own potential to explain variation in human behaviour satisfactorily, in several respects. First, irrespective of how genetic differences are regarded, there are genetic differences between people, and between groups of people (Rosenberg *et al.*, 2002). The universalism of Evolutionary Psychology hinders its ability to comprehend why people vary by dismissing one major source of variation. In the process, it prevents itself from exploiting certain potentially fruitful avenues of research (a point on which we elaborate below). If we consider the topics of greatest interest to evolutionary psychologists, it is apparent that people vary considerably with respect to their mating preferences, faithfulness, promiscuity, empathy, altruism, cooperativeness, sociality, innovativeness, intelligence, aggression and so forth, and it is highly likely that differences in each of these characters will be affected by genetic variation, alongside other factors. Yet, comparatively few of these have been explored, as traits underpinned by genetics, by evolutionary psychologists.

Second, the universalism also encourages an essentialist mindset, whereby, for instance, Evolutionary Psychologists frequently talk of fundamental properties of men and women, rather than exploring the systematic causes of variation in these properties. Below we use the example of cross-cultural variation in sex roles to illustrate this point.

Third, the combination of 'universal psychological mechanisms', and what is deemed a very rich specification of these by genes, generates a conception of the mind that leaves little role for anything else. All epigenetic, acquired, pre-natal, early-experience, developmental, environment and cultural effects are reduced to pushing alternative buttons on a 'jukebox' fully pre-programmed by genes. The jukebox metaphor is misleading in this respect: environmental and extra-genetic internal effects do not just flip human behaviour from one pre-specified programme to another; they play a massive role in building the mind in the first place, and maintain a constant and intimate interplay with genes to shape behavioural potential and output.

An example will help to expand these points. Heavily influenced by the classical experimental work of Bateman (1948) and theoretical work by Trivers (1972), Evolutionary Psychologists extensively refer to prescribed sex roles for human beings. Evolutionary theory is assumed to tell us that, because reproductive success is more closely linked to the number of mating partners in males compared to females and because females generally invest more in offspring than do males, men will have been selected to seek out multiple, young, fertile mates, while females will have been selected to be choosy in their mating partners, ensuring that they receive resources and/or good genes in exchange for sexual access (e.g. Buss, 1994). However, neither contemporary sexual selection theory nor data on variance in mating and reproductive success in current and historic human populations supports the notion of a single universal pattern (Brown, Laland and Borgerhoff-Mulder, 2009). To the contrary, comparatively recent theory (Kokko and Johnstone, 2002; Kokko and Monaghan, 2001) suggests that a number of factors, such as sex-biased mortality, population density and variation in mate quality, will affect how competitive, choosy or willing to invest in offspring males and females are. According to modern sexual selection theory, sex roles are therefore expected to vary considerably within and between societies.

A review of human datasets similarly reveals variation in how the basic assumptions underlying sex role evolution play out in human populations (Brown, Laland and Borgerhoff-Mulder, 2009). For instance, the assumption that male reproductive success varies more than female reproductive success does not hold across all human populations: males and females exhibit roughly equal variance in reproductive success in monogamous societies, whilst male variance significantly exceeds that for females only in small-scale polygynous societies (Brown, Laland and Borgerhoff-Mulder, 2009). While cultural influences are likely to play a huge role in the variation in sex roles both within and across populations, the possibility that genetic variation underlies some of these differences also cannot be dismissed. Although Evolutionary Psychologists have reported cross-cultural variation in mating strategies (e.g. Buss et al., 1990), the focus of research has generally been to extract the universal patterns of mate choice. We argue that, until the variation within and between populations is adequately incorporated, Evolutionary Psychological models of mate choice will provide an inadequate view of how evolutionary theory contributes to our knowledge of human behaviour.

The focus on universal patterns has distracted attention from this variation, depriving researchers of the opportunity for a rich research programme testing contemporary evolutionary theory and exploring the factors that generate different behaviour in different societies (Brown *et al.*, in press). We suggest the observed fluidity of behaviour across societies is not well served by a nativist theoretical framework, even with the 'condition-dependent strategies' that the jukebox metaphor is designed to capture. Contemporary Evolutionary Psychology has traditionally emphasised 'innate', context-specific structure in the mind, and the more flexible and variable the exhibited behaviour, the less explanatory power can be attributed to such structure. Ultimately, we strongly suspect that there will frequently prove to be insufficient 'innate structure' in the human mind to generate powerful nativist accounts of human behavioural variation.

HYPOTHESIS TESTING: ALTERNATIVE APPROACHES

There are some fine pieces of research within Evolutionary Psychology that we believe have fostered a deeper understanding of the workings of the human mind, and the best of Evolutionary Psychology is as rigorous and sophisticated as any research carried out in the general area of human behaviour and evolution. However, the discipline appears particularly vulnerable to weak studies that do little more than use a Pleistocene stereotype to contrive an evolutionary story that potentially explains a psychological finding. A major problem here is that the evolutionary hypothesis for the trait in question is rarely tested (Richardson, 2007).

Evolutionary Psychologists will no doubt be thinking that we are being unfair in implying that they rarely test their hypotheses; they would argue their journals are full of experimental tests of evolutionary hypotheses. However, such studies are typically tests of the *proximate* aspects of the hypothesis, not the ultimate aspects. Let us illustrate this with a familiar example. In a body of work that we esteem, Cosmides and Tooby (1992) propose the hypothesis that a history of reciprocal exchange between our hominin ancestors led to the evolution of a psychological module in the human mind dedicated to cheater detection, and tested this hypothesis with an extensive series of elegant experiments using the Wason Selection Task, generating findings consistent with their argument.

However, what such experiments test is the hypothesis that humans possess a cheater detection mechanism, not the explanation given for why it is there. An economist or social psychologist could have proposed the idea that individuals would benefit from a cheater detection mechanism, with no recourse to evolutionary thought at all, and such a hypothesis would also receive support. Naturally, we believe that credit is due to Evolutionary Psychology in general, and Cosmides and Tooby in particular, for actually formulating the hypothesis; we believe evolutionary biology to be an unusually rich source of ideas. But the fact remains that the Wason Selection Task does not test whether it was a history of reciprocal altruism in our Pleistocene ancestors that led to the evolution of a cheater detection mechanism.

One might equally argue, as Richerson and Boyd (2001, 2005) do, that a history of cultural group selection could have led to the emergence of this character. Moreover, until there is compelling evidence that any cheater-detection tendency is genuinely universal, one might equally argue that this attribute is a product of being raised in certain kinds of society. It is in this respect that Evolutionary Psychologists rarely test their hypotheses: psychologists are very good at determining whether psychological attributes or differences suggested by evolutionary thinking exist in contemporary human populations, and rather poorer at evaluating hypotheses regarding why such attributes are present. This leaves their evolutionary accounts vulnerable to the charge of 'storytelling'. Despite proposing that specific evolved psychological mechanisms are adaptations, Evolutionary Psychologists generally fail to test for adaptations in the same manner as evolutionary biologists, for example by measuring the heritability of a trait or determining whether a trait is derived or ancestral (Richardson, 2007). When Evolutionary Psychologists do attempt to address the question of universality (e.g. Buss *et al.*, 1990; Schmitt, 2005), the datasets often reveal large amounts of variation both within and between populations.

Evolutionary Psychology has produced its own version of how evolutionary hypotheses should be generated and tested. For instance, Cosmides and Tooby (1987) outline the steps that Evolutionary Psychological researchers should follow in order to carry out research. In brief, they suggest that researchers should (i) use evolutionary theory as a starting point to develop models of adaptive problems that the human beings had to solve; (ii) attempt to determine how these adaptive problems manifest themselves in Pleistocene conditions; (iii) use computational theory to determine the design features that any cognitive program capable of solving the problem must have; and (iv) eliminate alternative models with experiments and compare the model with manifest behaviour in modern conditions.

In a similar vein, Buss (2008) argues that two strategies are available for generating and testing evolutionary hypotheses: the 'theory-driven', or 'top-down', strategy, requires hypotheses to be derived from evolutionary theory (e.g. because women invest more in offspring than do men, women should be more choosy in their selection of mates), followed by empirical testing of predictions, while the 'observation-driven', or 'bottom-up', strategy allows researchers to make an observation about human behaviour (e.g. men base mate choice decisions on the physical attractiveness of potential partners) and then produce an evolutionary hypothesis to explain this observation, which is then tested empirically. As explained above, such methods do not actually make progress in testing the evolutionary aspects of these hypotheses, only the proximate aspects. Moreover, we have already questioned the reliability with which the adaptive problems faced by our ancestors can be characterised. Nonetheless, there is potentially some utility in using evolutionary theory to derive a number of competing hypotheses, ones that make alternative predictions about proximate mechanisms, and then choosing between these through careful experimentation or data analysis. The fact that this exercise intrinsically refutes evolutionary hypotheses, as well as deriving support for others, undermines any suggestion that Evolutionary Psychology is adaptive storytelling, and lends a rigour to the discipline.

Buss (2008) does point out that, once evolutionary hypotheses have been specified, several additional methods for testing these hypotheses are available, including cross-species and within-species comparisons. For researchers interested in human universals, cross-species comparisons do allow evolutionary hypotheses to be tested; for instance, if we believe that high levels of alloparental care characterise our own and other species (e.g. Hrdy, 1999), we can ask whether all of these animals share specific life history traits that may have a causal relationship with this trait. Ideally, comparative statistical methods would be deployed to address such questions rigorously (Harvey and Pagel, 1991). However, if we believe that a particular trait, such as language or strong reciprocity, is unique to human beings, we cannot use cross-species comparisons, as we only have a single data point. In this situation, researchers can use mathematical modelling to investigate the likelihood of our evolutionary hypothesis having been played out during our evolutionary history (e.g. Bowles and Gintis, 2004; Boyd *et al.*, 2003). Unfortunately, this option is missing from Buss's (2008) list, and is underexploited by Evolutionary Psychologists in general. In contrast human behavioural ecologists, cultural evolutionists and gene-culture co-evolutionists all use mathematical modelling extensively.

Where Evolutionary Psychologists refer to testing evolutionary hypotheses via intraspecific comparisons, they are usually referring to seeking 'condition-dependent' or 'situation-dependent strategies'. Currently, there would seem to be little consideration of the possibilities that variation between individuals may result from genetic differences between individuals. Nor is much credence given to the possibility that differences between people may be explained by transmitted culture; and where such variation is considered it is frequently dismissed as superficial, or non-functional (Tooby and Cosmides, 1992, 2005). Tooby and Cosmides (1992, p. 121) 'decompose the traditional concept of culture' into a universal 'metaculture', an 'evoked culture' where behavioural variation is generated by the differential triggering of psychological mechanisms by local circumstances, and an 'epidemiological culture' of socially transmitted elements. However, any such 'epidemiological culture' is largely ignored by Evolutionary Psychologists, who almost always explain variation as condition- or situation-specific-evoked culture (Brown *et al.*, in press). Tooby and Cosmides (1992, p. 118) essentially deny any substantive causal role for transmitted culture, since minds are deemed to filter and reconstruct acquired knowledge heavily.

Unfortunately, Evolutionary Psychologists rarely test whether behavioural variation is better characterised as condition-dependent or socially transmitted (although these categories are obviously not mutually exclusive). For instance, if human cultural variation is largely evoked, then environmental conditions should explain the bulk of the variation in human behaviour. Here, there are mixed results: behavioural ecologists regularly find that they can explain aspects of human behaviour as responses to ecological conditions (e.g. Cronk, Chagnon and Irons, 2000; Smith and Winterhalder, 1992), yet some studies report greater human behavioural variation to be explained by transmitted culture than ecology (e.g. Guglielmino *et al.*, 1995).

There are sufficient findings in the latter category to render the dismissal of transmitted culture problematic.

Evolutionary Psychologists seemingly fail to consider the possibility that the genetic constraints on human knowledge gain may be so broad that our evolved minds can acquire an endless sea of possible learned behaviour patterns, provided they are broadly adaptive (or only mildly maladaptive) in the current social context. As a result, an understanding of why a particular piece of information has been acquired as opposed to its alternatives may be better framed in terms of 'What is the local culture?' or 'Who is the transmitter?' than 'What is the evolved psychological mechanism?' Such social knowledge becomes essential in order to predict the information acquired by the learner. Moreover, in some contexts, we envisage that some quite general evolved psychological mechanisms (such as 'conform', or 'copy the most successful individual') could have been favoured, which do not greatly pre-specify information content. The important point here is that, while socially transmitted knowledge gain must be reliant on human evolved psychological mechanisms that detect and filter incoming information and reconstruct it in various ways, this does not mean (*contra* Tooby and Cosmides, 1992) that causality need not be attributed to social transmission.

Moreover, once researchers take the viewpoint that some of the variance in human behaviour is underlain by transmitted cultural variation and some by genetic variation, including functional psychological traits, a whole suite of methods for testing hypotheses becomes available. Here, we consider a well-researched example, namely the co-evolution of dairy farming and gene for adult lactose absorption, to highlight the methods that are currently being deployed in adjacent fields and which are potentially available to evolutionary psychologists to exploit.

Some, but not all, humans, particularly those in pastoralist societies, possess the capacity to digest milk and dairy products without getting sick, leading Simoons (1970) to propose the 'culture historical hypothesis', that ancestral dairy farming created the selection pressures that led genes for lactose absorption to become common in pastoralist societies (Durham, 1991; Simoons, 1970). Note this is an evolutionary hypothesis for a human attribute, logically equivalent to those proposed by evolutionary psychologists.

A variety of researchers, including anthropologists, archaeologists, demographers, geneticists and evolutionary biologists, have evaluated Simoons' hypothesis in various ways. A gene responsible for adult lactose absorption (LTP) has been identified, and statistical geneticists have confirmed that it exhibits strong signals of recent rapid selection (Bersaglieri *et al.*, 2004; Voight *et al.*, 2006). Bersaglieri *et al.* (2004) estimate that strong selection occurred within the past 5000–1000 years, consistent with an advantage to lactase persistence in dairy farmers. The selection coefficient associated with the adult lactose absorption trait has been estimated to be 0.09–0.19 for a Scandinavian population (Bersaglieri *et al.*, 2004). The variant of the LTP gene that confers adult lactase persistence has been found to be absent in ancient DNA extracted from early Neolithic European pastoralists (Burger *et al.*, 2007), supporting the hypothesis that culture came first. No fewer than four alleles facilitating adult lactase persistence have now been identified, in separate human populations

(Tishkoff *et al.*, 2007), providing compelling replication of the mechanism. Support can also be found in the pattern of geographical variation in milk protein genes in European cattle breeds, which covaries with present-day lactose tolerance in humans (Beja-Pereira *et al.*, 2003).

Durham (1991) predicted that human populations with traditions for consuming fermented milk products, such as cheese and yoghurt, but not fresh milk, should exhibit intermediary levels of adult lactase persistence, as these derived products have a lower level of lactose, a prediction that was confirmed. Gene-culture co-evolutionary models have been constructed that investigated the co-evolution of milk use and lactose absorption (Aoki, 1986; Feldman and Cavalli-Sforza, 1989), confirming that cultural processes could plausibly have modified selection, and revealing a contingency of gene frequency on the probability that the children of dairy-product users themselves became milk consumers. Holden and Mace (1997) applied comparative phylogenetic methods to a phylogeny of human cultural groups, finding no evidence for alternative explanations for variation in lactose digestion but support for the dairy-farming hypothesis. In addition, their analysis deployed statistical methods to confirm that dairy farming evolved first, which then favoured tolerance to lactose, and not the other way around.

Collectively, this body of evidence provides overwhelming support for this particular evolutionary hypothesis. Even though the link between genes and behaviour may be less straightforward, that is no excuse for failing to utilise the best available methods to explore the evolution of cognition. Such methods provide no quick fix, and will require many years of dedicated effort, frequently demanding interdisciplinary expertise that is only likely to be achieved through collaboration. Nonetheless, if adjacent disciplines such as evolutionary biology, neuroscience and behaviour genetics can engage in this kind of challenging research enterprise, why not evolutionary psychology? If we believe that genetic and cultural variation plays a role in variation between individuals in their psychological processing, we can use such methods to ask questions about human behaviour.

Why don't Evolutionary Psychologists (or evolutionary psychologists) adopt such methods? We suspect the answer to this question is that the dominant theoretical framework discourages Evolutionary Psychologists from exploring some of the rich possibilities for testing evolutionary hypotheses. Genetic variation affecting brain functioning has been identified, but Evolutionary Psychologists rarely explore the relationship between this and cognitive phenotypes, because their paradigm stresses genetic uniformity. Similarly, Evolutionary Psychologists rarely measure or estimate the fitness advantages of specific psychological attributes or behaviour patterns, because of the assumption that psychological mechanisms have evolved to function in past, but not present, environments, and 'counting babies' is unlikely to be productive (Crawford, 1993; Symons, 1990).

Gene-culture co-evolutionary analyses could be constructed to investigate the plausibility of specific Evolutionary Psychological hypotheses, but Evolutionary Psychologists typically do not exploit such methods, probably because of the assumption that the relevant selection took place back in the Pleistocene, before powerful culture existed, or perhaps because the mind-as-jukebox metaphor implies culture cannot direct evolutionary events. Comparative statistical and phylogenetic analyses could be deployed to investigate the factors that explain variation in human psychological attributes, but Evolutionary Psychologists generally do not deploy these methods; we suspect because they believe psychological mechanisms are universals. Deprived of these methods, Evolutionary Psychologists are left with little that they can productively do with evolutionary theory apart from using it to generate hypotheses. Contemporary Evolutionary Psychology is currently led into underusing evolutionary methods by its fundamental tenets – its universalism, its nativism, its gradualism.

A VISION OF THE FUTURE

It will be apparent that our vision of a future for the broader field of evolutionary psychology requires integration with adjacent approaches. We value such integration not because we are ecumenical but because it will strengthen the field and facilitate good science. The larger field of evolutionary psychology would greatly benefit from utilising the complete arsenal of evolutionary methods currently being deployed by human scientists. From human behavioural ecology, evolutionary psychologists can draw methods for studying variation in human behaviour (e.g. model development and testing, measuring fitness differentials); indeed, that should be comparatively easy, since many evolutionary psychologists already use these tools. From the fields of evolutionary biology, comparative phylogenetics and gene-culture co-evolution, evolutionary psychologists could draw methods for constructing evolutionary models, means of testing for adaptations, means of evaluating evolutionary hypotheses and ways of measuring selection coefficients. Gene-culture co-evolution has already been deployed by non-psychologists to address phenomena studied by psychologists, including the evolution of language, cooperation, learning, intelligence, sex differences and handedness (Laland *et al.*, 2010; Richerson *et al.*, 2010), while comparative statistical methods have been deployed to investigate language and the evolution of mating systems (Gray and Atkinson, 2003; Holden and Mace, 2003; Pagel, Atkinson and Meade, 2007). These advances would, however, require evolutionary psychologists to shed any commitment to the assumption, now known to be false, that all of the relevant selection on the human mind took place in the Pleistocene.

From cultural evolutionists, evolutionary psychologists could derive evolutionary methods for predicting, modelling and measuring how cultural phenomena change, and means for developing alternatives to gene-based evolutionary models that can be evaluated for their relative explanatory power. That would, however, require them to reject the ideological stance that cultural transmission is unimportant, that culture cannot evolve and that all culture does is push the buttons of the mind's jukebox. From geneticists, evolutionary psychologists could get extensive data detailing gene effects on the brain, genes thought to be responsible for human uniqueness, genes subject to recent selection and gene co-expression networks. It would, however, require evolutionary psychologists to reject any canonical commitment to universal patterns.

Evolutionary psychology needs to develop its understanding of non-universal psychological mechanisms, since evolution has delivered considerable variability to our species, as it has to all others. This would also require them to think about genes in ways they are not used to, as interactive entities that are elicited by environmental experiences, as variable entities that differ significantly between people. There will be aspects of human behaviour and psychology that are universal, that are no longer adaptive and that are switched on and off like the buttons of a jukebox, but evolutionary psychology must avoid the assumption that this is inevitably the case.

It is a moot point as to whether the field of evolutionary psychology has begun this journey and whether the problems that we attribute to narrow Evolutionary Psychology are characteristic of the larger field. Certainly, we do not believe that our portrayal of Evolutionary Psychology is entirely anachronistic, and we retain the view that the bulk of the central tenets of Evolutionary Psychology can be found in the discipline as a whole. In our judgement, the philosophical, conceptual and methodological structures developed by the leaders of Evolutionary Psychology in the 1980s remain the dominant influence on the field, and universalism, gradualism, domain specificity, EEA and so forth remain extremely widespread. They can, for instance, be found in some of the chapters in the present volume. Nonetheless, we see some positive signs, for instance, of integration between traditional Evolutionary Psychology and human behavioural ecology perspectives (see, for instance, Chapter 1 in this volume), of individual researchers utilising methods from across subdisciplines (see, for instance, Chapter 3 in this volume) and a wariness of EEA storytelling.

We suspect that, because of the mechanism-neutral stance of behavioural ecology, it is potentially more difficult to reconcile evolutionary psychology with cultural evolution than it is to reconcile either with human behavioural ecology (see Chapter 1 in this volume for an example of the integration of evolutionary psychology and behavioural ecology, and Chapter 6 in this volume for an example of the integration of behavioural ecology and cultural evolution). Evolutionary Psychologists have suggested that their field provides them with the tools to carve up the mind at its natural joints, that is to determine a non-arbitrary set of evolved psychological mechanisms that underpin human behaviour and cognition (Buss, 2008). However, while most cultural evolutionists would agree that there are evolved psychological mechanisms, their notion of these is frequently very different from that of an Evolutionary Psychologist's. Rather than psychological mechanisms for detecting cheaters, or for finding particular waist-to-hip ratios attractive, cultural evolutionists envisage evolved mechanisms for copying successful individuals or conforming to the local tradition. Moreover, the latter mechanisms potentially span across the domains described by contemporary Evolutionary Psychologists; one can conform with respect to what you find attractive, what you eat and with whom you cooperate.

Nonetheless, this is potentially an empirically accessible issue, and provided evolutionary psychologists are alive to the possibility of socially transmitted information differentially affecting behaviour, we see no reason why their perspective cannot be integrated with that of cultural evolutionists in the longer term. Swami and Salem (in Chapter 5 of this volume) argue that the best and the worst of evolutionary psychology is manifest in studies of attractiveness, particularly those studies investigating waist-to-hip ratios. One recent feature of this literature is the recognition that notions of attractiveness change over time, and vary from place to place, in a manner consistent with socially transmitted influences on mating preferences (e.g. Sear and Marlowe, 2009; Tovée et al., 2006). Both mathematical models (Laland 1994, 2008) and experimental studies (Jones et al., 2007; Little et al., 2008) support the argument that socially transmitted mating preferences can generate sexual selection on human physical and personality traits. Such findings hint at the possibility of a rapprochement. Further opportunities for synthesis may arise through evolutionary psychologists' utilisation of the cultural evolutionist's notion of content biases (see Chapter 10 in this volume), which can represent evolved predispositions favouring the acquisition of certain kinds of transmitted information.

The Evolutionary Psychology perspective has brought the study of the mind well and truly into the domain of evolutionary theory, bringing with it a welcome focus on proximate mechanisms. It has proven an enormously creative approach to the study of human behaviour, and has introduced a wealth of new ideas and methods. There can be no doubt that the Evolutionary Psychological literature has made important contributions to understanding many areas of psychology. However, the broader field of evolutionary psychology cannot afford to adhere to the theoretical framework of the past (Tooby and Cosmides, 2005), however fruitful that framework may have been. Pluralism is the engine of progress, since it generates variation and cross-fertilisation. Evolutionary psychology needs to become more outward-looking in order to make headway here, by deriving data, insights and methods from adjacent fields: its model of behavioural development should be that championed by developmental biologists; its understanding of genetic variation should be that described by molecular and population geneticists; its understanding of evolutionary biology should be that provided by today's evolutionary biologists. If it fails to accommodate such developments, evolutionary psychology risks being completely superseded by adjacent disciplines. Above all, evolutionary psychology needs to recognise that it is currently exploiting evolutionary theory in an impoverished manner, and that evolutionary biology has far more to offer than hypothesis-generation. We would like to see a future evolutionary psychology characterised as a rich, pluralistic, interdisciplinary field, at harmony with neighbouring disciplines, employing a multitude of theoretical and empirical methods, in a rigorous and disciplined manner. The time has come for evolutionary psychology to evolve.

ACKNOWLEDGEMENTS

This article was supported in part by grants to KNL from the BBSRC (BB/C005430/1) and EU (NEST-Pathfinder, Cultaptation) and by a Wellcome Trust career development fellowship to GRB. We are grateful to Rebecca Sear for helpful comments on earlier drafts of this chapter.

REFERENCES

Aoki, K. (1986). A stochastic model of gene-culture coevolution suggested by the 'culture historical hypothesis' for the evolution of adult lactose absorption in humans. *Proceedings of the National Academy of Sciences USA, 83*, 2929–33.

Bateman, A. J. (1948). Intra-sexual selection in *Drosophila. Heredity, 2*, 349–68.

Bateson, P. and Martin, P. (1999). *Design for a life: How behaviour develops.* London: Jonathan Cape.

Beja-Pereira, A., Luikart, G., England, P. R. *et al.* (2003). Gene-culture coevolution between cattle milk protein genes and human lactase genes. *Nature Genetics, 35*, 311–313.

Bersaglieri, T., Sabeti, P. C., Patterson, N. *et al.* (2004). Genetic signatures of strong recent positive selection at the lactase gene. *American Journal of Human Genetics, 74*, 1111–1120.

Boakes, R. (1984). *From Darwin to behaviourism: Psychology and the minds of animals.* Cambridge: Cambridge University Press.

Bowlby, J. (1969). *Attachment and loss: Volume 1: Attachment.* London: Hogarth Press.

Bowles, S. and Gintis, H. (2004). The evolution of strong reciprocity: Cooperation in heterogeneous populations. *Theoretical Population Biology, 65*, 17–28.

Boyd, R. and Silk, J. B. (2009). *How humans evolved* (5th edition). New York: Norton.

Boyd, R., Gintis, H., Bowles, S. and Richerson, P. J. (2003). The evolution of altruistic punishment. *Proceedings of the National Academy of Sciences USA, 100*, 3531–5.

Brown, G. R., Dickins, T. E., Sear, R. and Laland, K. N. (in press). Evolutionary accounts of human behavioural diversity. *Philosophical Transactions of The Royal Society of London B.*

Brown, G. R., Laland, K. N. and Borgerhoff-Mulder, M. (2009). Bateman's principles and human sex roles. *Trends in Ecology and Evolution, 24*, 297–304.

Burger, J., Kirchner, M., Bramanti, B. *et al.* (2007). Absence of the lactase-persistence-associated allele in early Neolithic Europeans. *Proceedings of the Royal Academy of Sciences USA, 104*, 3736–41.

Buss, D. M. (1994). *The evolution of desire.* London: Basic Books.

Buss, D. M. (1995). Evolutionary psychology: A new paradigm for psychological science. *Psychological Inquiry, 6*, 1–30.

Buss, D. M. (2008). *Evolutionary psychology: The new science of the mind* (3rd edition). London: Allyn and Bacon.

Buss, D. M., Abbott, M., Angleitner, A. *et al.* (1990). International preferences in selecting mates: A study of 37 cultures. *Journal of Cross-Cultural Psychology, 21*, 5–47.

Chiappe, D. and MacDonald, K. (2005). The evolution of domain-general mechanisms in intelligence and learning. *Journal of General Psychology, 132*, 5–40.

Chomsky, N. (1965). *Aspects of the theory of syntax.* Cambridge, MA: MIT Press.

Cosmides, L. (1989). The logic of social exchange: Has natural selection shaped how humans reason? Studies with the Wason selection task. *Cognition, 31*, 187–276.

Cosmides, L. and Tooby, J. (1987). From evolution to behavior: Evolutionary psychology as the missing link. In J. Dupré (ed.), *The latest on the best: Essays on evolution and optimality* (pp. 277–306). Cambridge, MA: MIT Press.

Cosmides, L. and Tooby, J. (1992). Cognitive adaptations for social exchange. In J. H. Barkow, L. Cosmides and J. Tooby (eds), *The adapted mind: Evolutionary psychology and the generation of culture* (pp. 163–228). Oxford: Oxford University Press.

Crawford, C. B. (1993). The future of sociobiology: Counting babies or studying proximate mechanisms? *Trends in Ecology and Evolution, 8*, 183–6.

Cronk, L., Chagnon, N. and Irons, W. (eds) (2000). *Adaptation and human behavior: An anthropological perspective*. New York: Aldine de Gruyter.

Daly, M. and Wilson, M. I. (1999). Human evolutionary psychology and animal behaviour. *Animal Behaviour, 57*, 509–19.

Dawkins, R. (1976). *The selfish gene*. Oxford: Oxford University Press.

Durham, W. H. (1991). *Coevolution: Genes, culture and human diversity*. Palo Alto, CA: Stanford University Press.

Endler, J. A. (1986). *Natural selection in the wild*. Princeton, NJ: Princeton University Press.

Feldman, M. W. and Cavalli-Sforza, L. L. (1989). On the theory of evolution under genetic and cultural transmission with application to the lactose absorption problem. In M. W. Feldman (ed.), *Mathematical evolutionary theory* (pp. 145–73). Princeton, NJ: Princeton University Press.

Foley, R. (1996). The adaptive legacy of human evolution: A search for the environment of evolutionary adaptedness. *Evolutionary Anthropology, 4*, 194–203.

Gangestad, S. W. and Simpson, J. A. (2000). The evolution of human mating: Trade-offs and strategic pluralism. *Behavioral and Brain Sciences, 23*, 573–644.

Garcia, J. and Koelling, R. A. (1966). Prolonged relation of cue to consequence in avoidance learning. *Psychonomic Science, 4*, 123–4.

Gilbert, S. F. (2003). *Developmental biology* (7th edition). Sunderland, MA: Sinauer.

Gould, S. J. (1981). *The mismeasure of man*. Harmondsworth: Penguin.

Gray, R. D. and Atkinson, Q. D. (2003). Language tree divergence times support the Anatolian theory of Indo-European origin. *Nature, 426*, 435–9.

Guglielmino, C. R., Viganotti, C., Hewlett, B. and Cavalli-Sforza, L. L. (1995). Cultural variation in Africa: Role of mechanism of transmission and adaptation. *Proceedings of the National Academy of Sciences USA, 92*, 7585–9.

Harvey, P. H. and Pagel, M. D. (1991). *The comparative method in evolutionary biology*. Oxford: Oxford University Press.

Hawks, J., Wang, E. T., Cochran, G. M. *et al.* (2007). Recent acceleration of human adaptive evolution. *Proceedings of the National Academy of Sciences USA, 104*, 20753–8.

Heyes, C. (2000). Evolutionary psychology in the round. In C. Heyes and L. Huber (eds), *The evolution of cognition* (pp. 3–22). Cambridge, MA: MIT Press.

Holden, C. and Mace, R. (1997). Phylogenetic analysis of the evolution of lactose digestion in adults. *Human Biology, 69*, 605–28.

Holden, C. J. and Mace, R. (2003). Spread of cattle led to the loss of matriliny in Africa: A co-evolutionary analysis. *Proceedings of the Royal Society B, 270*, 2425–33.

Hrdy, S. B. (1999). *Mother Nature: Natural selection and the female of the species*. London: Chatto & Windus.

Jensen, A. R. (1969). How much can we boost IQ and scholastic achievement? *Harvard Educational Review, 33*, 1–123.

Jones, B. C., DeBruine, L. M., Little, A. C. *et al.* (2007). Social transmission of face preferences among humans. *Proceedings of the Royal Society B, 274*, 899–903.

Karmiloff-Smith, A. (2000). Why babies' brains are not Swiss army knives. In H. Rose and S. Rose (eds), *Alas, poor Darwin* (pp. 144–56). London: Jonathan Cape.

Kingsolver, J. G., Hoekstra, H. E., Hoekstra, J. M. *et al.* (2001). The strength of phenotypic selection in natural populations. *American Naturalist, 157*, 245–61.

Klein, R. G. (1999). *The human career: Human biological and cultural origins* (2nd edition). Chicago: University of Chicago Press.

Kokko, H. and Johnstone, R. A. (2002). Why is mutual mate choice not the norm? Operational sex ratios, sex roles and the evolution of sexually dimorphic and monomorphic signalling. *Philosophical Transactions of the Royal Society B, 357,* 319–330.

Kokko, H. and Monaghan, P. (2001). Predicting the direction of sexual selection. *Ecology Letters, 4,* 159–65.

Laland, K. N. (1994). On the evolutionary consequences of sexual imprinting. *Evolution, 48,* 477–89.

Laland, K. N. (2008). Exploring gene-culture interactions: Insights from handedness, sexual selection and niche-construction case studies. *Philosophical Transactions of the Royal Society B, 363,* 3577–89.

Laland, K. N. and Brown, G. R. (2002). *Sense and nonsense: Evolutionary perspectives on human behaviour.* Oxford: Oxford University Press.

Laland, K. N. and Brown, G. R. (2006). Niche construction, human behaviour and the adaptive lag hypothesis. *Evolutionary Anthropology, 15,* 95–104.

Laland, K. N., Odling-Smee, F. J. and Myles, S. (2010). How culture shaped the human genome: Bringing genetics and the human sciences together. *Nature Reviews Genetics, 11,* 137–148.

Lickliter, R. and Honeycutt, H. (2003). Developmental dynamics: Toward a biologically plausible evolutionary psychology. *Psychological Bulletin, 129,* 819–35.

Little, A. C., Burriss, R. P., Jones, B. C. *et al.* (2008). Social influence in human face preference: Men and women are influenced more for long-term than short-term attractiveness decisions. *Evolution and Human Behavior, 29,* 140–146.

Lloyd, E. A. and Feldman, M. W. (2002). Evolutionary psychology: A view from evolutionary biology. *Psychological Enquiry, 13,* 150–156.

Lumsden, C. J. and Wilson, E. O. (1981). *Genes, mind and culture.* Cambridge, MA: Harvard University Press.

Nesse, R. and Williams, G. C. (1996). *Why we get sick: The new science of Darwinian medicine.* New York: Vintage Books.

Nielsen, R., Hellmann, I., Hubisz, M. *et al.* (2007). Recent and ongoing selection in the human genome. *Nature Review of Genetics, 8,* 857–68.

Odling-Smee, F. J., Laland, K. N. and Feldman, M. W. (2003). *Niche construction. The neglected process in evolution.* Monographs in Population Biology, 37. Princeton, NJ: Princeton University Press.

Oldroyd, D. R. (1980). *Darwinian impacts: An introduction to the Darwinian revolution.* Milton Keynes: Open University Press.

Pagel, M., Atkinson, Q. D. and Meade, A. (2007). Frequency of word-use predicts rates of lexical evolution throughout Indo-European history. *Nature, 449,* 717–720.

Pinker, S. (1997). *How the mind works.* London: Penguin.

Plotkin, H. (1997). *Evolution in mind: An introduction to evolutionary psychology.* London: Penguin.

Plotkin, H. (2004). Evolutionary thought in psychology: A brief history. London: Blackwell.

Richardson, R. C. (2007). *Evolutionary psychology as maladapted psychology.* Cambridge, MA: MIT Press.

Richerson, P. J. and Boyd, R. (2001). The evolution of subjective commitment to groups: A tribal instincts hypothesis. In R. M. Nesse (ed.), *Evolution and the capacity for commitment* (pp. 186–220). New York: Russell Sage Foundation.

Richerson, P. J. and Boyd, R. (2005). *Not by genes alone: How culture transformed human evolution.* Chicago: University of Chicago Press.

Richerson, P. J., Boyd, R. and Henrich, J. (2010). Gene-culture co-evolution in the age of genomics. *Proceedings of the National Academy of Sciences USA, 107,* 8985–8992.

Ridley, M. (2003). *Nature via nurture.* New York: HarperCollins.

Rose, M. R. and Lauder, G. V. (1996). *Adaptation.* San Diego: Academic Press.

Rosenberg, N. A., Pritchard, J. K., Weber, J. L. *et al.* (2002). Genetic structure of human populations. *Science, 298,* 2381–5.

Sabeti, P. C., Schaffner, S. F., Fry, B. *et al.* (2006). Positive natural selection in the human lineage. *Science, 16,* 1614–1620.

Sabeti, P. C., Varilly, P., Fry, B. *et al.* (2007). Genome-wide detection and characterization of positive selection in human populations. *Nature, 449,* 913–918.

Schmitt, D. P. (2005). Sociosexuality from Argentina to Zimbabwe: A 48-nation study of sex, culture, and strategies of human mating. *Behavioral and Brain Sciences, 28,* 247–311.

Sear, R. and Marlowe, F. W. (2009). How universal are human mate choices? Size does not matter when Hadza foragers are choosing a mate. *Biology Letters, 5,* 606–9.

Segerstråle, U. (2000). *Defenders of the truth: The battle for science in the sociobiology debate and beyond.* Oxford: Oxford University Press.

Simoons, F. (1970). Primary adult lactose intolerance and the milking habit: A problem in biological and cultural interrelations. II: A culture historical hypothesis. *Digestive Diseases and Sciences, 15,* 695–710.

Smith, E. A. and Winterhalder, B. (eds) (1992). *Evolutionary ecology and human behavior.* New York: Aldine de Gruyter.

Sober, E. and Wilson, D. S. (1998). *Unto others: The evolution and psychology of unselfish behavior.* Cambridge, MA: Harvard University Press.

Symons, D. (1990). Adaptiveness and adaptation. *Ethology and Sociobiology, 11,* 427–44.

Tishkoff, S. A., Reed, F. A., Ranciaro, A. *et al.* (2007). Convergent adaptation of human lactase persistence in Africa and Europe. *Nature Genetics, 39,* 31–40.

Tooby, J. and Cosmides, L. (1990). The past explains the present: Emotional adaptations and the structure of ancestral environments. *Ethology and Sociobiology, 11,* 375–424.

Tooby, J. and Cosmides, L. (1992). The psychological foundations of culture. In J. H. Barkow, L. Cosmides and J. Tooby (eds), *The adapted mind: Evolutionary psychology and the generation of culture* (pp. 19–136). New York: Oxford University Press.

Tooby, J. and Cosmides, L. (2005). Conceptual foundations of evolutionary psychology. In D. M. Buss (ed.), *The handbook of evolutionary psychology* (pp. 5–67). Hoboken, NJ: John Wiley & Sons, Ltd.

Tovée, M. J., Swami, V., Furnham, A. and Mangalparsad, R. (2006). Changing perceptions of attractiveness as observers are exposed to a different culture. *Evolution and Human Behavior, 27,* 443–56.

Trivers, R. L. (1972). Parental investment and sexual selection. In B. Campbell (ed.), *Sexual selection and the descent of man, 1871–1971* (pp. 136–79). Chicago: Aldine.

Varki, A., Geschwind, D. H. and Eichler, E. E. (2008). Explaining human uniqueness: Genome interactions with environment, behaviour and culture. *Nature Review of Genetics, 9,* 749–63.

Voight, B. F., Kudaravalli, S., Wen, X. and Pritchard, J. K. (2006). A map of recent positive selection in the human genome. *PLoS Biology, 4,* e72.

Wang, E. T., Kodama, G., Baldi, P. and Moyzis, R. K. (2006). Global landscape of recent inferred Darwinian selection for *Homo sapiens*. *Proceedings of the National Academy of Sciences USA, 103*, 135–40.

Williamson, S. H., Hubisz, M. J., Clark, A. G. *et al.* (2007). Localizing recent adaptive evolution in the human genome. *PLoS Genetics, 3*, e90.

Wilson, E. O. (1975). *Sociobiology: The new synthesis*. Cambridge, MA: Harvard University Press.

Index

abandonment, child 230
ability and intelligence 268–71
abortion 193, 240
absolute preferences for personality traits 257
acquired savant syndrome 286
adaptability driver 328–9
adaptation 5, 6, 76–7
adaptive ecological model 253
adaptive lag 203, 350
adaptive reasoning and modern reproductive
     behaviour 203
adaptive significance 254, 256
adrenocorticotrophic hormone (ACTH) 14
adult lactose absorption (LTP) 357–8
affordance learning 323
Agreeableness 26, 258, 259, 264–5
alleles 17
Allocation, principle of 184, 185
alloparents 192
altruism 17, 22
   definition 74, 75
   evolution of 330–1
   genetic kinship and 78
   see also reciprocal altruism
altruistic punishment 97
Angelman syndrome 295, 296, 298
anisogamy 110, 112, 217
anti-conformist bias 317
artificial fertility treatments 193
asocial learning 41–2
Asperger's syndrome 284, 285, 286, 297
   genetics and 298–9
assortative mating 258, 288
authoritarianism 267–8
autism 282, 284–5
   antithesis of mentalism in 288–92
   see also Asperger's syndrome
Autism-Spectrum Quotient (AQ) 287

autistic spectrum disorder (ASD) 282
auto-signal costly signalling 85–6, 87, 94

Baldwin effect 312, 328, 329
bats
   echolocation 4–5
   tit-for-tat strategy 9
Bateman's principle 123, 125
beauty
   intelligence and 133–4
   Pythagorean view of 132, 163
Beckwith-Wiedemann syndrome 294
behavioural drive hypothesis 328
behavioural ecology 345
behaviourism 344–5
belief-desire reasoning 56, 57
bet-hedging strategy 241
Big Five personality traits 26, 258–9
   cost-benefit analysis 262–7
biparental care 218, 219
bipolar disorder 301
birth order 230–4
   personality differences and 231–2
   reproductive value and 232–3
bodily attractiveness 138–9, 145–62
body mass index (BMI) 151
brain
   expansion and reorganisation 42–5
   interactive specialisation 45
   human 12
   modularity 34
brain size
   intelligence and 38–9
   and organisation 34
by-product mutualism *see* mutualism

Caenorhabditis elegans 12
cainism 189

central dogma of molecular biology 11, 13
central executive 38
cheating 22–3
child mortality 219, *220*, 221
chimeras 137
chimpanzees
  deferred imitation 53–4
  DNA 46–7
  inhibitory control in 48
  mental time travel 55
  social learning 56
  tool-use 49, *50*, 314
  understanding of intentions 57–60
  working memory 49–51, 51–2
coefficient of relatedness 76, 77
Cognitive Behavioural Therapy 294
cognitive revolution 345–6
collective action 91–8
  Greenbeard altruism as explanation
      for 95–6
    group selection as explanation for 96–8
    reciprocal altruism as explanation
        for 94–5
colour blindness 282
comparative psychology 345
complementarity theory 258
compositionality 320
Concorde fallacy 217
condition-dependent strategies 356
conditional cooperation 92
conditional mating tactics 117–18
conformist bias 317
Conscientiousness 26, 255, 258, 259,
    261, 265–7
conscious awareness 52–5
consensual preferences for personality
    traits 257
Contour Drawing Figure Rating Scale
    (CDFRS) 155
cooperation 8–9
  complex human 91–8
  definition 74–5
  evolution of 330–1
  individual-level theories of 76–7, 77–86,
      86–7, *86*
cooperative breeders 226

corticosteroids 14–15
corticotropin-releasing factor (CRF) 14
costly information hypothesis 316
costly signals, theory of 85–6, 108–9
creole 41
'criminal' face 139
critical-fat hypothesis 194
critical social learning 317
crystallised intelligence 37
cultural diffusion 321
cultural drive hypothesis 328
cultural niche construction 328
culture historical hypothesis 357
cumulative cultural evolution 312, 324,
      331–3
  human 332–3
cystic fibrosis 282
cytomegalovirus, schizophrenia and 300

'dark-side' disorders 271–6
Darwin, Charles 5
  On the Origin of Species 6
  on group selection 88, 89–90
  on sexual selection 108
Dawkins, Richard 7
Dayak tribal masks, symmetry in 135–6
de ClÈrambault's syndrome 290
declarative knowledge 37
delayed grief reactions 293
delusions of reference 291
demic diffusion model 321
demographic transition 196–8
differential psychology 252, 254–7
display, female 110–11
disposable soma theory 18
DNA 6, 7, 10, 13
do-as-I-do imitation 323, 327
dopamine 14
Down syndrome 134, 282, 287, 292
dual-inheritance theory 312, 313

eating disorders, reproductive
      suppression and 194
echolocation 4–5
ecology, definition 12
elective neutrality theories 254

electromagnetic spectrum 12
emulation 55, 322, 323, 324
emulation learning 322
environmental adaptation 321
epigenetics 12–16
episodic memory 46, 53
erotomania 290
erotomanic type delusional disorder 290
ethology 345
eusociality 78
evolutionarily stable strategy (ESS) 7, 316
evolutionary adaptedness (EEA) 32, 99,
        346, 347–51
evolutionary game theory 7
evolutionary psychology 21–5
exclusionary alliances 114
executive function 47
expensive tissue hypothesis 329
explicit awareness 52–5
explicit memory 53
extrastriate body area (EBA) 149–50
Extraversion 26, 122, 255, 257, 258, 259,
        263–4
extrinsic inheritance 11

facial attractiveness 112, 134–45
facial sexual dimorphism 141–4
facial masculinity 143–4
false-belief tasks 43, 44, 48, 56, 57
familial conflict 227–8
father absence, development and 20–1
fecundity, female 112–13
female-only care 218
female-philopatry 222
female sexual display 110–11, 114
    in humans 112, 113
fertility 18–21, 26
    cultural evolution of decline 198–9
    demographic transition 196–8
    maladaptation to novel contraceptive
            technologies 198
    optimisation mechanisms 193
    parental investment models of 199–204
    predicted optima and observed 194–5
    rate 20
fitness 16–21, 78

fitness maximisation 18
Five Factor Model of
        personality 252, 255
fluctuating asymmetry (FA) 134–8
    attractiveness of bodies and 138–9
fluid intelligence 37, 38, 42
FMR1 gene 302
foetal loss, age-related 113
folk biology 37–8, 37
folk physical systems 37–8, 37, 286
folk psychology 37–8, 37, 286
foraging patch choice model 123,
        124–5
Fragile X syndrome 282, 296, 302
free-rider punishment 92–4, 95
    and second-order problem 97–8
frequency dependence 254
fusiform body area (FBA) 149–50

game theory 17, 18, 22, 24
gaze, following 58, 59
gene-culture co-evolution (G-CG) 312, 313,
        325–33, 358–9
general intelligence hypothesis 34
generalist strategy 12
genes 6–7
    biochemistry of 7
    as replicators 76–7
genetic drift 6
genic self-favouritism 80–1, 83–4, 95
genomes 12
gestational diabetes 228
goal emulation 323
grandmother hypothesis of
        menopause 188, 227
grandmothers, role of 226–7
Greenbeard altruism 79–80, 81, 85, 90,
        95–6, 99
grooming behaviour 14–15
group selection 87–91
    collective action and 96–8

Hamilton's Rule 17, 78, 79
handicap models 109
haplodiploidy 78
'Happy Puppet Syndrome' 295

height
    as biomarker for physical health 186–7
    sexual selection 116
    'helpers-at-the-nest' 226–7
heredity, theories of 6
horizontal trait transmission 321
human family, form of 222
humour as sexual tactic 120–1
hunter-gatherers 100, 348–9
hypergyny 238
hyper-mentalism 292, 296, 304
hypo-mentalism 292
hypothalamic-pituitary-adrenal
        (HPA) axis 14, 27

IGF2 gene 294, 297, 298
imitation 322–3, 324
implicit memory 53
imprinted brain theory 282–305, *297*
inclusive fitness 78
indirect reciprocity 84, 95
individual optimisation hypothesis 193
infanticide 193, 230, 232, 238, 240
information-processing systems 37–8
inheritance 6, 11
inhibitory control 47–8
intelligence 254
    ability and 268–71
    beauty and 133–4
intentional states 326
intentionality 330–1
intentions, understanding of 57–60
interactive specialisation 45
intrinsic inheritance 11
IQ dispute 269, 351
    see also intelligence

'jack' mating tactic 122
jukebox metaphor 353, 354, 358

kin altruism 79
kin-influence hypothesis 199
kin recognition 79
kin selection 17–18, 77–9, 94
Kleinfelter syndrome 298
lactase persistence 313, 357–8

Lamarckian evolution 11, 13
language 324–5
    evolutionary origins 40–1
leg-to-body ratio (LBR) 152
life history theory 18, 19, 20–1, 123–5,
        183–205
    family size optimisation
        in modern societies 196–204
        in traditional societies 193–6
    trade-offs in 185–93
        between current reproduction and
            future success 187–8
        between growth and reproduction 186
        between quantity and quality of
            offspring 189–93
        methodological issues 185
local enhancement 55
love-is-blind bias 163
Lyonization 298

Machiavellian Intelligence Hypothesis *see*
        social brain hypothesis
major histocompatibility complex
        (MHC) heterozygosity and
        attractiveness 141
male births, maternal
        longevity and 188
male direct/indirect care childcare
        role 113–14
male-only care 218
male-philopatry 222
Malthusian catastrophes 5–6
marginal value theorem 123
massive modularity hypothesis 34, 39
mate choice copying 111–12
    in humans 115
maternal care 218, 219
    epigenetics and 14–15
mating tactics, alternative 117–18
    in human females 121–2, 123
    in human males 118–21
matrilocality 222
mechanistic cognition **301**
Mendel, Gregor 6
menopause 188
    grandmaternal effects and 188, 227

mental time travel 52–5
mentalism 288–92
mentalistic cognition **301**
middle-born disadvantage 231, 234
mimicry 55
mind, human 34–5
mirror self-recognition 52
modularity 34, **35**
molar epigenetics 13
molecular epigenetics 13
multiple births, biological cost of 187–8
mutation 6–7, 80
mutualism 75

n-person reciprocity 94
naive group selection 87
natural selection 6, 26, 75, 77
Neuroticism 26–7, 257, 258, 259, 264
'nice guy' sexual tactics 118–20, *120, 121*
niche construction 312, *333–4*
non-conformist bias 317
nuclear family 222

objective movement re-enactment (OMR) 323
Oncorhynchus spp. (Pacific salmon) 20
Openness to Experience 26, 122, 264
optimality modelling 108
other-signal costly signalling 85, 87, 94
oxytocin 14, 15

paraventricular nucleus (PVN) 14, 15
parental investment
    biased sex ratios at birth in humans 237
    birth order 230–4, *235*
    costs/benefits of parenting vs
        mating 223–5
    definition 216–17
    environmental quality and risk 241
    in human children 219
    human paternal investment 219–21
    in offspring 217–27
    interactions between birth order and sex
        biases 239–40
    nature of investment 228–9
    parental condition and investment 240–1
    paternity certainty 221–3

proximate mechanisms of paternal
        care 225–6
    sex biases in 234–9
partible paternity 223
patch choice models 123
paternal care 218, 219
patrilocality 222
pedagogy 325
personality and evolutionary
        imperative 257–62
    career success and resource
        acquisition 261–2
    fecundity, sexual behaviour, mate choice
        and relationships 257–60
    health and longevity 260–1
personality disorders 271–6
personality information, body size
        perception and 155
personality theory 255
phenylketonuria 282
phylogenetic relations among extant
        primates 33, *33*
pidgin 40–1
plasticity 12–16
polyandry 222, 227
polygeny 345
polygyny 222
polypeptide chain 7
positive assortation 95, 99
Prader-Willi syndrome 228, 282, 295–6
pre-eclampsia 228
prefrontal cortex 42–6
prefrontal lobotomy/leucotomy (PFL) 302
pre-natal care 228
prestige bias 318
primogeniture 233
Principle of Allocation 184, 185
Prisoner's Dilemma 8–9, 82
problem-solving mechanisms 35–7
programme-level imitation 323
proportional imitation rule 319
Pseudomonas fluorescens 90
psychophrenia 272
psychotherapy 293–4
psychotic spectrum disorders (PSD) 297
Psychoticism 257

psychotics 290
Pythagorean view of beauty 132, 163

r-k evolutionary theory 265, 270
race dispute 351
race, IQ and 269, 270–1
rape in humans 118, 119
ratcher effect 331
Raven's Progressive Matrices 284
reciprocal altruism 18, 75, 81, 82–3
  as explanation for collective action 94–5
  vs genic self-favouritism 83–4
red-imitation tasks 53
replacement fertility 20
replicators, genes as 76–7
reproductive suppression hypothesis (RSH)
    104, 194
reproductive value 112–13
  birth order and 232–3
resource dilution effect 230
Rett syndrome 282, 296
RNA 7
robot design and function 2–4, *3*, 26

savant syndrome 285–6, 300–1
schizophrenia 134, 282–3, 287, 297–8, 299
  gaze-monitoring in 289
  magical ideation in 291
  Openness in 264
schizotypy 264, 272, 283
'seeing is knowing' concept 58, 59
selective neutrality theory 254
self-awareness 32, 52
self-recognition 52, 327
self-reliance 43–4
self-representation 46
selfish gene theory 7, 345
semantic memory 53
sex differences in IQ 269
sex role evolution 353
sexual coercion in humans 118
sexual selection 5, 108–15
  human traits and 115–16
  within-sex differences 116–22
show-off hypothesis for hunting 224
siblicide 189

sibling competition 228
sibling rivalry 189
sign language 41, 43–4
Silver-Russell syndrome 294
similarity theory 258
situation-dependent strategies 356
16-factor model of personality 252
social action 75
social brain hypothesis 38, 326–9
social dilemma 92
social impact theory 318
social intelligence hypothesis *see* social
    brain hypothesis
social learning 39, 41–2, 46, 55–6
social learning biases
  context biases 317–19
    frequency-dependent biases 317
    model-based biases 317
  content (direct) biases 319–20
  selection for 316–17
social learning processes 322–3
social metaperception 162
social referencing 46
social status in humans 192
social transmission 315–25
  conditions favouring evolution of 315–16
  modes 320–2
  selection for social learning rules/
    strategies/biases 316–17
  social learning biases 317–19, 319–20
  social learning processes 322–3
sociobiology 16–21, 345
sociopathy 22, 26
sociotechnical assemblage 329
soft modularity 34
sperm competition in humans 114–15
spite 75
status-dependent mating tactics 118
stimulus–response association 57
strong reciprocity 90
suicide bombers 98
symmetry, preference for 134–5
synaesthesia 286

teenage pregnancy 20, 26–7
terminal investment hypothesis 240, 241

territorial defence 218
testosterone
    facial masculinity and 116, 143
    parenting effort and 225–6
    race differences 270
theory of mind 42, 43–4, 48, 56, 58, 326,
       327, 328, 329
thrifty genes 155–6
time allocation in mating 122–5
tit-for-tat strategy 9, 82
Tourette's syndrome 287
Toxoplasma gondii, schizophrenia and 299–300
tragedy of the commons 92
trait theories 255–7
traits 7
    sexually selected 109, **109**
    variation 5–6
Trisomy 14 134
Trivers-Willard hypothesis (TWH) 235–8,
    236, 240
tuberous sclerosis 282, 296
Turner's syndrome 282, 296

Ultimatum game 314
ultimogeniture 233

variation, explanations of 351–4
Venus figurines 156
vertical trait transmission 321
Vygotskian intelligence hypothesis 329

waist-to-hip ratio 112, 133, 145–9, 361
    applied to other research 152
    child sex prediction and 160
    critical tests 150–5
    cross-cultural and within-culture
        preferences 158–61
    health, fertility and 147–8
    importance to women 154
    mental modules and 149–50
    in paintings and sculptures 157–8
    sex judgements and 161–2
    temporal instability and 155–7
Wason Selection Task (WST) 23, *23*–4, 83,
    346, 354, 355
wealth and reproductive success 195–6
Williams, George 87–8
working memory 48–51
    social relations and 51–2

X trisomy 298